HM
19
B27
1961
v. 2

Date Due

The Library

_____

INDIAN VALLEY COLLEGES

Novato, California

BRO
DART   PRINTED IN U.S.A.

SOCIAL THOUGHT
FROM LORE TO SCIENCE

In Three Volumes. Volume II.
A History and Interpretation of Man's Ideas about
Life with His Fellows to Times when His Study
of the Past Is Linked with That of the Present
for the Sake of His Future

Third Edition

by HOWARD BECKER

Late Professor of Sociology, University of Wisconsin;
President, 1959-1960, American Sociological Association

and HARRY ELMER BARNES *with the assistance*

of Émile Benoît-Smullyan and Others

With an introductory note by Merle Curti, prefaces to all three editions,
1960 addenda for all chapters, a terminological commentary, a 1937-1960
appendix on contemporary sociology; 1960 bibliographies,
notes and subject indexes.

Dover Publications, Inc., New York

Copyright © 1938 by Howard Becker & Harry
Elmer Barnes.
Copyright © 1952 by Howard Becker.
Copyright © 1961 by Dover Publications, Inc.,
All rights reserved under Pan American and
International Copyright Conventions.

Published in Canada by General Publishing Com-
pany, Ltd., 30 Lesmill Road, Don Mills, Toronto,
Ontario.
Published in the United Kingdom by Constable
and Company, Ltd., 10 Orange Street, London
WC 2.

This Dover edition, first published in 1961, is an
expanded and revised version of the second (1952)
edition of the work originally published by D. C.
Heath and Company in 1938.

The work has been previously published in two
volumes, but the present edition is published in
three volumes. Volumes One and Two of this Dover
edition comprise the original Volume One, whereas
Volume Three of this Dover edition comprises
Volume Two of previous editions.

Professor Howard Becker's articles from the
various issues of the *Britannica Book of the Year*
are reprinted through the courtesy of Encyclo-
paedia, Britannica, Inc.

Standard Book Number: 486-20902-4
Library of Congress Catalog Card Number: 61-4323

Manufactured in the United States of America
Dover Publications, Inc.
180 Varick Street
New York, N.Y. 10014

To
Those Fulfilling Their Everyday Duties
in the Light of Kindly Purposes
Transcending Their Own Destinies

Authorship and editorial responsibility for each chapter and section is indicated by the following marks:

Barnes,   edited by Becker ....*
Becker,   "   "   "   ....†
Barnes and
    Becker, joint, "   "   "   ....‡
Others,   "   "   "   ....§

When chapter is not marked, see the section markings; when section is not marked, see the chapter marking.

CONTENTS

XV. The Transition to Objective Social Science and to Comte's Version of Sociology

XVI. The Quest for Secular Salvation: Social Reform in Relation to the Sociological Impulse

XVII. New Gospels: Revolutionary Socialism and the Winds of Doctrine

XVIII. Positivism Merges with Evolutionary Philosophy: Spencer and the Organismic School.*

XIX. Struggle over " The Struggle for Existence ":
Social Darwinism, Pros and Cons

XX. Deflation of Social Evolutionism: Prospects
for Sound Historical Sociology

A History and Interpretation
of
Man's Ideas about Life with His Fellows
to Times when
His Study of the Past Is Linked with That of the Present
for the Sake of
His Future

CHAPTER XII

Theories of the Natural State of Man

JUST SO STORIES AND SOBER FACT. — The problem of the state of man before the development of civilized society and political organization has been, as we have seen, one of the most debated questions in philosophy, theology, ethics, and social science. During much of the period of thought on this problem solutions were sought chiefly by speculative means. Although a few heirs of the Ionian enlightenment and the expansion of Rome, notably Herodotus, Strabo, Caesar, and Tacitus, made some little effort to study backward peoples on the fringe of the Classical world, most of those who discussed the question usually arrived at their conclusions in the effort to confirm some cherished doctrine. When the period of oversea explorations opened (about 1500), more concrete data about the life of primitive man began to reach Europe, and the discussions of the natural state of man, while still dogmatic and polemic, began to seek confirmation in the actual reports of explorers. The evolutionary hypothesis, as applied to man, emphasized the long human past which had existed before the period of civilized society and made the problem of the life of " primitive " man of real scientific and historical importance. The parallel development of ethnology and historical sociology made possible empirical study of the life of early man, and has substituted the verifiable facts of science for the dogmas and opinions of philosophers and moralists. It is the purpose of this chapter to review the more important typical interpretations of the life of early man — the condition of man in the so-called state of nature — from the earliest times to our own. Inasmuch as a great deal has already been said on this topic in preceding chapters, only the briefest summary of pre-medieval theories will be given; the lion's share of space will be devoted to later writers, and particularly to those of the seventeenth and eighteenth centuries.

Primitivism and the Normative Conception of Nature. — In order to understand the various theories about the natural state of man to be examined in this chapter it is necessary to relate them to the somewhat larger stream of thought which has been called "primitivism," and to realize their close dependence on the normative conception of "nature" which has played so important a rôle in the development of Western thought.[1]

Lovejoy, one of the chief authorities on this subject, distinguishes in the first place between two types of primitivism which he labels *chronological* and *cultural* primitivism, respectively. Chronological primitivism is a theory of history which asserts in a general way that the earlier phases of history have been more conducive to and productive of human welfare and happiness than the later phases, that the course of history has on the whole been downhill relative to human happiness, worth, or achievement.[2] Cultural primitivism, on the other hand, " is the discontent of the civilized with civilization or with some conspicuous or characteristic feature of it. It is the belief of men living in relatively highly evolved and complex cultural conditions that a life far simpler and less sophisticated in some or all respects is a more desirable life." [3] This is stated not only as an ideal but as a fact: it is assumed that either our prehistoric progenitors or our primitive or savage contemporaries or both have led or do in fact lead a life which is happier, more virtuous, or otherwise more desirable than the civilized life with which we are acquainted.

It is obvious that the beliefs in chronological and cultural primitivism are closely though not inextricably related, and that they have most frequently been held in common. The superiority of the life of our primitive progenitors is placed in sharp contrast to the inferiority of our contemporary civilized life, and the historical transition from the earlier to the later stage is then necessarily viewed as a descent or retrogression.

The motives for the acceptance of cultural primitivism are more diverse than has often been supposed, and in fact there have been two distinct and largely antithetical views as to the peculiar nature and virtues of primitive life, giving rise to two essentially different kinds of cultural primitivism which Lovejoy has called " soft " primitivism and " hard " primitivism, respectively. " Soft " primitivism has viewed savage life as easy, unconstrained, leisurely, and idyllic. In this view, the savage state has seemed to offer a life free from moral restraints and excessive toil. " Hard " primitivism, on the other hand, has in some respects tended to take a more realistic view of the picture; it has recognized that primitive life, judged by material standards, is a relatively poor one, that it is characterized by considerable exertion, hardship, and deprivation. But for the " hard " primitivist, the frugality, danger, and toilsomeness of primitive life have been held to be its greatest advantages. The reduction of desires to a minimum is viewed as the surest road to happiness and simplicity; toil and hardship are viewed as productive of great moral superiorities — in particular, of such virtues as self-restraint, discipline, and austerity.[4]

Upon analysis it becomes plain that the terms "nature" and "natural" as used in Western thought have been full of ambiguities, and these ambiguities have played the central rôle in certain of its developments. The use of "natural" in a normative or honorific sense has been in large part responsible for the glorification of the primitive; primitive life, as being "natural" or "according to nature," was *ipso facto* good and desirable. In analyzing any given theory about the natural state of man it is often difficult to be sure to what extent the theorist supposes himself to be describing the *facts* of primitive existence and to what extent he is merely indulging in ethical speculations as to the special character of the good life for mankind in general. In many cases, it is safe to assume that, as a result of the ambiguities inherent in the term "natural," this distinction is simply not perceived.

Lovejoy has clearly distinguished, with that analytical genius which is so particularly his own, sixty-six separate senses of the term "nature" as used in Western thought.[5] The logical relations of some of these senses and their bearing on the problem of primitivism he has excellently summarized in the following passage:

By virtue of its (probably) original signification, "nature" suggested the condition in which human society existed at its genesis: if, then, that which is "by nature" is *eo ipso* the best or the normal condition, the primeval state of man must have been his normal and best state. But this implication was greatly re-enforced by the sense of "nature" as that which is not made by man, not due to his contrivance, and the associated assumption that "nature" — as a quasi-divine power — does all things better than man. Cultural as well as chronological primitivism thus seemed to be in accord with the norm of "nature"; all man's alterations of or additions to the "natural" order of things are changes for the worse. The same conclusion was further facilitated by the fact that "nature" — in the sense of "original endowment" or "spontaneous tendency" — was in familiar usage [not only] antithetic to νόμος [custom or law], but also to art (τέχνη) and to culture or instruction (διδαχή). If "nature" is accepted as the name for what is "objectively right," or for what is "healthy," anything which is opposed to it becomes suspect; and therefore "art" and "the artificial" become disparaging terms, and whatever is acquired by deliberate teaching or cultivation seems, by definition, to be, at the least, inferior to the native intuitions or unsophisticated feelings of the mind. Finally, in so far as " nature " without a qualifying adjective, could serve as a name for what is fundamental and universal in man's own constitution, the beliefs and customs of primitive men could, on this ground also, be regarded as solely " in accordance with nature," and therefore as alone in keeping with an objective standard of truth or of morals. For it was . . . sometimes assumed in antiquity, and still more frequently in modern times, that the really universal elements in human nature are to be seen in their simplicity and purity only in savages or in primeval mankind; these were conceived as the least common denominators of humanity, while the " progress " of civilization has been characterized by the multiplication of differences: the religion, the moral ideas and customs, the entire cultures of the people who have departed from the state of nature appeared to have become increasingly dissimilar and conflicting. If, in short, it was taken for granted that there is a common *bond* of insights and impulses " natural " to man as such, and alone valid and needful, this manifestly could not be discovered, undisguised by the accretions due to divergent cultural developments, except among primitive folk.[6]

Lovejoy notes further that the term " state of nature " has at least seven different meanings:

1. The temporal state of nature. — The original or earliest condition of things and state of man.

2. The technological state of nature. — A state in which man is free from " art," in which only the simplest and most rudimentary practical arts are known.

3. The economic state of nature. — Human society without private property, i.e., economic communism.

4. The marital state of nature. — Community of wives and children.

5. The dietic state of nature. — Vegetarianism, a state in which man lived at peace with the animals.

6. The juristic state of nature. — Characterized by the absence of any but the " natural " government of family and clan, i.e., anarchism.

7. The ethical state of nature. — Control of human impulses " without deliberate and self-conscious moral effort, the constraint of rules, or the sense of sin." [7]

These senses are of course not mutually exclusive. A complete sense of nature might well include them all. In fact, however, most theorists dealing with the state of nature have had only one or a few of these senses primarily in mind. Thus for political theorists the state of nature has usually signified the *juristic* state of anarchism, a " state of intolerable evils of which the civil state is the necessary remedy." [8] Hence such thought has been predominantly anti-primitivistic. Among the thinkers of antiquity the technological and economic states of nature were those which were most frequently emphasized. The absence of arts and luxuries, as well as of private property, was held the most distinctive characteristic of man's natural state.

It is to be noted that cultural primitivism is by no means incompatible with a tendency to reform society. Communists, anarchists, pacifists, and many other critics of existing social standards and realities have commonly appealed to the conception of man's natural state to give moral authority to their views and programs. For example, it has often been felt much less effective to denounce the evils of war than to paint in glowing colors the happiness of those primitive societies in which war (supposedly) did not exist.[9] It must be observed, however, that when primitivism is converted into a program for reform it has necessarily been " a program of reform wholly through elimination and reversion. The way to improve society is not to continue a development already in process, not to add to gains which mankind has already won, but to undo the work of history, to scrape off from human life the accretions which have grown upon it." [10] Moreover, the primitivistic reformer has always supposed that his plans could be realized directly, immediately, and without any difficulty. Such plans have appeared to involve nothing more than a return to " nature's simple plan," which all men could immediately perceive if they freed their minds of " unnatural " prejudices and conventions. " This assumption of the essential simplicity of the social problem may be said to have been, both in antiquity and in the modern Enlightenment, the fundamental premise of most of those who looked forward with confidence to a radical amelioration of man's estate." [11]

Preliterate and Oriental Doctrines concerning the Natural Condition of Man. — One of the most interesting facts concerning preliterate peoples is that they often have elaborate " myths of origin " which trace their development from a distant past.[12] Many of these preliterate tales of human origins and development do not differ widely from those which have come down to us from Oriental sources. Nothing can demonstrate this better than the reading of the parallel collections of preliterate and Oriental creation tales which have been collected by Kroeber and Waterman in their *Source-Book in Anthropology.* Indeed, one may justifiably hold that the early Oriental accounts of human origins are but primitive creation stories which have assumed a position of unusual importance because of the peculiar relation of the religion, thought, and literature of the Orient to the cultural tradition of Western Europe and America.[13]

Although much time could be spent discussing the Osiris myth and the Gilgamesh epic, as examples of Oriental myths of genesis,[14] it is necessary in this place only to call attention to their many points of similarity to the Hebrew creation tales given in the Book of Genesis.

The Hebrew view of the natural state of man is of special historic significance because of the enormous influence it has exerted over the theology, ethics, and social science of Western Europe since the beginning of the Christian era. The Hebrew interpretation of human genesis, with some considerable infiltration of Greek philosophy, formed the basis for all orthodox Western views of social development down to modern times.[15]

The Israelites agreed with the Babylonians in believing that there had been ten antediluvian heroes who had lived extraordinarily long lives, and that ever since the flood, the span of life had been uniformly decreasing till the advent of historic times.[16] Reasoning backward, they concluded that there must have been a time at the beginning when man was happier and healthier than he ever was subsequently. Thus man was conceived to have been created by divine act some six thousand years ago and placed in a pristine paradise located in the land of Eden. He lived there in a technological and dietary state of nature — that is to say, devoid of the practical arts and crafts and at peace with the animals. From this paradise he was ejected because of yielding to the temptation of his female consort and Satan in the matter of varying from the dietary prescriptions of the Deity. This Fall of Adam and his descendants brought about the general degradation of the human race, which proceeded at an accelerated rate until God in his wrath destroyed by flood all save the family of the faithful Noah. The sons of the latter, departing from the ancestral household, peopled the world anew. A portion of the descendants of Shem, represented by Abraham and his successors, were chosen by God to bring to man the revelation of his Word, and, as a general leaven in the wicked mass of mankind, slowly to win back others from a life of sin and worldly interests.

Implicit in this account there appears to be a conception of world-ages. The first age was brought to an end by the flood, and the second age was to be concluded by a " cataclysm which was to destroy all mankind but a righteous remnant. The increasing wickedness of man after the initial creation, as well as after the Flood, is stressed." [17] All of these conceptions, however, are not distinctively Hebrew, but were common in Mesopotamia. Distinctively Hebrew, on the other hand, is the idealization of the nomadic life to be found, most especially, in the writings of the prophets. The later Israelites were continually being reminded by the prophets that their ancestors led a different (and a better) sort of life, that the increasing luxury, vice, oppression, and enslavement of the poor could be explained as the natural consequence of abandoning the nomadic *mishpat* for the settled urban and agricultural existence. This social protest dates from the eighth century B.C., after five generations of organized civic and commercial life productive of a considerable increase of wealth and luxury. While the Hebrew story of the creation may be set down as chronological primitivism, with some admixture of a " soft " cultural primitivism, the prophetic writings are characterized above all by the " hard " type of cultural primitivism.

Classical Theories of the State of Nature. — It will be recalled that all through the chapter on " Classical Theories of the Origin of Society and the State " reference was made to " the state of nature," although the topic was not explicitly treated. What we say here, as in several other sections, will therefore be slightly repetitious. Turning now to Greece, we find that in general the Greek thinkers held a view somewhat akin to that cherished by the Hebrews. Although the statement cannot be made without qualifications, nevertheless the majority of Greek writers on history and politics were chronological primitivists who believed that man had descended to his contemporary characteristics and circumstances from a previous golden or heroic age. As Bury has put it : " It is remarkable how the speculations of the Greeks on primitive civilization were bounded by that tradition of a decline from a golden age, which Hesiod expressed in his scheme of the five ages." [18]

Cultural primitivism also had a fairly wide distribution in antiquity. It was especially prominent in Cynicism, from which it was later passed to the Stoics. " The Cynic ethics may be said to reduce, in its practical outcome, almost entirely to primitivism. Cynicism was the first and most vigorous philosophic revolt of the civilized against civilization in nearly all of its essentials — except ' philosophy ' itself." [19] The two basic ideals of Cynicism were independence of external things and a life " in conformity with nature." These two ideals were more or less identified. From this it followed that the good was to be achieved primarily by limitation of desires. The development of the arts was therefore fiercely opposed (" technological " primitivism) as tending to increase artificially the number of desires. Associated with this was a sort of anti-intellectualism, an opposition to the arts and sciences as "unnatural." The primeval era which presumably had been uncontaminated by technical progress was viewed as the only "natural" one. Finally, only those desires are "natural" which are instinctive and basic, prompted not by vanity or emulation, but by irrepressible need, and which may ordinarily be satisfied easily by all men.

Although most of the writings of the original Greek Stoics have perished, we can gather a sufficient idea of their doctrines from their Roman disciples to be relatively certain that if they had any conception of a primitive "state of nature" it must have been a condition in which "social" relations prevailed, for a basic part of their doctrine was the dogma of the natural sociability of mankind.

The Epicureans, on the other hand, were the founders of those doctrines which were later to stand out so strongly in the philosophy of Hobbes. They held that the primitive state of mankind might be assumed to be one of violence and inconvenience, and that organized social relations had a utilitarian origin in the necessity of union for mutual defense and coöperation. It may be noted here that Epicureanism, in spite of the libels of its opponents, was by no means a doctrine for voluptuaries. In its conception of the simple life as the happiest one it bore striking resemblances to the Cynic and Stoic doctrines with which it has too often been contrasted.

Plato's position in respect to primitivism and the natural state of man is not entirely consistent.[20] There can be no doubt that he was a chronological primitivist. He states clearly that "the men of early times were better than we and nearer to the gods."[21] He displays, moreover, distinct leanings toward cultural primitivism, of the "hard" variety. He is definitely in favor of the austere and simple life characterized by few desires and the absence of luxury. Moreover, in the *Republic* he proposes economic and marital communism, and thus a return to a "state of nature" in at least two of its meanings. It is true, however, that his primitivistic proposals are to be confined to the highest social class (which is the only one for whom he assumed it to be possible).

On the other hand, there are at least three respects in which Plato is sharply anti-primitivistic. First, he was entirely out of accord with any claims for the superiority of the instinctive or unreflective type of life. He insisted that reason was the noblest part of man, should be the ruling faculty, and that only by the intensive and discriminating use of the intellect can man attain the higher levels of experience and achieve the good. Second, he is clearly opposed to the eulogistic use of " nature " in connection with the dyslogistic use of " art." " Law," he says, " and also art, exist by nature,"[22] i.e., art, or the use of reason, is also " natural " (in the sense of valuable, or fitting and proper for man, and in no way inferior to the non-artificial). Finally, Plato's view of human nature was such as to be clearly opposed to egalitarianism and the glorification of a juristic state of nature. Men are naturally unequal; they must be arranged in a hierarchy of innate worth and of corresponding authority, and they must all be equally subject to the control of a complex, unchanging, and authoritarian constitution.

Aristotle's position in respect to the state of nature must be classified as in the main anti-primitivistic. Though he occasionally used the term " nature " in a eulogistic sense of primeval, simple, and universal, what is most characteristic of him is that — taking a hint from Plato — he ended by using the word in a sense quite opposite to the usual one. " Natural " became for Aristotle the complex, the highly evolved, rather than the simple and original; i.e., not the first form of a thing but that which it tended to become.[23] There is implicit in Aristotle's thought a definite antagonism to chronological primitivism. His doctrine of the eternity of the world is incompatible with any supposition of an absolute beginning of things (whether glorious or ignoble). Moreover, his aversion to admitting any important change on a cosmic scale, his fundamental conservatism, made him opposed to any view of history as involving significant and continuous change in a single direction.

In Aristotle's view society " goes through a typical evolution which corresponds to, and results from, an increasing realization by men of the originally merely latent potentialities and needs of human nature — a gradual discovery of what 'a good way of living' for man is. The simplest and earliest form of social organization is the least excellent because it serves only the most rudimentary and least distinctively human of these needs. Man is 'by nature a political animal' in the sense that his specific nature can manifest itself fully only in the third stage, i.e., when he is a member of a *polis*."[24]

Aristotle has the lowest opinion of both the historical and contemporary forms of primitive men. "And of the foolish, those who are irrational by nature and live only by their senses are like barbarians."[25] Aristotle's celebrated defense of slavery rests in large part on the assumption that the barbarian is a lower order of being without the capacity for self-direction.

Technological primitivism is completely incompatible with the fundamental Aristotelian doctrine that the good life depends on a moderate degree of wealth, comfort, and leisure. The primitive arts could provide no more than a bare sustenance. Aristotle's celebrated criticism of Plato's proposals for economic and marital communism place him, in this respect also, in the anti-primitivist camp. And he shares with Plato the same glorification of reason and the intellect which, as we have seen, had already clearly marked off Plato from a genuine or thoroughgoing primitivism. (From this point on, because of scanty space, we shall cease to follow Lovejoy's elaborate analysis, confining ourselves largely to exposition.)

Although what remains in authentic documents of the doctrines of the Sophists is too slight to allow anyone to speak with certainty, many historians of Greek social thought are inclined to believe that, though they may have had no definite conception of a primitive state of man, they at least conceived of a pre-political stage out of which political society grew by means of a governmental compact.

Polybius, the last of the great Greek writers in this field, presents a view of the original condition of mankind which was strikingly like that of some of the members of the early modern " state of nature " school. He says:

> Originally, then, it is probable that the condition of life among men was this herding together like animals and following the strongest and bravest as leaders. The limit of authority would be physical strength and the name we should give it would be despotism. But as soon as family ties and social relations have arisen among such agglomerations of men, then is born also the idea of kingship, and then for the first time mankind conceives the notion of goodness and justice and their reverse.[26]

Roman political philosophy had its prototype in the various Greek thinkers and schools, and so, with the exception of the contributions of the Roman Lawyers, the political theory of the Romans was either an amplification or paraphrasing of the Greek antecedents. Although Cicero claimed to be an eclectic, his general inclination was toward the Stoics; his opinions concerning the original state of man were colored by the Stoic doctrine of the natural sociability of the human species. Thus he held that the earliest condition of the human race was a pre-political rather than a pre-social state.

Lucretius, it will be recalled, was the main representative of the Epicurean school among the Romans. In his view, the earliest type of human life was extremely wild, rough, and crude, but distinguished by the more elementary virtues of sympathy and admiration for strength and beauty. Although wild and simple, this life was at least tolerable. With the growth of wealth on the part of the leaders, however, enmity and jealousy were aroused. A period of violence followed, which was ended only by a mutual compact on the part of the people to put an end to this strife and submit to a common authority.

Although not so thoroughgoing an Epicurean as Lucretius, Horace held essentially the same views regarding the primitive state of human life. In fact, his description is so similar that the earlier poet may have provided the model for the later.[27]

The doctrines of the Stoic philosopher Seneca were among the most influential of Roman theories regarding the early conditions of mankind. He was the most notable Roman expositor of the theory of a primitive golden age from which mankind had subsequently declined. The origin of private property broke down this period of primitive felicity, and the consequent striving after wealth and position rendered political authority necessary to make the conditions of life tolerable.

The historian Tacitus had no particular theories of the origin of human society, but his method of turning to the Germanic tribes to get a picture of a life which seemed to him much more " natural " and virtuous than existence in imperial Rome was one which became very popular in the eighteenth century after the period of geographical discoveries had brought reports to the West of the existence of truly " natural " men in remote parts of the world.[28]

In formulating a distinction between the *jus naturale* and the *jus gentium,* the views of the Roman Lawyers of the imperial period seem to indicate a belief in the existence of a primitive state of nature like that pictured by Seneca. As pointed out in an earlier chapter, the *jus naturale* was apparently based upon usages assumed to be common to the primitive stage, and the *jus gentium* on the practices which it was believed had developed after the growth of the conventional institutions of organized society.

Medieval Views of the Original State of Man. — It is when we come to the views of the Patristic period that we first find the effect of Seneca's doctrine concerning the golden age of the primitive life of mankind. The Fathers transformed Seneca's notion of a primitive golden age into the conception of the condition of man-

kind before the Fall. While there was a certain logical problem
to solve in reconciling Seneca's conception of primitive social life
with a condition in which there were but two individuals in existence, still the heroic exegesis of the Fathers, with their never-
failing device of allegorical interpretation, was quite equal to the
task. It was through the Fall, as caused by the transgression of
Adam, that man passed from the state of nature into the miseries
of unorganized and unregulated life. Man was rescued from the
evils of this state only by the establishment of political society and
the acceptance of revealed religion. This " Christian anthropology " was very influential in the Middle Ages, as it furnished the
starting-point for most of the theological and political theories
regarding the primitive state of mankind.

Isidore of Seville (d. 636), the Spanish encyclopedist, forms
a sort of transition between the conventional Patristic period and
the ninth century. In the definition of " fortress " in his weighty,
but not very original, *Etymologies,* he says that " men were originally naked and unarmed, defenceless against the inclemency of
heat and cold, and the attacks of wild beasts and of all other men.
At last they learned to make for themselves huts in which they
might be sheltered and safe, and these were gradually collected in
towns." [29] Isidore thus combined the doctrines of Lucretius and
Cicero. This conception, taken from Classical writers, was handed
over by Isidore to the later encyclopedists of the Middle Ages and
was a very common starting-point for historical and political
theories. It is significant to note that he does not emphasize,
though he does not deny, the conception of a primitive golden
age.

In the social philosophy of that period of revival of intellectual interests generally known as the Ninth-Century Renas-
cence, there was little attention paid to the question of the original
state of mankind. The theories which were held were of a second-
hand sort gleaned from the earlier compendia, notably from that
edifying collection by Isidore mentioned above. Carlyle sums up
this period, as regards its theories concerning the primitive state
of man, as follows:

We find but little speculation or theory as to the beginnings of society
and the State. . . . In a treatise attributed to Alcuin, *De Rhetorica et
Virtutibus,* there is an interesting passage on the primitive conditions of
human life, drawn as the author says from ancient sources, in which man
is represented as having originally lived like the beasts, wandering about
in the fields, without any rational or moral principle or rule of life. A
great and wise man at last appears, and, recognizing the qualities and ca-

pacities of human nature, gathers men together into one place, and thus brings them to live a peaceful and humane life. We find a very similar statement of the primitive condition of man in Hrabanus Maurus' *De Universo,* taken from St. Isidore of Seville. . . .

In themselves, these statements are both too vague and too commonplace to enable us to fix very definitely the philosophic tradition to which they belong. We can hardly go further than this, that they represent a tradition which held that behind the period of the organized society of men there lay a time when there was no fixed order among mankind. It is a state of nature, but not, so far as these passages go, a good or ideal state, but rather one of disorder or misery. It would agree well enough with the conditions of human life as they might be pictured after sin and vice had come into the world, and before the great institutions, by which sin is controlled and checked had been developed.[30]

Beginning with the tenth and eleventh centuries, Roman law began to be revived as a study, particularly after 1088, when Irnerius began to teach at the University of Bologna in Italy. It made its way into Northern Europe and exercised an enormous influence upon both legal and political institutions and theories. As regards the theory of this revived Roman law concerning the primitive state of man, all that can be said is that the writers held essentially the views expressed by the writers of the *Digest* who have been mentioned above.[31]

About this same time canon law took a definite form in the *Decretum* of Gratian, published in 1142. The doctrine of the canon law was essentially similiar to the Patristic views concerning the original state of man: namely, that there was a primitive golden age which corresponded to the state of man before the Fall, and that this was followed by the period of violence incident upon Adam's transgression which rendered government necessary to establish order and endurable conditions of life.[32]

The scholastic social philosophy is perhaps best represented by Aquinas (1227–1274). He held, in harmony with the Aristotelian dogma of the natural sociability of man, that human society was the spontaneous product of man's inherent social instinct. Yet, owing to man's tendency toward evil unless restrained by authority, government was essential. This governmental authority, although rendered necessary by the demands of well-ordered social life, was nevertheless derived from God rather than based upon mere necessity.[33]

In his *Defensor pacis,* that brilliant adumbration of many later political theories of radical bent, Marsiglio of Padua (1270–1342) set forth his belief in a utilitarian basis of society. Society was essential to mankind for the carrying on of the coöperative activities so necessary to human comfort, and even for the very existence of human life. But unregulated society was prone to descend into disorder; hence the necessity of government to ensure order and justice. He says in regard to this:

> . . . it was necessary for men to congregate in order to acquire what is useful and escape what is injurious.
> Among men thus congregated, contention arises naturally. . . . It is therefore necessary to introduce into the community the rule of justice, and to set up a guardian or protector.[34]

Æneas Sylvius, who later became Pope Pius II (1458–1464), believed that the condition of mankind after the expulsion from Eden was the state of nature. After a period of bestial existence men perceived the value of social life, established social groups and cities, and invented the arts of life and pleasure. (Æneas Sylvius also seems to have originated the doctrine of the social contract as distinguished from the governmental compact.)

The State of Nature in Early Modern Social Philosophy. — The general social philosophy of the period from the fifteenth to the seventeenth century was colored chiefly by two somewhat divergent backgrounds: the Christian Epic, and the literature and philosophy of Classical antiquity which had been revived through the influence of the Humanists. Hence we find in the views of the state of nature expressed in this period a combination of Classical and Christian doctrines buttressed by frequent references to both Christian and pagan authorities.

Machiavelli's (1469–1527) discussion of the natural state of man was of an analytical and psychological nature rather than historical. It dealt with man's inherent characteristics as viewed by Machiavelli, rather than with his condition in the most remote historical period. As far as Machiavelli attempted to deal with man's historical development, he followed Polybius almost implicitly.[35]

In the *Vindiciae contra tyrannos,* the author (probably Duplessis-Mornay)[36] holds that men were "by nature free, impatient of servitude, and born rather to command than to obey." He follows Seneca and the Patristic writers in asserting that in the golden age government was in the hands of wise men, but that owing to the conflicts growing out of the struggle over private property, kings were chosen for their valor and diligence in order to suppress the struggles and confusion.[37]

George Buchanan, another anti-monarchist writer of the time, in his *On the Sovereign Power among the Scots,* followed Polybius in his view of the natural state of man in that he held that man in this period lived a rough animal-like existence without legal restrictions or any permanent habitation, but added a point in that he claimed that not only self-interest but also the divinely implanted social instinct must be assumed to account for the final development of human society.[38]

Jean Bodin, in his *Six Books Concerning a Republic,* does not develop the distinctive theory of a pre-social state of nature prevailing among mankind. Nevertheless he makes an advance toward this type of doctrine by holding that the life of primitive man was wild and violent and that the social instinct, first extending only to members of a family, and then expanding to include wider groups, was the only agency which made primitive life tolerable and finally rescued man from this state of confusion and violence. Although society thus originated in the social instinct, the state had its beginnings in force through the conquest of one group by another : [39]

Yea reason and the very light of nature leadeth us to believe very force and violence to have given course and beginning unto commonwealths.[40]

In another portion of his treatise he goes on in the following manner:

The first sort of men was most given to rapine, murder and theft, delighting in nothing more, nor accounting any honour greater than to rob and kill, and to oppress the weaker sort as slaves.[41]

He proceeds to cite Thucydides, Aristotle, and others regarding the alarming amount of robbery in historic Greece, and mentions how Aristotle apparently classifies robbery as a legitimate occupation.

Interpretations Offered by the Social Contract School and Others. — At no previous time had the alleged conditions of man in his natural state possessed such practical importance for social thinking as they came to assume in the seventeenth and eighteenth centuries. As we have seen, it was necessary to justify the existence of political society, the national state, and secular absolutism. The social philosophers, therefore, turned to " the natural state of man " to find sufficient reasons for the necessity of the establishment of orderly political life. It was held that this natural condition of man was either intolerably miserable or, at best, inconvenient and unsafe. To escape from such a situation political society was established. The instrument by which it was created

was, in the opinion of most of the writers of the time, the social
and governmental contracts. The growing importance of economic
factors in society, as a result of the developing Commercial Revolution and the "intervention of capital," is evident in the frequent
emphasis upon the relation of the rise of property to the necessity
for political protection, and also in the usual enumeration of the
right of possession as one of the "inalienable rights of man."

   Hooker: from Bad to Not So Bad. — Richard Hooker (1552–
1600), in his *Ecclesiastical Polity,* moves in the direction of
Hobbes in his description of the life of primitive man. He pictures the condition as anything but golden and gives thanks to
the Lord that even though things are bad enough in his time,
they are immensely better than in primitive days. He phrases his
conception thus:

> But neither that which we learn of ourselves nor that which others
> teach us can prevail where wickedness and malice have taken deep root.
> If, therefore, when there was as yet only one family in the world, no
> means of instruction, human or divine, could prevent the effusion of
> blood; how could it be chosen but that when families were multiplied and
> increased upon earth, after separation each providing for itself, envy,
> strife, contention, and violence must grow up amongst them? For hath
> not nature furnished man with wit and valor, as it were with armor,
> which may be used as well unto extreme evil as good? [42]

   Mariana and Echoes of the Fall. — If Hooker adumbrated
Hobbes, so did a Spanish Jesuit foreshadow Rousseau's *Discourse
on the Origin and Foundation of Inequality among Men.*[43] In his
work *On Kingship and the Education of a King,* Mariana (1536–
1624) describes a state of nature which was distinguished at first
primarily by rude simplicity and contentment. This condition was,
however, soon broken up by avarice (an attenuated version of the
Fall), and the violence which resulted was only done away with
through the submission of the group to political authority.[44]
Laures, our foremost contemporary authority on Mariana, thus
summarizes his doctrine of the state of nature and the origins of
civil society — probably the most complete and important treatment of the subject in his generation:

> According to Mariana men originally lived without a social organiza-
> tion, and without a positive law. They simply followed the law of nature
> and attended to nothing except supplying food for themselves and their
> families. Children obeyed their elders and the whole family, including
> children and grandchildren, lived together in perfect happiness until the
> death of the head of the family. Then the common home was broken up,

and the several members spread to adjacent districts. Each formed another large family, or rather a group of families which Mariana calls *pagi* (tribes).

Even at this stage men had no civil authority and no positive law. Nature gave freely what was needed for their maintenance. . . . They were guileless and honest; fraud and lying were unknown. They had no social obligations because there were no rich among them to bow to or to flatter. Ambition and war were unknown, and all lived peacefully and happily on equal terms. Nor had avarice claimed the goods of the earth from their common use as private property. All things belonged to all.

Unfortunately, this happy state of affairs did not last long. Men soon began to feel more and larger wants which they yearned to satisfy. This desire was good, for God had created men with manifold insufficiencies in order to induce them to combine into a perfect society. . . .

Primitive man needed above all protection from enemies, — wild animals and especially fellowmen whose rapacity had made them more cruel and dangerous than the beasts. The strong frightened the weak, robbed and killed them pitilessly. Murderous bands organized and pillaged neighboring tribes. Original happiness and harmlessness had disappeared, violence, robbery and theft reigned everywhere. Human life even was not respected.

Primitive man realized his helplessness. His Creator had purposely placed him in this condition in order that he might seek for help from his fellowman. The gift of speech enabled him to exchange ideas with his neighbors, to ask help and to give advice and assistance. Moreover, men observed how the weaker animals banded together to supplement by their number what was wanting in strength. When, therefore, the weaker individuals saw themselves surrounded by the violence of the strong and powerful, they resolved to look for a leader to protect them against their oppressors and enemies. They chose the most virtuous man from their midst and charged him to lead them to battle and to settle their quarrels and disputes. "Thus came into existence urban communities and the royal power. . . . Thus originated from the want of many things, from fear and the consciousness of frailty, human rights (by reason of which we are human beings) and the civil society under the control of which a good and happy life is led."

Such is Mariana's conception of the origin of the State.[45]

Grotius, Hither and Yon. — The doctrines of the first great exponent of international law, Hugo Grotius (1583–1645), concerning the state of nature are somewhat confusing. On the one hand, following the Stoics and Aristotle, he claims that man is by nature a social being and that man's natural state is therefore social. On the other hand, he frequently falls back upon a pre-political state of nature which he " identifies with the age of

Cyclopes and Autochthones of classic fable and with the patriarchal age of the Scriptures." [46] Dunning thus sums up his main
doctrines on this subject:

> At all events, while he declares the social life to be the "natural"
> condition of man, he as often recurs to the idea of an ante-political "state
> of nature," both as a logical concept and as an historical fact. This is
> the condition of man in which the pure law of nature rules, with every
> individual as executor of his own rights under it; for "public tribunals
> are due not to nature but to the act of man." By nature everyone has a
> right to resist a wrong; but when civil society has been instituted for
> the preservation of public tranquillity, this right becomes subject to the
> prescriptions of the sovereign. Against the sovereign the right of re-
> sistance is null, for the reason, among others, that those who instituted
> civil society deliberately willed their rights to the holder of supreme au-
> thority. It is indeed to be observed, Grotius says, in most explicit assertion
> of the contract theory, "that originally men, not by the command of God,
> but of their own accord, after learning by experience that isolated families
> could not secure themselves against violence, united in civil society, out
> of which act sprang governmental power. [47]

Hobbes and General Distrust. — Of the historic theories of the
state of nature none has been more famous or more quoted than
that of Thomas Hobbes (1588–1679). He made little attempt
to discover the actual state of early man, although he might have
learned much from reports of contemporary discoverers, but
rather sought to deduce it from the assumed universal traits of
human nature. The basic characteristic of man is "a general inclination, a perpetual and restless desire of power after power,
that ceaseth only in death." [48] Men are natural enemies, for they
potentially desire the attainment of the same ends or the possession of the same goods. Once in possession of goods, each man
lives in continual fear lest he be despoiled by his fellows. Then,
man's invariable pride and vainglory make him jealous of his
acquaintances. Hence the natural state of man is one of the war
of every man against every other man. Such a state of "force and
fraud" is one of universal misery. "In such condition there is
no place for industry; because the fruit thereof is uncertain; and
consequently no culture of the earth; no navigation, nor use of
commodities that may be imported by sea; no commodious buildings; no instruments of moving, and removing, such things as require much force; no knowledge of the face of the earth; no account of time; no arts; no letters; no society; and what is worst
of all, continual fear, and danger of violent death; and the life
of man, solitary, poor, nasty, brutish, and short." [49] Hobbes is

not insistent upon the historicity of this doctrine of the state of nature. If it is philosophically and logically sound, that is all that concerns him. Yet he contends that his view of man in the state of nature is not a historical impossibility, and cites the American Indians as an example of those who now live in such a condition. From the miseries of the state of nature man has escaped through the instrumentality of a social contract, by which he agreed to live an orderly and peaceful life in civil society under an organized government.[50]

Milton, Belated Church Father. — In his *Tenure of Kings and Magistrates,* John Milton (1608–1674) revived the old Patristic view which had been carried down through the Middle Ages and had received a new lease of life in the hands of the monarchomachs: namely, that men were born free, equal, and in a state of primitive bliss, but that owing to Adam's transgression they had lost their original privileges, had descended into a state of promiscuous violence, and, to rescue themselves from this situation, were forced to establish a common and superior political authority:

No man, who knows aught, can be so stupid as to deny that all men naturally were born free, being the image and resemblance of God himself, and were by privilege above all creatures, born to command and not to obey. And that they lived so, till from the root of Adam's transgression falling among themselves to do wrong and violence, and foreseeing that such courses must needs tend to the destruction of them all, they agreed by common league to bind each other from mutual injury, and jointly to defend themselves against any that gave disturbance or opposition to such agreement. Hence came cities, towns, and commonwealths.[51]

Spinoza and the "Logic of the Fish." — In his *Tractatus Theologico-Politicus,* published in 1670, Spinoza develops his doctrines concerning the state of nature and its implications. He begins, using an illustration reminiscent of Hindu theories, with the dogma that natural right is identical with power — in other words, in the state of nature, "might makes right." Desire is as legitimate a guide as reason in the state of nature. Whatever a man desires in a state of nature he has a right to obtain, and he may use any means whatsoever to secure the object of his desire. Nevertheless, it is far better to live by reason than by desire, for only through the guidance of reason is a social life with all its benefits possible; the man who lives in an isolated state, guided by mere instinct, must pass a most miserable existence. Therefore, men found it very advisable to join together in a civil society to

secure the advantages of a well-ordered social life. A few of the
more pertinent parts of Spinoza's treatment are the following:

> By the right and ordinance of nature, I mean merely those natural
> laws wherewith we conceive every individual to be conditioned by nature,
> so as to live and act in a given way. For instance, fishes are naturally
> conditioned for swimming, and the greater for devouring the less; there-
> fore, fishes enjoy the water and the greater devour the less by sovereign
> natural right. . . . Wherefore among men, so long as they are con-
> sidered as living under the sway of nature, he who does not yet know
> reason or who has not yet acquired the habit of virtue, acts solely ac-
> cording to the laws of his desire with as sovereign a right as he who orders
> his whole life entirely by the laws of reason. . . . The natural right of
> the individual man is thus determined, not by sound reason, but by
> desire and power.
>
> Whatsoever, therefore, an individual, considered as under the sway of
> nature, thinks useful for himself, whether led by sound reason or im-
> pelled by the passions, that he has a sovereign right to seek and take for
> himself as best he can, whether by force, cunning, entreaty, or by any
> other means; consequently, he may regard as an enemy anyone who
> hinders the accomplishment of his purpose.
>
> Nevertheless, no one can doubt that it is much better for us to live
> according to the laws and assured dictates of reason, for, as we have said,
> they have men's true good for their object. Moreover, everyone wishes
> to live as far as possible securely beyond the reach of fear, and this
> would be quite impossible so long as everyone did everything he liked,
> and reason's claim was lowered to a par with those of hatred and anger.
> There is no one who is not ill at ease in the midst of enmity, hatred,
> anger, and deceit, and who does not seek to avoid them as much as he
> can. When we reflect that men without mutual help, or the aid of reason,
> must live miserably, as we clearly proved, we shall plainly see that men
> must necessarily come to an agreement to live together as securely and
> well as possible if they are to enjoy as a whole the rights which naturally
> belong to them as individuals.[52]

Pufendorf and Feral Man. — The eminent German publicist
and social philosopher of the seventeenth century, Samuel Pufendorf (1632–1694), presented an elaborate study of the state of
nature. He developed two somewhat different treatments, one
speculative and the other historical. The state of nature, as a
speculative concept, is the condition in which " we may conceive
man to be placed by his bare nativity, abstracting from him all the
rules and institutions, whether of human invention, or of the suggestion and revelation of Heaven." [53] The following is Pufendorf's famous statement of the natural state of man as specula-
tively reconstructed:

Let us suppose a man bred up by another, just so far as to be able to walk, and without hearing a word spoken, insomuch that he shall be destitute of all instruction and discipline, and enjoying no knowledge, but such as sprouts naturally from the soil of his mind, without the benefit of cultivation; let us suppose the same man to be left in a wilderness or desert, and entirely deprived of the company and assistance of others; what a wretched creature should we at last behold! A mute and ignoble animal, master of no powers or capacities, any further than to pluck up the herbs and roots that grow about him; to gather the fruits which he did not plant; to quench his thirst at the first river, or fountain, or ditch that he finds out in his way; to creep into a cave for shelter from the injuries of weather, or to cover over his body with moss or grass and leaves. Thus would he pass a heavy life in most tedious idleness; would tremble at every noise and be scared at the approach of his fellow creatures, till at last his miserable days were concluded by the extremity of hunger, or of thirst, or by the fury of a ravenous beast. That mankind therefore do not pass their life in a more forlorn and a more deplorable condition than any other living thing, is owing to their union and conjunction, to their intercourse with the other partners and companions of their nature. The Divine saying, " 'Tis not good for Man to be alone," is not to be restrained to matrimony, but seems to belong in general to any society with other men. But now without law, it is impossible that any society should be either introduced or maintained in strength and quietness. And consequently, unless man had been designed for the basest and the most wretched part of the animal creation it was not by any means convenient that he should live loose from all direction and obligation of law.[54]

This speculative view of the natural state of man Pufendorf admits is not confirmed by historical observation. " We are ready," he says, " to acknowledge it for a certain truth that all mankind did never exist together in a mere natural state." This is evident from the Scriptures, for Eve was subject to Adam, and their children were subject to both. The closest actual historical approach to a state of nature came when these early men began to break away from their paternal households and establish separate homes. The smaller these family groups were, the nearer they approached the pure state of nature where men lived singly and without authority. There was authority within these family groups, but they lived in a state of nature with respect to each other, for they recognized no common superior. Yet even these independent communities enjoyed social contacts and coöperation, and knew nothing of the misery which must have existed in a state of pure isolation. Early patriarchal society was therefore the closest historical approximation to the speculative characteristics of the state of nature attained by man.[55]

Locke, Liberty, and License. — The conception of the state of nature held by John Locke (1632–1704) approached that of Pufendorf, as viewed in the historical sense of the latter's twofold conception, though Locke was more consistent than Pufendorf in maintaining that such a state was historical and was not a state of war but of peace. To Locke, the state of nature was rather pre-political than pre-social. Men had from the beginning lived in families and small social groups. Among the more important of Locke's descriptions of it are these:

> But though this [the state of nature] be a state of liberty, yet it is not a state of license. . . . Every one as he is bound to preserve himself, and not to quit his station willfully, so by like reason, when his own preservation comes not into competition, ought he as much as he can to preserve the rest of mankind, and not unless it be to do justice to an offender, take away, or impair the life, or what tends to the preservation of the life, the liberty, health, limbs or goods of another. . . .

> And here we have the plain difference between the state of Nature and the state of war, which, however, some men have confounded, are as far distant as a state of peace, goodwill, mutual assistance, and preservation; and a state of enmity, malice, violence, and mutual destruction are one from another. Men living together according to reason without a common superior on earth, with authority to judge between them, is properly the state of Nature. But force, or a declared design of force upon the person of another, where there is no common superior on earth to appeal to for relief, is the state of war. . . .

> God having made man such a creature, that in His own judgment it was not good for him to be alone, put him under strong obligations of necessity, convenience, and inclination, to drive him into society as well as fitted him with understanding and language to continue and enjoy it. The first society was between man and wife, which gave beginning to that between parents and children, to which, in time, that between master and servant came to be added. And though these might, and commonly did, meet together and make up but one family, wherein the master or mistress of it had some sort of rule proper to a family, each of these, or all together, came short of a " political society "; as we shall see if we consider the different ends, ties, and bounds of each of these.[56]

Bossuet, Ecclesiastical Lucretius. — The French apologist of monarchy, Bossuet (1627–1704), in his *Politics as Derived from the Very Words of the Holy Scriptures,* and his *Discourse on Universal History,* conceived of a state of nature prior to civil society which bore many points of resemblance to that pictured by Lucretius. The following is perhaps the best summary of Bossuet's view of the development of man from savagery:

To begin with, there have always been evidences of the origins of things, not merely in the earliest times, but also in far later periods. In reviewing this development one beholds laws being established, customs being refined and empires being created. The human race generally emerges from ignorance, is taught by experience, and invents and perfects the arts of life. Just in proportion as the numbers of men increase, the earth is populated from place to place. Men cross mountains and ravines; they traverse rivers and seas and settle new homes. The land, which was in the beginning nothing but a vast forest, became transformed. The levelled forests gave way to open fields, to pasture lands, to hamlets, to straggling villages, and, finally, to cities. Mankind then learned how to capture certain types of animals, and to domesticate some and adapt them to their use. At first men invented weapons, which man later turned against his own species. Nimrod, the first warrior and conqueror of history, is also called in the Scriptures a mighty hunter. Along with the animals man learned how to utilize fruits and vegetables. He further adapted metals to his service, and ultimately made all nature serve him.[57]

Vico and the sensus numinis. — The highly original Italian writer on history and jurisprudence, Vico (1668–1774), had rather a novel opinion concerning the original condition of mankind, for he held that the natural state of mankind was social and that any non-social condition was a fall or deviation from this natural state. He had two theories of the life of primitive man, one applying to the Hebrews and the other to the Gentiles. In both cases they originated in the same Paradise, and the same Fall and Deluge cursed both. That is to say, both were descendants of Adam. After the flood, however, there was a differentiation. The Hebrews continued their development, never passing through a period of barbarism. The Gentile nations, however, were plunged into the most wretched savagery after the Deluge and were rescued from this condition and brought into society only by the medium of a religious consciousness aroused by the common response to the terrors of nature. Flint has thus summed up Vico's doctrines concerning the Gentiles:

He imagined them to have lost the use of all the higher faculties characteristic of man; to have ceased to have any religious notions; to have become incapable of speech; to have taken to walk on all fours as frequently as on their legs; to have retained, however, their animal instincts and passions, and even, for reasons which are given, but which would be unprofitable to repeat, to have increased notably in bodily size and strength. Vico's giants, whom he identifies, of course, with the giants of the book of Genesis, the Cyclops of Homer, and the Titans of Greek mythology, are the descendants of men, but rather beasts than men, being not even distinguished from other animals by an habitually erect posture and bipedal progression, enormously strong, hairy, filthy, ferocious, solitary, speechless, godless, with no sense of duty, without bonds of marriage, not burying their dead. . . . The description of them and even of their surroundings — for they are supposed to have lived during a diluvial period among woods and marshes — closely resembles that given of primitive men by many modern ethnologists. . . .

As the diluvial earth dried up there were violent thunder storms, the terrors of which worked a mighty change in the minds of some of the giants, causing them to regard the heavens as angry, to feel that there was a supernatural power above them, and to take refuge, male and female, in caves and grottoes. The consciousness of a divine presence was accompanied by a sense of shame, which checked brutal lust, and led to the formation of families. Society had thus for its constitutive principle, religion. No other principle, it seemed to Vico, could reasonably be deemed sufficiently powerful to subdue savage men and to unite them into a social group. There could, he thought, be no tribes, no societies, without religion, and religion he supposed to have been occasioned, so far as it was of heathen origin, by terror.[58]

Montesquieu, Opponent of Hobbes. — The celebrated French *philosophe,* Montesquieu (1689–1755), took a view of the state of nature which varied widely from the conception held by Hobbes and those who represented " natural man " as a warlike and fierce being. Montesquieu pictures primordial man as a timid creature, frightened by the rude aspects of nature and guided only by the elementary instincts of self-preservation and reproduction. He held that the common response to the fear of natural phenomena would lead to social life, and that in due time this social life would have a stronger bond than instinct in the desire which man would acquire to live in society, once he had perceived its advantages. But when social life becomes well established, men lose the feeling of weakness which originally impelled them to society, and soon originate a state of war. With Montesquieu, therefore, the state of war is not a phenomenon of the state of nature but of civil society. He says in part:

Man in a state of nature would have the faculty of knowing before he had acquired any knowledge. Plain it is that his first ideas would not be of a speculative nature; he would think of the preservation of his being before he would investigate its origin. Such a man would feel nothing in himself at first but impotency and weakness; his fears and apprehensions would be excessive; as appears from instances of savages found in forests, trembling at the motion of a leaf, and flying from every shadow.

In this state, every man, instead of being sensible of his equality, would fancy himself inferior. There would, therefore, be no danger of their attacking one another; peace would be the first law of nature.

The natural impulse or desire which Hobbes attributes to mankind of subduing one another is far from being well-founded. The idea of empire and dominion is so complex and depends upon so many other notions that it could never be the first which occurred to the human understanding.

Hobbes enquires, " For what reason go men armed, and have locks and keys to fasten their doors, if they be not naturally in a state of war? " But is it not obvious that he attributes to mankind before the establishment of society what can happen but in consequence of this establishment, which furnishes them with motives for hostile attacks and self-defence?

Next to a sense of his weakness, man would soon find that of his wants. Hence, another law of nature would prompt him to seek for nourishment.

Fear, I have observed, would induce men to shun one another, but the marks of this fear being reciprocal, would soon engage them to associate. Besides, this association would quickly follow from the very pleasure one animal feels at the approach of another of the same species. Again, the attraction arising from the difference of sexes would enhance this pleasure, and the natural inclination they have for each other would form a third law.

Besides the sense of instinct which man possesses in common with brutes, he has the advantage of acquired knowledge; and thence arises a second tie, which brutes have not. Mankind have therefore a new motive of uniting; and a fourth law of nature results from the desire of living in society.[59]

Montesquieu, as probably the greatest advocate of the method of observation that had thus far appeared, manifests an attitude toward the natural man which was characteristic of his time. The results of oversea discoveries were becoming known to European thinkers, and they became superficially acquainted with the strange " men of nature " found in both worlds, with consequences much like those accompanying the Ionian age of discovery. For example, men now paid little attention to the attempt to locate the natural man in antiquity; they searched for him in the tales of travelers, who found audiences as receptive as those which greeted Herodotus. It was thought that there were survivals of the natural men still living in the woods, not only of remote countries, but even of Europe, and that if one of these could only be located, men could at last behold the object of age-long curiosity. Haddon, in discussing the work of Blumenbach, describes the most interesting example of this belief of the times and its final overthrow in the field of *scientific* thought. He says:

Within the species " Homo sapiens " Linnaeus included wild or natural man, " Homo sapiens ferus," whose existence was widely believed in at the time. The most authentic case was that of " Wild Peter," the naked brown boy discovered in 1724 in Hanover. He could not speak, and showed savage and brutish habits and only a feeble degree of intelligence. He was sent to London, and, under the charge of Dr. Arbuthnot, became a noted personage, and a subject of keen discussion among philosophers and naturalists. One of his admirers, more enthusiastic than the others, declared that his discovery was more important than that of Uranus, or the discovery of thirty thousand new stars.

Blumenbach alone, apparently, took the trouble to investigate the origin of " Wild Peter," and in the article he wrote on the subject disposed for all time of the belief in the existence of " natural man." He pointed out that when Peter was first met he wore fastened around his neck the torn fragments of a shirt and that the whiteness of his thighs, as compared with the brown of his legs showed that he had been wearing breeches and no stockings. He finally proved that Peter was the dumb child of a widower who had been thrust out of his home by a new step-mother.[60]

Salutary Scepticism: Hume. — Our shrewd Scot, David Hume (1711–1776), had no patience with any such conception as that of a state of nature prior to society, unless it was admitted to be a mere speculative figment constructed for the pleasure of intellectual activity. He held that the very characteristics and needs of human nature would make men social from the beginning, and that the conception of a pre-social state of nature was not different, as regards remoteness from reality, from the golden age hymned by the poets. The only difference between the two concepts was that the former described a mythical age of war; the latter an equally mythical condition of primitive bliss.[61]

Rousseau the Romantic. — As was usually the case with most of his opinions on philosophical subjects, Rousseau (1712–1778) showed considerable inconsistency (ably demonstrated by Lovejoy) in his doctrine of the state of nature. In his earliest treatment of the subject in the *Discourse on the Origin and Foundation of Inequality among Men,* he represents man in the state of nature as a free and easy-going savage, guided by instinct, devoid of cares and worries, and concerned merely with his own welfare. It was a blissful age of the purest savagery, devoid of any of the contaminations of civilization. With the exception of that short period centering about the origin of society and the industrial arts before inequality and private property had become permanently established, this natural state of man is represented to be the happiest of all the periods of human existence.[62] In his *Émile,* Rousseau attempts to discover the natural man by hypothetically removing from him all the additions that can be ascribed to the effect of society and its institutions. Taine has given the following graphic summary of Rousseau's attitude toward natural man as put forward in the *Émile:*

Strip off the artificial habits of civilized man, his superfluous wants, his false prejudices; scatter all systems, return to your own heart, listen to the intimate sentiments, permit yourself to be guided by the light of instinct and conscience; and you will rediscover that primitive Adam, like to a statue of incorruptible marble that, fallen into a marsh, has long been buried under a crust of mold and slime, but that rescued from its enclosing filth, can again be placed on its pedestal in all the perfection of its form and in all the purity of its whiteness.[63]

Nevertheless, Rousseau in his *Social Contract* represents the natural state of man as being essentially barbarous and unsafe, " so that the human race would perish unless it changed the manner of its existence." In fact, it is only by entering civil society that man really becomes human and gains that power of self-control which is the only true liberty.[64]

A few of the more pertinent of Rousseau's different descriptions of the state of nature appear below:

Let us conclude, then, that man in a state of nature, wandering up and down the forests, without industry, without speech, and without home, an equal stranger to war and to all ties, neither standing in need of his fellow-creatures nor having any desire to hurt them, and perhaps even not distinguishing them from one another; let us conclude that, being self-sufficient and subject to so few passions, he could have no feelings or knowledge but such as befitted his situation; that he felt only his actual necessities, and disregarded everything he did not think himself immediately concerned to notice, and that his understanding made no greater progress than his vanity. If by accident he made any discovery, he was the less able to communicate it to others, as he did not know even his own children. Every art would necessarily perish with its inventor, where there was no kind of education among men, and generations succeeded generations without the least advance; when, all setting out from the same point, centuries must have elapsed in the barbarism of the first ages; when the race was already old, and man remained a child.[65]

Contrast this with the following selections from the *Social Contract:*

I suppose men to have reached the point at which the obstacles in the way of their preservation in the state of nature show their power of resistance to be greater than the resources at the disposal of each individual for his maintenance in that state. The primitive condition can then subsist no longer; and the human race would perish unless it changes its manner of existence.

The passage from the state of nature to the civil state produces a very remarkable change in man, by substituting justice for instinct in his conduct, and giving his actions the morality they had formerly lacked. . . . Although in this state he deprives himself of some advantages which he got from nature, he gains in return others so great, his faculties are so stimulated and developed, his ideas so extended, his feelings so ennobled, and his whole soul so uplifted, that, did not the abuses of this new condition often degrade him below that which he left, he would be bound to bless continually the happy moment which took him from it forever, and instead of a stupid and unimaginative animal, made him an intelligent being and a man.[66]

Blackstone and the Patriarchal Family. — In his *Commentaries on the Laws of England,* Blackstone (1723–1780) expressly denies the existence of a pre-social state of nature and holds that the patriarchal family furnished the first basis of society. The patriarchal families grew and subdivided and in time became reunited into civil societies through "compulsion," "conquest," or "compact." He concludes that:

The only true and natural foundations of society are the wants and fears of individuals. Not that we can believe with some theoretical writers that there ever was a time when there was no such thing as society, either natural or civil; and that, from the impulse of reason, and through a sense of their wants and weaknesses, individuals met together in a large plain, entered into social contract, and chose the tallest man present to be their governor. This notion of an actually existing unconnected state of nature is too wild to be seriously considered: and besides it is plainly contradictory to the revealed accounts of the primitive origin of mankind, and their preservation two thousand years afterwards; both of which were effected by the means of single families. These formed the first natural society among themselves, which, every day extending its limits, laid the first, though imperfect rudiments of civil or political society: and when it grew too large to subsist with convenience in that pastoral state, wherein the patriarchs appear to have lived, it necessarily subdivided itself by various migrations into more. Afterwards, as agriculture increased, which employs and can maintain a much greater number of hands, migrations became less frequent, and various tribes which had formerly separated, reunited again, sometimes by compulsion and conquest, and sometimes, perhaps, by compact.[67]

The Physiocrats. — The group of French thinkers known variously as the Physiocrats or *Economistes,* probably influenced by Aristotle, used the term "natural" primarily in the sense of

" normal " and " perfect " rather than of " original " or " primitive." They believed in the existence of a natural order in the universe which had been revealed by Newton and his fellow-scientists; all that conformed to this was perfect and destined to succeed, while all that deviated was evil and abnormal just· in proportion as it departed from the natural line of procedure. According to this conception it was preposterous to advise a return to the primitive order to reach an ideal condition: all that was necessary was to discover the laws of the cosmic process and conform one's actions to them. Hence to the Physiocrats the state of nature meant a state of full and complete development and not a rude, primitive, or undeveloped condition.[68]

Ferguson the Profound. — One of the earliest and best applications of this doctrine of the natural state of man, viewed in the historical and analytical sense, was made by the Scottish writer, Adam Ferguson (1723–1816), in his *Essay on the History of Civil Society.*[69] This book has until very recently been sadly neglected, but it was unquestionably the most profound and accurate study of social development made in the eighteenth century — one which quite dwarfs Montesquieu's attempt from the standpoint of philosophic insight and historical accuracy in dealing with the fundamental problems of social development.[70] In this respect, it was probably matched only by Turgot's famous *Discourses* at the Sorbonne.

The chief reflections made by Ferguson on the state of nature may be summed up as follows: Many have foolishly considered man as being in the beginning different in kind from what he is at present, and have either pictured him as a mere beast or as excessively warlike. The natural historian, in treating all other members of the animal kingdom, collects concrete observations of actual conditions; when he comes to man, however, he thinks that he must substitute " hypothesis instead of reality, and confounds the provinces of imagination and reason, of poetry and science." If we want to know about man we must study him as we actually find him at present in the varied conditions of development; and if we want to know his real characteristics the thing to do is to study him under normal conditions, not in unnatural or forced circumstances. Hence, even if we could catch a wild man in the woods he would be no criterion by which to judge of the natural condition of mankind, but would be at the opposite pole from a natural human being. Ferguson reflects the theological anthropology and psychology of his time, however, by stating that man is different in kind from all other animals, and that therefore

nothing of his real characteristics can be discovered from studying the habits of animals.

Moreover, art (culture!) is not to be separated from nature,
for art as practiced seems to be the most natural characteristic
of man: he is continually endeavoring artificially to improve his
material conditions. The state of nature may be discovered where-
ever man is living naturally, in harmony with his surroundings,
as much in Great Britain as at the Cape of Good Hope or the
Straits of Magellan. Merely because man has begun to improve is
no reason to hold that he has left the state of nature; rather, the
more progress he makes the more natural he may be assumed to
have become. The terms "natural" and "unnatural" as applied
to human conduct are misnomers. All of the acts of man are natural. Really pertinent questions would be: What is just or unjust?
What is happy or wretched? What conditions are favorable or
unfavorable to the development of the better nature of mankind.[71]
On the whole, Ferguson was one of the first writers to anticipate
the modern anthropological tendency to minimize the difference
between "primitive" and modern man,[72] as well as to point out
some of the dangerous confusions implicit in the use of the vague
term "nature."

Burke the Uncertain. — Just what Edmund Burke (1729–
1797) thought about the state of nature is rather difficult to
determine, for his work on that subject, *A Vindication of Natural
Society,* was in the nature of an ironical satire upon the thinkers
of "the school of nature," particularly of the Rousseauan variety.
Burke first pictures the evils of the state of nature, and then
proceeds to show that the establishment of political society only
increased the misery. He points out how, in regard to external
relations, political society has inflicted countless wars upon man,
and how, internally considered, political society has ground man
down by means of the worst type of Machiavellian oppression.
All forms of government are more or less despotic, and their
evils far outnumber the good they are able to bestow. Finally,
civil society brings not only political oppression but also economic tyranny and the unequal distribution of wealth.[73] The whole
presentation is intended as a *reductio ad absurdum,* and although
it succeeds fairly well, still one may legitimately ask with Rogers
whether Burke "does not dismiss too easily the vision he has
conjured up." [74] Burke's description of the state of nature is of
the more common type, and runs as follows:

> In the state of nature, without question, mankind was subjected to
> many and great inconveniences. Want of union, want of mutual as-

sistance, want of a common arbitrator to resort to in their differences. These were evils which they could not but have felt pretty severely on many occasions. The original children of the earth lived with their brethren of the other kinds in much equality. Their diet must have been confined almost wholly to the vegetable kind; and the same tree, which in its flourishing state produced them berries, in its decay gave them an habitation. The mutual desire of the sexes uniting their bodies and affections, and the children which are the results of these intercourses, introduced first the notion of society, and taught its conveniences. This society founded on natural appetites and instincts, and not on any positive institution, I shall call natural society.[75]

Although Burke was no apologist for, but rather a fierce critic of, the view that this condition was the best in man's experience, still it seems reasonable to suppose that the above selection does not come far from presenting his real views regarding its concrete nature.

Original Sociability Once More: Paine. — In his *Common Sense* Thomas Paine (1737–1809) gives the familiar summary of social evolution which represents man as originally sociable because of the advantages of mutual aid, but without political control. This tends toward that condition of anarchy which renders the establishment of government a necessity for the restoration of order:

In order to gain a clear and just idea of the design and end of government, let us suppose a small number of persons settled in some sequestered part of the earth, unconnected with the rest; they will then represent the first peopling of any country, or of the world. In this state of natural liberty, society will be their first thought. A thousand motives will excite them thereto; the strength of one man is so unequal to his wants, and his mind so unfitted for perpetual solitude, that he is soon obliged to seek assistance . . . of another, who in turn, requires the same. . . .

Thus, necessity, like a gravitating power, would soon form our newly arrived emigrants into society, the reciprocal blessings of which would supersede, and render the obligations of law and government unnecessary while they remained perfectly just to each other; but as nothing but Heaven is impregnable to vice, it will unavoidably happen that in proportion as they surmount the first difficulties of emigration, which bound them together in a common cause, they will begin to relax in their duty and attachment to each other: and this remissness will point out the necessity of establishing some form of government to supply the defect of moral virtue.[76]

Kant's Similarity to Hobbes. — In considering the natural state of man Immanuel Kant (1724–1804) took practically the same ground as Hobbes. He held that men in an unregulated state of nature were in a state of violence and misery because of the anti-social and egoistic impulses of human nature. The only way to escape this was to establish civil society through a contract which was inviolable when once agreed to. The chief difference between his views and those of Hobbes was that Kant was even more in-clined to view the state of nature and the social contract as specu-lative postulates rather than as concrete historical realities.[77]

Utilitarian Analysis: Bentham. — A writer who has received considerable credit for his distinction between natural and politi-cal society is Jeremy Bentham (1748–1832), but it seems that all that is new in his conception is the elaborateness of his analysis. He asserts that the criterion for differentiating between the two states is the presence of the habit of obedience to a superior au-thority in the case of political society, and the absence of such a habit in a natural society:

> The idea of a natural society is a *negative* one. The idea of a political society is a *positive* one. 'Tis with the latter, therefore, we should begin.

> When a number of persons (whom we may style subjects) are sup-posed to be in the *habit* of paying *obedience* to a person, or an assemblage of persons, of a known and certain description (whom we may call *gov-ernor* or *governors*) such persons altogether (*subjects* and *governors*) are said to be in a state of *political society*.

> The idea of a *natural society,* is, as we have said, a *negative* one. When a number of persons are supposed to be in the habit of *conversing* with each other, at the same time that they are not in any such habit as men-tioned above, they are said to be in a state of *natural society*.[78]

This conception had been common in substance through the ages. What Bentham did was to give it more definite statement and qualification, and to analyze the meaning of the differentia-tion with greater acuteness than any predecessor.

Bentham may be taken as representative of the Utilitarian phi-losophers whose work culminated in John Stuart Mill, and who justified government by the material advantages conferred by it.

Ideas of Progress. — One of the most significant changes dur-ing the period from 1600 to 1850 was the gradual emergence of a theory of progress, as will be set forth in detail in the next chap-ter. Down to this time the prevailing view had been one of a decline from a primitive paradise or golden age. Now the attitude was gradually reversed, and writers came to conceive of man as having developed contemporary civilization from a lower and ruder type of culture. A more hopeful view of history thus became possible. Francis Bacon contended that the present generation was wiser than any of its predecessors, and presented an eloquent statement of the advantages which might come from the development of applied science.[79] Vico denied the Classical view of recurring cycles of development and postulated a spiral theory of progress.[80] Turgot, in his Sorbonne Discourse of 1750, set forth clearly the doctrine of the continuity of history and the cumulative nature of progress.[81] Kant endeavored to state the laws of progress and to demonstrate the reality of moral progress.[82] Condorcet formulated a theory of the development of successive stages of civilization and predicted remarkable advances in the century to come, as a result of the French Revolution and the application of science to human betterment.[83] Godwin expected much from the solution of human and social problems through the application of reason.[84] Saint-Simon advocated the creation of a science of social welfare, and Auguste Comte worked out in many of its major phases the first comprehensive scheme for the furtherance of what he conceived to be human progress.[85]

Summary of the Chapter. — We first noted the numerous meanings of "primitive" and "natural" and then considered the normative conceptions. Thereafter, with accompanying analysis, attention was called to the similarity of preliterate and Oriental tales of human origin and development. Through a combination of historical circumstances the Hebrew interpretation, somewhat modified by Greek philosophy, became the basis for all orthodox Western views of social evolution. For the most part, the Greeks conceived of a decline from a golden age which parallels somewhat the Hebrew fall from innocence; the views of the Epicureans seem Hobbesian in contrast to this. Lucretius, among the Romans, followed the Epicurean trend; Horace shared his views. Seneca was the chief Roman exponent of the theory of a primitive golden age and subsequent decline, and his ideas seem to have been followed by the Roman Lawyers in their distinction between the *jus naturale* and the *jus gentium.*

In the Patristic period, we find the Fathers incorporating Seneca's doctrine in their theology. Following this, interest in the primordial state of man lagged somewhat; but when canon law took a definite form in the twelfth century, Patristic views on the subject reappeared. Aquinas adhered to Aristotle's concept of the natural sociability of man. Marsiglio of Padua believed in a utilitarian basis of society; he agreed with Aquinas, however, in considering government necessary. Æneas Sylvius regarded the condition of mankind after the expulsion from Eden as the state of nature.

Coming to early modern social philosophy, we find Machiavelli's approach analytical and psychological rather than historical. Bodin approximated the idea of a violent pre-social state, followed by a period when the " social instinct " expanded to include groups wider than the family. All through this period views of the state of nature were influenced by both pagan and Christian doctrines.

Attempting to justify political society and the national state, social philosophers of the seventeenth and eighteenth centuries posited a natural condition full of misery and danger. Hooker, Mariana, Hobbes, and, less consistently, Grotius represented this point of view. Milton, in contrast, followed the Patristic tradition. Spinoza believed that in a state of nature any means were permissible to attain the object of desire, but that men gradually found it advisable to obtain the advantages of a well-ordered social life. Pufendorf developed two theories of the state of nature, but concluded that the historical did not bear out the speculative view. Locke was firm in his claim for the historicity of the natural state, thereby differing from Pufendorf. Bossuet's views were reminiscent of the Epicureans, Lucretius, and Hobbes. Vico's distinction between Hebrew and Gentile post-diluvial development diversified his theories. Montesquieu held quite different views, believing " natural man " to have been a timid creature who became warlike only after he had lost the feeling of weakness which was the basis for the origin of society. Hume discredited both a golden age and a pre-social state of nature, and declared that human needs made men social from the beginning. Rousseau's writings reveal at least two distinct doctrines of the state of nature: his well-known blissful age of the care-free savage, and a later description of the natural state as barbarous. Blackstone denied the pre-social state of nature, and conceived society as developing from the family.

The Physiocrats used the term " natural " to imply the normal and perfect rather than the original or primitive. Ferguson, with the same conception of the natural state, made a study of social development surpassing anything of the kind done in the eighteenth century; it appears quite recent in its minimizing of differences between " primitive " and modern man. Both Burke and Paine discussed the natural state, but made no outstanding contributions to the controversy. Kant followed Hobbes closely, but was much more dubious about the historicity of the state of nature and the social contract. Bentham made an elaborate but not particularly original analysis of the distinction between natural and political society.

These various theories all figured in one way or another in the development of the idea of progress.

Although it may be thought that speculative theories of man's natural state today have interest only for the antiquarian (and in some respects this is quite correct), it is not amiss to point out that such speculation exerts tremendous influence even now.

For example, Freud in his *Totem and Taboo* (1912) constructed an elaborate state of nature study in which he argues that the Oedipus complex which resulted from the practice of father-murder among certain tribal peoples gave rise to the institution of exogamy — incest taboo — among these peoples. Covering one aspect of what Lovejoy has termed the marital state of nature, Freud's story was repeated in his last book, *Moses and Mono-theism,* published in 1939, the last year of his life. Today, among orthodox Freudians, the story is gospel; through the inheritance of acquired charac-teristics *(sic)* all human beings whatsoever harbor the Oedipus complex. Here see Becker, *Man in Reciprocity* (New York: Praeger, 1956), chap. xvii, "The Freudian Family Romance and What It Is Worth," pp. 246-56.

Lovejoy's economic state of nature, together with the juristic and the tech-nological, are today offered as part of the orthodox Marxian package. Would anyone conversant with current events view that package as of no importance for social thought? For Marx, human society was originally classless because there was no private property, and it will again become classless, albeit at "a higher level," when private property is abolished. Here see the volume cited at the end of the preceding paragraph, chap. xx, pp. 280-99.

Interest in the natural state of man has also been manifested in fairly recent studies of "wild man" or feral man. Books by Singh and Zingg, Gesell, and others have been the result, and the very last article by W. F. Ogburn pub-lished in the *American Journal of Sociology* represented an attempt on his part to demolish what he called the myth of wild children — in particular, children presumably reared by wolves. The eighteenth-century Blumenbach has had a twentieth-century successor!

In one sense, of course, the studies just mentioned focus on the *un*natural state of man—that is to say, on children presumably brought up without normal sociation with other human beings. Kingsley Davis's well-known study of Anna falls in the same category; see his *Human Society* (New York: Macmillan, 1949), pp. 204-08.

CHAPTER XIII

The Rise of a Conception of Progress

ATTITUDE TOWARD PROGRESS BEFORE MODERN TIMES. — It is a fact worth noting that such actual advance in human culture as was achieved down to the close of the Middle Ages was effected without any clearly formulated theory of human progress. In preliterate societies, with their well-marked mental immobility, there is little if any opportunity for a doctrine of progress to arise. In Oriental antiquity much the same attitude prevailed as among preliterates — indeed, conservatism was more thoroughly organized and more consciously defended and maintained.

There were, however, at least two exceptions to this general rule. One was the social protest of certain Egyptians, writing near the close of the third millennium B.C., who denounced the injustices of their day and expressed their hope of a better future. Linked with this was the Messianic hope of the Jews, particularly as it developed during the days of their persecution following the Babylonian, Assyrian, and Greek conquests of Palestine. There was also doubtless some idea of progress in the reforms of the famous Amenhotep IV (Ikhnaton) of Egypt, designated by Breasted as " the first individual in history."

Among the pagans the dominating views were either those of a decline from a golden age, or those of the cyclical theory of history which represented human development as a series of repetitions of advance and decline forever returning to the first starting-point. The doctrine of a decline from a golden age, hinted at by Hesiod and Homer, was clearly enunciated by Seneca, and was later identified by the Christians with the period of Paradise and perfection before the Fall. The cyclical theory of history was best formulated by Plato, Aristotle, and others, in connection with Classical theories of the state. It was held that governments tended to pass from monarchy to tyranny, from tyranny to aristocracy, from aristocracy to oligarchy, from oligarchy to democracy, from democracy to anarchy, and from anarchy back to monarchy, thus starting the cycle afresh. Other Classical philosophers still further elaborated the notion and represented civilization as repeating itself in successive ages with great exactness. In the case of both the golden-age doctrine and the cyclical theory there was little place for the notion of progressive advances in civilization.

In their outlook upon secular affairs the Christians likewise offered little quarter to the theory of progress. They accepted the Hebraic doctrine of the Fall, and therefore placed the best period of human civilization in the remote past; perfection had existed at the outset and could never be regained in any appreciable degree. To be sure, the Christians held that even secular conditions had notably improved following the advent and triumph of Christianity. The best expression of this attitude was contained in Orosius's *Seven Books of History Against the Pagans;* here were contrasted the horrors and miseries of the earlier pagan civilization with the happier lot of mankind after the coming of Christianity. Yet the Christian writers never contended for a moment that any secular condition approximating paradise could be attained on this planet — indeed, there was a tendency to discourage interest in secular reforms for fear that they might distract the faithful from the much more important problem of spiritual salvation. In the place of the secular theory of mundane progress the Christians built up an elaborate eschatology; they looked forward to an imminent day of judgment after which the earth would pass away. Further, the belief that the end of the régime of man upon the earth was likely to come soon created a definite temporal obstacle to any belief or interest in progress. A theory of secular progress is only compatible with the parallel assumption of the long duration of the human civilization on our planet. In our own day ultra-Modernist Christians who have abandoned the older belief in eschatology and reject the orthodox conception of a literal heaven and hell accept the theory of progress with evangelical enthusiasm, but their attitude bears little resemblance to orthodox Christianity, Catholic or Protestant, up to the nineteenth century.

Early Anticipations of a Theory of Progress. — Perhaps the earliest symptom of a vision of mundane progress in Christendom may be identified in a curious letter written by Roger Bacon shortly after the middle of the thirteenth century. Although Bacon was interested in promoting the experimental method, he was primarily a medieval man at heart, and he proposed to make use of the newly acquired information for specifically medieval ends, such as getting out better editions of the Bible and Aristotle, clearing up problems in Scriptural geography and chronology, and locating heaven and hell more exactly. Nevertheless, in a letter on the ultimate effects of applied science he drew a striking picture of future technological progress, all of which has subsequently been realized. We herewith reproduce the more important sections of this remarkable prophecy:

> I will now enumerate the marvelous results of art and nature which will make all kinds of magic appear trivial and unworthy. Instruments for navigation can be made which will do away with the necessity of rowers, so that great vessels, both in rivers and on the sea, shall be borne about with only a single man to guide them and with greater speed than if they were full of men. And carriages can be constructed to move without animals to draw them, and with incredible velocity. Machines for flying can be made in which a man sits and turns an ingenious device by which skillfully contrived wings are made to strike the air in the manner of a flying bird. Then arrangements can be devised, compact in themselves, for raising and lowering weights indefinitely great. . . . Bridges can be constructed ingeniously so as to span rivers without any supports.[1]

The first appearance of theories of progress on any extended scale came in the seventeenth and eighteenth centuries. Two factors seem to have been chiefly responsible for this. One was the rise of modern natural science and the perception of the possibility of applying its results to human betterment; *all* seemed gold that glittered. A second strong stimulus to the growth of theories of progress was the effect of the oversea expansion: by observing mankind in different "stages" of cultural development philosophically-inclined persons were led to conceive of the reality of social evolution from primitive culture to modern times. In the eighteenth century the rising humanitarian movement supplied a strong incentive to the theory of progress, inasmuch as men were led to formulate plans for escaping from existing abuses by building a better social order.

The three great philosophers who first gave evidence of being influenced by the rise of modern science and the discoveries overseas, Montaigne, Francis Bacon, and Descartes, all made contributions of no little moment to the development of the conception of progress. Montaigne's chief contribution here lay in his insistence that the purpose of human learning should be to teach mankind how to live more successfully. This was a complete repudiation of the Christian objectives, and by implication involved a conviction that philosophy, if turned into secular channels, might be able to improve man's earthly circumstances. Another phase of Montaigne's independence was his capacity to criticize candidly those Classical writers whose ideas or style bored or irritated him. Although an enthusiastic Humanist, he was not bound down by the current theories attributing complete perfection to each and every ancient worthy.

Francis Bacon achieved a definite advance over the famous thirteenth-century bearer of his surname. Francis not only agreed with Roger in accepting the inductive and experimental methods as the only valid road to the acquisition of new knowledge, but he also rejected the medieval interest in theology as the prime center of intellectual activity. He not only accepted the scientific method, but proposed to apply its results to non-religious purposes: namely, the improvement of the secular estate of mankind. (We should overestimate Bacon's receptivity to innovation, however, if we were to forget his fear of "commixture of manners.") Bacon expressed his conception of the methods and limitations of the Scholastic philosophers in the following graphic words: "Having sharp and strong wits, and abundance of leisure, and small variety of reading, (but their wits being shut up in the cells of a few authors, chiefly Aristotle their dictator, as their persons were shut up in the cells of monasteries and colleges), and knowing little history, either of nature or time, they did, out of no great quantity of matter, and infinite agitation of wit, spin out unto us those laborious webs of learning, which are extant in their books." The futility of the speculative method as a means of acquiring new knowledge was aptly stated in the famous phrase: "Nature is more subtle than any argument." [2]

One of Bacon's most relevant contributions to the basis of a theory of progress lay in his denunciation of the current tendency to look back to the ancients as the source of extensive and infallible wisdom. Bacon correctly held that the latest generation is always the real collection of "ancients." As a mature man is considered wiser than a child, so with the development of civilization we may expect a greater accumulation of knowledge in recent generations than in those of antiquity. Bacon expresses this attitude toward the past in the following language:

Again there is another great and powerful cause why the sciences have made but little progress; which is this. It is not possible to run a course aright when the goal itself has not been rightly placed. Now the true and lawful goal of the sciences is none other than this; that human life be endowed with new discoveries and powers . . .

Again, men have been kept back as by a kind of enchantment from progress in the sciences by reverence for antiquity, by the authority of men accounted great in philosophy, and then by general consent. . . .

As for antiquity, the opinion touching it which men entertain is quite a negligent one, and scarcely consonant with the word itself. For the old age of the world is to be accounted the true antiquity; and this is the attribute of our own times, not of that earlier age of the world in which the ancients lived; and which, though in respect of us it was the elder, yet in respect of the world it was the younger. And truly as we look for greater knowledge of human things and a riper judgment in the old man than in the young, because of his experience and the number and variety of the things which he has seen and heard and thought of; so in like manner from our age, if it but knew its own strength and chose to essay and exert it, much more might fairly be expected than from the ancient times, inasmuch as it is a more advanced age of the world, and stored and stocked with infinite experiments and observations.

Now must it go for nothing that by the distant voyages and travels which have become frequent in our times, many things in nature have been laid open and discovered which may let in new light upon philosophy. And surely it would be disgraceful if, while the regions of the material globe, — that is, of the earth, of the sea, and of the stars, — have been in our times laid widely open and revealed, the intellectual globe should remain shut up within the narrow limits of old discoveries. . . .

Not is it only the admiration of antiquity, authority, and consent, that has forced the industry of man to rest satisfied with the discoveries already made; but also an admiration for the works themselves of which the human race has long been in possession.[3]

René Descartes's most important generalization bearing on the theory of progress was the declaration in his *Discourse on Method* to the effect that the philosopher must resolutely cut himself off from past authority and reject preconceived notions, for only by so doing can he expect to arrive at a sound and coherent body of knowledge. It is true, of course, that Descartes, like Bacon, was not entirely consistent. For example, he constructed his epistemology upon one of the most archaic and untenable of the fruits of speculation: namely, Anselm's ontological proof of the existence of God. Nevertheless, his enunciation of the principle of freedom from the illusions of the past was notable. We reproduce it in part:

As for eloquence and poetry, which are the subject of principal dispute between the ancients and moderns, although they are not very important in themselves, I believe that the ancients can have reached perfection, because, as I said, it can be reached in a few centuries, and I don't pretend to know exactly how many it takes. . . .

Were the great men of this century truly charitable, they would warn posterity not to over-admire them, and to aspire always at least to equal them. Nothing is such an impediment to progress, nothing hinders men-

tal development so much, as excessive admiration of the ancients. Because men had dedicated themselves to the authority of Aristotle and
sought for truth only in his enigmatical writings, and never in nature,
not only did philosophy wholly cease to advance but she plunged into
an abyss of bombast and unintelligible ideas, from which it cost a world
of pains to extricate her. Aristotle has never created a true philosopher;
but he has stifled a good many who might have become such had circumstances permitted. And the misfortune is that a prejudice of this
kind, once firmly established among men, is there for a long time; it
will take whole centuries to get away from it, even after its absurdity
has come to be recognized. Were men some day to develop an infatuation
for Descartes and put him in the place of Aristotle, there would be about
the same difficulty to contend with.[4]

Fontenelle, First Systematic Exponent of Progress. — It was
a disciple of Descartes, Bernard le Bouvier de Fontenelle (1657–
1757), who may be said to have formulated the first fairly
thorough and consistent theory of progress. His first work along
this line was his *Dialogues of the Dead,* published in 1683. It
was chiefly a dialogue between Socrates and Montaigne, in which
Socrates assumed that the moderns had advanced far beyond
the civilization of the ancients, whereas Montaigne denied that
this was true. The implied conclusion of the book was that civilization is essentially static. On the whole, although it contained many
interesting and satirical passages, it was rather an illogical and
disappointing performance, but it did at least abandon the conception that either the Christian or the pagan past was remarkably superior to the civilization of the seventeenth century.

Five years later, however, he published a brief but much more
trenchant work, *A Digression on the Ancients and the Moderns.*
He maintained therein the following five fundamental principles:
(1) from a biological standpoint the ancients were certainly not
superior to the moderns, for human nature has remained essentially the same since pagan times; (2) in the fields of science and
industry, where one achievement is built upon another, progress is
cumulative, and here the moderns have advanced far beyond the
ancients; (3) this does not mean that the moderns possess greater
innate capacity, but rather that they have been able to build upon
the original achievements of the ancients; (4) in the realm of
poetry and oratory, which are spontaneous expressions of human
nature, the ancients were great — perhaps perfect — but there is
no reason for doubting that the moderns can equal them; (5) at
all events, unreasoning admiration of the ancients is the chief
obstacle to human progress. The following passages embody representative examples of Fontenelle's ideas upon the above points:

If the ancients had intellects superior to ours, then their brains must have been better ordered, fashioned of firmer or more delicate fibres, filled with a higher percentage of animal spirits. But by virtue of what should the brains of that day have been better ordered than ours? Then the trees, too, would have been greater and more beautiful; for if nature was at that time younger and more vigorous, the trees as well as human brains, would certainly have felt the effects of that freshness and that vigor. . . .

The centuries produce no natural difference between men. The climate of Greece or of Italy and that of France are too nearly alike to cause any sensible difference between the Greeks or the Latins and ourselves. Even if they should produce a difference of some sort, it would be very easy to efface, and, finally, it would be no more to their advantage than to ours. We are all, then, perfectly equal, ancients and moderns, Greeks, Latins, and French. . . .

The ancients invented everything, to this fact their partisans point with triumph; hence they had intellects vastly superior to ours: not at all, they simply lived before us. . . . Had we been in their place, we should have done the inventing; were they in ours, they would add to what they found already invented: there is no question about that. . . .

And so, seeing that we are in a position to benefit by the discoveries of the ancients and by their mistakes even, it is not surprising that we surpass them. To merely equal them would mean necessarily that we were of a nature vastly inferior to theirs; it would almost mean that we were not men as well as they.

However, in order that the moderns may always continue to outdo the ancients, circumstances must be propitious. Eloquence and poetry require only a certain rather limited number of views in comparison with other arts, and they depend largely upon the keenness of the imagination. Now men can in a few centuries have accumulated a small number of such views; and the keenness of the imagination has no need of a long succession of experiences, nor of a great many rules, to reach all the perfection of which it is capable. But natural philosophy, medicine, and mathematics are composed of an infinite number of views, and depend upon accuracy of reasoning, which perfects itself very gradually, and is forever perfecting itself; it is often necessary even that they be helped along by experiences which are purely accidental, and which occur when least expected. It is evident that all this is an endless process, and that the most recent natural philosophers or mathematicians must naturally be the most skilled.[5]

Perrault, Believer in Seventeenth-Century Perfection. — An essentially similar view of the problem was set forth in the longer and more discursive work of Charles Perrault (1628–1703), *A Comparison of the Ancients and the Moderns,* which appeared

between 1688 and 1696. He too held that there has been little
or no biological change since ancient times — animals are as
strong and fierce and men as vigorous and intelligent as they ever
were. On the other hand, human knowledge is a cumulative affair;
hence, in the matter of human learning and its application to well-
being there has been remarkable progress since ancient times.
Each generation inherits all that its predecessors have possessed
and adds to this original inheritance such achievements as it has
been able to work out for itself. Perrault was not unpardonably
proud of the remarkable advances in science which had been made
in the seventeenth century — more notable, he said, than the sum
total of the performances in this field in the whole pagan period.
This eulogistic attitude led Perrault to regard his age as having
arrived at perfection, and this view of affairs naturally left little
hope for or interest in the future:

I admit that the ancients will always have the advantage of having
been the first to invent many things, but I shall maintain that the moderns have invented more ingenious and marvelous things. . . .

We need only read the French and English journals and glance over
the notable achievements of the Academies of these two great kingdoms
to be convinced that during the last twenty or thirty years more discoveries have been made in the science of nature than during the whole
extent of learned antiquity. I am not surprised that old men past the
age of receiving new ideas persist in their old prejudices, and prefer to
hold to what they have read in Aristotle than to that which men try to
teach them in their old age. . . .

As for myself, I confess I hold myself fortunate to know what happiness we enjoy, and that I take great pleasure in glancing back over all
the earlier centuries, where I see the birth and the growth of everything,
but where I see nothing which has not received new growth and new lustre
in the times in which we live. I rejoice to see our century arrived in
some sort at the highest perfection. And since for some years now progress has been much slower, and seems almost imperceptible, just as the
days seem to discontinue to lengthen as they approach the Solstice, I
have the further joy of thinking that very likely we have not many things
for which to envy those who will come after us.[6]

Vico, Philosopher of History. — With the Italian philosopher
of history, Gian Battista Vico (1668–1744), the discussion of
the idea of progress passed beyond the somewhat sophomoric debate concerning the merits of the ancients and the moderns and
attained the status of a preliminary effort to reconstruct the history of civilization and to formulate the principles which govern
the development of society. Flint gives him the honor of being the

first great writer on political and social theory to make a systematic application of the historical method:

The distinctive honour of Vico as a writer on jurisprudence was, that he was the first to expound and apply in an explicit, self-consistent, and systematic manner, the principles of the historical method. Aristotle, Machiavelli, Bodin, and others, had clearly taught that history is a source of political instruction; that the comparison of the constitutions and laws of governments of all forms, and under the most varied circumstances, is indispensable as a means of forming political science; and that the legislation which suits one age or nation will not suit another. By laying down these truths, they had certainly approximated to the historical method. But they only approximated to it. Vico actually adopted it, and adopted it as deliberately and decidedly as did Savigny.[7]

Vico's philosophy of history was psycho-sociological in essence, though he has been claimed by some as a geographical determinist and by others as a social determinist. His basic thesis was that the stages of social evolution are determined by the nature of the mental outlook and evaluations of man in the successive periods of his development. This is the doctrine of Comte and Lamprecht; namely, the interpretation of history in terms of the changes in the " collective mentality."

Vico grasped with great philosophic insight one basic doctrine: viz., that social development has been a general and comprehensive movement in which all factors have evolved simultaneously and not separately. As Flint tells us:

Vico took a particularly firm grasp of one of the truths most essential to the comprehension of history, yet one which even many recent theorists have ignored or inadequately recognized — the truth, namely, that all the constituent elements of human nature, all the great factors of human life, are evolved contemporaneously and not successively. He saw that social development is a general or collective movement, inclusive of a number of particular developments, which are not mere stages of the general development, but pervade it from beginning to end, running parallel to one another, and acting and reacting on one another. He saw that in order to know any one important phase of man's nature or history in a philosophical manner, all others must be in some measure known; that in history one faculty, or group of faculties, is not developed after another, seeing that humanity moves always and everywhere as a whole, the life of the whole flowing through each part.[8]

In one notable respect, however, his theory in this regard was erroneous. Although he comprehended social development as a philosophic unity, yet he contended that each nation had evolved its culture independently of all others, a proposition which is of only curious historical interest at present — unless one takes Spengler seriously.

Vico saw everything in history in a threefold division: " There were three kinds of nature, three types of character, three epochs of religion, three species of language, of writing, of governments, of natural law, of jurisprudence, of legal judgments, etc." [9] Although Flint would seem to contend that this was a more or less logical and tenable division, it appears more probable that, as Dunning says, " Vico's triopsis is at some points rather forced and unreal, yet he presents on the whole a very remarkable interpretation of institutions social and political, in connection with the various phases of human government." [10]

Quite in harmony with his threefold division of minor subjects was his three-stage theory of historical development. (This differed considerably from the famous scheme presented by Comte a century later, though the first stage in each plan was identical.) These stages are: first, the divine stage, or the age of the gods; second, the heroic stage; and third, the stage of man. These divisions Vico admittedly borrowed from Herodotus and Varro. Throughout all these stages certain great principles had operated which caused and conditioned social development:

The entire course of historical development he held to have been determined by certain principles, chief among which are the belief in Divine Providence, a sense of the need of some tie between the sexes, the reverence for the dead springing from a hope of future life. They have given rise to the institutions of religion, to marriage rites, and funeral ceremonies. These are the true *foedera humanitatis*. They are essential to the maintenance and progress of society. They draw individuals into, and retain them in, society. They attach earth to heaven; they link generation to generation; they connect the present with the past, and lead men onwards step by step into the future. Vico ingeniously describes how the principles mentioned have been gradually unfolded; how their manifestations have varied from age to age; and how, notwithstanding this, they have continuously kept in relation to one another.[11]

The divine stage was essentially identical with the myth-making period. " In this age man, he held, was rude, fierce, emotional. . . . It was the age in which the family was instituted, in which language originated, in which myths were produced, and in which the chief rudiments of civilization were brought to light." [12] The government was patriarchal. The whole of life was religious. The thunders frightened the people; they supposed that the gods were endeavoring to talk to them, and the anxiety or curiosity to know what message they desired to communicate led to divination, the first form of theology. It was also the age of poetry, the poets shaping the minds of others by their vivid pictures in words, and even believing themselves in their awful conceptions. This divine age passed gradually into the next or heroic age.

The heroic age came into being when the patriarchal rulers had conquered those remaining in a lower stage. This gave rise to political and social inequality and constant struggle between the governing and the governed. While the government of this period was essentially aristocratic, the tendency was for the democratic principle to assert itself more and more. Mythological language was in this period largely displaced by metaphorical, and wisdom was still in the hands of the poets. The great poet of this age was Homer, concerning whom Vico held the Wolffian theory: namely, that the Homeric poems are not the work of a single genius but the creation and revelation of a certain great age in human development. Says Flint:

> In spite of many faults and defects, many fanciful and disfiguring traits, Vico's picture of the heroic age must be pronounced a work of great, of unique genius. It surpassed all Greek and Roman fame, showing how little the classical world had comprehended even its own Homer, and how far from having been exhausted was the significance of that world itself. It displayed a combination of critical and constructive power, of sceptical courage and imaginative realisation, of which there had been no previous example in the department of history. It was a prophecy and prefiguration of the achievements alike of a Wolff and Niebuhr, and of a Walter Scott and Augustin Thierry. . . .[13]

The herioc age is in turn superseded by the third and last stage — the human. Flint has succinctly summed up what Vico taught regarding this period:

> In the third or human age writing is alphabetical; language is positive and precise; composition, alike in the form of prose and poetry, is natural and rational; manners are comparatively gentle and refined; civil and political equality are extended, and natural right more honoured than mere legality; justice is administered by tribunals; governments are democracies, or combinations of democracy and monarchy; myths fade away and are forgotten; religion is purified, and aims at diffusing morality, but tends also to extinction in scepticism, and to give place to philosophy.[14]

The human age also has its end. " Refinement issues in effeminacy. Even where civil equality is universally and fully attained, there will still be great inequality as regards wealth, and from that inequality will flow the most grievous evils — luxury and corruption in the rich, envy and aggression in the poor, general discord and disorder." For this state of affairs there are two possible cures, one internal and the other external. From within may arise a strong ruler like Caesar who will be able to restore order. But in case no such man comes to the fore, or if conditions have become so bad that he cannot cope with them, then there must come an external remedy in the shape of a barbarian conquest. Roman history exemplified both of these cases.

If the latter remedy — a barbarian conquest — was administered, the nation had to pass again through the stages from which it had emerged: " Thus, after the fall of the Roman Empire, the divine age reappeared in the dark ages immediately subsequent on the invasions, the heroic age in the middle ages, and the human age in modern times." (That there is perhaps more than a fanciful analogy between these two great cycles has probably been suspected by most modern students of history.) " In the dark ages," he goes on to say, " communication by articulate language to a large extent ceased, and men were intermingled as conquerors and conquered, who could only hold intercourse with one another by signs, gestures, and ceremonial observances. Writing became almost a lost art, the knowledge of it being preserved only in a separate class. Rites were multiplied, and felt to be of the most sacred significance. Religious wars, *purgationes canonicae,* ' judgments of God,' etc., testified of the return to a divine age. It was succeeded by a second age of heroes. The feudal chiefs resembled in many respects the heroic kings. Dante was another Homer. The ' Divina Commedia ' reproduced the second heroic age, as the ' Iliad ' and ' Odyssey ' had done the first. It closed one era and initiated another, the modern age of men."

At the same time Vico by no means contended, after the fashion of Spengler, that these recurring cycles were identical in all respects. Although perhaps more pessimistic than some philosophers of history, as a result largely of the influence of his personal experiences and surroundings, his general attitude was rather optimistic. He held that while there were marked resemblances between these great succeeding periods, the later periods showed many points of superiority over the earlier. As Flint says: " His whole attitude towards the future seems irreconcilable with the notion that he imagined that it would be the transcript of a page which had been already written. His belief in cycles or *ricorsi* was, indeed, inconsistent with a belief in continuous progress in a

470 RISE OF IDEA OF PROGRESS

straight line, but not with advance on the whole, nor with a gradually ascending spiral movement; and still less did it imply that any cycle was perfectly like another, and that history merely repeated itself."

In his monograph on the philosophy of Vico the great Italian critic, Benedetto Croce, has made it clear that Vico's theory of reflux in history is thoroughly compatible with the doctrine of progress as a spiral process in which each of the circles is made on a higher level than its predecessor:

Nor is the Vician law of reflux necessarily opposed, as has often been thought, to the conception of social progress. It would be so opposed if instead of being a law of mere uniformity it were one of identity, in agreement with the idea of an unending cyclical repetition of single individual facts which has been adopted by certain extravagant minds of both ancient and modern times. The reflux of history, the eternal cycle of the mind, can and must be conceived, even if Vico does not so express it, as not merely diverse in its uniform movements, but as perpetually increasing in richness and outgrowing itself, so that the new period of sense is in reality enriched by all the intellect and all the development that preceded it, and the same is true of the new period of the imagination or of the developed mind. The return of barbarism in the Middle Ages was in some respects uniform with ancient barbarism; but it must not for that reason be considered as identical with it, since it contains in itself Christianity, which summarises and transcends ancient thought.

Whether the conception of progress is formulated and thrown into relief by Vico is quite another question. Vico does not deny progress; he even refers to it in speaking of the conditions of his own time as an actual fact.[15]

At the same time, it must be said that Vico was not primarily a conscious or enthusiastic exponent of the doctrine of progress as such; it was incidental to his account of intellectual and social evolution.

Turgot, Anticipator of Modern Theories. — More profound and modern, and less fantastic in detail, was the philosophy of history sketched by the French statesman and publicist, Anne Robert Jacques Turgot (1727–1781). These views were embodied in the discourse (already discussed in a previous chapter) entitled "On the Successive Advances of the Human Mind," delivered at the Sorbonne, December 11, 1750. Conceived when the writer was only twenty-four years of age, it is almost unique in the history of social thought as a combination of precocity and profundity.

Turgot's philosophy of history was based upon a broad conception of the process of cultural evolution; he held that culture was the product of the interaction of geographical, biological, and psychological factors; the single-factor fallacy of attributing everything to race, or climate, or economic organization was thereby avoided. Like Fontenelle and Perrault, he held to the view of the biological fixity of human nature and the physical unity of mankind,[16] although he also recognized the great diversity of customs and institutions. His most original and enduring contribution to social science and the idea of progress occurs in an eloquent passage where he sets forth his conviction as to the unity and continuity of history:

> The succession of mankind . . . presents from age to age an ever-varied spectacle. Reason, the passions, liberty, continually give rise to new events. All the ages are linked together by a chain of causes and effects which unite the existing state of the world with all that has gone before. The manifold signs of speech and of writing, in giving to men the means of insuring the possession of their ideas and of communicating them to others, have made a common treasure-store of all individual knowledge, which one generation bequeaths to the next, a heritage constantly augmented by the discoveries of each age; and mankind, viewed from its origin, appears to the eyes of a philosopher as one vast whole, which itself, like each individual, has its infancy and its growth.[17]

In spite of the unity of mankind, historical development gives little evidence of uniformity or monotonous repetition. The reason for this is to be found in the inequalities of ability among both individuals and peoples, and in the diversification of the circumstances which play upon and coöperate with this differential capacity of mankind:

> Is not nature, then, everywhere the same? And if she guides all men to the same truths, if even their mistakes are akin, why do they not all advance at an equal pace along that path which is marked out for them? Doubtless the human mind contains everywhere the principle of the same progress; but nature, partial in her gifts, has endowed certain minds with an abundance of talents which she has refused to others; circumstances develop these talents or leave them buried in obscurity; and to the infinite variety of these circumstances is due the inequality in the progress of nations.[18]

In his explanation of social change and cultural development Turgot took a position in general outlines similar to that of many modern sociologists. It will be recalled that he maintained the chief cause of mental immobility and its accompanying lack of cultural innovation to be isolation, whereas the most dynamic factor in history he held to be the contact of cultures, whether induced by commerce, migrations, or war.[19] Turgot also contended that the evolution of civilization is a cumulative affair, that each cultural advance accelerates the rate of progress:

> Barbarism levels all men; and, in the earliest times, those born with genius find about the same obstacles and the same resources. However, societies are formed and expanded; national hatreds, ambitions, or rather avarice, the only ambition of barbarous peoples, multiply wars and ravages; conquests, revolutions, mix in countless ways peoples, languages, customs. Mountain chains, great rivers, seas, in arresting within certain bounds the migrations of peoples, and consequently their intermixture, produce common tongues, which become a tie between several nations and divide into a certain number of classes all the nations of the earth. Tillage gives greater permanency to settlements; it supports more men than it occupies, and hence imposes on those left idle the necessity for making themselves useful or formidable to the cultivators. Hence towns, commerce, industry, the polite arts even, the separate professions, difference in education, greater inequality in the conditions of life; hence that leisure whereby genius, relieved of the burden of caring for primal needs, emerges from the narrow sphere where they confine it and directs all its energies towards the cultivation of the sciences; hence that more vigorous and more rapid advancement of the human mind, which bears along with it all parts of society, and which, in turn, receives new energy from their perfection. The passions develop along with genius; ambition takes on new strength, political conditions lend it ever vaster outlooks, victories have more lasting results, and create empires whose laws, customs, government, influencing genius in divers ways, become a sort of common education for the nations, and create between nation and nation the same difference which education creates between man and man.[20]

Turgot not only espoused the doctrine of progress in the past; he anticipated the doctrine of " perfectionism " which was to be launched by Helvétius, Condorcet, and Godwin. The advances of the past were but preliminary to the realization of the perfections of the future. He was almost as exuberant over the cultural advances of his time as Perrault had been a half-century before him, but this did not, as with Perrault, prevent him from looking forward with keen anticipation to the greater achievements of the years to come.

Further, as Bury points out, Turgot definitely envisaged Comte's famous conception of the three stages of intellectual progress in the history of mankind, even though he did not construct his philosophy of history in terms of this conception:

He anticipated Comte's famous "law" of the three stages of intellectual evolution, though without giving it the extensive and fundamental significance which Comte claimed for it. "Before man understood the causal connection of physical phenomena, nothing was so
natural as to suppose they were produced by intelligent beings, invisible
and resembling ourselves; for what else would they have resembled?"
That is Comte's theological stage. "When philosophers recognised the
absurdity of the fables about the gods, but had not yet gained an insight into natural history, they thought to explain the causes of phenomena by abstract expressions such as essences and faculties." That is
the metaphysical stage. "It was only at a later period, that by observing the reciprocal mechanical action of bodies hypotheses were formed
which could be developed by mathematics and verified by experience."
There is the positive stage. The observation assuredly does not possess
the far-reaching importance which Comte attached to it; but whatever
value it has, Turgot deserves the credit of having been the first to
state it.[21]

Perhaps the best estimate of Turgot's significance in the history of the idea of progress is that offered by the foremost of
the English students of French rationalism, John Morley:

The characteristic merits of the second of the two discourses at the
Sorbonne may be briefly described in this way. It recognises the idea
of ordered succession in connection with the facts of society. It considers this succession as one, not of superficial events, but of working
forces. . . . Cause and effect, in Turgot's sense of history, describe a
relation between certain sets or groups of circumstances, that are of a
peculiarly decisive kind, because the surface of events conforms itself to
their inner working. His account of these deciding circumstances was
not what we should be likely to accept now, because he limited them
too closely to purely intellectual acquisitions, as we have just seen, and
because he failed to see the necessity of tracing the root of the whole
growth to certain principles in the mental constitution of mankind. But,
at all events, his conception of history rose above merely individual
concerns, embraced the successive movements of societies and their
relations to one another, and sought the spring of revolutions in the affairs of a community in long trains of preparing conditions, internal and
external. Above all, history was a whole. The fortunes and achievements
of each nation were scrutinised for their effect on the growth of all mankind.[22]

Condorcet, Incorrigible Optimist. — Doubtless the most elaborate and enthusiastic statement of the theory of progress prior
to the nineteenth century was contained in the *Outline of an Historical Picture of the Progress of the Human Mind,* composed by
Marie Jean Antoine Nicolas de Caritat, Marquis de Condorcet

(1743–1794) in 1793, and published in 1795. In this work, written when he was in hiding from the Jacobins during the French Revolution, Condorcet made a thorough effort to appraise the progress in the past, expressed a most optimistic opinion on the achievements of his own day, and presented a glowing picture of the much more striking advances which he anticipated in the future. His general attitude and his fundamental purposes are fairly apparent in the following passages from his work:

> I am attempting to sketch here an historical picture of the progress of the human mind, and not the history of governments, laws, morals, customs, or opinions among the different peoples who have successively occupied the globe. The details into which their almost infinite variety would compel me to enter are foreign to the object of this work. I must confine myself to selecting the general traits which characterize the various epochs through which the human race must have passed, which bear witness, now to its progress, now to its decline, which reveal causes, which indicate their effects.
>
> There will be found here no general history of the sciences, of the arts, or of philosophy, but simply such portion of that history as can shed light on the course which men have followed in passing, for example . . . from the vague observations of the first wise men on the progress of the intellect, on morals, on laws, to the profound analyses of men like Locke, Smith, and Turgot. . . .
>
> . . . I have simply wished to show how, by dint of time and of effort . . . [man] has been able to enrich his mind with new truths, to cultivate his intelligence, to develop his faculties, to learn the better to employ them both for his own well-being and for the common good. . . .
>
> . . . These observations, on what man has been, on what he is today, will lead us next to the means of assuring and accelerating the further progress for which his nature permits him to hope.
>
> Such is the object of the work which I have undertaken, the result of which will be to show, through reasoning and through facts, that nature has assigned no limit to the perfecting of the human faculties, that the perfectibility of man is truly indefinite; that the progress of this perfectibility, henceforth independent of any power that might wish to arrest it, has no other limit than the duration of the globe on which nature has placed us. Doubtless this progress can be more or less rapid; but never will men retrograde, so long, at least, as the earth occupies the same place in the system of the universe, and the general laws òf that system do not effect on this globe either a general destruction or changes which would no longer permit human kind to preserve or to exercise thereon the same faculties, and to avail themselves of the same resources. . . .[23]

He divided the history of the past into " epochs," in each case offering his estimate as to the progress which had taken place in that period. The French Revolution he regarded as the border-line between the past and the glorious future. The political and social achievements of the Enlightenment, which were then being brought to fruition in the French Revolution, together with the remarkable advances in pure and applied science, would inaugurate a new and happy era in human development. Bonar has thus described the scope and leading contentions of Condorcet's work:

He divides history into ten great epochs; 1st, that of hunters and fishermen; 2nd, that of shepherds; 3rd, that of tillers of the soil; 4th, that of commerce, science, and philosophy in Greece; 5th, that of science and philosophy from the conquests of Alexander to the decline of the Roman Empire; 6th, that of the decadence of science till the Crusades; 7th, from the latter date till the invention of Printing; 8th, from the invention of Printing to the attacks on the principle of Authority, by Luther, Descartes, and Bacon; and 9th, from Descartes to the French Republic, when reason, tolerance, and humanity were becoming the watchwords of all. In conclusion, he looks to the future, and sees not only enlightenment extending, but science more and more completely mastering nature. The progress of the race, in every respect, is without limit; and it will result in equality of material comfort and security of livelihood, as well as moral and intellectual perfection, universal peace, and political liberty. Industry, by aid of the sciences, will make the soil capable of yielding support without limit. He pauses to ask, Will not the increase of men be without limit, too? and answers, In any case, at a very distant time, and before that time arrives we shall no longer be prevented by " superstition " from limiting our numbers in ways obvious enough, but not now followed.

The equality of the sexes, which progress will certainly bring with it, will make this consummation more easy of fulfilment. Progress in the art of medicine will so prolong life, that death will be the exception rather than the rule. Persecuted philosophers may console themselves by looking away from the present to this glorious future.[24]

Our hopes for the future excellence of society, Condorcet held, lie in the prospect for improvement along three particular lines: (1) the inequality among nations must be destroyed; (2) equality must be assured among the people of any given nation; and (3) the nature of man himself must be perfected.

The first of these changes was to be realized by the abolition of national commercial monopolies, of international treachery, and of race or national prejudice — what Spencer called the "bias of patriotism." The brotherhood of nations must be brought about.

The three chief types of inequality within a nation, said Condorcet, are: (1) the inequality of wealth; (2) the inequality of condition between a man of permanent and assured income and a man whose income depends upon his ability to work; and (3) the inequality of instruction given to children. The inequality of wealth may be eliminated by removing the artificial and exclusive advantages which now exist in the legal rights of acquiring and transmitting property. The inequality of the second type may be lessened by the introduction of a system of annuities and insurance, and by an extension of the credit system. The inequality of instruction can be eliminated by progress in the selection of better subjects for study and in improved methods of instruction. While competent public instruction will not, as Helvétius contended, do away with the differences in natural capacity, it will make those of superior ability recognize their obligations to society and will cause the masses to admire and value high attainments.

There are many changes which will bring about the perfection of human nature. Laws and institutions will be constantly changed to keep pace with social improvement and to adjust the relations between society and the individual. With the abolition of hereditary dynasties the chief cause of war will be abolished. Learning will be facilitated by the adoption of a universal language, and teaching will be greatly improved by the proper combination and coördination of a large number of subjects. (In this last theory he foreshadowed the work of Herbart.) Finally, progress in the art of medicine will reduce the ravages of disease, sanitary knowledge will prevent epidemics, and the destruction of inequality will do away with misery and excessive wealth. Death will therefore become the result either of accident or of the ever slower wasting of vital energy — the life of man will never be without end, but it will doubtless be greatly prolonged.

In the following radiant and defiant paragraph, written when he was a fugitive in the shadow of the guillotine that finally dropped his head in the basket, Condorcet proclaims that this survey of the human past and prophecy regarding the human future constitutes the best consolation of the true philosopher and conjures up a vision which no enemy can snatch from him or posterity:

. . . And how admirably calculated is this picture of the human race, freed from all these chains, secure from the dominion of chance, as from that of the enemies of its progress, and advancing with firm and sure steps towards the attainment of truth, virtue, and happiness, to present to the philosopher a spectacle which shall console him for the errors, the crimes, the injustice, with which the earth is still polluted, and whose victim he often is! It is in the contemplation of this picture that he receives the reward of his efforts towards the progress of reason and the defense of liberty. He dares then to link these with the eternal chain of human destiny; and thereby he finds virtue's true recompense, the joy of having performed a lasting service, which no fatality can ever destroy by restoring the evils of prejudice and slavery. This contemplation is for him a place of refuge, whither the memory of his persecutors cannot follow him, where, living in imagination with man restored to his rights and the dignity of his nature, he forgets him whom greed, fear, or envy torment and corrupt; there it is that he exists in truth with his kin, in an elysium which his reason has been able to create for him, and which his love for humanity enhances with the purest enjoyments.[25]

Godwin, Philosophical Anarchist. — The next writer to be considered is the English scholar, William Godwin (1756–1836), whose work, *An Enquiry Concerning Political Justice,* created a great stir when it appeared in 1793. Accepting with all seriousness what Burke had intended as an ironical satire — namely, that government is an evil — he created a great sensation, at a time when the French Revolution was at its height, by the publication of a book which embodied this view as its central thesis. Salt has gathered some interesting samples of contemporary opinions evoked by the volume:

"No work of our time," says Hazlitt, "gave such a blow to the philosophical mind of the country as Godwin's celebrated *Enquiry concerning Political Justice.* Tom Paine was considered for the time as a Tom Fool to him; Paley an old woman; Edmund Burke a flashy sophist. Truth, moral truth, it was supposed, had here taken up its abode, and these were the oracles of thought." "Burn your books of chemistry," was Wordsworth's advice to a student, "and read Godwin on Necessity." "Faulty as it is in many parts," wrote Southey, "there is a mass of truth in it that must make every man think." We are told by DeQuincey that Godwin's book "carried one single shock into the bosom of English society, fearful but momentary." "In the quarto," he adds, "— that is the original edition of his *Political Justice,* — Mr. Godwin advanced against thrones and denominations, powers and principalities, with the air of some Titan slinger or monomachist from Thebes and Troy, saying 'Come hither, ye wretches, that I may give your flesh to the fowls of the air.' "[26]

The chief doctrines of this sensational treatise were: (1) that man has not made much progress in the past, that the present is in about as deplorable a condition as one could imagine, and that

all the evils of society arise from the detrimental effects of coercive and oppressive human institutions; (2) that all government, so far as it is coercive, should be abolished; (3) that the
ideal society is one which is composed of free individuals — free in
everything except the moral censure of their associates; (4) that
no coercive organization for social control larger than the parish
should be permitted; (5) that the unequal distribution of property should be done away with; (6) that marriage as an institution should be abolished; (7) that man is capable of unlimited
future progress; (8) that man is to be improved in the future
mainly through the influence of reason, that truth must ultimately
prevail; and (9) that the three chief agencies which will operate
to bring this about are literature, education, and political justice,
the last of which Godwin made the chief topic of his treatise.
Education, which is to inculcate the principles of reason, must be
given privately, not by public agencies. " Godwin's theory is the
apotheosis of individualism and (in a sense) of Protestantism; a
purified and enlightened individualism is not to him (as to Rousseau) the beginning, but the end of all human progress. He
is the father not so truly of philosophical radicalism as of
Anarchism." [27]

Godwin did not adopt the radical opinion which Rousseau held
in his earlier writings — namely, that all civilization had been
fraught with evil — but he held that the positive and coercive institutions which had grown up with civilization, particularly the
state and private property, were evil influences. Bonar sums up
his doctrine thus:

Godwin may be said to have extended to political philosophy the
doctrines which Adam Smith confined largely to trade. The institutions
of society are represented by Adam Smith as hindering the commercial
progress of nations; so in the *Political Justice* they are conceived as
hindering moral and intellectual progress. Like Adam Smith, Godwin
takes deep thought for the independence and originality of men, and
distrusts all associations. He would abolish government so far as coercive,
and would have no collective organization larger than the parish. Society
is to him only an " aggregation of individuals. Its claims and duties
must be the aggregate of their claims and duties, the one no more precarious and arbitrary than the other." Rousseau is wrong; civilization
has been a benefit and not an evil, but it is not identical with positive
institutions, which have been on the contrary an obstacle to all movement and progress. " Government, even in its best state, is an evil." [28]

Godwin's famous principle of justice greatly resembled the
Physiocratic " natural order " and Bentham's principle of utility.

That which secures the greatest amount of happiness for mankind is the essence of justice. Bonar says, quoting largely from Godwin:

> The true standard of the conduct of one man towards another is justice. Justice is a principle which proposes to itself the production of the greatest sum of pleasure or happiness. Justice requires that I should put myself in the place of an impartial spectator of human concerns, without regard to my own predilections. " Justice is a rule of the utmost universality, and prescribes a specific mode of proceeding in all affairs by which the happiness of a human being may be affected." . . . We must not think that we can justify political arangementa by referring to their historical origin; our only standard must be public welfare. . . . Whatever conduct secures the maximum of happiness to the world of men, generally — that is justice.[29]

That Godwin was not hostile to society in general, but was perfectly cognizant of its benefits to mankind, is evident from his answer to the criticism which was brought against his plan of individual freedom on the ground that man is intended by nature for society. Godwin makes plain his acceptance of this dictum, but goes on to show that this does not conflict in the least with his plan, for the ideal society is that composed of free and enlightened individuals. *This is the type of society for which nature intended man.* Few sociologists have been more eloquent than Godwin in their praise of the contributions of society to social progress, though their conception of society may have differed in many respects from his.

As has been mentioned above, Godwin advocated the equal distribution of wealth, and condemned the system of inequality:

> If justice have any meaning, nothing can be more iniquitous, than for one man to possess superfluities, while there is a human being in existence that is not adequately supplied with these [our animal necessities].

> Justice does not stop here. Every man is entitled, so far as the general stock will suffice, not only to the means of being, but of well being. It is unjust, if one man labour to the destruction of his health or his life, that another may abound in luxuries. It is unjust, if one man be deprived of leisure to cultivate his rational powers, while another man contributes not a single effort to add to the common stock. The faculties of one man are like the faculties of another man. Justice directs that each man unless perhaps he be employed more beneficially to the public, should contribute to the cultivation of the common harvest, of which each man consumes a share.[30]

At the same time, Godwin cannot be claimed by the socialists (either "utopian" or "scientific") by virtue of his economic doctrines any more than because of his political teachings. Common labor and common meals — two of the requisites of many socialistic utopias — were condemned explicitly by him; and he went even further than this and condemned all coöperation and division of labor — those principles which even the individualistic economist, Adam Smith, had assigned the chief place in the economic system, and which the "scientific" socialist also holds to be vital. Everything which is commonly understood by coöperation is evil, and the division of labor is the offspring of avarice.

As the abolition of government and all positive coercive institutions were the negative or destructive side of his program, so was its corollary, the perfectibility of man under a purely individualistic régime in which reason held full sway, his positive or constructive doctrine. He was not over-optimistic as to the immediate realization of his ideal, but he had perfect faith in its ultimate attainment. He looked for a gradual, evolutionary growth. Man is not capable of attaining absolute perfection, but is amenable to indefinite improvement — i.e., is perfectible:

There is no science that is not capable of additions; there is no art that may not be carried to a still higher perfection. If this be true of all other sciences, why not of morals? If this be true of all other arts, why not of social institution? The very conception of this as possible, is in the highest degree encouraging. If we can still farther demonstrate it to be a part of the natural and regular progress of mind, our confidence and our hopes will then be complete. This is the temper with which we ought to engage in the study of political truth. Let us look back, that we may profit by the experience of mankind; but let us not look back, as if the wisdom of our ancestors was such as to leave no room for future improvement.[31]

As a sort of concluding survey, let us see what Preston has to say concerning the probable sources of Godwin's views:

The doctrine of *Political Justice* is based on certain propositions, which, with the sources from which Godwin presumably received them, may be conveniently cited here.

1. The mind is not free, but plastic, acted upon by circumstances of heredity and environment, with certain, though inscrutable, results. This doctrine of materialistic determinism was probably first implanted in Godwin's mind by his early Calvinistic training. It was reinforced by later acquaintance with Jonathan Edwards's *Enquiry into the Freedom of the Will* (1754), with Hartley, and with d'Holbach's *Système de la Nature* (1770). Like Locke and Hume, Godwin denies the existence of

"innate principles and instincts." He holds that associations and experience far outweigh influences of heredity or of environment or of prenatal impressions, and consequently follows Locke in considering the pleasure of the greatest number the *summum bonum.*

2. The reason has unlimited power over the emotions; hence arguments, not an appeal to the emotions, and not force, are the most effective motives. Upon this psychological doctrine, derived partly from Helvétius and partly from Locke's statement that the law of reason, which all must obey, is the law of nature, is founded Godwin's theory of education and of the treatment of the criminal. In its earliest form, Godwin reduces the justice of the human sympathies and affections and of force to almost nothing. He explains our frequent failure to appeal to pure reason by citing Hartley's doctrine of voluntary and involuntary actions. From this proposition follows Godwin's condemnation of resistance to existent laws as a reprehensible appeal to violence. . . .

3. Man is perfectible; that is, man, though incapable of perfection, is capable of indefinitely improving. This optimistic and unqualified belief in human progress is at least implied in Helvétius, d'Holbach, Priestley, and Price. It was boldly stated in reasoned form by Condorcet (*Esquisse d'un Tableau Historique des Progrès de l'Esprit Humain,* 1793), who seems to have had a weighty influence on Godwin's revisions in the third edition.

4. Any individual is, in the eye of reason, the equal of any other. This democratic principle is as old, at least, as Jesus of Nazareth; it had more recently been set forth in the American Declaration of Independence, and before that had been promulgated by Helvétius. Godwin later retracted it.

5. The greatest force for the perpetuation of injustice is human institutions. Godwin's predecessors in this opinion are innumerable. He mentions in his preface Swift, and elsewhere Mandeville and the Latin historians (from whom he may also have derived his model of passionless stoicism). Price implies that government is an evil of which the less we have, the better; Priestley, Hume, and the later Utilitarians, weighing the good and evil effects of law, decide that the presumption is against law, and that government interference, except as a restraint where personal liberty interferes with the liberty of others, is inexpedient. The abstract right to be free leads Godwin to support the individual's right to private property.[32]

Kant's Moralistic Conception. — Important in the history of the idea of progress is the noted German philosopher, Immanuel Kant (1724–1804). Kant's reputation as a philosopher rests chiefly upon (1) his demonstration of the limited nature of rational knowledge and the validity of philosophical agnosticism in his *Critique of Pure Reason,* and (2) his foundation of Protestant modernism and a conception of morality based on an innate sense of duty in his *Critique of Practical Reason*. His contributions to the idea of progress were embodied in two other works much less widely known, *The Idea of a Universal History from a Cosmopolitical Point of View* (1784), and *On the Common Saying* (1793).

We may first consider Kant's philosophy of history as it is presented in the essay on universal history. In the first place, he says, whether the human will be free or not in metaphysical theory, its manifestations in human actions are as much determined by universal natural laws as are any other external events. When the plan of the human will is examined from the standpoint of a universal history, its movements may therefore be seen to follow a regular path of progressive development. Although this march of progress may seem tangled and unregulated in the case of individuals, the record of the achievement of the whole human species will be found to be a slow and gradual but nevertheless continually advancing development of its " original capacities and endowments." Individual men or even nations, in pursuing their personal or single ends, are unwittingly being guided by a great purpose of nature; they are unconsciously working toward an end which, if they knew, they might not think a matter of any great moment. The task of the philosophical historian, recognizing that no " rational conscious purpose " can guide the actions of mankind, is to see if he cannot discover the universal plan of nature in the paradoxical movements of humanity. Kant sought the clue to this plan of nature as revealed in history, in the hope that after he had discovered it someone would follow him who would fit this clue into a universal cosmic scheme in the same way that Newton had explained the discoveries of Kepler by the law of universal gravitation. Kant put his philosophy of history in a series of nine progressive propositions, each followed by a short explanation and elaboration.

I. All the capacities implanted in a creature by nature, are destined to unfold themselves, completely and conformably to their end, in the course of time. . . .

II. In Man, as the only rational creature on earth, those natural capacities which are directed towards the use of his Reason, could be completely developed only in the species and not in the individual. . . .

III. Nature has willed that Man shall produce wholly out of himself all that goes beyond the mechanical structure and arrangement of his animal existence, and that he shall participate in no other happiness or perfection but what he has produced for himself, apart from instinct, by his own reason. . . .

iv. The means which nature employs to bring about the development of all the capacities implanted in men, is their mutual antagonism in society, but only so far as this antagonism becomes at length the cause of an order among them that is regulated by law. . . .

v. The great practical problem for the human race, to the solution of which it is compelled by nature, is the establishment of a civil society, universally administering right according to law. . . .

vi. This problem is likewise the most difficult of its kind, and it is the latest to be solved by the human race. . . .

vii. The problem of the establishment of a perfect civil constitution is dependent on the problem of the regulation of the external relations between the states conformably to law; and without the solution of this latter problem it cannot be solved. . . .

viii. The history of the human race, viewed as a whole, may be regarded as the realisation of a hidden plan of nature to bring about a political constitution, internally, and, for this purpose, also externally perfect, as the only state in which all the capacities implanted by her in mankind can be fully developed. . . .

ix. A philosophical attempt to work out the universal history of the world according to the plan of nature in its aiming at a perfect civil union, must be regarded as possible, and as even capable of helping forward the purpose of nature. . . .[33]

Kant's most important proposition is the fourth, for this contains the dynamics of his theory of history and society. By the term " antagonism " Kant says that he means the " unsocial sociability of men "; that is, the struggle going on both in man and in society between altruism and egoism, between the love of society and others, on the one hand, and the love of self-achievement and independence on the other. This antagonism awakens all of man's latent powers, overcomes his natural indolence, and starts him on the road to progress. Without this struggle mankind might have led a happy and contented life of a rudimentary type, but never a developed and perfect existence. There would have been nothing to stir humanity into activity. Kant develops this theory as follows:

By this Antagonism, I mean the *unsocial sociability* of men; that is, their tendency to enter into society, conjoined, however, with an accompanying resistance which continually threatens to dissolve this society. The disposition for this lies manifestly in human nature. Man has an inclination to *socialise* himself by associating with others, because in such a state he feels himself more than a natural man, in the development of his natural capacities. He has, moreover, a great tendency to *individu-alise* himself by isolation from others, because he likewise finds in himself the unsocial disposition of wishing to direct everything merely according to his own mind; and hence he expects resistance everywhere just as he knows with regard to himself that he is inclined on his part to resist others. Now it is this resistance or mutual antagonism that awakens all the powers of man, that drives him to overcome all his propensity to indolence, and that impels him through the desire of honour or power or wealth, to strive after rank among his fellow-men — whom he can neither bear to interfere with himself, not yet let alone. Then the first real steps are taken from the rudeness of barbarism to the culture of civilisation, which particularly lies in the social worth of man. All his talents are now gradually developed, and with the progress of enlightenment a beginning is made in the institution of a mode of thinking which can transform the crude natural capacity for moral distinctions, in the course of time, into definite practical principles of action; and thus a pathologically constrained combination into a form of society, is developed at least to a *moral* and rational whole. Without those qualities of an unsocial kind, out of which this Antagonism arises — which viewed by themselves are certainly not amiable but which every one must necessarily find in the movements of his own selfish propensities — men might have led an Arcadian shepherd life in complete harmony, contentment and mutual love, but in that case all their talents would have for ever remained hidden in their germ. As gentle as the sheep they tended, such men would hardly have won for their existence a higher worth than belonged to their domesticated cattle; they would not have filled up with their rational nature the void remaining in the Creation, in respect of its final End. Thanks be then to Nature for this unsociableness, for this envious jealousy and vanity, for this unsatiable desire of possession, or even of power! Without them all the excellent capacities implanted in mankind by nature, would slumber eternally undeveloped. Man wishes concord; but Nature knows better what is good for his species, and she will have discord. He wishes to live comfortably and pleasantly; but Nature wills that, turning from idleness and inactive contentment, he shall throw himself into toil and suffering even in order to find out remedies against them, and to extricate his life prudently from them again. The natural impulses that urge man in this direction, the sources of that unsociableness and general antagonism from which so many evils arise, do yet at the same time impel him to new exertion of his powers, and consequently, to further development of his natural capacities. Hence, they clearly manifest the arrangement of a wise Creator, and do not at all, as is often supposed, betray the hand of a malevolent spirit that has deteriorated His glorious creation, or spoiled it from envy.[34]

Kant contended that the keener the struggle between these conflicting forces, the more rapid would be the progress of the race. (Recall the anticipation of this conclusion by Turgot: " Vehement fermentation is necessary for the production of good wines.") Consequently, the state which allows the greatest freedom for the operation of this struggle but at the same time prevents anarchy or oppression will do the most to promote the rapid development of society toward its final goal. The creation of a civil society that combines the greatest amount of legalized liberty with an irresistible coercive power is therefore the most indispensable achievement within the scope of human capacities.

This establishment of the ideal form of civil society is closely bound up with the securing of world peace. It is likely to prove futile to attempt to regulate the relations between men in a single state if the various independent states are to pursue their antagonisms unrestrained. Evils basically the same as those which afflict individuals in unrestrained freedom operate detrimentally upon nations whose external relations are not subject to legal control and adjustment. But here also, as in the case of the struggles of individuals within the state, nature is continually operating to effect that same ultimate harmony which she attempts to secure among the citizens of each separate state. The strain of preparing for wars and the devastation and exhaustion resulting from them are leading the nations toward the ultimate political unity — the federation of nations. Only through the realization of world peace can the rulers of separate states free themselves from the distractions of war and diplomacy and devote their attention to the perfection of the domestic institutions so essential to the regulation of the contending forces of collectivism and individualism and the realization of progress.

There are three possible ways, says Kant, in which this condition of world federation and world peace may be brought about: First, through the Epicurean scheme of the concourses of causes in action; i.e., the states, like particles of matter, will try all kinds of unions which will in turn be destroyed until the lucky combination is hit upon by chance — " a lucky accident which will hardly ever come about." Second, the desired end will be wrought by the gradual plan of nature; she will bring about this highest development in due time in her steady march of progress. Third, all the nations will be reduced to a universal despotic barbarism through the discord which is so prevalent among advanced societies. The second method seems by far the most likely to be used unless one is willing to concede that nature requires order and harmony in the parts of her universal scheme and not in the whole. The greatest need of the times, Kant says, is the cultivation of morality: the nations are even over-*civilized*, especially in the development of the various social forms of politeness and elegance, but a great deal of improvement is needed to bring about a condition wherein the people may be said to be *moralized*. Neither can any great moral progress be expected until nations cease wasting all their resources in vain external aggrandizement and begin to devote some time to the cultivation of good habits of thought and high character among their citizens. In other words, this much-needed moral culture must wait until the human race " shall have worked itself, in the way that has been indicated, out of the existing chaos of its political relations." [35]

Kant's conception of progress was therefore a moralistic view of the process of human development, in harmony with the growing protest against rationalism and its attendant interest in science and technology. In the latter part of his little book *On the Common Saying*, Kant admits that his conception of progress is a moral one, and reaffirms his belief that a definite moral progress of the human race can be demonstrated:

I will, therefore, venture to assume that as the human race is continually advancing in civilization and culture as its natural purpose, so it is continually making progress for the better in relation to the moral end of its existence, and that this progress although it may be sometimes interrupted, will never be entirely broken off or stopped. It is not necessary for me to prove this assumption; the burden of proof lies on its opponents. For I take my stand upon my innate sense of duty in this connection. Every member in the series of generations to which I belong as a man — although mayhap not so well equipped with the requisite moral qualifications as I ought to be, and consequently might be — is, in fact, prompted by his sense of duty so to act in reference to posterity that they may always become better, and the possibility of this must be assumed. This duty can thus be rightly transmitted from one member of the generations to another. Now whatever doubts may be drawn from history against my hopes, and were they even of such a kind as, in case of their being demonstrated, might move me to desist from efforts which according to all appearances would be vain, yet so long as this is not made out with complete certainty, I am not entitled to give up the guidance of duty which is clear, and to adopt the prudential rule of not working at the impracticable, since this is not clear but is mere hypothesis. And, however uncertain I may always be as to whether we may rightly hope that the human race will attain to a better condition, yet this individual uncertainty cannot detract from the general rule of conduct, or from the necessary assumption in the practical relation that such a condition *is* practicable.[36]

In conclusion, it should be pointed out that there is a foreshadowing of the " social telesis " of Lester F. Ward and others in Kant's ninth and final proposition: namely, that by formulating a tentative notion of the nature and principles of human progress one may hope to aid in some degree in guiding and accelerating it.

Herder and Early Romanticism. — Most of the writers referred to in the above sketch of the rise of the idea of progress in modern times were of the rationalist school. They laid primary stress upon reason; intellectual factors were regarded as all-important in the social process. They believed that it would be possible to revolutionize society rapidly by applying to its problems " the self-evident dictates of pure reason." Although recognizing that the present is rooted in the past, they did not believe it necessary for the present to be restrained by the past, particularly if man made a conscious effort to improve the present state of affairs. It was also held that the thinker could lay bare the past and indicate with clarity and precision the course, nature, and factors of human development.

There set in during the latter part of the eighteenth century a definite reaction against rationalism in the form of a movement in social and historical philosophy known as Romanticism. Romanticism in historical philosophy meant a decided shift in the direction of authoritarianism, and was a part of that trend in social philosophy which is chiefly identified with the names of Burke, DeBonald, DeMaistre, and Von Haller.

The basic premise of the historical philosophy of Romanticism was the doctrine of the gradual and unconscious nature of cultural evolution. The unique organic unity and development of all forms of national culture was stressed. There was a decided mystical strain in the thinking of the Romanticists; they maintained that the unconscious creative forces operated in a mysterious manner which defied rationalistic analysis. It was held that all were subject to the operation of these inscrutable forces of psychic power which went to make up the *Zeitgeist* (the spirit of the age). Great emphasis was laid upon tradition and other forces which constitute the spirit of the age and of the nation (the *Volksgeist*).

These conceptions naturally led to a doctrine of political fatalism which represented the individual or the nation as powerless before the mass of creative spiritual forces. Revolution was represented as particularly wicked, futile, and worthy of special condemnation. There grew up that philosophy of political " quietism " which fitted in excellently with the current *laissez faire* doctrines of the economists and political theorists. Out of this tendency there developed that notorious myth representing the

Anglo-Saxon peoples as the perfect examples of political quietism, and hence of inherent political capacity, while an equally erroneous doctrine pictured the French as the typical example of a revolutionary and unstable nation utterly devoid of all political capacity. This fundamental error did more than anything else to mar the accuracy of nineteenth-century political history and philosophy, and has not even yet been fully eradicated.

The idea of the pure, indigenous, and spontaneous nature of national culture led to a narrowing of the secular, cosmopolitan outlook of the rationalists and the centering of attention on purely national history. There thus developed a well-marked form of mental isolation. Further, for each nation the period of particular fertility for historical research was held to be the Middle Ages. This tendency was due in part to the strange misconception that this was the period of the fixing of the several national cultures, and in part to the intellectual affinity of the Romanticists with the medieval mental reaction to the problems of existence and causation. Language was believed to be the vital mark of nationality. This doctrine took deepest root in Germany, where language was almost the only bond of nationality, and it led to the great researches in philology associated with the names of Humboldt, Wolff, the brothers Grimm, and Lachmann. Because of the fact that the Romanticists maintained the hopelessness of any detailed analysis of historical causation, their philosophy of history ran in a vicious circle. Without giving any scientific explanation of the development of the spirit of a nation, they attributed the peculiarities of national institutions, laws, literature, and government to the genius of the nation, and then represented national character as the product of the art, literature, laws, and institutions of a people.

In spite of the archaizing tendencies and the all too frequent philosophical crudities of the Romanticists, they must be given credit for having done much to correct the crude catastrophic theory of the rationalists, and for having emphasized the element of unconscious growth in historical development, as well as the vital truth of the functional unity of any culture-complex. It was left for Lamprecht, nearly a century later, to take what was really valuable in the Romantic doctrines and work them over into his famous theory of historical development as a process of transformations and mutations within the " collective psychology " of both the nation and humanity.

The German philosopher of history, Johann Gottfried von Herder (1744–1803), was an early forerunner of Romanticism rather than a full-fledged Romanticist. He recognized the great influence of external factors, such as the physical environment, upon man, as we have already seen, but he also put much emphasis upon the operation of a complex of mysterious psychic forces affecting mankind which he included under the rather vague and elusive term *Geist* (mind or spirit). Indeed, the historical process was chiefly one of the gradual education of the race as it was impelled onward by the joint operation of *Geist* and geography. Herder went even beyond Turgot in stressing the continuity and unity of history:

> . . . his argument . . . has high value as a statement of the truth of the interdependence, or, as it is often now called, solidarity of men; a truth not only of essential importance in the philosophy of history, but, involved in the very conception of its possibility. Herder finds in this truth a warrant for faith in the progressive education of the race. " The history of mankind is a whole — that is, a chain of sociability and tradition, from the first link to the last. There is an education, therefore, of the human species; since every one becomes a man only by means of education, and the whole species lives solely in this chain of individuals." The title of Lessing's book notwithstanding, it was not Lessing but Herder who represented all history as a course of education, the whole earth as a school, — " the school," as he says, " of our family, containing indeed many divisions, classes, and chambers, but still with one plan of instruction, which has been transmitted from our ancestors, with various alterations and additions, to all their race." [37]

Herder was an essentially pious person, but he nevertheless believed that the historical development of man was a process strictly determined by the natural forces at work. Although God originated these forces, he did not interfere arbitrarily to modify or alter their operation. This doctrine bears a strong resemblance to the Deistic notions current at the time. Bury thus describes Herder's conception of historical determinism:

> The Deity designed the world but never interferes in its process, either in the physical cosmos or in human history. Human history itself, civilisation, is a purely natural phenomenon. Events are strictly enchained; continuity is unbroken; what happened at any given time could have happened only then, and nothing else could have happened. Herder's rigid determinism not only excludes Voltaire's chance but also suppresses the free play of man's intelligent will. Man cannot guide his own destinies; his actions and fortunes are determined by the nature of things, his physical organisation and physical environment. The fact that God exists in inactive ease hardly affects the fatalistic complexion of this philosophy; but it is perhaps a mitigation that the world was made for man; humanity is its final cause. [38]

Herder summarizes his views of the nature of human development in the following five propositions:

I. The end of human nature is humanity; and that they may realize their end, God has put into the hands of men their own fate.

II. All the destructive powers in nature must not only yield in time to the preservative powers, but must ultimately be subservient to the perfection of the whole.

III. The human race is destined to proceed through various degrees of civilisation, in various revolutions, but its abiding welfare rests solely and essentially on reason and justice.

IV. From the very nature of the human mind, reason and justice must gain more footing among men in the course of time, and promote the extension of humanity.

V. A wise goodness disposes the fate of mankind, and therefore there is no nobler merit, no purer or more abiding happiness, than to cooperate in its designs.[39]

DeMaistre, Reactionary and Critic of Progress. — But after all, Herder was in no sense a wholly anti-progressive thinker; that classification must be reserved for writers like Joseph De-Maistre,[40] perhaps the greatest of those reactionary[41] spirits who from time to time rise up to denounce the temper of their age, to condemn its general tendencies, and to preach the return to the past. The eighteenth century had believed fervently in progress, reason, liberty, and democracy. But these ideas had played no small part in bringing on the French Revolution, and no man could hate the French Revolution more intensely than DeMaistre. His position, therefore, would necessarily be anti-progressivist, anti-rationalist, authoritarian, and anti-democratic, and nowhere have these theses been more stoutly maintained or more cleverly argued.

The circumstances of DeMaistre's life played so important a part in molding his thought that it is essential that we give them brief examination. He was born at Chambéry in 1754, a thorough patrician, a member of the Savoyard hereditary magistracy, imbued, as Faguet penetratingly remarks, with a stronger patrician sentiment and spirit of caste than even the ordinary nobility. His education, which was at first superintended by the Jesuits, was intensive, arduous, and characterized by a spirit of absolute obedience. Even as a student at the University of Turin he never read any book without first securing permission from his mother to do so. His legal studies completed, he held various official positions in the government of Savoy, and settled down contentedly to a career in the judiciary. His life as a bureaucrat further confirmed in him a love of order, stability, and obedience, a fear of individual variation and initiative as conducive of anarchy, and a faith in the exclusive and sovereign power of legal coercion to control men and to preserve social order. He was a settled man in his middle thirties with family responsibilities and with his ideas completely fixed when the French Revolution suddenly burst upon him like a thunderbolt, negating all his essential ideals, destroying the system by which he lived, and driving him into exile. For many years he and his family suffered the bitterest privation, and were even for a time threatened with beggary. At a later period he was appointed Sardinian ambassador to Russia, and was separated from his family for fifteen years. These facts help to explain his hatred of the Revolution and its ideals, as well as the profound pessimism which inspires his religious and philosophic views.

At the core of DeMaistre's thought is a deep-seated distrust of reason. Though his method is dialectical rather than empirical, he uses reason only in the end to refute reason. The basic dogmas of his thought (notably those of religion) he never descends to discuss, and his analyses always lead in the end to conceptions or propositions which defy clear formulation, to say nothing of rational demonstration. In obvious opposition to the eighteenth-century *philosophes,* who believed fervently in discussion, he denied entirely the social rôle of reason. He asserted that discussion and argument are fatal to stability, that a constitution or social order which is rationally achieved and understood is by that very fact incapable of winning the support and obedience upon which social order and stability rest. Men obey only what they venerate but cannot understand. Thus DeMaistre is completely opposed to written constitutions and to parliamentary government. Societies must be ruled by customs and institutions, the origins of which are lost in the mists of history. Laws must be the edicts of a king which are accepted blindly, not on their merits, but as emanating from a source of authority divinely ordained.

DeMaistre had seen the tides of social change sweep away all that he held dear, unseat the nobility, execute the king, strip the church of her powers. What men call progress was thus anathema to him, and his whole objective was to restore the *ancien régime* in such a fashion that never again would it be shaken. Stability was for him the all in all; change was viewed as unnecessary and undesirable, and those forces productive of change he wished to bind up securely, never to be set free. Here again his opposition to reason and to discussion springs forth. Discussion has an unsettling effect, it leads to doubt — and doubt is for DeMaistre the unpardonable sin, for doubt leads to criticism, to suggestions for unsettling change, to disastrous attempts at improvement.

Individualism, also, is strongly opposed by DeMaistre, on the basis of a well-developed sociological realism. Society is real in itself, wholly above and apart from its members. Indeed, it is more real than its members, and it legitimately demands their sacrifice in its interests. Rousseau's " rights of man " are contemptuously dismissed. Man cannot exist prior to society, and in society he has not rights but duties. So, too, democracy or any concessions to the democratic spirit are indignantly repudiated as tending to divide sovereignty and dissipate it among the masses. For DeMaistre, on the other hand, power, authority, must be concentrated if it is to be effective, and thus in his opinion an absolute monarchy is the only possible form of government. Not only does it supply the maximum concentration of authority, but in the person of the king it provides a perfect symbol for the society as a whole, a rallying-point for collective sentiments, a proper object of awe and veneration. Moreover, hereditary transmission of authority assures its continuity, symbolizes the continuity of the society, and when long maintained assures respect for such authority as is legitimate.

Finally, there is the bitter attack on liberty. Essential in De-Maistre's thought is the organismic doctrine. Societies are real organisms; individuals are only parts of these organisms, living in and through them. The demand for individual liberties is " mad egoism "; it is the part revolting against the whole. The healthy organism demands proper subservience of its parts to the efficient functioning of the whole. Individuals may have a relative degree of freedom as to just how they will make their social contributions, but only because and in so far as this enables them to contribute more fully and ably. Freedom has absolutely no value in itself, and we should talk not of individual liberties, but of individual efforts which may be allowed and encouraged when they are worthy. Moreover, DeMaistre, with his complete distrust of reason and discussion, could see little point in such dangerous business as freedom of speech and press. Since all that mattered was stability, and since (as he thought) the surest method of achieving stability is the imposition of dogma, the unquestioning acceptance by all of tradition, he could certainly not see the point of allowing dissenting opinions the opportunity of expressing themselves. Logically carried through, this implies a state religion and the suppression of heresy by inquisition. DeMaistre cheerfully accepted the implication. He was a convinced Roman Catholic, and looked back to the Middle Ages with unmixed admiration. Protestantism he denounced with frank hatred. It introduced the spirit of individualism and was responsible for the division of Europe into two armed camps. " It is the first step toward anarchy."

To defend a position of this sort DeMaistre was forced to elaborate a philosophy of religion. (There is space for only the briefest sketch of his ideas on this point.) In the first place, De-Maistre's king is not the tyrant he appears to be. His reign is legitimated because he himself is responsible to something higher; namely, to the church. If the king strays from the path of righteousness the pope has the power to release his subjects from their obligation of obedience. DeMaistre's thought is thus ultimately theocratic. Authority, secular as well as strictly religious, comes from God, but is dispensed on this earth by the pope.

In the second place, he disposes very readily of the criticism that his system is founded on injustice and is inevitably productive of countless particular injustices. This criticism he does not deny: he admits it gladly, even insists upon it. But he removes the sting from it by elaborating a whole religious philosophy which makes injustice fundamental, ubiquitous, the central law of life. He dwells upon the importance of murders, warfare, bloody sacrifices, tortures, and legal executions. War is " the habitual state of the human race," and " human blood must flow uninterruptedly on the earth somewhere or other." [42] Nations are societies formed for the express purpose of committing injustices upon one another, and within society, the criminal ceaselessly commits injustices and the hangman as ceaselessly punishes and commits new injustices in turn. The hangman is a particular favorite of DeMaistre, and is apostrophized by him as the very cornerstone of society.

This pessimism has certain obvious roots in DeMaistre's own life. He had lived what by his standards was a blameless life; yet he had been severely afflicted and made to suffer deeply. Since he possessed an essentially supernaturalistic type of mind, for him it had to be seen as a part of a divine plan. So viewed it was manifestly unjust, and the only way to justify this particular injustice was to generalize it, to make it seem merely an episode in the universal injustice behind all life. There is still of course the religious difficulty of reconciling this universal injustice with the conception of a merciful, kindly, and just God. The problem of evil is the perennial religious problem, and as DeMaistre's answers are neither original nor conspicuously successful, we may perhaps be excused from burdening our pages with them.

Before discussing the influence of DeMaistre's thought on the development of sociology, it seems well to consider the work of another reactionary thinker whose name is usually associated with DeMaistre and whose contributions are of the same type and of almost equal importance.

DeBonald, Traditionalist and Scholastic. — Joseph DeMaistre once wrote to the Vicomte DeBonald: [43] " I have never thought anything which you have not written, and I have never written anything which you have not thought." In their fundamental sentiments and presuppositions, as well as in their social and political conclusions, there is a resemblance between the two men so close as almost to constitute identity. Nevertheless, they differed greatly in temperament and in approach. DeBonald was a typical French *émigré* whose life was singularly devoid of interest and untouched even by personal danger or suffering. He began writing at Heidelberg shortly after the Terror, and with the restoration he returned to France and held various political offices. In temperament he was optimistic and somewhat stolid, lacking both the fire and the deep-seated pessimism of DeMaistre. His method, also, was more pedantic and laborious; the reiteration of a single idea under myriad aspects, the endless piling up of illustrative examples, take the place of DeMaistre's brilliant sophisms and paradoxes.

In short, DeBonald has neither the intellectual keenness nor the stylistic brilliance of DeMaistre and has therefore been much less widely read. But for the student of social theory he is well worth independent study, as he built up a far wider basis of sociological theory for his ethical and political generations, and it will be this part of his thought with which we shall be mainly concerned.

One of the most striking characteristics of DeBonald's thought is the central place allotted to the number three. He had a somewhat scholastic conception that the world was made up of innumerable trinities, of which the general formula ran as follows: the cause is to the means as the means is to the effect. Cause, means, and effect are the three elements in every system. Let us now view some of the illustrations of this principle which, as we shall see, were dearer to DeBonald than the principle itself. What, he asks, is man? A cause: the mind — means: the body and its organs — and an effect: conservation and reproduction. What is the family? Cause: the husband — means: the wife — and the effect: children. What is society? Cause: the king — means: the minister and nobility — effect: the conservation and reproduction of the people. For the formula cause, means, effect, DeBonald sometimes substitutes the formula power, ministers, subjects. Thus in the family the husband is the power, the wife his minister, and the children his subjects. In society the king is the power; the nobility, clergy, and judiciary are ministers; and the people his subjects.

This general formula — which DeBonald elevates to the status of a natural law — he claims to generate empirically from a study of many particular instances. But in fact it is not difficult to discern that he has done no more than to erect his royalism into a system. He passionately desires a state of society in which there is an absolute king, nobles who advise the king and carry out his decrees, and a people who are no more than his passive and obedient subjects. Such a society is "natural" or conformable to the "order of nature." In his use of these expressions, however, DeBonald falls into a typical confusion. A monarchical system is natural or "a law of nature" in the sense that it is (or then seemed to be) the normal or most usual form of society, historically speaking. But DeBonald, who had seen his king executed, was quite well aware that men do not *always* live in a monarchical society. The term "natural" then takes on its ethical or evaluative sense. Monarchy is natural in the sense of "good," or "proper," or "appropriate," and any deviation from it can be dismissed as a temporary aberration arising from human wickedness. DeBonald's "law of nature" is thus at the same time a purported description of objective uniformities in history, and an ethical norm in terms of which deviations from these uniformities can be condemned.

A large part of DeBonald's sociology rests, then, upon an extensive series of analogies between the individual body, the family, and the society as a whole. Having perceived a certain relationship between two elements in the individual, he assumes that a similar relationship does or should exist between analogous elements in the family and society — and *vice versa*. This ignores the difference between the biological or organic, and the social levels of reality, but for DeBonald this difference is non-essential, for society itself is an organism. From this assumption springs an anti-individualism which is as intense as DeMaistre's and works along the same lines. Society is prior to the individual and is the real creator of civilization. Great men are those who adequately reflect the society in which they live. Originality, far from being desirable, is a potent source of evil. It leads to attempts at changing society, which are inevitably tragic in their outcome. Individualism is the first step toward anarchy. For DeBonald there is no halting-ground between unreasoning acquiescence to authority and refusal to accept any bounds whatsoever to the expansion of the ego. At bottom his argument rests on a conception of natural human depravity (here taking the form of asociality) which requires control by a code externally imposed.

In defense of his anti-individualistic or " sociologistic " conceptions, DeBonald develops several types of arguments of considerable importance in the history of social thought. The first of these is the philological. Ideas, he asserts, presuppose language. Thinking is impossible without words. Words enable us to make those distinctions without which thought is an impossibility. The thinker does not know what he means until he can think of the words which express it. Now it is obvious, DeBonald continues, that language is not an individual invention. To invent language it would first be necessary to have the idea of language, but, as has already been demonstrated, it is necessary to have language before one can have any ideas. Therefore we must conclude that man acquires language from the society into which he was born, and that *ab initio* language was not invented, but created by a divine source and presented ready-made to society.

DeBonald argues that what is true of language is also true of all the other social institutions. They could not have been invented; they must have been created by supernatural means. The individual man is entirely in error when he imagines that he has the power of invention or creation. We are all of us merely particular expressions of *society,* which is the thought of God. The ideas which we combine or recombine are those which are already in the social tradition and which are manifestly of divine origin (as their dependence on language clearly indicates). Man lives in and through social traditions. When those are weakened man suffers a general disorientation and *malaise:* when they are destroyed, he perishes. To live healthily we must live according to the laws and traditions which we inherit from our ancestors and which were originally given to society by God.

There can be no doubt that religion plays a central rôle in DeBonald's sociology. He insists that religion is an essential — one might even say *the* essential — factor in achieving social stability. This stability, as we have previously seen, depends on a moral consensus, on a tradition which must be accepted by all. Now religion is of value here precisely because of its mystical and non-rational character. It is a matter purely of faith and dogma, admittedly not amenable to reason, and it thus lends to tradition and to morality a sanction which is absolute and beyond the reach of discussion. Religion also has indirect effects of similar value and importance. DeBonald admits as axiomatic that for the vast majority of men life will be so afflicted with toil and misery as to make it a heavy burden. Religion is of value in that it helps them to bear that burden. First, it ennobles man's sufferings by interpreting them as divinely ordained; second, it focuses man's attention on the life to come. By taking the edge off human misery, religion inhibits social change.

DeBonald's ideas on the family are also worth brief examination. The family, not the individual, is the real unit of society. The individual is only a single point in an enormous succession of lives; he has significance only as the member of a family. The sole function of the family is reproduction; society must be maintained in spite of the death of individuals. The general character of the family follows from the natural law of its trinitarian structure. The father as cause must have both moral authority and physical power. Thus in primitive society the father has the right of life and death over his wife and children, and the " unwritten law " still gives him the right to kill a wife who has been unfaithful. The wife, as means, has the function of reproduction and, standing between the father and the child, she obeys the former and commands the latter. The child as subject has no function but obedience. There are two types of family: the *famille ordinaire,* and the *famille noble.* The first type is sunk in the cares of daily existence. Its whole function is economic and reproductive. It takes no real part in the higher forms of social existence, and forms a broad base on which the few aristocratic families rest. These families are properly relieved of the cares of material existence and are given the comforts and luxuries which enable them suitably to fulfill their functions. These functions are in general the study of social problems, the directing and guidance of society, and its defense against enemies. In this way DeBonald attempts a justification of what at bottom is the class structure of the *ancien régime.* For the rising bourgeoisie DeBonald had only distrust and dislike. The rural family seemed to him infinitely superior to the urban family, and he had a well-founded suspicion that industrialism and division of labor would lead to an increase of individualism. The urban *milieu* seemed also to be too productive of variation in thought to be anything other than dangerous.

The Significance of the Traditionalists. — It is impossible in a brief space adequately to evaluate or criticize the work of De-Maistre and DeBonald. What they have accomplished, above all, is an excellent analysis of an ideal type of the traditionalist society in general and of the *ancien régime* in particular. Any superficial criticism of DeBonald and DeMaistre is bound to be useless. It is of no value to show that they are on particular points involved in self-contradiction, since they are frankly contemptuous of reason, and base their systems on dogmas and sentiments. It is of no value to show that the march of history has left their sort of society behind, since recent events have shown that reverse movements are equally possible. What is needed is a thorough and systematic analysis of the whole set of presuppositions upon which their theories rest, and any attempt of this sort would constitute a formidable task.

It is necessary, however, to indicate at least briefly the great and important influence which their work has had upon the development of social thought. Through Saint-Simon many of their essential ideas were passed on to Comte, the father of modern sociology. Among these it may suffice to mention the following: the idea that society rests on a moral *consensus;* that individualism is " the disease of Western civilization "; that the individual has no rights, but duties; that the family rather than the individual is the true social unit; that society is a reality above and beyond its constituent individuals; that the reëstablishment of social stability rests upon the disciplining of the individual and a restoration of respect for authority; that religion is an essential and indispensable instrument of social control. Ideas of this sort have been passed on through the tradition of sociologistic positivism. In the neo-positivism of DeRoberty we have a " biosocial hypothesis " which makes the bare fact of association responsible for the emergence of human personality, and which revives DeBonald's argument that thought depends on language and that language could not be individual creation or invention. This hypothesis was taken up and expanded by Espinas and, particularly, by Izoulet. In the work of Durkheim, the spiritual descendant of Comte and the most influential of recent French sociologists, many ideas of DeMaistre and DeBonald reappear in a new and somewhat more scientific guise, but without any fundamental change of nature. Society is a reality *sui generis;* the individual is merely a partial expression of this larger reality and is powerless to effect any social changes on his own account; social institutions and traditions cannot be given an individualistic explanation since they are " social things "; the central social problem is that of social control, which is to be achieved solely by securing the individual's submission to the moral rules of the group externally imposed; society is in essence something external to and constraining the individual; the liberation of the individual from the constraining influences of the group is a source of social danger and personal disorganization leading even to suicide; the surest guarantee of social integration and stability lies in a body of dogma which is generally accepted; and religion is essential in this connection, for it has the basic function of revivifying group sentiment and reaffirming traditional standards and values.

These ideas form the basic framework of most of the work done by the Durkheim school in French sociology. Outside of academic sociology the influence of DeBonald and DeMaistre has been even more direct. The revival of traditionalism and royalism in France, in the works of Brunetière, Bourget, DeVogué, Le Maître, Maurras, Barrès, *et al.*, is not only inspired by the general spirit of DeBonald and DeMaistre, but is very little more than a new, and often inferior, restatement of their arguments.

Hegel and the Dialectic Conception. — Another absolutistic tendency in the interpretation of human progress of a quite different type is to be found in the philosophy of history set forth by the ponderous and abstruse German metaphysician and dialectician, Georg Wilhelm Friedrich Hegel (1770–1831). He organized his scheme of historical analysis upon the foundation of the evolution of human liberty, but his conception of liberty was much like that of the Duke of Alva in *Egmont:* " What is the freest freedom? Freedom to do right! " (with Alva determining the right). Dunning admirably characterizes Hegel's view of the world-process:

> The final channel through which the state is revealed as perfected free will is, according to Hegel, world history (*Weltgeschichte*). To him the process of events is an unfolding of universal spirit (*Geist*). The culture of every people — its art, religion, political institutions — expresses a particular stage in the activity and revelation of the absolute idea. Each successive age in world history since civilization began offers to view some people in whose spirit (*Volksgeist*) is reflected the world-spirit (*Weltgeist*) so far as that has been revealed. The process of revelation and realization of the idea, according to the principles of the Hegelian dialectic, is a fourfold process. It is not surprising, therefore, that Hegel's survey of general history detects four great world-historic political systems (*Reiche*) in whose successive careers the idea of freedom has progressed to perfect realization. These four systems are the Oriental, the Greek, the Roman and the German. With benumbing legerdemain the philosopher makes the commonplace facts of familiar history fit themselves nicely at the word into the categories and relations of his logic, and shows us mankind through all the ages marching steadily but unconsciously along Hegelian lines toward the Germanic perfection of the nineteenth century. In the modern world freedom is revealed to be the

universal principle of state life. "The Orient knew and to the present day knows only that *One* [*i.e.* the despot] is free; the Greek and Roman World, that *Some* are free; the German World knows that *All* are free."

Such is Hegel's generalization of the world-historical process. It displays the usual tendency of a philosophy of history — to represent the thinker's own time and place as the climax and summation of progress. But with whatever qualifications we judge the speculation and conclusions of Hegel, it is impossible to deny that the scope and coherency of his system of political science and the boldness and vast sweep of his historical inductions reveal a mind of titanic power.[44]

In addition to his general conception of the historical process as the gradual realization of liberty within the absolutist state, Hegel made one other important contribution to the idea of progress; namely, his theory of the so-called " dialectic of development." He held that the process of advancement is essentially the following: an affirmation or a movement — the thesis — appears; it is immediately countered by the emergence of an opposing contention or movement — the antithesis; and the conflict between the thesis and the antithesis results ultimately in a creative achievement, the synthesis of the best in the struggling principles or movements. The synthesis, however, immediately becomes the next thesis, to be opposed by a new antithesis, and the process again runs its course. This doctrine has more than curious interest, for it was adopted by Karl Marx as the basis for the theory of development embodied in the Marxian views of history and economics, and is even today responsible for much verbal fireworks in certain left-wing circles.

Hegel, in his attitude toward progress past and future, occupied a position almost the direct opposite of Godwin's. The latter held that there had been very little progress in the past, but hoped for almost infinite advancement in the future. Hegel contended that there had been a great deal of progress in the past — so much, indeed, that man had attained perfection in Hegel's own time, and therefore little was to be expected or desired from the future. Bury has well characterized this aspect of Hegel's doctrine:

. . . with Hegel the development is already complete, the goal is not only attainable but has now been attained. Thus Hegel's is what we may call a closed system. History has been progressive, but no path is left open for further advance. Hegel views this conclusion of development with perfect complacency. To most minds that are not intoxicated with the Absolute it will seem that, if the present is the final state to which the evolution of Spirit has conducted, the result is singularly inadequate to the gigantic process. But his system is eminently inhuman. The happiness or misery of individuals is a matter of supreme indifference to the Absolute, which, in order to realise itself in time, ruthlessly sacrifices sentient beings.

The spirit of Hegel's philosophy, in its bearing on social life, was thus antagonistic to Progress as a practical doctrine. Progress there had been, but Progress had done its work; the Prussian monarchical state was the last word in history. Kant's cosmopolitical plan, the liberalism and individualism which were implicit in his thought, the democracies which he contemplated in the future, are all cast aside as a misconception. Once the needs of the Absolute Spirit have been satisfied, when it has seen its full power and splendour revealed in the Hegelian philosophy, the world is as good as it can be. Social amelioration does not matter, nor the moral improvement of men, nor the increase of their control over physical forces.[45]

The Theory of Progress Merges with Sociology. — The idea of progress was probably the leading strain in early sociology — in other words, in the sociology of the nineteenth century. The chief interest of most of these sociological or quasi-sociological writers lay in discovering the nature of progress and the means of its realization. We shall analyze their views much more at length later, and hence shall rest content here with a brief summary of the leading points of view.

The need for sociology as a means of social planning and guidance was set forth early in the century by an enthusiastic devotee of the idea of progress, Count Henri de Saint-Simon. His belief in the possibility of progress is amply attested by the following eloquent paragraph:

The imagination of poets has placed the golden age in the cradle of the human race. It was the age of iron they should have banished there. The golden age is not behind us, but in front of us. It is the perfection of social order. Our fathers have not seen it; our children will arrive there one day, and it is for us to clear the way for them.[46]

He held that the rapid transformation of social and economic conditions which was being brought about by the scientific and industrial revolutions necessitated the creation of a real science of social progress, based upon thoroughly positivistic grounds. He called this essential new social science *la science politique,* but his disciple, Auguste Comte, was soon to christen it *sociologie.* He accepted the law of the three stages of intellectual progress, anticipated by Turgot and Burdin and later to be elaborated in great detail by Comte. Saint-Simon was thoroughly committed to the scientific and technological interpretation of history, and expected great things from applied science. At the same time, he was one of the first to understand that any advancement in this field would have to be paralleled by comparable progress in institutional re-adjustment to that same advancement if it was to prove permanent and trustworthy. This change could not be brought about through the application of emotionally dominated schemes for social re-form; it would require the intervention of a genuine social science, thoroughly informed and rigorously positivistic in attitude and methods. In his practical scheme for social reorganization, Saint-Simon advocated (1) the socialization of Christianity as a dy-namic emotional force, and (2) the placing of the control of the material destiny of society in the hands of technological experts, of social engineers who could master and apply the dictates of the new social science. Dunning thus summarizes Saint-Simon's spe-cific plan for socio-political reconstruction:

> The new social order must rest on the political leadership of the useful class. Capacity rather than possessions must become the qualification for control of the public service. The producers must supplant the mere consumers — the bees the drones — in political authority. For the real-ization of which end in France Saint-Simon sketched out the reorgan-ized political system. Without requiring the abolition of the monarchy, he called for a government with supreme power in a new species of parlia-ment. This body should include, first, a house of invention, consisting of civil engineers, poets (*ou autres inventeurs en littérature*), painters, sculp-tors, architects and musicians; second a house of examination, consisting of physicists and mathematicians; and third, a house of execution, con-sisting of captains of industry (*chefs des maisons d'industrie*), unsalaried, and duly apportioned among the various kinds of business. The first house would present projects of law, the second would examine and pass upon them, and the third would adopt them.[47]

Auguste Comte took up the views of Saint-Simon and developed them all in great detail. He accepted the argument for the neces-sity of a science of social reconstruction, described with great thor-oughness the stages of intellectual and social progress, and worked out a massive positivistic utopia based upon his sociological doc-trines. In his *Positive Philosophy* Comte set forth his views on the three great stages of the mental evolution of the race: the theo-logical, the metaphysical, and the positive or scientific. Many writ-ers have imagined that this trilogy of intellectual stages repre-sented Comte's conception of the stages of civilization and have criticized him for so narrow a view of the historical process. In his *Positive Polity,* however, one finds a much more comprehen-sive scheme cast in terms of historical rather than exclusively intellectual stages. Here he divides history into three great epochs: the Theological-Military, the Metaphysical-Legalistic, and the Scientific-Industrial. Each of the three stages was elaborately subdivided and minutely analyzed. In his positivistic utopia (to be considered at length in a later chapter) wisdom for social guidance was to be supplied by the sociologist-priests, moral stimulus was to be produced by the influence of women, and administrative acumen was to be made available by the captains of industry. Religion was to be divorced from supernaturalism and transformed into a collective emotion-building force supporting secular reforms and social justice.

In the thought of Herbert Spencer the idea of progress was merged with the notion of cosmic evolution. Everything in the universe was in a state of evolution, a conception in which Spencer envisaged both progress *and* decline. Nevertheless, he was a cosmological optimist; when talking about evolution he usually meant progress manifesting itself in accordance with his well-known laws of integration of matter and differentiation of form and function. Spencer did not, however, believe that man could coöperate effectively in hastening the process of evolution through positive legislation. He defended *laissez faire* on the grounds of cosmic evolution much as the Physiocrats had championed it on the basis of the socio-theological deductions from Newton's celestial mechanics. He contended that social evolution, like cosmic and organic development, was a purely naturalistic and genetic process which man could not hasten by lawmaking, but which he might seriously retard or distort. Among sociologists the Spencerian position was upheld by William Graham Sumner and many others, notably Ludwig Gumplowicz and Jacques Novicow. The opposite thesis was defended by the German *Kathedersozialisten* (" socialists of the chair " or " professorial socialists "), Lester F. Ward, Albion W. Small, and Leonard T. Hobhouse — to name only a few of the most prominent. Ward admitted that social evolution had thus far been for the most part purely naturalistic or genetic, but he contended that with the growth of human knowledge and social science man could gradually assume charge of the processes of his own development and supplant the wasteful genetic method of development by the more rapid and economical method of telesis or planning.

The latest phase of the discussion of the theory of progress among sociologists has been devoted to a critical analysis of the term, its implications, and its validity. Many sociologists now maintain that conceptions of progress have tended to be subjective or one-sided, with no objective tests or standards. Consequently it has seemed to such writers better for the time being to abandon the term " social progress " and to use instead a phrase that begs no questions, such as "social change." To illustrate: though we can demonstrate unprecedented progress in material complexity during the past hundred years, we cannot assume, as did the promoters of the "Century of Progress," that this is a proof of the progress of humanity in general. If this material progress ends by creating a civilization so complex that mankind proves helpless in the face of the problems of controlling it, then it is plain that the advances in technology since the early nineteenth century will not have been indicative of human progress. Certain writers, among them Tenney, Bossard, Kelsey, and Ellwood, have proposed the formulation of a comprehensive and objective set of tests of progress, so that we may begin to deal with the subject in a scientific and discriminating manner.

It is also interesting to note that the Classical theory of the cyclical nature of history has been recently revived by Oswald Spengler in his influential work, *The Decline of the West*. Pitirim Sorokin's profound and highly original work on *Social and Cultural Dynamics* shows traces of the Classical writers, but also of Ibn Khaldūn, DeMaistre, DeBonald, Durkheim, and others. For him the course of history is in some respects a " trendless flux " of "ideational," "sensate," and "idealistic" social and cultural configurations. (We shall consider this significant modern theory at length in Chapter Twenty.) Progress, in its nineteenth-century meaning, is summarily ushered out.

Summary of the Chapter. — Not until the seventeenth and eighteenth centuries did theories of progress become a really absorbing subject of speculation. Montaigne, Bacon, and Descartes began to divert attention from the ancients and medieval theology, thus making a definite start toward the idea under consideration here. Fontenelle was the first to formulate a systematic theory of progress; he maintained that moderns were neither biologically superior nor inferior to the ancients, but that since progress is cumulative in science and industry, the moderns far surpass the ancients. Perrault's views differed chiefly in that he considered that his age had already arrived at perfection, and consequently he had negligible interest in the future.

Vico, who has been credited with being among the first great writers on social theory to make systematic application of the historical method, attempted to formulate the principles which govern the development of society. His analysis was made in the form of stages and cycles; opinions differ as to whether or not these are compatible with a belief in progress. It can safely be said, however, that if he held such a belief it was simply a by-product of his analysis of intellectual and social development.

Turgot's most profound contribution in this connection was his assertion of the unity and continuity of history. His views on the effects of culture contact and related matters were surprisingly in advance of his time. He also definitely anticipated Comte's conception of the three stages of intellectual progress. In a very elaborate and sanguine description of the past and prophecy of the future, Condorcet viewed each of his numerous epochs as an unequivocal advance over the preceding one, and regarded his age as the threshold leading to a consummate degree of happiness and realization of human potentialities. Godwin believed that although man was capable of unlimited future progress through the influence of reason, oppressive human institutions had kept him from making progress in the past. The end of human progress was enlightened individualism, and the chief instruments were literature, education, and political justice.

During the latter part of the eighteenth century, the Romantic school began partially to displace the rationalist, to which most of the above-mentioned writers had belonged. The Romanticists arrived at a doctrine of political quietism, and a mystical strain colored all their thinking; on the other hand, they correctly emphasized the non-rational elements in historical development, called attention to the functional unity of culture-complexes, and exposed the fallacies in the crude catastrophic theory of the rationalists.

Herder was a connecting link between these two periods: he emphasized the mysterious psychic forces affecting mankind, and at the same time declared that human welfare rested solely on reason and justice. He declared that the destructive powers in nature must ultimately give way to the perfection of the whole. Kant's idea of progress, which was a moral one, contained germs of social teleology. He believed the human species as a whole to be ever more closely approximating its potentialities, and considered moral progress demonstrable.

The direct antithesis of such optimistic theories was set forth by the reactionary and traditionalist writers DeBonald and De-Maistre. They both regarded the " progress " culminating in the French Revolution as a great catastrophe, and hoped for the restoration of the *ancien régime*. They exercised much influence on Saint-Simon, Comte, and like successors.

Another authoritarian emphasis was introduced by Hegel, who viewed the historical process itself as the gradual realization of liberty. His dialectic contributed directly to the notion of progress through the young Hegelians, but his historicism and his belief that mankind had attained perfection in his own time were basically anti-progressive.

During the early nineteenth century, sociology began to take form, and the " climate of opinion " in which it grew was primarily determined by the idea of progress. Saint-Simon argued the necessity for the creation of a science of social progress, and expected applied science to usher in a golden age. Comte followed him closely in all his ideas, especially the emphasis on the necessity of a scientific basis for social reconstruction. Comte's means of attaining his positivistic utopia included secular reforms and social justice. Spencer seems to have believed that in general cosmic evolution makes for progress; he differed from such later sociologists as Ward, Small, and Hobhouse in considering social evolution a purely " natural " process which could not be furthered by lawmaking or planning.

The most recent development in the discussion of this subject is a critical analysis of the term and its implications; advances in technology are no longer being equated with human advance. There is a tendency to substitute the term " social change " for " social progress," and even to develop cyclical theories of a kind that implicitly or explicitly deny the possibility of progress.

In everyday life, at least in the United States, progress as not only inevitable but also desirable is accepted with little question except among those who fear atomic annihilation.

Further, a substantial number of American sociologists cherish a doctrine of progress under the Ogburnian disguise of "cultural lag." Cultures grow, as it were, but some parts grow more rapidly than others. Progress is attributable to the more rapidly growing parts; failure to progress, to the slower. Technology, in particular, outpaces the other parts, such as law or religion, and in so doing imposes strains on the latter that forces them to adjust or to dwindle still further. This bears some resemblance to Marxian substructure-superstructure conceptions, and in addition serves as a convenient means of slipping value-judgment cards into the scientific deck. There can be no objection to studies of the relation of technology, for example, to other parts of a culture, but there can be objection to viewing as "good" or "bad" whatever discrepancies in "growth" may be discovered. Cultural lag is at bottom a term of moral disapproval with regard to anything that is found to lag.

The present chapter deals adequately neither with the doctrine of progress attributable to Hegel nor with the range of variations found among right-wing and left-wing Hegelians. In a later chapter (xvii), dealing with Marx at some length, this deficiency is partially remedied.

CHAPTER XIV

Unity in Diversity: Sociological Aspects of
the Rapidly Differentiating
Social Sciences

GROWTH OF SPECIALIZATION. — The increase in the division of labor that is both cause and consequence of increase in the complexity of culture was strikingly manifest in Europe after the series of changes that ushered in early modern times — breakdown of isolation, growth of money economy, advance of secularization, and so on — was well under way. Not only was the handicraftsman who made his product from start to finish slowly supplanted by the merchant who organized whole communities of home-workers along highly specialized lines, not only did the factory make its appearance (even before the introduction of steam), but in the learned world as well the division of labor gradually increased its scope. During the " Thirteenth, Greatest of Centuries," a Thomas Aquinas could write *summae* that almost covered the full range of human knowledge at that time, but the joint impact of " a smaller earth and a larger world " so shattered the old framework of learning that it could no longer aid in compressing the vast bulk of new knowledge to manageable size. More and more men resigned themselves to the onerous task of extracting irreducible elements of knowledge from the landslide of fact, perhaps in the hope that these elements might some day enter into a new secular synthesis that should utterly dwarf the once majestic edifice of the Age of Faith. The forerunners of the specialized anthropogeographer, economist, psychologist, political scientist, and sociologist entered upon the scene of their labors.

It must of course be remembered that specialization was not far-reaching during the period under consideration (extending roughly from Bacon to Comte). Most of the writers with whom we shall deal focused on but one aspect of social life, true enough, but nearly all of them thought that they could interpret all the significant phases of society by continually tracing their manifestations to the one aspect they chose as most important. Even the cautious Adam Smith did not wholly escape this particularistic fallacy; although he did not base his doctrines on the analysis of one aspect alone, he thought that two were sufficient, as we shall see, and with the keys of self-interest and sympathy he sought to unlock every door in the mansion of the social sciences. But we should not be too exacting in our standards, especially in view of the fact that a great many modern social scientists flirt with the same particularistic fallacy, and sometimes fall prey to its wiles.

In this chapter we shall deal with the early modern stages of human geography, economics, psychology, history, political science, and jurisprudence in so far as they have a bearing on social thought in general and sociology in particular.

Human Geography Gets under Way. — The advances brought about by the specialized study of the influence of the physical environment upon man and human society between the beginning of the seventeenth and the early nineteenth century were remarkable indeed. During this period the transition was effected from the astrological absurdities of Bodin to the beginnings of truly scientific physical geography and anthropogeography with Karl Ritter. Only a little more than half a century after Bodin, Jean Chardin began to gather together anthologies of travelers' stories about the strange lands of the East and the New World which had recently been discovered. These collections furnished the theoretical writers with an abundance of illustrative material; Montesquieu, for example, drew very heavily upon Chardin's *Travels*. In Alexander von Humboldt and others of his type about a century and a half later, we find the first really scientific explorers; they made observations sufficiently precise and extensive to enable their reports to be used with some assurance by the geographers and "political philosophers." Richard Mead and John Arbuthnot illustrate the combined effects of the discoveries in the physics of atmospheric pressure and the post-Vesalian physiological attitude toward bodily processes and their conditioning by external factors. Montesquieu, Herder, and Ferguson, in their attempt to view social processes in something of a comparative fashion, naturally endeavored to assess the relative importance of geographical influences. Bernhardus Varenius laid down the framework for the science of geography, and Karl Ritter, building upon the work of predecessors and the accurate reporting of geographical data by Humboldt and others, not only established modern physical geography upon the foundations of wide knowledge and sound methods, but also laid the basis of modern anthropogeography —

most of the great anthropogeographers of the generation of Ratzel had been Ritter's students.

The Travelers and " Social Meteorologists." — Jean Chardin (1643–1715) was the son of a rich Frenchman. Dominated by a passion for adventure and travel, he made two trips to Persia in 1665 and 1667, and published an account of his experiences in his *Travels in Persia,* one of the most highly prized of the early modern works on distant lands. His observations on the domestic customs of the Persians and on the Persian government were the chief sources from which Montesquieu derived his conceptions of polygyny and Oriental despotism. Chardin's work was representative of a number of books of this sort which were eagerly used by descriptive and theoretical writers on the subject of history and political philosophy.

Much more important was the descriptive work of great scientific explorers like Alexander von Humboldt (1769–1859). They described the configuration of the earth and climatic conditions with detailed accuracy, and indicated with precision and insight the relation between these physical factors and the distribution and character of plant and animal life. Such careful work in the field of description and classification in geography was necessary before men like Ritter and his successors could systematize physical geography and lay down the beginnings of scientific anthropogeography.

Richard Mead (1673–1754) was an English physician of great eminence in England during the first half of the eighteenth century. He took cognizance of the progress in physiology which had begun with Vesalius's study of anatomy and Harvey's discovery of the circulation of the blood; consequently, he discarded the greater part of the Hippocratic speculations concerning the four humors and their admixture. Likewise, he had familiarized himself somewhat with the recent advances in atmospheric physics signalized by Torricelli's barometer and the rudimentary laws concerning the pressure of gases set forth by Boyle. His important work on the subject of atmospheric influences was entitled *A Treatise Concerning the Influence of the Sun and Moon on Human Bodies,* in which he assigned differences in atmospheric pressure to the pull of the sun and moon, particularly the latter, upon the atmospheric band which surrounds the earth. If the moon exerted an influence upon the oceans and caused tides, said Mead, it must also affect the air. He held that the maximum pull of the sun and moon on the atmosphere came at the time of new and full moons, when the attraction of both sun and moon was combined.

The changes in atmospheric pressure produced by the pull of the sun and moon on the air profoundly affect the bodily processes, Mead contended, and he attempted to work out an extended theory of the correlation between physiological processes, mental states, and the courses of diseases on the one hand, and lunar periods on the other. Both Mead's meteorology and his physiology were lamentably weak and misleading, when compared with modern knowledge, but his work represented the first important step which was to lead students of this subject from the morass of astrology to precise statistical studies showing just how much (or how little) can be claimed for meteorological influences.

Rather more scientific and comprehensive was the work of another British physician, John Arbuthnot (1667–1735), whose *Essay Concerning the Effect of the Air on Human Bodies* appeared in 1733. Arbuthnot did not remain content with the study of atmospheric pressure, but also dealt with other " qualities of the air," such as heat, cold, and dryness. He found that these characteristics of the atmosphere, singly and in combination, greatly affected the physiological processes of man. Climatic influences on man and society were of particular interest to him, and he held to a theory of climatic determinism, contending that the institutions of any area remain essentially unchanged even when there is a shift of the inhabiting races. Further, said he, institutions must be adapted to geographical conditions; it is impossible to legislate successfully in the face of environmental opposition. His views were in singular accord with those of Montesquieu (1689–1755), the great author of *The Spirit of Laws* to whom we have many times referred; and the French scholar, Dedieu, has contended that Montesquieu derived the greater number of his theoretical views from Arbuthnot, as he did much of his illustrative material from Chardin.

Montesquieu, Herder, and Ferguson as Anthropogeographers. — During this period a number of writers made an effort to present a panoramic and comparative view of social processes and human development. In so doing they felt themselves compelled to consider the geographical influences which operate on man and society. Of this type of writer, decidedly the most important was Montesquieu. As we have pointed out above, his descriptive material was drawn from Chardin and other compilers of books of travel and history, and his theoretical doctrines were based chiefly upon the writings of Arbuthnot. He is also said to have worked out a crude experiment as to the actual effect of heat and cold upon animal fibres by heating and cooling the tongue of a

sheep, observing the effect of such procedure meanwhile. Whatever we may think of this Laputa-like method for discovering the
effect of climate on world-civilization, at least the mentality it
manifested marked an advance over the astrological credulity of
Bodin.

The purpose of *The Spirit of Laws* was to lay down the fundamental principles of legislation. These Montesquieu found to be
primarily: (1) the adaptation of institutions and legislation to
the character of the peoples for whom they were intended; and
(2) the harmonious interaction of the various institutions, laws,
and other devices for ensuring social control and well-being applied by any group. Such a view led him to consider the factors
which produced the diverse physical and cultural characteristics
to be observed among the various peoples of the world, and he
defended the position that the main cause of the diversities among
human types and cultures was geographical influences, especially
climate. By examining the effects of geographical factors, he held,
one could discover the traits of the different peoples of the world
and thus be in a position to determine the appropriate laws and
institutions for each type of man. Montesquieu frankly abandoned
the conventional view that there was some absolutely best state,
religion, form of family, or moral code, and entirely adopted the
comparative approach. That institution was "best" which was
best adapted to the conditions of the people for whom it was intended. Climate and other geographical factors have created the
various types of man, said he, and it is the function of the wise
legislator to discover just what these types and traits are and to
legislate accordingly. To illustrate: Montesquieu maintained that
a despotism was best adapted to the type of peoples dwelling in
warm climates, a limited monarchy to those in temperate climates,
and a republic to the dwellers in cold areas. Mohammedanism was
eminently suited to those living in the tropics, Catholicism to
those in intermediate climates, and Protestantism to those in
colder zones. Polygyny was particularly fit for the tropics,
whereas monogamy was indicated in temperate and cold regions.
Drinking should be tabooed in the warm climates, because no
stimulus is needed to produce vivacity, but heavy drinking may be
tolerated in cold areas because of the need of internal heat and a
stimulation of the senses and of playfulness among the "phleg-
matic peoples of the north."

Johann Gottfried von Herder, in his *Ideen zur Philosophie der
Geschichte der Menschheit* (1784), also accepted the view that
great influence was exerted upon the course of the historical de-

velopment of mankind by geographical forces, especially topographic and climatic conditions. Nevertheless, he was far more restrained and qualified than Montesquieu, for to him the driving forces in history were the innate tendencies of man as a manifestation of organic nature. (How these innate tendencies arose and functioned he admitted he could not wholly explain, and finally had recourse to *Geist.*) Civilization-building was a process whereby this dynamic factor of human nature was modified and conditioned by the environmental surroundings. As we noted in the chapter on culture contact, Herder cautioned against sweeping generalizations with regard to geographic conditioning, and called attention to the need of recognizing exceptions and variations. Moreover, he also departed from the common tendency to regard geographical influences as invariably exerted in some direct or immediate fashion, and showed how such environmental conditions might operate quite indirectly, by affecting the life and habits of the peoples and in this way reacting upon their physical nature.

In his *History of Civil Society,* Adam Ferguson (1723–1816) also laid much stress upon the conditioning influence of climate, but, like Herder, he was inclined to be more cautious than Montesquieu. His most notable thesis was the superiority of the temperate climates as the physical environment for the higher cultures, and right or wrong, it was the first argument for this point of view which was free from the astrological hypothesis and from other mystical conceptions which had come down from antiquity.

The Founding of the Specialized Branches of Geography.— The general problems and framework of scientific geography were laid down by the brilliant young Dutch geographer, Bernhardus Varenius, in his *Geographia Generalis* (1650). He divided geography into three major departments: (1) absolute geography, dealing with the dimensions of the earth and its movements in space, a precise mathematical science; (2) relative geography, or the study of the causes and influences of climatic zones, seasonal changes, and the like; and (3) comparative geography, comprising a study of the grand divisions, precise location by latitude and longitude, and the physical features of the earth. Varenius thus made possible a more exact pursuit of geographical knowledge and the better classification and organization of geographic facts as they were subsequently accumulated.

Both scientific physical geography and reputable anthropogeography are usually and rightfully held to have been founded by Karl Ritter (1779–1859). Physical geography was established in his massive *Die Erdkunde im Verhältnis zur Natur und zur Geschichte der Menschen,* while his anthropogeographical conceptions were embodied in the introduction to the *Erdkunde* and in three lectures delivered before the Berlin Academy in 1833, 1836, and 1850.

There is a vast gap between the anthropogeographical views and conclusions of Ritter and those of any predecessor, not excepting even Herder. Ritter possessed an unrivaled knowledge of the facts of geography, together with a constructive imagination. Moreover, his professional interests linked him as closely to history as to geography, and this enabled him to place " geographical influences " in a genetic and cultural perspective. As a consequence the cardinal sins of anthropogeography find no exemplar in Ritter; he did not neglect the human element in history, he did not attempt to force the doctrine of geographic determinism, he was always qualified in his generalizations, and he fully recognized that changes in culture modify the effect of environmental factors. Some modern exponents of " cultural sociology " hold that they alone are guiltless of these high crimes and misdemeanors; hence we shall quote Ritter's views on the relation of geography to man, and on the necessity of taking account of the connections between history and geography:

Man cannot be regarded as dissociated from those things which cover the earth and occupy space. He belongs to the earth, and to the three natural kingdoms, the mineral, the vegetable and the animal, having, by virtue of his material form, characteristics found in all of these. And yet man, whether regarded as an individual or as having collective, national existence, is not bound to one spot as are the members of the three natural kingdoms; still he is very much modified by his surroundings, both in his physical and intellectual nature. Thus it results that the effects of situation, however great they may be, upon the inanimate world as well as upon living forms, and the spiritual development in special of human beings and nations, of the whole human race indeed, is an important part of the themes which fall within the province of geographical science. But, though laws do not change, the elements which make up the earth's surface are in constant change. All the surroundings which condition life are in never-ceasing flux and reflux; obeying the great promptings of the earth, they manifest a constant movement and advance; they are all obedient to great and harmonious laws of progress. But man, although following the laws of development which have their home in his soul, yet, so long as he is a creature moving upon the surface of the earth, is brought into conflict with the unceasing movement of his surroundings. And thus reflex influence of place upon the life of man, and the moulding of the human race, physically and spiritually, become the crowning task of geographical science. . . .

We have to keep constantly in mind that there is such a truth as the contemporaneous existence of things, as well as their chronological sequence. The science which embraces the affairs of place can just as little do without a measure of the order of events in point of time, as the science which embraces the affairs of time can dispense with a theatre of observation where those affairs can be brought before the eyes of men. History demands such a theatre for its own development; it must, whether it declares the need or not, have a geographical department, — a field where it may display its events; it must give a prominent position to that science which concerns the *places* where events occur, whether in the writings of such men as Thucydides and Johannes Müller, who open their works with a broad geographical survey, or in the writings of Herodotus, Tacitus, and other masters in this department, who give geographical delineations in the course of their historical progress, and by way of illustration; or, again, in the writings of such as only tinge their works with geographical tints, as it were. In the philosophy of history, as Leibnitz and Bacon have outlined it, and as Herder has carried it into fulfilment, the bearing of geography has of course a doubly conspicuous place.

But, on the other hand, geographical science can just as little dispense with the historical element, if it wishes to take rank as embracing all the relations of extents on the earth's surface, — not as an imperfect and partial thing, the mere frame and rafters of a structure, but the whole perfected dwelling itself, comely, shapely, and in every part complete.[1]

We should not conclude this brief summary of the early phases of anthropogeographical doctrine without once more calling attention to David Hume's vigorous assault upon the geographical determinists (especially Arbuthnot and Montesquieu, though he does not mention them by name), and his defense of social and cultural determinism. (See Chapter XI, pp. 407–409.) It is true, of course, that although Hume's strictures possessed great relevance when directed against the type of analysis presented by Montesquieu, they are not so annihilating when applied to Ritter's carefully qualified hypotheses.

The Birth of Modern Economics in Mercantilism. — The period from 1600 to 1800 (or thereabouts) witnessed the beginnings of modern economic science. In the Middle Ages it had been primarily a branch of applied theology and ethics, but in the early modern period it emerged as an independent science of the acquisition and uses of wealth. The evolution of economic science in this period is primarily associated with three phases of doctrine:

(1) Mercantilism, which flourished from about 1600 to 1750; (2) the Physiocratic doctrine, which developed in the middle of the eighteenth century as a revolt against the restrictions of the Mercantilist system; and (3) the quasi-synthesis of the then existing economic theories by Adam Smith in *The Wealth of Nations.*

The first notable writer to advance the body of ideas known as Mercantilism was Antonio Serra, an Italian authority who in 1613 published a book entitled *A Brief Treatise on the Causes which make Gold and Silver abound where there are no Mines.* Other eminent Mercantilists were Sir Thomas Mun (1571–1641), Sir William Petty (1623–1687), Sir Josiah Child (1630–1699), and Sir Charles Davenant (1659–1714).

The commercial expansion of this era, with its various subordinate results, had a direct and important effect upon the political tendencies of the time, particularly the growth of large territorial states and the trend toward secular absolutism. With the increased resources of the royal treasuries as a result of the income from privateering, customs duties, and fees for chartering monopolistic companies, the kings became more powerful, and were able gradually to make good their aspiration for ascendency over feudal lords. The possibility of maintaining a paid army and officialdom loyal to their source of supply was a basic factor in creating the early national dynastic states. This fresh access of income was also used by many states to extend their territories in Europe and overseas through warfare. Again, the various activities of the state in connection with commercial monopolies and maritime regulation served greatly to extend the notion of its importance and the scope of its activities. Finally, the narrowly conceived commercial policy known as Mercantilism helped to create a feeling of national separatism and jealousy, thus stimulating the nationalistic trend.

The Commercial Revolution produced a very important development in the commercial theories and policies of Western Europe. Interference by central governments in economic life had not been unknown in the medieval period, but the relative weakness of the secular state had prevented such control from assuming any very significant proportions. With the combined and parallel growth of world-commerce and the national dynastic state, there evolved the policy and practice of the most complete governmental regulation of economic activities. This new policy, though varying in detail and extent of application, was known as Mercantilism in England, as Colbertism in France, and as Cameralism in Germany. It rested upon the projection into economic life of the current narrowly nationalistic conceptions and practices. Every state was assumed to be the potential commercial enemy of every other, and the prosperity of each was supposed to depend upon a narrow, exclusive policy of monopolizing the trade of its colonies and at the same time doing everything possible to restrict or injure the commerce of its neighbors.

Doctrines and Policies of the Mercantilists. — The fundamental assumptions of this Mercantilist system were roughly as follows: (1) The available supply of precious metals is the all-important measure of the wealth of a nation. (2) Aside from mining of ore, trade is the chief means of accumulating these precious metals in the shape of specie. (3) In order that this trade may be profitable, in order that specie may be accumulated, there must be a favorable balance of exports over imports. (4) To furnish markets for these exports and thus to create a favorable balance of trade for the mother-country, colonies are valuable, if not indispensable. (5) In order that the colonies may furnish markets for finished products and a source of supply of raw materials, manufacturing must be forbidden in the colonies, lest they supply their own necessities and exhaust their stock of raw materials. (6) The colonies must thus be looked upon primarily as profitable commercial enterprises of the mother-country.

We now know that this Mercantilist argument was erroneous in many of its premises, particularly the notions that the supply of specie is the chief mark of national prosperity and that a favorable balance of trade necessarily means an increase in the volume of available specie. We further know that these policies and practices greatly restricted the commercial activity and prosperity of the various European states. Inevitably, the sum of the small injuries they inflicted on each other did some damage to the European family of nations as a whole. These facts were not understood at the time, and this attitude of the state toward economic life persisted with little mitigation until the second quarter of the nineteenth century.

Along with those aspects of Mercantilism which related to commercial and colonial policies went very important extensions of state activity in economic affairs within the home boundaries. In England such things as the Statute of Apprentices introducing state control of labor and its conditions, the establishment of the price-fixing power of the justices of the peace, and the state control of industrial life by public proclamation are significant cases in point. In France the state enforcement of guild practices and mores, the digging of canals, the erection of public buildings, and the reclamation of land are achievements associated with Colbert and his assistants and successors.

Cameralism and Social Planning. — Even more thoroughgoing was the state intervention in the field of national economic life and public finance in Prussia, guided by the German Cameralists and most thoroughly executed under the aegis of Frederick the Great. This trend was colored by the peculiar semi-feudal circumstances which still existed in the Germanic states as compared with commercial states like England, France, and Holland. The problem of foreign trade was not overwhelmingly important at that date in Germanic countries, and the philosophy of extensive state intervention was naturally turned in the direction of domestic problems, and this brought up the question of the technique of social improvement by means of state regulation and control. Evidently the answer to the question was that improvement through state intervention was feasible, for the number and influence of the Cameralists, who favored state control, increased by leaps and bounds. The leading Cameralists were Veit Ludwig von Seckendorff (1626–1692), Johann Joachim Becher (1635–1682), Wilhelm Freiherr von Schroeder (1640–1684) Julius Bernhard von Rohr (1688–1742), Georg Heinrich Zincke (1692–1768), Johann Heinrich Gottlob von Justi (1717–1771), and Joseph von Sonnenfels (1733–1817). The chief student of Cameralism from the sociological point of view has been Small, and we offer in the following quotation his estimate of the significance of the Cameralists in the history of social thought:

This system of ideas and of practice had been developing since 1555. It did not correspond in its subdivisions with later academic definitions of the social sciences. It started not as general theory but as formulation of administrative expediency. It set forth with the frank purpose of subordinating everything within the control of the state to the state's problem of existence. The central question to which cameralism elaborated answers was: The ruler being all-powerful over his territories and his subjects, what policies, and what details of practice in pursuance of the policies must he adopt, in order to make his rule most secure at home, and in order to provide most abundant means of asserting himself against other rulers? It would require but little reflection to prepare against surprises at what happened. Under the circumstances of the time, this question necessarily led to answers which amounted to prescribed programs covering the entire outward life of the subjects of German rulers. It soon became evident to the advisers of those rulers, and to the administrators of their states, that their problem involved not merely physical factors, but that it was a question of training the whole population for all the different sorts of useful work of which human beings are capable.

From generation to generation the men who developed cameralistic theory and practice saw more and more clearly that if the rulers of German
states were to command abundant resources, they must rule over re-
sourceful people. This meant that the people must be trained physically,
mentally, morally and technically. In the end, therefore, cameralistic
theory covered everything in the lives of the citizens, from farm work
to religious worship. The machinery for administering this theory grew
more and more complex. In detail its organization differed in one state
from that in another. Its main purpose was everywhere the same, viz.,
to make the people as amenable as possible to all the discipline necessary
to insure maximum performance of all the physical, mental and moral
processes tributary to the strength of the ruler.[2]

The Revolt against Mercantilism. — The restrictions imposed
upon the complete freedom of trade and industry by the state-
intervention policies of Mercantilism soon engendered a revolt
against this type of doctrine and practice. The philosophical justification of this revolt was discovered in the naturalistic philosophy
based upon the scientific discoveries of men like Sir Isaac Newton.
(The effect of these discoveries upon Berkeley has already been
discussed.) Newton had shown that certain definite cosmic
"laws" governed the physical universe, and those desiring to
combat Mercantilism maintained that equally few and simple laws
controlled human society. Man should therefore cease attempting
to control social processes; the social order should be left to the
beneficent control of God, which would only yield the maximum
of beneficence if there was no interference from human legislation.

These writers, considered in the aggregate, were the real founders of modern economics, though Adam Smith is usually accorded
this honor, and they soon dropped the name *Physiocrates* and took
that of *Economistes*. There is perhaps a good analogy between
the history of sociology and that of economics: the Physiocrats
might be compared to Comte, and Smith to Spencer, as far as their
place in the development of the two sciences is concerned. In saying this we should not overlook the fact that the Physiocrats
thought that they could interpret virtually all the significant
phases of society by reference to *l'ordre naturel*. This circumstance justifies their inclusion in a history of social thought — if
any justification is needed.

The Physiocratic Exaltation of Normal as Natural. — The
fundamental doctrine of the Physiocratic school was the belief
in the existence of a *natural order* in the workings of the universe
of which man is a part. Anything which conformed to these nat-

ural laws was destined to succeed, whereas that which ran counter to them was bound to be handicapped and to end in ultimate failure. All that was necessary to bring about human happiness was to learn what constituted this universal plan of nature and to conform oneself to it. As Higgs puts it:

The general plan of creation had provided natural laws for the government of all things, and man could be no exception to the rule. He needed only to know the conditions which conduce to his greatest happiness and to follow and observe them. All the ills of humanity arise from ignorant opposition to these laws, study of which will show that the welfare of each member of society is inseparably bound up with the welfare of others, and the attainment of this common welfare will dispose mankind to grateful adoration of the beneficent Being by whose order this perfect cosmos is maintained.[3]

The conception of the natural as the normal rather than as the primitive was a real contribution, for modern scientific usage attaches a similar meaning to the term. Once this point of view was accepted, it followed that it was not necessary to return to the rude primitive state in order to reach the ideal condition. One needed only to conform to the natural laws of the cosmic process. It was this idea, more elaborately developed, which was given great vogue by Herbert Spencer in his dogma that the evolutionary process was a natural and automatic development. It is easy to see that this conception is at variance with the doctrine of Rousseau and others who held that man was free only in the state of nature and that he sacrificed much in entering society, although he might receive some compensatory benefits by so doing. The Physiocrats, quite on the contrary, claimed that man gained tremendously by passing from the stage of savagery into that of civilization. To quote a passage from Gide and Rist on this subject:

The worship of the "noble savage" was a feature of the end of the eighteenth century. It pervades the literature of the period, and the cult which began with the tales of Voltaire, Diderot, and Marmontel reappears in the anarchist writers of to-day. As an interpretation of the Physiocratic position, however, it must be unhesitatingly rejected, for no one bore less resemblance to a savage than a Physiocrat. They all of them lived highly respectable lives as magistrates, *intendants,* priests, and royal physicians, and were completely captivated by ideas of orderliness, authority, sovereignty, and property — none of them conceptions compatible with a savage state. "Property, security, and liberty constitutes the whole of the social order." They never acquiesced in the view that mankind suffered loss in passing from the state of nature into the social state; neither did they hold to Rousseau's belief that there was greater freedom in the natural state, although its dangers were such that men were willing to sacrifice something in order to be rid of them, but that nevertheless in entering upon the new state something had been lost which could never be recovered. All this was a mere illusion in the opinion of the Physiocrats. Nothing was lost, everything was to be gained, by passing from a state of nature into the civilised state.

In the second place, the term " natural order " might be taken to mean that human societies are subject to natural laws such as govern the physical world or exercise sway over animal or organic life. From this standpoint the Physiocrats must be regarded as the forerunners of the organic sociologists. Such interpretation seems highly probable because Dr. Quesnay through his study of " animal economy " (the title of one of his works) and the circulation of the blood was already familiar with these ideas. Social and animal economy, both, might well have appeared to him in much the same light as branches of physiology. From physiology to Physiocracy was not a very great step. At any rate, the Physiocrats succeeded in giving prominence to the idea of the interdependence of all social classes and of their final dependence upon nature. And this we might almost say was a change tantamount to a transformation from a moral to a natural science. . . .

To sum up, we may say that the " natural order " was that order which seemed obviously the best, not to any individual whomsoever, but to rational, cultured, liberal-minded men like the Physiocrats. It was not the product of the observation of external facts; it was the revelation of a principle within. And this is one reason why the Physiocrats showed such respect for property and authority. It seemed to them that these formed the very basis of the " natural order." [4]

Property, Government, and Laissez Faire. — Their social and political philosophy was in entire harmony with this conception of the natural order in the universe. The very organization of man shows that he was meant for society and a social life. Society is made up of a number of individuals who have the same natural rights. Though all may not be equal in capacity, yet each is better equipped than anyone else to pursue his own interests. The immediate object of society is the increase of wealth, which means increased happiness. Property is essential to man's preservation, and the liberty to use it as seems fit must be held as an integral part of property rights. Government is a necessary evil, is based upon a contract, and must be limited to the least amount of interference which is essential to prevent anyone from interfering with the rights of others. As far as industry is concerned, this rule must guarantee to the laborer the full fruits of his labors. Freedom of trade should be secured, competition should be unrestricted, and all monopolies should be abolished.

The two organs of government are to be: first, a body of magistrates who put into execution such laws as they think just; and second, a "tutelary authority" or a sort of patriarchal despot, who is a co-partner with his subjects in the wealth of his realm, and thus has no incentive to rule unjustly, but on the contrary has every inducement to govern with discretion. He should give out the laws, since the Physiocrats, by an ingenious logic, argued that a legislative body was undesirable. If the members of a legislature disagreed, then all could not be perfectly wise, while if they were in harmony, this meant that one person would be just as good if not better. A strange form of government was thus provided: the judges were to assume both judicial and executive power, whereas the supreme law-giving power was to be lodged in a single monarch deprived of executive powers. Legal despotism was thus considered the best form of government, while arbitrary despotism was thought so infinitely bad that a true nation could not exist under its sway.

The government, it was held, should keep out of economic affairs entirely except for negative interference for the purpose of securing the free operation of the natural order of things. Its motto should be the famous phrase *laissez faire*. The origin of this classic maxim is usually assigned to Gournay, but, says Higgs, " a study of Turgot's *Éloge de Gournay* shows that the expression *laissez faire* is really due to Le Gendre, a merchant who attended a deputation to Colbert about 1680 to protest against excessive state regulation of industry, and pleaded for liberty of action in the phrase ' *Laissez-nous faire.*' "[5] Higgs admits, however, that it was probably Gournay who popularized the phrase and brought it into general use.

Agriculture, Sole Source of Wealth. — We may now turn to what was the most important doctrine of this school, as far as the history of social thought is concerned: namely, their interpretation of social development in terms of agriculture. Only agriculture, including mining, was, according to their view, productive. " Civilization began with agriculture. ' The first wheat sown in the earth was the germ of empires.' With agriculture came settled life, property, and political government. There followed too a great increase of people, for ' men only multiply in proportion to the wealth necessary to their subsistence; and so it is that agriculture, which is the only source of the wealth of empires, occasions a rapid increase of population.' "[6] Gide holds that this preference of the Physiocrats for agriculture had a theological basis, since the creation of agricultural products was the work of God, while commerce and manufacture were the work of man — God alone being able to create anything. Still, he says, the predilections of the Physiocrats may be excused, since Lavoisier had not yet shown by his work in chemistry that nothing could be created or destroyed, but only transformed.

Ingram points out that their partiality for agriculture was due to the prevailing sentiment in favor of nature and primitive simplicity.[7] Probably both of these influences played their part, but they were only two out of many, among the most important of the others being their hostility to the Mercantilist theories and their indignation at the poverty and wretchedness of France. Perhaps this last was the most important of all the causes for their emphasis upon agriculture, and it found utterance in their famous maxim, " Poor peasants, poor kingdom; poor kingdom, poor king."

The Net Product and the Single Tax. — The Physiocrats' conception of production was the creation of a surplus over cost rather than the mere creation of commodities. The land produces a surplus over and above the necessities of the laborers who aid in its utilization, and it is this surplus which makes possible commerce and the professions and stimulates industry. This surplus due to the bounty of nature, of production over cost, was termed the *produit net,* and upon its amount depended the prosperity of a country and the possibility and rate of social evolution. It was to secure the greatest amount possible of this *produit net* that the Physiocrats advocated the abolition of special privileges and the reign of free competition. This was necessary in order that each producer might have the best possible conditions under which to carry on his work of extracting the *produit net.*

In harmony with their general theory of the importance of agriculture was their theory of a single tax or *impôt unique;* this tax, to be laid upon the land, was not to exceed one-third of the surplus of production — i.e., of the *produit net.* Their argument was that the weight of the taxes ultimately fell upon land under any method of levying, and that by putting it upon the land at the outset, the expense of collection and the opportunity for corruption would be greatly lessened. They differed from Henry George and his followers, however, in that they did not advise the abolition of private property in land, but rather strove to guarantee this right. (Land nationalization as a remedy for social evils was later recommended by Charles Hall, a learned English physician, who published his *Effects of Civilisation* in 1805.)

Adam Smith, Founder of " Classical Economics." — The most distinguished and influential book which grew out of the movement of economic liberalism was the classic work of Adam Smith. Smith was acquainted with the work of the Physiocrats and derived much from contact with them. Yet he added much that was original and he is usually regarded as the founder of systematic economics. " In the year 1776, Adam Smith published his *Wealth of Nations;* which, looking at its ultimate results, is probably the most important book which has ever been written, and is certainly the most valuable contribution ever made by a single man toward establishing the principles on which government should be based." [8] Henry Thomas Buckle thus described the significance of the work of the eminent leader of the British school of classical economists. While the exponents of the now popular theory of extensive state activity would be inclined sharply to differ with Buckle's estimate of the importance of *The Wealth of Nations* as an expression of political and economic philosophy, there can be no doubt that this work was more effective than any other in producing the generally accepted economic theory which dominated the mid-Victorian era in which Buckle wrote his *History of Civilisation in England.* Whatever may be the opinion of the modern social reformer with respect to the validity of Smith's individualistic and *laissez faire* social theory, it is undeniable that a work which for more than half a century was able to shape the political and economic thought of a great European country, as well as of a considerable portion of continental Europe, is worthy of serious consideration by any student of the evolution of social thought. Inasmuch as Smith's major work involved both political philosophy and economic theory, it may increase the clarity of this summary analysis to treat these two phases of his doctrines separately (though in Smith's mind they formed a single unified and coherent body of thought).

Smith's Political Doctrines. — In his political theory Smith followed the teachings of Locke, Montesquieu, and Hume, combined with the doctrines of the Physiocrats, regarding the proper scope of state activity. It is his concern with the latter which is of chief importance in this analysis, as he here exerted his greatest influence. Accepting the doctrine which the Physiocrats had taken over from contemporary scientists and *philosophes* — namely, that there is a natural and beneficent order which pervades the universe and of necessity extends to the domain of social phenomena, an order which man cannot and therefore should not attempt to alter — Smith launched a violent attack upon the restrictive state activity which had been advocated by the Mercantilist writers who had dominated political and economic theory and practice for more than a century prior to 1776. It was his fundamental thesis that human happiness and " the wealth of nations " can be most rapidly and effectively increased by bringing about complete industrial and commercial liberty, and it was at this point that his political philosophy merged with his economic theory and made possible a unified and coherent body of doctrine, though it prevented Smith from separating politics from economics as effectively as he had divorced ethics from economics.

Smith enumerates the three classes of duties which it falls to a state to perform or to guarantee the execution thereof, and beyond which it should not proceed. These are: (1) the protection of the citizens against foreign states; (2) the administration of law and justice; (3) the establishment and maintenance of public works and the provision of education, academic and religious. But he would have even the last two types of functions exercised as far as possible by the citizens acting voluntarily in the light of self-interest; the state should intervene in these fields only when voluntary activity fails to function in an effective manner. It is needless to add that he vigorously urged the immediate abolition of all restrictive state regulation of industry and commerce, and the immediate initiation of that régime of unhampered competition which would presumably allow economic affairs to harmonize with the beneficent order of nature and bring the full measure of happiness and prosperity to the human race. These *laissez faire* theories were adopted and reëmphasized by Smith's disciples, and were the leading factor in securing that abolition of industrial and commercial restrictions which characterized the régime of " economic liberalism " and " political individualism " which dominated Europe during the first half of the nineteenth century, after the publication of *The Wealth of Nations*.

Smith's Economic Theories. — In his strictly economic doctrines Adam Smith has had as wide an influence as through his political theories. Though not the founder of modern political economy, he was its first great systematizer, and *The Wealth of Nations* stands toward modern economics in much the same way that Comte's *Positive Philosophy* does to present-day sociology.

The most conspicuous element in Smith's system of economic doctrines was his emphasis on the factor of *labor,* which he conceived to be the ultimate source of all wealth and the true measure of value (herein he was followed by Ricardo and Marx). In his theory of production, his emphasis upon the importance of the division of labor has been most influential in the history of economic thought. Smith's treatment of this subject was the first extensive analysis it had received since the appearance of the *Republic* of Plato, and in many respects it has never been improved upon. Smith's analysis of value and exchange centered about the well-known labor theory of value, and he maintained that the actual measure of value was the quantity of labor which a given commodity could command in exchange. His theory of distribution initiated the conventional discussion of wages, profits, interest, and rent. Wages are the return to labor and are determined by the demand for, and the supply of, labor. Profits are the return to capital and are determined by the amount of capital stock invested, varying inversely in proportion to the amount of the stock. Interest is that part of profits which is derived from the lending of capital. Finally, rent (and here in part he anticipated Ricardo) is the return to the landowner, and may exist as soon as all free land is occupied. It normally equals the residue from the gross income of the renter after he has deducted profits and wages.

The Significance of The Wealth of Nations. — Though these specific phases of economic analysis in *The Wealth of Nations* were of great importance for the subsequent development of economic theory, they have scarcely stood the test of more refined and scientific analysis, and they have done far less than his more general contributions to secure for Adam Smith the pontifical position which he still occupies in the history of economic thought. These general contributions were: his epoch-making attack upon Mercantilism; the accompanying advocacy of the initiation of the régime of *laissez faire* and unhampered industrial competition; and his production of the first great systematic treatise on political economy. The significance of *The Wealth of Nations* for posterity has been thus expressed by Walter Bagehot: "The life of almost every one in England — perhaps of every one — is different and better in consequence of it. No other form of political philosophy has ever had one-thousandth part of the influence on us."[9]

The most competent and thoroughgoing appreciation of the sociological significance of Smith's economic doctrines is contained in Small's *Adam Smith and Modern Sociology*. According to Small, *The Wealth of Nations* was in reality a treatise on sociology with a special interest in the economic processes of society. As Small says:

If one were to come upon *The Wealth of Nations* for the first time, with a knowledge of the general sociological way of looking at society, but with no knowledge of economic literature, there would be not the slightest difficulty nor hesitation about classifying the book as an inquiry in a special field of sociology. . . . Smith set a new standard of inquiry into the economic section of the conditions of life, while life presented itself to him as, on the whole, a moral affair, in which the economic process is logically a detail. . . . Modern sociology is virtually an attempt to take up the larger program of social analysis and interpretation which was implicit in Adam Smith's moral philosophy, but which was suppressed for a century by prevailing interest in the technique of the production of wealth.[10]

Psychological Theories: Social Contract and Rationalistic Optimism. — Though scientific psychology can scarcely be said to have had its beginning before the publication of William James's *Principles of Psychology* in 1890, and though we are not yet in possession of an integrated survey of the whole field of psychology that can readily take its place in the equipment of the social scientist, yet there were very significant inclinations in the direction of a psychological interpretation of society in the two hundred years from about the middle of the seventeenth century onward. This was characterized by two widely divergent attitudes. The first was strictly intellectualistic, and found expression in such doctrines as the social contract theory, the rationalistic hypothesis of rapid and revolutionary reform through the application of a few self-evident dictates of pure reason, and the Benthamite " felicific calculus." The other group of writers laid primary emphasis upon emotional factors, and their theories ranged from the exaltation of " the folk-spirit " and the non-rational by the Romanticists to the dispassionate analyses of the social rôle of sympathy by Spinoza, Hume, and Adam Smith. The intellectualistic current exerted greater influence in the period under consideration, but the study of the non-rational factors in social behavior was far more in harmony with later developments in the " psychology of society."

We have amply described the nature of the social contract doctrine in earlier chapters, and it will suffice at this place to indicate again that this theory assumed the complete dominance of rationalistic considerations. Human beings were represented as eminently capable of recognizing and of making their conduct conform to their interests. While the emotional processes, particularly those connected with the love of property and of prestige, created those disturbances and conflicts that made escape from the state of nature desirable, yet the intellectual powers of man came quickly to the rescue and pointed the way to adequate relief through the establishment of civil society. We need only to recall here how thoroughly Hume disposed of the assumptions underlying this brand of psychological doctrine.

The second type of intellectualistic interpretation of society characteristic of the period was that associated with the optimism of the rationalists, who for the most part held that geographical and racial factors were less important than cultural, contended that adherence to a few basic principles of pure reason would suffice to reconstruct society, maintained that many of the inequalities of mankind were due solely to differences in opportunity, and put their faith in the application of reason through education and legislation as the method of ensuring social progress.

Helvétius, Sieyès, and Godwin: Optimists All. — Perhaps the three most representative and conspicuous exponents of the potency of reason in reconstructing human relations and social institutions were Claude Adrien Helvétius, the Abbé Sieyès, and William Godwin. Helvétius was the most optimistic of the social environmentalists of the eighteenth century; he believed that men were essentially equal and that perfection might be attained through the inculcation of reason by means of education. Bury has thus described the setting and nature of Helvétius's doctrine:

> The optimism of the Encyclopaedists was really based on an intense consciousness of the enlightenment of their own age. The progressiveness of knowledge was taken as axiomatic, but was there any guarantee that the light, now confined to small circles, could ever enlighten the world and regenerate mankind? They found the guarantee they required, not in an induction from the past experience of the race, but in an *a priori* theory: the indefinite malleability of human nature by education and institutions. This had been, as we saw, assumed by the Abbé de Saint-Pierre. It pervaded the speculation of the age, and was formally deduced from the sensational psychology of Locke and Condillac. It was developed, in an extreme form, in the work of Helvétius, *De l'esprit* (1758).
>
> In this book, which was to exert a large influence in England, Helvétius sought, among other things, to show that the science of morals is equivalent to the science of legislation, and that in a well-organised society all men are capable of rising to the highest point of mental development. Intellectual and moral inequalities between man and man arise entirely from differences in education and social circumstances. Genius itself is not a gift of nature; the man of genius is a product of circumstances — social, not physical, for Helvétius rejects the influence of climate. It follows that if you change education and social institutions you can change the character of men. . . .
>
> It followed from the theory expounded by Helvétius that there is no impassable barrier between the advanced and the stationary or retro-

grade races of the earth . . . and consequently that there is no people
in the world doomed by nature to perpetual inferiority or irrevocably
disqualified by race from playing a useful part in the future of civilisation.[11]

Of the writers in France during the Revolutionary period the
most ardent exponent of the social therapy of reason was the Abbé
Sieyès, who embodied his constructive theory in his *Qu'est-ce que
le Tiers État?* (1789). He here advocated the solution of French
problems by the inculcation of those self-evident dictates of reason which were relevant to the circumstances. Specifically, this
would lead to representative government, the emergence of a
national will, and rational legislation. In this way reason would
lead not only to personal enlightenment but also to the solution of
all problems facing the statesman. As Dunning puts it:

> To settle the controversies then current in France Sieyès contended in
> his fifth chapter that a few simple principles of pure reason would serve
> better than the delicate and complex devices of great statesmen. Such
> principles he proceeded to set forth. They were the principles of Rous-
> seau's *Contrat Social,* with the addition of representative government,
> which Rousseau repudiated. Individuals will to unite into a community;
> *ipso facto* the nation exists. A general will thereupon takes the place
> of all the individual wills. When the number and dispersion of the
> individuals become so great as to make difficult the expression of the
> general will, that part of the national will and power necessary to provide
> for public needs is confided to certain of the people. Such is the origin of
> representative government.[12]

We have already dealt with Godwin's eulogy of the potentialities of reason in the chapter on progress. Like Sieyès, he believed
in the power of reason to effect human enlightenment and social
justice, but he proposed to put reason into operation by radically
different means. Sieyès was chiefly interested in representative
government and the functions of constitutional conventions,
whereas Godwin was an advocate of the elimination of all forms
of government except local units, upon which he would confer very
limited powers. Sieyès devoted himself to proclaiming how the
national state might function more adequately; contrariwise, Godwin bent his efforts to the description of the nature and results of
a system of anarchism that should supersede the national state.
Brailsford has stated the strength and weakness of Godwin's
attitude toward society as follows:

> Godwin and his school set out to show that the human mind is not
> necessarily fettered for all time by the prejudices and institutions in

which it has clothed itself. When he had done stripping us, it was a nice question whether even our nakedness remained. He treated our prejudices and our effete institutions as though they were something external to us, which had come out of nowhere and could be flung into the void from whence they came. When you have called opinion a prejudice, or traced an institution to false reasoning, you have, after all, only exhibited an interesting zoölogical fact about human beings. We are exactly the sort of creature which evolves such prejudices. Godwin in unwary moments would talk as though aristocracy and positive law had come to us from without, by a sort of diabolic revelation. This, however, is not a criticism which destroys the value of his thinking. His positions required restatement in terms of the idea of development. If he did not anticipate the notion of evolution, he was the apostle of the idea of progress. We may still retain from his reasonings the hopeful conclusion that the human mind is a raw material capable of almost unlimited variation, and, therefore, of some advance towards " perfection." We owe an inestimable debt to the school which proclaimed this belief in enthusiastic paradoxes. . . .

Precisely because of its revolutionary *naïveté*, its unscientific innocence, there is in Godwin's democratic anarchism a stimulus peculiarly tonic to the modern mind. No man has developed more firmly the ideal of universal enlightenment, which has escaped feudalism, only to be threatened by the sociological expert. No writer is better fitted to remind us that society and government are not the same thing, and that the State must not be confounded with the social organism. No moralist has written a more eloquent page on the evil of coercion and the unreason of force. *Political Justice* is often an imposing system. It is sometimes an instructive fallacy. It is always an inspiring sermon. Godwin hoped to " make it a work from the perusal of which no man should rise without being strengthened in habits of sincerity, fortitude and justice." There he succeeded.[18]

Bentham's Human Calculating Machine. — By all odds the most important and influential version of the intellectualistic fallacy in the societal psychology of this period was the famous " felicific calculus " of Jeremy Bentham (1748–1832). Bentham held that man is essentially unaffected by social considerations or pressures in his choices. He accepted the hedonistic premise that man always chooses between pleasure and pain, and that he consciously selects that type of conduct which will bring him a maximum of pleasure and a minimum of pain; i.e., that he " calculates felicity." Carried out to its logical social conclusion, this produced Bentham's social ideal, " the greatest happiness of the greatest number," a phrase which perhaps was first formulated by Beccaria, but which was given currency, if not immortality, by Bentham.

This intellectualistic interpretation of human behavior, so completely divorced from fact because of its ignoring of custom, convention, fashion, habits, and a host of other social factors which distort at the source or at the least frustrate rational decisions, had enormous influence on psycho-sociology in the nineteenth century. It was explicitly or implicitly adopted by Stanley Jevons, Karl Menger, Friedrich von Wieser, Eugen Böhm-Bawerk, John Bates Clark, and other members of the so-called psychological school of economists, whose view of human nature and economic choices remained unpunctured until the contemporary work of Thorstein Veblen, Wesley Mitchell, Max Weber, and other sociological economists. It was also basic in political philosophy from Bentham to Bryce; indeed, it was not demolished until Graham Wallas wrote his *Human Nature in Politics*. It influenced many sociologists, such as Spencer, Ward, and Sumner, but the ministerial derivation of most early American sociologists saved them from Bentham because of the unholy nature of his frank hedonism. At the same time, they purchased their immunity at the price of an essentially theological view of human nature, still another stage removed from man as he is. Wesley Mitchell has thus summarized the essentials of Bentham's view of human nature and his conceptions of social progress:

The ideal of science which men then held was represented by celestial mechanics; its hero was Newton, whose system had been popularized by Voltaire; its living exemplars were the great mathematicians of the French Academy. Bentham hoped to become " the Newton of the Moral World." Among the mass of his papers left to University College Halévy has found this passage:

" The present work as well as any other work of mine that has been or will be published on the subject of legislation or any other branch of moral science is an attempt to extend the experimental method of reasoning from the physical branch to the moral. What Bacon was to the physical world, Helvétius was to the moral. The moral world has therefore had its Bacon, but its Newton is yet to come."

Bentham's way of becoming the Newton of the moral world was to develop the " felicific calculus." There are several expositions of this calculus in his *Works;* but the first and most famous version remains the best to quote.

" Nature has placed mankind under the governance of two sovereign masters, *pain* and *pleasure*. It is for them alone to point out what we ought to do, as well as to determine what we shall do. On the one hand the standard of right and wrong, on the other the chain of causes and effects, are fastened to their throne. . . ."

1. Human nature is hedonistic. It is for pain and pleasure alone "to determine what we shall do. . . . They govern us in all we do, in all we say, in all we think: . . ." These words from the first paragraph of *Principles of Morals and Legislation* put simply the leading idea. "Nothing," — Bentham remarks in *A Table of the Springs of Action*, " nothing but the expectation of the eventual enjoyment of pleasure in some shape, or of exemption from pain in some shape, can operate in the character of a *motive*. . . ."

2. Human nature is rational. There is nothing in the felicific calculus " but what the practice of mankind, wheresoever they have a clear view of their own interest, is perfectly conformable to. . . ."

3. Human nature is essentially passive. Men do not have propensities to act, but are pushed and pulled about by the pleasure-pain forces of their environments. . . .

4. Since men ought to follow the course which will secure them the greatest balance of pleasure, and since they do follow that course so far as they understand their own interests, the only defects in human nature must be defects of understanding. . . .

5. Since whatever is amiss in the opinions or conduct of mankind is due to "intellectual weakness, indigenous or adoptive," education must be the one great agency of reform. And since the understanding is made up of associations among ideas, the forming and strengthening of proper associations must be the great aim of education.[14]

Romanticism and the Non-Rational. — We have already called attention to the fact that during the latter part of the eighteenth century a philosophical and psychological revolt against the intellectualistic position of rationalism had set in under the form of Romanticism. This philosophy of human behavior rejected the interpretation of conduct in terms of rational considerations and laid almost exclusive stress on emotional and traditional aspects. It had both a good and a bad effect on psycho-sociology and social philosophy. It broadened the current conception of human nature and called attention to the many non-rational influences which operate upon man. On the other hand, over-emphasis on tradition and historical continuity often led to mental immobility among its adherents — in situations where such immobility was no asset. Moreover, its mystical tendencies, perhaps admirable from some points of view, often degenerated into obscurantism. Randall has characterized the tenets of Romanticism in these words:

Fundamentally, that tendency or attitude to which we have given the name of Romanticism was a reaction against a too narrow construing of human experience in terms of reason alone. It was an emphasis on the less rational side of human nature, on everything that differentiates man from the coldly calculating thinking machine; and correspondingly a revolt against viewing the world as nothing but a vast mechanical order. It was the voicing of the conviction that life is broader than intelligence, and that the world is more than what physics can find in it. It was the appeal from science alone to the whole breadth and expanse of man's experience; its creed, if so formless a persuasion can be said to have a creed, has been admirably summed up by him who is perhaps the foremost living romanticist, Bergson: " We cannot sacrifice experience to the requirements of any system." Experience, in its infinite richness and color and warmth and complexity, is something greater than any intelligible formulation of it; it is primary, and all science, all art, all religion, is but a selection from a whole that must inevitably slip through whatever human net is set to catch it. In this sense, even our science, in breaking from the narrow and fixed forms of eighteenth-century mechanics and mathematics, and becoming frankly inquiring and experimental, has felt the romantic influence; while our knowledge of nature and human nature has been vastly heightened and deepened, and under its spur has almost added a whole new dimension. The virtues of the romantic attitude are its open-mindedness, its receptivity to whatever of truth and whatever of value any experience may reveal; as William James put it, although the past has uniformly taught us that all crows are black, still we should continue to look for the white crow. Its besetting vice is that it may lead men to disregard all standards of truth and value, to refuse to make any of the distinctions that are essential to an ordered life; like the drunken man, who accepts all things as of equal worth, the romanticist often fails to criticize his experience, and in the mere joy of living remains oblivious to the greater joys of living well.[15]

As the more eminent contributors to the doctrines of Romanticism, and its view of human nature, we should certainly mention the following: Johann Gottfried von Herder (1744–1803), Edmund Burke (1729–1797), Johann Gottlieb Fichte (1762–1814), Louis DeBonald (1754–1840), Joseph DeMaistre (1754–1821), Joseph von Schelling (1755–1854), Friedrich von Schlegel (1772–1829), Adam Müller (1779–1829), Friedrich Schleiermacher (1768–1834), Karl Christian Krause (1781–1832), Franz Baader (1765–1841), François de Chateaubriand (1768–1848), and Joseph Görres (1768–1848).[16]

Spinoza, Hume, and Smith: Sympathy Theorists. — Of more immediate importance, in all probability, than the abstruse Romanticist theories were those earlier psycho-sociological contributions associated with the study of the influence of sympathy in building up social relations and structures. Although other writers — Hutcheson, for example — contributed to this subject, we shall select, as most representative, Baruch Spinoza, David Hume, and Adam Smith.

In his *Ethics* Spinoza sets forth the important theory of conscious or reflective sympathy. This theory involves the contention that when one person beholds another person like himself doing something or giving expression to some emotion, the spectator is immediately seized with a desire to imitate the action or to express the same emotion. The following is that part of the *Ethics* in which the idea is developed:

> By the fact that we imagine a thing which is like ourselves, and which we have not regarded with any emotion, to be affected with any emotion, we are already affected with a like emotion.

> Proof: — The images of things are modifications of the human body the ideas of which represent to us external bodies as present, that is the ideas of which involve the nature of our body and at the same time the nature of the external body as present. If, therefore, the nature of an external body is similar to that of our own, then the idea of the external body which we imagine will involve a modification of our body similar to the modification of the external body: and consequently if we imagine any one similar to ourselves to be affected with any emotion, this imagination will express a modification of our body similar to that emotion. And therefore from the fact that we imagine a thing similar to ourselves to be affected with any emotion, we are affected in company with it by that emotion. And if we hate a thing similar to ourselves, we shall to that extent be affected with it by a contrary emotion not a similar one.[17]

Hume, definitely the most "psychological" of the eighteenth-century philosophers (in spite of Berkeley's priority of doctrine — 1713 *vs.* 1740), develops the doctrine advanced by Spinoza, making sympathy, if not the prime cause of society, at least the fundamental factor in adaptability. It makes itself plainly manifest even among animals, leads men to share one another's pains and pleasures, causes imitation and the reduction of a nation to a general type, and varies directly in intensity with the degree of relationship and likeness. Hume thus paved the way and possibly furnished the inspiration for his friend Adam Smith's theory of sympathy. Hume thus expresses his conviction of the importance of sympathy as a social factor:

> No quality of human nature is more remarkable, both in itself and its consequences, than that propensity we have to sympathize with others, and to receive by communication their inclinations and sentiments, however different from, or even contrary to our own. This is not only con-

spicuous in children, who implicitly embrace every opinion proposed to them; but also in men of the greatest judgment and understanding, who find it very difficult to follow their own reason or inclination, in opposition to that of their friends and daily companions. To this principle we ought to ascribe the great uniformity we may observe in the humours and turn of thinking of those of the same nation; and 'tis much more probable, that this resemblance arises from sympathy, than from any influence of the soil and climate, which, tho' they continue invariably the same, are not able to preserve the character of a nation the same for a century together. A good-natur'd man finds himself in an instant of the same humour with his company; and even the proudest and most surly take a tincture from their countrymen and acquaintance. A cheerful countenance infuses a sensible complacency and serenity into my mind; as an angry or sorrowful one throws a sudden damp on me. Hatred, resentment, esteem, love, courage, mirth and melancholy; all these passions I feel more from communication than from my own natural temper and disposition.[18]

A more thorough treatment of the social significance of sympathy is contained in Adam Smith's *Theory of Moral Sentiments* (1759). He says that no man can be so selfish that he is not interested in the welfare of others. That one weeps over the grief of others is a fact too obvious to take the trouble of proving. Yet, since one cannot experience the feelings of others, this sense of mutual sorrow must arise from one's imagining himself in the place of the suffering person, and as being subject to the same emotions. This changing places with the sufferer, then, Smith asserted to be the only source of the fellow-feeling for the sorrow of others. Not only is this a general impression, but it extends to particular parts of the individual organism. If one is about to be injured or has been injured in a certain part of his body, the observers are immediately afflicted with a sense of shrinking or of pain in a similar part of their own anatomy. Not only pain and sorrow but also pleasurable emotions produce a similar feeling in the mind of the spectator, who puts himself, through the power of imagination, in the place of the person observed. Although " pity " is the term generally used to describe fellow-feeling for a person afflicted with sorrow or pain, Smith consistently employed the term " sympathy " since it may be applied to fellow-feeling for both pleasant and unpleasant emotions. Sight or knowledge of affliction will stir up this fellow-feeling, and in many cases simply the expression of the face which conveys the impression of a certain emotion may set up a comparable one in the spectator.

"*Increasing Knowledge Increaseth*" . . . *Sympathy.* — In order for this sympathy to be fully developed, however, the cause of the emotion must be known, for as a matter of fact, said Smith, sympathy does not arise so much from the sight of the emotion as it does from a knowledge of the situation under which it has been brought forth. Indeed, one may by putting himself in another's place feel for him emotions which the original person could never have experienced. For instance, a cultured person may be greatly embarrassed at the actions of a boor, whereas the latter may be wholly unconscious of his improprieties. Again, the man who appears happy in insanity may stir up within the spectator the deepest pity of which the human senses are capable, since insanity is usually considered the greatest of human ills and, by the same token, the one which the spectator himself most dreads. Sympathy therefore is not a reflection of the sentiments of the person observed, but the effect of reflective consideration on the part of the spectator as to what would be his sentiments under similar conditions.

To look at this principle of sympathy from the other side: It is true that there is nothing more pleasing than to detect in another a fellow-feeling with the emotions which rule oneself, and likewise nothing is more distasteful than disagreement with one's sentiments. Philosophers of the strict utilitarian persuasion are wont to account for this state of affairs by saying that, since man is conscious of his own needs and the value of the assistance of others, he rejoices at their expression of emotions similar to his own, for he then feels sure of their assistance. For the same reason, he grieves when they possess different sentiments, since this indicates that he is to be deprived of their help. Even if several doubtful assumptions are granted, however, the utilitarians are wrong, for the pleasures or the pains which arise from another's having the same or different emotions occur so suddenly, and often are caused by such trivialities, that they could not have their origin in studied self-interest.

The Reciprocal Relation of Spectator and Actor. — It is impossible, said Smith, for the spectator ever to bring his feelings up to the same pitch as those of the person observed, whereas the latter will not be satisfied unless the spectator's sympathy is complete — unless the concord of their emotions is perfect. It should be clear, however, that the person observed can never hope for such a condition — unless he lowers the intensity of his feelings to correspond with those of the spectator, which is tantamount to saying that there can never be perfect correspondence. Nevertheless, there may be sufficient concord for the harmony of society. To bring about this harmony (Smith here invokes the *deus ex machina*), "Nature" has "taught" the spectator to assume by imagination the condition of the person observed, and conversely, it teaches the latter to put himself in the situation of the spectator. This influence of the sentiments of spectators upon him makes the person observed more moderate in his emotions than he would otherwise be, says Smith; society and conversation, therefore, are the most powerful means of restoring tranquillity to the mind. As to the degree of sympathy expected from others, the deciding factor is the closeness of the relation between the spectator and the observed. The greatest sympathy is expected from a friend, less from a common acquaintance, and still less from strangers. The person afflicted will therefore lower his emotion to correspond with that of the group with which he comes in contact; he will be most self-controlled when among strangers, less so in the presence of acquaintances, and least of all when friends alone observe him.

Sympathy is of great influence in social relations in still another way. The emotions of an individual are viewed as correct or incorrect by the spectator in accordance with their correspondence with or divergence from his own; hence gratification of the wish for recognition or approval ultimately rests upon that same foundation of sympathy. The principle of self-approval is also based upon sympathy, inasmuch as the only way in which we can sanction or condemn our own conduct is to put ourselves for the moment in the place of the spectator, and reflect as to whether we would approve or disapprove of such procedure in another. Without society man could form no opinion of his own character or conduct; society, on the other hand, furnishes him with a mirror in which to view his behavior. Thus, said Smith, there is in every person this dual relation of spectator and actor.

The same principle operates in the desire of praise and praiseworthiness, according to our sage, for everyone governs his actions by the thought of the light in which others will view them. Inasmuch as everyone desires to be worthy of praise, he will do those things which he imagines will attract the admiration of others, and if this result is obtained he is pleased with the confirmation of his own self-approval by the approval of others. The love of praise and the love of praiseworthiness are to be differentiated, since the first should be the outgrowth of the latter. No one is likely to rejoice in praise for things which he has not accomplished; to do so would indicate the greatest superficiality and vanity. Smith concludes by observing that the person who loves praise for its own sake without being worthy of it is weak and vain — a value-judgment which is obvious enough, but which does not add much to our understanding of the phenomenon.

The Ulterior Significance of Smith's Doctrine. — Giddings attempted to derive modern sociology, on its psychical side, from the discussion of sympathy in Smith's *Theory of Moral Sentiments.* To Giddings this phase of Smith's thought appeared to be fully as significant as Smith's socio-economic views seemed to Small, and he thus expressed his sense of obligation to Smith's writings on sympathy:

At the same time, I intimated that there was more to be discovered in fellow-feeling than previous writers had observed. If I had not believed that the facts called for a new description, I should have put into my first chapter a paragraph contending that Adam Smith was the true founder of sociology, because it was from Smith's " Theory of Moral Sentiments " that I derived the suggestion which presently grew into my conception of the consciousness of kind. Were I now re-writing the sketch of the development of social theory, I think I should indeed claim for Adam Smith the first place among sociologists.[19]

Although Giddings's claim and his use of the Scotsman's doctrine of sympathy may well be questioned, there can be no doubt of the fruitfulness of Smith's analysis. Many persons have been puzzled, however, by the apparent contradiction between *The Wealth of Nations* and *The Theory of Moral Sentiments,* between self-interest and sympathy. Indeed, this difficulty has found its way into German social thought under the title of *das Adam Smith-Problem.* In a review of the preface of a recent German translation of *The Theory of Moral Sentiments* this supposed problem is dealt with substantially as follows:

There is no " Adam Smith problem " in the sense of a formal reconciliation between the supposed altruism of *The Theory of Moral Sentiments* and the supposed egoism of *The Wealth of Nations.* . . . The *Wealth* seems, superficially considered, a typical bit of eighteenth-century individualistic theory, in which a society of neat, rounded-off, self-contained human units carry on their wealth-producing activities; the economic order is a prettily contrived mechanism in which each part automatically serves the ends of the whole. But the economic work presupposes the ethical work published years earlier! The *Moral Sentiments,* with its sources in the British and Scottish school of moral philosophy known as " sentimentalism," regards the facts of individuality as relative to social facts and as dependent upon explanatory principles which transcend the individual.

Instead of taking the individual as " given," and moved by a single purpose only, Smith, in the *Moral Sentiments,* finds that man is not born human, that he is in the deepest sense a social being. It is because he is the product of his society that his acts are in accord with the social welfare. His very interests (also pointed out by Small in *Adam Smith and Modern Sociology*) are those which have been instilled by his social milieu; and hence, in pursuing his own interests he also pursues those of his community or society. The sharp and indefensible distinction between *ego* and *alter* is thus broken down. The very reason why the individual strives for his own welfare is that he wishes the approval and admiration of his fellowmen (*Moral Sentiments,* Part IV, chap. i), so that even the motive of self-interest is not individual but social in its origin. The *Moral Sentiments*, Smith's first and most highly valued work, upon the revision of which he spent the last months of his life, shows the inner organic relation that exists between all the single parts of a society and the plurality pattern which constitutes them and which they constitute.[20]

It should be noted, in closing, that there has been extensive criticism of Smith's somewhat naïve psychologizing in the *Moral Sentiments;* we shall consider one of the chief attacks upon his doctrine when discussing the work of Max Scheler. Nevertheless, we should not be too critical of Smith; he was head and shoulders above most of the thinkers of his day, not only in economics but also in his knowledge of the psychical aspects of social life.

Phrenology and Sociology. — An illuminating commentary on the development of psychology in the last hundred years lies in the fact that the work of the phrenologist, Franz Joseph Gall (1758–1828), represented one of the most valuable contributions to the progress of psychology during this period. He helped to put an end to the mystical conception of thought as an emanation from the human soul, for he suggested that the brain was the seat of thought, insisted that the mind had a definite physical basis, and held that the mental faculties were amenable to scientific investigation. It is revealing as to the state of the psychological basis of sociology at the close of the period under discussion to learn that Auguste Comte laid more stress upon the doctrines of Gall, upon "cerebral physiology," than upon those of any other student of mental processes in his day.

The Philosophy of History. — The chapter on the origins of the theory of progress contained much material bearing on the development of the historical attitude toward the study of human society. The historical or genetic approach was especially evident in the various theories of cultural advancement, continuity of history, and stages of civilization. Another notable contribution during the early modern era was embodied in the philosophy of history, which, as we have seen, was engendered by the same processes that gave rise to theories of progress. To be sure, it was based upon very inadequate information, and was constructed under the influence of warping biases, but it possessed no little significance as the beginning of an effort to appraise the nature and significance of changes in material and non-material culture.

The chief contributors to the philosophy of history in the period under discussion were Vico, those Romanticists mentioned in connection with the revolt against the intellectualistic psychology of rationalism, Hegel, and Auguste Comte. Unquestionably the most influential of the Romanticists was Friedrich Schlegel, and in addition to overshadowing those of his own school of thought, he was even more widely recognized (among historians, at least) than the redoubtable Hegel. His work was thoroughly theological in its presuppositions: for example, the very existence of history was held to be regrettable, because if man had not sinned but had remained in Paradise, there would have been no history. History, like civil government, was rendered necessary by the Fall, and was therefore a testimony to the weakness and sinfulness of mankind. With this sorrowful start Schlegel made the best of his task, and his work was for more than a half-century the fount of wisdom in all Western countries on the course and meaning of history. Burgess, who did more than anyone else to found scientific history in the United States, was first stirred to an interest in history by certain lectures of President Seelye of Amherst College in which the secrets of Schlegel were expounded. (We briefly indicated the nature of Hegel's philosophy of history in the chapter on the idea of progress, and we shall describe Comte's contributions in a later chapter summarizing his system of sociological doctrines.)

Voltaire, Exponent of the History of Civilization. — The study of the history of civilization was really established by Voltaire, who was not only a great essayist and crusader for enlightenment, but also one of the finest historians among eighteenth-century writers. His two important books in this field were his *Siècle de Louis XIV* and his *Essai sur les Mœurs.* The first of these volumes was an intensive piece of work which surveyed the civilization of the brilliant reign of Louis XIV in a comprehensive fashion. His *Essai* was the first real history of civilization. It was planned as a vast *Kulturgeschichte* of all ages and peoples. Although Voltaire did not possess the knowledge or leisure requisite for its completion, and though the book is marred by serious omissions and a sad lack of proportion, still it is one of the great landmarks in the development of historiography. It was the first real universal history; it was the first European work written after the rise of Christianity in which recognition was given to the non-Christian contributions to civilization; it first put political history in its proper relation to economic, social, and cultural history; and it constituted a powerful attack upon the theological and providential interpretation of history which had prevailed from Orosius to Bossuet. Gibbon, greatest of eighteenth-century historians, built upon ideological foundations laid by Voltaire.

Gibbon, Secularized Historian. — Although Gibbon (1737–1794) chose a somewhat more restricted field than the general history of civilization, his *Decline and Fall of the Roman Empire* marked a decisive step in the direction of modern historical tendencies. Especially important was the secular vein in which he composed his work. He was the first writer to treat of the rise and triumph of Christianity in a truly historical and systematic fashion. Whenever his urbanity and detachment failed him, his animus *against* Christianity was usually responsible. He attempted, quite successfully, to explain the success of the Christian church on the basis of secular issues and events; i.e., without in any sense assuming special supernatural intervention in its behalf. His rationalistic approach to Christian origins greatly shocked the orthodox, but it was a great impulse to more accurate historical writing (in spite of certain biases inherent in rationalism). Likewise, in treating of the rise of Mohammedanism, he restricted himself to a calm and dispassionate narrative, making no attempt to teach a great moral lesson through contrasting the unique truth and merit of Christianity with the indescribable forgeries and depravity of the Moslem cult.

German Contributions to Historical Penetration. — In his highly original work on the *Origins of Sociology,* Small lays special stress on the rise of what he calls a drive toward objectivity and accuracy in history during the first quarter of the nineteenth century. He means by this (1) an effort on the part of the more advanced historians to obtain a better supply of accurate facts through the use of reliable documentary sources, and (2) a parallel attempt to free themselves from the subjectivity of the Romantic philosophy of history. To illustrate the various tendencies in this general movement toward objectivity Small selects the great legal historian, Friedrich Karl von Savigny (1779–1861), as the best example of recognition of continuity in cultural and institutional development; Karl Friedrich Eichhorn (1781–1854) as the man who most fully recognized the complexity of historical factors in the record of human advancement; Barthold Georg Niebuhr (1776–1831) as the most competent critic of historical sources and of the earlier mythological interpretations of cultural and national origins; and Leopold von Ranke (1795–1886) as the master of the new science of historical documentation. He also rightfully calls attention to the work of Georg Heinrich Pertz in editing the *Monumenta Germaniae Historica* and thus initiating the first great collection of the sources of national history.

Although the fanfare of trumpets heralding the economic interpretation of the historical process did not blare forth until the time of Karl Marx, this interpretation was quietly ushered in by the famous Göttingen professor, Arnold Hermann Ludwig Heeren (1760–1842), to whom we have already referred. His masterpiece, *Ideen über die Politik, den Verkehr, und den Handel der vornehmsten Völker der alten Welt,* was the first distinguished historical work which fully recognized the effect of commerce and industry upon the course of historical development. Moreover, he formulated for the first time one of the most indispensable conceptions of the institutional historian: namely, that of the state system and the interrelations of state systems. Further, he showed that the state system was not only something which rested upon definite types of political assumptions, policies, and institutions, *but was also something which depended to no small degree upon the basic economy of the state.*

In all of the historical works just discussed, however, the historical interest held the upper hand; the sociological insights were by-products. It is hardly too much to say that the only eighteenth-century writing that can justifiably be included in the category of historical sociology was done by Turgot, Montesquieu, Herder, and especially Adam Ferguson. The writer last named is famous for his remarkable *Essay on the History of Civil Society.* (We shall not consider this book here, however; it can best be dealt with in one of the following sections devoted to description of the development of methods and outlook in social analysis during this period of incipient specialization.)

Revolutionary Presages and Aftermaths. — During the century pivoting about the French Revolution, the most significant phases of the analysis of political processes and institutions were: (1) the controversy between Edmund Burke and Tom Paine concerning the merits, theories, and processes of the French Revolution; (2) Montesquieu's elaboration of the comparative method in politics and his theory of the foundation of political liberty in the separation of governmental powers; (3) Ferguson's successful application of the historical method to the explanation of political origins; and (4) the development of the idealistic theory of the state, with its repudiation of the negative attitude toward political institutions, by Kant, Fichte, and Hegel.

The French Revolution has long been regarded as a unique and heroic event in human history, but recent analysis has proved it to be but a final phase of the reaction of the Commercial Revolution on France.[21] Henry IV, Richelieu, and Mazarin, with the aid of the new middle class, had destroyed the political power of feudalism and, paradoxically enough, had also successfully stifled the growth of representative or democratic institutions in France. The French Revolution marked that stage of development in which the bourgeoisie put an end to even the economic and social vestiges of feudalism and terminated irresponsible royal despotism. The social revolution achieved by the French between 1789 and 1795 consisted mainly in the despoiling of the feudal landlords and the elevation of the business class. The latter not only attained political power, but also secured legislation giving a large measure of freedom to business enterprise. No other class profited materially from the revolution, and it is well known that the nobility and the clergy were greatly reduced in wealth, power, and prestige. The programs of social reform put forth as part of this movement varied all the way from the advocacy of limited constitutional monarchy by Lafayette and Sieyès to the fantastic radicalism of the Mountain and the openly avowed socialistic proposals of François Babeuf. (The latter might perhaps be classed as somewhat akin to the utopian writers of the preceding century.) But in spite of radical programs of social reform and some mob violence by the proletariat, the lower classes, particularly in the cities, failed to profit to any marked degree through the revolution, for it was above all a bourgeois movement. The peasantry, to be sure, gained a good deal by the ending of economic feudalism, but for the elevation of the city workers, three additional revolutions and the growth of modern industrialism were required.

Burke vs. Paine. — The fundamental contribution of the political philosopher and orator, Edmund Burke (1729–1797), was his eloquent and commanding statement of the corporate unity of society. He ruthlessly criticized the *a priori* and rationalistic political philosophy of his time; he declared that the construction of governments was not a matter of reason but of historic growth and long experience. Burke's view of history, however, was not dynamic; it was to him chiefly an instrument to support or to defend existing institutions and to combat change. Although he accepted a modified version of the contractual basis of society, he maintained that this contract was universal in scope and application and binding in perpetuity, and bitterly assailed the versions which justified revolution. We quote his famous passage on the organic unity of civil society, for it is his most noted generalization in the field of social theory and one of the greatest formulations of the conservative philosophy of the age:

Society is indeed a contract. Subordinate contracts for objects of mere occasional interest may be dissolved at pleasure — but the state ought not to be considered as nothing better than a partnership agreement in a trade of pepper and coffee, calico or tobacco or some other such low concern, to be taken up for a little temporary interest, and to be dissolved by the fancy of the parties. It is to be looked on with other reverence; because it is not a partnership in things subservient only to the gross animal existence of a temporary and perishable nature. It is a partnership in all science; a partnership in all art; a partnership in every virtue, and in all perfection. As the ends of such a partnership cannot be obtained in many generations, it becomes a partnership not only between those who are living, but between those who are living, those who are dead, and those who are to be born. Each contract of each particular state is but a clause in the great primaeval contract of eternal society, linking the lower with the higher natures, connecting the visible and invisible world, according to a fixed compact sanctioned by the inviolable oath which holds all physical and all moral natures, each in their appointed place. This law is not subject to the will of those, who by an obligation above them, and infinitely superior, are bound to submit their will to that law. The municipal corporations of that universal kingdom are not morally at liberty at their pleasure, and on their speculations of a contingent improvement, wholly to separate and tear asunder the bands of their subordinate community, and to dissolve it into an unsocial, uncivil, unconnected chaos of elementary principles. It is the first and supreme necessity only, a necessity that is not chosen, but chooses, a necessity paramount to deliberation, that admits no discussion, and demands no evidence, which alone can justify a resort to anarchy. This necessity is no exception to the rule; because this necessity itself is a part too of that moral and physical disposition of things, to which man must be obedient by consent of force: but if that which is only submission to necessity should be made the object of choice, the law is broken, nature is disobeyed, and the rebellious are outlawed, cast forth, and exiled, from this world of reason, and order, and peace, and virtue, and fruitful penitence, into the antagonist world of madness, discord, vice, confusion, and unavailing sorrow.[22]

Burke's forthright criticism of the French Revolution called forth a vigorous rebuttal from Tom Paine (1737–1809), in his

Rights of Man and his *Dissertation on the First Principles of Government*. According to Paine, man was by nature social because of his social instinct and the necessity of coöperative activities. The state of nature was not pre-social, but one in which men possessed the natural rights of liberty and equality. This had to be abandoned, and governmental authority established, because of human imperfections which made unregulated existence intolerable. Government was created by a contract between the members of society, not between the governed and the governors. His view of monarchy was directly opposed to that held by props of the throne such as Bossuet, and he was one of the most ardent advocates of democracy and popular sovereignty in the eighteenth century. Especially important was his doctrine that the minority should be protected by constitutional checks that would prevent an absolute majority rule.

The Comparative Method in Politics: Montesquieu. — Our French philosopher made important contributions to social philosophy, both in general method and in specific analysis of various aspects of social processes. His general method was objective and descriptive, and his work was a conspicuous example of the comparative method of approach to social and political problems revived by Bodin and his contemporaries. There had been plenty of descriptive matter in the works of writers before Bodin, but after the ascendency of Christianity it had been mainly a study of Biblical and Classical mythology and history, in which the exploits of Seth and Enoch and the heroes of Homer and Livy had been much more conspicuous than an analysis of contemporary societies. Montesquieu based his comparisons primarily on the data of the discoveries of the two previous centuries. As a result, he presented a far more complete interpretation of social processes in terms of environmental influences than had been developed by any other writer, as an earlier section of this chapter may have done something to show.

His specific contributions were equally important. Although still adhering to the term "state of nature," he attacked the idea that the natural state of man was one of war, and insisted that the tendency toward association was strong enough to be designated as a law of nature. War was a product of civil society, not of the state of nature.

But the fame of Montesquieu in the past has been due more than anything else to his widely adopted theory that political liberty can best be secured in a governmental system in which the three departments of government are sharply differentiated and

perfectly coördinated, each exerting a check upon the unlimited
power of the others. This doctrine of checks and balances was
drawn from a misinterpretation of the British government, and
was made the basis for the construction of the federal government
of the United States.

Adam Ferguson and Historical Sociology. — The contributions of the Scottish philosopher, Adam Ferguson (1723–1816),
to the development of historical sociology have not been sufficiently acknowledged. French and German writers, like Comte,
Gumplowicz, Stein, and Sombart, have recognized his importance,
but until very recently English and American students of the subject have generally minimized or entirely overlooked the genuine
worth of his work (Lehmann and Bryson are honorable exceptions). If anyone before Saint-Simon and Comte has the right to
be designated as the " father of sociology," it is not Adam Smith,
but Adam Ferguson. Indeed, aside from certain formal distinctions and terminology originated by Saint-Simon and Comte,
Ferguson's *Essay on the History of Civil Society,* which appeared
in 1765, is quite as much a treatise on sociology as is Comte's treatment of " social physics " in his *Positive Philosophy.*

That Ferguson was moving in the right direction may be seen
by the fact that he combined the descriptive and historical method
of Montesquieu with the psychological and critical procedure of
Hume. His treatment was thus both concrete and analytical. He
rejected all *a priori* methods, as well as the ideas of a state of
nature and a social contract; he insisted on studying society as it
is. The dynamic element was very strong in the work of Ferguson:
he ridiculed the ideas of Aristotle and Hobbes that social stability
and peace were the chief ends in society, and laid such stress upon
the value of competition and conflict in social development that
Gumplowicz has claimed him as the first outstanding apostle of the
" group struggle " theory of social development. This is too flat-
tering an estimate, as our discussion of Ibn Khaldūn, Turgot, and
Herder may have done something to show, but Ferguson was
nevertheless of great importance. Certain it is that his work is the
most complete study of political origins prior to the writings of
Auguste Comte and Ludwig Gumplowicz, to say nothing of his
other contributions.

Lehmann has given us a clear-cut and balanced appraisal of
the main features of Ferguson's work:

> We . . . count it sufficient to claim that Ferguson appreciated the fact
> and the meaning of society and brought it into the center of his field of
> vision and attention in a way that was at least remarkably realistic,

critical, and essentially empirical; that he keenly appreciated the organic nature of society or the socio-historical process in its static and still more in its dynamic aspects, and treated it from a point of view that was at once psychological and historical; that as a result he presented a thoroughly evolutionistic analysis that at least deserves our most serious attention; that he developed the concept of a division of labor in society in a way that remarkably anticipates later writers; that he perceived the interdependence of the various fields of human interest and activity in a way that would logically call for sociology as a science more comprehensive in its scope than the other social sciences; that he moved on a plane of humanistic or psycho-cultural interpretation that might still challenge many a writer in sociology today; and finally, that he anticipates such specific theories, as in particular the conflict theory of human society, in a way that should alone give him a place in the history of social theory if not of sociology itself.[28]

Kant's Theory of the State. — The renowned German philosopher, Immanuel Kant (1724–1804), was a zealous advocate of universal peace, though some critics, such as Dewey in his *German Philosophy and Politics,* have attempted to show that the Kantian ethics, with its sharp distinction between the world of sense and necessity and the supersensible world of moral freedom and duty, probably had a good deal to do with the German militaristic and nationalistic philosophy so strikingly manifest during the World War and now showing signs of recrudescence. Kant maintained that genuine progress would go on most rapidly in that country which allowed the greatest freedom to opposing views and yet secured individual liberty, protection, and the equitable administration of law. Such a condition, he asserted, could not be attained until the external relations between societies had been put on a firm, stable, and peaceful basis and the resources of the nations set free to undertake the great program of progress and enlightenment. The only way to arrive at such a state of international peace would therefore be to establish a universal federation of nations. Looking back over history, Kant thought that he could see the gradual working out of this very plan of federation and peace. He was an optimist and believed that progress was continually going on; the criticisms of contemporary conditions were explained as simply manifestations of a more refined moral conscience.

Like Blackstone, Kant believed in the social contract as the philosophical basis of political obligations, though he denied its historicity and declared, with Burke, for the perpetuity of the contract.

Fichte and Hegel, Nationalistic Idealists. — The post-Kantian German idealists had an important influence on the development of social philosophy and political thinking. Fichte is noted mainly for three contributions. In the first place, he carried the theory of a social contract to a greater extreme than any other adherent of that doctrine, and represented a republicanism rather radical in the Germany of his day. Secondly, his *Der geschlossene Handelsstaat* was one of the earliest presentations of a doctrine of state socialism, though the basis of Fichte's conception was idealistic and not economic, as in the case of Marx. In fact, Fichte's doctrine has been adopted by the National Socialists, who certainly are not Marxian. Finally, in his *Reden an die deutsche Nation* he set forth the highly patriotic but exaggerated conception of the superior quality and exalted mission of the German people. This notion was absorbed and transmitted with great effect by Hegel, and in turn was taken up and elaborated by the nationalistic German historians of the nineteenth century — Droysen, Von Sybel, and Treitschke. At the same time, it is all too easy to exaggerate Fichte's nationalism in the unwarranted manner evident in many writers familiar only with the *Reden*. Engelbrecht, author of the definitive study of Fichte's nationalism, says this:

During his lifetime Fichte was a Jacobin and revolutionary to his contemporaries and remained such for the Prussian reactionaries even in the 1820's. After 1840, and especially after 1862, he was thought of chiefly as a nationalist and a patriot, though the Socialists and liberals did not forget him. And now, after the World War, we again find all shades of interpretation represented — extreme nationalism to revolutionary bolshevism.[24]

The ponderous but profound dialectician Hegel played a more important part in educating the German people as to their superior mission in the world. He conceived of society as the means of developing and setting free the human will and personality. He believed that this freedom was progressively realized, not only in the different stages of society from the family through civil society to the state, but also in the different periods of history. In the stages of society the family represents the reproductive organ; civil society embodies the economic aspect of social organization; and finally, the state, the highest and most perfect of the grades of society, is an almost ineffable entity — the synthesis of universal and individual will, of objective and subjective freedom — something for unrestrained adulation. The state was for Hegel the philosophical realization of perfected rationality and freedom, the earthly embodiment of the Absolute Idea, and in similar vein he hymned the German people as its supreme, never-to-be-surpassed historical manifestation. The *Weltgeist*, after having temporarily sojourned among the Oriental and Classical nations, had seen fit to take up its abode among the Germans, whose mission it was to bring to the world the conception that freedom is the prerogative of every man:

The History of the World is the discipline of the uncontrolled natural will, bringing it into obedience to a Universal principle and conferring subjective freedom. The East knew and to the present day knows only that *One* is Free; the Greek and the Roman world, that *Some* are free; the German World knows that *All* are free. The first political form therefore which we observe in History is *Despotism*, the second *Democracy* and *Aristocracy*, the third *Monarchy*.[25]

One has only to reflect upon Hegel's philosophic preëminence in Germany and the significance of his conceptions to understand his widespread influence on the nationalistic tendency of nineteenth-century thought in Germany. Aside from this phase of his influence, his emphasis upon society as *process* of realization has been important in German sociology, and is evident in the work of Ratzenhofer and a number of later writers.

The idealistic theory of the state, developed chiefly by Kant, Fichte, and Hegel, exerted a powerful effect on actual German political practice as represented in German social legislation in the last half of the nineteenth century. It was brought from the Continent to England by Matthew Arnold, Thomas Hill Green, and Bernard Bosanquet. Through its influence on Hobhouse and others it contributed not a little to the conversion of British Liberalism from *laissez faire* and state inactivity to the comprehensive social reform policy of the Liberal Party following 1905. No one has better summarized this attitude toward the state and its duties than the brilliant English writer, Ernest Barker:

Not a modification of the old Benthamite premises, but a new philosophy was needed; and that philosophy was provided by the idealist school, of which Green is the greatest representative. That school drew its inspiration immediately from Kant and Hegel, and ultimately from the old Greek philosophy of the city-state. . . . [It met] the new needs of social progress, because it refused to worship a supposed individual liberty which was proving destructive of the real liberty of the vast majority, and preferred to emphasise the moral well-being and betterment of the whole community, and to conceive of each of its members as attaining his own well-being and betterment in and through the community. Herein lay, or

seemed to lie, a revolution of ideas. Instead of starting from a central
individual, to whom the social system is supposed to be adjusted, the
idealist starts from a central social system, in which the individual must
find his appointed orbit of duty.[26]

Political Science and Sociology. — To conclude this section on
sociological tendencies in political philosophy during the era of
intellectual differentiation, we could not do better than call attention to the growing conception that political science is not co-
extensive with sociology. Saint-Simon had insisted upon the necessity of a basic and fundamental science of social reconstruction,
far broader than political philosophy, and his disciple, Auguste
Comte, had outlined such a science in his system of positive philosophy. Even more significant was the dawning comprehension,
among political scientists themselves, that in addition to political
science there was a definite need for a broader and more comprehensive science of society. This was best recognized by two German political scientists, writing in the first half of the nineteenth
century, Heinrich Ahrens and Robert von Mohl. Von Mohl's recognition of the relevance and value, even necessity, of sociology
is well set forth in the following paragraph:

At this moment the sciences of the state have reached . . . a turning
point. That the state is the unitary organism of the total life of the people,
and therewith that the science which embraces and interprets it is in
antithesis with the science of the individual life, has been clear and recognized since human relationships have been grasped in their nature and
have been logically expounded. Public law and private law; public finance and private thrift; civic history and description of life; have for
thousands of years been regarded as distinct areas of thought and knowledge. It would accordingly be wholly superfluous to rehearse here the
long familiar conceptions in order to be clear to oneself and to one's
readers about the boundary lines of political science on this side. The
case is different with a differentiation between the life of the state and
the life of society, and with precise definition of conceptions and determination of boundaries between the respective sciences. Only now has
this become possible, and consequently it has become a demand. Only
quite lately have we arrived at a definite recognition that the life which
men lead in common by no means has its existence in the state alone;
but that intermediate between the sphere of the single personality and
the organic unity of the life of the people there are many life circles which
likewise have communitary objects as their aim, which do not originate
from or through the state, even if they are already present in it, and
are of the highest significance for weal or woe. These two circles of
thoughts and doctrines, which for more than two thousand years have
appeared to be similar, or at most as part and whole, have now shown

themselves as essentially different, and must also be treated separately, so that henceforth they may exist side by side as dissociated but equally privileged divisions of human knowledge.[27]

Jurisprudence and Social Philosophy. — The confusion between the state and society, just referred to by Von Mohl and frequently mentioned in previous chapters, had as an inevitable consequence confusion between the regulations of rational domination — i.e., laws — and the everyday relations of social intercourse. This claim we must reject, but it is nevertheless true that much of sociological importance can be learned from a study of jurisprudence as it was when it applied to a much greater area of human life than is now the case. Sorokin, among others, has frequently stressed this point, but it has not been sufficiently heeded.

The main trends in jurisprudence during the eighteenth and early nineteenth centuries were: (1) the establishment of the comparative method by Montesquieu and François Charles Louis Comte; (2) Beccaria's epoch-making proposals in criminal jurisprudence; (3) Blackstone's contributions to analytical jurisprudence and his defense of the British legal system; (4) Bentham's conception of legislation as a method of " social engineering " — the application of the science of social reform; (5) the solid founding of the historical approach by Burke and Savigny; and (6) Thibaut's forcible demand for the discriminating criticism of systems of law and the codification of national law.

François Comte, Follower and Critic of Montesquieu. — We have already shown how Montesquieu attempted to find a valid basis for legislation in the conception that laws should be made to suit the civilization of the people for whom they are intended. Geographic conditions, especially climate, determine the character of peoples and the resulting institutions appropriate to them. It is the task of the legislator to familiarize himself with these divergent cultures and to formulate his codes of legislation accordingly. There is no absolutely best code or system of laws; that code is best which is most perfectly adapted to the conditions of the population for which it is compiled and enacted. This, at least in a rudimentary form, is the basic assumption of the early comparative school of jurisprudence.

A much more discriminating effort in this direction was embodied in the work of the French writer, François Charles Louis Comte, who in 1826 published his *Traité de législation ou exposition des lois générales suivant lesquelles les peuples prospèrent, dépérissent ou restent stationnaires.* Although in general harmony with the view of Montesquieu that geographic factors create the physical types and cultural conditions to which sound laws must conform, he held that Montesquieu's study of environmental influences had been woefully inadequate and one-sided. Montesquieu had relied upon inadequate and unreliable information and had narrowed down geographical factors all too much by concentrating almost exclusively on climate. François Comte held that at least six geographical factors must be taken into account by the student of the interrelation of laws and environment, namely: (1) configuration and exposure of the soil; (2) latitude; (3) elevation; (4) location relative to bodies of water and internal waterways; (5) temperature and humidity; and (6) distribution and variation of the seasons. He also insisted on the necessity of making allowance for racial traits as well as geographical influences in the determination of culture. Only on the basis of a comprehensive and discriminating survey could the legislator hope to draw up a sound and adequate system of laws.

Beccaria on Crime and Punishment. — Next to the work of Montesquieu, there is little doubt that the most famous and influential work in the field of jurisprudence in the eighteenth century was the *Essay on Crimes and Punishments* by the Italian publicist and humanitarian, Cesare Beccaria (1738–1794). The framework of Beccaria's thought was provided by his intensive cultivation of the French and English rationalists of this period; he freely confessed his indebtedness to them. He was familiar with the writings of the whole group, but a few in particular seem to have had a special influence on his thinking and aspirations. Montesquieu's *Persian Letters* stimulated him to take cognizance of the oppressive nature and absurdity of many European institutions of his time, and especially to note the barbarities in systems of criminal procedure. The same writer's *Spirit of Laws* impressed upon him the relativity of the excellence of laws, for it showed how largely they depend on their adaptability to the people and the times. From Hume and Helvétius he derived much of his humanitarianism, his hedonism, and his utilitarian view of ethics, and the Encyclopedists supplied a broad comprehension of eighteenth-century learning and enlightenment. Voltaire, as well as Montesquieu, drew his attention to the notorious abuses and cruelties in the body of criminal law and in the prevalent methods of treating criminals. Finally, his intimate friend, Alessandro Verri, was a prison official in Milan. Beccaria frequently visited Verri's institution, and the revolting scenes which he invariably beheld during these visits furnished the clinical information for and the moral stimulus to the execution of his *Dei Delitti,* a work which had more practical effect than any other treatise ever written in the long campaign against barbarism in criminal law and procedure.

Beccaria was in no sense a professional lawyer, jurist, or technical student of criminology. He was therefore equally free from the paralyzing weight of tradition and convention and the limited perspective of professional activity. He wrote as an intelligent layman who, completely divorced from tradition, viewed the problem with all the humanitarianism, enlightenment, and courage of contemporary rationalism. His classic work was written in collaboration with his friend Pietro Verri (the brother of Alessandro), who was a man of marked literary ability; he actually wrote parts of the *Dei Delitti* and carefully revised the whole work.

In order to appreciate the timeliness and novelty of the book it is necessary to recall the situation at the time, characterized as it was by secret accusations, almost complete absence of provision for the defense of the accused, extensive use of the most savage types of torture, an incredibly large number of capital crimes, and barbarous lesser punishments, such as whipping, branding, and mutilation. In comparison, the Code of Hammurabi does not fare badly. Space does not permit close analysis of his famous essay, but we may summarize concisely the essentials of the system which he recommended:

(1) The basis of all social action must be the utilitarian conception of the greatest happiness for the greatest number. (2) Crime must be considered as an injury to society, and the only rational measure of crime is the extent of this injury. (3) Prevention of crime is more important than punishment for crimes; indeed, punishment is justifiable only on the supposition that it helps to prevent criminal conduct. In preventing crime it is necessary to improve and publish the laws so that the nation may know what they are and be brought to support them; to reward virtue; and to improve education both as to legislation and life. (4) In criminal procedure secret accusations and torture should be abolished; there should be speedy trials; the accused should be treated humanely prior to trial and must have every right and facility to bring forward evidence in his behalf; and turning state's evidence should be done away with, as it amounts to no more than a "national authorization of treachery." (5) The purpose of punishment is to deter persons from the commission of crime and not to secure social revenge. Not severity, but certainty and speediness of punishment best secure this result of deterrence. Punishment must be sure and swift, and penalties must be determined

strictly in accordance with the social damage wrought by the crime. Crimes against property should be punished solely by fines, or by imprisonment when the person is unable to pay the fine. Banishment is an excellent punishment for crimes against the state. There should be no capital punishment, for it does not eliminate crime; life imprisonment is a better deterrent. Capital punishment is irreparable, and hence makes no provision for possible mistakes and later rectification. (6) Imprisonment should be more widely employed, but its mode of application should be greatly improved through providing better physical quarters and by separating and classifying the prisoners as to age, sex, and degree of criminality. His conclusions state his viewpoint with clarity and conciseness: " In order that every punishment may not be an act of violence committed by one man or by many against a single individual, it ought to be above all things public, speedy, necessary, the least possible in the given circumstances, proportioned to its crime, dictated by the laws." Excepting only the modern psychiatric analysis of the criminal, with its substitution of the conception of treatment for punishment, one may safely say that Beccaria's little treatise envisaged the major criminological advances during the next century and a half.

Beccaria's brochure had an enormous influence on his contemporaries and successors, only the outstanding phases of which can be mentioned here. The French rationalists, especially Voltaire, welcomed it with great enthusiasm. Voltaire proclaimed that it would assure its author immortality and would work a revolution in the moral world. Eminent writers on law and criminal reform, such as Sonnenfels in Austria, Filangieri and Renazzi in Italy, and Blackstone, Howard, Bentham, and Romilly in England, were profoundly influenced by Beccaria's doctrines and freely acknowledged their indebtedness to him. Much in the way of practical reform of criminal jurisprudence also grew out of his essay. Among such changes in greater or lesser degree influenced by Beccaria may be mentioned the reforms in Austria under Maria Theresa and Joseph II, those carried out by Leopold of Tuscany, the criminal code of the French Revolution, the abolition of the barbarous criminal code of England, and the reform of the criminal law in the United States after 1776. Catherine the Great was much impressed by Beccaria's work and invited him to St. Petersburg to aid her in drawing up a new set of laws, but he was obliged to decline because of delicate health.

Blackstone vs. Bentham. — The most famous of British jurists of the eighteenth century was Sir William Blackstone (1723–

1780). He is especially noted for his complete satisfaction with
the British legal system and for his doctrine of legal sovereignty,
later so important for Austin and the analytical school of jurists.
Great Britain had gradually worked out a body of legislation
reasonably well adapted to the needs of the new commercial era
and capable of realizing what Locke had defined as the chief end
of the state: namely, the protection of property. Blackstone consequently felt that British legislation and jurisprudence left little
to be desired this side of the heavenly realm. This complacent attitude, stirred Jeremy Bentham to the deepest indignation, and
his withering *Fragment on Government* soon appeared. Blackstone's view of the attributes of sovereignty as supreme, irresistible, absolute, and uncontrolled power was not only utilized by
the analytical jurists, but was in line with the even more comprehensive and fundamental view of political sovereignty which culminated in the work of the American scholar, John William
Burgess.

Jeremy Bentham, while often regarded as the precursor of
John Austin and the analytical school of jurists, is viewed in truer
perspective as the leading exponent of the utilitarian interpretation of politics and legislation. His *Fragment on Government* was
a relentless attack on Blackstone's social and political philosophy.
This work is important in social theory for its acute differentiation
between natural and political society, its detailed criticism and
rejection of the social contract and natural rights doctrine, and its
justification of any type of government or legislation on the basis
of the principle of utility; i.e., of their relative contribution to
the increasing of the greatest happiness of the greatest number.
Although Bentham's place in the history of jurisprudence is usually
based on his formulation of the theory of sovereignty (which was
adopted with modifications by Austin and the analytical jurists),
it would seem that from the point of view of social theory he was
far more significant as one of the first to conceive of law as a form
of social technology: he held that sound legislation was the logical
avenue to social reform. This doctrine lies at the basis of his
Introduction to the Science of Morals and Legislation, and there
is little doubt that Bentham's fertility in proposing reform measures entitles him to rank as the foremost " social inventor " in human history. His works were adapted for Continental readers by
his disciple Pierre Étienne Louis Dumont (1759–1829), who
translated or paraphrased most of Bentham's important treatises.

*Historical Jurisprudence and the Thibaut-Savigny Contro-
versy.* — Closely related to the comparative approach to juris-

prudence, so emphasized by Montesquieu, was the historical attitude, best represented in this period by Burke and Savigny. In his *Reflections on the French Revolution* Burke contended with great eloquence that valid and workable laws could not be drawn up overnight. Laws were the product of national character, developing slowly as a result of experience and becoming an integral part of the whole organism of national culture. It was unthinkable to attempt to separate the legal system from the rest of the cultural complex or to hope to transfer such systems from one country to another. Legal codes Burke held to be one of the most subtle expressions of national genius.

Much more profound and technical in this connection was the work of the great German jurist, Friedrich Karl von Savigny, universally conceded to be the real founder of historical jurisprudence. In addition to his wide influence as a writer on legal history and similar subjects, Savigny attracted much attention through his memorable debate with another German jurist, Anton Friedrich Justus Thibaut, who in 1814 set forth an eloquent plea for the examination, sifting, and codification of German law. So convinced was Savigny of the genetic, living, and organic nature of law that he denied the very possibility of codifying law without necessarily destroying its very life. His perpetual refrain was: "It must grow, it must grow!" Savigny thus formulated the essential doctrine of historical jurisprudence:

The basis of the entire historical system is the tracing of this common element through all its transformations until its origin is reached, the origin which comes to it from the character of the nation, of its destiny, and its needs. This anterior element is not a dead letter, as it seems to the opposing school, a fact accomplished, whose persistence is stated without comprehension of the reason. It is living. It is one of the forces, one of the modes of activity of the nation. The general principle of the historical doctrine is that in every state, and especially in regard to its civil law, a people is not an accidental individuality, but an individuality which is essential, necessary, controlled by its entire past; that consequently the search for a common law is as foolish as the search for a general language which will replace all the actual and living languages. This does not mean, however, that this school does not recognize in humanity certain uniform tendencies, which may be called the philosophical element of all positive law.[28]

Through this and similar utterances Savigny founded that historical tradition in jurisprudence which has been so ably carried on since his day by Sir Henry Sumner Maine, Frederick William Maitland, Sir Frederick Pollock, and others.

We have already called attention to the controversy between Savigny and Thibaut following the latter's proposal to institute a systematic codification of German law, applicable to the nation as a whole. Thibaut stated his case as follows:

I am of the opinion . . . that our civic law (under which I have always understood the civil and criminal law and procedure) needs a complete revision, and that the Germans cannot be prosperous in their civic condition unless all the German governments, with united energy, seek to accomplish the composition of a code withdrawn from the arbitrariness of the separate governments, and issued for entire Germany.

Two demands may and must be made for all legislation: (1) that it should be formally and substantially complete, with its specifications presented clearly, unambiguously and comprehensively; (2) that it should set in order the civic arrangements wisely and appropriately, in accordance with the needs of the subject. Unfortunately there is no single country in the German empire where a single one of these demands is half satisfied. . . . Accordingly our whole native law is an endless waste of mutually contradictory and destructive rules, wholly fitted to separate the Germans from one another and to make it impossible for judges and magistrates to reach a thorough knowledge of the law. . . .

Taking all this together, the wish must impress itself upon every friend of the Fatherland that a simple code, the work of our own energy and activity appropriate to our civic conditions and to the needs of the peoples, may be established; and that a patriotic session of all German governments might promote for the whole realm the benefaction of such a civic constitution for all time.[29]

Although Savigny had the better of the controversy at the time, Thibaut's views ultimately triumphed when, after 1871, the magnificent German imperial code was prepared. It is possible, however, that Savigny would have advocated the imperial code, for, after all, the nation had become a unity and hence was ready for a unified body of laws. No real violence was done to his precept of " It must grow."

But, as Small says:

It does not fall within the scope of our argument to answer the question: To what extent and in what sense, if at all, did Savigny establish his thesis? That is primarily a matter for the legal historians. . . . The important matter is that Savigny and the historical school put such emphasis upon the fact of *survival* or *continuity* of historical causation that it thenceforth became an element which demanded a share of consideration in every social science problem. . . .

Expressed in another way, from 1814 the historians, and with them social scientists in general, had possession of a clue to the mystery of the scheme of things human which was comparable with Darwin's generalization, nearly a half-century later, of the scheme of things physical. In their own way the historians had arrived at perception of a fact to which they might have given the name *evolution*.[30]

Summary of the Chapter. — In this chapter we have been witnessing the gradual splitting up of all-inclusive systems of social philosophy and the consequent rough-hewing of separate timbers that eventually were built into the framework of what we now know as human geography, economics, psychology, history, political science, comparative jurisprudence, and sociology.

Human geography began to abandon the Hippocratic doctrines, dominant as late as the time of Bodin, as soon as the travelers and " meteorological determinists " of the seventeenth and eighteenth centuries had an opportunity to bring the field of their interest in line with the developments in physics, chemistry, and physiology. Chardin, Mead, and Arbuthnot were representative of this group. Montesquieu drew upon the work of these and other predecessors, and a sweeping panorama of man's development and conduct as influenced by geographic factors was the result. His emphasis on these factors was excessive, however, and Herder and Adam Ferguson, who wrote along similar lines, laid much less stress on the direct social effect of climate and topography. Only, however, with the development of scientific geography through the work of systematic thinkers such as Varenius, and through the observations of travelers equipped to conduct genuinely scientific researches such as Alexander von Humboldt, did it become possible for the earlier errors and exaggerations to be left behind. The outstanding exponent of both the new physical and human geography was Karl Ritter, a genius who anticipated much of the critical stock in trade of present-day cultural sociologists, and who consequently was relatively uninjured by Hume's justified attack on extreme geographic determinism.

The beginnings of modern economic science were associated with three notions: (1) the theory that the state should control economic life in every particular in its own interest as over against that of other states — a theory variously known as Mercantilism, Colbertism, and Cameralism; (2) the ideological revolt, sponsored by the Physiocrats (the real founders of modern economics), against this policy of state restriction and regulation; and (3) the temporarily valid integration achieved as a consequence of Adam Smith's pronouncement that human happiness and " the wealth of nations " could be most rapidly and effectively increased through the adoption by all national states of a policy of complete commercial and industrial liberty.

The early phases of psycho-sociology also became distinguishable from social philosophy in this period (approximately from the middle of the seventeenth to the middle of the nineteenth century). Although most modern psycho-sociology lays greatest stress on non-rational processes affecting social relations, intellectualistic emphases, exemplified by the exponents of social contract doctrines and the rationalists, were more pronounced during this early period. Nevertheless, notable contributions toward the study of the social rôle of sympathy, a non-rational impulse, were made at an early date by Spinoza, Hume, and Adam Smith. It must be admitted, however, that even these analyses of sympathy were conducted along somewhat rationalistic lines; not until the Romanticists appeared on the scene was there a really sweeping reaction against intellectualistic theories. The Romanticists concerned themselves almost exclusively with those emotional and traditional aspects of human behavior not amenable to intellectualistic interpretation, and in spite of all their exaggerations and fallacies, notably deepened current psycho-sociological insights. The phrenologist Gall, in his insistence that there was a definite physical basis for mental activity, did much to counteract the spiritualistic trends in Romanticism, and at the same time greatly helped to encourage scientific psychological investigation.

In the realm of the philosophy of history cognizance was taken of the nature and significance of changes in material and non-material culture. Voltaire established the study of the history of civilization, and for the first time political history was put in its proper relation to " social," economic, and cultural history. Gibbon, in the late eighteenth century, and a number of eminent German historians, in the first quarter of the nineteenth, strengthened the trend toward a more secular, dispassionate, and accurate view of the historical process.

It was approximately at this time also that the controversy concerning the theories and merits of the French Revolution raged, that Montesquieu's important work in comparative politics was done, that the historical method was applied to the study of political origins, and that the idealistic theory of the state was developed.

Meanwhile sociological insights were resulting from the changed emphasis in historical method, and in political science there was definite recognition of the need for a basic science of social relations.

The eighteenth and nineteenth centuries also witnessed the establishment in jurisprudence of the principle of the comparative method, together with recognition of the necessity of the adaptability of laws to the people concerned. A new conception of criminal jurisprudence arose, carrying with it widespread consequences in Austria, France, England, and the United States. Important innovations in analytical jurisprudence were made by Blackstone; and his tenets were attacked by Bentham, who set forth a utilitarian interpretation of political behavior and legislation. Finally, the Thibaut-Savigny controversy brought to the fore the idea of historical continuity, not only in legal institutions but in all of social life, thus anticipating later applications of the idea of evolution.

Part of the title of this chapter is the well-worn phrase, "unity is diversity," but the unity is occasionally far to seek. It might therefore be well to indicate, if not points of unity, at least points of possible profitable emphasis for the sociologist.

In view of the wide vogue of ideas, many of them vague, about transference, sympathy, empathy, and so on, study of writers such as David Hume and Adam Smith might yield worthwhile results even today. At the very least, it might serve as useful introduction to the works of Lipps, Scheler, Moreno, and others who have dealt with similar themes, and might also help to put the assumptions of Schopenhauer, Eduard von Hartmann, and Freud and his followers in proper perspective. Here see Becker, "Empathy, Sympathy, and Scheler," *International Journal of Sociometry*, vol. i, 1 (Sept., 1956), pp. 15-22. Let it be emphasized, however, that this article is no substitute for the study of Scheler's writings, in particular, at first hand. Fortunately there is now an excellent English version of one of Scheler's major works, *The Nature of Sympathy* (London: Routledge & Kegan Paul, 1954). Peter Heath did the very able translating; the enlightening introduction is by Werner Stark.

Another point of emphasis might be on the legal aspects of social control, or on sociology of law. Distinctions between proverbial, prescriptive, principial, and pronormless societies (see p. 42) basically involve the ways in which social control in the form of various kinds of law (other forms of social control are not so immediately relevant here) actually operates. The sections of the present chapter on François Compte, Beccaria, Blackstone, Bentham, Thibaut, and Savigny offer useful leads.

Still another rewarding emphasis might have to do with Adam Ferguson. Although mentioned frequently in the present treatise and although dealt with at length by Bryson and Lehmann, he is still not sufficiently exploited as a source of stimulating suggestions. A good recent start has been made by Herta Joglund, *Ursprünge und Grundlagen der Soziologie bei Adam Ferguson* (Berlin: Duncker und Humblot, 1959), containing an excellent bibliography.

CHAPTER XV

The Transition to Objective Social Science and to Comte's Version of Sociology

L OOKING BACKWARD: *Eighteenth-Century Achievements.* —
About the beginning of the eighteenth century a new era
seemed to be dawning in social theory. The older interpretations of society in purely speculative terms were being gradually abandoned, though there was a temporary recrudescence in
the works of Rousseau, Hegel, and similar writers. Vico presented
a theory of progress and a new attitude toward the study of early
society. Berkeley and others manifested the influence of the Newtonian natural science. Montesquieu produced the first great descriptive treatise in sociology. Voltaire gained elbow-room for the
new social knowledge by his assaults on obscurantism. Fontenelle,
Turgot, Kant, and Condorcet were among the first conspicuous
advocates of the doctrines of continuity in history and the possibility of indefinite human progress, and, along with Herder and
others, gave a great impetus to the philosophy of history. Hume
presented the first great psycho-sociological interpretation of society, annihilated the social contract doctrine, and suggested a
naturalistic study of religion as a form of human behavior. Ferguson and Herder combined several methods of analyzing social
processes, but granted a large place to empirical evidence. Economic influences were analyzed in detail by the Physiocrats, Adam
Smith, and the classical economists. The ideologists of the French
Revolution emphasized to excess the doctrines of the amenability
of social processes to rational direction. The scientific historical
approach to the study of social institutions was embodied in the
work of Eichhorn, Savigny, Niebuhr, Ranke, and Guizot. Finally,
Saint-Simon classified the sciences and pointed out the need of an
as yet non-existent science of society to furnish a basis for reconstructing the social order.

The various lines of approach to the interpretation of social
processes which were to converge in sociology were thus all in
process of development during the eighteenth century and the

first quarter of the nineteenth, and, when one reflects upon the situation, it appears neither miraculous nor even strange that Comte was able to conceive and partially formulate the principles of a system of social philosophy bearing some of the earmarks of what we now call sociology. At best, however, his achievement consisted primarily in the combination of a number of the interpretations of social life current during his time.

Another Retrospect: Influences on the " Drive toward Objectivity." — The situational influences on social philosophy during the period of its transition into sociology are not difficult to discover. The older tendencies, clustering about the creation of the national state, furnished the center of orientation for the doctrines of the Mercantilists and the Cameralists, whose influence lasted well into the eighteenth century. The reaction against their excessive emphasis on the paramount importance of the interests of the state and on the value of state activity found expression in the *laissez faire* doctrines of the Physiocrats and the English classical economists.

Natural science, which had received its most striking expression in Newton, reacted powerfully on eighteenth-century political and social philosophy. Inasmuch as Galileo and Newton had been able to interpret the physical universe in terms of such simple formulas as the laws of " falling bodies " and " inverse squares," it seemed probable to the social philosophers that equally simple formulas could be found to explain and to furnish the means of controlling social and political phenomena. Whether or not this tendency had any influence upon the development of the contract theory it is difficult to determine, but it is certain that it was a foundation of the prevalent eighteenth-century doctrine that a few " self-evident dictates of pure reason " were adequate to interpret and to adjust social relations, and particularly of the basic philosophy which buttressed the *laissez faire* tenets of the Physiocrats and Adam Smith.

The critical spirit of the eighteenth century, which found its ablest representatives in Voltaire, the Encyclopedists, Hume, and Paine, can be traced to a number of sources. Bacon and Descartes, in the previous century, proclaimed the futility of a dependence on the past. The development of natural science contributed to a general spirit of scepticism and curiosity. The increasing geographical discoveries and explorations kept up that process of the contact of cultures which is the most potent agency in awakening criticism of prevailing institutions. The Deists emphasized the necessity of introducing reason into religion, the very possibility of which had been denied by Luther. All these forces and tendencies gave rise to that destructive criticism of old theories and institutions which was necessary to clear the ground for a new, secular study of society. Shaftesbury, Pope, and other Deists attacked the current theological view of inherent depravity and hopeless wickedness, and made possible the conception of man as a worthy subject for scientific analysis, thus justifying the social sciences in a way which now seems unnecessary but which at that time was of vital psychological importance.

The critical spirit, the Deistic conception of the worthiness of man, and the "dynamic" type of mind created by further development of science, commerce, and industry made possible that idea of the future progress of mankind so rapturously expressed by Fontenelle, Turgot, Condorcet, and Godwin.

The Industrial Revolution, one of the greatest transformations in the history of humanity, broke down the foundations of the older social system even more completely than the Commercial Revolution had destroyed the medieval order. Out of the confusion, as an aid in solving the newly created social problems, there came a further development and differentiation of the special social sciences, and pervading them all was a type of thought that eventually issued in sociology.

This recapitulation of the outstanding achievements in social theory produced, for the most part, between 1700 and 1825, makes it clear why it is customary to view this period as transitional. We have already noted the growing tendency to abandon the comprehensive field of social philosophy, dealing as it did with economics, politics, sociology, jurisprudence, and ethics, and to make at least definite beginnings toward specialization both in sociology and in the other social sciences. In other words, it was the age which witnessed the differentiation of social philosophy into the social sciences as we now understand them. Moreover, not only did this period witness the growth of specialization, but it also marked a very definite trend toward greater objectivity and the triumph of empirically based and comparative methods in social science. The older reliance on *a priori* and speculative notions was gradually abandoned; greater insistence was laid on controlled observation of social phenomena and their careful analysis according to scientific criteria.

New Shoots on Old Stems: the Sociologically Relevant Sciences Push Forward. — In addition to those antecedents which have just been summarized (most of them falling in the eighteenth century), it may be of value to provide a brief inventory of tendencies in social science during the period in which Comte was developing his system — a period characterized by new and remarkable activities in every phase of social science.

In the same year (1848) that the *Communist Manifesto* was published, there appeared another work which indicated a line of approach to sociological problems which is now considered by many to be the most promising of all. This was the *Du système social et des lois qui le régissent* of Adolphe Quetelet (1796–1874). This work and his earlier *Sur l'homme* (1835) and his later *Physique sociale* (1869) were the first widely noticed attempts to apply the statistical method to the analysis of collective behavior. Although his modern disciples are no doubt oversanguine in their anticipation of the amenability of social phenomena to statistical *interpretation,* there can be no doubt that it is destined to be one of the most effective means of bringing empirical sociological generalization up to a high level of reliability.

The geographic factors in social organization and evolution were analyzed, with a thoroughness never before approached even by Heeren, in the writings of Ritter (1779–1859), especially in his *Die Erdkunde im Verhältnis zur Natur und zur Geschichte der Menschen,* which first appeared in 1817–18; in Guyot's (1807–1884) *Earth and Man;* and in Buckle's (1821–1862) *History of Civilization in England.*

The influence of the doctrine of organic evolution on sociology was first exerted by Lamarck (1774–1829), who, in his *Philosophie Zoölogique* (1809), stated his belief in the mutability of species through the inheritance of acquired characteristics. The principle enunciated by Lamarck was further developed in the lectures of Sir William Lawrence (1783–1867), in Chambers's *Vestiges of the Natural History of Creation* (1844), and in Spencer's early writings; it reached its classic exposition in Darwin's *Origin of Species* (1859), only to be modified by the later investigations of Mendel, Weismann, DeVries, Morgan, and a host of others.

Anthropometry, ethnology, and prehistoric archaeology were beginning to assume that form which renders them so valuable to sociology in the work of Blumenbach (1752–1840), Retzius (1796–1860), Broca (1824–1880), Prichard (1786–1848), Bastian (1826–1905), and Boucher de Perthes (1788–1869).

Scientific historiography was taking form in the writings of Mignet (1796–1884) and Guizot (1787–1874) in France; Niebuhr (1776–1831) and Ranke (1795–1886) in Germany; and Hallam (1777–1859), Palgrave (1788–1861), and Grote (1794–1871) in England.

In economics, the impetus given by the Physiocrats and Adam Smith was carried on by Sismondi (1773–1842) in France; Rau (1792–1870) and Thünen (1783–1850) in Germany; and Ricardo (1772–1823), McCulloch (1789–1864), and James and John Stuart Mill in England.

In socio-political theory and organization the outstanding figures were DeBonald (1754–1840), Cousin (1792–1867), Constant (1767–1830), and DeTocqueville (1805–1859) in France; Hegel (1770–1831), Krause (1781–1832), Leo (1799–1878), Ahrens (1808–1874), and Von Mohl (1799–1875) in Germany; Von Haller (1768–1854) in Switzerland; and Bentham (1748–1832) and Austin (1790–1859) in England.

The socialistic and social reform tendencies of early nineteenth-century thought were best reflected in the works of Robert Owen (1771–1858) in England; Saint-Simon (1760–1825), Cabet (1788–1856), Fourier (1772–1837), Louis Blanc (1811–1882), and Proudhon (1809–1865) in France; and Lassalle (1825–1864) and Rodbertus (1805–1875) in Germany. Their doctrines were in the main all motivated by the misery attendant upon the social transformation which followed the Industrial Revolution, as we shall see in a later chapter. Although the earlier of these writers commonly advocated a refined type of utopian communism, Louis Blanc, Proudhon, Lassalle, and Rodbertus criticized such schemes as visionary, and proposed what they held to be more practical and immediately applicable remedial measures. They may rightly be regarded as the main figures in the transition of socialism from the stage of utopian schemes to the " scientific " socialism of Marx (1818–1883) and Engels (1820–1895). From the appearance of Marx's *Holy Family* in 1845 and his joint work with Engels, the *Communist Manifesto,* in 1848, dates the formal launching of scientific socialism, with its basic premise that man can directly control his social relations and the total process of sociation, and its doctrines of the economic interpretation of history, the labor theory of value, the theory of surplus value, class struggle, ultimate economic revolution, and state control of industry.

Saint-Simon: Precursor of Comte. — Count Henri de Saint-Simon (1760–1825) anticipated the main theoretical positions in the sociological system of Auguste Comte. If one substitutes " sociology " for " political science," a term used by Saint-Simon with practically the same connotation that Comte gave to sociology, then Saint-Simon may be said to have formulated Comte's chief theses, though even he himself merely collected and systematized the doctrines current at the time.

Alengry enumerates the following as Saint-Simon's fundamental doctrines: (1) Science must be distinguished from art in all departments of knowledge. (2) The sciences must be classified in the order of their increasing complexity, and a new science — *la science politique* — should be put at the head of the hierarchy. (3) This *science politique* must be based on the solid inductions of history and observation, and must be animated by the conception of development and progress. (4) The general law of progress is that formulated by Turgot and Burdin — namely, the law of the three stages of the psychological evolution of the race: the conjectural, the " miconjectural," and the positive. (5) All sociological theories of progress must be founded upon this fundamental law. (6) The practical conditions of social life, and not supernatural sanctions, must be made the basis of a new secular morality; and increased happiness for mankind must be realized through a transformation of the present social order rather than in heaven. (7) This transformation requires a new industrial organization, a new social and political system, and a union of Europe in a new fraternity, *Le Nouveau Christianisme*. One who is familiar with Comte's system need not be told that all that remained was for him to expand and systematize the outlines laid down by Saint-Simon, and the best critics agree that such was the primary contribution of Comte to sociology.

There was extremely little that was original in the theoretical content of Comte's work, as we have already hinted and shall later show in detail. His main contribution was to give systematic form to a few of the somewhat detached and incoherent doctrines current in his time. As a matter of fact, Comte was greatly behind the scientific achievements of his age in many ways (he practiced " cerebral hygiene " by reading no scientific works after 1826), and quite failed to absorb many of the most important developments of the period which have since entered into sociological thought. At the same time, Comte cannot be denied a certain degree of genius, for there have been few minds able to grasp in a more comprehensive manner the vast number of factors involved in the organization and development of social life.

When Did Sociology Emerge? — This cursory enumeration of the chief tendencies in the study of social phenomena in the earlier part of the nineteenth century gives a basis for examining some apparently contradictory assertions concerning the origin of sociology. Small long contended that sociology did not emerge in isolation from the other social sciences, but that the latter had faced and partially solved many of the most important problems of sociology before Comte gave it a name. Giddings, on the other hand, apparently ignoring his partiality for Adam Smith, maintained that a new and definitely sociological type of approach to the study of social phenomena was "predicted" if not created by Auguste Comte, and developed directly through the writings of Spencer, Ward, and the sociologists of the present generation.

There has been an attempt to reconcile these conflicting views of the matter by calling attention to the conceptions of the nature of sociology held by each of the writers mentioned. If one accepts Small's earlier contention that sociology is the philosophical synthesis and organization of the results of the special social sciences, then his view that the "drive toward objectivity" beginning about 1800 is the source of the sociology that achieved fairly sharp differentiation about 1880 may be regarded as valid. On the other hand, if one agrees with Giddings that sociology is the elemental and basic social science, distinguished by its investigation of society as a unity in its broadest and most fundamental aspects, then one must grant that the initial formal differentiation of sociology as a distinct science began with the quasi-sociological systematization of earlier doctrines by Auguste Comte. If, as Ellwood and Vincent have contended, both views are tenable because complementary, the conflict of opinions is of course more apparent than real, and one may simply place the origins of sociology as such in the last century, both in the work of avowed sociologists and in the increasing tendency of the other social sciences to assume the sociological method of approach to their problems.

Another point of view is held by the exponents of "systematic sociology," who maintain that not until well into the fourth quarter of the nineteenth century did sociology emerge as a specialized discipline. Leopold von Wiese is the most outspoken advocate of this position, and he puts his case thus:

. . . the evolution of sociology hitherto has been a very gradual process of self-limitation. It has fulfilled and is fulfilling itself through a steady contraction of the far-flung boundaries of its original domain, through greater precision in the formulation of its problems, and through the development of a more and more independent method. Simultaneously, such changes mean severance from social philosophy, from doctrines of general culture, from ethics, and from the other special social sciences in neighboring fields. But since this movement toward freedom and independence has taken place only in the relatively immediate present, it may be said to be a demonstrable proposition that all sociology in Germany before Tönnies and Simmel, in France before Tarde, in America before Small and Giddings, may be referred to the preliminary period of its history. *In fact, we assert that sociology as a clearly defined, independent social science is only today coming into existence.*

The first efforts to reach this standpoint, however, began a century ago. We shall therefore distinguish first of all a long preliminary period in the history of the science. We place in this era antiquity, the Middle Ages, and the succeeding period down to the close of the eighteenth century. Then comes the first stage of sociology proper. At this time (nineteenth century) it is characterized as a universal science, and seeks to make good its claims as an independent discipline by choosing the question: What is society? as its basic and essential problem. This very question, however, blocked the path to fruitful knowledge, since in answering it too many questions had to be dealt with which were not sociological even though they were closely related to general social science or social philosophy. Finally, there follows a second stage, covering the period from the late nineteenth century to the present [1925], in which sociology slowly ripens into an independent and closely delimited science, although the boundary between the two stages is vague, depending as it does on the importance attributed to one or another writer.[1]

Regardless of the choice of opinions one may make, however, the fundamental fact is that the essence, if not the name, of sociology was (1) an inevitable result of the growing conviction that an adequate science of society was a necessity, as well as (2) an equally inevitable product of a gradually improving method of analyzing social phenomena. Above all, it was *not* the fortuitous and questionable invention of one man, nor the perishable and exotic ideology of a brief period in the history of Western Europe. At about the time when the general social situation and the advances in positive knowledge and scientific method first made possible such a thing as a science of society, and when this possibility was already being exploited by a large number of writers, Auguste Comte, an enthusiast with a flair for assimilation and systematization, appeared on the scene and gave a name and a peculiarly personal, warped expression to an already powerful tendency. That sociology would have come into existence in its present nature and strength, though perhaps under a different name, is an incontestable conclusion to anyone who knows of.the work of the long line of thinkers we have passed in review, or who has investigated the development of social science since 1850. And now that we have taken the proverbial look before the leap, let us plunge directly into an examination of the social theory of Comte.

Comte's Life and Works. — Isidore Auguste Marie François Xavier Comte (1798–1857), scion of a Catholic Royalist family, was born in Montpellier, and received his higher education at the *École Polytechnique.* During six years of his young manhood he was a close friend and ardent disciple of the heterodox French thinker, Henri de Saint-Simon, whom we have already discussed. In 1824 there came a sharp break [2] which led Comte into a somewhat ungracious disavowal of his former master. They differed chiefly in their attitudes toward the revolutionary philosophy and tendencies of the times; the pupil, true to his family background and his veneration of the Romanticist DeMaistre, was inclined toward a much more conservative position than his teacher. Comte's earliest work of importance was the famous prospectus of his social philosophy: *Plan des travaux scientifiques nécessaire pour réorganiser la société* (1822). In 1826 he worked out in lectures, given in his own home, the first formal exposition of the principles of the Positivist philosophy, and was honored by the attendance of such distinguished men as the scientist Alexander von Humboldt. Shortly thereafter he experienced a severe mental crisis and attempted suicide; unfortunately, as we shall see in the next section, this crisis was not the last.

Comte's first great work — the *Cours de philosophie positive* — appeared between the years 1830 and 1842. From 1836 until 1846 he was an examiner for the *École Polytechnique.* After his dismissal from this position he was supported chiefly by contributions from his disciples and admirers. His friendship with Clotilde de Vaux flourished during 1845–46; it doubtless contributed strongly to certain features of his *Polity,* particularly his eulogy of women. He founded the Positivist Society in 1848. Comte's last and most important work — the *Système de politique positive* — appeared between 1851 and 1854. He died three years later.[3]

In the first of his chief works — the *Philosophy* — Comte worked out, in more detail than in his earlier sketches and essays, his main theoretical positions. These include: the hierarchy of the sciences; the necessity for, and the nature of, sociology, with its two main divisions of social statics and social dynamics; and the law of the three stages of universal progress. The *Polity* was a detailed expansion of his theoretical doctrines, and their practical application to the construction of a " positive " or scientifically designed commonwealth. Although many are inclined to maintain that the *Philosophy* contains all of Comte's important contributions to sociology, such is far from the case.[4] Though the *Polity* is verbose, prolix, involved, and repetitious, nearly all his chief postulates are developed in it with far greater maturity and richness of detail than in the *Philosophy*.

Comte's Mentality. — So much for the bare outlines of Comte's life and work; now for a bit of precautionary comment. Here and there in the foregoing paragraphs mention of Comte's mental instability has been made. In these days of psychiatric enthusiasm, it is all too easy to assume that because a writer has particular mental quirks his work is therefore useless. Such an assumption is unwarranted; the quirks may be the very reason why the person in question succeeds in analyzing processes to which normal men and women devote no attention. The validity or invalidity of a system of concepts must be determined by reference to the rules of logic and the empirical data available, not by psychological probing into the writer's "unconscious." True, this probing may give us hints as to the places where flaws in the logical structure of the system may be discovered, or as to the utilization of scanty or inadequate data to bear burdens beyond their powers — *but* the logic and the data must be examined, not merely the psychological processes. As Jaspers puts it, "Propositions are valid or invalid regardless of their origins." The fact that a good husband, father, and citizen is the epitome of everything that is normal in his community is no warrant that his thinking is of high quality; conversely, the fact that Comte manifested many abnormal traits is no reason for dismissing his social theories as so much moonshine.[5] With these warnings in mind, let us examine the evidence regarding Comte's mentality.

Dumas, in his remarkably able study, *Deux messies positivistes,* has analyzed at length the Messianic delusions of Comte. He errs, however, as Devolvé has pointed out,[6] in attributing too much importance to crises of mania such as those which determined his attempt at suicide and his belated infatuation. After all, these crises were but the cyclical culminations of a constant state of mental maladjustment that characterized Comte's whole life.

This maladjustment appeared at a very early age: he was always abnormally detached from his surroundings — a condition which appears to have been due to poor coördination of his emotional and intellectual life. He manifested great intellectual precocity, but at the same time showed well-marked delusions of oppression and persecution; his perpetual insubordination as a student derives largely from this source. Temperamentally, Comte was not the detached, aloof, unemotional creator of pure thought which one might assume him to be when reading his elaborately systematized and pompously phrased discourses, for there was a wide gap between his intellectual activity and his emotional life. The former got under way at such an early age that the latter never really caught up; at a period when his rational processes were highly complex, the emotional phases of his social relations remained rudimentary and crude.

His sexual life, for example, was gross and almost wholly devoid of the refinements of sentiment until his belated attachment to Clotilde de Vaux. This diagnosis is borne out by his letters to Valat and other friends. The unintegrated nature, amounting to virtual duality, of Comte's personality was the fundamental reason for his extraordinary lack of tact in dealing with his English supporters (Mill and others) and with his superiors in the *École Polytechnique*. To this circumstance was also due his violent breach with Saint-Simon and with his wife. Lack of tact was also the source of the peculiar rationalistic utopianism characteristic of Comte; he tended to identify his personal predilections with the precepts of universal wisdom, and was quite blind to the idiosyncrasies of other persons. As a consequence his utopia is so thoroughly rational as to be virtually inhuman. It should also be noted that the strange discrepancy between the intellectual powers of his wife and himself derives from the same source; his marriage took place at a period in his development when the breach between his rational and emotional life was at its widest, and the woman he chose as his wife was nothing more than a means for the immediate gratification of his crude sexuality.

Comte also had a strong tendency toward dereistic or autistic thinking. After he experienced the mental breakdown of 1826 he resolved not to do any reading that might overtax his mind, but this resolve was probably a rationalization of a tendency to ignore the theories of other persons when they conflicted with the elaborate systematic structure he was incessantly building up in his autistic reveries.

The most strongly marked period of dissociation in Comte's life extended from 1826 to 1845; the latter date marks the beginning of a new period infused by his love for Clotilde de Vaux — a love which has all the earmarks of being the first he had ever experienced and which consequently seems almost like the calf-love of late adolescence. At the same time, this new emotional experience served a useful function in that it produced a measure of integration in Comte's personality; his thought was no longer so wholly isolated from his emotional experiences.

It is significant that after 1845 Comte constructed his *Polity*, a semi-utopian system making much use of exalted sentiments for the maintenance of social order. Highly sentimentalized passion caused him to attempt the application of his utopia to all the affairs of life, particularly to his "secular religion" of humanity, that "Catholicism without Christianity" guided by priests but inspired by women, which we shall soon survey.

Warnings previously given must be recalled at this point: merely because Comte's *Philosophy* was probably engendered in and through dereistic thinking, merely because his *Polity* was a blend of earlier autistic reveries and newly emergent emotionalism, we are not absolved from the necessity of examining these elaborate systematic structures if we wish to assess their scientific value. Enough has now been said about Comte's frailties; let us now turn to the work for which he has become famous, making what allowance we individually choose for possible lapses in logic or unwarranted generalization from inadequate evidence.

Synthesizing Power. — It is generally conceded by the foremost students of Comte's social philosophy that his chief contribution lay in his remarkable capacity for synthesis and organization, rather than in the development of new and original social doctrines. (This marked synthesizing power seems to show that his autistic reveries were of great help.) He drew much from writers on social philosophy. Plato furnished him with his fundamental notion as to the basis of social organization: namely, the distribution of functions and the combination of efforts. From Hume, Kant, and Gall he received his conceptions of positivism in method and his physiological psychology. Hume, Kant, and Turgot were the sources of his views of historical determinism, and Bossuet, Vico, and DeMaistre are to blame for his somewhat divergent doctrine of the providential element in history. From Turgot, Condorcet, Burdin, and Saint-Simon he derived his famous law of the three stages in the intellectual development of mankind. Montesquieu, Condorcet, and Saint-Simon provided his conception of sociology as the basic and directive science which must form the foundation of the art of politics: each of the three had made special contributions to this subject, for (1) Montesquieu had introduced the conception of law in the social process, stressing particularly the influence of the physical environment; (2) Condorcet had emphasized the concept of progress; while (3) Saint-Simon had insisted upon the necessity of providing a science of society sufficiently comprehensive to guide the process of social and industrial reorganization. It was the significant achievement of Comte to work out an elaborate synthesis of these contributions of the thought of the previous century and to indicate the bearing of this new social science upon the problems of European society in the nineteenth century.[7]

Comte's outstanding doctrines — namely, the hierarchy of the sciences with sociology at the head; he division of this subject into statics and dynamics; the " law " of the three stages of universal progress; and the conception of the organic nature of society, with its corollary of society as a developing organism — have been so often repeated in résumés of sociological theory that they have become commonplaces. Even a cursory reading of Comte's major works, however, is bound to impress the reader with the fact that he had much more to offer than can be intelligently summarized under the above headings. There are few problems in social theory or history upon which he did not touch.[8]

Methodology. — His fundamental methodological position is that if human knowledge is to be extended in the future this must be accomplished through the application of the positive or scientific method of observation, experimentation, and comparison. Sociological investigation must follow this general procedure, with the addition that when the comparative method has been applied to the study of consecutive stages of human society, a fourth method, the historical, will have been developed, from which may be expected the most notable results.[9]

Comte constructed a hierarchy of the sciences, beginning with mathematics and passing through astronomy, physics, chemistry, and biology to the new science of sociology, which was to complete the series. The fundamental theoretical foundations of this classification were: first, that each science depends upon those below it in the series; second, that as one advances along the series the subjects become more specific, more complex, and less amenable to scientific measurement and prediction; and finally, that the difficulties of sociology are due to the greater complexity of the phenomena with which it deals and the contemporary lack of proper investigation and measurement of these phenomena, rather than to any generic difference in desirable or possible methodology or procedure.[10]

The Social Organism. — Although Comte did not elaborate to any great extent the organismic conception of society, he may be said to have offered suggestions for the later school of so-called " organicists," and undoubtedly held that the organismic doctrine was no mere analogy but a reality. " It is the individual who is an abstraction rather than the social organism." Organismic doctrines found in the *Philosophie positive* have thus been summarized by Coker: Society is a collective organism, as contrasted with the individual organisms or plant, and possesses the primary organismic attribute of the *consensus universel*. There is to be seen both in the organism and in society a harmony of structure and function working toward a common end through action and reaction among the parts and upon the environment. This harmonious development reaches its highest stage in human society, which is the final step in organismic evolution. Social progress is marked by an increasing specialization of functions and a corresponding tendency toward an adaptation and perfection of organs. Finally, social disturbances are maladies of the social organism, and hence are the proper subject-matter of social pathology.[11] In the *Polity* Comte elaborated the similarity between the individual and the social organism. In the family may be found the social cell; in the social forces may be discerned the social tissues; in the state (city) may be discovered the social organs; in the various nations are to be detected the social analogues of the systems in biology.[12] The great difference between the individual organism and the social organism lies in the fact that the former is essentially immutable, while the latter is capable of immense improvement, if guided according to scientific principles. Another distinction is that the social organism, in contrast to the individual, allows a far greater distribution of functions combined with a higher degree of coördination of organs.[13]

Social Order and Social Progress. — Sociology was defined by Comte in two ways: specifically, as the science of social order and progress; generally, as the science of social phenomena.[14] It is closely related to biology: the subject-matter of the latter is organization and life; homologously, sociology deals with order and progress.[15]

Comte divides sociology into two major departments: social statics, or *théorie générale de l'ordre spontané des sociétés humaines,* and social dynamics, or *théorie générale du progrès naturel de l'humanité.*[16] He finds that the underlying basis of social order is the principle of the distribution of functions and the combination of efforts (which he assigns to Aristotle, though it probably belongs more rightfully to Plato): the distribution of functions is engendered in the specialization and division of labor in society, and the combination of efforts is realized through the institution of government.[17]

The governing principle in social progress is to be found in the law of the three stages of intellectual advance.[18] (Comte possessed almost as great a love for triads as did Vico. Thus, he finds three stages of intellectual progress, three divisions of cerebral functions, three types of social forces, three grades of society, three social classes, three stages of religion, and three classes of regulating power in society.) Through each of these stages — the theological, metaphysical, and scientific — there must pass the proper development and education of the individual, the various realms of human knowledge, and the general process of social evolution. None of these stages can be eliminated, though intelligent direction may hasten the process and lack of wisdom retard it.[19] Each stage is the necessary antecedent of its successor, and any period is as perfect as the condition of the time will allow; hence, institutions are relative in their degree of excellence and none can hope to attain absolute perfection.[20] Objectively considered, progress may be regarded as consisting in man's increasing control over the environment.[21] Again, progress may be broken up into three constituent parts: intellectual, material, and moral. Intellectual progress is to be found in the law of the three stages; material progress in " an analogous progression in human activity which in its first stage is Conquest, then Defense, and lastly Industry "; and moral progress " shows that man's social nature follows the same course; that it finds satisfaction, first in the Family, then in the State, and lastly in the Race." [22] In securing progress the desires and emotions are the driving forces, and the intellectual factors are the guiding and restraining agencies — a theory that robs Ward's doctrine of conation and telesis of much of its supposed originality.[23]

Although Comte's philosophy of history has been criticized by many for being too one-sided because it supposedly stresses intellectual factors alone,[24] most of his critics have overlooked those passages in which he foreshadows Spencer and Giddings by describing the three great stages of human progress as the Military-Theological, the Critical-Metaphysical, and the Industrial-Scientific.[25]

Comte laid great stress upon the family as a fundamental social institution and upon religion as one of the most important regulating agencies in society. Although somewhat utilitarian as regards the social application of religion, his exposition of the principles of the Positivist creed, developed in great detail in the *Polity,* is stimulating and suggestive. His doctrines regarding the basic importance of the family and religion, appreciated by Ward, have been recently revived by Ellwood,[26] and form part of the standard teachings of most American sociologists.

Finally, as Ward pointed out, Comte holds that the great practical value of sociology is to be looked for in its application to scientific social reform, and in his most elaborate work he develops at great length what he believes will be the ultimate type of social organization — if society is wise enough to study and apply the science which investigates the laws of its organization and progress.[27] A great part of the social reform effort in contemporary American sociology is rationalized on this basis.

Sociology and Political Science. — Comte makes no clear distinction between political science and sociology. Indeed, he seems to regard sociology as the perfected political science of the future. At the same time, however, he clearly differentiates sociology from the older political philosophy dominated by metaphysical doctrines. Sociology has nothing in common with the *a priori* method that characterized the earlier political philosophy; it must be based on the assured scientific procedure of observation, experimentation, and comparison.[28] It is even doubtful whether Comte conceived that a science of the state, distinct from the general science of society, was at all possible.[29] At any rate, his political theory is inextricably connected with his psychology, theology, ethics, and economics, and these are included within his sociology. In general, Comte denied that the special social sciences are true sciences; he held that society must be studied as a whole by a unitary science — sociology. In other words, he contributed not a little to the development of so-called " encyclopedic " sociology.[30] Political science, to Comte, was that part of his sociology which was concerned with the history of the state and the theory and practice of its organization, but he rarely if ever treated these subjects in isolation; each was dealt with as a part of social evolution and organization as a whole.[31]

The Nature of the State. — Comte's ideas concerning the nature of the state and its distinction from society, nation, and government are vague and uncertain, but in this he was no different from other writers of his time — indeed, not a few modern social scientists are equally hazy. Moreover, Comte was too much interested in the ultimate Positivist society of the future to devote his attention to an elaboration of the theoretical foundations of the contemporary national bourgeois state. Furthermore, he regarded this as but a transitory form of social organization at best: " Between the city, uniting man and his dwelling place, and the full development of the Great Being around a fitting centre, a number of intermediate forms of association may be found, under the general name of *states*. But all of these forms, differing only in extent and permanence, may be neglected as undefined." Comte's whole position would have made it hard for him to conceive clearly of such a network of interhuman relations as society politically organized, as distinct in practice, at least, from its other non-material and its material aspects. His own theory of society was so all-inclusive (with its mixture of family ethics, theological dogmas, economic arrangements, and politics) that it was not favorable to clearly differentiated concepts in the political realm. The only point on which he may be said to be unmistakably clear is his dogma that there can be no social relations of any permanence without political organization — i.e., a government. The first principle of positive political theory, he says, is that " society without a government is no less impossible than a government without society. In the smallest as well as in the largest associations, the Positive theory of a polity never loses sight of these two correlative ideas, without which theories would lead us astray, and society would end in anarchy." [32] When Comte begins to discuss the governmental arrangements in his state or society, however, he immediately introduces conceptions quite foreign to orthodox notions of governmental organization by his advocacy of increasing governmental rectitude through the influence of family morality, and by entrusting its encouragement and surveillance to the priests of the religion of Humanity. In short, it seems that he regarded the state as the organ for the direction of the general material activities of society, but although this is the most frequent connotation of the term " state " as employed by Comte, he often uses it in senses identical with the nation and with society in general.[33]

Upon the question as to what constitutes the fundamental attributes of the state, Comte is a little more clear. In fact, he quite agrees with what are now considered the indispensable attributes of any state or political society: namely, population, territory, a sovereign power, and a governmental organization. He is particularly insistent upon the territorial prerequisite of the state.[34] His belief in the indispensability of government has just been referred to above. Finally, in his unequivocal statement of the necessity of adequate social control in any stable society and the recognition that political organization ultimately rests upon force, Comte makes it plain that he discerned the necessity of a sovereign power for the creation and maintenance of a permanent political society.[35] Comte also anticipated modern trends in political science by stressing the importance of the psychical and economic factors in the state. He sums up his position on these points very briefly in the following passage:

When Property, Family, and Language have found a suitable Territory, and have reached the point at which they combine any given population under the same, at least the same spiritual government, there a possible nucleus of the Great Being has been formed. Such a community, or city, be it ultimately large or small, is a true *organ* of Humanity.[36]

In addition to being an epitome of Comte's doctrines regarding the fundamental elements of any state, this passage is an admirable example of how he was wont to introduce sundry visionary notions of ethical and theological character into political thought. Here again, however, he cannot be said to be markedly different from others of his time; moreover, later writers such as Schäffle, Lilienfeld, and Spann were — and are — quite as fantastic.

Principles of the Genesis of Political Structures. — Comte treated the subject of the origin of society, state, and government in both an analytical and a historical manner. In his analytical treatment he based his procedure on the Aristotelian dogma of the inherent sociability of mankind; hence, he declared the notion of a state of nature mere metaphysical nonsense and the contract theory of political origins untenable.[37] Man, he held, prevailed over the other animals because of his superior sociability; and the prolongation of human infancy was perhaps the most important factor in developing this sociable (gregarious or associative) " human nature." [38]

The unit of society, according to Comte, is not the individual but the family. The great function of the family in history has been to generate the basic elements which ultimately produced the state. The growth and perfection of language was the main factor making it possible for the state to develop from the family:

A *society*, therefore, can no more be decomposed into individuals than a geometric surface can be resolved into lines, or a line into points. The simplest association, that is, the family, sometimes reduced to its original couple, constitutes the true unit of society. From it flow the more complex groups, such as classes and cities. . . .

During the whole continuance of the education of the race, the principal end of the Domestic Order is gradually to form the Political Order. It is from this latter, finally, that the critical influence originates, whereby the family affections are raised up to their high social office, and prevented from degenerating into collective selfishness.[39]

Although society, in a psychological sense, is ultimately based upon the social instinct, expressed mainly in the family, the wider and more highly developed forms of social organization, as exemplified by the state and society, are based upon the Aristotelian principle of the distribution of functions and the combination of efforts. It is this coöperative distribution of functions which marks off the political society from the domestic association, which is based upon sympathy.[40] The great point of superiority of the social organism over the individual organism is that it allows of a higher degree of distribution of functions, coördinated with a more perfect adaptation of organs. The perfect distribution of functions and coördination of organs in society is the ultimate goal of social evolution, and it is in a study of the relation between these two principles that one is to look for the relation between society and government. The reason for this is that too much specialization, although it leads to the development of a great skill and a high degree of interest in narrow fields, is likely to result in the disintegration of society through a loss of the conception of the unity of the whole and of the mutual relations between the individual and society. It is the function of government to coördinate human activities, and to guard against the dangerous elements in specialization, while at the same time conserving its beneficial effects.[41]

Integrating Processes in the State and Society. — In proportion as a distribution of functions is realized in society there result natural and spontaneous processes of supraordination and subordination, the principle being that those in any occupation come under the direction of the class which has control over their general type of functions; i.e., the next class above them in the hierarchy of industrial differentiation. Government tends naturally to arise out of the controlling and directing forces, which are at first centered in the smaller functional groups of society. In the past, war has been the chief factor in amalgamating this divided governmental power into one central unit. Industry, however, is coming more and more to be the source of social discipline and governmental control. " The habits of command and of obedience already formed in Industry have only to extend to public spheres, to found a power in the State capable of controlling the divergencies, and regulating the convergencies, of the individuals within it." [42]

This material basis of government in the principles of the division of labor, combination of efforts, and supraordination and subordination [43] harmonizes, says Comte, with those psychic characteristics of humanity which lead some to command and others to obey. While it is necessary to recognize the almost universal desire to command, it is no less essential to observe that people find it very agreeable to throw the burden of expert guidance upon others.[44]

But one must go beyond this distribution of functions and combination of efforts, even though it provides the fundamental analytical basis of the state, if a complete system of social philosophy is to be constructed. With the Aristotelian axiom must be combined the Hobbesian notion of force as the ultimate foundation upon which governmental organization rests. " Social science would remain forever in the cloud-land of metaphysics, if we hesitated to adopt the principle of Force as the basis of Government. Combining this doctrine with that of Aristotle, that society consists in the Combination of efforts and the Distribution of functions, we get the axioms of a sound political philosophy."

The Unifying Rôle of the Positivist Religion. — To the doctrines of Aristotle and Hobbes, however, Comte adds his own more specific notions. He finds that, in addition to the requirements just named, an efficient general regulating power or system of social control is a vital requisite. " Close study, therefore, shows us that there are three things necessary for all political power, besides the basis of material Force: an Intellectual guidance, a Moral sanction, and lastly a Social control." This regulating power is to be found in the religion of humanity and is to be administered by the priests of that cult. In the perfect state, therefore, three grades of society are necessary: (1) the family, based on feeling or affection; (2) the state or city, based on action; and (3) the church, based primarily on intelligence but in practice synthesizing all three.[45] These grades of society correspond to, and have their basis in, the three fundamental powers or functions of man's cerebral system [46] (which Comte took from Gall's phrenology and made the basis of his psychology and much of his social science).

The final element, the church, with its universal surveillance and guidance of all social activities, will make possible the dissolution of the great tyrannical states and the completion of the social organism without any danger of anarchy or license. In place of the conventional political state there is to be a group of cities united in and through the common religious tutelage provided by the worship of humanity as administered by its priests. Such political patterns, to Comte's way of thinking, are probably as large as any which can be constituted without the entry of tyranny; his doctrine therefore tended partially to revive the localism and municipal character of the utopias of Plato and Aristotle, and to a certain degree anticipated LePlay and modern regionalism:

The foundation of a universal Church will enable the gradual reduction of these huge and temporary agglomerations of men to that natural limit, where the State can exist without tyranny. . . . No combination of men can be durable, if this is not really voluntary; and in considering the normal form of the State we must get rid of all artificial and violent bonds of union, and retain only those which are spontaneous and free. Long experience has proved that the City, in its full completeness and extent of surrounding country, is the largest body politic which can exist without becoming oppressive. . . . But besides this, the Positive Faith, with its calm grasp over human life as a whole, will be sufficient to unite the various Cities in the moral communion of the Church, without requiring the help of the State to supplement the task with its mere material unity.

Thus the final creation of a religious society whereby the great organism is completed, fulfils all the three wants of the political society. The intellectual guidance, the moral sanction, and the social regulation which government requires to modify its material nature, are all supplied by a Church, when it has gained a distinct existence of its own.[47]

Outlines of the Positivist Philosophy of History. — In his treatment of the origin and development of the state from a historical point of view, Comte reminds one of Hegel's tale of the successive migrations of the *Weltgeist* until it finally settled permanently among the Germanic peoples.[48] Comte ranges over the history of humanity and traces the stages through which the race has passed in preparation for the final goal of its evolution — the Positivist utopia. One considerable difference between Hegel and Comte, however, is that the latter presented a much more accurate interpretation of the facts of history than did Hegel. Indeed, when viewed in the light of his times, Comte is by no means so devoid of historical information as some modern historical critics might seem to indicate.[49] He seems to have been acquainted with Gibbon and Hallam, for instance, and he grasped the significance of many fundamental movements in history, particularly in the field of economic development, which escaped many later and more erudite "political historians." A comprehensive grasp of the vital factors at work in history is as essential to a true conception and interpretation of history as a detailed knowledge of objective events. Judged by this criterion Comte was really a more precise historian than many of the extremely careful and critical "political historians " of the nineteenth century.

It is beyond the purpose of this chapter to present in detail Comte's philosophy of history. All that will be attempted is a brief statement of his fundamental principles and a summary of the portions dealing with the evolution of political institutions.

Comte's philosophy of history is based on as ingenious a system of triads as distinguished the work of Vico.[50] In the first place, social evolution, like social organization, is based on the tripartite functions of man's cerebral system — feeling, action, and intellect. Feeling or emotion, which is the basis of morality, passes through three stages in which man's social nature finds satisfaction: first in the family, then in the state, and finally in the race. Or, as he puts it in other words, altruism in antiquity is domestic and civic, in the Middle Ages collective, and in the Positive period universal. Still another way of describing this type of evolution is his assertion that the sympathetic instincts of humanity advance through the stages of attachment, veneration, and benevolence. There is a close relationship between these different views of moral evolution, for fetishism, which founded the family, also developed the feeling of attachment; polytheism, which founded the state, fostered veneration; and monotheism, with its universality, favored the sentiment of benevolence.[51] Man's activational evolution proceeds through the stages of conquest, defense, and industry. Finally, the evolution of the intellect follows the famous three stages — theological, metaphysical, and positive or scientific. In this process emotion is the dynamic power, action the agent of progress, and intellect the guiding force.[52]

In view of the foregoing, it can be confidently asserted that Comte did not base his philosophy of history exclusively on the single element of intellectual evolution, although many commentators on his doctrines have given such an impression. Even the law of the three stages of intellectual progress aimed at a larger synthesis which would include material and spiritual factors, although the religious element probably played a predominant part in his scheme. The periods of intellectual development (in broad outline) posited by Comte were the theological, divided into fetishism, polytheism, and monotheism; the period of the "Western Revolution," 1300 to 1800; and the beginnings of the Positive period, from 1800 onward. Each of these periods was further subdivided.

The Stages of Social Evolution. — In the period of fetishism, or what in the late nineteenth century was called animism,[53] the family or private society was instituted, and with it that fixity of residence which made the later development of the state possible. In the first polytheistic period, that of theocratic or conservative polytheism (i.e., the period of the great Oriental empires), the great political contribution was the founding of the city (i.e., the state) and the development of the institution of landed property.

Its great defect was the attempt to found a church before civic life had been perfected. Another unifying and disciplinary feature of this period was the wide development of the caste system.[54] In the next period, that of intellectual polytheism (i.e., the Greek age), there were no important political contributions except in a negative sense. The service of the Greeks was intellectual and was rendered by freeing humanity from theocratic influences. National solidarity was impaired by the attacks of the Greeks upon property and upon caste without providing other unifying influences, and their political life was mainly the rule of demagogues. If the Greeks made any political contribution at all it was in repelling the Persian advance.[55] In the Roman period, or the age of social monotheism, there were several phases of political progress. The most important was the development of the conception of "Fatherland," which Comte defines as "the permanent seat of all those moral and intellectual impressions, by whose unbroken influence the individual destiny is moulded." "Nothing is so well adapted to consolidate social ties as their habitual consolidation around a material seat, which is equally appropriate to relations of Continuity as to those of Solidarity." The world is therefore indebted to Rome for the first definite step toward sociocracy. Again, Roman law tended toward sociocracy, inasmuch as it substituted social sanctions for supernatural sanctions in the administration of its law to a considerable degree.[56] Finally, when Roman warfare was transformed from conquest into defense, it naturally resulted in the transformation of slavery into serfdom and of the Empire into small-state systems, thus opening the way for the development of feudalism, the germs of which are to be found in the cession of Roman territory to barbarian chieftains.

The next period was that of defensive monotheism or the Catholic-feudal transition — the period of the establishment of the church, as contrasted with the foundation of family and state in earlier periods. "The distinguishing feature of medieval civilization was the two-fold nature of the aims in view and the combination of two heterogeneous elements for its attainment." The general purpose of the period was to regularize and systematize all phases of social life, and this, the task of the church, for the most part failed. The special "purpose" of the age was the emancipation of women and laborers, and this, primarily the work of feudalism, was in large measure successful. Inasmuch as the religion of this period was universal, whereas political power was local, there resulted the indispensable separation of church and state. At the same time warfare was finally transformed from aggressive to defensive.[57] Mariolatry, with its idealization of woman, was an advance toward sociolatry or the worship of humanity. Great steps in advance were taken with the separation of employers from employed, the rise of the guilds, and the emancipation of the serfs.

Yet in spite of these important contributions, this period of defensive monotheism did not directly inaugurate the Positivist régime. Another period, that of the " Western Revolution," had to intervene; this corresponds to the metaphysical period of mental development. The eight main forces operating to bring about this revolution were: the influence of women; scientific advances; modern industrial improvements; art; the development of the state; the decay of the church; the work of the civil lawyers (légistes) in adapting Roman law to the needs of the time; and finally, the negative contributions of the metaphysicians.[58] In this period industry became consolidated, for employers and employed joined forces against the other classes in order to further their own mutual interests. Government, in turn, began to patronize industry because it recognized that its development was essential to the furnishing of the wealth needed for maintaining military activities; and this reacted upon the rulers by making them responsible administrators of the public wealth. This double process marked the real entry of industry, as the chief end of the modern polity, into Western politics; civilization, hitherto military, now became increasingly industrial in character.[59] The whole period, and particularly that of the French Revolution, was one of disintegration and of preparation for Positivism.[60]

In the preliminary work of the next or Positive period, important beginnings had already been made before Comte, as he himself admitted. Condorcet had laid the philosophic foundation for sociology; DeMaistre had renewed the veneration for the " best elements " in the Middle Ages; scientific advances had been made by Lamarck, Bichat, Broussais, Cabanis, and Gall. The time was ripe for Comte's discovery of the two fundamental laws of sociology, and he felt that still greater advances were made when his system, which was " too intellectualistic " in the Philosophy, was rounded out on its emotional side through his friendship with Clotilde de Vaux, and appeared in a more complete form in the Polity. On the side of preparatory theory, then, Comte believed that everything was ready for the institution of the Positivist system. Strangely enough, at just this time the coup d'état of 1851 had revived the institution of the dictatorship, which was held to be the great preliminary step in the political field preparatory to the inauguration of Positivism; greatly excited by the prospect of the imminent realization of his prophecies, Comte held himself ready to assume the office of supreme pontiff of the new religion.[61] Man's fundamental make-up and the struggles of ages had apparently conspired to render the Positivist system as inevitable as it was desirable. In this last stage of social evolution, "Family, State, and Church are finally to be distinguished and harmonized, or fixed in their proper organic relations to each other, so as to preclude forever their warfare or intrusion upon each other's provinces." [62]

Forms of State and Government. — Although Comte was familiar with the conventional Aristotelian classification of the forms of the state and government, he held it to be of minor importance, or merely superficial significance. To him there were only two fundamental types of society, state, and government — theocracy and sociocracy.[63] The former was the government of theologically oriented priests, in which temporal power was subordinated to spiritual. The latter was the condition to be reached in the Positivist state, where spiritual and temporal power were to be separated and properly coördinated, and in which social organization was to be based on the principles of Comte's sociology. To effect the transformation from the former to the latter, says our naïvely self-centered genius, has been the problem of the greater part of human history,[64] a problem " now fortunately solved."

Sovereignty. — In a system of social control like that proposed by Comte, a system in which authority was to be divided into moral, material, and intellectual realms, each to have separate organs of enforcement, and in which this enforcement, although of paramount importance, was to be administered through persuasion and suggestion, it is easy to see that there was no place for any such concept as that of political sovereignty in its conventional modern sense.[65] Probably the directors of material activities — that is, the leaders of the employer class — came the nearest of any of Comte's proposed governing agencies to having sovereign power: at least they were to possess the functions of ordinary civil government. He discusses the problem of sovereignty to only a limited extent, and seems to mean by it nothing more than participation in government; [66] the nearest he gets to a positive theory of sovereignty is his express approval of Hobbes's doctrine that government has an important basis in force.[67] In speaking of popular sovereignty, he says that the portion of Positive theory bearing on this point separates the elements of truth in the metaphysical doctrine from its errors. Two different conceptions of popular sovereignty thereby win Comte's favor: one a political connotation applicable in special cases, the other a moral interpretation suitable in all cases. By the political application he means that the voice of the people should be appealed to in cases which concern the practical interests of the whole community and are intelligible to the masses, such as " declarations of war and the decisions of the law-courts." On the other hand, says Comte, it would be manifestly absurd to have the whole people decide on questions of particular interest requiring special and trained judgment. The moral aspect of popular sovereignty consists in his proposition that the efforts of the whole of society should be centered on the common good; that is, there should be a " preponderance of social feeling over all personal interests." [68]

The Positivist Scheme of Social Reconstruction. — It is difficult to grasp the full significance of Comte's theory and plan of social organization without a preliminary statement of the historical background of his doctrines. He was witnessing the deterioration, as a result of the French and Industrial Revolutions, of the old social order, and was keenly conscious of the evils of the new, though still transitional, society. Quite in contrast to Say, Bastiat, and the French optimists, Comte joined with Sismondi in condemning the new capitalistic order. His indictment of the new bourgeois age is well stated by Lévy-Bruhl:

Comte saw the bourgeoisie at work during Louis Philippe's reign, and he passes severe judgment upon it. Its political conceptions, he says, refer not to the aim and exercise of power, but especially to its possessions. It regards the revolution as terminated by the establishment of the parliamentary *régime,* whereas this is only an " equivocal halting-place." A complete social reorganization is not less feared by this middle class than by the old upper classes. Although filled with the critical spirit of the eighteenth century, even under a Republican form it would prolong a system of theological hypocrisy, by means of which the respectful submission of the masses is insured, while no strict duty is imposed upon the leaders. This is hard upon the proletariat, whose condition is far from improving. It " establishes dungeons for those who ask for bread." It believes that these millions of men will be able to remain indefinitely " encamped " in modern society without being properly settled in it with definite and respected rights. The capital which it holds in its hands, after having been an instrument of emancipation, has become one of oppression. It is thus that, by a paradox difficult to uphold, the invention of machinery, which *a priori*, one would be led to believe, would soften the condition of the proletariat, has, on the contrary, been a new cause of suffering to them, and has made their lot a doubly hard one. Here, in brief, we have a formidable indictment against the middle classes, and in particular against the political economy which has nourished them.[69]

Yet in Comte's mind the problem was not one of capitalism as such, or of its abolition. It was not the industrial or financial technique of the new industrial order which he felt to be at fault, but rather the failure to develop a new industrial and social morality which could exert proper control and discipline over the modern industrial system:

That there should be powerful industrial masters is only an evil if they use their power to oppress the men who depend upon them. It is a good thing, on the contrary, if these masters know and fulfill their duties. It is of little consequence to popular interests in whose hands capital is accumulated so long as the use of it is made beneficial to the social masses.

But modern society has not yet got its system of morality. Industrial relations which have become immensely developed in it are abandoned to a dangerous empiricism, instead of being systematized according to *moral* laws. War, more or less openly declared, alone regulates the relations between capital and labour.[70]

What is needed, then, is a new industrial and social morality, to be inculcated through the Positive educational system — according to the father of Positivism — for this will be far more effective than state-socialistic schemes and paternalistic legislation. Comte's scheme of social reconstruction was thus one which rested more on a moral than a political basis. The socialization of the modern order " depends far more upon moral than upon political measures. The latter can undoubtedly prevent the accumulation of riches in a small number of hands, at the risk of paralyzing industrial activity. But these tyrannical proceedings would be far less efficacious than the universal reproof inflicted by positive ethics upon a selfish use of the riches possessed." " Everything then depends upon the common moral education, which itself depends upon the establishment of a spiritual power. The superiority of the positive doctrine lies in the fact that it has restored this power." " Once common education was established, under the direction of the spiritual power, the tyranny of the capitalist class would be no more to be feared. Rich men would consider themselves as the moral guardians of public capital. It is not here a question of charity. Those who possess will have the ' duty ' of securing, first, education and then work for all." [71] In turning, in the following paragraph, to a more detailed consideration of Comte's scheme for a new social dispensation, we must bear in mind that his chief aim was to develop a new social morality; he believed that this would be the only force adequate to solve the problems of modern industrialism.

Comte's theory of social reconstruction, like his doctrines of social organization and his philosophy of history, rests ultimately upon the threefold division of the human personality into action, intelligence, and feeling. This is clearly shown in his analysis of the social forces; they are: (1) material force, based on action and expressed in numbers and wealth; (2) intellectual force, founded on speculation and expressed in conception and expression; and (3) moral force, based on affection and expressed in command prompted by character and obedience, which in turn are inspired by the heart. It is the supreme task of social organization, as well as its chief difficulty, to combine these forces in the right proportion without the undue predominance of any one.

In the state, says Comte, one finds that the fundamental social classes are founded on this same general principle. " In the smallest cities capable of separate existence, we find these classes: the Priests who guide our speculation; the Women who inspire our highest affections; and the practical Leaders who direct our activity, be it in war or in industry." The agency needed to connect and harmonize these three fundamental orders is to be found in the mass of the people or the proletariat, " for they are united to the affectionate sex by domestic ties; to the Priesthood through the medium of the education and advice which it gives them; and to the practical Leaders through common action and the protection afforded them."

Every social class, except the women, should be ranked on a hierarchical scale based upon the principle of importance and specialization of function. " Our ultimate state will exhibit a classification of society more distinct than any we know in all sides of human life. From the High Priest of Humanity down to the humblest laborer, society will show the same principle at work distributing ranks: generality of view decreasing as independence of life increases." [72]

In Comte's state the directive power, or what might perhaps be called the function of government, was to be centered, in all essentials, in the priests of the Positive religion and in the leaders of industry. His scheme of social, economic, and political reorganization derived, in its major outlines, from Saint-Simon. The temporal and military power of the past was to give way to the principle of *capacité industrielle,* as applied to material government; and *capacité positive,* as applied to intellectual direction and moral surveillance.[73]

The Supreme Importance of the Priesthood. — The most important class in the Positivist state was to be the priesthood, or those distinguished by positive capacity.[74] *It should be understood at the outset that Comte's priests were not theologians, but sociologists.* They were to be the scientific directors of society, selected for their special talent and their immediate and extensive acquaintance with those sociological principles upon which enlightened social policy depends. They were to interpret to man the religious, or rather sociological, doctrines of Positivism, of which the principle was love; the basis, order; and the end, progress. Aside from special training, the priesthood must be eminent for the qualities of courage, perseverance, and prudence.[75] Of the organization of the Positive priesthood, which Comte describes in the most minute detail, only the most general outline can be given here. It suffices to say that there were to be some twenty thousand priests for Western Europe, presided over by a High Priest of Humanity with his headquarters at Paris. He was to be assisted by seven national chief priests, and this number was to be increased to forty-nine at the final regeneration of the world and its conversion to Positivism. The remainder of the priesthood were to be priests and vicars attached to the local temples, which were to be distributed in the proportion of one to every ten thousand families. The priests were to be paid a fixed salary, so low as to preclude pecuniary reasons for desiring service in the profession.[76]

It is difficult to say just what Comte considered the fundamental function of the priesthood, as he enumerates in various places several " supreme duties " of this class. It seems, however, that he regarded their duties in general as comprising several vitally important functions. They were above all to be the systematic directors of education. Further, they were to judge of the worth of each member of society and, relying primarily upon suggestion rather than force, to attempt to place him in society according to his merits and capacities. This, Comte admits, is a rather difficult achievement, as one can hardly judge of the capacity of an individual until his career is over, but the priesthood should do its best to arrive at a correct preliminary estimate.[77] Again, the priests should foster the feeling of continuity between different generations and of solidarity between the different social classes by teaching men their relation to nature, to the past, and to other men. Once more, the priests should be the general moral censors of the community, using the force of their opinions in keeping men aware of their social duties and obligations, and warning them in case of deviation. Finally, they should be the general fountain-spring of useful social and scientific knowledge and advice. In short, the priests should constitute the ideal aristocracy of intellect, exemplars of the philosopher-kings for whom Plato longed.

The priests should not, however, presume to possess one iota of temporal power. It was the mixture of spiritual and temporal power which was the great defect of antiquity, to Comte's mind, and it was the great contribution of Christianity that it separated the two. The powers of the priesthood were rather to be employed in the following extra-legal manner: in the first place, they were to exercise their influence through the medium of their teaching and preaching; secondly, they were to give a proper direction to public opinion; again, they might give their formal condemnation to any act; finally, they were to have a most important consulting function in all affairs of civic life. They might suggest action by the " secular arm of the law," but must never undertake such action on their own responsibility and initiative.[78] It seems that Comte, like Jefferson before him, relied upon the principle that " the people " would sufficiently admire and respect superior intellectual and moral ability to ensure their willing submission to the guidance of the priesthood — a noble belief, perhaps, but something which history has thus far shown to be seldom if ever realized, except when buttressed by a sacred order or by supernaturalism, or, most frequently, by both.

The Possessors of Temporal Power. — The material or industrial power, and the actual functions of civil government as well, were to be divided among the employing class, with its various subdivisions of bankers, merchants, manufacturers, and agriculturists, each ranked on the hierarchical scale and all possessing *capacité industrielle*. As the most influential and least numerous of the employers, the bankers were to possess the most authority.[79] The general principle of concentration of power among the employers is that there should be but a single manager for every field of industry which one man can personally direct.[80] Although the employers have the legal right to fix their incomes at any figure they may deem desirable, still they will be checked in excessive consumption by their greater need for and desire of public esteem, and it is a function of the Positivist priests to make the wealthy realize their social responsibility. In this manner Comte hoped to assure both industrial efficiency and social justice. In their relations to their employees the leaders of industry were always to keep in mind the following principles: " that everyone at all times should be the entire owner of everything of which he has the constant and exclusive use "; and " that every industrious citizen shall be secured in the means of fully developing his domestic life." The transmission of wealth and industrial function was to be regulated thus: each individual was to have the right to nominate his successor seven years before the date of his expected retirement and to submit this nomination to the judgment of public opinion; and testamentary disposition of wealth was to be allowed in all cases.[81]

With regard to moral authority in the Positive state, our sage maintained that domestic morality should be guided by the women and public morality safeguarded by the priesthood.[82] The moral influence of woman was to be ensured by the Positivist rule of indissoluble monogamous marriage and perpetual widowhood [83] — again " Catholicism without Christianity."

The problem of foreign relations in the Positivist society held no terrors for Comte, inasmuch as he was convinced that it would be largely solved through the adoption of the Positivist religion, with its universal priesthood and its tendency to dissolve the greater nations into non-tyrannical city-states.[84]

He was equally unconcerned about the matter of individual liberty and the principles of state interference, for he erected no constitutional barriers to tyranny. The ordinary citizen had to trust in the influence of the moral exhortations of the priesthood upon the governing class. Again, the citizen had no private sphere of rights which was free in any sense from invasion by some organ of the directing power of society.[85] Duties, rather than rights, were the central feature of Comte's political philosophy. In fact, the separate person, as such, was practically ignored and all attention was centered upon the " social organism "; even universal suffrage and parliamentary government were condemned.[86] He thus solved the problem of the reconciliation of sovereignty and liberty by failing to provide for assurance of either.

The upshot of Comte's intellectual travail in the field of social theory was that his stillborn state was an odd combination of religious and intellectual idealism with benevolent though partly non-political paternalism in the interests of " organic welfare." This, more than anything else, separates his doctrines from those of his individualistic successor in the field of sociology — Herbert Spencer.

Public Opinion and Social Control. — Comte laid considerable stress upon the value of public opinion as an effective agent of social control. He held that it was practically the sole guaranty of public morality, and maintained that without an intelligently organized public opinion there could be little hope of any extended reform and reconstruction of social institutions. The requisite conditions for the proper organization of public opinion are: " First, the establishment of fixed principles of social action; secondly, their adoption by the public and its consent to their application in special cases; and, lastly, a recognized organ to lay down the principles and to apply them to the conduct of daily life." He believed that the workingmen's clubs, which were then in the first flush of enthusiastic beginnings (i.e., during the Revolution of 1848), were likely to be one of the great instrumentalities in securing the adoption by the public of rules of " social conduct." But, to be effective, public opinion must have an able and recognized organ of expression, for its spontaneous and direct enunciation by the people is rarely possible. Once more Positivism would come to the rescue, with all the needed apparatus for an effective public opinion! Its doctrines would supply the proper rules of social conduct; the proletariat would furnish the necessary power; and the priest-philosopher-sociologists of the Comtist régime would offer an unrivaled organ for the proper expression of public opinion. All three requisite conditions for healthy public opinion were then in existence, but not yet in a proper relation to each other. The necessary progressive step was a " firm alliance between philosophers and proletaries."

Finally, says Comte, the influence of public opinion will probably become much greater in the future: " All views of the future condition of society, the views of practical men as well as of philosophic thinkers, agree in the belief that the principal feature of the State to which we are tending will be the increased influence which Public Opinion is destined to exercise." When it has become the great regulator of society it will eliminate revolutions and violent disputes by " substituting peaceable definition of duties." [87]

It is perfectly obvious that in a state like that designed by Comte, with its hierarchical arrangement of governmental agents and its hereditary transmission of function, there could be no such institution as the modern political party. The nearest possible approach would be a group of agitators or propagandists attempting to direct public opinion in some definite manner. (The study of " pressure groups " conducted since 1933 under the auspices of the Social Science Research Council shows how effective such " direction " of " public " opinion may sometimes be.)

The Nature of Social and Political Progress. — In his views of the nature of social evolution and the laws governing its progress, Comte was about midway between the positions of Spencer and

Ward, though the latter regarded him as the founder of the principle of " social telesis." He held, on the one hand, that the general tendencies of social evolution and the basic lines of its progress were subject to invariable laws and confined to certain fixed stages which could not be fundamentally altered by human interference. At the same time, he maintained that social development might be slightly modified and considerably accelerated by the coöperation of mankind if such coöperation were based upon an understanding of the great laws of social evolution — that is, if his philosophy of history were generally understood *and* followed! All schemes of social reform, to be successful, must be in harmony with the general march of civilization and not too far ahead of the conditions of the time. It is the function of social science to gather together all the relevant facts concerning the course of social evolution in the past, so that the political and social policy of the present may accord with what seem to be universal laws of development. While society need not blindly obey the laws of social evolution, but may hasten progress by intelligent action, still nothing could be more foolish than to imagine that social systems can be reconstructed in a day by the drawing up of a new constitution. Comte defended his own measures by contending that they were not his own arbitrary schemes of reform, but merely explicit statements of the teachings of history and social science concerning the evolution and future state of society.[88] Some of the more significant of his statements follow:

It appears, therefore, from the preceding remarks that the elementary march of civilization is unquestionably subject to a natural and invariable law which overrules all special human divergencies. . . .

Political science should exclusively employ itself in coördinating all the special facts relative to the progress of civilization and in reducing these to the smallest possible number of general facts, the connection of which ought to manifest the natural law of this progress, leaving for a subsequent appreciation the various causes which can modify its rapidity. . . .

But society does not and cannot progress in this way (i.e., by making constitutions for social reform as in the French Revolution.) The pretension of constructing offhand in a few months or even years, a social system, in its complete and definite shape, is an extravagant chimera absolutely incompatible with the weakness of the human intellect.

A sound political system can never aim at impelling the human race, since this is moved by its proper impulse, in accordance with a law as necessary as, though more easily modified than, that of gravitation. But it does seek to facilitate human progress by enlightening it. . . .

There is a great difference between obeying the progress of civilization blindly and obeying it intelligently. The changes it demands take place as much in the first as in the second case; but they are longer delayed, and, above all, are only accomplished after having produced social perturbations more or less serious, according to the nature and importance of these changes. Now the disturbances of every sort, which thus arise in the body politic, may be, in great part, avoided, by adopting measures based on an exact knowledge of the changes which tend to produce themselves. . . .

Now in order to attain this end, it is manifestly indispensable that we should know, as precisely as possible, the actual tendency of civilization, so as to bring our political conduct into harmony with it.[89]

Summary of the Chapter. — Comte's sociology has been called by some writers a prolegomenon to the subject rather than an initial venture in that science as such.[90] Similarly, it would not be inaccurate to declare that the same relationship exists between his theories of society and the state and those advanced by most later sociologists. Some of his doctrines most influential in subsequent developments are: (1) the sociological view of the state, and the thesis that political activities and institutions must be studied in their wider social relationships; (2) the pseudo-sociological, organismic theory of society, later developed by Spencer, Schäffle, Lilienfeld, Fouillée, Kjellen, Worms, Spann, *et alii;* (3) the more tenable sociological doctrine that neither the state nor society is an artificial product of rational perception of utility ("perceived utility"), but that both state and society, past and present, are beyond reasonable doubt the natural results of social necessity and historical growth; (4) the theory that the only rational limits of state activity are to be determined by a study of sociological principles and not by an appeal to "natural" laws; (5) a proper recognition of the all-important function of the broader social and extra-legal methods of social control — a line which has been exploited by such writers as Ross, Cooley, Giddings, and Sumner; (6) a clear statement of the necessary conformity between measures for social amelioration, the fundamental characteristics of human nature, and the principles of sociology — a matter to which sociologists are constantly calling the attention of social technologists; (7) a comprehensive view of the historical process through which the present political organization has been reached that is particularly suggestive because of its emphasis on the transition of the state from a military to an industrial basis — a view made much of by Spencer and later writers.[91]

Comte's immediate influence was not great, however, and devoted followers were few. Except for Littré and his French disciples and Frederic Harrison and his group in England, the Positive social philosophy was not enthusiastically adopted. Moreover, Darwinism made its appearance a few years after the publication of the *Polity*. This, together with Spencerian evolution, turned sociology in large part either into the social Darwinism of Gumplowicz and his school or into the much less fertile field of the biological analogies developed by Schäffle, Lilienfeld, Worms, and others. Spencerian sociology lent its great prestige to the defense of *laissez faire* and to the denunciation of social planning. French sociology after Comte developed chiefly in the more restricted fields of social anthropology and psycho-sociology. Sociology in America was, for the first generation, based either on Spencerianism, as with Giddings, or upon the German *Klassenkampf* doctrines, as with Small and his school, or upon the French psycho-sociology, as with Ross. Only Lester F. Ward took Comte seriously, and Ward diverged so widely from Comte in his system of social philosophy that most of his readers forgot his tribute to the Frenchman. Finally, the well-nigh complete bourgeois domination of Western society tended to discourage the cultivation of the doctrines of a writer so critical of unregulated capitalism as was Comte. Whether doctrines akin to his will have any considerable vogue in the construction of future plans of social reorganization is a problem of prophecy and not of the history of social theory, but it seems safe to say that no less grandiose a scheme can even be conceived to be adequate to the reorganization of the whole social order.

Comte was one of the great representatives of encyclopedic sociology, and for this reason, if for no other, is not today highly regarded among social scientists in general and sociologists in particular.

Nevertheless, a basic feature of encyclopedism—the effort to attain a comprehensive view of society with the intent of exerting control—is still with us. Comte's *savoir pour prévoir, prévoir pour pouvoir* has not really been cast aside. Witness: the unity of science movement; foundation support of the three "behavioral" sciences — anthropology, social psychology, and sociology; recent stress on interdisciplinary research; and the attempted development of deductive models of entire societies for the purpose of deriving hypotheses that can be at least tentatively proved or disproved by the aid of electronic computers. Further, take account of the establishment by contemporary historians of *Society and History: a Journal of Comparative Studies* and similar publications; and of programs such as that of the 1959 annual meeting of the American Historical Association, in which some sessions were obviously more sociological than historical. Philosophers have developed sociological interests; so also have theologians.

A modern social-scientific Marcellus would be wrong were he to declaim that no spirit walks abroad. In less elevated vein, it may be said that Comte still haunts us; we are confronted by an old ghost with new sheets.

CHAPTER XVI

The Quest for Secular Salvation:
Social Reform in Relation to the
Sociological Impulse

THREE ASPECTS OF THE INDUSTRIAL REVOLUTION. — The
background of many contemporary social doctrines and
problems must be sought in that remarkable transformation of material culture and social institutions known as the Industrial Revolution. This began in England in the first half of the eighteenth century, *and is still in process of rapid development* — many writers speak of a " second Industrial Revolution."

The term should not be confined, however, to any single line of economic development in modern times. Rather, the conception adopted must be sufficiently broad to include all the diverse economic changes which have produced contemporary material culture, together with the alterations in social institutions that have followed these economic transformations. For the sake of clarity in analysis, the Industrial Revolution may be divided into three main phases or aspects: (1) the revolutionary technological changes in the methods of manufacturing, in the modes of transportation, and in the facilities for the communication of information; (2) the rise of the factory system as a new method for the organization of industry and the discipline and application of labor; and (3) the general economic, social, and cultural results of the new technology and the factory system, as they have reacted on Western civilization.

The technological changes which formed the basis for the other aspects of the Industrial Revolution rested to no small degree upon the advances which had been earlier made in natural and applied science. In the broadest sense, the revolution in technique consisted first of all in a transition from a handicraft to a machine technique.[1] There probably has never been a more revolutionary transition in human society than was embodied in the abandonment of the tool economy and the entry into the machine age. Man now was able to subjugate nature through the power of an iron slave. A new machine technique was provided for the manufacturing of textiles, and cheaper and more effective methods for the large-scale production of metal products were also developed. New types of motive power were found to drive the new machinery and the new agencies of transportation. The steam engine, the internal combustion engine, and the electric motor supplanted the ox, the ass, and the horse. Electricity has not only been exploited in the interest of transportation facilities, but it has also been made the basis for a marvelous revolution in the communication of information, so that facts (and fancies) may be communicated over any distance known to this planet, with the practical elimination of the time element. Finally, the information thus transmitted is more or less effectively disseminated through the medium of the cheap daily newspaper and the household radio.[2]

Equally significant was the appearance of the factory system, for it initiated a new method of industrial organization and labor discipline. The old guild and putting-out systems had been primarily based upon personal relationships between the employer and the employee in industry. Both of these systems were compelled to give way to the modern factory system, once the machine technique had been introduced. It should be noted that the factory system is often quite incorrectly identified with the mechanical technique of manufacturing; as a matter of fact, the factory system relates not to the technique of " machinofacture " but to a specific method whereby labor is applied and disciplined.[3] A sort of factory system appeared several times in history before the development of the modern mechanical methods of manufacturing. It existed in Babylonia, in Greece and Rome, and even in eighteenth-century England, along with handicraft methods of manufacturing. In the latter country and period, various wasteful aspects of the putting-out or domestic system led to the installation in many places of factories or central shops. Here large numbers of workers were gathered together to carry on their activities under common supervision, but they still relied upon the old handicraft methods of spinning, weaving, and so forth. Once the mechanical technique had been provided, however, it was absolutely necessary to establish the factory system, because the expensive new machinery with its complicated processes could not be installed in the households. The factory system provided a radically different type of industrial discipline. Far larger numbers of individuals were brought within one establishment, women and children entered industry on a large scale, the personal relations between the employer and the employee tended to disappear, and the worker became regimented in all of his activities and was essentially at the mercy of his employer until the labor organizations had provided a means for collective bargaining and proletarian defense.[4]

Finally, the Industrial Revolution meant not merely a changed technique and a new type of industrial organization, but also deep-seated and extensive economic, social, and cultural reactions. The mechanical technique, carried on under the factory system, led to an enormous increase in the production of commodities, stimulated commerce, called for a much larger application of capital, reduced labor to a condition of general dependence on the capitalist class, produced larger and improved banking and credit institutions, created corporations and other forms of industrial organization,[5] and stimulated large-scale business combinations tending toward monopoly. Social conditions were also altered: civilization began to change from a predominantly agrarian to an urban basis; the problems of the modern city were heaped on those already piled up by urban life; population increased so rapidly that the number of people living in Europe in 1900 was roughly double that in 1800; and great international shifts of population took place as a result of emigration from industrially backward countries and settlement in more highly developed areas.[6]

The intellectual results of the Industrial Revolution were likewise notable. The individual could receive information from all over the world as a result of the new methods of communication. Further, the gradual development of a consciousness of his interests on the part of the worker and his advocates brought the beginnings of free public education. Along with these general intellectual and cultural advantages of the Industrial Revolution went a number of serious disadvantages: the nervous strain of the modern urban age was for many city dwellers far greater than that of the earlier and simpler life of the country; culture tended to become standardized in terms of the machine technique; and the laborer became merely a cog in a great industrial machine. To a certain extent, in evolving the machine, man was himself brought into bondage to the economic and social system which the machine technology created.

The political life of Europe and the world was also profoundly altered by the Industrial Revolution. The middle class became almost all-powerful in the era of the industrialized state, and provided for the proper political protection of their interests through legislation based on the sanctity of property rights and through parliamentary and constitutional government. Their ascendency was soon challenged, however, by the wage-earning class, whose partial successes in political participation have created what we have of modern democracy. The development of the modern mechanism for transmitting information made it possible for citizens of each of the great national states to feel and think alike as a result of subjection to common stimulation. In this way, the popular aspects of nationalism and patriotism, which had been initiated by the French Revolution, were now made relatively permanent and enduring. Finally, the greatly increased productivity brought about by the new machine and factory system led to the search for new colonies and markets in oversea areas, a movement which we speak of in history as modern national imperialism.

In brief, the accessible secular society took shape in an empirical guise almost parallel with the ideal-typical formulation presented in the " Abstract Epitome " of Chapter One.

The Industrial Impetus to Humanitarianism. — The Industrial Revolution was one of the most severe social crises which had thus far taken place in the history of human society. It tangled and tore the whole web of social life in the Western world, and forced extensive readjustments to meet the new conditions of living. The misery and suffering which resulted led to a large number and variety of proposals for social and economic reconstruction. Nothing which had previously taken place gave so tremendous an impulse to the humanitarian movement. For the most part these plans of social reform and reconstruction rested more upon profound sympathy with the unfortunate classes than upon any scientific conceptions of society and methods of securing social reform. In due time, however, many students of the social problems of the age became convinced that if social reform (we shall use the term in this chapter to include proposals for radical social reconstruction as well) was not to be wasteful and misguided, it would have to rest upon a " science of society " which would indicate the nature of and the limitations upon social betterment. We need not necessarily agree with nineteenth-century humanitarianism, nor with any of the specific programs associated therewith, to recognize that in the following quotation Small has clearly indicated the interrelationship between these early social reform movements and the rise of sociology:

How did it come about that sociology is in the world at all?

This is something more than a mere matter of historical curiosity. The answer to the question goes far toward explaining very prevalent confusions about sociology itself. The subject sometimes seems to be utterly abstract speculative philosophy. As it is represented by other men, it knows nothing whatever of logic or philosophy, and is simply a scheme of sentimentally benevolent experiment. How does it come about that such different things can pass under the same name?

The answer is, in a word, that in all probability the sentimental philanthropic impulse has done more than the scientific impulse to bring sociology into existence. Men of the type of St. Simon (1760–1825), Fourier (1772–1837), and even Comte (1798–1851), in France; Robert Owen, Ruskin, Maurice, Kingsley, Robertson, and Mill, in England; the socialists in all countries; a group of earnest so-called " social-scientists," and especially certain types of philanthropists, in this country, so industriously advocated *the improvement of social conditions* that presently attempts to develop a scientific sociology became inevitable. The various agitations for social reform or improvement worked in this way: People of philanthropic temper decided that something was wrong and ought to be righted. It might be the existence of paupers; or of competent workmen out of work, or of long hours, low pay, and bad sanitary conditions for those who did work; or of private ownership of what might have been owned by the public; or a hundred other things. Earnest people declared that these things ought not so to be. Then obstinate conservatives were roused to opposition. They said: " Nonsense! These people are crazy. Sentimentalism has gone mad in them. They mean well, but they are trying to do the impossible. It is paternalism. It is contrary to the laws of political economy to attempt to help people who do not help themselves. There is no scientific ground for these visionaries to stand on." There was some truth on both sides. Evils were being allowed to take their course which the proper amount of attention could have mitigated, if not wholly remedied. On the other hand, schemes of reform were being promoted without serious attempt to find out what their consequences would be, outside of a very narrow circle. As Herbert Spencer has shown, in his essay on *The Sins of Legislators,* laws were passed, in the most confident spirit, which time and again produced greater evils than they were devised to remove. All this tended to educate people of a different type; people who could see the evils, on the one hand, but, on the other hand, could see that our knowledge of social relations is too meager to be a safe guide in attempts to reorganize society. These men said: " Yes, the sentimentalists are right that we ought to do better, but the conservatives are also right that we ought to look before we leap. We must be sure we are right before we go ahead; or, at least, if we cannot be sure, we must study society deeply enough to justify our beliefs that courses of action are reasonable, and in the direction of progress."

600 SOCIAL REFORM AND SOCIOLOGY

It followed that a few people accepted the logic of the situation and marked out a course of study accordingly. Lester F. Ward, the author of *Dynamic Sociology,* is the best illustration. His position was, in brief, that men may make human life vastly more rational, profitable, worthy, and satisfying, if they will train the same sort of study upon life as a whole which they now devote to more or less meaningless abstractions from life. The shortest and surest route to better doing in the end is more thorough knowing. There is work for a few students who will devote themselves to patient study of human society as a whole, without impatience about the length of time which will be required to reach practical results. There is work for men who will consent to be sneered at as dreamers, who will be patient while people revile and ridicule them as impractical transcendental philosophers. There is work for men who will run large surveys of life in its ultimate meanings, and will discover general principles that are always valid in society. This will in the end prove the most practical sort of work, for it will furnish the only possible rational basis for intelligent programs of social action. Meanwhile nobody is fit for this grade of work who cannot devote himself to it with patience and persistence, in spite of probability that during his lifetime it will yield very meager returns which can be put to any practical use.

Essentially, search for fundamental or general social principles is the most practical sort of social work that can be undertaken. Superficially, immediately, and to the person capable of appreciating only concrete details, it is bound to seem a sterility and a mockery. Yet sociology has come into being from this deep loyal impulse of social service. Its whole animus is constructive, remedial, ameliorative. Even its most abstract and technical refinements have their final meaning as ultimate contributions to the art of life. Of course, it is true in sociology, as everywhere else in the scientific world, that men get swamped in technicalities and forget the larger interests which alone make the technicalities worth while. In spite of these individual lapses, sociology is through and through a plan to lay the necessary foundations of knowledge for the most enlightened program of human life which it is possible for men to propose. It is not dead embalmed science. It is an attempt to reach vital insight for the sake of efficient action. It is at the same time a consistent protest against action, or agitations for action, in advance of ability to furnish morally conclusive reasons for the action.

After what has been said, it is to be hoped that two things have been made clear: First: The program of sociology aims finally at the most thorough, intense, persistent, and systematic effort to make human life all that it is capable of becoming. Second: This thoroughly social and constructive impulse is held in restraint by scientific sociology until a philosophy and a theory of action can be justified. There is nothing in sociology, therefore, for people who are not able and willing to consider today's practical affairs in their relation to the largest generalizations of human conditions and actions that the mind can reach. The impulse is humanitarian. The method is that of completely objective science and philosophy.[7]

It is the interrelation so admirably indicated in the statement by Small that gives us warrant for surveying a great number of social reform movements that seem at first glance to have had nothing to do with the development of sociology. These movements fall into two great groups: (1) those considered in this chapter — movements that in their actual inception *or their ideological foundations* antedate the rise of Marxian socialism; and (2) those dealt with in the succeeding chapter, entitled "New Gospels: Revolutionary Socialism and the Winds of Doctrine" — movements that followed the abortive revolutions of 1848 and the *Communist Manifesto,* when it began to appear that the classes disadvantaged by the Industrial Revolution would not have an easy task in setting up a society more in accordance with their aspirations.

In view of the importance attributed to the Industrial Revolution, it may seem that we have little to learn from any of the programs and movements that preceded it. Those which followed of course do bear most directly on the development of sociology as a science, but if our conspectus of the history of social thought has been of any value, it should have demonstrated that the indirect effects of doctrines hoary with age may at times be considerable, and that occasionally theories apparently decrepit or dead may be revived with surprising consequences. Let us therefore proceed to an examination of certain ancient proposals.

Social Reform Movements in Antiquity and the Middle Ages. — Programs and movements for social reform date back almost to the dawn of written history. Oppression of certain classes existed in the first societies of which history has any record, and it is not surprising that some of the earliest literature reflects the growth of unrest among subject groups (the chapters on social thought in the ancient Far and Near East, it will be recalled, deal with this point here and there). As Seligman has shown, the desire to improve the social environment has ever been the impulse behind the evolution of economic and political doctrines, though it is quite true that theories once acclaimed as harbingers of progress may later be reviled as ideological bulwarks of the *status quo.* Proposals for the betterment of social conditions have appeared at all times, but they have been most numerous after great upheavals which have altered the relative standing of different classes and have brought an abnormal amount of misery to those most seriously affected by the transition. As Flint has said: " It is in their times of sorest depression that nations usually indulge most in dreams of a better future and that their imaginations produce most freely social ideals and utopias." [8]

For example, when Athens was undergoing the stresses of rapid commercial expansion, protracted warfare, and internal strife, Plato produced his *Republic*. It was not the first social reform program, by any means, but it is perhaps the earliest scheme for social reconstruction that has remained a classic. Here was proposed a society resting fundamentally upon a social division of labor, an elaborate plan of eugenics, and rigid control by the wisest members of the community.

Even Plato, however, recognized the futility of hoping for the adoption of a social system so inhumanly rational; moreover, it was marred by another serious defect because it was designed to apply only to the upper classes; the others, it was hoped, would be reduced to a still more severe and permanent state of subjection. Among the Romans, one might mention the schemes of the Gracchi brothers, who made an attempt to check the growing power of the plutocracy, but were thwarted by the " vested interests."

The Apostolic Christians, living in the hope of an imminent return of Christ, developed communistic tendencies and doctrines, but the special circumstances under which they were conceived prevented them from having any considerable significance in the history of social reform programs. Although other-wordly conceptions had been somewhat weakened by the time of the later Patristic period, they were still strong enough to paralyze any social initiative. The faithful were warned against undue concern over earthly conditions, lest they thereby forfeit entry into the Kingdom of Heaven. The poor were regarded as a part of the divine order existing for the spiritual edification of rich almsgivers. The Patristic outlook, coupled with the static nature of the quasi-caste system which developed as the basis of feudalism, and the general immobility of medieval civilization, made the Middle Ages a period designed to discourage any radical movements in social reform.

It nevertheless should not be forgotten that the more radical religious movements of the medieval period, associated with the Waldensians, the Albigenses, the Franciscans, and the Lollards, carried with them varying degrees of revolt against prevailing social and economic conditions as well as against religious institutions and legal practices. It is probable that of all the medieval programs of social reform the most interesting and "modern" was that set forth by Pierre DuBois at the opening of the fourteenth century in his *De Recuperatione Terre Sancte,* with which Powicke and Power have familiarized English and American readers and which we have already examined (pp. 280–285). Finally, the discussions of the Conciliar Movement perhaps bear some vague relation to the problem of social reform in so far as that is related to the development of representative government.

The Commercial Revolution and Social Reform. — We have already seen how this great commercial transformation brought with it the decline of the feudal order, the rise of the merchant class in the political as well as the economic field, and the gradual development of the modern national state, at first purely dynastic but later becoming more and more a semi-representative if not a democratic institution. At first the new merchant class or bourgeoisie supported the kings in their attack on the feudal nobility, but once the feudal lords had been coerced, the middle class arose against the monarchs and imposed constitutional limitations on the royal prerogatives. The social and economic effects were no less important. The manorial system was undermined or completely shattered, and the guild system was weakened or wholly supplanted by the "domestic system." [9] These changes profoundly affected all social classes, bringing the severest consequences to those whose status was reduced by the transformation.

The social theories engendered by the Commercial Revolution bore a close relation to the political, social, economic, and intellectual setting created by it. To retrace our steps: In the field of political theorizing, the *de facto* royal absolutism was accompanied by the divine right doctrine associated with the names of Filmer and others, whereas the rise of the bourgeoisie against despotism produced the left wing of the social contract school, with its apologies for revolution, in the writings of Sydney, Locke, Rousseau, and their followers. The social and economic changes, with their accompanying misery to the lower classes, gave rise to theoretical attempts to construct ideal societies which would embrace none of the evils of existing conditions; i.e., to the utopias. (We shall consider early Poor Laws — most of them a direct outcome of the Commercial Revolution — after we have paid some attention to a number of other movements, and particularly to Christian socialism.)

The growth of rationalism, which set in somewhat later, was especially significant for the development of social reform programs. Although the rationalists were seldom violent political or social revolutionists, their very scepticism concerning current views of the nature and significance of natural and social phenomena inevitably led to a critical attitude toward social institutions and the gradual development of a " spirit of reform." Particularly important in this respect, it will be recalled (Chapter Nine), were the English Deists and their numerous followers among the French *philosophes*. The Deists held, in radical contrast to the theological views of Augustine and Calvin, that man as man is worthy of study in the effort to improve his secular lot. This doctrine did more than anything else to remove obstacles to social self-improvement (real or chimerical), and was also very effective in producing the growth of the humanitarian spirit. Strangely enough, however, a part of the cosmic and social philosophy of the Enlightenment became a great barrier to social reform after the Industrial Revolution got under way, for as we shall see, the notion of " natural order " was adopted by the adherents of economic liberalism to form the metaphysical basis of their defense of *laissez faire*.

Contemporary Remedies for the Evils of the Early Industrial Revolution: Economic Liberalism. — This set of theories, more generally known as the economic doctrine of *laissez faire*, or the political theory of individualism, cannot be properly appraised unless the historical circumstances surrounding its origin and diffusion are taken into consideration. It began before the Industrial Revolution as an attack on the archaic legislative restrictions which had grown up as a part of the Mercantilistic commercial and colonial doctrine, and in so far as it helped to clear away these obstructions, it contributed to the coming of modern industrial society. After the Industrial Revolution had arrived, however, its later adherents utilized the *laissez faire* concepts to defend the new capitalistic order and as far as possible to prevent the solution, through remedial legislation, of the grave evils it created.

The founders of economic liberalism were that group of French writers in the middle of the eighteenth century, known as the Physiocrats, whose theories we have dealt with at length (Chapter Fourteen). Their general ideas concerning individualism and state inactivity, except in the field of abolishing restrictive legislation, received the support of the distinguished French economist, sociologist, and statesman, Anne Robert Jacques Turgot (1727–1781), and of the first great systematic writer on political economy, the Scotsman, Adam Smith (1723–1790). The chief significance of Adam Smith for the history of social reform is that he embodied the *laissez faire* thesis in his *Wealth of Nations* (1776). But in spite of his acceptance of the general Physiocratic position on the proper functions of the state, Smith abandoned to a considerable degree the Physiocratic laudation of agriculture, and emphasized the value of commerce and manufactures. Especially did he revive the Platonic doctrine of the importance of the division of labor in increasing productivity, and his emphasis on the part played by labor in production paved the way for the later views of Ricardo and the socialists respecting the " labor theory of value." His advocacy of free trade on the basis of international industrial specialization and division of labor is one of the most forceful arguments ever advanced.

Smith died before the Industrial Revolution had fully developed even in England, and there is good evidence for holding that he did not even foresee the course of this transformation, much less stand out as an apologist of the new capitalist class.[10] His doctrines, however, were of a sort which fitted in admirably with the policy of non-interference which the capitalist manufacturers desired to have prevail in order that they, if not their employees, might enjoy the " blessings of the perfect freedom of contract." His notions were therefore expanded and utilized by the middle class, and economists sympathetic therewith, to furnish authoritative theoretical opposition to social legislation designed to advance the interests of the industrial proletariat.

The Development of Economic Liberalism in Britain. — The most extensive development of Smith's concepts naturally took place in Great Britain, where that industrialism which was most congenial to his views was the furthest advanced, but he was honored by reverent disciples in every important European country and in the United States. His most distinguished British disciples were Thomas Robert Malthus (1766–1834); David Ricardo (1772–1823); James Mill (1773–1836); John Ramsay McCulloch (1789–1864), and William Nassau Senior (1790–1864). The one thing which in particular distinguished the doctrines of Smith from those of his disciples was his greater optimism, a difference which may perhaps be explained by the great change in the economic environment in the interval which had elapsed. The later version of economic liberalism, sometimes termed Manchesterism, was even called the " dismal science," and was strikingly caricatured in Dickens's *Hard Times*.

While the chief importance of Smith's disciples was their elaboration of the theory of economic individualism, each contributed some special interpretation of more or less originality and significance. Malthus held that remedial legislation was not only harmful, as interfering with the natural order of things, but was also useless so far as any hope of improving the poorer classes was concerned. He maintained that even if the distribution of wealth were equalized, no permanent good could result, because population tends to increase more rapidly than the means of subsistence; hence the disparity between population and available means of support would ultimately be restored, and with it would come a return of poverty and misery. Through an excessive birthrate the proletariat created its own misery, and the only hope of permanent relief lay in the artificial control and restriction of the birthrate through the postponement of marriage and the " moral check." [11]

Ricardo paid particular attention to the subject of distribution. From the Physiocratic notion that the wages of agricultural laborers tend toward the minimum of subsistence, and from Malthus's doctrine of population, he derived his famous " subsistence theory of wages." According to this theory, wages inevitably tend toward that level which allows the laboring class to exist and perpetuate itself without either increase or decrease. The folly of legislation designed to enlarge the income of the proletariat was held to be patent, for the resulting increase of population, it was assumed, would prevent any diminution of poverty and misery. Moreover, higher wages would lower profits, curtail industrial initiative, increase unemployment, and augment poverty and misery. Further, Ricardo attacked the landlords by maintaining that rent tended to absorb an ever greater share of the social income, and that the interests of the landlords were opposed to those of all other economic classes. Finally, he laid the basis for the Marxian theory of value by holding that value is determined (within certain definite limitations) by the amount of labor involved in production. [12]

James Mill brought into economic liberalism the Utilitarian philosophy of Bentham regarding the greatest good for the greatest number; Mill and his associates confidently believed this end to be attainable through the operation of the principles of economic liberalism. Mill's clearly written treatise did much to popularize the theories of Ricardo, who was a prolix and involved writer. Of all this group, Mill had the most naïve and limitless confidence in the benevolence of the middle-class manufacturers and merchants.

McCulloch was chiefly a systematizer of the principles of the school, and was that member of the group most sympathetic toward the laboring classes, being a supporter of Place and Hume in the attempt to legalize trade-unionism. He is most widely known for his elaboration of the " wages fund " doctrine — the notion of a semi-mystical fund reserved for the support of labor in the industrial process.

Senior represented the final and most extreme stage of economic liberalism through his attempt to perfect economics as a purely abstract and objective science — a science of wealth and not of welfare — and by his ardent opposition to even the mildest form of legislation likely to be beneficial to the laboring classes. Contending that profits were made in the last hours of the working day, he warned against legislation shortening the hours of labor, lest it destroy all industrial initiative.

In the writings of John Stuart Mill (1806–1873), there came a break with the most cherished traditions of economic liberalism. Mill held that the processes of production alone, and not those of distribution, were subject to the control of natural law and hence not to be disturbed by human legislation. This view of course opened the way for any type of legislation regulating wages, interest, rent, and profits.[13]

Although most of these writers took little active part in politics, their ideal of " perfect competition for the employers and subjection for the workers " was eagerly adopted by Cobden, Bright, and other members of the " Manchester School " and the Liberal Party in their effort to reduce the power and privileges of the landed aristocracy. Their notions were widely popularized, and their general views were as much the order of polite conversation in British parlors as notions of the state of nature had been in the French *salons* of a half-century before.

The Spread of Economic Liberalism in France, Germany, and America. — The later version of economic liberalism was espoused by a number of French economists, the most notable of whom were Jean Baptiste Say (1767–1832) and Frédéric Bastiat (1801–1850). Say's position was very similar to that of Senior. He maintained that political economy was purely a descriptive science, not in any way a practical art. The economist should simply study and formulate economic laws, never usurping the functions of the statesman. Reversing the position of the Physiocrats, he laid greatest stress on the social contributions of manufacturing, and he was the most enthusiastic of all the eulogists of the new era of mechanical industry. He was the French bourgeois economist of the period in the same way that Guizot was the historian and statesman.

Bastiat revived the optimism of Adam Smith and, as an ardent admirer of Cobden, devoted his attention chiefly to the advocacy of free trade. The function of the state, he held, was solely to maintain " order, security, and justice." So enthusiastic were Say and Bastiat over the importance and beneficial activities of the manufacturing and commercial classes [14] that some of their less scientific followers came to deny that poverty or misery existed.

In Germany economic liberalism was defended by Johann Heinrich von Thünen (1783–1850) and Karl Heinrich Rau (1792–1870).[15] In America Henry C. Carey (1793–1879) first introduced the classical political economy, though he differed from Smith's disciples by reviving the optimism of Smith and attacking the pessimism of Malthus.[16] Moreover, he advocated national protectionism in contrast to the free trade doctrines of the others of the school.

The Effects of Laissez Faire. — Though it will be evident that economic liberalism was as distinctly a capitalistic movement as socialism has been a proletarian agitation — that, as Cliffe Leslie has said, its exponents " created a science for wealth rather than a science of wealth " — nevertheless it cannot be denied that their efforts accomplished much that was good. Before national-state activity to solve the problems created by the Industrial Revolution could begin in an effective manner, it was necessary that the antique rubbish of Mercantilism should be cleared away. This was the great contribution of the economic liberals and their political adherents, even though they offset much of the value of their destructive efforts by obstruction of subsequent progressive legislation. In passing, it should also be pointed out that the economic liberals were aided, paradoxically enough, by the contemporary philosophy of Romanticism, with its denial of the possibility of artificially accelerating the rate of political progress, and by the political individualism which had been set forth by Wilhelm von Humboldt and later taken up by John Stuart Mill (in his earlier days) and Herbert Spencer.

In England the more notable practical effects of economic liberalism were: (1) the growth of free trade, associated with the work of Huskisson, Cobden, Bright, Peel, and Gladstone; (2) the abolition of such archaic political restrictions as the Test and Corporation Acts; (3) the increase of the political powers of the middle class in the central and local government by the Reform Bills of 1832 and 1835; (4) the abolition of slavery in the colonies through the efforts of Wilberforce and Buxton; (5) the

repeal of the savage criminal code as a result of the work of
Romilly, Mackintosh, Buxton, and Peel; (6) the development
of a policy of preventive treatment in the handling of the problem
of poor relief, evident in the revision of the Poor Law of 1834 (to
be discussed in detail later); (7) and the first anticipation of a
more liberal policy of imperial government through the leadership of Lord Durham, Gibbon Wakefield, and others. In France,
serfdom and the guild monopolies were abolished before the close
of the eighteenth century; Guizot directed the Orleanist régime
solely in the interests of the capitalists; and Bastiat's doctrines
were able to win Napoleon III for free trade.

In Prussia, Stein and Hardenberg secured legislation looking
toward the complete abolition of serfdom and guild monopolies
and the development of municipal self-government. Following
1819, a more liberal economic and commercial policy was embodied in the famous *Zollverein,* the work of Maassen, Bülow,
Eichhorn, and Von Motz.[17] Most of the other German states followed Prussia in this liberalizing policy, and some, like Baden,
quite outdistanced it. Quite obviously, however, none of this legislation materially benefited the proletariat. Indeed, some of the
legislation of the period was specifically designed to paralyze all
efforts of the laborers at self-improvement, and the agitators for
the abolition of Negro slavery in the colonies failed to notice a
far worse type of slavery at home, among their own countrymen.
Such a body of doctrine could not long endure unchallenged in the
face of the growth of modern industrialism and the increasing
misery of the proletariat.

English Philosophical Radicalism and Utilitarianism. — Utilitarianism, a term used by Jeremy Bentham and given currency by
John Stuart Mill, is the designation usually applied to the school
of writers headed by Bentham (1748–1832) and including,
among others, James Mill, George Grote, John Austin, Alexander
Bain, and John Stuart Mill. They represented primarily the spirit
and tenets of economic liberalism in political theory, and their
work constituted the only significant contribution of England to
this field between the time of Burke and that of Spencer. Essentially, they were a further development of that philosophical radicalism in England, growing out of English sympathy with the
French Revolution, represented by William Godwin, Thomas
Paine, William Cobbett, Francis Place, and the group of literary
men, such as Shelley, Byron, and Wordsworth, with whose works
and ideas Brailsford and Brinton have recently made us familiar.[18]

This group stood in direct opposition to the satisfaction of Blackstone and Burke with the alleged perfection of British institutions, and maintained the necessity of radical changes.[19]

In his earlier years Bentham might have been classed with this group, for, as we have seen in Chapter Fourteen, his first notable work — *A Fragment on Government* (1776) — was a violent attack on the complacency of Blackstone. He gradually developed a general philosophy of reform, however, and thus molded radicalism into Utilitarianism. But his practical program of reform indicated that, like the economic liberals, he regarded unrestricted competition and enlightened self-interest as the chief avenues through which his Utilitarian program could be realized. His chief concern was with the abolition of restrictive legislation, but he did urge some positive reforms, such as education of the masses, the extension of savings institutions, public health legislation, and prison reform. Further, though Bentham and his immediate followers might seem to have regarded the " greatest good to the greatest number " as best attainable through conferring " the greatest amount of goods upon the business classes," his terminology, if honestly interpreted, was an excellent basis for a large amount of positive remedial legislation in behalf of the proletariat.[20]

This evolution of Utilitarianism is evident even within the circle of its own adherents, for John Stuart Mill eventually changed from an exponent of marked individualism into a vigorous advocate of social legislation and a not unappreciative student of distinctly socialistic proposals. Probably the only important achievement of this group in the way of " aiding the lower classes " was the work of Francis Place and Joseph Hume in securing the temporary legalizing of trade-unionism and some indirect benefits from political reforms and health legislation, but they made important contributions to securing that abolition of obstructive legislation which was described above in connection with the practical results of economic liberalism.

Opposition to Economic Individualism: Criticism by Economists. — There were several theoretical difficulties in economic liberalism which called forth the opposition of political economists. Although Smith probably thought that his work was really more concerned with the wealth of a " nation " than of a class, it is nevertheless true that his followers seemed to be chiefly concerned with the wealth of the new business class rather than with the problem of increasing the prosperity of the entire nation. This brought upon the school the criticism of economists who pre-

sented a national or social theory of wealth; they maintained that
the increase of the wealth of individuals or classes was no safe
criterion for judging of the value to the state or society of an
economic, social, or political policy. This was the point of view
especially of the Scotsman, Lord Lauderdale (1759–1839), and
the Scottish-Canadian, John Rae (1786–1873). By appealing to
authorities from Aristotle to his own day, as well as by logical
analysis, Rae proved to his own satisfaction that state activity
was more in harmony with the principles of nature and society
than *laissez faire* and pure competition.

The contention of the economic liberals generally, and of Senior
and Say in particular, to the effect that the economist should maintain his science as a purely abstract and descriptive discipline,
refraining from the advocacy of any positive policy of statesmanship or social reform, was vigorously attacked by Jean
Charles Leonard de Sismondi (1773–1842), an itinerant Italo-
Swiss scholar. In his own time he was the most distinguished and
effective exponent of the notion that economics has a distinct function in promoting general prosperity and social reform, a point
of view since urged with vigor by economists such as Wagner,
Schmoller, Brentano, Gide, Pigou, Webb, Hobson, Tawney,
Patten, Fetter, and Seager. He firmly believed that economics
should be intimately concerned with the problems of practical
statesmanship, and more than any other writer of his time he
foreshadowed modern social or "welfare" economics. Moreover, his practical program of reform embraced most of what is
now included in trade-unionism, factory legislation, and social
insurance. He was a somewhat solitary figure for a time, but his
doctrines were later accorded respect as the vogue of economic
liberalism waned.[21]

The economic liberals, it will be recalled, were internationalists
and exponents of free trade. This attitude was attacked by the
early nationalistic economists, Adam Müller (1779–1829),[22]
Friedrich List (1789–1846), and Henry C. Carey (1793–1879),
who defended the policy of a national protective tariff to give
national autarchy and prosperity. The nation rather than individuals, classes, or human society as a whole received their special
solicitude. They were not inflexibly dogmatic in this position,
however; List in particular held that, after the Industrial Revolution had thoroughly reconstructed a country, free trade might
be beneficial, but to aid "infant industries" in the first stages of
industrial development a protective tariff was indispensable.

Finally, the economic liberals were charged with too great an abstraction and absolutism in economic doctrines. It was asserted that they generalized too much from contemporary conditions and were too confident of the universal and eternal applicability of their economic " laws." The early representatives of the historical school of economics, chiefly Richard Jones (1790–1885), Bruno Hildebrand (1812–1878), Wilhelm Roscher (1817–1894), and Karl Knies (1821–1898), held that their approach was the only corrective of this alleged defect.[23] The predominance of the Germans in this group has led to the practical identification of the historical school with German economists. These writers ridiculed the element of absolutism in the classical economic doctrines, maintaining that any type of economic theory could be assumed to be true only for the society from which the facts or premises were drawn. Economic theories must therefore change with historical alterations in the economic constitution of societies; hence, said the members of the historical school, there can be no invariable economic laws, nor any valid economic theory which ignores the element of economic change.[24] Their emphasis on the necessary relation between fact and theory suggested careful statistical studies of actual social and economic conditions, which frequently led to advocacy of remedial legislation.

Political Opposition: The Assault of Tory Humanitarianism. — It has been shown that economic liberalism was primarily an economic philosophy and a political program designed in the interest of the capitalists, who in politics adhered to the Whig or Liberal Party. It was but natural, therefore, that it should be assailed by the one powerful existing party whose economic and political interests were diametrically opposed to the business element, namely, the landed proprietors who made up the bulk of the Tory or Conservative Party. The Tories had a number of reasons for disliking the capitalists. In the first place, there was the social aversion of the aristocrats for what they regarded as the upstarts eager to break into their ranks. Next, they felt that the new industrialism had destroyed forever the " Merrie England " in which the landlords were supreme. Again, they entertained a jealousy of the growing political power of the middle class, especially after the latter had forced through the Reform Bill of 1832. Finally, the economic interests of the two classes were fundamentally opposed; the Tories desired a continuation of the Corn Laws to keep the price of grain high, whereas the business class desired their abolition in order to secure cheap wheat and therefore, according to the current economic reasoning, cheap labor.

The Tories were fortunate in finding a point of attack on the capitalists which enabled them, consciously or unconsciously, to cloak their political and economic aims under the mantle of humanitarian sentiments and also to increase their political following among the proletariat. The avenue of assault decided upon by the Tories was factory legislation, which would reduce the prosperity of the manufacturers by compelling them to grant higher wages or shorter hours and to introduce better physical conditions and appliances in their factories. Probably too much has been made of this point of self-interest by recent writers, who have followed Arnold Toynbee in emphasizing the political and economic selfishness that motivated the landlord factory reformers. Doubtless many of the leaders in this movement were governed by real humanitarian impulses, but it can at least be said that they were especially favored in finding a line of social reform which harmonized particularly well with their economic and political interests.[25]

The leaders in the earlier stages of this " Tory social reform " were Anthony Ashley Cooper, Seventh Earl of Shaftesbury (1801–1885), Michael Thomas Sadler (1770–1835), Richard Oastler (1789–1861), and John Fielden (1784–1849), a public-spirited manufacturer. They secured the appointment of the investigating commissions that have furnished the present generation with most of their sources of information concerning the conditions among the laboring classes in England during the first half of the nineteenth century, and obtained much remedial legislation designed to alleviate or eliminate these temporary evils.

It is impossible in the space available to describe in detail the contents of this legislation, but its general character can be indicated. The Factory Acts of 1802, 1819, 1831, 1833, 1844, 1847, 1850, and several minor laws of the 'sixties secured for the laboring classes in practically all factories the ten-hour day, proper factory inspection, safety appliances, better sanitary conditions, and a general discouragement of child labor. Women and children were excluded from mines, and better hours and safety devices were provided for in the acts of 1842, 1855, and 1872. The distressing evils in the employment of juvenile chimney-sweeps were eliminated by laws of 1834 and 1840. The results of the efforts of Ashley, in particular, were the important Factory Act of 1833 and the famous " Ten-Hour Bill " of 1847.[26]

Thus political jealousy and economic rivalry between the upper and middle classes were able to achieve for the advancement of proletarians much more than the latter were able to obtain for themselves. Although Shaftesbury may have been motivated by some genuine humanitarian impulses in his campaign for social reform, it is doubtful if the same can be said for the continuer of his policy, Benjamin Disraeli (1804–1881). That he thoroughly understood the oppression of the peasantry and the industrial proletariat no reader of his *Sybil* can doubt, but little evidence exists that he was touched by any real personal sympathy for the oppressed, and one is led to the conclusion that his advances to the lower classes were founded upon purely partisan and personal motives and ambitions. In part, he continued Shaftesbury's social legislation, but his appeal for the support of the proletariat was primarily political. By the Reform Act of 1867 he extended the suffrage to the more prosperous portion of the urban laboring class.

This type of social reform again appeared in England during the Conservative-Unionist régime of the 'nineties, when it was particularly associated with the name of Joseph Chamberlain. This benevolent paternalism, born of political rivalry, was confined in its earlier stages chiefly to England, for there alone had the new business class attained sufficient proportions to attract the organized opposition of the landed interests. It later appeared in other European states, most notably in the case of the Bismarckian social insurance legislation.

The Early Christian Socialists. — The new capitalism and industrialism and its theoretical apologists among the economic liberals were frequently identified with the philosophy of materialism and rationalism, and this inevitably led to opposition from the religious elements. Although programs of social reform hostile to economic liberalism were put forward by Catholics, High Churchmen, Broad Churchmen, and Dissenters, one unifying purpose ran through all of their work: namely, the desire to socialize Christianity and thereby to capture social reform for the church and to win the gratitude and favor of the proletarian classes.

The origins of modern Christian socialism may be traced to *The New Christianity* (1825), written by the French thinker Saint-Simon, mentor of Auguste Comte. In this work the contrast between the social doctrines of Jesus and the traditionalism and ritualism of the church was clearly drawn and a striking appeal made for the socialization of religion. In the field of Social Catholicism there were a number of interesting developments, particularly in France under the Bourbon restoration and the Orleanist monarchy. The movement began in the monarchical, romantically reactionary doctrines (no value-judgment implied!) of

François René de Chateaubriand (1768–1848), Louis Gabriel
Ambroise DeBonald (1754–1840), and Joseph DeMaistre
(1753–1821), but the growth of democracy affected church as
well as state in France, and the leaders of the religious revival
clearly understood that if they were to make any headway they
would have to liberalize the Catholic standpoint. This was partially achieved by Antoine Frédéric Ozanam (1813–1853), who
founded the Society of Saint Vincent de Paul and linked up Neo-
Catholicism with practical philanthropy; by Alphonse de Lamar-
tine (1790–1869), who attempted to connect the Catholic movement with the growth of republican sentiment in France; by
Robert de Lamennais (1782–1854), who tried ineffectively to
harmonize Catholicism and the principles of the French Revolution and political democracy; and by Phillippe Joseph Buchez
(1796–1865), who shared the historical viewpoint of the German
school of economists, tried to prove that the spirit of Christianity
was revolutionary, anticipated the " guild socialism " of Bishop
von Ketteler and Franz Hitze, and advocated a scheme of co-
operative production and distribution.

The Protestants in the group of Christian social reformers
called into action by the Industrial Revolution have usually been
the only members labeled " Christian socialists," but there seems
no doubt that this title could with equal accuracy be extended to
the Catholic reformers. The leaders in this movement were
chiefly Anglican clergymen of the Broad Church party, though
some support was accorded by the Unitarians. The most prominent members of the Christian socialist group in England were
John Frederick Denison Maurice (1805–1872), Charles Kingsley (1819–1875), and Thomas Hughes (1822–1896). Others
having some influence who adhered to their general point of view
were John M. F. Ludlow (1821–1911) and John Lalor (1814–
1856).

Maurice, conventionally regarded as the founder of the movement in England, was especially interested in promoting the cause
of the education of the laboring class. Kingsley analyzed the social
problems of his day in powerful sermons and in telling books such
as *Alton Locke, Yeast,* and *Water-Babies.* Like Buchez, he also
urged the formation of workingmen's organizations and coöperative associations. Probably the most enduring contribution of
English Christian socialism to social reform was the impulse it
gave to the organization of coöperative and profit-sharing societies, of which the one based on the work of Owen — the famous
Rochedale Pioneers — has endured to the present day. The co-

operative movement spread rapidly on the Continent, and has developed particularly in Denmark and Belgium. The Christian socialists actually imported their ideas on associations and co-operation from Buchez's work in France, as Owen's work in England was then thought to be outrageously anti-Christian. The other important effects of Christian socialism in this first stage were its aid to proletarian education and the arousing of the interest of the Anglican Church in social reform.

The impulse to social reform originated by the Christian socialists within the Anglican Church attracted even members of the High Church party. The leaders of that effort at religious resuscitation known as the Oxford Movement, among them such influential persons as Whately, Arnold, Froude, Hurrell, Newman, Keble, and Pusey, lent their support to the development of trade-unionism and the betterment of housing conditions among the poor. Finally, even the dissenting sects, particularly the Quakers and the newer evangelical organizations, took a very significant part in agitating for remedial legislation for the poorer classes. This social impulse in Christianity spread to the United States, where much interest was shown by the New England Unitarians and Transcendentalists and others.[27]

Relief of the Poor. — It is of course common knowledge that long before the Christian socialists appeared on the scene, the church had a definite attitude toward the lower social strata, and particularly toward those below the poverty line. For a long time, however, there was no effort to obtain social legislation in their behalf; private benevolence was enjoined, but that was all. This is not to say that such benevolence always took the form of a direct relation between donor and recipient: even the early Christians collected alms and distributed them through officials of the church, and with the spread of Catholicism the monasteries became the agencies through which Christians, collectively organized in the church, " the bride of Christ," administered relief to the poor. The bishops later tried to have the parish priest take care of the destitute of his congregation with funds collected from the other members of the parish, and although this measure soon failed, the parish for a long time remained the administrative unit for relief-giving. In both of the methods mentioned, the poor were visited and cared for, with few exceptions, in their own homes; this localized type of " outdoor relief," as the social technologists later termed it, was the parent form from which other measures sprang.

As the Commercial Revolution, corruption of the church,

eviction of small farmers, and other aftermaths of the Crusades began to exert their disorganizing effects, there was a marked decline in the feeling of social responsibility, and a rapid spread of pauperism was the consequence. Giving to the poor had always been a Christian virtue, but with the rise of the mendicant friars the belief in the peculiar meritoriousness of giving to beggars, regardless of the effect on the beggar, gained a much firmer foothold. A vicious circle was thereby completed, and despite occasional exhortations against indiscriminate giving, pauperism steadily increased.

About the beginning of the sixteenth century a few far-seeing leaders, both Protestant and Catholic, began to see the damaging results of such " grace-gathering benevolence," but their protests were largely unavailing; little change in practice resulted.

Public Outdoor Relief in England. — The first English legislation bearing on the pauper did not arise as a result of charitable intentions, but out of a scarcity of labor, and was essentially repressive. The first " statute of laborers " was enacted in 1349, following the Black Death, and became the basis of English Poor Law. (We should consider the Poor Laws of other countries as well, but space does not permit.) Its purpose was to control the labor supply, and hence to suppress vagrancy: all persons able to labor and without other means of support were to be compelled to serve those who had need of them at the wages prevailing before the Black Death, and giving alms to beggars was made illegal. Following this came a law prohibiting laborers from traveling about the country (this was apparently the source of More's prohibition of wandering in his " turn-back-the-clock utopia "). In 1359 London passed a law compelling visitors to the city who were below a certain rank to leave immediately or be put in the stocks.

The first important English law dealing with the poor as such was passed in 1536. In it England expressed the tendency of all Europe to handle the problem in a more fundamental way than did the statutes of laborers. Although England followed Continental patterns in this matter, internal conditions probably occasioned the immediate action. During the first half of the sixteenth century there was a decided growth in all sorts of distress — a result, in part, of the indiscriminate giving already mentioned. Other conditions, however, greatly aggravated the situation: (1) the cessation of the civil wars left many soldiers without occupation; (2) the agrarian changes deprived large numbers of the population of their customary means of support; (3) the shift from tillage to sheep-raising had dispossessed many yeoman farmers; (4) from 1527 to 1536 England experienced a series of bad harvests; and (5) the debasement of the coinage by Edward VI and Henry VIII made it impossible for many honest laborers with low wages to live by following their usual trades. The ranks of the wandering beggars and vagrants were tremendously increased. To remind our readers of the parallel previously drawn when discussing the mass unrest that preceded the Crusades: "Aimless wandering became so prevalent that it took on the aspect of genuine collective behavior; tension and unrest carried thousands of hapless souls up hill and down dale, looking for they knew not what, *just as they did in the England of More's time*" (page 260) — the time we are now discussing.

The statute of 1536 went further than any of the others in stating that it was illegal to beg, thus placing the obligation to support the destitute directly on the parish. At first funds were raised by voluntary contributions, but when this source dried up, as it soon did, the justices were authorized in 1572 to make direct assessment for the support of the poor and to appoint special overseers to distribute the money. In 1576 the "honest poor" (i.e., those who did not move about) were given work to do on stocks of wool, hemp, flax, iron, and other materials, in order that they might be made self-supporting. This was the beginning of the workhouse system, one of the first steps toward the partial shift from "outdoor" to "indoor" relief that culminated in the reform of 1834. Legislation followed, seeking to find employment for the "honest poor," and efforts of this kind finally brought about the 43rd Act of Elizabeth in 1601. Its outstanding provisions were as follows:

I. Overseers of the poor shall be named by the justices of the peace each year, which shall include, besides the church wardens, from two to four substantial householders, according to the size of the parish.
The duty of these overseers is:

1. To take such measures with the consent of two justices as may be necessary to set children to work whose parents are unable to maintain them.
2. To set adults to work who have no means of support in order that they may earn a livelihood.
3. To raise weekly by taxation of every inhabitant and occupant of a holding, such sums as are necessary:
   (a) To obtain convenient stock of flax, hemp, wool, and other necessaries for the employment of the poor.

(b) For the relief of the lame, impotent, blind, and others un-
    able to work.

(c) For placing out poor children as apprentices.

4. The overseers must hold meetings at least once a month and at
   the end of the year prepare a statement of their transactions.

II. This section empowers the justices, where a parish cannot afford
    to bear the burden of its own poor, to levy a tax from other
    parishes in the same hundred or even in the same county. The jus-
    tices can collect the tax, and on neglect to pay may imprison the
    defaulter in the county jail.

III. This authorizes the binding out as apprentices of boys under their
     twenty-fourth year and of girls until their twenty-first year or
     until marriage.

IV. The establishment of workhouses is provided for in this section.

V. Appeals to the Court of Quarter Sessions against the tax levied are
   made possible.

VI. Section 6 regulates legal responsibility for the maintenance of
    parents, grandchildren, and children.[28]

The major features of this act are important because of their
subsequent effect on the Poor Laws of England and the United
States. In England the essential clauses remained virtually unchanged up to the reform of 1834. Even then the only sweeping
alteration was to make the workhouse the keystone of the system — and provision for the workhouse was already contained in
the Elizabethan act. Further changes were recommended by the
Poor Law Commission of 1909, but no extensive revision took
place. Only with the accession of the Labor Party to power, beginning in the 1920's, did the recommendations of the Webbs
and others have much direct effect. The English colonists who
settled the eastern shore of what is now the United States of
course brought with them institutions which prevailed in the England of their time; hence the relief of the poor was based on the
laws of the fifteenth and sixteenth centuries, particularly on the
" 43rd Elizabeth." Down to the present day many of the eastern
States, particularly in New England, have this act as the basis
of their poor relief. Only since the Federal government has begun to play a larger part in the administration of relief has
there been substantial modification, and this has been as much
through the ignoring of older laws as through their express abro-
gation.

Let us now turn to a consideration of unofficial efforts, largely
without even the help of legislation, to alleviate the worst conse-

quences of the English Poor Law; in so doing, we really turn our attention to the early forms of social case work.

The Beginnings of Social Case Work: Thomas Chalmers. — There were no professional social workers in feudal society. It is true that there were people who " went about doing good," but the specialization of production, the division of labor, and the concentration of impersonal groups had not yet created the demand for professional social workers, much less case-workers (although the " censors " of Vives, the fifteenth-century Spanish reformer, foreshadowed later developments — see Chapter Twenty-eight).

The term " case work " has been in use in its present connotations only a relatively short time, perhaps not more than two or three decades, but the term " case " is of older standing and was freely used at least as early as the writings of Thomas Chalmers (1780–1847), a Scottish divine. In 1819 he became minister of the church and parish of St. John's, Glasgow, where he was singularly successful (from the viewpoint of his era) in dealing with the problem of poverty, and from 1820 to 1826 he published the three volumes, in which " case " frequently occurs, of his *Christian and Civic Economy of Large Towns.* His great importance in the history of social work therefore comes largely from his writings, and to a lesser degree from the experimental demonstration of his theories which he undertook in the latter period of his life.

Like his successors in social case work in Great Britain, his point of contact with the problem came in the field of the English Poor Law administration, forced upon Scotland by the Act of Union. He was bitterly opposed both to its principles and to its practice. As we have seen, it provided for poor relief, financed by taxation, to all those whom the authorities deemed indigent in the economic sense. In the course of economic and administrative development, certain notions and interpretations had grown up and gained a certain amount of popular acceptance, such as, for example:

    I. That a considerable proportion of the population was bound to be dependent.

    II. That in view of the fluctuations of economic conditions it was impossible to differentiate between those who could find work but would not, and those who could either find no work or would be unable to undertake it if found.

    III. That those incapable of self-support were entitled to relief, and that " indoor relief," i.e., institutional " care," usually in close connection with the workhouse, was the best way of providing it.

iv. That the work test in established workhouses served to segregate the able-bodied willing but jobless from the able-bodied who were unwilling to work.

v. That it was a proper burden upon the tax rates to take care of those who were unable to work and those who were able but could not find employment. Poor relief then became a simple mechanical arrangement by which those found unable to work were assigned to institutions, while among the able-bodied the automatic functioning of the workhouse separated the sheep from the goats — the former being a proper charge on the public while the latter were dismissed from further consideration.

It is plain that these commonly accepted interpretations developed in the same " climate of opinion " as that which helped economic liberalism to flourish. There were many points in this Poor Law system which were abhorrent to Chalmers and which he attacked with vigor and consistency. He considered the mechanics of the system inadequate for weeding out those who could but would not work, and who therefore ought not become a burden on the commonwealth. He insisted that the careful investigation of each applicant rather than an automatic testing device would best distinguish those who needed help from those who did not, and would also show what kind of help was needed, if any; and that the investigation itself, and public recognition of the fact that aid depended on the outcome of the investigation, would act as a deterrent upon application from those who really were not in need.

Early Case Work and Economic Liberalism. — Chalmers was by no means a thoroughgoing opponent of economic liberalism, however; in fact, his *Political Economy,* published in 1832, shows distinct traces of the current *laissez faire* ideology. Even in his earlier writings he demanded that state outdoor relief be entirely discontinued and the burden removed from the taxpayer. It was his opinion that the cost of relief, whether through taxation or through voluntary contribution to the parish authorities, would be greatly reduced by the principle of individual investigation of each case. In accord with modern theory, he held that there is no such thing as poverty in the absolute sense, but that it is relative to habits, places, and times. The influence of the current economic liberalism becomes still more apparent in his insistence that those actually in need of relief would find ample resources in the " natural environment " of family, relatives, and friends, without recourse to state or parish. " Charity does not aim at the abolition of poverty, but of the evils which are often associated with it, one of the worst is pauperism." " . . . judgment must be brought into action as well as your sympathy." [29]

For all of Chalmers's linkage with the *laissez faire* doctrines of his time, however, his opinions nevertheless represent something substantially new: namely, a theory which substitutes for the simple idea of poverty as merely an economic minus sign the more complex concept of poverty as a resultant of unwise legislation, misguided generosity, unintelligent administration, bad habits, disregard of community solidarity, and slovenly thinking on the part of recipient and giver. He paid no attention to possible maladjustments or downright defects in the structure of the prevailing economic system, but no one man can be a universal genius — it is not in this sense that the medieval maxim, *Homo est quodammodo omnia,* is true.

The Glasgow Experiment. — Chalmers's ideas might have found less acceptance had he not taken the bold step of testing his theories by the experiment conducted in St. John's parish in Glasgow in 1822. He had succeeded, as responsible head of the parish, in obtaining official consent to the practical suspension of the administration of the Poor Law within his district. He then assumed the responsibility of meeting all needs that might be found through the resources of the parish and of the population itself. In this experimental district cases already " on the rates " were to be continued, but no new cases were to be brought before the poor relief authorities.

The essential parts of the experiment centered about the following proposals: (1) the parish was to be divided into districts, with a deacon responsible for each district of some four hundred persons, with whom he was expected to become thoroughly acquainted; (2) to this deacon was reported any case of need, and he was to be responsible for both the investigation and the subsequent treatment; (3) only such funds were to be used as were raised in voluntary contributions by the church; (4) the funds actually available to the deacons were to be kept as restricted as possible in order that the resources naturally abiding within the population itself — resources which were conceived to be of a more normal nature and of far greater potentiality than recognized resources — might be drawn upon by the persons requiring aid. As already noted, it was Chalmers's belief that the deliberately planned investigation, with all that it implied, would be — in the sense in which a test was desirable — much more accurate than the mechanical workhouse test. Along with these somewhat negative principles he stimulated thrift, habits of industry, and mutual helpfulness by such practical devices as encouraging savings deposits and extending facilities for instructing boys and girls in reading, sewing, and other useful attainments. The experiment came to an end before it provided the necessary proof or refutation of Chalmers's theories, but apparently they had been sufficiently tested, or had made a sufficient appeal, to establish a great readiness on the part of those who became interested in the charity organization movement in the 1860's to look back to his work as the basis of both their theoretical and practical principles.

The Charity Organization Movement. — Although she was prominent among the other pioneers of social case work, Octavia Hill is better known for her work in housing reform. Edward Denison of London was associated more intimately with the humanitarian movement as a whole, and perhaps the settlement field owes a greater immediate debt to him than does case work. Both Denison and Hill, however, were actively interested in the establishment and promotion of the Charity Organization Society of London, and were perhaps the most important interpreters of that venture. Of the two, Hill was by far the more articulate; she spoke and wrote abundantly, and continued to call attention to the significance of the Charity Organization Society after Denison's premature death.

Hill, as did Chalmers, emphasized the supreme importance of investigation in each case, but the goal of investigation was no longer conceived principally as the elimination of impostors, or the reduction of deliberate imposition and calculated pauperism; it was rather for the ascertaining of the more deeply hidden causes of destitution and the finding of methods of treatment more constructive than the " unkind doles."

Without using present-day phraseology, both Denison and Hill emphasized the importance of understanding the complete personality of the client in any attempt to help him. Many of the important phrases and ideas that have come to build up the concept of case work as a method of dealing with complete personalities came from Octavia Hill and, to a lesser extent, from Edward Denison.

The principal vehicle for the evolution of the concept and practice of social case work has been the charity organization movement, and particularly its first representative, the Charity Organization Society of London. Sir Charles S. Loch, its secretary for many years, was the teacher, promotor, and educator through whom for a long time the ideas of social case work, more usually thought of as Charity Organization Society ideas, were developed and extended. His writings deal mainly with the charity organization movement, and clearly mark the transition from the ideology of poor relief to that of social case work.

Influence in the United States. — It was natural that important social developments such as those represented by the charity organization movement should have been transplanted. Americans interested in philanthropy were consistent students of European experience, and some of Octavia Hill's important essays were reprinted by the State Charities Aid Association of New York in 1875. One of the active participants in the early work of the Charity Organization Society in London, S. H. Gurteen, was himself personally associated with the first Charity Organization Society in this country, in Buffalo, New York. As a result of these and other influences, the charity organization movement as such, rather than any outstanding interpreter of it, was responsible for the development of social case work during its early period in the United States. It was not until the twentieth century that Edward T. Devine and Mary E. Richmond began to interpret case work in print. Devine, a prolific author, covered the field from various angles, but with the focus still resting in the realm of poor relief and charity organization. It remained for Richmond to formulate, for the first time and in a comprehensive way, the meaning and function of social case work as a distinct theory in itself, dissociated, except historically and incidentally, from the agencies by which it is practiced. Her *Social Diagnosis,* published in 1917, still remains one of the best systematic treatments of social case work as a scientific procedure.

Even with the literary activity noted, however, it is true that the persons just named made their contributions to the development of social case work in part, and in many cases in large part, through the promotion and extension of the charity organization movement, which, to repeat, was the earliest and most important vehicle for the theory and practice of social case work. Other movements have contributed, especially in recent days, but their share has been chiefly in the augmenting and refining of a concept already formulated. The juvenile court system in the United States, medical social work, psychiatric social work, and child guidance are among these later contributory institutions.[30]

In close conjunction with the more recent phases of the development of social case work went another institution not as yet discussed: the social settlement. A brief sketch of its genesis is therefore in order.

The Social Settlement. — We can hardly express the aims of the settlement movement more adequately than in the language

used by Jane Addams more than thirty years ago when addressing
a body of social workers.

I have divided the motives which constitute the subjective pressure
toward social settlements in three great lines: the first contains the
desire to make the entire social organism democratic, to extend democracy beyond its political expression; the second is the impulse to share
the race life, and to bring as much as possible of social energy and the
accumulation of civilization to those portions of the race which have
little; the third springs from a certain Renaissance of Christianity, a
movement toward its early humanitarian aspects.[31]

The settlement has been defined in the following way:

. . . a center in which men and women of education, wealth, and
leisure may meet on terms of neighborly friendliness the less fortunate
citizens of their community, where each may learn from the other, and
through friendship render service to each other resulting in enlargement
of vision, development of personality, and united action for social
betterment.[32]

When we compare this definition with the statement of the
" subjective pressure " toward social settlements it becomes apparent that Jane Addams was right in her emphasis on democracy,
humanitarianism, and " socialized Christianity " as the background of the movement. There was another element, however,
which may be called " the aesthetic revolt " (to be discussed
later) ; many early settlement residents were as much impelled by
a desire to save those among whom they worked from what the
residents conceived (and perhaps quite rightly) to be appalling
ugliness as from poverty and squalor.

It is difficult to say when or how the settlement idea got under
way. In 1860 Frederick Maurice founded the Workingmen's
College in London, where classes were taught by Cambridge students during their spare time. In 1867 Edward Denison, already
mentioned in connection with the charity organization movement, went to live as a student among the poor of the parish of
John Richard Green, the historian, who was the vicar of St.
Philip's, Stepney. Denison died shortly afterward, but not before
he had interested a number of other students in the struggles
of the poor; and through his indirect influence Canon Barnett, an
Oxford graduate, in 1873 accepted a parish in the slums of East
London which was described by the bishop as " the worst parish in
my diocese, inhabited mainly by a criminal population, and one
which has, I fear, been much corrupted by doles." Barnett applied
the principles of Chalmers to his work, and many university students, among whom was Arnold Toynbee, came to help him. His

personality attracted a wide range and variety of talent, and as a result of favorable public comment, the notion of a settlement to be staffed by university students developed. Under the direction of Barnett, the necessary funds for the settlement house were raised, and in 1885 Toynbee Hall — named for Arnold Toynbee, who died in 1883 — was dedicated.

This institution may rightly be termed the first full-fledged settlement in the world, and Canon Barnett was unquestionably the dean of social settlement workers until his death in 1915. Yet, it is probably true that his direct influence by no means accounts for the surprising rapidity of the development of the settlement movement in the United States: the problems of the old and the new immigration and rapid urbanization made American cities an even more fertile soil than the centers of the Old World.

In 1887 Stanton Coit, a clergyman, organized the Neighborhood Guild (later known as the University Settlement) in East Side New York; this was the first settlement in the United States. In 1889 Jane Addams, as a result of a visit to East London and Toynbee Hall, rented an old mansion in slum Chicago and opened Hull House, one of the most famous settlements in America. From this time on the movement grew rapidly, and to-day (1937) there are over seven hundred settlement houses, more than five hundred of which are in the United States.

There seems no immediate prospect of settlements either declining appreciably in number or securing all of their professed objectives, but their aim, so we are told, is to "work themselves out of a job" and turn over their functions to self-perpetuating community organizations. In fact, Robert Wood, one of the prominent recent leaders of the movement, has always declared that the settlement is not an institution but an attitude. Nevertheless, a recession of humanitarianism — and signs of such a recession are not wanting — would inevitably force the settlements into an institutional routine of ministering only to the material needs of the lower economic strata. But Federal aid to work projects, such as those sponsored by the WPA, has for a time at least, and perhaps permanently, lessened this tendency. Moreover, the Social Security Act will undoubtedly diminish the strictly economic load on the settlements. Consequently, the statement quoted below is not so badly outmoded as it would have been in 1932 or thereabouts:

. . . we may say that the past of the settlement gives the impression of a neighborhood organized under the direction of cultured persons who take up residence in the community. Its spirit is that of the altruism and idealism so characteristic of college and university life, but its opposition to the old doctrine of *laissez-faire* does not involve it in enterprises which pauperize. The aims of the settlements are characterized by emphasis on some one such activity as health, education, religion, or music, but nearly all attempt several lines of activity, among which the most common are educational, health, political, charitable, recreational, and scientific.

The settlements have been met by many criticisms, but most of such criticisms arise from sources which make them a tribute to the activity of the residents. In the future the settlement may serve as a department of our social work for introducing new ideas or methods, training leaders, and interpreting city life in human terms to the prospective leaders of business, politics, education, and religion.[38]

And again let us call attention to the notions of democracy, humanitarianism, and socialized Christianity — the above summary once more shows how much influence these essentially nineteenth-century ideals still exert in the settlement movement. We have already noted the part played by another element: namely, the aesthetic protest; it is now possible to consider this in its own right.

The Aesthetic Revolt against Materialism and Misery. — Although the Industrial Revolution has produced nearly all the material comforts of modern life and created many new forms of art and beauty as well, there can be no doubt that in its first stages, at least, the new industrialism, with its dismal factories, clouds of smoke, and filthy tenements, was extremely ugly and repulsive to the aesthetic temperament and to humanitarian impulses. The new order of things and its supporters among the economic liberals therefore sustained a vigorous attack from the representatives of the literary and artistic standards of the age. This so-called aesthetic revolt against the origins of the modern industrial order was of a rather varied sort, ranging all the way from the purely cultural protest of men like Matthew Arnold to the espousal of openly socialistic programs by leading literary figures like George Sand and William Morris. Although nearly all the leading figures in art and literature during the second third of the nineteenth century were in some way involved, a few can be singled out as the leaders in the aesthetic protest. Among these were Robert Southey (1774–1843), Thomas Carlyle (1795–1881), Samuel Coleridge (1772–1834), Charles Dickens (1812–1870), Charles Reade (1814–1884), John Ruskin (1819–1900), Matthew Arnold (1822–1888), William Morris (1834–1896), Ralph Waldo Emerson (1803–1882), George Sand (Madame

Dudevant; 1804–1876), and Leo Tolstoy (1828–1910). Of this group the most important were Carlyle, Ruskin, George Sand, Tolstoy, and Arnold.

Carlyle is significant chiefly as a critic of materialism and the economic abstractions of the classical school. He had no constructive program of reform beyond a willingness to wait for some unique genius, some " hero," to appear with a ready-made solution. Ruskin was as bitter as Carlyle in his criticism of the new industrial society and its ideals, but over and above this he offered at least the rudiments of a program through his advocacy of the dignity of labor and of a régime of industrial coöperation, state education, government workshops, and state insurance for the working classes. A part of his program bordered on the guild socialism of a slightly later period, but he set education above all other types of remedy. A trace of the temptation to a utopian flight appears in his " Guild of St. George."

George Sand, of a slightly earlier period, imbibed freely the utopian and revolutionary socialism of the 1840's in France, and by her writings did much to popularize these notions, in particular the doctrines of Pierre Leroux. Tolstoy penned his protests at a much later date, but the peculiarly retrospective nature of his reform program gives us warrant for considering him here. His " flight into the past " was not so disconnected from his contemporary setting, considering the agrarian background of Russia, as it would have been had he written in the midst of Western industrialism. He advocated a complete abandonment of the new industrialism, a return to an agrarian age, and the organization of the agrarian economy according to the principles of the Russian *mir,* with its communistic and coöperative practices considerably expanded. In spite of this obvious " flight from the present," his powerful emotional appeal gripped a number of early settlement leaders, among them Jane Addams. Arnold, an admirer of the authoritarian Prussian state, helped to lay the literary basis for the introduction of the Hegelian theory of the state into England.

Although one can appreciate the real and valid motives for this revolt of the aesthetic temperament against the repulsive features of modern industrial society, little in the way of workable, constructive reforms was offered. Few except those who went over to socialism had any tangible program. Further, even those who, like Ruskin, had some program to offer, were scarcely in harmony with the aspirations of contemporary labor; they desired the establishment of some sort of authoritative and benevolent paternalism. In spite of all this, the aesthetic protest was a real contribution to the reform cause, for it effectively insisted that an increase in material gain was no complete justification of a new order of civilization, that modern industrialism must make a place for the ideal and the aesthetic. The more recent circle of literary critics of the social order — Émile Zola, Anatole France, Bernard Shaw, H. G. Wells, John Galsworthy, Maurice Maeterlinck, Sinclair Lewis, Theodore Dreiser, John Dos Passos, Upton Sinclair, and a host of others — differ from most of their predecessors, for instead of favoring a return to a more primitive economy and social order, they are among the most ardent exponents of reconstruction. Only a few, keenly aware of the best that older civilizations offered and equally sensitive to the darkest phases of the present order, have looked back with longing eyes to an image of a bygone age.[34]

Utopian Socialism. — It has already been noted that the schemes of social reform conventionally known as utopian appear in great number after some " time of troubles " which brings with it an abnormal degree of misery. The Industrial Revolution, one of the greatest of all such transitions, and probably the most productive of accompanying misery, brought forth an unprecedented number of utopian plans for the solution of existing social problems, but all of these programs were more realistic and practical than the somewhat fanciful utopias of the seventeenth century.

In the most fundamental sense, utopian socialism of the first half of the nineteenth century was a revolt against the semifatalism which had represented society as the product of natural laws, had accused the proletariat of being the sole authors of their own miseries, and had sharply denied the possibility of improving conditions " artificially " through constructive legislation.

Utopian socialism denied these assorted premises of Romanticism, individualism, and economic liberalism, and revived the notions of the French Revolution to the effect that human intelligence and ingenuity are fully equal to the task of forging a new social order. Its advocates held that human nature is primarily the product of the social environment, and that the remedy for the contemporary evils is therefore to be found in the creation of a better set of social institutions. They maintained that man can by rational thought determine his own social relations, and some, like Fourier, even claimed that by well-conceived legislation the normal course of social evolution can be anticipated.

Saint-Simon's Utopia. — The initiator of the utopian schemes of this period is conventionally assumed to be Count Henri de Saint-Simon (1760–1825), though there is no doubt that other

utopias would have appeared had Saint-Simon never written.[35]
We have already dealt with him as the formulator of the chief
theses of the Comtean sociology and as a forerunner of Christian
socialism. His disciples developed his various notions: Enfantin
and Bazard emphasized the communistic principles found in that
primitive Christianity which Saint-Simon had so much admired;
Leroux defended the notion of the social and moral equality of
men and the essential solidarity of society; and Comte attempted
to systematize the new social science of which Saint-Simon had
seen the need.

Fourier, Utopian Numerologist. — The most thoroughgoing
of the French utopians was Francois Marie Charles Fourier
(1772–1835). He was one of the firmest believers in the possibility of reforming mankind through the creation of an ideal social
environment. This he believed would be found in an " apartment-
house utopia " — a coöperative community or phalanstery comprising some eighteen hundred persons. He hoped to see human
society reconstituted as a world-federation of phalansteries, the
capital of which was to be located at Constantinople. Fourier did
not plan a society which would wholly abolish all private property
or attempt to equalize all classes and individuals, but meticu-
lously worked out in a manifestly psychopathic manner what he
believed to be a proper fractional distribution of the social income between labor, capital, and enterprise.[36] He did not profoundly affect France, but no other utopian attracted so large and
sympathetic a following in America. Many Fourierist groups
were established, the most famous of which was Brook Farm,
conducted by some of the most noted members of the " Brahmin
caste " of New England literary lights. Another French utopian
reformer was Étienne Cabet (1788–1856), whose followers established an experimental community, first in Texas and later in
Nauvoo, Illinois.[37]

Owen, Utopian Practitioner. — The leading English utopian
socialist was Robert Owen (1771–1858), who came into the field
of utopian theorizing fresh from a practical demonstration of
the possibility of establishing an ideal industrial community. At
the cotton mills in New Lanark he had organized a unique industrial community which, in the early nineteenth century, possessed many of the features characterizing the most advanced industrial organizations of the present day. While Owen gave his
support to almost every type of constructive philanthropy current
in his day, he is known especially for his agitation in the cause of
factory legislation and trade-unionism, his vigorous advocacy of

industrial coöperation, and his concrete plan for ideal industrial communities. Though his plan was adopted in several places in the United States, most notably at New Harmony, Indiana, it had little practical success here, and the enduring mark which Owen left on social reform consists chiefly in his catholic support of virtually every means then extant of wiping out existing evils, and in his emphasis on the peculiar virtues inhering in coöperation.[38] More recent echoes of the utopian movement have been William Morris's *News from Nowhere,* Edward Bellamy's *Looking Backward,* several semi-utopian novels of H. G. Wells, and the writings of Ralph Borsodi.

Hall and Land Nationalization. — Although the great majority of the utopian socialists were concerned chiefly with the reformation of the new industrial society, there was one writer, the learned British physician, Charles Hall, who anticipated Henry George and Franz Oppenheimer in contending that the cause of all the evils of the age was private property in land and its concentration in great estates. In his *Effects of Civilization,* published in 1805, Hall argued for the nationalization of land as the remedy for the abuses and oppression of his age. Beer has thus summarized his doctrines:

> The diversion of land into large dominions, and the inequality consequent upon that division, gave to the rich an absolute power over the non-possessors, whom they use for the purpose of increasing the stock of wealth. Private property in land led to manufactures, trade, and commerce, by which the poor are made poorer still, and the small possessors are deprived of the little they possess and thrown into poverty.
>
> The division of the land being thus the original cause of the evil, the reform of society must evidently start by removing the cause. The land, therefore, should be nationalized and settled with small farmers. The land should be restored to the nation, and the nation to the land. Agriculture should be the main occupation of all. Of the sciences and arts only those should be preserved and promoted that are necessary for the prosperity of agricultural pursuits.[39]

Significant as were the premises and the achievements of utopian socialism in emphasizing the ability of society consciously and planfully to solve its own problems, this type of socialism could scarcely lead directly into Marxian socialism, as has sometimes been maintained. It was too impractical and, from the standpoint of the Marxian, it was not sufficiently proletarian. In a very real sense it was as much the forerunner of modern French " solidarism " as of Marxian socialism. Between utopian and Marxian socialism there intervened the stage of " transitional socialism " by which socialism was made a revolutionary and proletarian movement. Before we can discuss this stage, however, it is necessary to say something about a widely different sort of program.

Philosophical Anarchism. — It might be thought that the economic liberals had attained the most perfect apotheosis of the individual, but they were exceeded in this respect by another contemporary school: namely, the earliest philosophical anarchists. The economic liberals proposed to retain the state for at least the function of preserving life and protecting property, but the anarchists declared for the total abolition of the state and all other coercive institutions.

The first of this group was William Godwin (1756–1836), with whose *Inquiry Concerning Political Justice* (1793) we have already dealt (pp. 477–481); this work was probably the best example of the adoption of the extreme notions of the French Revolution by an English social philosopher. Pierre Joseph Proudhon (1809–1865), a French heir of the same upheaval, inveighed mightily against the bourgeois state, which he regarded as wholly an institution for exploitation and oppression. His ideal society was to be founded upon a combination somewhat difficult to effect, to say the least: namely, "the union of order and anarchy." He believed that if the obligations of contract were adhered to, society would function perfectly, but he allowed no weight to the contention that there can be no certain enforcement of contractual obligations without the force of the law behind them. Although both Godwin and Proudhon had rejected the utility of the state they had stressed the importance of society and of the concept of humanity. It was left for the German writer, Max Stirner (1805–1856), in *The Ego and His Own* (1844) to exalt the individual above even humanity and society, to assert that the individual constitutes the only extant reality, to maintain that the only limitation upon the rights of the individual is his power to obtain what he desires, and to contend that "the only right is might." While these early anarchists were guilty of many excesses of statement and offered no well-reasoned substitute for the state which they proposed to destroy, they did perform a real service by insisting that the state, at least as long as it was undemocratized, might be unjustly oppressive and hence a legitimate object for the suspicion of those who were excluded from participation in it.[40]

Transitional Socialism. — The most important figures in the so-called transitional socialism already referred to were the English "Ricardian socialists," William Thompson (1785–1833),

John Gray (d. *c.* 1850), Thomas Hodgskin (1787–1869), and John Francis Bray (*c.* 1840); the Frenchmen, Louis Blanc (1813–1882) and Pierre Joseph Proudhon (1809–1865); and the Germans, Wilhelm Weitling (1808–1870) and Ferdinand Lassalle (1825–1864) — though Proudhon played a more prominent part in founding modern philosophical anarchism and Lassalle was equally distinguished as an advocate of state socialism.

As far as his practical reform program is concerned, Thompson was a disciple of Robert Owen, but his *Inquiry into the Principles of the Distribution of Wealth most Conducive to Human Happiness* (1824) contained a very clear statement of the famous Marxian doctrine of " surplus value." He maintained that labor produces all value and should get the whole product, but under capitalistic society it is exploited out of a great part of its just income. Gray criticized the bourgeois society of his day, accepted the labor theory of value, and advocated state intervention. Hodgskin turned the theory of the natural order against the economic liberals by attempting to show that capitalism is an artificial and not a natural product.[41] Bray elaborated the economic interpretation of history as well as the labor theory of value.[42]

Louis Blanc was one of the first to insist that the only effective help which the proletarians could expect must come from their own efforts. They themselves must make effective their most basic claim, the right to labor. He believed that the laboring classes would have to triumph through an economic revolution, either peaceful or violent, and his post-revolutionary program consisted of " social workshops " — tantamount to initial state support and control of industry according to a democratic plan of organization. In the revolution of 1848 his plan was ostensibly tried in France, but as it was operated by enemies who desired to discredit it, the scheme proved a hopeless failure. Certain phases of Blanc's doctrine resemble some aspects of the program of syndicalism and guild socialism. (It should never be forgotten, however, that Lenin shared Marx's detestation of the mere "Blanquist," i.e., of the advocate of *coup d'etat* revolution.)

Proudhon made an especially bitter attack on the institution of private property, or rather on the abuses of private property which then existed. He was equally critical, however, of doctrines of economic egalitarianism; he proposed to base the income of everyone solely upon the amount of labor performed, the unit value of which was to be equal and uniform among all members

of society. Those who worked most were to get most. He attempted to secure the establishment of a national banking system
founded upon labor scrip following the revolution of 1848, but
he failed utterly in this. Standing at the opposite pole from Say
and Bastiat in his attitude toward modern capitalism, he is chiefly
significant for his effective onslaught upon the abuses of the bourgeois régime.[43]

Weitling, a Magdeburg tailor who later came to the United
States, anticipated Marx by a comprehensive and trenchant review of the evils which modern capitalism had brought to the
workingmen and by an eloquent appeal to the proletariat, urging
them to rise in their own behalf and overthrow their capitalistic
oppressors. His program was a curious combination of proposals
similar to certain notions of Fourier, Saint-Simon, and Proudhon:
namely, Fourier's conception of " attractive industry "; Saint-
Simon's idea of expert direction of society; and Proudhon's proposal for an exchange-bank based on labor scrip.[44]

Lassalle, a German Jew of great ability, made important historical, legal, and philosophical attacks on capitalism and private
property, stressed the fact that the laborers could escape from
bondage only through political activity, and assumed a leading
part in the formation of the first significant labor party in Germany. His concrete plan for reform was the establishment of
state workshops much like those proposed by Louis Blanc,
but this phase of his doctrines had little subsequent influence.[45]
From even this brief survey it can readily be seen that transitional socialism in many ways prepared Europe for Marxian
socialism.

Summary of the Chapter. — The upheaval in economic, social,
political, and " cultural " life which accompanied the Industrial
Revolution gave an unprecedented impetus to the humanitarian
movement, and this eventually had a great deal to do with the rise
of social sciences directed toward melioristic goals. In fact,
the humanitarian motive probably had more to do with the
growth of sociology than did the quest for knowledge for its
own sake.

We passed in rapid review such early schemes for social reconstruction as those of Plato, the Gracchi, and a few radical religious movements of the medieval period, and noted that the
social and economic changes entailed by the Commercial Revolution engendered a host of utopias of escape. Later, the growth of
rationalism had a profound effect on the development of social
reform programs, and the doctrines of the Deists were particu-

larly effective in removing obstacles to what was believed to be social improvement.

The *laissez faire* ideology of economic liberalism served to block for a time the remedial legislation called forth by the enormous amount of social disorganization attendant upon the early Industrial Revolution. Throughout this period there was an acceleration of the phenomenal growth of the powers of the middle class and, in the struggle with the remnants of feudalism, the abolition of slavery, serfdom, guild monopolies, and the privileges of crown and clergy came about. The beginnings of a policy of preventive treatment in handling the problem of poor relief were seen, but none of the legislation of the period notably benefited the proletariat, and much of it was definitely subversive of their interests. The Utilitarians advocated a large amount of positive remedial legislation in behalf of the laboring classes. The most effective source of proletarian advance, however, was the rivalry between the conservative landlords among the Tories and the representatives of the manufacturing and commercial interests in the Whig or Liberal Party. The Tories gained several of their points designed to disadvantage the Whigs, and the partial result was the passage of several factory acts which limited the number of hours of labor, provided certain safety precautions, and gave special protection to women and children.

Attempts at " the socialization of religion " in France of an earlier period had brought about the foundation of the Society of Saint Vincent de Paul; and in the same country the origins of modern Christian socialism may be traced in part to the writings of Saint-Simon. In England there was an obvious attempt in many branches of the church to secure the allegiance of the laboring classes by sponsoring programs of social reform; these included free education, the launching of coöperative societies, and even support for trade-unionism. The earliest forms of relief for the poor after the collapse of the Roman Empire in the West had been through the church, and for a long time the parish remained the administrative unit. The combined effect of the Commercial Revolution, the Crusades, and other associated factors was to increase pauperism tremendously. Early legislation aimed at mendicancy placed responsibility for support on the parish, and led gradually to the famous Elizabethan Act of 1601 — famous because of its enduring effects on subsequent legislation in England and the United States.

The beginnings of social case work can best be dated from Chalmers's protest against the principles and practice of the

English Poor Law. This arose from his conviction that poverty was the result of unwise legislation, indiscriminate charity, poor administration, bad habits, and a host of other factors. The early sponsors of the charity organization movement in London continued Chalmers's emphasis on the investigation of each case, but the end of investigation was seen to be the laying bare of the causes of destitution rather than mere prevention of deception. Chalmers's ideas also influenced the pioneers of the settlement movement — a movement proceeding from notions of democracy, humanitarianism, and socialized Christianity.

An impassioned aesthetic revolt was occasioned by the materialism and misery which followed in the wake of the Industrial Revolution. A glance at the names of the writers involved indicates that little in the way of clearly formulated and consistently advocated reforms resulted from this revolt.

The utopian socialism of the first half of the nineteenth century denied the validity of the doctrines of Romanticism, on the one hand, and of economic liberalism on the other, and emphasized the supposed effectiveness of rational thought and social institutions constructed in accordance with it in creating a new social order.

The early philosophical anarchists had their most important representatives in Godwin, Proudhon, and Stirner. The first two urged the abolition of the state, but emphasized the claims of life in society. Stirner, however, went further, proclaiming the individual as the paramount factor and his self-sufficiency as the only goal worth striving for.

Meanwhile, socialism was undergoing a transformation at the hands of the Ricardian socialists, as well as through the writings and actions of Thompson, Hodgskin, Blanc, Weitling, and Lassalle, and this paved the way for revolutionary socialism. The transformation came about through the enunciation of the doctrines of surplus value, the labor theory of value, and the belief that the only effective help for the masses must come through their own economic and political efforts directed toward a revolutionary objective. The stage was set for the new heralds of the dawn of secular salvation, Marx and Engels. The gospel of revolutionary socialism was soon to find its Paul and Silas.

Many results of the social ferment just described still exert influence, but most of them are best considered in specialized treatises on social work, labor legislation, etc. Some will concern us when the history of professional sociology is presented, but in the present context many that are relevant are treated in the next chapter.

CHAPTER XVII

New Gospels: Revolutionary Socialism and the Winds of Doctrine

IMPORTANCE OF THE MARXIAN ORIENTATION. — In the foregoing chapter we made a rapid survey of movements for social reform and reconstruction that in their actual inception or their ideological foundations antedated the rise of Marxian socialism. The present chapter deals with movements that followed the ineffective, spasmodic revolutions of 1848; which is to say, with movements that either were carried in the wake of Marxian doctrine, or struck out on similar courses, or endeavored to make head against it, but that always in some way were oriented with regard to it. For better or for worse, revolutionary socialism had appeared on the horizon, and it entered into all calculations that had as their aim the charting of the future course of the social order. In attributing this degree of importance to Karl Marx (1818–1883) and his disciples, we do not necessarily subscribe either to his theories or to his program: our only point is that Marxian notions have made a difference in the intellectual climate that affects everyone, and particularly the social scientist. Small certainly overestimated Marx's significance, but his statement is worth quoting here because it shows why a history of social thought *must* grant a niche to the patron saint of revolutionary socialism:

> Marx was one of the few really great thinkers in the history of social science. . . . Up to the present time the appellate court of the world's sober second thought has not given him as fair a hearing as it has granted to Judas Iscariot. . . . I do not think that Marx added to social science a single formula which will be final in the terms in which he expressed it. In spite of that, I confidently predict that in the ultimate judgment of history Marx will have a place in social science analogous with that of Galileo in physical science.[1]

So much by way of preliminary. It is now necessary to turn to a consideration of historical and doctrinal detail. This will carry us far afield, both theoretically and chronologically, but it never-

theless seems preferable to the alternative of dealing with these
matters in the chapters on sociology proper.

The " watershed year " of 1848 has already been mentioned
several times: in the winter and spring of that year the masses
throughout central, western, and southern Europe revolted in
the hope of gaining political liberty and thereby freeing themselves from oppression. In the Germanic states freedom from political autocracy was desired; in the Hapsburg realms and in
Italy not only political liberty but also freedom from the social
burdens of feudalism were aimed at; in France political participation and the overthrow of bourgeois oppression were the goal;
and in England the Chartists hoped to achieve economic betterment and that part in the world of politics which had been denied
them by failure to remove all limitations of the franchise in the
Reform Bill of 1832. For various reasons, but primarily because
of the division of the revolutionists resulting from national, party,
or economic rivalry, the movements failed in every country,
though the abolition of serfdom in the Hapsburg possessions was
a permanent achievement. The failure of these *political* revolts of
the masses turned the energies of many into *economic* channels of
attack upon what they regarded as the forces of privilege. " Scientific " socialism and a number of related theories were accorded
a wide hearing.[2]

The Growth of "Scientific" Socialism. — This variety of socialism is generally and correctly associated with the work of
Marx and his aide, Friedrich Engels (1820–1895). As Russell
has said:

Socialism as a power in Europe may be said to begin with Marx. It is
true that before his time there were Socialist theories, both in England
and in France. It is also true that in France, during the Revolution of
1848, socialism for a brief period acquired considerable influence in the
State. But the socialists who preceded Marx tended to indulge in Utopian
dreams and failed to found any strong or stable political party. To Marx,
in collaboration with Engels, are due both the formulation of a coherent
body of socialist doctrine, sufficiently true or plausible to dominate the
minds of vast numbers of men and the formation of the International
Socialist movement, which has continued to grow in all European countries throughout the last fifty years.[3]

The International Workingmen's Association took its origins
from a conference of laborers at the London International Exhi-
bition of 1862. It was organized at London two years later, and
its principles were drawn up by Marx and adopted at the Geneva

conference of 1866. A German wing was started by Wilhelm Liebknecht in 1864, and under his leadership and that of August Bebel it grew into the Democratic Workingmen's Association at Eisenach in 1869. In the meantime a German General Working-men's Association had been organized and its program enunciated in 1863 by Ferdinand Lassalle, of whom we have already spoken. These two groups coalesced at Gotha in 1875, and created the German Social Democratic Party. Persecuted by Bismarck from 1878 to 1890, it grew in numbers and power until the party commanded 110 out of 397 votes in the Reichstag of the pre-War German régime.[4] As might have been expected, the bureaucratic sops thrown to deserving members corrupted the party. This was especially true after the World War, when the Social Democrats came into power: the bureaucracy grew by leaps and bounds, and the vested interest in political stability that resulted made the party vacillating and pusillanimous when quick decisions and forti-tude were necessary. Moreover, the Social Democrats unwisely gave credence to the war-guilt myth and assumed the onus of the " policy of fulfillment " *vis-à-vis* the Treaty of Versailles. Finally, they slaughtered some of the most courageous of German radicals when they put down the Spartacist revolt — radicals whose *Tap-ferkeit* might have done something to stem the charge of the National Socialist storm troopers who in 1933 finally ousted the effete Social Democratic trade-union and Reichstag leaders.

The beginning of the modern French political organization of labor dates back to 1878; two years later French Marxism took form under the leadership of Jules Guesde. The French socialists, however, were for a long time unable to arrive at the same unity that characterized the party in Germany. Numerous sects de-veloped and much bitter feeling grew up, particularly between the Marxians led by Guesde, and the revisionists or opportunists led by Jean Jaurès, perhaps the most striking figure in the history of modern parliamentary socialism. An effort to unite these fac-tions failed in 1899, but met with more success in 1905, and the United Socialist Party was able to elect 102 out of 602 members of the Chamber of Deputies in 1914, besides eighteen members of the allied Independent Socialist Party. As in other European countries, most of the French radicals succumbed to the national-ism fanned into fiercer flame by the World War; the earlier inter-nationalism has distinctly lost ground. Indeed, only the Commu-nists, those heirs of genuinely revolutionary socialism, still place the concept of class above that of *la belle France*.

Socialist party organizations affiliated with the Second International made rapid progress before the World War in a number of the other chief European countries, notably Austria, Italy, and Russia, and reached remarkable strength in some of the lesser states, particularly Finland, Sweden, Denmark, and Belgium. In part, this was the result of the increased strength of the proletariat, and in part the effect of a dilution of socialistic proposals. This dilution attracted many left-wing democrats who could not quite bring themselves to accept the doctrine of class conflict, but who were swayed by the socialistic critique of capitalism and the aspiration to ground production on the motive of " social service " rather than private profit.

The Sources and General Nature of Marxian Doctrine. — It would probably be futile to attempt to indicate all the sources of Marx's views, for he read deeply in the literature and was in contact with most of the tendencies of his period, but a few of his more conspicuous obligations may be set down: (1) To Hegel he was indebted for his dialectical system and his faith in state activity; (2) general information about socialism and communism in France and elsewhere he probably encountered for the first time in the writings of Lorenz von Stein, from whom he also received, in all probability, the ideas of " civil society " and of social classes; (3) his historical materialism he took in part from Feuerbach and another portion, perhaps, from Heeren; (4) the labor theory of value was derived from Ricardo, Rodbertus, and the Ricardian socialists; (5) the doctrine of surplus value he found in the writings of Thompson; (6) the notion of class conflict and the necessity of a proletarian upheaval was emphasized in the works of Louis Blanc, Proudhon, and Weitling; (7) from Sismondi he received his conviction that the capitalists would be weakened by the progressive concentration of wealth in the hands of a few men; (8) his ideas of primitive " classless society " seem to have come from his Hebraic *mishpat* heritage and certain " natural rights " theories — Morgan merely provided later " confirmation "; (9) from Rodbertus he may have derived the thesis that continually recurring crises are a necessary phase of economic life under capitalism; (10) from his reading of the Old Testament may have come his faith in a future golden age of quasi-Messianic character; and (11) last but by no means least, his notions of revolutionary tactics (to be dealt with at length) came in part from Danton and other Jacobin leaders of the French Revolution.

The *Communist Manifesto,* a document drawn up by Marx and Engels for the German Communist League in Paris in January, 1848, contains the essence of Marxian socialism. This begins with the economic interpretation of history: namely, the contention that the successive systems of the production and distribution of wealth have primarily conditioned the accompanying social and cultural institutions. Then comes the labor theory of value; i.e., the contention that labor produces all value. From this is derived the doctrine of surplus value by pointing to the difference between the total social income and that received by labor. This difference is asserted to be the surplus value created by labor, out of which it is cheated by the capitalist in the form of rent, interest, and profits. Hence arises the notion of an inevitable and irreconcilable struggle between the proletariat and the capitalists. This can only terminate in the final overthrow of the latter, for they are being continually weakened by the steady concentration of wealth in the hands of their more powerful representatives and by disastrous repeated crises, whereas the proletariat will become progressively stronger through economic solidarity and party organization. When the proletariat shall have finally perfected their organization and when " objective conditions " are suitable, they will rise up and expropriate their oppressors and institute the régime of social and economic collectivism which Marx predicted but refrained from describing in detail.[5] These doctrines were elaborated with greater thoroughness, although in more technical and difficult terminology, in the work called *Das Kapital,* largely written by Marx but in part edited after his death by Engels.

The Present Status of Marxian Theory. — Some of the enduring theoretical contributions of Marx are his stress on economic factors in historical development, his restatement and amplification of the " internal conflict " theory of the state, his extremely effective criticism of the individualistic industrialism of the first half of the nineteenth century — the reading of which " cannot but stir into fury any passionate working-class reader, and into unbearable shame any possessor of capital in whom generosity and justice are not wholly extinct " — and his shrewd analysis of revolutionary tactics. Few if any of Marx's other major doctrines are now regarded as of substantial validity, but as a contributor to the science of economics he is generally regarded as the instigator of " institutional economics " as since cultivated by Max Weber, Sombart, Hobson, the Webbs, Hammond, Veblen, Tawney, and others. With occasional exceptions, English and American writers who have dealt with Marxian theories have confined themselves primarily to such topics as economic " determinism," surplus value, and the relation of non-material to material culture (*Überbau und Unterbau*). German and Russian writers, on the contrary, have paid considerably more attention to the Marxian theory of the state, to the class struggle, and to political strategy. Such subjects have the merit of subsuming virtually everything of sociological relevance falling in the group first mentioned, and in addition of calling attention to the dynamic elements in Marxian thought — which, it must be insisted, " aims not to interpret the world, but to change it." A similar line of analysis is followed here: the theories of Marx (and in some minor instances, of Engels) will be examined in so far as they bear upon the rôle of revolution in social change. That this emphasis upon the supreme importance of the revolutionary process in Marx's thought is not peculiar to the present writers is amply borne out by the following quotation from Gray, one of England's foremost students of Marx (who is not himself a " Marxian ") :

Marx . . . held that revolution was the fundamental mode of social development, not the incremental, cumulative, and co-operative march of technology and science, although he made a very valuable contribution to social science in stressing the significance of these factors. It is an irony that modern sociologists, under the guidance of natural science, should single out as Marx's main contribution to the thought of the nineteenth century what he himself regarded merely as an adjunct to his essential doctrine.

It has been German social democracy which has fathered the notion of " economic determinism " as a complete sociological law, not Karl Marx. The doctrine of Kautsky, the German equivalent of English Methodism, assured the exploited masses that the social millennium would come without any effort on their part, simply by the irresistible march of economic events. The views of Marx . . . were not so necessitarian. They were saved from that fatal political defect by the conception of the dialectic and by the theory of the class struggle . . . he believed in the power of the human will to force the pace of social change, to bring a revolution about in one place rather than another, at one time rather than another. The dialectic is not a determinist philosophy. It is a statement of the general pattern by which men change the world.[6]

The Prerequisites of Revolution. — Marx's theory of social development rests upon the following propositions: (1) in every epoch concerning which history provides trustworthy information, the prevailing methods by which wealth is produced and exchanged constitute the most important conditions of social organization and strongly influence, in particular, political arrangements and ideologies; (2) every social organization, considered as a whole, is subject to ceaseless change and finally develops to a point where its political patterns and other institutions check further growth, with the consequence that such institutions are overthrown in a violent upheaval and are replaced by new ones more in accord with the " social relations of production "; (3) on the other hand, no part of the social organization can ever be set aside as long as it bears an intrinsic relation to the economic substructure, and hence new modes of production and distribution never appear before the economic order has exhausted all its possibilities of growth and expansion within the prevailing framework; (4) all complex social organizations are inevitably stratified, and are therefore pervaded by the struggle of the strata or classes — it is always in the interest of the propertyless to overthrow the old order, whereas the propertied find it to their advantage to uphold it. When the subjugated classes succeed in conquering their former masters the social revolution in its outward form is thereby manifested.

From the foregoing, it is apparent that Marx held that revolutions are inevitable *once their prerequisites have materialized,* but that the latter proviso must be given full weight. A cycle of " want " → " outworn   institution "   unrest → " forcible   repression " → greater unrest → further repression → violent revolution has been going on, said Marx, ever since " the original classless tribal organization, with its communism in land," was disrupted. Moreover, he maintained that the cycle will perpetually recur until the workers become the controllers of society and, by an unprecedented " leap into freedom," all exploitation, oppression, and class struggle forever cease.

Obviously enough, an extensive change in what the denizens of contemporary culture regard as " human nature " will be necessary before the return to the golden age can be effected, but in justice to Marx it must be said that he was fully aware of this difficulty, and at least attempted to indicate the way in which the change would take place, as the following excerpt shows:

For the widespread generation of the communist consciousness, and for the carrying out of the communist revolution, an extensive change in human beings is needed, which can only occur in the course of a practical movement, in the course of a revolution, so that the revolution is not only necessary because the ruling class cannot be overthrown in any other way, but is also necessary because only in a revolution can the uprising class free itself from the old yoke and become capable of founding a new society.[7]

In other words, revolution has the rôle not only of overthrowing the old, but of preparing for the new; the revolutionary process is central in Marx's thinking, and his system cannot be understood until the nature and *modus operandi* of revolution are made clear.

Thus far we have referred to the prerequisites of revolution only in extremely general terms applicable to any historical epoch; let us now see what they must be in the present era of capitalism.

To begin with, the capitalist system of production and distribution must have reached a high state of development and concentration; it must fully have established itself as the thesis of which, in true Hegelian fashion, the proletariat is the antithesis: the factor which effects the dialectic fusion of these polar opposites is the revolutionary process issuing in the ultimate establishment of " a classless society." Because of its dialectic function, therefore, the high development of productive forces promoted by capitalism may be regarded as " one of the civilized sides of capitalism." [8] From the same standpoint it may be said that the capitalist as " personified capital " is " respectable." [9]

Next, it necessarily follows that a powerful class of capitalist magnates is an indispensable adjunct.[10] Further, an indispensable prerequisite of revolution in the capitalist era is the discipline and organization enforced upon the working class by the capitalist mode of production. Trade-unions formed in self-defense, strikes against starvation wages, and other manifestations of working-class organization inevitably accompany the factory system. And, says Marx, " Now and then the workers are victorious, but only for a time. The real fruit of their battles lies, not in the immediate result, but in the ever-expanding union of the workers." [11]

Finally, an intense class-consciousness is essential. The way in which this develops was hinted at in the previous paragraph: capitalism itself inevitably engenders the conditions which make class-consciousness possible. Mark, it does not create class-consciousness automatically; it merely affords it opportunity for growth.

Historical Chance and the Active Element. — And here we come to a point often overlooked by both friends and foes of Marxian theory; such words and phrases as " inevitable," " dialectic necessity," and " natural law " have hypnotized some persons into the belief that human volition plays no part in the rise of class-consciousness and the revolutionary mood. It must be granted that many of Marx's utterances, superficially considered, appear to point in this direction.[12] He seems to posit consciousness as a powerless epiphenomenon, as a fleeting shadow cast by the wheels of an onrushing car. But note the following aphorism:

> Man makes his own history, but he does not make it out of the whole cloth; he does not make it out of conditions chosen by himself, but out of such as he finds close at hand.[13]

This concise utterance, which could be paralleled by others, indicates that Marx recognizes human volition as both a caused and a causal factor in the revolutionary process; it is an indispensable link in the revolutionary chain. This has been strikingly put: " Circumstances may be altered by men " [14] and " revolutions are the locomotives of history." [15]

From Marx's standpoint it may be said with equal warrant that a given revolution is *inevitable* and that it is *volitional*. The pseudo-dilemma vanishes when ultimate and proximate causes are distinguished. It is from the standpoint of its ultimate cause that a revolution is inevitable, and it is from the standpoint of its proximate cause that it is volitional. Human desires undeniably play a vital rôle in history by availing themselves of the right moment for their realization, but the methods of production (or productive forces) provide both the opportunities for and the limiting conditions of such realization.

What does this mean in concrete terms? In terms of personality? Of leadership? Of the part played by chance? The Marxian reply is this:

> . . . it [world history] would be of a very mystical nature if " accidents " played no role. These accidents naturally fall in the general process of development of their own accord and are compensated again by other accidents. But hastening and retarding are very much dependent upon such " accidents," among which the " accident " of the character of the people who stand foremost at the head of the movement also figures.[16]

" The character of the people who stand foremost at the head of the movement " ! Here indeed is the crucial issue, an issue of which Marx was keenly aware, and to which he devoted much intellectual effort, as the statement of no less an authority than Lenin indicates:

> Marx, during all his life, alongside of theoretical work, gave unremitting attention to the tactical problems of the class struggle of the proletariat. An immense amount of material bearing upon this is contained in all the works of Marx and in the four volumes of his correspondence with Engels, published in 1913. This material is still far from having been collected, organized, studied, and elaborated.[17]

Except, we might add, in so far as it was concentrated and endowed with new energy in the mind of Lenin himself. At this point, however, it is necessary that we ourselves attempt to collect and organize Marx's discussions of tactics.

The Art of Insurrection and the Bourgeoisie. — A good point of departure would seem to be Marx's exhortations on the art of insurrection:

> . . . Firstly, never play with insurrection unless you are fully prepared to face the consequences of your play. Insurrection is a calculus with very indefinite magnitudes, the value of which may change every day; the forces opposed to you have all the advantage of organization, discipline, and habitual authority; unless you bring strong odds against them you are defeated and ruined. Secondly, the insurrectionary career once entered upon, act with the greatest determination, and on the offensive. The defensive is the death of every armed rising; it is lost before it measures itself with its enemies. Surprise your antagonists while their forces are scattering, prepare new successes, however small, but daily; keep up the moral ascendency which the first successful rising has given to you; rally those vacillating elements to your side which always follow the strongest impulse, and which always look out for the safer side; force your enemies to a retreat before they can collect their strength against you; in the words of Danton, the greatest master of revolutionary policy yet known, *de l'audace, de l'audace, encore de l'audace!* [18]

These resounding words were written shortly after the reaction that followed the revolution of 1848. In his earlier writings Marx had not shown himself keenly aware of the danger of the counterstroke that seems to follow virtually every revolution. But after '48, he lost no opportunity of giving warning.[19] The Paris Commune (1870) provided an even more sharply enforced lesson. It will be recalled that the Commune arose during the Franco-Prussian War when, after the defeats at Sedan and elsewhere, the Second Empire under Napoleon III was overthrown and the new republican government of Thiers seated in Versailles had not yet succeeded in establishing itself. Inasmuch as most of the Paris bourgeoisie had fled before the city was besieged, the workers had practically everything to·themselves, particularly because the armed force of Paris, the National Guard, was itself overwhelmingly proletarian. Although the Versailles government offered opposition, the Paris Commune was proclaimed after the general municipal election of March 26, and was ushered in without bloodshed. The forces of the Versailles government, although frustrated in their attempt to control the election, were permitted to remain intact.[20] The Communards did not seem to realize the

vital part played by force. Instead of preparing to meet the attacks of their opponents by determined and disciplined resistance,
they wasted precious time in ideological squabbles and in jockey-
ing for petty privileges. In the meantime, the astute leaders of
the bourgeois counter-revolution were busy preparing for action,
and their wisdom was demonstrated after a stubborn struggle,
in which the Communards were disastrously defeated and the
counter-revolutionary desire for revenge abundantly gratified.

If the lesson of 1848 was taken to heart, how much more that
of 1870! In conjunction, the two catastrophes served to render
explicit the meaning latent in these words of the famous *Manifesto:*

> Though not in substance, yet in form, the struggle of the proletariat
> with the bourgeoisie is at first a national struggle. The proletariat of each
> country must, of course, first of all settle matters with its own bour-
> geoisie.[21]

So much for the national aspects of revolution. Inasmuch as
the "workingmen have no country," the international aspects
offer little difficulty. When in any country the proletariat acquires
political supremacy, rises to be the leading class of the nation, it
thereby constitutes itself the nation. As a consequence, national
barriers vanish (potentially or actually) before the proletarian
onset. This is the reason that "the Communists everywhere support every revolutionary movement against the existing social and
political order of things." [22] The compelling necessity of " settling " with the bourgeoisie of one's " own " nation ineluctably
leads to settling with the bourgeoisie the world over.

Marx's Advocacy of Violent Revolution. — Even if we were
to take into account only the statements already quoted, it is quite
apparent that Marx had but one idea in mind when he spoke of
" settling " with the bourgeoisie; physical force was in his mind
the *ultima ratio,* the final arbiter. In view of the frequency with
which the assertion that Marx sanctioned the use of force is con-
tested, however, it seems advisable to adduce further evidence.
Let us begin with the famous passage from the *Manifesto:*

> The Communists disdain to conceal their views and aims. They openly
> declare that their ends can be attained only by the forcible overthrow
> of all existing social conditions. Let the ruling classes tremble at a Com-
> munist revolution. The proletarians have nothing to lose but their chains.
> They have a world to win.[23]

Further, in criticizing the Gotha Program in 1875, Marx vigorously stated the claims of the revolutionary method, and de-

nounced peaceful demands such as universal suffrage and direct legislation as " a mere echo of the middle-class People's Party." [24] Four years later, when referring to the Zürich Social Democrats, he contended that Wilhelm Liebknecht, who admitted avowed pacifists to the party, thereby became an active agent in its demoralization, and on this and other grounds attacked the compromise tendencies of the Zürich group with great severity.

In other words, Marx was as fiery a combatant in his old age as he was in his younger days, although on at least one occasion he made a grudging admission that a peaceful overturn of the social order might be possible.[25] For every such reluctant and half-hearted concession to the reformist wing of the party, however, he made at least ten vigorous denunciations of reformism, so that there can be no doubt as to the quarter in which his real convictions lay.

Engels a Proponent of Force. — Moreover, the faithful Engels was just as ardent an advocate of forcible measures as was Marx. In support of this contention let us again follow a chronological sequence. First comes a drastic utterance written in 1847 [26] in which he attempts to show that violent revolution is necessary, in spite of intimations that peaceful procedure, if it were possible, would be more desirable. As between an improbable ideal and a revolutionary necessity, however, Engels did not hesitate for a moment; he joined Marx in championing violent revolution both in the first (1848) edition of the *Manifesto* and in the preface to the new German edition written in 1872. There can be little doubt that his occasional concessions [27] to the reformists were at the most merely tactical. Chang has shown conclusively that Engels time and again advocated violent methods up to the very year of his death, and that the German Social Democrats with Revisionist tendencies have been guilty of falsifying, by striking out inconvenient passages, the whole tenor of Engels's later writings. In the light of such evidence, there can therefore be little doubt that Marx and Engels remained consistent advocates of violent revolution to the very last stages of their career. This point established, let us turn to specific phases of the doctrine.

Conflict and Parliamentarism. — One of the most interesting of these phases is Marx's idea of the way in which force was to be applied. Did he envisage it as the more or less decorous threat of force implied in the sheathed saber of the proletarian gendarme, or did he anticipate a chaotic clash akin to the Jacobin rushes of the first French Revolution and the barricade carnage of its successors? There can be little doubt that he predicted the

latter alternative. For, as he queries: " Would it . . . be a matter for astonishment if a society, based upon the *antagonism* of
classes, should lead ultimately to a brutal *conflict,* to a hand-to-
hand struggle as its final dénouement?" This seems forthright
enough, but he concludes with words still more drastic: " On the
eve of every general reconstruction of society, the last word of
social science will ever be: — ' *Le combat ou la mort; la lutte
sanguinaire ou le néant. C'est ainsi que la question est invincible-
ment posée.*' " This quotation was taken from George Sand and
in English it runs thus: " Combat or death; sanguinary struggle
or extinction — this is the form of the unavoidable dilemma." [28]

With all of Marx's stress on the likelihood, or rather necessity,
of spontaneous, chaotic, man-to-man struggle, however, he had
very definite ideas as to the most fruitful points of attack. That is
to say, he foresaw that violence would be applied in unpredictable
ways, but he also had sharply defined convictions about the points
where it should be applied as part of a carefully worked-out
policy. This policy was the *shattering* of the machinery of the
state.[29] It can therefore occasion small wonder when we find Marx
rejecting parliamentarism, appeal to the courts, and all other attempts to utilize the existing state machinery in the workers' interests.[30] He also rejected such legalistic and reformist measures
as universal suffrage,[31] factory legislation,[32] and so on. To be
sure, he gives them his approval so long, and only so long, as they
are *not* viewed as substitutes for revolution by force but merely
as auxiliary means for the overthrow of the bourgeois state; that
is to say, such measures are to be utilized for destructive purposes
only. This means that the hope of the " petty bourgeois " for a
peaceful realization of his " doctrinaire socialism " is destined to
be shattered on the unyielding rock of " genuinely revolutionary
socialism." [33] The relations of the proletariat with other groups
during the revolution must be uncompromisingly hostile; where
there is no common interest, there can be no common cause (although, as we shall see later, there may be *joint* attack on
enemies).

The Varieties of Revolution. — The chief reason for the hostility, latent or active, of the proletariat toward other revolutionary groups such as the bourgeoisie is the fact that revolutions are
of more than one kind. There are bourgeois revolutions, and
there are communist revolutions, and these differ widely in their
ultimate bearings. In spite of these points of variance, however,
there may be occasion for " joint attack on enemies," as was
noted above. When a class deriving its power from feudal rela-

tions is still dominant, for example, both bourgeoisie and proletariat may march against the oppressor,[34] and when victory
is gained, the proletariat must exploit the joint victory on *its own
account alone;* if need be, the revolution is to be prolonged and
the bourgeois democrats are to be pushed to extremes far beyond
the goals they regard as desirable.[35] Obviously the bourgeois
democrats will not long endure the terrific pressure thus applied.
Sooner or later the transitory alliance will be dissolved and class
warfare will begin afresh on a new plane, as Marx clearly saw:

> But it is the fate of all revolutions that this union of different classes,
> which in some degree is always the necessary condition of any revolution,
> cannot subsist long. No sooner is the victory gained . . . than the victors
> become divided among themselves into different camps, and turn their
> weapons against each other. It is this rapid and passionate development
> of class antagonism which, in old and complicated social organisms, makes
> a revolution such a powerful agent of social and political progress; it is
> this incessantly quick upshooting of new parties succeeding each other
> in power, which during those violent commotions makes a nation pass in
> five years over more ground than it would have done in a century under
> ordinary circumstances.[36]

Such tremendously accelerated development gave Marx some
warrant for believing that in the Germany of his day the interval
between revolutions might be greatly reduced. As he put it,
" After the fall of the reactionary classes . . . the fight against
the bourgeoisie itself may *immediately* begin." [37] In other words,
bourgeois revolutions may be but preludes to proletarian revolutions. In his address to the League of Communists in 1850, Marx
envisaged this probability, and outlined the tactics to be followed
with such clarity that the Russian Bolshevists must have profited
greatly by his prophetic advice.[38]

Party Organization. — We have now blocked in the rough outlines of Marx's revolutionary method, but in order to make the
picture more sharp, we must consider other tactics and measures
that contribute to the same revolutionary end.

One of the most important of these is the organization of the
proletariat into a political body: " The immediate aim of the
Communists is the same as that of all the other proletarian parties; formation of the proletariat into a class, overthrow of the
bourgeois supremacy, conquest of political power by the proletariat." [39] Inasmuch as the proletariat is already a class, it is
evident that Marx means the formation of a class-conscious party.
Textual exegesis is not necessary to establish this point; the

change in tactics of the International when under Marx's control (1862) shows the goal he had in view.[40]

As was the case with virtually all his tactical proposals, this emphasis on political organization rooted deep in Marx's basic theory. In the early struggle against Proudhon, he had proclaimed that " *Social evolutions* will cease to be *political revolutions* " only when " there will be no longer classes or class antagonism." [41]

International Solidarity. — As an inevitable corollary of the fundamental importance attributed to the political struggle conducted by the proletarian party, there appears the Marxian emphasis on international solidarity. Patriotism in the nationalistic sense of the term was granted no positive function in Marx's scheme of things.[42] This might lead one to the conclusion that Marx was devoid of historical sense, that he failed to recognize the important economic, political, and historical rôle of the national state. This is only partly true; even in the *Manifesto* he traced the steps by which the bourgeoisie created the national state, and mocked at the young enthusiasts who thought they could brush aside the nation as an obsolete prejudice. Nevertheless, later developments showed that he had considerably underestimated the unifying force of national feeling; his assumption that economic dividing lines would prove more effective than national boundaries has not yet been justified by the event. But after all, we are here concerned with Marx's tactics as such, not with the empirical adequacy of those tactics, and we may therefore proceed further in our exposition.

An exceedingly important phase of Marx's emphasis on international solidarity is its utter remoteness from the liberal or democratic ideal of the brotherhood of man; in fact, he found fault with the original Gotha Program because " it borrowed from middle-class Leagues of Peace and Freedom the phrase of the international brotherhood of peoples, whereas it was necessary to promote the international combination of the working classes in a common struggle against the ruling classes and their Governments." [43] Marx had no confidence in the international pacifism of the bourgeoisie, for he believed that such pacifism was the fruit of fear — fear that if the bourgeois weakened themselves by international strife they would be unable to resist their proletarian antagonists. Proof of this was afforded Marx by the Paris Commune; as he put it, " the national governments are one as against the proletariat." [44]

" Class culture," the loss of which the bourgeois lament, is for the enormous majority a mere training to act as a machine.[45] Engels says that morality is "class morality,"[46] that "the good of the whole society" is the good of the ruling class and that the "exploitation of one class by another" is the basis of civilization.[47] Religion and order are "vital conditions"[48] of bourgeois rule. All the "brave words" about freedom in general "have a meaning, if any, only in contrast with restricted buying and selling." Individuality applies only to capital in bourgeois society.[49] Equality is bourgeois equality.[50] For the proletariat equal right is only the right to sell labor for the bare means of subsistence.[51] The right to work is a "contradiction, a miserable pious wish."[52] This is all implicit in the famed *Manifesto,* where we learn that since "the Communist revolution is the most radical rupture with traditional property-relations . . . no wonder that its development involves the most radical rupture with traditional ideas."

Marx's Theory of the State. — Implicit in this relentless attack on abstractions and their associated reforms is a theory of the nature of that basic political organization called the state. We have now reached a point where we can consider Marx's explicit treatment of this institution. In the *Manifesto*[53] he states that "political power, properly so-called, is merely the organized power of one class for oppressing another," and in *Capital* he says that "the State power is the concentrated and organized force [*Gewalt* — physical force] of society."[54] The capitalist state is merely a specific form of an institution that has had a long and checkered history:

> At the same pace at which the progress of modern industry developed, widened, intensified, the class-antagonism between capital and labor, the State power assumed more and more the character of national power of capital over labor, of a public force organized for social enslavement, of an engine of class despotism.[55]

From these definitions it is plain that Marx did not long imitate Hegel in deifying the state; following Stein, he soon came to regard it as a mere institution of society. His breach with Hegelian conceptions became evident in his *Vorwärts* controversy with Ruge in 1844, where he renounced state socialism and explicitly declared the state to be "an institution of society."[56] — indeed, to be subordinate to society. This may seem an academic question, but it nevertheless has proved profoundly important in the actual course of events, for from it has developed the idea of the dictatorship of the proletariat.

The corollary to the effect that the state is always a class state is in sharp conflict with the ideology of nineteenth-century bourgeois democracy, with its fervent faith in universal suffrage and parliamentary government — it challenges the belief that as democracy becomes more pure the state loses its oppressive character. Far from allowing that bourgeois democracy is in any way the rule of the people as a whole, Marx maintains that the more apparently pure the democratic forms of government are, the more naked is the class rule of the bourgeoisie.[57] Far from admitting that one of the state functions is the managing of " the common interests of society," both Marx and Engels believed this idea absurd and impossible.[58]

In the cases so far considered a certain Machiavellian self-knowledge is attributed to the proponent of democracy; he is supposed to know that his " ideals " are merely smoke-screens for his class interests. Manifestly such sophistication is relatively rare; most bourgeois democrats fondly imagine themselves to be working for the good of all.[59] But whether sophisticated or naïve, the democrat is always a representative of a class, and to Marx at least one of the greatest of all fallacies was the belief that democracy could ever be anything but class rule. The democratic state is still a class state.

The Dictatorship of the Proletariat. — This doctrine of the nature of the state undoubtedly played a large part in shaping the doctrine of the dictatorship of the proletariat, and this latter is of literally tremendous significance in the Marxian tactics. Unless the dictatorship of the proletariat is understood in its remotest theoretical implications, no real comprehension of its practical bearings can be achieved. For this reason, it seems well to discuss the idea of dictatorship in accordance with its chronological development, for its importance warrants the additional space necessary.

The term " dictatorship of the proletariat " as such does not appear in the *Manifesto,* but in that document there is frequent reference to raising " the proletariat to the position of ruling class," to " the state, i.e., to the proletariat organized as the ruling class," and most striking of all, the injunction that the proletariat wrest *all* capital from the bourgeoisie [60] (an injunction that cannot but remind one of the stifling pressure intermittently but none the less fiercely applied to private enterprise by the Soviets).

In spite of these phrases, however, it must be admitted that the idea still remains exceedingly abstract; it was not until the French experience of the revolutionary years after 1848 that

Marx succeeded in giving a more concrete meaning to the idea of the dictatorship of the proletariat. Curiously enough, this concrete meaning was achieved in immediate conjunction with his first recorded use of the term itself; in commenting on the June collapse of the 1848 French revolution, Marx says:

> The Paris proletariat was provoked and lured into the June insurrection. . . . The proletariat itself did not feel the immediate need for the forcible overthrow of the bourgeoisie. . . . The *Moniteur* declared plainly enough that the time was passed when the republic could be induced to pay honour to the illusions of the workers; and it needed the June defeat to convince them of the truth that it was Utopian to expect even the slightest improvement of their conditions within bourgeois society. . . . In the place of the reform demands . . . the bold battle cry was heard: *Overthrow of the bourgeoisie! Dictatorship of the proletariat!* [61]

For a long time after the French revolutionary events of 1848–1851, relatively little occurred that would cause Marx to re-emphasize what he had already so forcefully stated. Not until the Paris Commune came into view, with its sanguinary civil warfare and actual dictatorship of the proletariat, did Marx again place himself on record. First of all, he approved the use of force during the Paris Commune.[62] Second, the experience of the Commune led him to emphasize afresh the idea of destruction of the bourgeois state machinery. In his work on the Commune (written in 1871), he remarks, " the working class cannot simply lay hold of the ready-made State machinery and wield it for its own purpose." [63] From the context it is quite plain that Marx meant that it must *destroy* the old machine and construct one of its own. This program of shattering and building afresh is of course directed to the end of effective proletarian dictatorship, which in its turn is a means to the attainment of the final communist commonwealth in which there is to be neither oppressor nor oppressed, bourgeois nor proletarian.

But let us return to the proximate. In his *Criticism of the Gotha Program* (1875), Marx hints at the measures to be followed under proletarian dictatorship, and some idea of the nature of the *transitional* state emerges:

> The means of production will gradually be socialised, production will be placed on a co-operative basis, education will be combined with productive work, in order to transform the members of society into producers. So long as the transition period lasts the Communist maxim, " From each according to his capacity, to each according to his needs,"

cannot become operative. For this period is in every respect — economic, social and intellectual — still tainted with the marks of the old society, and " rights cannot transcend the economic structure of society, and the cultural development which it determines." [64]

In the third edition of the *Manifesto* (1883) there are a number of concrete suggestions that make still more clear the implications of a real rule of the workers:

For the most advanced countries the following measures might come into very general application:

1. Expropriation of landed property, and application of Rent to State expenditure.

2. Heavy progressive taxation.

3. Abolition of inheritance.

4. Confiscation of the property of all emigrants and rebels.

5. Centralisation of credit in the hands of the State by means of a National Bank with State capital and exclusive monopoly.

6. Centralisation of means of transport in the hands of the State.

7. Increase of national factories, instruments of production, and reclamation and improvement of land according to a common plan.

8. Compulsory obligation of labour upon all; establishment of industrial armies, especially for Agriculture.

9. Joint prosecution of Agriculture and Manufacture, aiming at the gradual removal of the distinction of town and country.

10. Public and gratuitous education for all children; abolition of children's labour in factories in its present form; union of education with material production.[65]

Nowhere in the writings of either Marx or Engels is to be found a retraction of any of these principles. They did add to the list, however, the expropriation of the whole means of production for the benefit of the state, and insisted upon this measure as indispensable.

The Withering Away of the State. — So fervent was Marx's advocacy of the dictatorship of the proletariat that we are in grave danger of losing sight of the fact that he regarded it as essentially transitional. In spite of the fact that this proletarian state is a *Gemeinwesen*, a commonwealth,[66] it is not the highest phase of communism, for in this highest phase all the vestiges of the state wither away. This theory is hinted at but not explicitly stated in the *Manifesto*.[67] Only about four years after its publication, however, Marx wrote a letter to a friend in which the doctrine latent in that document was brought out in sharp relief:

As far as I am concerned, the honor does not belong to me for either having discovered the existence of classes in present society or of the struggle between the classes. Bourgeois historians a long time before me expounded the historical development of this class war and the bourgeois economists the economical structure of classes. What I did, was to prove the following: (1) That the existence of classes is connected only with certain historical struggles which are characteristic of the development of production. (2) That class war indispensably leads to the dictatorship of the proletariat. (3) That this dictatorship is only a transition to the destruction of any classes and to society without classes. . . .[68]

This third stage has since come to be known as the " withering away of the State," a vivid phrase which Marx himself did not use — it occurs first in the writings of Engels.[69] But after all, the phrase is not the most important thing; the essential idea is to be found in the writings of Marx, as the evidence we have already adduced demonstrates, and as the following excerpt from the *Critique of the Gotha Program* (five years prior to Engels's phrase) conclusively proves:

In the highest phase of Communist society, after the disappearance of the enslavement of man caused by his subjection to the principle of division of labor; when, together with this, the opposition between brain and manual work will have disappeared; when labor will have ceased to be a mere means of supporting life and will itself have become one of the first necessities of life; when with the all-round development of the individual, the productive forces, too, will have grown to maturity, and all the forces of social wealth will be pouring an uninterrupted torrent — only then will it be possible wholly to pass beyond the narrow horizon of bourgeois laws, and only then will society be able to inscribe on its banner: " From each according to his ability; to each according to his needs." [70]

In justice to Engels, however, it must be said that he furnished the first detailed and connected discussion of the process by which Communists believe the withering away of the state will take place. Witness the following:

The proletariat seizes political power and turns the means of production into State property.

But in doing this, it abolishes itself as proletariat, abolishes all class distinctions and class antagonisms, abolishes also the State as State. Society thus far, based upon class antagonisms, had need of the State. . . . When at last it (the State) becomes the real representative of the whole society, it renders itself unnecessary. As soon as there is no longer any social class to be held in subjection, as soon as class rule, and the individual struggle for existence based upon our present anarchy in production, with the collisions and excesses arising from these, are removed, nothing more remains to be repressed, and a special repressive force, a State, is no longer necessary. The first act by virtue of which the State really constitutes itself the representative of the whole of society — this is, at the same time, its last independent act as a State. State interference in social relations becomes, in one domain after another, superfluous, and then withers away of itself. . . .[71]

And again, it is Engels who has furnished what is perhaps the classic statement on the subject:

When organizing production anew on the basis of a free and equal association of the producers, Society will banish the whole State machine to a place which will then be the most proper one for it — to the museum of antiquities side by side with the spinning-wheel and the bronze axe.[72]

From these and similar utterances it is clear that Marxian theory incorporates the notion of a double golden age — one before the " primitive classless society " was disrupted by private property and exploitation, and another when present-day class society and its accompanying state shall have passed into the discard. It is also interesting to note that the idea of the " withering away of the state " makes the final goal of Marxian social development the same as that cherished by the philosophical anarchists: namely, a society without coercive institutions of any kind. (Needless to say, here as elsewhere we are not setting forth those phases of Marxian doctrine which we regard as valid; our method is simply that of straightforward exposition and not of critical evaluation, either positive or negative.)

The English Fabians and the Growth of Revisionist Socialism. — In spite of the mass of plausible and persuasive theory which we have hastily surveyed in the foregoing pages, and in spite of the success of Marxian socialism in attracting a following sufficient to make it a social movement of the greatest importance, it nevertheless possessed certain theoretical difficulties, which Marxian scholars could explain to at least their own satisfaction, but which gave enemies a vulnerable point of attack and embarrassed some of its less ardent supporters. These weaknesses (real or illusory) were chiefly the dogma of economic determinism as developed by " orthodox " Marxians (in a way Marx himself did not sanction), the labor theory of value and the deductions from it, and the refusal of some stiff-necked Marxians to " co-operate " with existing governments in securing remedial legislation for the proletariat.

The consequences of the resulting defections from simon-pure

Marxism first became apparent in the formation of the Fabian society in England. These English radicals repudiated revolutionary socialism and strove to make socialism " an evolutionary rather than a revolutionary movement." [73]

Although the Fabians originated many of the tenets of " opportunism," the spread of this Marxian heresy was primarily due to the work of Eduard Bernstein (1850–1931). Under his leadership so-called Revisionism came into being. He had lived in England during the period when the anti-socialist laws of Bismarck were in effect in Germany, and was converted to the ideas of the Fabians. As the result of his *Evolutionary Socialism,* he did a great deal to transform German socialism from a proletarian party of revolution into a party of social reform which could attract the support of the " liberal " element.[74]

The general history of socialism after the death of Marx and Engels has been much like that of German socialism: Marxism has served as the entering wedge of propaganda, and the growth of the movement has led to the domination of Revisionism. Only in Russia did the Marxians remain in the majority.

The Expansion of State Socialism. — Closely related to the principles and program of Revisionism is so-called state socialism. The same general program of remedial legislation is followed by both, although their final aim is quite different. The Revisionist hopes for an ultimate proletarian state just as does the Marxist, whereas the state socialist hopes to retain the capitalistic system while at the same time making concessions to the laboring classes.

State socialism received considerable impulse from Lassalle, Rodbertus, and Dupont-White. Moreover, it drew support from professorial champions of social reform within the capitalistic state, the so-called " Socialists of the Chair," such as Schäffle, Wagner, and Schmoller in Germany; Bouglé and Gide in France; the Webbs, Hobson, and Hobhouse in England; and Small, Patten, and Fetter in the United States.

State socialism in actual legislative achievement made the greatest progress in Germany, where an elaborate program of social legislation in the interests of the laboring classes, and also a great deal of direct governmental and municipal ownership, were instituted. Austria followed the example of Germany to a considerable extent in this movement. France made extensive progress in the direction of state socialism in the latter half of the period of the Third Republic, and after 1900 much remedial legislation was also passed in Italy. The home of economic liberalism, England, was the scene of a rapid rise of state socialism under the leadership of David Lloyd George and others. In the United States, state socialism made scant progress until the administration of Wilson, after which time change in this direction was marked. Hand in hand with this secular collectivization went a good deal of Christian socialism which carried forward the religious and ethical demand for more equitable distribution of economic goods already noted in the previous chapter.

The Newer Anarchisms. — Of the two great leaders of modern anarchism, Michael Bakunin (1814–1876), the great opponent of Marx in the First International, was the revolutionary propagandist and terrorist. To him the state appeared as a great machine for oppressing human beings, and he devoted his life to the task of bombing it off the earth. Once the state was destroyed, according to Bakunin, the task of building a new world on anarchistic principles could safely be left to posterity. Peter Kropotkin (1842–1921) was the chief systematic and constructive writer of modern philosophic anarchism. For him the noncoercive community, without private property, functioning perfectly through the operation of the principle of mutual aid, was the supreme goal of human effort. To support his position he made a historical study — *Mutual Aid a Factor in Evolution* — of the beneficent rôle of coöperation from the earliest animal societies to his own time.

The economic program of the anarchists is not greatly different from that of the socialists, so far as the ultimate fate of private property is concerned, but their political ideals are diametrically opposed. The socialist proposes a vast increase in state activity, whereas the anarchist desires the complete extinction of political authority in order that voluntary coöperation may have a free hand in re-creating human nature. The coöperative movement, of a more moderate character than anarchism, has gained wide support and has achieved remarkable results, especially in some of the smaller agrarian states of Europe.[75] It was powerfully aided by early utopian and Christian socialism.

Syndicalism and the Radical Labor Movement. — The early part of the nineteenth century saw the repeal of laws against combination and criminal conspiracy in Great Britain and elsewhere, and the modern labor movement emerged. There can be little doubt that this did a great deal to advance the material interests of the laboring classes, but in spite of this, labor unionism as such was bound to be unsatisfactory to those who did not believe in merely alleviating the misery of the proletariat, but who hoped to overthrow the whole capitalistic system. As a consequence there developed a tendency to abandon conventional labor unionism and go over to the more radical labor movement which found its greatest strength in syndicalism. This originated in France in the '80's and '90's of the last century, and found in Sorel, with his *Reflections on Violence,* its most significant ideologist.

The syndicalists eschew any attempt to come to favorable terms with their employers in any permanent settlement. They aim frankly and openly at conducting a class war by the method of " direct action," the two chief types of which are sabotage and the general strike. The former is regarded as a temporary instrument to be used until the general strike finally drives the capitalists from the field. This strike is not thought of as a mere suspension of labor to improve local conditions, but as a general " cessation of work, which would place the country in the rigor of death, whose terrible and incalculable consequences would force the government to capitulate at once." If the syndicalists should be successful in destroying the capitalistic order they would institute a communistic economic society and a governmental organization based on the industrial system. They believe in a local or communal government, and their state is a glorified trade-union whose activities are confined to economic functions; their nation is simply a collection of federated communal trade societies. In other words, they would take government out the front door of the state and bring it in by the back door of industrial regimentation.

Beginning about 1910 there was an effort to arrive at a compromise between socialism and syndicalism. This is known as guild socialism, which in its essence is a system of economic decentralization coupled with the revival of industrial associations somewhat like the medieval guilds. To many, guild socialism seems the most promising of modern reform policies because it is a clever synthesis of some of the most attractive radical programs. Others deny the possibility of any real separation of political and industrial associations such as is necessarily involved. Although the popularity of the doctrine has considerably waned in recent years — largely because some of its features have been adopted by Mussolini and Hitler — it still attracts many persons repelled by the harshness of revolutionary socialism or undiluted syndicalism. Moreover, it embodies a certain ethical and Romantic appeal.

A great deal more might be said about this and the other

movements " that either were carried in the wake of Marxian doctrine, or struck out on similar courses, or endeavored to make
head against it, but that were always oriented with regard to it
in some way," but we should then be carried even further out
of our historical and theoretical frame of reference than we
have already been. More extended consideration, in other words,
belongs in a more specialized book. We have stepped outside
long enough to feel the buffeting of " the winds of doctrine ";
it is now time that we return.

Marx's Relation to Evolutionary Thinkers. — In the next
chapter we shall deal with the early advocates of the theories
of cosmic and organismic evolution, and inasmuch as some writers
regard Marx's idea of the struggle of the classes as a piece of
the same cloth from which the evolutionary idea of the struggle
for existence and the survival of the fittest was cut, it may be
well to show why he has been dealt with here instead of A (fter)
D (arwin). To quote again from Gray:

A generalised theory of the process of social development cannot be
found in Marx's writings. This is partly because of the absence in his
time of ethnological and anthropological studies that would have necessitated a longer backward view, and partly owing to the lack of any
social science with claims to explain exhaustively the nature of man's
social behavior, deriving from a basis of experimental knowledge pre-
dictions that might give a more accurate picture of the social future. It
would also be true to say that Marx, no more than Hegel, shared the modern sceptical temper of science, with its perspective of eons of time, man
being regarded as only in the beginning of his journey. The full repercus-
sions of the Copernican revolution have been felt only in very recent years
among other than physical thinkers. Marx was still anthropomorphic
enough to believe that the millennium lay, not, indeed, in the present of
the Prussian State, where Hegel placed it, but just round the corner in
the communist society of tomorrow. There is abundant evidence that
he held the view, common to the Rationalist perfectionists of the previous century and the anarchists of his own, that under communism not
only would classes and divisions of economic power entirely disappear,
but there would be no more scarcity or inequality or injustice in the
world. In this connection his thought was teleological, and when he
spoke of evolution he meant development (*Entwicklung*) to a goal already known or decided in advance to be desirable, not a verifiable and
potentially modifiable generalisation of what has occurred under certain
conditions, would hold in the future only under the same conditions, and
had not, by itself, any ethical status at all.[76]

Summary of the Chapter. — The setting for the revolutionary
socialism of Marx and Engels was briefly sketched in the discus-

sion of traditional socialism in the preceding chapter. Not until the time of Marx and Engels, however, was socialist doctrine so formulated as to constitute a working theory which appealed to and dominated vast numbers of followers. In the analysis of the part played by material culture in historical development, in the further formulation of the " internal conflict " theory of the state, and in the devastating criticism of the industrialism of the first half of the nineteenth century, Marx and Engels (particularly Marx) made theoretical statements of lasting influence.

Marx's emphasis on the revolutionary process as a fundamental mode and method of social development was marked by a considerable degree of originality. He regarded the collapse of capitalism as inevitable, at the same time recognizing that the proletarian revolution could not dispense with the element of human volition. The revolutionary process was further characterized, in his thought, by both international " inter-classism " and intranational class conflict issuing in violence; parliamentary reform was eschewed except for propaganda purposes. The most important weapon in the revolutionary arsenal was held to be the organization of the proletariat into a class-conscious body.

The theory of the state espoused by revolutionary socialism is in sharp contrast with that underlying the " bourgeois revolutions " and nineteenth-century parliamentary democracy: Marx regarded it as the organized power of a class, and therefore declared the state to be a " *class* state." Out of this theory grew his idea of the dictatorship of the proletariat during the phase transitional to what was believed to be " the highest phase of Communist society," a condition in which the state has " withered away," and hence is identical with the society desired by the philosophical anarchists.

Revolutionary socialism never made much headway in England; the Fabians bent every effort to make socialism an " evolutionary " movement there — perhaps because of the fact that the great philosopher of cosmic evolution, Herbert Spencer, and the great empirical exponent of organismic evolution, Charles Darwin, were Englishmen and gained their first audience in that country. Through Bernstein, who was markedly influenced by the Fabians, Revisionism transformed the German Social Democratic organization into a reform party, a development paralleled in many other countries. Revolutionary socialism has without doubt played its greatest rôle in Russia.

State socialism, a program whereby the capitalistic system is retained, with some modifications in favor of labor, had already taken form in the governmental and economic structure of pre-War Germany, France, England, Italy, and, in considerably lesser degree, the United States. The post-War world has seen a greatly accelerated growth of state socialism, even in those countries previously most resistant — notably in the United States.

The later anarchist movement incorporated an economic program approximating that of the revolutionary socialists, but their political ideals were at opposite poles. Bakunin for the terrorists and Kropotkin for the philosophical anarchists were the best-known nineteenth-century representatives.

Syndicalism, now or until recently quite strong in France, Belgium, Italy, and other Romance countries, represents the radical movement most committed to violent " direct action " which has developed since the emergence of Marxian socialism (with which it has little in common). Guild socialism resulted from the attempt to reconcile socialism and syndicalism; its cardinal feature is the separation of economic and political powers in government, and it is precisely this feature which renders its effectiveness doubtful. Moreover, the fact that Fascism and Naziïsm have both erected façades with guild socialist or syndicalist motifs has diminished the popularity of these latter doctrines among left-wing ideologists.

It now seems necessary again to indicate, somewhat more clearly if only in a negative way, the relation of the revolutionary socialism of Marx to the philosophy of evolution, the theme of the first part of the next chapter. In the following quotation, which gives us the means to " indicate somewhat more clearly," mention is made of idealist moral philosophy and of naturalism, but nothing is further from our present purpose than to contrast them to the derogation of either; in so far as they are *both* philosophies of life and action, it is not our province as *sociologists* to criticize them:

> . . . it must be borne in mind that Marx, like Hegel, was satisfied, as a philosopher of history, with one great dialectical process whose end was in sight; it was never intended to be a process outgrowing into an endless future. For this reason, if no other, it is inaccurate to compare Marx with Spencer and Darwin as a pioneer in the field of historical evolution. It was not primarily as a naturalist that Marx studied history. It was as an idealist moral philosopher.[77]

The originator of the greater part of the present chapter, Frances Bennett Becker, is now engaged in a study of Marxism-Leninism in conjunction with Howard Becker and Daniel Kubát. The results of this study, well along toward completion, confirm her 1938 presentation in all but trivial details.

CHAPTER XVIII

Positivism Merges with Evolutionary Philosophy: Spencer and the Organismic School

SPENCER'S LIFE AND WORKS. — Comte's work in the field of sociology was taken up and greatly amplified by the philosopher who, better than anyone else, summed up the main currents of nineteenth-century thought — Herbert Spencer (1820–1903). This does not mean that Spencer regarded Comte as his scientific precursor. In fact, quite the opposite was the case, for Spencer claimed to have published his first sociological treatise, *Social Statics,* before he had any detailed knowledge of Comte's ideas, and it seems that in many respects the similarity between the two writers was due to their participation in the same culture base. After all, the calculus is not the only example of duplicate invention. However, it is hard to agree entirely with Spencer in his attempt to prove his complete independence of Comte and his fundamental divergence from the views of the latter,[1] although the verdict of Michel is probably too severe: " *Il ne suit pas que les Principes de Sociologie puissent être sincèrement regardés comme un livre original, par quiconque a lu les Opuscules* [i.e., early essays] *de Comte. Toutes les idées directrices, et jusqu'à la méthode de Spencer se trouvent dans les Opuscules. Comte a tracé les cadres: Spencer n'a fait que les remplir."* [2]

Of feeble health as a child, Spencer was taught at home; he never received any public education, thus having at least one point in common with his famous contemporary, John Stuart Mill. His failure to accept a university career doubtless tended to contribute strongly to the failure of academic circles in England to take a lively interest in his teachings, and his lack of a socialized existence in early life certainly had not a little to do with his extreme individualistic tendencies as an adult. Aside from these more strictly personal elements, Spencer's non-conformist inheritance from his family, and his reaction against the radical revolutionary doctrines of his youth, are matters which must be taken into consideration in attempting to get an insight into the sources of his philosophic tendencies and an understanding of his intellectual predispositions.[3]

Spencer early acquired a taste for mechanics, and in 1837 he became chief engineer of the London and Birmingham railroad. He resigned from this position in 1848 to become sub-editor of the *Economist,* and during the four years that he served in this capacity he produced (1850) his first important contribution to sociology, *Social Statics.*[4] During the next eight years he developed the basic tenets of his system of synthetic philosophy and published them in the *First Principles* in 1862. No one can understand Spencer's philosophy if he has not read this work, any more than one can appreciate Comte's fundamental ideas without reading his early essays. In this volume Spencer disposed of theology by relegating its field of study to the realm of the ultimately unknowable; outlined his theory of universal evolution; and indicated the main lines of its application to the totality of human knowledge. He did not, as has frequently been asserted, attempt to apply the theories of Darwin to a restatement of science and philosophy, but rather applied to this field his own theory of evolution, which had been formulated prior to and independent of that of Darwin. Spencer's theory is based upon a thoroughly distinct, though harmonious, set of fundamental propositions.[5]

His Rank as an Original Thinker. — This is not the place to attempt to pass judgment on the merits of Spencer's system as a whole. It certainly suggested the general line of approach which dominated the latter part of the nineteenth and the early twentieth century — namely, the evolutionary viewpoint — however much Spencer's particular view of evolution failed to bear the tests of later and more specialized inductive and quantitative studies. If his system is more open to criticism with the advance of knowledge than are the systems of earlier philosophers, it is because he dealt with tangible matters capable of verification or disproof through the extension of knowledge and the refinement of scientific methods. Further, there can be little doubt that for original productivity of mind Spencer is quite unequaled. It requires a remarkable man, for instance, to produce a book like Sombart's *Modern Capitalism,* in which the author seems to have a good acquaintance with all the important literature on his subject, but, though such an erudite treatise may be infinitely more valuable from a scientific point of view, it requires less genius to produce it than a work like Spencer's *Principles of Psychology*. This remarkable analysis was written after its author had read less formal psychology than the average elementary teacher in an American public school. In short, whatever in Spencer's system may be destroyed by subsequent scientific progress (and it seems that much of it has even now passed into the realm of rhetoric), still he may claim the honor of having placed many phases of scientific study on the road to new knowledge through having made their guiding principle that of evolution. The late William Graham Sumner thus stated the significance, for at least the thinkers of his day, of Spencer's establishment of the evolutionary principle in social science:

Mr. Spencer addressed himself at the outset of his literary career to topics of sociology. In the pursuit of those topics he found himself forced to seek constantly more fundamental and wider philosophical doctrines. He came at last to the fundamental principles of the evolution philosophy. He then extended, tested, confirmed, and corrected these principles by inductions from other sciences, and so finally turned again to sociology, armed with the scientific method which he had acquired. To win a powerful and correct method is, as we all know, to win more than half the battle. When so much is secured, the question of making the discoveries, solving the problems, eliminating the errors, and testing the results, is only a question of time and of strength to collect and master the data.[6]

The Evolutionary Formula. — As Spencer's whole system of social science was built up from his " laws " of evolution in general, it is essential to understand the fundamental propositions involved in his doctrines on this point. This is incomparably more important in Spencer's sociology than his development of the organismic analogy, though most critics of his sociology have dwelt almost exclusively upon the latter. Spencer's laws of universal evolution are found in their complete development in the second part of his *First Principles*. In the first place, he finds three fundamental truths or propositions. Of these the basic one is the law of the persistence of force, which means the existence and persistence of some ultimate cause which transcends knowledge. The two remaining basic principles are the indestructibility of matter and the continuity of motion, both being derived from the principle of the persistence of force. There are in turn four secondary propositions. The first is the persistence of the relations among forces, or the uniformity of law. The second is the transformation and equivalence of forces; namely, that force is never lost but is merely transformed. The third is the law that everything moves along the line of least resistance or of greatest attraction. The fourth and final law is that of the rhythm or alternation of motion. To render this system complete some law must be found which will govern the combination of these different factors in the evolutionary process. This want is supplied by the law that, with an integration of matter, motion is dissipated and with a differentiation of matter motion is absorbed, and that the process of evolution is characterized by a passage from an incoherent homogeneity to a coherent and definite heterogeneity.[7] Working from these foundations, he summarizes his complete law of universal evolution as follows: " Evolution is an integration of matter and concomitant dissipation of motion; during which the matter passes from an indefinite, incoherent homogeneity to a definite, coherent heterogeneity; and during which the retained motion undergoes a parallel transformation." [8] Adding to this basic foundation of his evolutionary system such important corollaries as the instability of the homogeneous, due to the incidence of unlike forces; the spread of differentiating factors in a geometrical ratio; the tendency of differentiated parts to become segregated through a clustering of like units; and the final limit of all the process of evolution in an ultimate equilibrium, Spencer's system of evolution stands complete in outline. As the reverse of evolution we find dissolution, in which the process of evolution is undone through a reversal of stages in the process.[9] Spencer briefly applied this formula to all phenomena in the remaining portion of his *First Principles,* and the application to social processes therein to be found is the vital portion of Spencer's sociological system. The detailed extension of this preliminary application found in the *First Principles* constitutes Spencer's system of *Synthetic Philosophy.*

   Giddings's Summary of Spencer's Sociological Theories. — Spencer's formal treatment of sociology, aside from the outline of his system in the *First Principles,* is to be found in *The Study of Sociology* — a sort of prolegomenon to the subject, and still an indispensable introduction — and in the three large volumes of the *Principles of Sociology.* While Spencer gave an excellent summary of his whole philosophical system (see the Preface of F. H. Collins's *Epitome of the Synthetic Philosophy*), he failed to present a succinct digest of his sociological theory. Giddings attempted to supply this want, and performed the task in a manner satisfactory to Spencer. His lucid and comprehensive summary follows:

Societies are organisms or they are super-organic aggregates.

Between societies and environing bodies, as between other finite aggregates in nature, there is an equilibration of energy. There is an equilibration between society and society, between one social group and another, between one social class and another.

Equilibration between society and society, between societies and their environment, takes the form of a struggle for existence among societies. Conflict becomes an habitual activity of society.

In this struggle for existence fear of the living and of the dead arises. Fear of the living, supplementing conflict, becomes the root of political control. Fear of the dead becomes the root of religious control.

Organized and directed by political and religious control, habitual conflict becomes militarism. Militarism moulds character and conduct and social organization into fitness for habitual warfare.

Militarism combines small social groups into larger ones, these into larger and yet larger ones. It achieves social integration. This process widens the area within which an increasingly large proportion of the population is habitually at peace and industrially employed.

Habitual peace and industry mould character, conduct, and social organization into fitness for peaceful, friendly, sympathetic life.

In the peaceful type of society coercion diminishes, spontaneity and individual initiative increase. Social organization becomes plastic, and individuals moving freely from place to place change their social relations without destroying social cohesion, the elements of which are sympathy and knowledge in place of primitive force.

The change from militarism to industrialism depends upon the extent of the equilibration of energy between any given society and its neighboring societies, between the societies of any given race and those of other races, between society in general and its physical environment. Peaceful industrialism cannot finally be established until the equilibrium of nations and of races is established.

In society, as in other finite aggregates, the extent of the differentiation and the total complexity of all the evolutionary processes depend upon the rate at which integration proceeds. The slower the rate the more complete and satisfactory is the evolution.[10]

Better known than Spencer's interpretation of society in terms of the laws of evolution, though not so vitally linked with his system, is his development of the analogy between society and an organism. This analogy was by no means original with Spencer, as it is to be found in numerous ancient Oriental, Classical, and early Christian writings; it was common throughout the Middle Ages,[11] and had been considerably elaborated by Comte, Krause, and Ahrens, among others. It was reserved for Spencer, however, to present the first *systematic* development of the theory.[12] (This will be dealt with at length in later sections.)

The Present Significance of Spencer's Sociology. — These two fundamental theories of society — the evolutionary and the organismic [13] — comprise the major theoretical contributions of Spencer to sociology. His remaining voluminous works on the subject are primarily descriptive, though in many cases they present a keen analysis of social processes. Just how Spencer's sociological system will rank in the future, when more refined systematic and psycho-sociological studies have allowed the general body of sociological theory to assume something like a stable form, it is difficult to say. It seems safe to hold that as a *physical interpretation* of society his system will remain in general outline a fairly consistent statement of the subject. The organismic analogy will doubtless be accepted as an interesting bit of description, but will be discarded as possessing little value as an explanation of social processes. How much of his historical sociology will remain can probably be stated definitely at present as virtually none. Already the researches of the more critical ethnologists like Ehrenreich, Graebner, and Thurnwald in Germany; Durkheim, Hubert, and Mauss in France; Rivers, Marett, and Malinowski in England; and Boas and his disciples and successors in America have overthrown almost entirely the highly orderly and almost mechanically systematic anthropological schemes of the classical school of anthropology, of which Spencer was one of the most thoroughgoing exponents. If, however, one can no longer hold with Carver that not to have read Spencer's *Principles of Sociology* would disqualify one from discussing the subject to a degree greater than that which would be caused by the neglect of any other treatise,[14] still it would probably be accurate to say that, viewed from the standpoint of the historical development of the subject, Spencer's contribution is the most far-reaching in its influence that has yet been made. Small summarized the significance of Spencer's position, particularly as set forth in the *Principles of Sociology:*

Spencer's scheme is an attempt to give name, and place, and importance to the meaning [*sic*] factors in human association. It is not a system of speculative conceptions. It is an attempt to represent in language the literal facts of society in the relations in which they actually occur in real life. It is a device by means of which, in proportion as it is adapted to its purpose, we should be able more truly, more comprehensively, and more profoundly to understand, for instance, the life of the people of the United States, than we could without the aid of such description. The fair test is, not to ask whether this scheme leaves nothing in the way of social exposition to be desired, but whether it lays bare more of essential truth about society than is visible without such an interpretation; not whether there is a remainder to be explained, but whether more appears in the confusion of everyday life than is discovered before it is seen in terms of these symbols.

Judged by this test the Spencerian scheme is certainly an approach to truth.[15]

Social Reform and Sociology. — Great as was the significance of " the English Aristotle " in the field of pure science, his importance as an exponent of concrete social policies was almost equally great. Spencer's writings on the subject of social reform were prolific and spirited; so also were those dealing with the proper field of state activity. (In fact, these questions are but different sides of the same problem.) As the foundation of his doctrine concerning the latter was equal freedom, natural rights, and negative regulation, so in regard to the former his central dictum was that results are not proportional to appliances.[16] Not that Spencer denied the need of reform or the tendency of all social structures to become conservative and resist change; in his *Principles of Sociology* [17] Spencer gives an illuminating discussion of how social institutions become immobile. It was not the need of reform that he questioned; it was rather the efficacy of the methods and principles of reform then proposed. What Spencer desired to emphasize was that it was futile to expect that any measure directly designed to remedy a certain situation would be successful unless it took into consideration the general cultural complex of which the particular defect was a part, and allowed for the interdependence of social forces and institutions. Writers have accused Spencer of dealing with " straight men " and formulating a " political arithmetic," but in this field of social reform, at least, he was sufficiently conscious of the actual conditions which confront the social reformer. His classical statement of this principle is contained in the following paragraph:

You see that this wrought-iron plate is not quite flat; it sticks up a little here toward the left — " cockles," as we say. How shall we flatten it? Obviously, you reply, by hitting down on the part that is prominent. Well, here is a hammer, and I give the plate a blow as you advise. Harder, you say. Still no effect. Another stroke? Well, there is one, and another, and another. The prominence remains, you see: the evil is as great as ever — greater, indeed. But this is not all. Look at the warp which the plate has got near the opposite edge. Where it was flat before it is now curved. A pretty bungle we have made of it. Instead of curing the original defect, we have produced a second. Had we asked an artizan practised in " planishing," as it is called, he would have told us that no good was to be done, but only mischief, by hitting down on the projecting part. He would have taught us how to give variously-directed and specially-adjusted blows with a hammer elsewhere: so attacking the evil not by direct but by indirect actions. The required process is less simple than you thought. Even a sheet of metal is not to be successfully dealt with after those commonsense methods in which you have so much confidence. What, then, shall we say about society? "Do you think I am easier to be played on than a pipe?" asks Hamlet. Is humanity more readily straightened than an iron plate? [18]

Nevertheless, Spencer was not a complete and unqualified advocate of *laissez faire*. What he was trying to combat was the all too prevalent tendency to repose perfect trust in the efficacy of direct, "hammer and tongs" legislation as a cure for social ills. As a spirited advocate of the opposite school he naturally went too far. What he wanted to impress upon society was the necessarily small part which an individual or even a generation can hope to achieve in changing the direction of social evolution. He did not desire to discourage either individual or collective effort toward reform, provided it recognized the necessary limitation on the scope or results of such action. He sums up this position well in the following paragraph:

Thus while admitting that for the fanatic some wild anticipation is needful as a stimulus, and recognizing the usefulness of his delusion as adapted to his particular nature and his particular function, the man of the higher type must be content with greatly moderated expectations, while he perseveres with undiminished efforts. He has to see how comparatively little can be done, and yet find it worth while to do that little: so uniting philanthropic energy with philosophic calm.[19]

Although few would wait so patiently for the impersonal laws of evolution to work out a program of reform as Spencer felt willing to do, still few can doubt the wisdom of his advice to beware of the fatal doctrine of manufacturing progress by "ordering-and-forbidding" legislation.[20] A law which is not based on the widest possible knowledge of the sociological principles involved will almost certainly do more harm than good.[21] This is the lesson which sociologists are still trying to impress on well-meaning but ill-informed philanthropists and legislators.[22]

Necessitarian Inclinations and Negativism. — With the possible exception of his thesis that social reform could not be expected from direct legislative measures, the most famous part of Spencer's social theory was his analysis of the legitimate sphere of state activity. As one eminent sociologist recently observed, Spencer was so busy throughout his life attempting to formulate a doctrine of what the state should not do that he failed to develop any coherent, positive theory of the state. Spencer's well-known vigorous opposition to extensive state activity or positive remedial social legislation seems to have been based upon two main factors: (1) the view of the necessitarian nature of social evolution which was current in the middle and third quarter of the nineteenth century; and (2) the negativistic traits of his neurotic constitution, which made the authority of the state abhorrent to him.

The idea that social development and the proper working of the social process is an automatic and spontaneous affair had long been accepted before the time of Spencer. In its earliest modern form it grew out of the reaction of Newtonian cosmic mechanics on the social science of the eighteenth century. The English Deists and the French *philosophes* developed the notion that social institutions are governed by the same " natural laws " that Newton had shown to dominate the physical universe. Their preliminary assumption was taken up and incorporated in social science by the French Physiocrats and the classical economists, the latter employing it as a philosophic defense of the new capitalistic system produced by the Industrial Revolution. Though this conception was shown to be unsound early in the nineteenth century by Rae, Hodgskin, and Sismondi, it prevailed very generally throughout the century. (As we have seen, Kautsky imposed it upon the *anti*-necessitarian theory of Marx.) With the development of the evolutionary philosophy a new " naturalism " was provided. It was believed that the highly organized types of animal life had developed from lower forms in an automatic and independent manner. It was easy to assume a direct analogy between organismic and social evolution, and to assert that social evolution was a wholly spontaneous process which " artificial " human interference could in no way hasten, but might fatally obstruct or divert. Spencer, more than any other writer, set forth this necessitarian view of social development as an argument against state activity — a position which Lester F. Ward, to name no others, later challenged.

Spencer seems to have derived from some source what certain recent psychologists would designate as an extreme " anti-authority complex." Coupled with what is known regarding his early life, especially his early domination by male relatives, and his confirmed neurotic tendencies, it is not impossible that his persistent and ever-growing resentment against the ex-

tension of governmental activity may have been personally motivated by a neurotic reaction. It must also be remembered that
Spencer came from a dissenting family and was reared in that
atmosphere. It seems on the whole that his attitude in this respect
must have had a very deep-rooted emotional foundation, as
it diverged materially from some of the vital premises of his
general philosophy, and this inconsistency was continually causing him trouble and entailing considerable labor in patching up
a reconciliation.[23] Be this as it may, his attitude in respect to
the question of state activity may quite well have been originated
— and it certainly was abundantly nourished — by the political
conditions of his lifetime. The revolutionary ideas of the early
nineteenth century, with their doctrines of the efficacy of hasty
and violent political reform, and the great volume of proposed
remedial legislation designed to solve the problems which the
disorganization of the older social control by the Industrial Revolution had presented, were admirably adapted to awaken sentiments like those entertained by Spencer and to prevent them from
becoming dormant.[24] (At this point it seems well to repeat what
we have already insisted upon in the case of Comte: " Propositions are valid or invalid regardless of their origin." The
mere fact that Spencer was negativistic does not *disprove* his
theories.)

The Proper Sphere of State Activity. — Spencer published his
first essay on this subject, entitled *The Proper Sphere of Government,* in 1842; eight years later appeared his first elaborate
treatise, *Social Statics.* The fundamental principle of this work is
Spencer's law of equal freedom, which is but a revival of Rousseau's definition of liberty: each individual shall enjoy as perfect
a degree of freedom as is compatible with the equal privilege of
other individuals.[25] In this work Spencer states his famous theory
of the state as a joint-stock company for the mutual protection
of individuals,[26] and presents his catalogue of activities from
which the state should refrain, with a detailed analysis of his
views in support of his position. This list of *interdicted* activities
includes the following, some of which are rather startling: commercial regulation, state religious establishments, charitable activities tending to interfere with natural selection, state education,
state colonization, sanitary measures, regulation and coining of
money, postal service, provision of lighthouses, and improvement of harbors.[27] The real duty of the state is to administer
justice, which consists theoretically in maintaining the law of
equal freedom, and practically in protecting the life and property

of the citizens from internal robbery and fraud and from external invasion.[28]

In *The Study of Sociology* (1873) Spencer repeats his fundamental notions regarding political *laissez faire,* especially in the justly famous opening chapter on " Our Need of a Social Science," and in the equally excellent chapter on "The Political Bias." In one passage in his *Study of Sociology,*[29] Spencer approaches the view of Sumner regarding the Forgotten Man as the small taxpayer who bears most of the financial burdens of state activity and gets the least benefit from this legislation. His political theories, expressed in the *Principles of Sociology,* are mainly historical and analytical, and, with the exception of the contrasts between military and industrial society, deal only incidentally with the question of the amount of state activity. Between 1850 and 1884, when he published his *Man versus the State,* Spencer contributed to various journals a large number of articles on the subject of non-interference. These have been for the most part gathered together in the third volume of his *Essays: Scientific, Political, and Speculative* (New York, 1891). Perhaps the most important among them is his " Specialized Administration " (1871), issued in answer to Huxley's attack on Spencerian doctrines in his essay on *Administrative Nihilism* (1870). By the doctrine of specialized administration Spencer means the relinquishment by the government of its function of positive regulation of human activities and the perfection of its negatively regulating function.[30] He published a telling attack upon socialism under the title "From Freedom to Bondage."[31] The second essay in his *Man versus the State,* " The Coming Slavery," is also mainly devoted to a refutation of socialistic propositions. Finally, in *Man versus the State*[32] and in *Justice*[33] one may look for Spencer's final word on the subject. In *Man versus the State* he discharges a fiery blast against the socialistic tendencies of the age, the attempted intrusion of family ethics into the field of state activity, and the contemporary dogma of the sovereignty of Parliament as the representative of the majority. His final doctrine regarding the proper sphere of government is that it should be limited to the provision for safety from physical assault, the freedom and enforcement of contracts, and the protection of the individual from foreign aggression; in other words, the state should be concerned purely with negative regulation.[34] In the postscript to the final edition of *Man versus the State,* he admits that he is fully aware that his theory of state activity is far in advance of his age and that it will not be adopted for generations to come, but justifies his devotion to the cause on the ground that society must have an ideal to guide it toward realization.[35]

Taking into account both those theories we have already dealt with and those we have had to leave practically unmentioned, Spencer's salient political doctrines, all of which relate directly or indirectly to the question of the proper scope of state activity, may be summarized as follows: (1) He revived the contract (agreement) doctrine to account philosophically for the justification of political authority; (2) he put forward a strong sociological statement of individualistic political philosophy, in which the state was completely subordinated to the individual, and was regarded simply as an agent for securing a greater degree of freedom for the individual than was possible without its " negative interference " with human conduct; (3) he denied the possibility of securing social progress by direct remedial legislation (at least of the type with which he was familiar), and asserted that society must wait for the automatic working of the general laws of evolution to effect permanent progress; (4) he developed a philosophy of social evolution based on the purposes toward which organized society functions, finding these purposes to have been, first, military expansion, and second, industrial development; (5) finally, Spencer made the important contribution of correlating the state with society in general, in the attempt to estimate its position and function in the wider social process. In short, he approached political problems from the point of view of the sociologist, however inconsistent and inadequate may have been his application of the principles of his science to the solution of those problems.[36]

Summary of Spencer's Sociological Theories. — There are a number of other aspects of Spencer's work almost if not quite as important as those we have dwelt upon; hence it seems well to call attention to them by giving the substance of Hankins's concise and cogent analysis (abridged and adapted) by way of critical summary, instead of merely recapitulating our own discussion:

We may deal with Spencer's sociological theories under the following headings: (1) the validity of the evolutionary viewpoint; (2) the data of sociology; (3) the institutional analysis; (4) the origin of religion; (5) individuation versus genesis; (6) evolution from militarism to industrialism; (7) the organismic conception.

(1) Spencer's approach to sociology was from the basis of a general philosophy. We cannot argue here questions of such broad import. But, even if the entire formula of Spencerian evolution be applicable to so-

ciety, it does not suffice for an understanding of social processes. The broad formula of evolution remains substantially without meaning until given substance and content by translation into biological, psychic, and social data. Moreover, Spencer was continually betrayed by the formula itself, for while the doctrine of evolution is at bottom a theory of perfected adjustment or adaptation, it does not necessarily imply " progress " in the sense of more perfect realization of human ideals and valuations. Thus Spencer himself says: " Evolution is commonly conceived to imply in everything an *intrinsic* tendency to become something higher. This is an erroneous conception of it . . . change does not necessarily imply advance." [37] And yet, oddly enough, Spencer continually uses the term " social evolution " as implying advance, and over and over again, especially in the chapter " Retrospect and Prospect," he interprets social processes as working for the realization of certain ideal ends. Thus Evolution becomes God.

(2 and 3) Spencer found the data of sociology in primitive man and his physical environment and the reaction of these one on the other. He conceived primitive man as representing retarded stages of evolution, and, on the principle that the character of the society is determined by the type of the component individual,[38] he viewed early institutions as essentially inferior. His description of primitive man as long-armed, short-legged and pot-bellied successfully demolished the " noble savage " of tradition but failed to do justice to the extraordinary range of variation among primitive types. Moreover, his easy assumption that primitive men were essentially inferior in natural psychic powers, while doubtless true for many cases, is equally untrue of others. Spencer's greatest error here was in assuming a close relation between the state of cultural advancement and inherent mental and character traits. Finally, his theory that the character of the component unit determines the character of the society, while containing an element of truth, is less important than the obverse truth that society shapes the individual as set forth by Tarde and Durkheim.

(4) The Spencerian ghost theory of the origin of religion [39] was put out about the same time as E. B. Tylor's largely similar theory.[40] Spencer made fear the primary religious emotion; derived the idea of soul from the experiences of the shadow, echo, sleep, and dreams, and the idea of ghost from that of soul or " other-self "; and made ancestor worship the universal form of earliest religion. In his view the mind of primitive man worked logically on a high level of reasoning power, but with false assumptions due to ignorance of causation in the scientific sense. This and related hypotheses now appear untenable or only partially adequate. For example, that the idea of a double or " other-self " was the first suggestion of spirit now seems doubtful, for Lévy-Bruhl has shown that in some primitive communities the idea of several souls precedes that of one. His theory of totemism as arising from the custom of nicknaming has proven wholly inadequate, if not ridiculously erroneous. Again, instead of ancestor worship being universal, it is found nowhere among

very primitive peoples. Fear is doubtless an element in religious control, but that it constituted the emotional tap-root is at least doubtful.[41]

(5) Another Spencerian theory, dealt with in Part V of his *Biology,* is that there is an opposition between Individuation and Genesis. From it Spencer drew the conclusion that human evolution would after many generations arrive at such a perfect adjustment to conditions of life on the globe that the natural unrestricted fertility would be about two per couple or just enough to sustain the population in a static state. Had this theory been generally accepted, it would not only have allayed all Malthusian fears but also would have revived the rosy visions of the Perfectionists. Even in Spencer's own presentation of the theory, however, serious difficulties arose, and modern biological research has shown it to be untenable.

(6) Little need be said of the generalization that society evolves from militarism to industrialism. This was in fact another piece of Spencerian apriorism; a rationalization of one of his deepest and most pious wishes. He contemplated the evolution of man toward a state of perfect adaptation; this involved a continuous reduction of primary conflicts, an increased rule of reason and toleration, and the achievement of that moral perfection which every philosophical anarchist conceives himself to have attained and which he imagines would enable each individual to govern himself in the full light of an effulgent reason and free from every form of social constraint. Spencer thus attached great moral significance to the advancement of peace and worked heroically to that end.[42]

(7) In the minds of many students Spencer is almost exclusively identified with the organismic concept. This is strange, almost paradoxical, in view of the fact that the philosophy of individualism received its final and most complete formulation in his writings. This paradox is not without some possibility of explanation. He did not in fact hold society to be an organism but a super-organism, and introduced his analogies only as aids to the imagination. This he makes clear in the conclusion of Part III of his *Principles* [as we shall note in following sections]. It cannot be successfully denied, however, that Spencer was attached to his biological conception of society, for he clung to it even when Huxley and others showed that it was in fundamental contradiction to his philosophic anarchism.[43]

And now let us consider this organismic analogy in detail, both before Spencer and after.

Early Organismic Analogies. — The theory of a resemblance between classes, groups, and institutions in society and the organs of the individual is as old as social theory itself. We have already noted its presence in Hindu social thought, and have also called attention to the fact that Aristotle, in Book IV of his *Politics,* sets forth this organismic analogy with precision and clarity. The same conception appears clearly in the writings of Cicero, Livy, Seneca, and Paul.[44] In the Middle Ages elaborate anthropomorphic analogies were drawn by John of Salisbury and Nicholas of Cues.[45] In the early modern period, Hobbes and Rousseau contrasted the organism and the state, holding that the organism was the product of nature while the state was an artificial creation.[46] In the late eighteenth and early nineteenth centuries fanciful notions of the social and political organism appeared with such writers as Hegel, Schelling, Krause, Ahrens, Schmitthenner, and Waitz.[47] Following them came another school of writers who dwelt at length on the supposed " personality " of the state. Among these were Stahl, Stein, Lasson, and Gierke.[48] Another significant application of the analogical doctrine was that which compared the psychical ages of the state with stages in the life of the individual. The more important writers in this group were Welcker, Rohmer, and Volgraff. The most famous of the group was Theodor Rohmer, whose *Theory of Political Parties* was published in 1844. In it he compared the ages of political parties with the life ages of man. Each individual passes through four periods, boyhood, youth, manhood, and old age. There are four types of political parties which are related to and characterized by the psychical tendencies most prominent in each of these four ages. In boyhood, man is radical; in youth, he is liberal; in manhood, he is conservative; and in old age, he is absolutist. There are, then, four natural types of political parties, the radical, the liberal, the conservative, and the absolutist.[49]

Another school of organicists were those who, though they wrote before the emergence of modern evolutionary biology, turned to natural science to discover data which would support the comparison between the organism and the state. The leaders in this group were Zacharia, Volgraff, Frantz, and Bluntschli. The most extreme and influential of these writers was Johann Caspar Bluntschli. He went further than any other writer, before or since, in claiming the identity of the state and the organism. Bluntschli selected sixteen parts of the human body and compared them in detail with sixteen organs of the body politic. He also determined the sex of the social organism, stating that it was scientifically demonstrable that the state was masculine and the church feminine.[50] On account of the fact that Bluntschli was one of the most influential political scientists of the nineteenth century, his notions about the state and the social organism had a great effect on the development of social thought, in Germany at least, for two generations after 1850.

The Biologizing of Social Theory. — The middle of the nine-teenth century was preëminently the period of great biological discoveries. It was in that century that the use of the microscope made known the similarity in cellular construction of all organized beings; that protoplasm began to be recognized as the physical basis of life and the seat of all vital activities; that most contagious diseases were traced to microscopic organisms and, as a consequence, that medicine and surgery were reformed; that the belief in the spontaneous origin of life under present conditions was given up; and finally, that the researches of Goethe, Lamarck, Von Baer, Wallace, and Darwin gave an empirical basis for the philosophy of evolution propounded by Spencer and his numerous forerunners and followers.

The result of the astounding victories of biological science was very much as one might expect: workers in other fields began to look to this youthful giant for leadership and aid. Among social theorists, in particular, this took the form of elaboration of the notion of the resemblance between the biological organism and the " social organism." This differed from the earlier anthropo-morphic and mystical analogies, as well as from the quaint " political anatomy " of Bluntschli, for it rested upon the new scientific knowledge of biological structure and processes, and attempted to show how these were also exemplified by social institutions and social processes. Though we now regard these attempts as sterile, except for purposes of rhetorical description, they represent the final completion of the organismic theory of society. Among the progenitors of sociology in this group were Comte, Spencer, Lilienfeld, Schäffle, Worms, and Fouillée.[51]

Comte and the " Reality " of the Social Organism. — Although Comte did not elaborate to any great extent the organismic conception of society, he may be said to have offered many suggestions for the later school of so-called organicists, and is notable for holding that the organismic doctrine is no mere analogy but a description of reality. It is the individual who is an abstraction rather than the social organism. Coker has summed up in the following manner the organismic doctrines to be found in the *Positive Philosophy:*

Society is a collective organism, as contrasted to the individual organism or plant, and possesses the primary organismic attribute of the *Consensus Universel.* There is to be seen in the organism and in society a harmony of structure and function working toward a common end through action and reaction among its parts and on the environment. This harmonious development reaches its highest stage in human society, which is the final step in organismic evolution. Social progress is characterized by an increasing specialization of functions and a corresponding tendency toward an adaptation and perfection of organs. Finally, social disturbances are maladies of the social organism and the proper subject-matter of social pathology.[52]

In the *Polity* Comte elaborated the similarity between the individual and the social organism. In the family may be found the social cell; in the social forces may be discerned the social tissues; in the state (city) may be discovered the social organs; in the various nations are to be detected the social analogues of the apparatus of biology; and, finally, one may behold in the social classes the analogue of the systems in biology. The great difference between the individual organism and the social organism lies in the fact that the former is essentially immutable, whereas the latter is capable of great improvement through social effort and control.[53]

Spencer, Organicist and Individualist. — At length we have returned to Spencer: as we have several times remarked, it was reserved for him to present the first systematic development of the organismic theory.[54] He enumerates six fundamental similarities between society and organism. First, both are distinguished from inorganic matter by an augmentation of mass and visible growth during a greater part of their existence. Second, as both increase in size they increase in complexity of structure. Third, progressive differentiation of structure in both is accompanied by a like differentiation of functions. Fourth, evolution establishes in both social and animal organisms not only differences, but definitely connected differences of such character as to make each other possible. Fifth, the analogy between a society and an organism is still more evident when it is recognized that conversely every organism is a society. Finally, in both society and the organism, the life of the aggregate may be destroyed and the units still continue to live on for at least a little while.

On the other hand, there are three important differences to be noted between society and the organism. In the first place, in an individual organism the component parts form a concrete whole, and the living units are bound together in close contact, whereas in the social organism the component parts form a discrete whole and the living units are free and more or less dispersed. Again, and even more fundamental, in the individual organism there is such a differentiation of functions that some parts become the seat of feeling and thought and others are practically insensitive, whereas in the social organism no such differentiation exists; there is no social mind or sensorium apart from the individuals that make up the society. As a result of this second difference there is to be observed the third distinction: namely, that, while in the organism the units exist for the good of the whole, in society the whole exists for the good of the individual members.[55]

Now Spencer did not regard these differences as inconsequential, nor did he ever assert, as Comte did, the reality of the social organism. He merely introduced the analogies of sustaining, distributing, and regulating systems, social structures and functions, and social metamorphoses, not as explanations or even descriptions, but as parallels aiding the imagination. This he points out in the final chapter of Part II, where he says in substance: " There exists no analogy between the body politic and a living body, save those necessitated by the mutual dependence of parts. The social organism, (1) discrete instead of concrete, (2) asymmetrical instead of symmetrical, (3) sensitive in all its units instead of having a single sensitive center, is not comparable to any single type of organism. If the parallels be dispensed with, the inductions still hold true. Societies grow. Etc." And in a footnote he exclaims: " This emphatic repudiation of the belief that there is any special analogy between the social organism and the human organism, I have a motive for making. A rude outline of the general conception . . . was published by me in the *Westminster Review* for January, 1860. In it I expressly rejected the conception of Plato and Hobbes, that there is a likeness between social organization and the organization of a man, saying that ' there is no warrant whatever for assuming this.' Nevertheless, a criticism on the article . . . ascribed to me the idea which I had thus distinctly condemned." [56]

Unfortunately for Spencer, however, his persistence in the use of the analogy after such misunderstanding had shown how likely it was to lead to false interpretations, and his incautious use of headings like that of Chapter 2, Part II, " A Society Is an Organism," resulted in his doctrine becoming practically indistinguishable, in its actual effects, from those of the genuine organicists. The biologizing of sociology thus proceeded apace.

Lilienfeld, Organismic Extremist. — The first writer after Spencer to develop the organismic theory of society, and the most voluminous author of that school, was the Russo-German scholar, Paul von Lilienfeld (1829–1903), whose five-volume work, *Gedanken über die Socialwissenschaft der Zukunft,* appeared in Mitau between 1873 and 1881. His later works of major importance were *La Pathologie Sociale* (Paris, 1896), and *Zur Vertheidigung der organischen Methode in der Sociologie* (Berlin, 1898). This last work is an excellent epitome of his system.

Although Lilienfeld's work appeared about the time of Spencer's formal treatise on sociology, and after his first extended use of the organismic analogy, it seems that he developed his fundamental doctrines independently of the work of Spencer. While Spencer had argued that the relation between the organism and society was chiefly an illuminating analogy, Lilienfeld insisted that there was a real identity between society and the organism. He held that if there was any difference it was merely in degree and not in kind, society being the third or highest form in the organismic realm, ranking above the plant and animal kingdoms.

Lilienfeld enumerates five fundamental characteristics of an organism which correspond to analogous attributes in society. In the first place, there is an intense and varied interaction of forces in both. The difference is that " society is a more many-sidedly developed organism, in which purposivity, spirituality, and freedom prevail over causation, materiality, and necessity in a higher degree than in all other organisms of nature." In the next place, both are characterized by an inner unity — a cohesive attraction of an aggregation of particles toward a center of gravity. Again, in both society and the organism matter and force act in a purposive manner. Social action, especially, is never without a definite purpose: it always pertains to the interaction of individuals or social groups, or is directed against the forces of nature, and is easily the most purposive of all organic action. Further, society best exemplifies the characteristic of structural perfectibility common to it and the organism. By this is meant the increasing specialization of outer and inner parts, and of the functions pertaining to them, through successive adjustments of the organism to the environment. Finally, society is superior to the organism in their mutual characteristic of the process of " capitalization ": namely, the storing up of materials and energies for future consumption.

There are some minor differences between society and the organism, but they are by no means as important or numerous as the identities. These differences are: first, organization finds a higher development and complexity in society; and second, the relation of the parts to the whole varies as between society and the organism. In the plant kingdom neither individuals nor parts move; in the animal kingdom the individual moves independently but not the parts; in society both the individual and the aggregate are capable of independent movements.

The structure of the social organism is made up of cellular and intercellular substance. The first is composed of social cells or the individual nervous systems of men, and social tissues or social groups, classes, and professions. Society is a superior sort of organism in having only nerve cells and tissues. By " intercellular substance " Lilienfeld means the total social and physical environment in which man is placed, as well as the transformations he is able to effect in this environment.

In every social group three fundamental spheres of activity may be detected: economic, juridical, and political. These correspond to the physiological, morphological, and unitary spheres of the organisms of nature. Political life is thus the unifying force in the hierarchy of social forces, and government may be designated as the brain of the social organism — the organ of unification and coördination. " The government, as the sovereign power, as the incorporation of social unity, takes up into itself the wills of the individual members of society and reflects back upon them the collective will, directly or through the agency of various intermediate organs. But the government . . . can receive only a small part of the whole sum of reflexes which are going on among the individual wills traversing the organism. The more highly developed the society is, the more variously and with greater fullness does the government receive the reflexes from all parts of the organism, and therefore the more actively and effectively does it react upon the parts." The forms of government simply determine the manner in which the society achieves unity through the coördinating organs. They have no correlation with the degree of development of a society, but simply provide convenient categories for distinguishing social groups.

The general law of the evolution of the social organism is to be found in the process of progressive integration and differentiation of the social forces. Political development is characterized by " an intenser concentration of forces combined with a greater independence of parts."

Finally, the social organism is subject to sickness and decay. Maladies of the social organism are usually localized in the cellular substance, altering the character of the cells. Government is the great therapeutic agent in treating the maladies of the social organism.[57] " Social pathology " is no mere figure of speech.

Elsewhere we have referred to Lilienfeld as follows: " His

later works were little more than variations on the organismic motif set by the *Gedanken,* and he regarded his doctrine that society is a real organism as his great contribution to sociology. . . . Although Lilienfeld possessed considerable erudition (his writings abound with references to Darwin, Tylor, Waitz, and others not usually cited as early as the 1870's), his intellectual gifts were not of the highest order. Much of his work is mere journalistic prattle. His importance was negative; for sociologists of the late nineteenth century he was a horrible example of the consequence of taking seriously his own dictum: *Sociologus nemo nisi biologus.*" [58]

Schäffle, Psychical Organicist. — Albert G. Fr. Schäffle (1831–1903) must in many respects be classed with the organismic school, but as Wiese has pointed out, it would be at least as correct to place him with the social philosophers of idealistic tendency. At heart he was closer to Schelling and Hegel than to Darwin, Spencer, or Haeckel. Nevertheless, all his works except his posthumous *Abriss der Soziologie* are pervaded by the terminology of biology, and as he made much use of the organismic analogy, we shall deal with him here.

Schäffle published his chief work and most influential contribution to sociological literature, *Bau und Leben des Socialen Körpers,* in seven volumes between 1875 and 1878. The most compact statement of his final version of sociology, in which he sought to free himself from the bounds of biologism, is to be found in the posthumous work already mentioned, *Abriss der Soziologie von Dr. Albert G. Fr. Schäffle,* edited by Karl Bücher and published in 1906. [59]

Schäffle's use of the biological analogy in explaining social processes is much more qualified than was the case with most other members of the school. He maintained that society is not a real organism, but is rather a life union of individuals which is spiritually (or psychically — here we have the familiar ambiguity of *Geist*) and not physiologically constituted. At the same time he believed in the general usefulness of the organismic analogy and his method is primarily biological, though there is a large amount of acute psycho-sociological reflection to be found throughout the work.

The study of the forms and functions of society falls under the headings of social morphology and physiology, dealing with individuals, national possessions, and their combination; and social psychology, which deals with the mental life of society.

Schäffle finds five general types of social tissue. The first is designated as " arrangements of domiciliation " such as buildings, streets, roads, and so forth; these have no " homologue " in the organic kingdom. The next type is the protective tissues such as clothing, roofs, safes, and fortresses, and is homologous to the epidermal tissues in the individual organism. The third type of tissue is the economic or household arrangements, such as the economic arrangement of family, social, religious, political, and cultural life. The homologous tissues in the organism are those which supply its nourishment. Next are the practical or technical social arrangements, such as the various means for the generation and application of social power as exemplified by the army, police, state officials, and business administration, and having for their homologue the muscular tissues in animals. The fifth and final type of social tissue is the psycho-physical, such as the institutions of intellectual activity manifested in all the agencies of public and private control and direction. These have as their organismic homologue the nerve tissues. Schäffle epitomizes his theory of society in the following paragraph:

The social body takes up into itself all human, animal, vegetable and inorganic materials and forms of movement of the whole earth body, comprehends them into one historical life-community, and leads them towards the last, most universal, and most many-sided equilibrium of human, spiritual, and bodily development with all the external influences of our planet. The universality and high degree of spiritualisation of its stuff and its movements are the distinctive characteristics of the social body.

There are three main groups of social organs. The first group includes the " institutions of outer national life," such as production, trade, transportation, and protection. The second group comprehends the " institutions of inner national life," such as sociality, education, culture, science, literature, art, and religion. These two groups are united, controlled, and coördinated by the third group — the state. " The state is thus the regulative central apparatus for coördinating all the elements of general social activity, and the organ of positive interference for preserving the social aggregate. Its task is the centralised integration of all social will and action in the interest of the maintenance of the whole and of the essential parts thereof. In the central universal corporation — the State — the whole nation attains unity and individuality."

The structure of the state may be analyzed on the basis of the same fivefold set of tissues which characterize society in general.

A combination of these tissues makes up the " organ-system " of the state. This system may otherwise be divided into the constitutional holders of public authority, made up of the magistrates, electorate, and representative body, and the political agencies affecting the above, such as political parties. Again, each of these may be subdivided as central and local in scope of action.

The genesis of the state is a result of the struggle for existence and natural selection in respect to both individuals and groups, and the process of evolution itself is progressive integration and differentiation. Schäffle thus combined Darwinian and Spencerian conceptions. There are five stages in the evolution of the state: the primitive patriarchal constitution; the class constitution, such as control by the military, priestly, feudal, or monarchical class; the city-state constitution; the territorial constitution; and the modern national constitution. In this process of evolution the struggle for existence becomes less violent as society develops, since " adjustment replaces annihilation." [60]

Fouillée and the " Contractual Organism ". — Spencer was not without followers among the French scholars, and in 1880 Alfred Fouillée (1838–1912) published his suggestive work, *La Science sociale contemporaine,* in which he attempted to combine effectively the doctrines of the social contract and the social organism, both of which are to be found in Spencer's writings, though he devotes more space to an elaboration of the latter.[61] Society to Fouillée was thus a " contractual organism " — both a " natural " and an " artificial " product.[62]

In pointing out the similarities between society and the organism, Fouillée enumerates five characteristics which are common to both, namely: concurrence of dissimilar parts; a systematized structure allowing a functional distribution of members; organic vitality of the constituent elements; spontaneity of movement; and an exemplification of the processes of development and decay. In his proof of his position he follows Spencer closely.

There are, however, some important qualifying differences between society and an organism. In the first place, the social organism alone has the quality of " inner finality "; in other words, only in the social organism do the constituent elements recognize each other and coöperate to promote the common end of their organic composite. The main bonds in society are psychic, resting upon sympathy of the members and pleasure in association with like members. Again, there is, strictly speaking, no social brain. Although the scientists, philosophers, and rulers in a society may offer a close analogue to a social brain, there is no single and separate social consciousness. Fouillée's emphasis on the absence of a social sensorium is perhaps the most characteristic mark of his theory of the social organism. Finally, Fouillée includes within his conception of the social organism the element of conscious volition. " In fact, at what moment does an assemblage of men become a society in the true sense of the word? It is when all the men conceive, more or less clearly, a type of organism which they can form through uniting themselves, and when they do effectively unite themselves under the determining influence of that conception. We have thus an organism which exists because it has been thought and wished, an organism born of an idea; and since that common idea involves a common will we have a . . . contractual organism."

Fouillée based his political doctrines upon this dual conception of society. Government must be an art which takes into account the nature of the social organism. The legislator must always be aware of the interrelation of the different parts of the social organism, and must even refrain from attempting to improve one part if such action will be accompanied by the infliction of a greater injury upon the remaining parts. No comprehensive plan of social reform should be undertaken unless some general social movement and organization of public opinion have indicated the necessity of such reform and the direction it should take. Moreover, a comprehensive scheme of social reform should conform to the wishes of at least a majority of the society, and all changes should be made as gradually as possible so as to conform to the general laws of evolution. Revolution, however, may be at times unavoidable to remedy long-standing social evils, but any revolution should be a manifestation of the general will of society and should promote the general welfare of the society as a whole. Fouillée thought that Spencer trusted too much to the automatic action of social organs and, for his part, maintained that society might successfully undertake directive social reconstruction. The state itself might be regarded as the system of directive organs in society.[63]

René Worms and the Super-Organism. — Another French scholar, René Worms (1869–1926), was perhaps the most extreme exponent of the organismic school, throughout the greater part of his life, among the French adherents of that variety of sociology.[64] Worms defines society as " an enduring aggregation of living beings, exercising all their activity in common." Worms finds four characteristics which pertain to both society and an organism: their external structures are variable in time and irregular in form; their internal structures are undergoing constant changes through assimilation and integration, and disassimilation and disintegration; there is a coördinated differentiation among their parts; finally, both have the power of reproduction. He proceeds to develop the organismic conception of society under the heads of the anatomy, physiology, origin, development, classification, pathology, therapeutics, and hygiene of society, all of these topics being treated in technical biological nomenclature. Not only did Worms develop the organismic concept at great length and with real precision, but he also offered a long refutation of the conventional objections to the doctrine.

His final conclusion was that while there is a " very profound and close analogy between society and the organism," still there is not an identity of nature. The bond which unites social elements is primarily psychical, whereas the bonds of union in an organism are material. Again, society is more plastic, adaptable, and better able to replace a loss of its members. Finally, society is more complex in its constitution than the organism; it is a " super-organism."

As to the state, that is a high form or expression of society — one which has become conscious of its unity and has attained a degree of personality. It is " a being having its own life, distinct from that of its members, though resulting from it; so distinct and superior that it at times demands the sacrifice of some one of those subordinate existences, and almost always obtains it." From this conception of the state several deductions may be made in regard to political conduct. Radical individualism is to be condemned as opposed to the essential nature and purpose of the state. Since society is subject to the laws of evolutionary development, any idea of progress and reform is prohibited as not taking into account the natural laws and stages of development.[65]

The Developing Idea of the Organic Unity of Society as a Product of Mental Interaction: Mackenzie. — Lilienfeld, Schäffle, Fouillée, and Worms in his earlier writings, together with Spencer as commonly understood (or misunderstood), constituted the classical organismic school of sociologists. As a development of the conception of the vital unity and organization of human society, this school emphasized an important proposition in social theory, but as an explanation of social processes or an attempt to understand the basic principles of social causation through using the magical abracadabra of biology, organismic contributions were of little value. Indeed, they exemplified highly pedantic elaborations upon the mere analogy as analogy that were quite out of proportion to the valid results obtained.[66]

At the same time, their lucubrations served at least one useful purpose: eventually several members of the school unconsciously abandoned the rigid biologism with which they began, and slipped into the use of psycho-sociological terminology. This was particularly true of Schäffle, Fouillée, and Worms: they tacitly shifted from biological, *organismic* notions to psycho-sociological, *organic* ideas. At about the time that this tendency became clearly marked, there appeared a work which made it evident that, in spite of all the extremism or even arrant nonsense of the organismic school, the metaphysicians and philosophers had been stimulated by such theories to the extent that they were once more becoming interested in the organic interpretation of society. The work referred to was the *Introduction to Social Philosophy* of J. S. Mackenzie,[67] an eminent Scottish philosopher. This work attempts to discuss in a rather systematic way the chief problems connected with modern society and the construction of a comprehensive social philosophy which can be adjusted to modern needs. It is not too much to say that while it usually evades any direct and concrete solution of the problems it suggests, either by referring them to specialists in different social sciences or by applying to them vague philosophical generalities, it is nevertheless one of the best syntheses that have yet appeared from the hands of recent philosophers. He distinguishes at great length between the mechanical, chemical, and organic types of unity. He sums up his conclusions on this point in the following paragraph:

A mechanical system is a collection of parts externally related; it changes by an alteration of its parts; and has reference to an end which is outside of itself. A chemical system is a compound of parts which are absorbed in a whole; it does not change except by dissolution; and it has no end to which it refers. In an organism, on the other hand, the relations of the parts are intrinsic; changes take place by an internal adaptation; and its end forms an essential element in its own nature. We see, in short, that an organism is a real whole, in a sense which no other kind of unity is so. It is *in se ipso totus, teres, atque rotundus.* . . . We may define it, therefore, as a whole whose parts are intrinsically related to it, which develops from within, and has a reference to an end that is involved in its own nature.[68]

The assumptions in this definition, which have been reached *a priori*, are next tested by determining whether their concrete application to society will substantiate their validity. The results of such a test seem eminently satisfactory to Mackenzie. He then proceeds to analyze the end toward which the social organism functions. This he finds to be true self-realization for the individual, which can only be achieved through man's contact with society. Self-realization suggests the proper social ideal, which may be resolved again into three subordinate and specific ideals: those of liberty, equality, and aristocracy. What is needed is to synthesize these ideals in one all-inclusive organic ideal, which Mackenzie describes as follows:

> The first point we have to note about such an ideal is, that it must to some extent include all the elements which are represented by the other three. It must include such a degree of freedom as is necessary for the working out of the individual life. It must include such a degree of socialism as is necessary to prevent exploitation and a brutalizing struggle for existence, as well as to secure to each individual such leisure as is required for the development of the higher life. It must include such a degree of aristocratic rule as is necessary for the advance of culture and for the wise conduct of social affairs.[69]

True social progress consists in working out this organic ideal through the subjugation of nature, social organization, and personal development. As to the functions which a state may assume, Mackenzie lays down the following fundamental propositions: It should not undertake anything which will tend to deaden the sense of individual responsibility, which is not open to public criticism, or the limits of which cannot easily be defined. As to its interference with functions which it does not undertake but which are exercised by private or voluntary organizations, he simply mentions a few possible fields of interference, such as property restrictions, and passes the final answer of the question over to specialists in the social sciences. He finds no conflict between the organic doctrine and a rational individualism. To quote:

> That there is no contradiction between the independence which is now claimed for the individual and the fact of his social determination, becomes evident when we consider the nature of that determination and of that independence. That the individual is determined by his society means merely that his life is an expression of the social atmosphere in which he lives. And that the individual is independent, means merely that the spirit which finds expression in him is a living force which may develop by degrees into something different.[70]

The organismic theory was not at once abandoned in the face of criticism by the new and growing school of mental interactionism (of which Tarde was the most powerful exponent in sociological circles). It was defended, with certain qualifications admitting a strong psycho-sociological current, by DeGreef, the famous Belgian syndicalist-sociologist, and was the basic working hypothesis of the Russo-French group of sociologists represented by Novicow, DeRoberty, and others whose contributions appeared in the *Annales de l'Institut International de Sociologie* before the Great War. Worms, for a long time in control of this publication, also continued his organismic train of thought well into the twentieth century, but as we shall note in the concluding section, finally went over to the camp of the mental interactionists. None of the later organismic thinkers just mentioned made any substantial contribution to the original body of doctrine; they merely added more biological jargon and got further and further from concrete social life.[71] In England and the United States, the terminology of the organismic school lingers in a general way among writers on social problems, but it is now used mainly as a means of emphasizing the essential unity of society rather than as a means of pseudo-analysis, and in many respects the result is virtually indistinguishable from the organic doctrine of which Mackenzie has provided an example.[72] A number of English socialist writers, among them J. Ramsay MacDonald, have used organismic terminology as a method of defending the contentions of reformist socialism,[73] and there can be little doubt that it is a more logical aid to this type of thought than to the individualistic doctrines of Spencer. In Germany organicism is now rampant: the racial evangelists, the school of *Geopolitik,* and a number of pseudo-sociologists have revived the doctrine. Italy also has incubated a new crop of organismic writers, of whom Corrado Gini is most representative.

Summing Up: Assessment of the Significance of the Organismic Theory. — Present-day scientific sociologists give little or no attention to the elaborate discussions of the analogies between the organism and society. The only service to sociology which they concede to have been made by this line of doctrine is that it emphasizes the interdependence of the various specialized groups in society and the necessity for their harmonious growth and adjustment. Hobhouse has very well summarized this:

Social development involves the harmonious development of the constituent members of society. This is one of the elements of truth contained in what is called the organic conception of society. To speak of society as if it were a physical organism is a piece of mysticism, if indeed it is not quite meaningless. But the life of society and the life of an individual do resemble one another in certain respects, and the term

692   POSITIVISM MERGES WITH EVOLUTIONISM

"organic" is as justly applicable to the one as to the other. For an organism is a whole consisting of interdependent parts. Each part lives and functions and grows by subserving the life of the whole. It sustains the rest and is sustained by them, and through their mutual support comes a common development. And this is how we would conceive the life of man in society in so far as it is harmonious.[74]

What Hobhouse is saying here is in line with our distinction between "organic" and "organismic"; the former has some sociological standing, the latter none. The most conclusive verdict, however, has probably been rendered by Worms, for in his earlier writings he was probably one of the most consistent organicists, and in his later years he retracted a great deal of what he had written, as the following statement from his last important work shows:

Study, experience, and reflection have taught us to qualify the approval we at first gave to the principles of the organismic theory, or at least to put in their place statements of sufficient clarity.[75]

Not only this: Worms finally joined the group which maintains that if society is in any sense a unity, that unity lies on the psycho-sociological, not the biological plane. Worms's theory runs somewhat as follows: Societies come into existence on the same level as organisms, and at first function according to the same laws. Then they advance in a peculiarly human way by working toward an ideal constructed by the mind: an ideal of justice, freedom, enlightenment (here he parallels Mackenzie). In this way they come to seek for the creation of equality and contractual solidarity (here he revives Fouillée's conception) among their members. From the organismic to the social level there is a smooth and continuous progression brought about by the mediation of the psychical level.[76] From this statement it can be seen that he practically scuttled his earlier biologism in favor of a psycho-sociological interpretation. In his thinking the fundamental social fact finally became "the mental meeting of human beings" ("La rencontre mentale des êtres, voilà pour nous le fait sociale originaire").[77] Worms steps into the same company as James Mark Baldwin, Cooley, Mead, and a host of other exponents of the theory of society as an organic unity *mentally* constituted.

Organismic analogies, some of them crude in the extreme, are still with us. On the other hand, some sociologists who once viewed with favor the theory of society as an organic unity mentally constituted have grown weak in the faith, on the ground that the available empirical evidence shows that few if any societies are ever one piece. See Becker, *Man in Reciprocity* (New York: Praeger, 1956), pp. 189-190.

CHAPTER XIX

Struggle over "The Struggle for Existence": Social Darwinism, Pros and Cons

NINETEENTH-CENTURY UNREST: MALTHUS. — The rapid industrialization of Europe, and particularly of England, brought into high relief those features of poverty and its attendant evils that are present in the background of every complex society. We have already seen how numerous and varied were the programs for gradual or sweeping social reconstruction in the late eighteenth and early nineteenth centuries; men could not shake off the conviction that the world was out of joint. Even those who opposed alterations in the *status quo,* for whatever reason, felt the need of showing why alterations could not be made without wreaking more havoc than could be remedied; they spoke in phrases much like the following lines, in which the voice is that of Masefield's " old purple parson " but the thought is that of Burke:

> You think that Squire and I are kings
>> Who made the existing state of things,
> And made it ill. I answer, No,
>> States are not made, nor patched; they grow,
> Grow slow through centuries of pain
>> And grow correctly in the main,
> But only grow by certain laws
>> Of certain bits in certain jaws.[1]

Protests of this kind against the optimistic rationalism of Helvétius, Condorcet, Godwin, and Paine were fairly common, but at about the turn of the century a new mode of attack made its appearance. Malthus, a clergyman in the Established Church and an economist by avocation, published in 1798, just four years after the works of Godwin and Condorcet had come off the press, a pamphlet in which he called upon the learned public to discount these writers severely. As Ingram puts it:

To their glowing anticipations Malthus opposes the facts of the necessity of food and the tendency of mankind to increase up to the limit of the available supply of it. In a state of universal physical well-being, this tendency, which in real life is held in check by the difficulty of procuring a subsistence, would operate without restraint. Scarcity would follow the increase of numbers; the leisure would soon cease to exist; the old struggle for life would recommence; and inequality would reign once more. If Godwin's ideal system, therefore, could be established, the single force of the principle of population, Malthus maintained, would suffice to break it down.[2]

We are here dealing with Malthus in detail because of his importance in the genealogy of the Darwinian theory, and it seems necessary to trace the biological background out of which the Malthusian doctrines developed. In so doing, we shall also be tracing the other antecedents of Darwin.

Biology before Malthus. — Although the truly scientific study of the biological processes which underlie human society dates from Darwin, Huxley, Claude Bernard, Haeckel, Galton, and others of their age, the preparation for their work was laid by the developments in biology between Vesalius and Lamarck. Not only was the biological knowledge necessary to any basic understanding of society rendered more precise and comprehensive by the technical students of various aspects of biology, but, with Malthus and his predecessors, an ever greater interest was taken in the application of biological principles to social problems.

We may first briefly notice some of the more remarkable advances in biological science which served to give students a better idea of the nature of man and of the relation between his physical endowments and social processes and institutions. Leonardo da Vinci (1452–1519) was the first in Western Europe to begin a concrete and realistic study of the human body, but he worked by himself and had little influence on posterity. The beginning of the systematic study of anatomy is usually associated with the work of Andreas Vesalius (1514–1564). Vesalius's impulse to the study of human anatomy was broadened into the investigation of the comparative anatomy of man and other animals by such investigators as Georges Cuvier (1769–1832) and John Hunter (1728–1793). Work such as this was of much value in founding the Darwinian hypothesis. Physiology may be said to date from the discovery of the circulation of the blood by William Harvey (1578–1657), and it was notably forwarded by the innovations and researches of Albrecht von Haller (1708–1777), Johannes Müller (1801–1858), and Claude Bernard (1813–1878). The first important work in the microscopic study of organic matter was done by Robert Hooke, who published the results of his earlier researches in 1665. He was the first to learn of the cellular nature of organic tissue. This type of activity was markedly advanced in the generation immediately following Hooke by Jan Swammerdam, Antony van Leeuwenhoek, Marcello Malpighi, and Nehemiah Grew. The cell theory was established by Bichat, Schleiden, and Schwann in the first half of the nineteenth century. The work in microscopic anatomy and cytology, together with the establishment of embryology by Karl Ernst von Baer (1792–1876), laid the foundation for the study of genetics, so important for social biology and eugenics. The evolutionary hypothesis was also prepared for through the work of John Ray (1628–1705) and the Count de Buffon (1707–1788) in natural history, of Alexander von Humboldt (1769–1859) on the relation between geographical factors and the distribution of the flora and fauna of the earth, of Carl Linnæus (1707–1778) in biological classification, and of Georges Cuvier in paleontology. In the writings of Geoffroy St. Hilaire (1772–1844), Erasmus Darwin (1731–1802), Jean Baptiste Lamarck (1744–1829), and Johann Wolfgang von Goethe (1749–1832), we find preliminary formulations of the evolutionary point of view, which were soon to be confirmed and extended by Darwin, Wallace, Romanes, and others. Finally, we must not overlook the origins of physical anthropology and the study of racial traits by Johann Friedrich Blumenbach (1752–1840), Peter Camper (1722–1789), and Anders Retzius (1796–1860). The more significant aspects of the application of biology to human society awaited the activities of Malthus and the Neo-Malthusians; of Galton, Pearson, and the eugenists; and of Topinard, Martin, Keith, and the physical anthropologists; but all subsequent progress in both biology and biological sociology rested upon the work done from the middle of the sixteenth to the middle of the nineteenth century, work which marked the passage of biology from a branch of theology to a positive science characterized by exact methods and an ever-growing body of subject-matter.[3]

The origins of one quantitative aspect of human biology — namely, the study of population problems — are usually associated with the work of Thomas Robert Malthus (1766–1834), but Gonnard and Stangeland have shown that there was a veritable swarm of writers who dealt with the problems of population before Malthus. There was little if anything original in his work, but he drew attention to the problem in a way and at a time which led to the definite association of his name with the beginnings of the study of the relation of population and food supply. Stangeland's summary makes plain the setting and significance of the work of Malthus:

From about the time of the Restoration in England, and from the days of Colbert (but also before, as in Bodin's *Commonwealth*) in France, and from the Peace of Westphalia in Germany, and concurrently in most other countries, with the growing dominance of mercantilist influence and the increasing rivalry among the nations for political preeminence, — the doctrine that a great and increasing population is always desirable became universally accepted. Populousness, national wealth, and popular welfare were regarded as interdependent.

Toward the end of the seventeenth and to the middle of the eighteenth century more rationally developed theories found acceptance, not as replacing but as supplementing the ordinary mercantilist, nationalist doctrine. Great populations were still desired, but with the reservation that the people be comfortable, employed and healthy. Some ideas of the limitations to increase by the amount of means of subsistence obtainable were expressed; — governments should seek to develop commerce first and agriculture secondly, so that the masses could find employment and thereby be enabled to increase effectually and without an unnecessary increase of misery or a too great increase of pauperism.

From about the middle of the eighteenth century to the time of Malthus, the modern, so-called "Malthusian," doctrine, that population tends to increase more rapidly than the food supply, found almost universal acceptance; — among French writers, by Montesquieu, Brückner, and others, besides the Physiocrats and political and philosophical writers generally; in England and America in the works of Franklin, Hume, Wallace, Steuart, Smith, Paley, Chalmers, and others; in Germany in the discussions of Möser, Schloezer, and Herrenschwand, especially; and among Italian writers quite generally.

The part of the theory which maintains that population tends to increase at a geometrical ratio, while the means of subsistence tends to increase more slowly was announced in the works of Graunt, Petty, Saxe, Brückner, Mann, Suessmilch, Ortes, and several others. This part of the theory owes its origin mainly to the comparative study of birth rates and mortality tables of various cities on the continent as well as of London. Positive and preventive checks to increase were acknowledged by most writers; but it was often believed that many of these hindrances to increase could be removed by wise and benevolent governmental regulation.

The theories of the last fifty years before Malthus are frequently parts of protests against governmental abuses and the special privileges and wanton luxury of the rich and the nobility, with a disregard of the interests and welfare of the many, the peasants. A more equitable distribution of wealth as well as more intelligent and better methods of administration of fiscal burdens were desired. This would relieve the poor and encourage increase; edicts and laws which did not take the economic well-being of the people into account could never effect an increase.[4]

The first edition of Malthus's essay was merely a polemic screed which grew out of an argument with his father, who was an ardent admirer of Rousseau, Godwin, and Condorcet. It was revised and greatly improved and expanded in the second edition, published in 1803, entitled *An Essay on the Principle of Population: or a View of Its Past and Present Effects on Human Happiness; with an Enquiry into our Prospects Respecting the Future Removal or Mitigation of the Evils which It Occasions.* That the central idea of Malthus — namely, the tendency of the population to increase beyond the means of subsistence — was a novel or original theory, neither he nor any other scholar has ever contended; both Plato and Aristotle had foreseen the action and result of this principle and had proposed preventive methods. The distinctive contribution of Malthus was the scientific formulation and elaborate statement of this principle with many of its implications.

The Tendency to Outbreed the Food Supply. — Malthus sets forth his purpose in the second essay in the following words:

The principal object of this present essay is to examine the effects of one great cause immediately united with the very nature of man, which, though it has been constantly and powerfully operating since the commencement of society, has been little noticed by the writers who have treated this subject. The facts which establish the existence of this cause, have, indeed, been repeatedly stated and acknowledged; but its natural and necessary effects have been almost totally overlooked; though probably among these effects may be reckoned a considerable portion of the vice and misery, and of that unequal distribution of the bounties of nature, which has been the unceasing object of the enlightened philanthropist in all ages to correct.

The cause which I allude to, is the constant tendency in all animated life to increase beyond the nourishment prepared for it.[5]

The check to this tendency is easy among plants and animals, since the lack of room or nourishment, or the consumption of one variety by another, tends to shut off undue increase. With man the checks are somewhat more complicated, as we shall see.

Malthus then proceeds to analyze the comparative rate of increase between population and the means of subsistence. He says that the experience in America has been for the population to double itself each twenty-five years, though other distinguished authorities have maintained that the doubling process might take place as often as once in from ten to fifteen years. He concludes that in making the comparison, it would be safer to take the lowest estimate; namely, twenty-five years. On the other hand, it would be a most extravagant estimate to consider that the produce of the earth could increase each twenty-five years by an amount equal to that now produced. In short, a conservative estimate of the rate of increase of population puts it as doubling each quarter of a century — that is, an increase in a *geometric* ratio; while a most sanguine estimate of the rate of the increase of the means of subsistence would put it as but an increase in an *arithmetic* ratio. Malthus then sums up the argument and shows its consequences:

Taking the whole earth . . . and, supposing the present population equal to a thousand millions, the human species would increase as the numbers 1, 2, 4, 8, 16, 32, 64, 128, 256, and the subsistence as 1, 2, 3, 4, 5, 6, 7, 8, 9. In two centuries the population would be to the means of subsistence as 256 to 9; in three centuries as 4,096 to 13, and in two thousand years the difference would almost be incalculable.

In this supposition no limits whatever are placed to the produce of the earth. It may increase for ever, and be greater than any assignable quantity; yet still the power of the population being in every period so much superior, the increase of the human species can only be kept down to the level of the means of subsistence by the constant operation of the strong law of necessity, acting as a check upon the greater power.[6]

Checks on Population Increase. — There are two great checks, says Malthus, which tend to keep down the disproportionate increase of population: viz., the preventive and the positive. The first or preventive check may be otherwise classified as moral restraint, and consists in prudence and restraint in marrying and begetting children before one possesses the material means of supporting them. This discretion may lead to temporary unhappiness for the person who exercises it, but such consequences are negligible as compared with the misery which would certainly result from failure to practice self-control. The preventive check, in other words, may grow into a positive check in some regrettable cases, for the restrained passion prevented from finding a matrimonial outlet may lead to immorality and prostitution, which are among the greatest causes of misery and positive checks to propagation. There are, however, a number of other positive checks, as Malthus shows:

The positive checks to population are extremely various, and include every cause, whether arising from vice or misery, which in any way contribute to shorten the natural duration of human life. Under this head therefore may be enumerated all unwholesome occupations, severe labor and exposure to the seasons, extreme poverty, bad nursing of children, great towns, excesses of all kinds, the whole train of common diseases and epidemics, wars, pestilence, plague, and famine.

On examining these obstacles to the increase of population which are classed under the heads of preventive and positive checks, it will appear that they are all resolvable into moral restraint, vice, and misery.[7]

The checks to population being thus reduced to these three, Malthus points out that it is not hard to discern that the first is much less objectionable than the others, and goes on to paint an idyllic picture of an imaginary society in which this principle of restraint holds sway: (1) the supply of labor in the market would be diminished and wages would therefore rise; (2) restraint in the sexual sphere would be accompanied by restraint in expenditure of wages, and therefore a sum for contingencies would be in possession of every family. This would make private charity or public relief unnecessary except in the case of those persons " who had fallen into misfortunes against which no prudence or foresight could provide." [8]

No Relief from the Struggle for Existence. — Malthus and his disciples were compelled to admit, however, that there was no immediate prospect of realizing this idyllic condition, and that the positive checks would continue to operate as they had in the past. " The short and simple annals of the poor " would consist largely of the record of the bitter, unrelenting struggle for the bare means of existence. The deductions drawn from this inescapable conclusion (" inescapable " in view of the premises) served to buttress the opposition of the economic liberals to remedial legislation for the working classes, and played the chief rôle in the formulation of the famous " iron law of wages," according to which it was held impossible for wages to rise permanently above that amount just sufficient to keep the laborers alive and reproducing. These and many more consequences of a clergyman's argument with his father might be dealt with in detail, but we are here concerned with Malthus primarily as he exerted influence, through his emphasis upon the struggle for existence, on the theory of natural selection propounded by Charles Darwin.

Darwin and the Process of Organismic Evolution. — In preceding pages it has been shown that the idea of evolution as a general guiding principle was by no means new in Darwin's time,

700 SOCIAL DARWINISM, PROS AND CONS

and that Herbert Spencer, in particular, had published in 1857 an essay in which he announced his theory of universal evolution as a cosmic process of equilibration of organism with environment.[9] The only thing lacking was tangible empirical evidence of the way in which this process operated. This lack was soon to be supplied by Darwin, Wallace, and a host of other biologists all over Europe.

Darwin had been particularly fortunate as a young man in having made a voyage around the world, during which he had ample opportunity for observation and collection of specimens.[10] Reflection led him to accept the theory of the gradual modification of species rather than adhere to the older notions of special creation and fixity, and he also came to see the rightness of Lamarck's contention that adaptation had taken place, although he rejected the latter's explanation. Finally, he had made a study of the variation and selection of domestic animals and plants. The only question for which he could find no answer was this: How could the modifications produced by the conscious or " artificial " selection of the breeder and fancier occur under natural conditions? In his autobiography he tells the story of the way in which the answer came to him:

In October 1838, that is, fifteen months after I had begun my systematic inquiry, I happened to read for amusement *Malthus on Population*, and being well prepared to appreciate the struggle for existence which everywhere goes on from long continued observation of the habits of animals and plants, it at once struck me that under these circumstances favorable variations would tend to be preserved, and unfavorable ones to be destroyed. The result of this would be the formation of new species. *Here, then, I had at last got a theory by which to work.*[11]

What have the sponsors of Pure Induction to say to this " mere theory " ? The stubborn problem was about to be solved. If empirical evidence could be brought to show that variation was a universal process, that reproduction was vastly in excess of survival, that this discrepancy was due to the rigors of the struggle for existence, and that the survivors underwent similar variation and selection until finally, after many generations, a new type emerged, the theory of natural selection as the mode of organismic evolution could be regarded as proved. Darwin at once set to work to assemble the evidence needed to bear out his working hypothesis, and in 1856 began to prepare a lengthy work which was to set this hypothesis and the evidence before the public. At about the same time Alfred Russel Wallace, another biologist, arrived at a theory in all respects similar to Darwin's, and after taking counsel with friends, Darwin and Wallace published their discovery together in the summer of 1858. Little general notice was taken of their joint product, and following the urgent advice of fellow-scientists, Darwin took the manuscript he had begun in 1856, condensed it, added new evidence, and brought it out in November, 1859, under the title of *The Origin of Species*. This immediately attracted attention, and a battle of far-reaching significance began, which became more intense when in 1871 he published *The Descent of Man,* a work in which he applied the hypothesis contained in his major work to the question of the origin of man. Eventually the theory of organismic evolution won acceptance from the greater part of the scientific world (although not in the precise form in which it was first set forth), and man's kinship with "the lower orders of creation" became common knowledge. As a result of the campaign of popularization carried on by Huxley and others, the phrases "the struggle for existence," "natural selection," and "the survival of the fittest" were scattered hither and yon, taking root almost everywhere.

Darwin Not a "Social Darwinist." — The great biologist did not himself systematically extend his hypothesis to the explanation of social phenomena; that was a task reserved, perhaps unfortunately, for others who did not all possess his keenly critical type of mind and his willingness to follow the evidence. If by "social Darwinism" is meant the glorification of the struggle for existence and the belief that the upper classes in the present social order have survived because of their peculiar fitness in the moral or ethical sense, then it may be said categorically that Darwin was not a social Darwinist. Had he lived long enough he might have given us an aphorism to set beside Marx's "*Je ne suis pas un marxiste.*"

Indeed, Darwin was inclined to emphasize a contrast between the processes of organismic evolution and of social evolution, or at least to maintain that while the factors of natural selection had produced the physical basis for man's higher nature, social selection had developed the more important moral qualities. In general, however, Darwin avoided any dogmatic social philosophy. He expressed himself as uncertain whether the nomenclature, mechanisms, and processes of biological or organismic evolution could be transferred without serious modification to the social field. That which characterizes all types of so-called social Darwinism, however divergent in nature and content, is a common and uniform lack of justice and accuracy in the claim to

Darwinian approval for their doctrines. As Ernest Barker says, " On the whole, Darwin devoted his thoughts to natural science, and never set himself up to provide a social philosophy. What has happened to his doctrine is that would-be social philosophers have pressed it willy-nilly into their service; and in this manner it has been enlisted under the different banners of anti-clericalism, and imperialism, socialism, and militarism." [12]

" External Conflict " Theories. — In the latter part of this chapter we shall call attention to the part played by the popular champion of Darwin, Huxley, in stressing the antithesis between natural and social selection that Darwin had tentatively formulated, and shall also devote considerable space to the writings of Novicow, who opposed the social Darwinism of his time on the ground that no moral qualities inhere in the mere fact of natural selection — a contention of which Darwin himself might have approved. Before doing this it is necessary to discuss at length certain outstanding types of social Darwinism, particularly those that made the development of the central political institution, the state, their point of focus. In analyzing the theories of Marx and Engels, we have already referred to the " internal conflict " doctrine of the origin and maintenance of the state; i.e., to the notion that the state develops *within* any community as soon as it becomes necessary to consolidate the position of an exploiting class. The ideas we shall now examine may first of all be classed under the head of " external conflict " theories; i.e., they advance the conception that the state is a product of conquest (although they also pay some attention to internal conflict). A group previously dwelling *without* the confines of a given community conquers the latter, and the conquerors become a ruling caste who stay in the saddle by the use of force. In so far as this ruling caste may be regarded as winners in the struggle for existence, they fall within the formula of the social Darwinists; " natural selection " has led to " the survival of the fittest." The inference then is, often enough, that the winners " ought " to survive; ethical sanction is added to the naked fact of superior might. We are getting ahead of the story, however; we must first examine the basic postulates and the antecedents of the external conflict theory.

Fundamental Requisites of Conflict Theories. — The question as to the manner in which the state arose is one that has concerned thinkers from earliest times, as we are by this time fully aware. In spite or because of the long duration of the problem and of the many and varied attempts throughout all the ages to solve it, there is no unanimity of agreement now, nor has there ever been, upon either the distinctive characteristics of that institution we term the state, or the cause and process of its development.

Certain answers have been given with relative frequency, however, and one of the most frequent we shall now consider. All the way from Polybius to our contemporary, Franz Oppenheimer, there have been scholars who have deemed conditions resulting from conflict between ethnocentric societies as the primary element in the origin of the state. The adherents of this theory may be classified as members of the external conflict school. (From this point on in this chapter we shall drop " external "; by " conflict " or " combat " we shall mean external conflict.)

This group of theorists has set up, either explicitly or by implication, three requisites which must be fulfilled before a human society can be considered a state:

(1) Social stratification must take place as a consequence of the fact that a superior minority ("superior" in the sense of ability to gain their ends) has gained and organized control over a large majority of the people.

(2) The economic system of private ownership of property must be established among both the supraordinate and subordinate groups; hence the former must have obtained coercive power to enforce its decrees over the latter. The subordinate group must be continually seeking to become dominant itself.

(3) Both the master and the subject groups must be settled in a definite territorial area, an area over which the ruling class or " the state " exercises sovereignty.

It is plain that the state as conceived by the conflict school is a class state; it is an institution with two broad social divisions of widely divergent rank and power, one possessing and the other seeking to obtain control of the coercive elements which came into existence at the very time of the establishment of the state. In the words of Oppenheimer: " Every state in history was or is a state of classes, a polity of superior and inferior social groups based on distinctions either of rank or of property."

This viewpoint of the nature of the state manifestly is not peculiar to the conflict school; its especial stamp is derived from its conception of the process by which this type of state is believed to have come into being. The contention of the school is that stratification and its political consequent, the state, originated through the conquest of one *unstratified* group by another, the conquering group imposing itself on the conquered as a privileged, exploiting, social class. Thus the state is the political product which issued from circumstances directly due to the conquest of one " primitive tribe " by another. And it is this very conquest which, it is claimed, precipitated out those three distinctive elements — establishment of superior and inferior classes, rule of the superior class, and sovereignty over a specific area — that set the state apart from the social order immediately preceding it.

Here an important distinction must be made: It is not conflict in and of itself that has given rise to the state; rather its source is to be found in the *conquest* of one group by another, after conflict in the form of physical *combat* has occurred between them. To sum up the fundamental position of the conflict school in regard to the nature and origin of the state: the state is a class state; it has originated through conflict indirectly and conquest directly.

Thus the processes of conflict and conquest, the second growing out of the first, led to the rise of the state, but these processes presumably took place among " primitive," unstratified societies, and the conflict school considers these to have had certain definite characteristics. They are similar in essence to the community with " mechanical solidarity " of Durkheim and the *Gemeinschaft* of Tönnies. The bond of union among members of such a social unit is kinship, not territorial contiguity. Further, social stratification has not set in to destroy the homogeneity of these sacred societies; the persons who make them up are mentally, morally, and socially similar. The force which controls the life of the community is the force of tradition; the " cake of custom " has fixed itself almost unshakeably upon them. So binding are the social decrees of the community, so deeply are they ingrained into each and every member, that, although the elders may occupy positions of control, overt coercion to enforce the prevailing code is rare. The members, moreover, are very group-conscious; they enter into almost no relations with genuine " outsiders," whom they almost always deem inferior to themselves. Such, then, is the nature of the social groupings whose struggles and conquests have resulted in the origin of the state, according to the viewpoint of the conflict school. With this fundamental position of the school in mind, let us now turn to a somewhat more detailed survey of the theories that have been advanced by some of its forerunners and its more important members.

Classical and Medieval Adumbrations. — The general notion that conflict and struggle have played a vital part in both cosmic and social evolution is an old one. As early as the close of the sixth century B.C., Heraclitus of Ephesus is reputed to have re-marked in a strain quite " social Darwinian " that " War is common to all and strife is justice, and all things come into being and pass away through strife." [13] The concept of " war as deter-miner," then, dates back almost to the dawn of human reflection on the problems of development and progress, and its persistence through the centuries is but a reflection of the persistence of combat. Herodotus (c. 484–424 B.C.) considered the Persian Wars as the collision of two fundamentally opposed civilizations, and had no doubt that the victory of the Greeks was an unmis-takable proof that the gods had expressed their approval of the Hellenic virtues.[14] Although he was compelled to witness the actual submerging of Hellenic localism by the Macedonian Em-pire, Aristotle (384–322 B.C.) opposed the policy of territorial expansion, set forth the patriarchal theory of political origins, regarded the small city-state as the ideal political unit, and held that stability was the chief criterion for judging of the excellence of the administration of particular states.[15]

All this, however, was but a vague foreshadowing of the con-flict theory; Polybius (203–121 B.C.), one of the greatest his-torians, sociologists, and political scientists of antiquity, may properly be considered the originator of the historical theory of the origin of the state through the use of force. Drawing his con-clusions from his detailed study of the development of the Roman Republic through military expansion, he contended that political evolution was a social process which was initiated by war and conflict, but which was progressively tempered by the introduction of the elements of reason, reflection, and consent,[16] à la Pax Romana. The Epicureans among the Greeks, as well as their Roman followers, such as Lucretius and Horace, took from Heraclitus the doctrine of the origin of all things in conflict and strife, but held that the inconveniences of warfare and anarchy in society led to the establishment of a stable political order and the introduction of the " reign of law." [17] The epic poet, Virgil, and the epic historian, Livy, both sang the praises of the Roman expansion, the gradual absorption of smaller states by the Roman administrative machine, and the " peaceful blessings " of the re-sulting centralization of power.[18]

Though the Christian theologians expanded the Stoic doctrines emphasizing the essential brotherhood of mankind, historical con-ditions made it inevitable that the Dark Ages, the first centuries of the Christian domination of the Western world, should wit-ness a prevalence of warfare unparalleled since the conquests of early Rome. This social environment reacted on the writers of the period, who represented the development of political institutions as a perpetual struggle to substitute law and stability for strife and disorder.[19] With the development of scholasticism in the thirteenth century and its revival of Aristotelian social theory, the patriarchal theory of political origins again became popular, and persisted until the disintegration of the scholastic philosophy with the new intellectual impulses which came from the Crusades, the trade with the Levant, and the ensuing Commercial Revolution.[20]

Ibn Khaldūn, Eulogist and Elegist of Nomadic Hardihood. — In the chapter on " The Meeting of East and West " considerable attention was paid to the learned Berber of Tunis, who witnessed the upheaval of Moorish culture and the disorganization of urban life attending that expansion and contraction of the Mohammedan world which antedated the European developments by at least two centuries. Our interest in him, however, was primarily with reference to theories of migration, mobility, and culture contact, although by implication some aspects of his thinking about political institutions were noted. His *Prolegomena to History* was our *pièce de résistance,* and it is also in the *Prolegomena* that the material is to be found which places this astonishingly fertile thinker among the conflict theorists. In that work the point is made that people who live from the produce furnished by their herds are usually addicted to nomadic life, whereas agriculturists tend to congregate in towns and villages. Under settled conditions, however, vice, luxury, and immorality abound, with the inevitable consequence that the moral fiber of the inhabitants decays. Living behind gates and walls in perfect security, with troops posted on the outskirts of the community, the population as a whole renounces the bearing of arms and soon loses its pristine bravery, ferocity, and pride in independence. Moreover, each sedentary sybarite pursues his own individual interest without regard to the welfare of his neighbors; communal solidarity is superseded by extreme individuation. Among the nomads, on the other hand, the hard, rigorous life of the desert engenders simplicity of manners and physical ruggedness and endurance. The constant moving about and the ceaseless raiding and counter-raiding of desert tribes develop a strong tribal discipline and intense *esprit de corps;* the commands of leaders are instantly obeyed, and each combatant has but one thought, the protection of tribe and family. Further, all the members of the unit are bound together by kinship ties. Thus nomads in the desert are

characterized by abstemiousness, discipline, united action, fight-
ing ability, bravery, and ferocity. Hence Ibn Khaldūn frames the
generalization that any pastoral nomad group can always van-
quish a sedentary community of equal man-power.

This leads to a continual conquest of towns and cities by the
brave and hardy desert dwellers, who, attracted by the ease and
luxury and bountifulness of city life, abandon their sparse grass-
lands to sweep down upon the settled agricultural districts. This
overcoming of tillage peoples means the establishment of a state
or empire. The nomads, on becoming sedentary, soon lose their
distinctive characteristics. They drift toward all the customs of
sedentary life and promptly form sedentary habits. Becoming
habituated to abundance, well-being, and softness, they gradually lose their courage and ferocity. Contact with the alien inhabitants of the city, leading to a mixture of institutions and of
blood, enfeebles family relationships and domestic ties. Finally,
the deep-rooted *esprit de corps* is entirely obliterated. Having
taken on civilized manners, the wild tribal group loses much of
its erstwhile valor and strength, and in its turn falls an easy prey
to some nomadic tribe fresh from the desert. In this way the
empires established by nomads undergo a constant cycle, a rise
to power and then a collapse.

This very brief restatement (see Chapter Seven for details)
of Ibn Khaldūn's theory relating to the origin of states or empires is incomplete; yet it is perhaps sufficient to recall to mind
his trenchant analysis and to show that he properly belongs to
the conflict school.

He believed that in nomadic tribes observed by him neither
class stratification nor private property had set in, and also that
bonds of blood kinship tied together all the members of the
group, marked as it was by rigid social control and an intense
tribal spirit. Hence all the attributes of "mechanical solidarity"
attach themselves to these and similar nomad groups. It is also
true that among sedentary urban or semi-urban peoples the
original homogeneity of culture and fixed social control frequently gives way to disunion and individuation.

It must be admitted, however, that Ibn Khaldūn ascribed the
origin of states to the conquest of *stratified* tillage communities
by nomadic tribes. From this it follows that he does not regard
the state as the product of two similar, unstratified groups, and
thus he is somewhat at variance with other conflict theorists in
this respect.

Nevertheless, the crucial point that states arise through group

conflict and conquest is adhered to strictly. Further, in these
" conquest " states or empires class differentiation definitely takes
place; the conquering nomads become rulers over the subject
peoples within the limits of the conquered domain. The great
Moslem's conceptions of the rise and fall of empires, and of the
reasons for the cyclical recurrence of this rise and fall, make still
more plain his position as a conflict theorist, and in addition reveal him as a thinker who emphasized causal principles in history
at a time when " providential " viewpoints everywhere held sway.

Machiavelli. and Machtpolitik. — Once more we turn to the
West, where we again view that process of fourteenth- and
fifteenth-century exploration and commercial expansion which
marks the dawn of modern history. Along with the mushroom
growth of commerce came the general suppression of the feudal system and the rise of the modern dynastic national states
through the struggle of the kings against the feudal lords — an
environment admirably suited to the production of theories of
social conflict.[21] As Italy was first affected by the development of
commerce in the later medieval period, it is not surprising that
the earliest modern exponent of *Machtpolitik* was the Italian,
Nicolo Machiavelli (1469–1527), whose social theory mirrored
the continual intercity strife of the Italy of his day. A great
admirer of Polybius, he adopted the latter's theory of political
origins, but was not willing to stop at this point: he insisted that
the state not only originated in force, but that it must continue to
expand or perish. He not only rejected the Aristotelian notion
of the virtue of political stability, but also departed from Classical and Christian precedents by ejecting ethics from the domain
of political philosophy. Maintaining that considerations of individual morality have no relation to the acts of the state, he thus
revealed himself as an expositor of *Realpolitik* as well as of
Machtpolitik.[22]

Bodin, Defender of Forcible Amalgamation. — The French
publicist, Jean Bodin (1530–1596), reflected the process of
national unification in France manifesting itself in the civil wars
of the sixteenth century which culminated in the coronation of
Henry IV He viewed society and the state as an aggregate of
lesser social groups, and held that the state was and should be
produced by the forcible amalgamation of these smaller social
entities.

In his philosophy of society, Jean Bodin indicated three types
of social organization: the family, the civil society, and the state.
He agrees with Aristotle that all society has a natural origin in

the family: " The beginnings of all civil societies are derived from
a family which is itself a natural society, and by the father of
nature itself first founded in the beginning together with mankind." (For references on the general social theory of Jean Bodin,
see Chapter Nine.) Although the family is a natural society,
and existed before the civil society, still the former contains the
germ of the latter. This arises from the fact that civil society
arose because reason, ingrafted by God in man, made him desir-
ous of society and speech with other men as well as causing him
to take pleasure in the propagation and increase of families.

Civil society has its origin in the social nature of man, but the
state originates quite differently: " Force, violence, ambition,
covetousness, and desire of revenge have armed one [civil so-
ciety] against another; the issues of war and combat giving
victory unto the one side made the other to become unto them
slaves. Then that full and entire liberty of nature given to every
man, to live as himself best please, was altogether taken from the
vanquished. So the words of Lord and Master, Prince and Subject, before unknown unto the world, were first brought into use.
Yea, Reason and the very light of nature leadeth us to believe
very force and violence to have given course and beginning unto
Commonweale." Thus Bodin presents the idea of a free and
equal civil society antecedent to politically organized society, and
anticipates Gumplowicz in his concept of struggle as responsible
for the origin of the state.[23]

It cannot be said that the social philosophies of Ibn Khaldūn
and Jean Bodin are similar; their details are considerably at variance, but the basic principles underlying both have much in common. There is at least some suggestion of similarity between the
nomad tribe and the civil society. Both are groupings relatively
lacking in social stratification, and in each the individual members
are practically on equal footing. According to Bodin, after a
period of violence and war among just such groups the chances
of combat lead to conquest and the establishment of the state,
in which the conquerors rule and the vanquished are enslaved.
In contrast with this, Ibn Khaldūn does not indicate that the
tillage peoples, subjugated by the desert tribes, are forced into
a condition of slavery. Whether or not the conquered population
is placed in servitude, it is clear that the states of Ibn Khaldūn
and Jean Bodin are both class states founded by conquest.[24]

*Hobbes, Hume, and Ferguson, Founders of Modern Conflict
Theories.* — The English absolutist, Thomas Hobbes (1588–
1679), was an early member of the modern conflict school. To

discredit the revolutionary theories of his day in England, he emphasized the great value of political authority by dwelling at length on the evils of the incessant warfare which must always be a concomitant of anarchy and the absence of authoritative political control. Although he is conventionally regarded as a great exponent of the contractual theory of political origins, Hobbes argued that this contract need not be voluntary, but might be forced by a conquering group upon a conquered people.[25]

Important and interesting as the above anticipations of the modern conflict school may be, it seems fairly clear that the modern version of the historical theory of political origins must be credited to David Hume (1711–1776). In his destructive criticism of the social contract theory, Hume offered as a substitute the doctrine which had been foreshadowed by Polybius and Bodin: namely, that the state and government originate in force, but come to rest more and more upon consent as the subject citizens begin to appreciate the value of political control and institutions.[26] Hume was a philosopher and a psychologist, however, rather than a historian; his doctrines were expressed only in a fragmentary manner, and his contemporaries, Millars and Linguet, were not notably successful in their efforts at systematization. It remained for his disciple, Adam Ferguson (1723–1816), to present the earliest successful systematic elaboration of the historical theory of social evolution.[27] So strongly did he stress the importance of conflict and competition that Gumplowicz has maintained that he was the first great exponent of the theory of social and political development, viewed as the product of the struggle of social groups.[28] This is undoubtedly claiming too much for Ferguson, but his great importance is beyond question.

Hegel, Comte, and Spencer. — Hegel's conception of the development of society and civilization as a process of conflict was an important contribution to this type of doctrine, though Hegel's emphasis was upon the psychical rather than the physical aspect of strife.[29]

The founders of sociology under its present name, Auguste Comte and Herbert Spencer, while accepting the historical theory of political origins in the primordial struggle and amalgamation of social groups, did not push this doctrine to an extreme. Comte held that not only force but also the Aristotelian doctrines of the inherent sociability of man and the social division of labor must be assumed as necessary to explain the origin and growth of the state.[30] Spencer, in drawing his famous contrast between military and industrial society, contended that although society, the state,

and government originated in the primeval warfare that produced the amalgamation and integration of primitive social
groups, there was an inevitable tendency to substitute an industrial for a military basis of social life and political activity, and
to replace warfare by industrial competition.[31]

We have several times pointed out that the Spencerian philosophy of cosmic evolution was not the same as the Darwinian
hypothesis of organismic evolution, but it would be folly to deny
that Spencer had been influenced by Darwin. In fact, it is highly
probable that Spencer's conflict theory (outlined above and dealt
with in detail in a subsequent section) was partially inspired by
the writings of Walter Bagehot (1826–1877), a follower of
Darwin who made the first systematic application of his hypothesis to the social field. Let us therefore see what Bagehot had to
say before discussing Spencer further.

Bagehot, First Avowed Social Darwinist. — This brilliant
English writer was eminent in at least four fields: politics,
science, economics, and sociology. It is in the last-mentioned field
that he made his application of Darwinian principles. The subtitle of his *Physics and Politics* (1873) — " Thoughts on the Application of the Principles of ' Natural Selection ' and ' Inheritance ' to Political Society " — indicates clearly enough his objective in this work. He divided the history of human society into
three basic stages. The first of these was the custom-making age
in which group mores (customs, etc. — Bagehot never used the
term " mores ") gradually took shape and assumed ascendency
over thought and action. This was the period of the fixing of
various types of mores as they evolved to meet certain definite
conditions in the social and natural environment. The second
stage was that of the conflict of groups which had adopted these
diverse sets of mores — the so-called nation- or state-making age
— in which a victorious group would conquer others and force
upon them the mores of the conquerors. This was the period of
political origins. It also illustrated in a social sense the analogue
of the biological struggle for existence. The groups with the
best customary codes were those which survived. These early
military-religious states, however, tended to develop cultural stagnation and arrested civilization unless variation and progress
were ensured through a growing prevalence of government by
discussion. Discussion served to dissolve antiquated customs, develop tolerance, and open the way for innovations. But discussion
was never able to destroy the old entirely; so civilization has been
characterized by the social heredity of the best customs from the

past, with the opportunity through discussion and tolerance to add new, change-causing elements to culture and institutions.

Though Bagehot wrote his *Physics and Politics* to illustrate the social applications of the new biology, his work was quite as much psycho-sociological as biological in its analysis and implications. He was as much a forerunner of Gabriel Tarde as a social Darwinist.[32] Moreover, he did not lay great stress on strictly biological and racial factors — a stress which is characteristic of full-fledged social Darwinists, like Gumplowicz — nor did he exalt the social rôle of conflict. All in all, he belongs only on the margin of the conflict school proper, and his chief significance here is his probable influence on Spencer.

Spencer's Theory of Political Origins. — In his theory of social evolution Spencer introduces a line of analysis very similar to that of Bagehot. His main conclusions regarding the evolution of political organization may be summarized about as follows: At the outset society may be assumed to exist as an undifferentiated and unorganized horde. The beginning of authority and political organization was the temporary submission of the group to a leader in time of war. The natural prowess of this leader in war was augmented by his supposed power to control ghosts and obtain their aid, thus bringing a supernatural sanction to his rule. In due course of time, with the improving organization of society, the more continuous periods of warfare and the better organization of military activity, this temporary war leader evolved into the chief or king who held his power for life. In turn, the difficulties and disorder which occurred at the death of a leader and the period of the choice of a successor tended to establish the principle of hereditary leadership. In this manner the stability of leadership was provided for. Along with this development of the ruler went the parallel evolution of the consultative and representative bodies. First merely spontaneous bodies meeting in times of necessity, they evolved into formal senates and assemblies.

The processes of integration and differentiation are exhibited in the development of political organization as well as in evolution in general. The great period of military activity which characterized the earlier stages of political evolution brought about the consolidation of the petty primitive groups and their respective territory. As the best organized groups tended to win in the struggle, the process of the integration of society and the extension of the range of power of the successful state was a cumulative matter. With the integration of political authority both in scope of application and increase of area of control, there went a corresponding increase in differentiation and coördination. The differentiation of society, which begins in the family, is extended through the periods of conquest that characterize early political progress until it has created the classes of wealthy rulers, ordinary freemen, serfs, and slaves. As political power becomes centered in a definite ruling class, and is increased in scope and applied over a larger territory, it has to be delegated in order to be administered with efficiency. All of the vast machinery of modern government with its ministries, its local governing agencies, its judicial, revenue, and military systems, is but the further differentiation and coördination of the earlier fundamental germs of government expressed in the simple triune structure of chief, council, and assembly.

The state at first centers all its attention on military organization, conquest, and territorial aggrandizement, but as time goes on its attention is turned more and more toward the development of industry. From this time on the process of political evolution is one of a transformation of the military state into the industrial state. This process is still under way. The purely industrial state, however, is not the goal of social evolution. The ultimate stage to be hoped for is one in which the resources of a developed industrialism may be turned toward the perfection of human character in the higher aspects of moral conduct.[33]

It is clear that the famous " homogeneity to heterogeneity " formula of cosmic evolution plays the leading part in this theory, but it is equally plain that Darwinian notions of the type popularized by Bagehot are by no means absent.

Gumplowicz, Most Extreme of the Conflict School. — In the development of social Darwinism in the stricter sense there can be no doubt that the most influential figure was the eminent Austrian sociologist, political scientist, and jurist, Ludwig Gumplowicz. Entertaining the same aspiration in regard to sociology that Buckle had manifested concerning history, Gumplowicz made a resolute and consistent effort to reduce sociology to a natural science. He attempted to base it upon certain definite universal or cosmic laws applicable to social life. The core of his system was the doctrine that social and cultural evolution was wholly a product of the struggle of social groups, inter-group war being the social analogue of the struggle for existence and the survival of the fittest.

In applying this hypothesis to the origin of the state, two assumptions are made: an inherent, deadly hatred among different groups, peoples, and races; and the polygenetic origin of mankind. Gumplowicz maintains that the sociologist cannot discover the ultimate origin of society but must assume the existence of social groups to start the social process. The prehistoric period was characterized by the birth and differentiation of heterogeneous social units. This polygenetic viewpoint is supported by two types of evidence: (1) "good authorities"; and (2) the observation that history shows a steady decrease in the number of stocks and a constant amalgamation of tribes into larger structures. Gumplowicz assumed at the outset of the historical process of social and political development a large number of small social groups or hordes, each united by consanguinity and identity of economic interests, and living in sexual promiscuity and equality of social position.[34] The eventual emergence of the matriarchate, and later of the patriarchate, provided a crude type of organization for these groups.[35]

This elementary period of social evolution was broken down by the development of war, of inter-group conflict, and thus was initiated the eternal process of social conflict which can never have an end. In external relations the groups have continually attempted to effect further conquests, and within each expanding group there has been a ceaseless struggle going on between an ever-increasing number of competing social classes.[36]

The fundamental motive of group conquest throughout history has been the desire for an improvement of economic well-being:

The motive force in the establishment of primitive political relations was economic, as has been seen; higher material welfare was sought. But this force never fails; the innermost nature of man keeps it in ceaseless operation, promoting the development of the state as it laid its foundation. Investigate the cause of any political revolution and the result will prove that social progress is always produced by economic causes. Indeed, it cannot be otherwise, since man's material need is the prime motive of his conduct.[37]

In the earliest type of group conflict the conquered were exterminated, but in the course of time there was instituted that fundamental transformation in social evolution whereby slaughter was transmuted into slavery and economic exploitation.[38]

In this process of the superimposition of one social group upon another and the subjection of the weaker is to be found the origin of sovereignty and the state.[39] No state has ever arisen except through the conquest of one stock by another. The state is invariably a composite of heterogeneous racial and social elements. " No state has arisen without original ethnical heterogeneity; its unity is the product of social development." [40]

The minority of conquerors was able in the first instance to conquer and later to exploit the conquered majority because of superior unity and discipline, for unity and discipline are the chief source of the strength of all social groups.

As soon as the first political relations were established through group conquest resulting in the exploitation of a subject majority by a sovereign minority, the process of social conflict was transformed from an external strife between groups into a struggle between classes within the state. This intra-group conflict, in addition to its fundamental economic motive, was also stimulated by the " necessity for satisfying ambition, love of glory, the interests of a dynasty, and various other ideals; and the life and death struggle between hordes anthropologically different becomes a contest between social groups, classes, estates, and political parties." In other words, external conflict gave rise to internal conflict, to the Marxian class struggle.

The earliest class conflict was the struggle for adjustment between the sovereign and subject classes. This relatively simple process was soon interrupted, however, by the development of a class of foreign merchants whose appearance marked the beginning of that extremely important element in every population, the middle class or bourgeoisie. In response to the growing needs of the developing civilization, there differentiated from these primary or original classes of rulers, merchants, and exploited masses, such secondary or derived classes as the priesthood, professional classes, and artisans.[41]

The necessity for securing loyalty and unity to withstand outside foes forces the ruling class to grant certain concessions, and thus comes into existence the concept of " rights." From this idea of legal rights there comes forth a system of law. The class in power soon realizes that it can most easily hold and expand its sway by the establishment of political and legal institutions, backed by coercion, so that to gain control of these becomes the object of formation of state policy and the advancement of the interests of the ruling classes. Hence we can see that according to Gumplowicz political rights are the legal statement of the actual conditions that exist in any political society at a given time.[42]

The generalized account of political evolution which has been summarized above is in reality oversimplified, for a large and highly developed state is rarely or never the product of a single conquest, but is normally the result of many processes of conquest and partial or complete assimilation and amalgamation.

A unified folk-state rarely remains such for any considerable period of time, for a state has an inevitable tendency to expand or decline. New conquests bring in another set of heterogeneous elements, and the process outlined above must begin anew. No limit can be set to the extent of the possible or desirable expansion of a state. The natural tendency is for a state to increase until its strength fails from external resistance or internal disruption. This last part of Gumplowicz's theory is exactly similar to Ward's. There is a further point of similarity that does not appear in the earlier writings of Gumplowicz: late in life he was compelled to admit that behind polygenism lay the process of differentiation through which the human race of common heredity and single birthplace was broken up into " innumerable homogeneous hordes . . ." and this, as we shall see, is the position of Ward.

As was pointed out above, Gumplowicz maintains that ethical considerations have no relation to the conduct of states in a process of expansion. The state is a product of nature and is ruled and guided by the laws of nature, and is thus not amenable to ethical judgment.[43]

While no authoritative student of anthropology, with the possible exceptions of Klaatsch, Dixon, and a few others, would today accept Gumplowicz's extreme doctrine of the polygenetic origin of the several branches of the human race, it is generally agreed that the chief contribution of Gumplowicz to sociology consisted in his systematic elaboration of what has come to be widely, although by no means universally, accepted as the historical theory of the origin of the state and political sovereignty. Few would doubt, however, that he underestimated the pacific and coöperative factors which played at least some part in that process. His other doctrines were less striking, and he was antedated by Marx and a number of other scholars in his analysis of political activity within the state as a process of ceaseless struggle and continuous adjustment and readjustment between groups and classes which have their constituent principle in a common interest or policy. The undoubted importance of Gumplowicz in the sociological spread of this theory springs from his connections with that other Austrian sociologist, Ratzenhofer, and their joint influence on Small, Oppenheimer, et al.

Ratzenhofer, Military Man and Conflict Theorist. — This social philosopher, like Gumplowicz an interesting example of the ethnic strife that rent the Dual Monarchy, also held that the state arose through conflict of blood-relationship groups, but there is a deep-seated contrast between the theories of the two men. Gumplowicz not only considered the individual entirely as a group product, but also made the group the starting-point of the social process. On the other hand, the individual was the focus of Ratzenhofer's sociological investigations; the social process is a process of individual phenomena. The concern of Gumplowicz is the group as a whole; the concern of Ratzenhofer is the single unit, which, with other units, makes up the group.

Ratzenhofer, like his predecessors, set up a universal principle to explain all sociological phenomena, and for him " it is the key of *interests* that unlocks the door of every treasure house of sociological lore." Every individual is endowed with certain inner forces of vital and psychic character which are termed " interests." The whole social process is the incessant reaction of persons urged on by interests that in part conflict, and in part coincide, with the interests of their fellows. Hence the relations among various individuals are of two types: those caused by conjunction of interests, and those caused by conflict of interests. Ratzenhofer places the innate interests in the following categories: (1) the sexual interest, which is the basis of family and race and ensures continuance of the species; (2) the physiological interest, which deals with the food quest; (3) the individual interest, which drives the human being to fulfill his personal impulses regardless of all else; (4) the social interest, originally due to relations of consanguinity which cause subordination of selfish desires to group welfare; and (5) the transcendental interest, which looks to the ultimate and unseen where struggle between individual and collective interests has ceased. (Small based on this classification his famous series of " health, wealth, sociability, beauty, knowledge, rightness.")[44] Building upward from this foundation, Ratzenhofer states: " The social process is a continual formation of groups around interests and a continual exertion of reciprocal influences by means of group action."

Reversing the assumption in Gumplowicz's earlier writings, the monogenetic origin of the human race is assumed by Ratzenhofer. The first groups arise because of community of origin of certain individuals, and this blood-bond silences for a time the interests of the individual, which would otherwise render him absolutely hostile to all other men. Through increase in numbers and quest for food these primitive clans are forced into spatial separation, and this gradually leads to race differentiation. The fulfillment of such interests as are dominant in the savage tribe produces a certain structural and functional arrangement, and thus the rudiments of social authority arise.

And now the social process goes on among these early structures, marked by consanguinity, by a willingness of the individual to merge his interests with those of the entire tribe, and by a certain communal authority. The patterned plurality, manifesting as it does the dominant dispositions of its members (to control food sources and reproduce without limit), inevitably clashes with others which, like itself, are moved by the same interests. The struggle for existence has broken out in inter-group hostility and warfare, an identical state of strife being checked in the individuals of the inimical groupings by the restraints of blood kinship. From this stage on, Ratzenhofer is like all the other conflict theorists. Struggle among these primitive tribes results in victor and vanquished. At first the defeated are killed; later they are enslaved. Thus the state comes into being, with its classes (hostile to each other), laws, and sovereignty. Conflict accordingly falls into two divisions: class struggle for control of internal politics, and the efforts of the community to extend its holdings and to secure them from foreign attacks — internal and external conflict.

As a consequence of the processes just described, an extensive differentiation of social structures begins. The social process goes on as a continuous rhythm of the individualization of structures arising anew out of others already in existence, and of the socialization of structures already existing. Coincidentally the form of state gradually evolves. After conflict has established the state, there follows a period when peaceful interests predominate; this results in an attempt to reconcile a limited creative freedom of individuals with control over the subjugated. As this effort succeeds, the "culture state" supersedes the "conflict state." The ultimate dominance of the culture state means the complete socialization of man and political, social, and industrial equality through perfection of the social organization.[45]

Ratzenhofer's system has been interpreted to American readers through its critical exposition and analysis by Small, and has been applied to the analysis of the operation of the American government by A. F. Bentley in what is probably the most valuable contribution made by an American writer to the analysis of the deeper processes of government since Calhoun published his *Disquisition on Government*.

Ward, Conflict Theorist and Social Optimist. — Lester F. Ward, " the Nestor of American sociology," may also be reckoned among the conflict theorists. In presenting that part of Ward's system which has to do primarily with the state and its origin, it may be well to begin with his concept of structure: " A structure implies a certain orderly arrangement and harmonious adjustment of the materials, an adaptation of the parts and their subordination to the whole." [46] Every type of structure — inorganic, organic, or social — is held to come about through the action of a single principle: they are all products of the interaction of antagonistic forces. Through the workings of this universal law structures do not remain static; they pass from a primordial stage of great simplicity into a more complex secondary stage. These are called protosocial and metasocial respectively.

Unlike Ibn Khaldūn and Gumplowicz, who do not tell us how their tribal groupings first came into being, Ward says that the origin of his conflict groups is the simple propagating couple. Very soon there is a small family consisting of parents and children of both sexes; these grow to maturity, pair off, and thereby produce families of the second order. After several generations the group has attained a size sufficient for it to be termed a horde or " clan." At length the clan becomes overgrown and splits up into several lesser units which more or less separate territorially, but live in comparative peace with each other. Because of continuous reproduction the clans multiply rapidly, so that there results a wider and wider spatial separation, until finally certain clans have become so far removed from the original center of dispersion as to lose all connection with it. In this way Ward pictures a great area of the earth's surface sparsely peopled by a host of clans which have spread out along territorial lines of least resistance, with each clan in contact only with the few nearest by.

There now comes into play the process of social differentiation, a process which after a sufficient length of time has elapsed makes different races, in all essential respects, of clans that once dispersed from a single source. Local variations, naturally undergone by the groups in the course of their migrations, have slowly but surely changed the common speech of all into a series of different languages. Likewise local variations have rendered increasingly dissimilar their customs and beliefs. The clans are now structures of the protosocial stage; altogether similar elements compose each group. The fact that they have all developed from a single source has resulted in a repetition of like groups without any evolution in form or structural advance, although differentiations

— e.g., in speech, customs, and beliefs — have taken place. We may say, then, that the protosocial stage is marked by a large number of isolated communities.

Social differentiation is succeeded by social integration as a result of the " interaction of antagonistic forces." Social evolution has reached the stage in which innumerable alien hordes each occupy a certain territorial area. Each has members motivated by inherent gustatory and sexual appetites to perform the functions essential to life, nutrition, and reproduction. Inevitably mutual encroachment produces hostility among groups; war results, and one clan proves superior and conquers its foe or foes. The metasocial stage commences with the union of one or more simple hordes into an amalgamated group. The first step in the whole process is brought about by conquest.

The initial effect of this subjugation is the establishment of a system of caste, the conquering race assuming the rôle of a superior or noble caste and the vanquished race being relegated to the position of an inferior or ignoble caste. The greater part of the conquered race is enslaved and compelled to work; thus begins labor in the economic sense. The conquerors parcel out the lands to the leading military chieftains; thus the institution of private ownership of land has its origin. Mutual race hatreds arising from resentment and friction cause perpetual uprisings by the vanquished race requiring constant suppression by the military power. This is costly, dangerous, and precarious, and wisdom soon dictates a form of systematic treatment for offenders. Personal regulation gradually gives way to general rules, and these ultimately take the form of laws. Government by law gradually succeeds arbitrary military commands.

To step aside from the exposition of theory for an instant: It will be noted how much less positive Ward is than Gumplowicz. The former attributes the rise of group conflict to encroachments rather than to inherent hatreds, gives the fluctuating chances of combat as the cause for victory on one side or the other, and makes the separation between the master and subject elements much less distinct.

The effect of the rise of castes, of private property, and of laws is nothing less than the origin of the state. In the words of Ward: " The state is a spontaneous genetic product, resulting like all other structures from the interaction of antagonistic forces, checking and restraining one another and evolving a great social structure. . . ." [47] The state having been founded, the forces which carry on the process of social integration continue their action and bring forth the nation. First, the great majority, of both subject and master groups, is engaged in a struggle for subsistence. In the intense economic activity fostered by the new order, with its law, private property, and division of labor, this sameness of essential interest causes commingling and coöperation among the two races, with a consequent decline of hatred and prejudice. Second, however great the antipathy between the two groups may be, still it is not sufficient to prevent intermarriage. Miscegenation therefore begins immediately, and steadily becomes greater with the passage of time. The final outcome of the action of these forces is the production of a people. There then comes a realization by all the population that they are " one people " and coincidentally an attachment for country and land arises — thus a nation comes into being.

It should be remembered that this type of nation, the development of which has just been traced from the very beginning of society, is not a modern nation, but one that probably existed in prehistoric times. Struggle between two states of this type brings with it conquest and amalgamation, and a state slightly higher in the scale of social structures arises. With each step upward greater social efficiency is acquired. This process of conquest and amalgamation and slow progress has been repeated again and again in the case of every nation of which history tells us. Thus Ward adheres to his conflict theory position to the end. To conflict between unstratified clans is due the origin of the state; to conflict between states is due the march forward to greater social efficiency and higher civilization. (In contrast with Gumplowicz, Ward holds to the monogenetic theory of the origin of races, and attributes the rise of different races to their inheritance of qualities caused by local variations.)

In spite of his emphasis on conflict, Ward believed that the process of social evolution could be modified by the " natural force of the human intellect." [48] In fact, so much did he deal with the psychic factor in human society that Ellwood regards him as a founder of " psychological sociology." [49]

Oppenheimer, Reviver of the Theories of Ibn Khaldūn. — In the recent past, the most prominent advocate of the conflict theory has been Franz Oppenheimer — in fact, he is still turning out voluminous tomes designed to buttress the doctrine he laid down over twenty-five years ago. Although he follows in the footsteps of the earlier members of the conflict school, particularly Gumplowicz, he has made a more or less original effort to explain the historical fact that in some regions there have been isolated sacred communities not yet in the stage of statehood, whereas elsewhere and at other times this step has been taken. Moreover, although the modern thinkers who preceded Oppenheimer were preoccupied with finding the causes of those inter-group conflicts which give rise to the state, it remained for him, following in the footsteps of Ibn Khaldūn, to show why such conflicts have not been historically universal.

The fundamental theory of Oppenheimer is contained in his early work, *The State* (1910; 2nd ed., 1926; our references here are all to the first edition because of its historical importance). We shall quote extensively from this volume because of the lucidity of Oppenheimer's exposition even when greatly condensed:

The state is an organization of the political means. No state, therefore, can come into being until the economic means has created a definite number of objects for the satisfaction of needs, which objects may be taken away or appropriated by warlike robbery. For that reason, primitive huntsmen are without a state; and even the more highly developed huntsmen become parts of a state structure only when they find in their neighborhood an evolved economic organization which they can subjugate. But primitive huntsmen live in practical anarchy. . . .

[Further] . . . within the economic and social conditions of the peasant districts, one finds no differentiation working for the higher forms of integration. There exists neither the impulse nor the possibility for the warlike subjection of neighbors. No " State " can therefore arise; and, as a matter of fact, none ever has arisen from such social conditions. Had there been no impulse from without, from groups of men nourished in a different manner, the primitive grubber would never have discovered the State. . . .

Herdsmen, on the contrary, even though isolated, have developed a whole series of the elements of statehood; and in the tribes which have progressed further, they have developed this in its totality, with the single exception of the last point of identification which completes the state in its modern sense, that is to say, with exception only of the definitive occupation of a circumscribed territory. . . .

The huntsman carries on wars and takes captives. But he does not make them slaves; either he kills them or else he adopts them into the tribe. Slaves would be of no use to him. The booty of the chase can be stowed away even less than grain can be " capitalized." The idea of using a human being as a labor motor could only come about on an economic plane on which a body of wealth has developed, call it capital, which can be increased only with the assistance of dependent labor forces.

This stage is first reached by herdsmen. The forces of one family, lacking outside assistance, suffice to hold together a herd of very limited size, and to protect it from attacks of beasts of prey or human enemies. Until the political means is brought into play, auxiliary forces are found very sparingly. . . . The few existing labor forces, without capital, are not sufficient to permit the clan to keep very large herds. . . .

For that reason, the developed nomad spared his captured enemy; he can use him as a slave on his pasture. . . .

With the introduction of slaves into the tribal economy of the herdsmen, the state, in its essential elements, is completed, except that it has not as yet acquired a definitely circumscribed territorial limit. The state has thus the *form* of dominion, and its economic basis is the exploitation of human labor. Henceforth, economic differentiation and the formation of social classes progress rapidly. . . .

Thus the herdsman gradually becomes accustomed to earning his livelihood through warfare, and to the exploitation of men as servile labor motors. . . .

. . . tribes of herdsmen increase faster than hordes of hunters. This is so, not only because the adults can obtain much more nourishment from a given territory, but still more because possession of the milk of animals shortens the period of nursing for the mothers and consequently permits a greater number of children to be born and to grow to maturity. As a consequence, the pastures and steppes of the old world became inexhaustible fountains, which periodically burst their confines letting loose inundations of humanity, so that they came to be called the *vaginae gentium*. . . .

Hunters, it may be observed, work best alone or in small groups. Herdsmen, on the other hand, move to the best advantage in a great train, in which each individual is best protected; and which is in every sense an armed expedition, where every stopping place becomes an armed camp. Thus there is developed a science of tactical maneuvers, strict subordination, and firm discipline. . . .

The same tried order, handed down from untold ages, regulates the warlike march of the tribe of herdsmen while on the hunt, in war and in peaceable wandering. Thus they become professional fighters, irresistible until the state develops higher and mightier organizations. Herdsman and warrior become identical concepts. . . .

An identical development takes place with the sea nomads, the " Vikings," as with the land nomads. This is quite natural, since in the most important cases noted in the history of mankind, sea nomads are simply land nomads taking to the sea.[50]

The stages in the development of the primitive state Oppenheimer has divided as follows:

The first stage comprises robbery and killing in border fights, endless combats broken neither by peace nor by armistice. It is marked by killing of men, carrying away of children and women, looting of herds, and burning of dwellings. . . .

Gradually, from this first stage, there develops the second, in which the peasant, through thousands of unsuccessful attempts at revolt, has accepted his fate and has ceased every resistance. About this time, it begins to dawn on the consciousness of the wild herdsman that a murdered peasant can no longer plow, and that a fruit tree hacked down will no longer bear. In his own interest, then, wherever it is possible, he lets the peasant live and the tree stand. The expedition of the herdsmen comes just as before, every member bristling with arms, but no longer intending nor expecting war and violent appropriation. The raiders burn and kill only so far as is necessary to enforce a wholesome respect, or to break an isolated resistance. But in general, principally in accordance with a development of customary right — the first germ of the development of all public law — the herdsman now appropriates only the surplus of the peasant. . . .

The moment when first the conqueror spared his victim in order permanently to exploit him in productive work, was of incomparable historical importance. It gave birth to nation and state, to right and the higher economics, with all the developments and ramifications which have grown and which will hereafter grow out of them. . . .

The third stage arrives when the " surplus " obtained by the peasantry is brought by them regularly to the tents of the herdsmen as " tribute ", a regulation which affords to both parties self-evident and considerable advantages. By this means, the peasantry is relieved entirely from the little irregularities connected with the former method of taxation, such as a few men knocked on the head, women violated, or farmhouses burned down. The herdsmen on the other hand, need no longer apply to the " business " any " expense " and labor, to use a mercantile expression; and they devote the time and energy thus set free toward an " extension of the works ", in other words, to subjugating other peasants. . . .

The fourth stage . . . is of very great importance, since it adds the decisive factor in the development of the state, as we are accustomed to see it, namely, the union on one strip of land of both ethnic groups. . . . From now on, the relation of the two groups, which was originally international, gradually becomes more and more intranational.

This territorial union may be caused by foreign influences. It may be that the stronger hordes have crowded the herdsmen forward, or that their increase in population has reached the limit set by the nutritive capacity of the steppes or prairies. . . . In general, however, internal causes alone suffice to bring it about that the herdsmen stay in the neighborhood of their peasants. The duty of protecting their tributaries against other " bears " forces them to keep a levy of young warriors in

the neighborhood of their subjects; and this is at the same time an excellent measure of defense since it prevents the peasants from giving
way to a desire to break their bonds, or to let some other herdsmen become their overlords. . . .

As yet the local juxtaposition does not mean a state community in its
narrowest sense; that is to say, a unital organization. . . .

In case the country is not adapted to herding cattle on a large scale —
as was universally the case in Western Europe — or where a less un-
warlike population might make attempts at insurrection, the crowd of
lords becomes more or less permanently settled, taking either steep places
or strategically important points for their camps, castles, or towns. From
these centers, they control their " subjects ", mainly for the purpose of
gathering their tribute, paying no attention to them in other respects.
They let them administer their affairs, carry on their religious worship,
settle their disputes, and adjust their methods of internal economy. Their
autochthonous constitution, their local officials are, in fact, not interfered
with. . . .

The logic of events presses quickly from the fourth to the fifth stage,
and fashions almost completely the full state. Quarrels arise between
neighboring villages or clans, which the lords no longer permit to be
fought out, since by this the capacity of the peasants for service would
be impaired. The lords assume the right to arbitrate, and in case of need,
to enforce their judgment. In the end, it happens that at each " court "
of the village king or chief of the clan there is an official deputy who
exercises the power, while the chiefs are permitted to retain the appearance of authority. The state of the Incas shows, in a primitive condition,
a typical example of this arrangement. . . .

The necessity of keeping the subjects in order and at the same time
of maintaining them at their full capacity for labor, leads step by step
from the fifth to the sixth stage, in which the state, by acquiring full
intra-nationality and by the evolution of " Nationality ", is developed
in every sense. The need becomes more and more frequent to interfere,
to allay difficulties, to punish, or to coerce obedience; and thus develop
the habit of rule and the usages of government. The two groups, separated to begin with, and then united on one territory, are at first merely
laid alongside one another, then are scattered through one another like
a mechanical mixture as the term is used in chemistry, until gradually
they become more and more of a " chemical combination." They inter-
mingle, unite, amalgamate to unity, in customs and habits, in speech and
worship. Soon the bonds of relationship unite the upper and the lower
strata. In nearly all cases the master class picks the handsomest virgins
from the subject races for its concubines. A race of bastards thus develops, sometimes taken into the ruling class, sometimes rejected, and
then because of the blood of the masters in their veins, becoming the
born leaders of the subject race. In form and in content the primitive
state is completed.[51]

The six stages Oppenheimer describes may be conveniently epitomized as follows: (1) extermination; (2) appropriation of surplus; (3) tribute-giving; (4) occupation; (5) regulation; and (6) amalgamation.

Ibn Khaldūn asserted that empires were born through the triumph of pastoral nomads over sedentary agriculturists; Oppenheimer has devoted himself to probing into the reasons why this particular type of conquest engenders the state, and concludes that the pastoral nomads have already developed all the essentials necessary to the creation of the state *before* any lasting triumph over the tillers has been achieved, simply as a consequence of occasional raids. These essential prerequisites are: (1) the fundamental economic basis for the exploitation of human labor; (2) the existence of classes; and (3) a certain degree of familiarity with the utilization of slaves. It remains only for definite conquest to pour these tendencies in rigid molds and to add to them that necessary element, a territorial area with fixed boundaries. Above all, it is through his insistence on the preëminence of economic factors that Oppenheimer explains, to his own satisfaction at least, the proposition that " the primitive State is born in and through nomadic conquest."

The Present Status of the Conflict Theory of Political Origins. — Heretofore nothing but straightforward expositions of the theories that distinguish the school have been given; it is now necessary to discuss briefly instances of favorable and adverse criticism. Further, historical evidence bearing on the conflict theory should at least be mentioned.

The opponents of the conflict theory do not contend that it is utterly untenable; they are usually willing to accept it as *one* thesis among many, but they reject it as *the* single explanation for the genesis of every — or, let us say, almost every — state in history. The present writers have not included in the exposition of Oppenheimer's conflict theory certain qualifications that attempt to account for the genesis of nations like the United States and other obvious exceptions to the general thesis. An examination of the literature of the past decade, however, shows that American sociologists are not in accord with Ward's overconfident opinion: " Gumplowicz and Ratzenhofer have abundantly and admirably proved that the genesis of society as we know it has been through the struggle of races. . . . We at last have a true key to the solution of the origin of society. . . . It is the only scientific explanation that has been offered of the facts and phenomena of human history." [52]

In tracing the development of the state most emphasis has been laid upon the manner in which that institution first came into existence; it is to be remembered, in considering historical support for the conflict theory, that the school does not contend that the complex states of antiquity and of today are the outcome of a single conquest. On the contrary, such states are deemed the product of countless conquests that have occurred successively among earlier states, each later nation being more complex than those immediately before it on the time scale. Oppenheimer gives a list of states that have originated through conquest:

Everywhere we find some warlike tribe of wild men breaking through the boundaries of some less warlike people, settling down as nobility and founding its State. In Mesopotamia, wave follows wave, state follows state — Babylonians, Amoritans, Assyrians, Arabs, Medes, Persians, Macedonians, Parthians, Mongols, Seljuks, Tartars, Turks; on the Nile, Hyksos, Nubians, Persians, Greeks, Romans, Arabs, Turks; in Greece, the Doric States are typical examples; in Italy, Romans, Ostrogoths, Lombards, Franks, Germans; in Spain, Carthaginians, Visigoths, Arabs; in Gaul, Romans, Franks, Burgundians, Normans; in Britain, Saxons, Normans. In India wave upon wave of wild warlike clans has flooded over the country even to the islands of the Indian Ocean. So also is it with China.[53]

To this list might be added the Frankish states in Syria (established during the Crusades) and the Hungarian state. The countries named above do not by any means constitute all the nations founded by conquest; yet the number is sufficient to make clear that the conflict theory has ample historical justification for at least some of its hypotheses.

If the three requisites — class stratification, coercive enforcement of upper-class control, and delimited territorial area — that distinguish the state as such, according to the conflict school, are accepted, then the validity of the theory depends upon whether or not these three characteristics could have come into being without conflict and conquest. (There are, of course, other points in the conflict viewpoint which can be and have been attacked, without serious threat to the entire theory.) In his section on Gumplowicz, Sorokin, author of *Contemporary Sociological Theories*, has a criticism which he applies to the whole school, but which should perhaps be limited to the author with whom he directly deals. Sorokin holds that consolidations of groups have been achieved without warfare, and that different ethnic groups are not necessarily hostile. These objections do not seem vital: first, because the state is something quite different from mere consolidation; and second, because the lack of " absolute " hostility in Gumplowicz's sense does not preclude conflict, conquest, and the rise of the state. Sorokin also writes that social stratification is a close correlate of any human society; he states: " We do not know any single example where, in a group of men more or less permanently living together, and having no war, social stratification did not exist." [54] Here again the criticism is beside the point; Oppenheimer, for example, is anxious to show that social stratification exists prior to the establishment of the state. It is not a question of stratification as such, but of the *kind* of stratification. He also claims that the ruling upper classes have not always been composed of the victorious conquerors. Further, he denies that laws, juridical institutions, and customs have originated through conquest, although he grants a facilitating rôle to the factor of warfare. The argument that law (in the *strict* sense of Chapter One) has developed without conflict and conquest constitutes a grave criticism of the conflict theory if it can be supported, but the cases and authorities cited by Sorokin are not altogether convincing because the definition of law is too loose. Oppenheimer, on the other hand, defines law as *positive* law.

The Origin of the State, by W. C. MacLeod,[55] takes a position diametrically opposed to the conflict theory, but is based on data from aboriginal North America only. Now Oppenheimer explicitly recognizes that conditions in North America require a modification of his theory. In the New World, where no herdsmen existed, hunting tribes conquered the agriculturists, and in those areas in which roving huntsmen only were to be found, these peoples were eliminated but not subjugated by their conquerors, who imported men to be exploited from afar. In those European colonies in which importation of slaves was forbidden, the growth of the state is explained by the fact that the men to be exploited imported themselves from other countries where their position was unbearable — there was an " infection " with " statehood " from abroad. Despite these modifications by Oppenheimer, MacLeod holds that the conflict theory is untenable for North America because: (1) there is no evidence that an unstratified social group ever conquered another like group and superimposed itself as a ruling class; (2) many communities evolved social stratification through internal processes; (3) the " infection with statehood " from " conflict state " source is pure speculation. MacLeod further contends that primitive tribes have definite boundaries, speaks of the " myth of absolute hostility " of early groups, and asserts that the ideology of inferior classes, expropriation of lands, laws, and tribute must have existed in the conquering group before such institutions were imposed on defeated groups. Several of these points are at least partially met by Oppenheimer, for he describes the process by which herdsmen develop the institutional prerequisites for statehood, shows that stratification exists in the conquering group *before* conquest takes place, and makes no use of Gumplowicz's notion of absolute hostility.

Therefore, in spite of the deflation of social evolutionism (to be discussed in Chapter Twenty), and the criticisms noted, it seems safe to subscribe to the opinion voiced by Lowie in his *Origin of the State,* which is in effect that while the position of the conflict theory is far from unassailable, still it is of great value in accounting for the genesis of many if not all states, rests on concrete evidence, and explains much otherwise not readily intelligible.[56] In saying this, we are by no means committed to the social philosophy that frequently accompanies social Darwinism of this type, and which we shall now view through the eyes of some of its opponents.

Conflict within the Conflict School: Critiques of Gumplowicz. — As has already been pointed out, the chief immediate influence of Darwinism upon sociology, aside from stimulating research into the early history of mankind, consisted in leading many writers to attempt to construct systems of sociology on the foundation of the Darwinian formulas carried over into the realm of social phenomena without a proper modification. Thus there arose a pseudo-Darwinian sociology bristling with misleading dogmas, though in certain instances emphasizing social processes which had hitherto been neglected. Among the sociologists of this type, Gumplowicz and his followers were the most conspicuous, and with them were allied certain statesmen and political scientists who employed pseudo-Darwinism as a cloak for their militaristic aims. Perhaps the best method of gaining insight into the implications of the system of Gumplowicz is explicitly to compare it with the doctrines of those members of the so-called conflict school who have written since Gumplowicz set forth his theories in the *Rassenkampf* and the *Grundriss.* Not another theorist of this school, as we have seen in the cases of a few of them, accepts his bald parallelism between biological and social evolution or approves of his notion that the struggle of races, states, and social groups must continue without termination or mitigation. All either contend that the conflict is transferred from the crude and elementary physical plane to a higher level of competition, or maintain that conflict ultimately ends in adaptation or coöperation. Loria, Vaccaro, and Oppenheimer have emphasized the fact that the primordial physical struggle between groups is transformed into an economic conflict.[57] Novicow (whose theories are discussed in the next section) has held that a study of social evolution reveals the fact that the primitive physical contest is progressively commuted through the alliance and federation of groups, and through the substitution of intellectual competition. This field of psychic strife has been explored with acumen by Tarde, Sighele, and Williams.[58] According to De Greef social evolution is a process of gradual substitution of contract and consent for the force of more primitive times.[59] Spencer and Tarde, but more especially Vaccaro, have built up systems of sociology based on the thesis that conflict ultimately terminates in an equilibrium or in adaptation.[60] Finally, Ratzenhofer and Small have insisted that conflict is continually tempered by socialization and is transformed into coöperation, and that the " conquest state " of early days is superseded by the " culture state " of the modern age.[61]

Therefore, even many of the adherents of the conflict theory are generally agreed that the transformation of conflict into alliance and coöperation seems to be a function of social evolution, and would apparently support the notion that war must be followed by an ultimate international adjustment which will forever exclude the recrudescence of the crude process of physical warfare. But all this lies in the realm of the abstract. Even if it be conceded that these theories are valid (a concession we do not necessarily make), it may legitimately be asked if we must wait for the tardy and expensive methods of allowing this final era of alliance and coöperation to be brought about by the automatic processes of social evolution. Cannot man anticipate this development and by legislation secure the benefits of peace in advance? The doctrine that man may anticipate the normal course of social evolution by well-considered legislation was one of the few doctrines contained in the fantastic social philosophy of the French utopian socialist, Fourier,[62] to outlive the sporadic outburst of phalansteries. It was revived and made the cornerstone of the sociological system of America's earliest and most voluminous writer on sociological matters, Lester F. Ward. In a later chapter we shall deal with his doctrine of " social telesis " in detail; suffice it to say here that he confidently looked for the ultimate extinction of crude physical combat through rational planning.

Sociological Opponent of Social Darwinism: Novicow. — Although the biologists themselves, particularly Wallace and Huxley, had pointed out the fallacies involved in a direct transference of the Darwinian biological terminology into the field of sociological investigation, few sociologists heeded their warnings. They either rushed into the camp of the social Darwinists or remained silent. The Russian writer Jacques Novicow (1849–1912) was the first avowed sociologist to devote his life and system of sociology to a refutation of the doctrine that an unmitigated physical struggle for existence is the chief factor in the social process and the mainspring of human progress.

The experiences of Novicow's own life doubtless did much to determine the nature of his sociological theories. His own cosmopolitanism must have had an important influence on his fundamental doctrines regarding the value of a federation of nations and the necessity of the cultural assimilation of peoples before attempting to make them a part of any political group. Coming to France as a young man, Novicow used the French language as a medium of expression, and many of his ideas reflect the influence of the Western European environment. This is particularly apparent in his anti-militaristic doctrines and his frequent attacks on Bismarck and the policy of " blood and iron " which the latter represented. (Bismarck represented much more than this, to be sure — but we are here dealing with Novicow.) The Franco-Prussian War and the seizure of Alsace-Lorraine are constantly utilized to illustrate the folly, perfidy, and injustice of militaristic statesmanship. At the same time, his earlier life in Russia left its imprint in making him an implacable enemy of despotism and of all interference with the free and spontaneous development of the human mind and the unhampered spread of ideas. Like Thomas Jefferson, he had apparently sworn " eternal enmity to every form of tyranny over the mind of man." His Russian environment also served to stimulate his emphasis on coöperation and mutual aid as socializing factors.

Novicow's first important work was entitled *La Politique internationale.*[63] According to Eugene Véron, who furnished the introduction to the work, it was the first coherent and comprehensive exposition of a theory of international political organization. Probably this is rather an extreme statement for, as Darby and others have shown, from the days of Dante occasional isolated writers have from time to time expressed more or less vague ideas of a union of nations, but there can be little doubt that Novicow's work was one of the first scientific modern treatments

of the subject.[64] The first portion of the work is devoted to an
analysis of the organismic theory of society and to a discussion
of the nature and mutual relations of the state and the nation.
The second part is a prelude to his major work, *Les Luttes entre
sociétés humaines,* and states his fundamental contribution to sociology: namely, that although the struggle for existence is the all-
important process in social evolution, this struggle becomes in
society primarily an intellectual rather than a physical type of
conflict. This work contains the suggestions and theses which
were elaborated in *Les Luttes,* and afterward further developed
in a number of separate volumes.

Novicow's chief treatise, and the one which embodies all his
vital conceptions, is entitled *Les Luttes entre sociétés humaines
et leurs phases successives.*[65] The basic thesis is that the course
of human evolution has been characterized by struggles and alliances which, in a serial succession, have been primarily physiological, economic, political, and intellectual. Novicow devotes his
first book of *Les Luttes* to a brief survey of the fundamental
propositions, the expansion and elaboration of which constitute
his sociological system. At its close he summarizes them conveniently as follows:

The universe is an arena of endless combats and alliances.

It is impossible to fix any limit to the possible extent of association.

The struggle for existence is a universal phenomenon. It is in turn and
successively chemical, astronomical, biological, and social.

Between plants and animals the struggle takes two principal phases:
elimination and absorption.

But even among animals we may distinguish economic and mental
struggles.

Alliance does not necessarily exclude the possibility of struggle within
groups, but it modifies the nature of the struggle.

The result of the struggle for existence is adaptation to the environment.

From the psychological point of view, adaptation to the environment
furnishes the most exact formula for comprehending the nature of the
universe.

The struggle for existence, in eliminating those least adapted to the
cosmic environment, brings about an increasingly perfect harmony between the subject and the object.

Pleasure consists in a harmony between the external and the internal
world.

Finally, progress is simply an acceleration of the process of adaptation.[66]

With these general propositions in mind, Novicow's analysis of the chief historic types of human conflict may be examined in greater detail. Each of the four phases of human struggle — physiological, economic, political, and intellectual — appears under two different manifestations: a slow and irrational type, and the more advanced, rapid, and rational variety.[67] He formulates certain fundamental deductions and generalizations regarding these four main types of struggle with their various manifestations. First of all, it is maintained that human struggles in society are but a continuance of the earlier chemical, astronomical, and biological conflict.[68] These four types of conflict form a logical sequence, and progress consists in increasing the scope and influence of the higher forms and in substituting within each general type of conflict the rational and rapid manifestation for the slow and irrational expression.[69] This progressive transformation is to a certain extent brought about automatically by the operation of the universal biological law that all living beings tend to avoid pain and seek pleasure.[70] The lower and more elementary types of conflict are obstructive to progress if introduced into the field of the higher phases of conflict. This explains the folly of an attempt on the part of the state to interfere with the various manifestations of intellectual conflict. The future developments of civilization will not bring about a cessation of conflict, but will tend rather to produce a greater amount of strife within society. The conflict, however, will become increasingly intellectual in character, and the growth in its volume will thus be beneficial, as social evolution is most rapid in those societies which provide the widest scope for intellectual conflict. Not only will conflict in the future increase in volume and tend to become predominantly intellectual, but it will be accompanied by an increase of justice and sympathy and a decrease of hatred. It will develop in the direction of competition, tempered by mutual esteem and tolerance. This series of struggles has the effect of bringing about the survival of the best individuals, and this survival of the best may be regarded as the essence of justice in its broadest signification. Justice is thus the real goal of the cosmic and social processes, which find their final and most perfect expression in the intellectual struggles of humanity.[71]

The subject of the waste and disorder in modern society, particularly as due to the expenditures in wars and militaristic measures and the bungling interference of the government in economic matters, is discussed by Novicow in his work entitled

Les Gaspillages des sociétés modernes.[72] The indictment of war and its advocates is carried still further in his *La Guerre et ses prétendus bienfaits.*[73] It examines briefly the physiological, economic, political, intellectual, and moral effects of war. In the concluding portion he develops the thesis that social Darwinism is a product of a theoretical misunderstanding and of a misapplication of Darwinian biological theories to an interpretation of social processes.

The possibility of a federation of European states and the advantages which would accrue from such a movement — a proposal to be found in all of Novicow's works — is treated in a specific and extended manner in *La Fédération de l'Europe* (1901). The first part of the work is devoted to the economic, political, and general advantages of a federation of European states; the second portion, to an analysis of the chief obstacles to international federation; and the third, to the factors which favor federation. In the concluding sections he analyzes the methods by which the federation is to be achieved, the progress which has already been made in this direction, and the probable character of future international federal institutions.

Novicow's most direct attack on " pseudo-Darwinian sociology " is embodied in his *La Critique du darwinisme social.*[74] This work is devoted to a thoroughgoing criticism of the exponents of the theory that group struggle on a physical basis is the chief motive power in social progress. Spencer and Renan are criticized to a certain extent, but Ward and Ratzenhofer receive the brunt of the attack. Gumplowicz, the most flagrant of the offenders in this respect, is for some reason passed over with almost no reference. Although Novicow's criticism is as one-sided as the theories of his opponents, and although neither school shows an assiduous application to the study of the latest researches in biology, anthropology, and ethnology, no one should attempt to defend the doctrines of the Gumplowicz-Ratzenhofer-Ward-Oppenheimer group without first having considered the objections which Novicow so skillfully marshals.

Novicow's last comprehensive work, *Mécanisme et limites de l'association humaine,*[75] a fitting conclusion and summary of his literary activity, is an elaboration of his oft-repeated doctrine that there is no logical or practical limit to the possible extent of human association, and is specifically directed toward the destruction of the " spoliation illusion," and the demonstration of the feasibility of international federation and the abolition of the class struggle.

Biological Darwinists but Dissenters from Social Darwinism: Huxley and Wallace. — Thomas Henry Huxley (1825–1895), who was to the Darwinian doctrine what Giordano Bruno was to the Copernican theory, and whom some of the English churchmen of his time would doubtless have liked to see share the fate of his illustrious predecessor, rejected the notion that society is an organism, and maintained that it is an artificial product based upon an implied contract. Likewise, as we have already noted, he continued the tradition of Darwin that there is a fundamental difference between the processes of organismic evolution and those of social evolution. The rule of organismic evolution is a ruthless struggle for existence and a survival of those who are fittest to survive under the conditions imposed by nature. Like Hobbes, he maintained that there is no moral standard in the processes of nature, but then went on to say that society must seek a moral standard outside the realm of the purely " natural." The following pronouncements are characteristic of Huxley's point of view:

Social progress means a checking of the cosmic process at every step, and the substitution for it of another, which may be called the ethical process; the end of which is not the survival of those who happen to be the fittest, in respect of the whole of the conditions which exist, but of those who are ethically the best.[76]

Let us understand, once for all, that the ethical progress of society depends, not on imitating the cosmic process, still less in running away from it, but in combating it. It may seem an audacious proposal thus to pit the microcosm against the macrocosm and to set man to subdue nature to his higher ends; but I venture to think that the great intellectual difference between the ancient times . . . and our day, lies in the solid foundations we have acquired for the hope that such an enterprise may meet with a certain degree of success.[77]

The natural factors which form the connecting link between the organismic and the social world are, according to Huxley, the family instinct and man's inherent tendency toward the imitation of his fellow-men. Although man is a part of nature, it is his function as a member of society to direct social institutions so that they combat the biological struggle and secure a survival of the morally best. " Man arrests the cosmic process of struggle in the interests of an ethical process directed to the survival of those who are ethically best." [78] It is the function of the state to guarantee those moral rights which have their origin in society, and to promote the general good of the community. The general welfare must override any such consideration as so-called " natural rights." [79] This goal of the common good cannot be fixed in an absolute sense, but must be reached empirically at any given time and place according to the conditions that exist, but there can be no limitations placed upon state activity short of this goal and achievement.

The development of political institutions may be regarded as simply the advance of the artificial methods of social control in opposition to the sway of the laws of organismic evolution. While the state must remain aware of the biological factors in man's nature and try to strike a balance between man's natural tendencies toward self-assertion and his social instincts, still the social welfare must always predominate over the natural tendencies in any rational public policy. Huxley was thus hardly an unqualified exponent of either anarchism (as Spencer really was) or an excessive extension of governmental activity, but in general his philosophy tended to favor the latter at the expense of the former. The social process was essentially a struggle between the social and the natural in man, and it was the main weakness in the doctrines of Huxley that he failed to effect a reconciliation between these two factors. " A certain dualism, and with it a certain pessimism, remain as the conclusion of the whole matter." [80]

The co-discoverer with Darwin of the doctrine of natural selection, Alfred Russel Wallace (1823–1913), was also inclined to believe that there were many and far-reaching contrasts between the processes of organismic and social evolution. He held that man's moral qualities are so different in kind from anything in the animal kingdom that they cannot be explained on any purely materialistic basis, and resorted for their explanation to an obscurantic theory; namely, that at the time of the emergence of man from the animal kingdom he received " some influx from the unseen world of spirit." [81] As far as his political theories were concerned, Wallace leaned toward socialism. He opposed the ideas of the eugenists that progress is to come through an improvement in the human stock, and maintained that what is needed is to improve the social environment so that human nature and natural selection can operate unhampered. Such a philosophy in his hands lent its support to a decided extension of state activities.[82]

The Prolongation of Infancy, Parental Affection, and Sympathy: Fiske and Sutherland. — The American philosopher, John Fiske (1842–1901), chiefly famous for his *Outlines of Cosmic Philosophy,* has the distinction of being one of the first social theorists to attack the problem raised by Bagehot, Huxley, and Wallace; viz., the origin of the difference between natural and social evolution. Darwin had explained gregariousness, and Bagehot had pointed out that family relationships were an indispensable prerequisite of civilization, but Darwin had not indicated the way in which mere gregariousness became sociality, nor had Bagehot done anything beyond asserting that the process by which the family originated was " inscrutable."

Here was Fiske's opportunity; he combined existing ideas into a system in which the prolonged helplessness of the human infant as contrasted with the young of the less intelligent animals played the central rôle (an idea as old as Anaximander), and in which the supporting parts were played by the necessity for extended parental care, the enforced association of the parents, the growth of adjustive behavior, and the final development of "moral-altruistic" qualities. Lichtenberger summarizes Fiske's contention thus:

> Psychic changes have superseded in importance the physical changes in human evolution. Psychic adaptation producing necessary physical adjustment results in prolongation of human infancy. This in turn transforms the human family into a permanent relation in which sympathy develops and supplementing other bonds, converts gregariousness into sociality.[83]

Giddings held that Fiske made an important contribution to social theory, but that his work was deficient in that he failed to assign the proper causes to the fact of the prolongation of infancy:

> Admitting that the prolongation of infancy was probably a factor in the evolution of stable family relationships, and therefore played a part in strengthening the social sentiments, we must remember that the actual social life and solidarity of the gregarious group was probably a chief cause of the prolongation of infancy itself. Demanding, as it did, a relatively keen exercise of brain and nervous system in communication, imitation and coöperation, it operated to select for survival those individuals that varied in the direction of high brain power and its correlated long infancy. But that is to say that society was a factor in the evolution of man before man became a factor in the evolution of society, and the difference is important.[84]

The Anglo-Australian philosopher, Alexander Sutherland (1852–1902), followed a line of analysis somewhat like Fiske's, as the following excerpt from the introduction to his *Origin and Growth of the Moral Instinct* shows:

Throughout its earlier chapters, — my book will follow the growth of sympathy; it will show, how in due course, parental care must have made its beneficent appearance as an agency essential to its emergence, the survival and subsequent ascendency of the more intelligent types amid a world of ceaseless competition. Having shown how sympathy thus entered on its first humble existence, I hope in succeeding chapters to indicate how it has developed and expanded, and how there has arisen from it the moral instinct with all its accompanying accessories, the sense of duty, the feeling of self-respect, the enthusiasm of both the tender and the manly ideal of ethic beauty.[85]

The Survival Value of Religion: Kidd. — With the publication in 1894 of *Social Evolution,*[86] by Benjamin Kidd (1858–1916), there appeared a novel development in social Darwinism, and in the organismic analogy as well. One of Kidd's fundamental propositions is the Darwinian doctrine and the Neo-Darwinian revision of that theory by Weismann to the effect that progress comes only through that natural selection which results from the struggle for existence, and that if progress does not take place not only stagnation but also actual retrogression will set in.[87] Another important premise is that for the progressive development of the social organism there is no rational sanction. Kidd's interpretation of reason, however, is very arbitrary, since he makes it practically synonymous with egoism. In other words, there is a basic and eternal struggle between the interests of the individual and those of the social organism, and progress comes only in proportion as the former are subordinated to the latter. Likewise, the social conditions of any given time as part of the progressive development of humanity are without any foundation in reason. In short, reason and all its implications and consequences are anti-social and retrogressive. He says in one typical paragraph: " While our evolution is in the first place preëminently a social evolution, the most profoundly individualistic, anti-social, and anti-evolutionary of all human qualities is one which, all other things being equal, tended to be progressively developed in the race; namely, reason." This is indeed vastly removed from the social theory of those philosophers who, two centuries before, had sought to deduce all the principles of social progress and conduct from the " dictates of right reason."

If reason has not guided the progressive development of society, what has been responsible for this process? Kidd is prompt with his answer: it is not reason nor the automatic working of evolutionary laws; it is *religion* which furnishes an " ultra-rational sanction " for those modes of human conduct which are conducive to progress and opposed to reason. Again, this religion cannot be of the type proposed by Comte; namely, rational doctrine of social duties. It must be supra- or ultra-rational. As a matter of fact, no religion can be rational, as such an assumption is a mere contradiction of terms. He sums up the matter as follows: " A religion is a form of belief, providing an ultra-rational sanction for that large class of conduct in the individual where his interests and the interests of the social organism are antagonistic, and by which the former are rendered subordinate to the latter in the general interests of the evolution which the race is undergoing." The social organism, then, according to Kidd, is a religious organism comprehending not a single society or generation, but an entire type of civilization.

Having reached these conclusions, Kidd attempts to verify them through an appeal to the concrete facts of history, which he treats with the same easy legerdemain that he had already employed in dealing with metaphysics, psychology, and biology. He examines the development of Europe, which he characterizes as " Western Civilization." In general, he accepts Spencer's differentiation between military and industrial society as well as his characterization of both types. The nations of antiquity, Greece, and Rome were military states, and with their monarchical or aristocratic systems, their sumptuary regulation of life, and their institution of slavery they stifled the action of social selection and passed into decay. Civilization was thus about to collapse when Christianity appeared with the two requisites for rapid social progress: a strong ultra-rational sanction for conduct and an altruistic ethical system. The task of " Western Civilization " as directed by Christianity was to break down the military systems of antiquity and by emancipating and enfranchising the masses to raise the selective struggle from the crude inter-group basis to the more socially advantageous strife between equals within the society.[88]

There is a great deal more of this sort of thing in *Social Evolution* and the other works of Kidd, but it all revolves around the peculiar blend of the anti-rationalist strains of Romanticist social philosophy with the teachings of evolutionary biology. Society is viewed as a socio-religious organism, and the Darwinian hypothesis becomes the struggle for the existence of the organism, the natural selection of those who subordinate their own welfare to that of the organism, and the survival of the fittest organism.

Kidd's doctrines were popular for a short time (about the turn of the century) with a certain section of the populace, but the biologists resented his emphasis on religion and his denial of the value of reason, while the religiously-minded were shocked by his characterization of religion as irrational. What popularity his writings enjoyed was among those who wished to believe in both religion and evolution, but the task of reconciliation was performed much more clearly and convincingly by Henry Drummond and Alexander Sutherland. Nevertheless, there is probably a kernel of sound sociological theory in the mass of chaff that Kidd perpetrated; Giddings, at least, was of that opinion. To quote from his review of Kidd's posthumous book, *The Science of Power* (which was a more forceful and consistent restatement of his earlier thesis as to the superior social value of non-rational conduct) :

This faith by which a race, a family, or an individual lives, is not anti-rational, nor yet super-rational. It is rather sub-rational or proto-rational. It is deeper, more elemental, than reason — a fact of instinct and feeling. It is *faith in the possibilities of life,* born of actual survival in the struggle for existence. The question, therefore, which Mr. Kidd should have asked, and which we, in reviewing his work, must ask in his stead, is this: May we identify our elemental faith in the possibilities of life with the tremendous social phenomenon of religion, which, in all the ages of man's progress, has been one of his supreme interests? Shall we perhaps find that, when reduced to its lowest terms, to its essential principle, religion is not, as has been supposed, a belief in gods, or in a supernatural, in any way conceived, but is rather that primordial faith in the possibilities of life which was born, and generation after generation is reborn, of success in the struggle for existence; which may gather about itself all manner of supplementary beliefs, including a belief in spirits and in gods, but which will persist as the deepest and strongest motive of life after science has stripped away from it all its mystical and theological accretions? . . . So believing, I accept as a positive contribution to the theory of human evolution Mr. Kidd's proposition that religion, a thing deeper and more elemental than reason, has been a chief factor in social evolution.[89]

Summary of the Chapter. — A strong reaction against the boundless optimism of some apostles of the French Enlightenment soon set in, and one of the most vigorous exponents of this reaction was Malthus. He maintained that it was impossible ever to better the condition of the laboring classes because their rate of reproduction would inevitably reduce their wage to a mere subsistence level — unless they themselves applied a moral check to their concupiscence. Moreover, the failure to apply this moral check would not only lower wages, but would bring on a bitter struggle for existence and the elimination of the weak through vice, misery, and other " positive checks."

Darwin ran across the Malthusian doctrines early in his biological career, and applied them to all forms of life. The consequence was his theory of natural selection, the logical outcome of the struggle for existence. Those naturally selected were of course those " fittest " to survive under the prevailing circumstances, and thus was rendered possible the conception, not held by Darwin, that the human survivors were in some way of special moral excellence as well.

Another application of Darwinian doctrine was in theories of intergroup struggle and survival, here termed external conflict theories. This type of thought has a long history — among its outstanding early representatives were Ibn Khaldūn and Jean Bodin — but it received a tremendous impetus when *The Origin of Species* appeared. Shortly thereafter Bagehot published his " thoughts on the application of ' natural inheritance ' and ' selection ' to political society," and in spite of Bagehot's own reservations, social Darwinism was fairly launched.

Only a short time after this, Spencer brought out his theory of political evolution, in which the main stress was laid on the " homogeneity to heterogeneity " formula, but in which the example given by Darwin and Bagehot was by no means ignored; the struggle for group existence was implicitly given due weight. The most explicit and extreme of the social Darwinists, however, was Ludwig Gumplowicz; for him all of history could be resolved into the struggle between originally disparate racial groups, a struggle in which the fitter became the upper classes and castes of ever larger political organizations or states. Ratzenhofer developed an external conflict theory much like that of Gumplowicz, but he did not make the group the unit in the struggle for existence; the pursuit of individual interests was his explanatory thesis, and as a consequence he also contributed largely to the development of " internal conflict " or *Klassenkampf* doctrines.

The American sociologist, Ward, enthusiastically adopted the theories of Gumplowicz and Ratzenhofer, modifying them to fit into his schema of cosmic evolution and his gospel of social telesis. Another disciple of these conflict theorists is Oppenheimer, who has combined the earlier insights of Ibn Khaldūn with theirs, and at present is the outstanding defender of the thesis that the state originates in and through the struggle of contending groups, primarily those constituted by tillers and by nomads. In spite of many untenable elements in his theory, Op-

742 SOCIAL DARWINISM, PROS AND CONS

penheimer is generally regarded as having notably furthered sociological knowledge of political origins and processes.

The extreme social Darwinism of some members of the conflict school, particularly Gumplowicz, soon evoked determined opposition, both from other members of the school and from outsiders. Among the latter was Novicow, who virtually devoted his life to the refutation of the doctrine that an unmitigated struggle for existence is the chief factor in the social process and the sole means of human progress. Several of the biological Darwinists also dissented from the tenets of social Darwinism; among them were Huxley and Wallace, who asserted that there is a fundamental difference between natural and social evolution.

One of the first social theorists to attack the problem of the origin of this difference was Fiske, who found the answer in the prolongation of human infancy and the consequent development of " moral-altruistic " qualities. Sutherland followed a similar line of analysis, and arrived at substantially the same conclusion.

A novel development in social Darwinism and in the organismic analogy as well was represented by Kidd's attempt to demonstrate the survival value of religion. The Darwinian hypothesis was transformed into the struggle for the existence of the socio-religious organisms of which their members are but cells, the natural selection of those who subordinate their own welfare to that of these organisms, the survival of the fitter organisms, and with them, of their members. *Ergo,* religion aids in the struggle for survival; let us then be religious. Right or wrong, this is incontestably a long way 'round from the Malthusian notions of positive and negative checks with which " the struggle over the struggle for existence " began.

Probably because of the unabashed espousal of social Darwinism by the Nazis, resulting in their inhuman extermination policy and practice, renewed attention has been given to the doctrine, notably by Richard Hofstadter in his excellent book, *Social Darwinism in American Thought,* rev. ed. (New York: Braziller, 1959). For the Nazi references, especially with regard to the social-Darwinistic indoctrination inflicted on the veriest children, see Becker, *German Youth: Bond or Free* (London: Routledge & Kegan Paul, 1946), using index and bibliographies.

It should, of course, be noted that not any and every kind of struggle within and between groups can justifiably be tossed into the hopper of social Darwinism. There must be some explicit ideology that not only specifically refers to the struggle for existence (although not necessarily by use of the phrase itself), but also that lends it moral sanction as furthering, through evolution, some supreme end such as progress, a superior human race, or the like. Several aspects of the present chapter should be scrutinized in this light.

CHAPTER XX

Deflation of Social Evolutionism: Prospects for Sound Historical Sociology

SCOPE OF HISTORICAL SOCIOLOGY. — There is a very close relation between the general theme of this book and the topic of the present chapter, for practically every thinker who has concerned himself with social matters has at one time or another attempted to answer questions like the following, all of which fall within the compass of historical sociology: (1) What was the earliest condition of mankind, and how was that condition altered? (2) What has been the general trend of the whole process of social development? (3) By what sequences or stages have the various branches of the human race arrived at their present states of societal organization? (4) Are there really cycles in social affairs which when discovered will demonstrate the truth of the maxim that "History repeats itself"?

Obviously enough, very few thinkers distinguished between these four separate problems. As our summary of theories advanced before the time of Spencer and Darwin will show, all four questions were asked in the same breath, as it were, by virtually everyone, and the answers returned almost invariably referred to more than one problem. Only in comparatively recent times has there been any attempt to deal with each problem separately, and it may well be doubted whether complete separation has been, or can be, or should be effected. For didactic purposes, however, we shall so far as possible consider them in the order given, leaving the question as to their interrelation to be answered implicitly by the accompanying discussions of method.

Summary of the Period before Spencer and Darwin. — Our chapters on the social thought of the ancient Far and Near East, Classical ideas of the origin of society and the state, theories of the natural state of man, conceptions of progress, and a few others, all have a direct bearing on several of the questions listed. We shall again summarize them, however, from a slightly different viewpoint; namely, with regard to the answers therein returned to two of our questions, " What was the earliest condition of mankind, and how was that condition altered? " and " By what sequences or stages did the various branches of the human race arrive at their present state of social organization? "

Preliterates often account for social origins by saying that a culture hero, sometimes a sort of trickster, sometimes a wise old man, sometimes a divinely inspired or definitely divine lawgiver, was the means through which their present altogether admirable institutions and practices were initiated; and in a number of instances, a complete creation myth is also involved. Among the historical peoples, familiar examples of this type of thought are the Osiris myth, the Gilgamesh epic and its Hebrew derivative in Genesis, and the numerous stories of racial and tribal origins which flourished among the Greeks and Romans. Practically all these accounts have the common characteristics of a very slight measure of rationality and a disregard of causal sequences observed in everyday life, and are to that extent strikingly similar to those products of mental immobility with which modern folklore and ethnography have made us familiar.

Perhaps the first group of thinkers who rationally considered the problem of the origins of organized society were the Greek " talemakers " and their successors, the Metics and Sophists of the fifth century B.C., those mentally mobile " strangers " in the sacred societies of their day. They seem to have believed in an unregulated state of nature, which was ended when civil society was created through a governmental compact. At odds with these thinkers, and yet agreeing with them in some respects, was Plato, who set forth, in Book III of his *Laws,* one of the most complete accounts of social genesis produced in ancient times. In this account he assumed much of the chronological measure of modern geology and biology when he stated that " every man should understand that the human race either had no beginning at all, and will never have an end, but will always be and has been, or that it began an immense while ago." Aristotle gave very little attention to the problems of social genesis, and his brief " solution " was analytical rather than historical. Chiefly concerned with demonstrating the social nature of man, he traced the progressive expression and realization of his " social instinct " in the family, the village, and the state. An approximation to the historical and comparative method is to be seen in his alleged study of 158 constitutions as the basis of his *Constitution of Athens.* One of the most neglected, and yet one of the most striking, of the early discussions of social and political development is that contained in the sixth book of Polybius's *History of Rome,* in which he foreshadowed the later conflict theorists in his doctrine that the state originated in violence, antedated Sumner by more than two thousand years in his postulate as to the customary basis of morality, and anticipated Spinoza, Hume, and Adam Smith by his discussion of reflective sympathy as a social force. Infinitely the most Spencerian of Classical theories of the history of society was that offered by the great Epicurean poet, Lucretius, in his effort to indicate the evolutionary and naturalistic character of the development of the universe and society independent of any aid or interference from the gods. The Roman Stoic philosopher, Seneca, is significant for having carried further even than Plato the notion of the idyllic life of early man.

One of the most significant results of the development of this doctrine by Seneca was its adaptation by the Christian Fathers to serve as the accepted Patristic view of the course of social evolution. The Fathers identified Seneca's golden age with the state of man before the Fall, and held that the subsequent period of misery, confusion, and disorder was none other than that which followed the expulsion from Paradise. This conception of the history of society prevailed throughout most of the Middle Ages, though the writers often tended to forget the original felicity and to stress chiefly the miseries of existence before the establishment of the Christian polity.

The most remarkable contribution to historical sociology between Lucretius and Adam Ferguson was embodied in the *Prolegomena to History* of the Berber scholar and statesman, Ibn Khaldūn, with whom we have recently dealt at length. He not only produced what is regarded by some scholars as the first adequate theory of history, but also, in his description of pastoral nomadism in North Africa, contributed one of the best studies of preliterate life down to the rise of modern ethnography.

In the latter part of the seventeenth century there appeared two important contributions to historical sociology in the writings of the French publicist, Jean Bodin, concerning whose theories we have recently been reminded, and of the Spanish Jesuit, Juan de Mariana. The latter's view of social and political development was strangely like that of Seneca.

The most prevalent type of historical sociology during the seventeenth and eighteenth centuries was that which traced the development of society and the state through a social and governmental compact. The historical and psychological weaknesses of the social contract theory, as presented in its classical form, were attacked by three writers who may be said to have been the first to restore the historical point of view in sociology to the place it had held with Plato, Polybius, Lucretius, and Ibn Khaldūn. (1) Vico, while not devoting himself particularly to the demolition of the social contract, emphasized the necessity of pursuing an inductive and historical approach to social problems. The possibilities of such procedure he himself demonstrated in the fields of philology and jurisprudence. (2) Hume showed that the social contract theory was a philosophical monstrosity, a psychological impossibility, and a fantastic figment denied by the concrete facts of history. (3) Even more " anti-contract" in viewpoint was Adam Ferguson's surprisingly modern *History of Civil Society*. He stated the idea of the origin of the state in conquest and force, and foreshadowed Boas and the critical school of anthropologists by insisting that we must discard preconceived notions as to the nature of " primitive man " and his institutions and study the life of the " simpler peoples " at first hand.

The next impulse to historical sociology came from the philosophy of history and the history of civilization to which Vico was an early contributor. Voltaire, Turgot, Condorcet, and Saint-Simon represent the more important French contributors to this field, and were all tinged by more or less rationalism, scepticism, and optimism. In the works of Herder, Fichte, Schelling, Adam Müller, and Hegel one finds, along with a rationalistic streak here and there, the Romantic trend in the German philosophy of history, with its emphasis on tradition and national character, the indwelling of *Geist,* and the emotional nature of man. It undoubtedly was somewhat deficient in logic and clarity at times, but nevertheless the Romantic impulse was, as Lord Acton has well insisted, remarkable for the scope of the historical interests which it stimulated. In the work of Auguste Comte rationalism and Romanticism of a French brand were combined to furnish the historical background of the first system of doctrine to bear the name of sociology, and in this system were incorporated several " laws " of social and mental development. While there is little doubt that historical sociology is different in method and content from many if not most forms of the philosophy of history, as we shall later show, yet the latter, in its attempt to find some meaning and significance in the flow of events in the past, contributed much in the way of both impulse and data.[1]

No little importance must also be assigned to the development of critical historical scholarship through the work of Ranke and his disciples and students in many countries. Although there was little of the sociological orientation or interest in most of the scientific history of the nineteenth century, yet by improving the mechanism of research it did much to advance and refine the inductive method of research in historical sociology, and it brought forth a vast amount of concrete material which has either been utilized or still awaits exploitation by the historical sociologist.

The last of the pre-Darwinian impulses which may be said to have influenced the development of historical sociology was the initial interest in historical economics and economic history evident in the work of Heeren, Sismondi, Hildebrand, Roscher, and Knies. The genetic point of view which characterized the group brought them exceedingly close to the borders of historical sociology.[2]

Historical Sociology after the Rise of Evolutionary Doctrine. — Unquestionably the most potent influence contributing to the development of historical sociology was the Darwinian theory of organismic evolution and its reaction on social science, with Spencer's grandiose formulas running a close second. The idea became firmly rooted that human society, as well as organismic life, was the natural product of evolutionary forces operating over an immense period of time. The historical sociology thereby engendered followed two major lines of development — the social Darwinism of Gumplowicz and others, and the comparative or classical anthropology of Lubbock, McLennan, Tylor, Lang, Frazer, Letourneau, Post, Lippert, Kovalevsky, and Morgan.[3]

What may be narrowly and technically described as the systematic historical sociology of the latter half of the nineteenth century was both created by, and based upon, the classical anthropology (strictly speaking, ethnology) just mentioned. This is particularly apparent in such specialized works as those by Westermarck and Howard, and is still evident in the more modern contributions of Webster, Hobhouse, Sumner-Keller, and Briffault. One of the most ambitious syntheses of historical sociology produced in this period, Book III of Giddings's *Principles of Sociology*, was based essentially upon both the method and the data of the comparative school — as indeed it had to be when written.

The classical school assumed that there is an organismic law of development in social institutions. The theory of unilinear evolutionary growth was adhered to, along with its implications of gradual and orderly changes, largely the same world over, and, in general, proceeding from simple and confused relations to complex and well-coördinated social adjustments. On account of the assumed unity of the human mind and similarities in the geographical environment, it was held that we must expect parallelisms and similarities in culture and institutions among peoples widely separated in their geographic distribution.

The "Comparative" Method of the Classical Anthropologists. — From the initial assumptions just noted grew the so-called "comparative" method (better termed "illustrative"). It was considered valid, in reconstructing the record of social development, to link together a series of isolated examples of any type of culture. These examples were taken from the most diverse regions and periods of time, irrespective of the totality of the cultural complex from which each was lifted, and were forced into a prearranged schema of evolution. The result was held to be proof of the "natural course of social evolution" and cultural growth.[4] Among sociologists who espoused the comparative method Herbert Spencer was, with the possible exception of Letourneau, unquestionably the one who accepted it in its most extreme form and the one whose writings have been most influential. His somewhat naïve description or, perhaps better, confession, of his method of procedure in tracing social evolution is outlined in the following passage from his *Autobiography:*

With the entry of this new division of my work, the marshalling of evidence became a much more extensive and complicated business than it had hitherto been. The facts, so multitudinous in their numbers, so different in their kinds, so varied in their sources, formed a heterogeneous aggregate difficult to bring into the clear and effective order required for carrying on an argument; so that I felt much as might a general of division who had become commander-in-chief; or rather, as one who had to undertake this highest function in addition to the lower functions of all his subordinates of the first, second, and third grades. Only by deliberate method persistently followed, was it possible to avoid confusion. A few words may fitly be said here concerning my materials, and the ways in which I dealt with them.

During the five and twenty preceding years there had been in course of accumulation, extracts and memoranda from time to time made. My reading, though not extensive, and though chiefly devoted to the subjects which occupied me during this long interval, frequently brought under my eyes noteworthy facts bearing on this or that division of Sociology. These, along with the suggested ideas, were jotted down and put away. The resulting mass of manuscript materials remained for years unclassified; but every now and then I took out the contents of the drawer which received these miscellaneous contributions and put them in some degree of order — grouping together the ecclesiastical, the political, the industrial, etc.; so that by the time I began to build, there had been formed several considerable heaps of undressed stones and bricks.

But now I had to utilize the relatively large masses of materials gathered together in the *Descriptive Sociology*. For economization of labor, it was needful still further to classify these; and to save time, as well as to avoid errors in re-transcription, my habit was, with such parts of the work as were printed, to cut up two copies. Suppose the general topic to be dealt with was "Primitive Ideas." Then the process was that of reading through all the groups of extracts concerning the uncivilized and semi-civilized races under the head of "Superstition," as well as those under other heads that were likely to contain allied evidence — "Knowledge," "Ecclesiastical," etc. As I read I marked each statement that had any significant bearing; and these marked statements were cut out by my secretary after he had supplied any references which excision would destroy. The large heap resulting was joined with the kindred heap of materials previously accumulated; and there now came the business of re-classifying them all in preparation for writing. During a considerable preceding period the subdivisions of the topic of "Primitive Ideas" had been thought about; and various heads of chapters had been settled — "Ideas of Sleep and Dreams," "Ideas of Death and Resurrection," "Ideas of Another Life," "Ideas of Another World," etc., etc. Taking a number of sheets of double foolscap, severally fitted to contain between their two leaves numerous memoranda, I placed these in a semi-circle on the floor around my chair; having indorsed each with the title of a chapter, and having arranged them in something like proper sequence. Then, putting before me the heap of extracts and memoranda, I assigned each as I read it to its appropriate chapter. Occasionally I came upon a fact which indicated to me the need for a chapter I had not thought of. An additional sheet for this was introduced, and other kindred facts were from time to time placed with this initial one. Several sittings were usually required to thus sort the entire heap. Mostly too, as this process was gone through some time in advance of need, there came a repetition, or several repetitions, before the series of chapters had assumed its final order, and the materials had all been distributed.

When about to begin a chapter, I made a further rough classification. On a small table before me I had a large rude desk — a hinged board, covered with green baize, which was capable of being inclined at different angles by a movable prop behind. Here I grouped the collected materials appropriate to the successive sections of the chapter; and those which were to be contained in each section were put into the most convenient sequence. Then, as I dictated, I from time to time handed to my secretary an extract to be incorporated.[5]

Lewis H. Morgan is somewhat difficult to classify, but it seems best to regard him as primarily a member of the classical school. Although Morgan was much more systematic and thorough than Spencer in his study of "primitive" social institutions, Lowie has recently shown that his method was essentially the same and his conclusions quite as unreliable. His *Ancient Society,* as we shall later show in detail, has probably done more both to stimulate and to distort historical sociology than any other work.

The next notable example of method in systematic historical sociology after Spencer's *Principles of Sociology* was Book III of Giddings's *Principles of Sociology,* which, although dominated by a number of the classical preconceptions, was much less naïve in its assumptions, procedure, and results than the works of Spencer and Morgan, and showed an unusual acquaintance, for a sociologist, with the best works then available in the fields of anthropology and history.

The introduction of even greater qualifications in accepting the extreme methods and conclusions of comparative ethnology was evident in the critical introduction and summary comments of W. I. Thomas's *Source Book for Social Origins.*[6] Much of the illustrative material cited was from writers of the comparative school, but the editor did not hesitate to point out the limitations of this approach to social evolution, and gave some indication of an acquaintance with the earlier critical work of Boas and his school. Moreover, he introduced several valuable concepts, among them the highly significant " crisis." Other works on historical sociology accepting the comparative method, albeit somewhat gingerly, were Hobhouse's *Morals in Evolution* (1st ed.),[7] and C. E. Hayes's *Introduction to the Study of Sociology* (1st ed.).

Durkheim's Rejection of the Comparative Method. — The first sociologist of note thoroughly to reject the comparative method in a published work of significance was Émile Durkheim. In his *Les Formes élémentaires de la vie réligieuse* (English translation by J. W. Swain) he rejected the procedure of the comparative school in attempting to derive the laws of social evolution from the study of many social institutions as they have appeared in diverse regions and periods of time. He contended that any valid conclusions as to social evolution must rest rather upon an intensive study of but one social institution on the basis of its manifestations in a single and definite cultural area. For his own work he selected the development of religion in Australia. Critics have insisted, however, that Durkheim introduced quite as many methodological errors as he had rejected. Further, Australian ethnography and ethnology have not been pursued with sufficient critical care to make the available data of sufficient reliability to justify generalization even for that continent alone.

As Goldenweiser has well said of this aspect of Durkheim's work, " the fact itself that the author felt justified in selecting the Australian area for his intensive analysis shows plainly enough how far from realization still is the goal which his own life-work has at least made feasible, the rapprochement of ethnology and of sociology." [8] It seems to be agreed that, as a basis for generalization, Durkheim's study of primitive religion is as unreliable as the results of Frazer's studies, pervaded by a far different method. The value of his book must be found in the sociological and psychological acumen and not in the reliability of the method of investigation or of the ethnographic material adduced to substantiate the conclusions.[9]

Statistics Used to Buttress the Comparative Method. — An interesting innovation in method was the attempt of Hobhouse and his collaborators to introduce the method of statistical correlation into an investigation of the evolution of social institutions in their relation to the progress of material culture. In an earlier work, *Morals in Evolution,* Hobhouse had relied upon a critical utilization of the comparative method, which may perhaps have impressed upon him its risks and questionable assumptions. In his *Material Culture and Social Institutions of the Simpler Peoples* (executed in collaboration with G. C. Wheeler and Morris Ginsberg), he introduced a new method of investigation through the means of statistical correlation of the stages in the progress of government and justice, the forms of the family, and the nature of war and its reaction upon social structure, with the epochs in the development of material culture. This was, Hobhouse frankly admitted, but an elaboration of the method proposed by Tylor in 1889, in his famous essay, " On a Method of Investigating the Development of Institutions: Applied to the Laws of Marriage and Descent." [10] Hobhouse offered the following criticism of the comparative method, and indicated the difficulties of establishing valid generalizations concerning social evolution:

Theories of social evolution are readily formed with the aid of some preconceived ideas and a few judiciously selected corroborative facts. The data offered to the theorist by the voluminous results of anthropological inquiry on the one hand, and by the immense record of the history of civilization on the other, are so vast and so various that it must be an unskilled selector who is unable, by giving prominence to the instances which agree and by ignoring those which conflict with his views, to make out a plausible case in support of some general notion of human progress. On the other hand, its theories are easily made, they are also easily confuted by a less friendly use of the same data. That same variety of which we speak is so great that there is hardly any sociological generalization which does not stumble upon some awkward fact if one takes the trouble to find it. Anyone with a sense for facts soon recognizes that the course of social evolution is not unitary but that different races and different communities of the same race have, in fact, whether they started from the same point or no, diverged early, rapidly, and in many different directions at once. If theorizing is easy when facts are treated arbitrarily, a theory which would really grow out of the facts themselves and express their true significance presents the greatest possible difficulties to the inquirer. The data themselves are vast but chaotic, and at every point incomplete. They fall into two main divisions. On the one hand, there is the historical record of the civilizations; upon the other there is the immense field of contemporary anthropology. In both alike the data are equally difficult to ascertain with precision, and when ascertained to reduce to any intelligible order. In the history of civilization we have full studies of many institutions, and we can learn something, not only of what they were at any one moment, but of their development in time, their genesis, their rise, their maturity, their decay. But even here the information often breaks off short at the most interesting point. Beginnings are frequently matter of conjecture. The nature of institutions, as they appear on paper, may be known to us, while we are left to reconstruct their actual working from casual examples, hints, and references that leave much to the imagination. We find them decaying without intelligible cause, and often enough we are faced with the fact that more thoroughgoing inquiry has completely revolutionized our view of an institution which had been taken as thoroughly explored and fully interpreted by earlier schools of historians. So is it also with the anthropological record. Here indeed we have a handful of monographs made by trained and skilled observers in modern times, which leave nothing to be desired excepting that the work had been carried out three or four generations ago before contact with the white man or with other more civilized races had begun to corrupt the purity of aboriginal institutions. Outside these monographs we have a vast mass of travellers' reports, good, bad, and indifferent, data which it is impossible to ignore and yet which can seldom be taken at their face value. Moreover, all anthropological data of this kind, however simple the life of the people with which they deal, are modern: with the exception of the few available references that we have to the peoples that surrounded the Greeks and Romans in Herodotus, Tacitus, and other writers of antiquity, the great bulk of anthropological inquiry dates from the last three or four centuries, and it is sometimes forgotten that the peoples of whom they treat must have lived as long, must in a sense have had as extensive a tradition behind them, and to that extent are as far removed from the true primitive as civilized man himself.[11]

Critics soon called attention, however, to certain serious defects in the execution of Hobhouse's project, while admitting the excellence of the method if the data were adequate and the detailed application rigid. They alleged that by his arbitrary division of primitive peoples into the lower and higher hunters, and so forth, he inevitably obtained from his study what he had assumed at the outset in his preliminary classification. Again, his selection of the " tribe " as the statistical unit was said to make specific accuracy and definiteness impossible, because of the great variation in the nature of the tribe.[12] The most damaging criticism, however, was commonly agreed to be the author's own admission that the ethnographical data gathered by skilled and critical investigators were not sufficient to warrant the undertaking of any such enterprise; if he meant what he said he should have been unwilling to use the highly unreliable material gathered by missionaries and travelers in the absence of trustworthy information.[13] Further, a survey of the authorities used indicates that, like Durkheim, Hobhouse did not realize the serious methodological errors that had been involved in compiling the material for Spencer and Gillen's monographs on the Australian data. In other words, not only did he fail to limit himself to reliable ethnographical sources, but he also failed to discriminate critically between the relative reliability of the various records available.[14]

Moreover, it may be quite true, as Lowie has gone far to show, that there is no close correlation between material culture and specific forms of social organization. Yet social institutions are a part of the general cultural complex of any group, and their development and changes may follow general patterns as yet undiscovered or inadequately formulated. In any event, the historical sociologist must be aware of the *Problematik*, no matter what he thinks of the possibilities of solution.

The Chief Theories of Cultural Growth. — There have been advanced by ethnologists some three chief doctrines of explanations of cultural growth and change.[15] The first was that expounded by the comparative school; namely, the theory of independent origins and transformation. They held that cultural and institutional similarities and parallelisms have an independent origin, due to the unity of the human mind and also to environmental similarities. Changes in social institutions are likewise due to causes arising independently of any contiguous cultural group. This dòctrine, of course, embodied the apotheosis of human initiative and capacity for invention.[16]

At the opposite from this school of writers was that group which accounted for cultural growth and transformation on the basis of contact and diffusion. They held that the instances of invention and independent origins of culture are very few indeed, and that changes in culture are almost entirely the result of the introduction of new cultural traits or elements from without. This view of cultural evolution was anticipated by Tylor and Ratzel and was elaborated by Frobenius, Graebner, and Elliot Smith. It has been accepted by Rivers, Foy, Ankermann, and in a modified form by Schmidt and Koppers. It may possess some validity as an explanation of the spread of material culture, but it has many weaknesses from psychological and geographical viewpoints.[17]

Recognizing the defects of these older theories, Ehrenreich in Germany and Boas and his school in America substituted a critical or historic-analytical procedure. They assigned full credit to the theory of independent development and invention as the cause of many cultural origins and changes, but also recognized that diffusion is an important factor in accounting for cultural transformations. Particularly significant was their searching analysis of alleged cultural parallelisms from the historical and psychological point of view.[18] The revolutionary significance of such positions, once understood, cannot fail to be obvious to any thoughtful historian or sociologist; if they were fully realized such works as Breysig's *Vom geschichtlichen Werden*, certain volumes in Henri Berr's *L'Evolution de l'Humanité* series, Briffault's *The Mothers*, or Müller-Lyer's *History of Social Development* would never have been perpetrated. Let us now offer some justification for these harsh words.

The Deflation of Social Evolutionism as Illustrated by Studies of the Family and Social Organization. — The nineteenth century's first outstanding attempt to trace the historical development of social origins through tribal society rested on a theory, of Biblical origin and sanction, which had been " confirmed " by the generalizations of Aristotle, Bodin, Pufendorf, Locke, and Blackstone: namely, that the patriarchal organization of society was the earliest form of familial, social, and political life. This thesis received its ablest presentation and defense in the *Ancient Law* and other monumental contributions to historical jurisprudence and politics from the pen of Henry Sumner Maine.

This point of view was attacked by J. J. Bachofen in his *Das Mutterrecht,* published in 1860. He maintained the existence of a primordial promiscuity in sexual relations and a subsequent development of a matriarchate, or a polity dominated by females. But he was a follower of the methods of Vico rather than those of Darwin and Morgan, for he based his generalizations on data drawn from a study of Classical mythology and tradition. This line of approach was soon abandoned for what has come to be known as the "evolutionary" approach to historical sociology. A group of distinguished scholars, most notable among them being Sir John Lubbock, J. F. McLennan, Herbert Spencer, Andrew Lang, W. Robertson Smith, Albert H. Post, Edward B. Tylor, Lewis H. Morgan, James G. Frazer, Charles Letourneau, and Daniel G. Brinton, brought the evolutionary principles of Darwinian biology to bear on the reconstruction of the early history of human society, and reached results equally disruptive of the position of Maine. While there were important differences of opinion in matters of detail among these writers, they were in general agreement on essentials of method and results.

Applying these methods and assumptions, described elsewhere, to the study of early society, these writers arrived at a series of definite conclusions. The monogamic family shows a slow but distinct development from original promiscuity, and the family of any type is a late product, developing within the older kinship or gentile organization of society. In the development of gentile society, certain definite and successive stages can be isolated and their sequence correlated with the development of material culture. The first type of extensive human grouping was found in the endogamous horde, where there were neither fixed family relations nor others of wider extent. This stage was followed by the appearance of definite kinship or gentile society, associated with the exogamic clan which was usually if not always connected with a totemic complex. The earliest form of gentile society was the maternal clan, which was in time invariably succeeded by the paternal clan, this transformation in the basis of relationship being definitely correlated with progressive advances in material culture. The paternal clan was gradually strengthened into a patriarchal organization of society, which, through the development of property and the infiltration of foreigners induced by economic attraction, was in time superseded by the abolition of kinship principles and the establishment of the territorial state and civil society. This orderly synthesis of social and political evolution was most comprehensively organized and most effectively set forth in the famous work on *Ancient Society* by Louis Henry Morgan.

Since Morgan's day new methods of ethnological investigation and synthesis and more thorough studies of existing preliterate societies have served to discredit the principles of investigation followed by the evolutionary or classical school of ethnologists

and to disprove the conclusions which they reached by the employment of these methods. In fact, more careful investigation, even
according to the old methods, enabled Westermarck to prove
inaccurate the assumption of a primitive promiscuity.[19] The basis
for the newer point of view was laid by very painstaking studies
of preliterate cultural areas with the attempt to study the data in
an objective manner. Space forbids the mention of more than a
few of the earlier examples of this type of indispensable ethnographical research. In any such enumeration would come the
studies of Australian data by Cunow, Brown, and N. W.
Thomas; Rivers's great monographs on *The Todas* and the
History of Melanesian Society; Seligman's survey of the Ved-
das; the Torres Straits investigations undertaken by A. C. Haddon and a group of English scholars; the investigation of African
data by Roscoe and Pecheul-Loesche; Thurnwald's meticulous
description of the Banaro; and, particularly, the careful studies
of American areas by the participants in the Jesup North Pacific
Expedition, and by Boas and those influenced by him. These unparalleled data, together with a more objective and scientific attitude toward their interpretation, not only brought about more
reliable doctrines concerning social evolution, but also showed
that the facts of social development are far different from what
was earlier supposed. The more critical school proved that the
assumption of a universal law of evolution from the simple to the
complex is not invariably true with respect to culture or social
institutions. It showed that parallelisms in culture and social organization in different areas do not imply identical antecedents
or necessitate similar subsequent developments. Similarities may
grow out of "cultural convergencies," proceeding from widely
varied antecedents, or they may be produced by imitation of a
common pattern.[20]

The application of this more scientific method to the study of
preliterate society has been nothing short of revolutionary;
among American sociologists only the Sumner-Keller school still
cling desperately to the old " grab-bag " practices.[21] The universality of gentile society cannot be proved; many groups have
developed to a relatively high stage of culture without any relationship system wider than the family. Where gentile society
exists there is no general tendency for relationships to change
from a maternal to a paternal basis; in fact it may be doubted
if there are more than three or four well-authenticated examples
of independent change in kinship from maternal to paternal in
the whole range of preliterate society. Further, there is no evi-

dence that maternal kinship is correlated with lower material culture or paternal with more advanced economic life. Finally, totemism has been in large measure dissociated from exogamy. It is evident that the whole fabric of the scheme of social evolution provided by the evolutionary school has perished, and Lowie has well expressed its obituary notice:

> To sum up. There is no fixed succession of maternal and paternal descent; sibless tribes may pass directly into the matrilineal or the patrilineal condition; if the highest civilizations emphasize the paternal side of the family, so do many of the lowest; and the social history of any particular people cannot be reconstructed from any generally valid scheme of social evolution but only in the light of its known and probable cultural relations with neighboring peoples.[22]

Ethnographized Sociology and the Way Out. — The aftereffects of the deflation of social evolutionism have been both good and bad. The good is apparent enough — anyone will admit that the destruction of an erroneous theory is a service to science. The harmful aspects of the collapse are not so easily stated, but at least one merits our attention here: the growth of extreme historicism.

This is most apparent in American ethnology; the reaction against the grandiose and fantastic formulas of the nineteenth century has gone so far that one American ethnologist (strictly speaking, an ethnographer only) has revived Maitland's dictum: " By and by anthropology will have the choice between being history or nothing." [23] This means that the attempt to find explanatory principles applicable to widely varying cultures has been abandoned, and that the effort now is simply to describe a given people with the minute and scrupulous accuracy of the historian — and to stop there. Radin is the most extreme representative of this trend, but it is everywhere in evidence. One simply tells everything one knows about the Yurok or the Tlingit or the Winnebago, and the story is its own best reason for being. No ulterior considerations, such as relevance to a particular problem, comparability with another culture, or whatever, can be granted a controlling influence; it must be " ethnography for ethnography's sake." The consequence is chaos; to apply Vincent's phrase in another connection, the ethnologist becomes " an intellectual kodak fiend." No sociologist who has passed beyond the anecdotal stage can grant any place in his work to such extreme historicism; he must achieve generalization of some kind if he is to fulfill his scientific function.

The first thing that must be done if a sound historical sociology is to be built up is to attach proper weight to historical data. This sounds paradoxical, and perhaps it is: nineteenth-century historical sociology drew a tremendous proportion of its materials from the so-called primitives, and paid altogether insufficient attention to the " historical peoples." Sociology was ethnographized, and the consequences we have witnessed.

This ethnographized sociology was destroyed, but curiously enough, the prestige of the destroyers, who were themselves ethnographers, was so great that American sociologists continued to purvey ethnographized sociology: *all they did was to change their allegiance from Morgan to Boas, and to stress differences in culture rather than similarities.* They became vaguely aware that the preliterate does not necessarily represent the primitive, but they continued to study the " simpler peoples " (who are in many respects as complex as ourselves) in the hope of gaining insight into the processes of their own society. This was all very well, if they had not ignored historical data; something was undoubtedly gained, but a great deal more was lost. Let us try to see why.

To begin with, even if the sources were equally good, information about the course of social development in Western Europe and America is of more value, in understanding contemporary social matters, than similar information regarding Hidatsa society (to choose a well-worn example). And, to carry the fight closer home: even if ethnologists were willing to abandon their extreme historicism and admit that a study of the Hidatsa might yield features comparable with those of peasant life in Roumania, let us say, the resulting generalizations would necessarily be inferior to those arrived at through the use of *first-class* historical data. One of the chief reasons lies in the fact that there is a surprisingly small number of really good ethnographies — works by Thurnwald, Nordenskiold, Boas, Rivers, Radcliffe-Brown, Kroeber, Lowie, Wissler, Malinowski, Radin, Herskovits, and a few others exhaust the list now deemed acceptable *by American ethnographers themselves.* Further, most of these are valueless for historical sociology, for they cover much too short a period — three or four generations at best. Moreover, even the best ethnographies suffer from the fact that in the majority of cases the " document " and the " interpretation " necessarily derive from or through the same person — in spite of all efforts, there are few *complete* sets of sources stemming solely from relatively naïve participants, and hence description and analysis tend to coincide. Again, there are few preliterate groups unaltered by Western culture, and within a generation these probably will be vastly changed, so that few or no real comparisons can be made. Finally, preliterate language obstacles make it virtually impossible for any considerable number of ethnographers to check the work done by any one investigator, so that when some later field-worker casts doubt on the accuracy of his predecessor, it is almost a case of "You're another!" with no possibility of decision.

Certain it is that historical data are blemished in many ways, but the careful student who delves equally deep in both fields will almost certainly come to the conclusion that the shards yielded by ethnography are frequently inferior, for the purposes of historical sociology, to the marred or broken, but recognizable and richly figured vases turned up on history's soil. *This is not to say that the sociologist should neglect the attested data of ethnography* — if he does not make the fullest possible use of it he is committing a scientific crime — but it most emphatically is to say that he who neglects the treasure-trove of history will find himself poor indeed.

The Relation of History and Sociology. — In thus asserting the importance of historical data, not only for historical sociology but for all sociology, we are automatically confronted by a fundamental problem in the logic of the social sciences: What is the relation of history and sociology? How can the data of history be used by sociology at all? The traditional answer has been in terms of the Windelband-Rickert distinction between the idiographic and the nomothetic disciplines: history depicts the unique, the non-recurrent, the empire of *Napoleon;* sociology sets forth the causal laws of the common, the recurrent, the *empire* of Napoleon and similar rulers. Simple, clear, persuasive. And yet. . . .

Can historical data — which is to say, social data — be torn out of their full context? Dare we assume when we begin an investigation that we can tear a closely woven tapestry apart, sew the fragments on a "timeless" background, and get anything but a crazy quilt for our labor? As one of the present writers has put the case with regard to a specific problem:

In order for separate characteristics . . . to have meaning, they must be considered with reference to the whole problem and to each other — they must be considered as a configuration united by the logic of internal relationships. . . . The configuration constitutes the parts just as the parts constitute the configuration; neither can be considered in isolation. Consequently . . . ["timeless" classifications] must not be regarded as anything more than convenient tools for dissecting purposes; to this end they are well adapted, but if we use them so unskilfully that the configuration is destroyed, we shall have nothing left but a scattered collection of *disjecta membra* that helps us to explain nothing.[24]

Neglect of such elementary methodological precautions landed earlier historical sociologists in the morass of the so-called comparative method. This much we can grant the historicist: the sociologist should not approach his data with the intention of forcing them, willy-nilly, into a Procrustean bed of "timeless" categories that are *a priori* generalizable.[25] True, he *can* do this if he wishes, but in nearly all cases he will find that the result yields purely taxonomic or classificatory satisfaction rather than explanatory power. If his concepts are to have the latter quality, they must be worked out without primary regard to their generalizability; if they prove to be generalizable *in spite of* the fact that they are intended to be fully adequate to the shorthand description and analysis of the social processes and structures permeating and, as it were, sustaining a *particular* historical happening, era, or what not, so much the better, but such generalizability must not be the controlling aim of the endeavor.

In the field of the sociology of religion, for example, the concepts of the ecclesia, the sect, the denomination, and the cult [26] are designed primarily to render possible the sociological comprehension of a particular series of historical occurrences which we call the development of Christianity. They are not intended to explain the genesis and interaction of all religious structures, or of social structures in general, but are expressly limited to specific Western European and American phenomena. If, upon comparison with other culture case studies, there appears a generalizable essence or aspect (as indeed there does), this is a welcome consequence but not the guiding desideratum.

A Genuinely Comparative Method. — "Upon *comparison* with other culture case studies!" Yes, just that; here we go beyond the historicist. What has already been called the illustrative method must not be confused with a *genuinely* comparative method. Let us indicate what is meant by the latter phrase, following in part the lines laid down by Robert E. Park.

Suppose that the problem is the relation of culture contact to social change. In examining historical data with an eye to this connection, one is likely to be struck by the fact that instances appear in which there is little evidence of some of these phenomena over a relatively long period. Conversely, there are to be found certain noteworthy examples in which culture contact and social change reach what seems to be a maximum: the social

organization of early fifth-century Sparta on the one hand —
the social organization (or shall we say disorganization?) of
parts of the metropolis of New York on the other.

Such cases give us a line of approach that seems likely to yield
a valid basis for selection and comparison. The study of a culture,
in the full particularity of its time and place, where the phenomena denoted by the problem are at a *minimum,* would yield
a sort of control case, a marginal case. One point thus fixed, it
would then be necessary only to find an instance where the
phenomena denoted by the problem are at a *maximum,* and two
points of reference would then be established. As the logicians
say, these marginal cases would then give the determining orientation; between these two extremes any additional number of
cases could be placed. If a sufficient number were examined, a sort
of continuum could be built up; if the number were very large,
transition from one to the other would be so slight as to be almost
imperceptible, and yet in either direction would lie the limiting
extremes, giving significance to even the minutest variation. The
extremes, it will be recalled, are on the one hand a social order in
which the phenomena denoted by the problem — culture contact
and social change — are at the empirically discoverable minimum,
and on the other, one in which the same phenomena are at the
empirically discoverable maximum. When, as the result of intensive culture case study and comparison, *followed by ideal-typical
formulation,* the processes correlated with transition toward one
or the other extreme have been discovered, the problem has been
solved.

The chart on the next page summarizes the preliminary phase
of such a comparative study partially completed by one of the
present writers. (In order to give point to the contentions advanced regarding the richness of historical data, only material
of this type has been included, but ethnographical material could
have been used with advantage in some instances.) Obviously
this chart must not be taken too seriously; the full implications of
a series of culture case studies become apparent only when the
studies themselves are read.[27] Nevertheless, a word or two of
comment may not be amiss.

First of all, it should be noted that reference to mental mobility as a *comparable* aspect of all the cases does not necessarily
mean that it is a *generalizable* factor, for it may be only the
known outcome of a series of unknowns having little or nothing
in common. At the same time, the fact that mental mobility has
emerged as the result of focusing on the same problem in seven

SPARTAN	GYPSY	NOMADIC	GERMANIC	ATHENIAN	RENAISSANCE ITALIAN	MODERN URBAN
(Sources scanty but fairly good from *Kulturgeschichte* standpoint)	(Sources surprisingly full, as witness Black's *Gypsy Bibliography*)	(For pastoral nomads bordering Fertile Crescent, sources adequate though not as complete as could be wished. See Cowan, *Master-Clues in World History*)	(Rather good sources, from *Kulturgeschichte* viewpoint, for several tribes. See Steinhausen, *Geschichte der deutschen Kultur*.)	(Sources and their adequacy for some problems too well known to need comment)	(For Florence, and one or two other city-states, sources excellent)	(Wealth of material, but as yet insufficiently sifted. For present problem this is not a serious drawback)
Minimum of culture contact	Minimum of effective culture contact	Minimum of effective culture contact even though combat contacts are frequent	Moderate degree of culture contact	High degree of culture contact in form of vicinal, social, and mental accessibility	Very high degree of culture contact in form of vicinal, social, and mental accessibility	Maximum of culture contact in form of vicinal, social, and mental accessibility
Appears in conjunction with vicinal isolation and its retarding, stabilizing, fixating, and exclusive effects	Appears in conjunction with social isolation resulting from high cultural and biological visibility, and high degree of social control resulting from kinship grouping and family unity	Appears in conjunction with routine migration, social immobility, and routine raiding pattern; high degree of discipline and combat efficiency	Appears in conjunction with following: Nomadic migrations; conquest of tillage peoples; rise of one form of territorial state; shattering of kinship bonds and consequent disorganization; breakdown of social control and consequent individuation; reorganization	Appears in conjunction with frontier settlement of Ionia and its reflex effects; commerce, colonization, the intrusion of the stranger, rise of rationalism and secularization	Appears in conjunction with extreme release, preceded by the following: reorganization, inhibition, and unrest; "milling" and emergence of "the crowd that acts"; cataclysmic culture contact (Crusades) and more gradual conquest, with consequent disorganization	Appears in conjunction with very high degree of differentiation and contactual mobility, affording opportunities for gratification of segmental cravings, acquisition of urbanity, compartmentalization of personality; high degree of vicarious movement and vicarious mobility
Minimum of social change	Minimum of social change	Very low rate of social change	High rate of social change but subsequent rigid reorganization	High rate of social change	High rate of social change	Maximum of social change
Comparable aspect: Mental immobility	Comparable aspect: Mental immobility	Comparable aspect: Mental immobility	Comparable aspect: Mental mobility in transitory form	Comparable aspect: Mental mobility	Comparable aspect: Mental mobility	Comparable aspect: Mental mobility

Isolated Sacred Societies   Accessible Secular Societies

historical cases ranged in sequence renders it probable, although by no means certain, that the formula which explains such mobility, all variables taken into account, in each of the seven cases will also explain it, *mutatis mutandis,* in all other cases.

Second, let it be emphasized that such an explanatory formula does not appear in the chart, for it can be arrived at only through the conceptual utilization of the outcomes of these culture studies.[28] When this is done, the result is the construction of ideal types resting firmly on the granite of history, and yet transportable between certain points of the historical terrain. Such ideal types are never wholly " timeless " if they have any explanatory value; the necessary presence of some degree of " historical saturation " is thoroughly demonstrated by the work of Max Weber, for example, in spite of the fact that he rendered lip-service to the Windelband-Rickert theory. Instances in point are his ideal-typical forms of domination (of which we have made extensive use) : traditional, charismatic, and rational. Each of these is manifested in *clear-cut* fashion only in a particular type of historical configuration, and the attempt wholly to eliminate their historical reference deprives them of almost every vestige of explanatory power. Moreover, as Löwith has recently shown,[29] virtually all of Max Weber's ideal-typical formulations have the red thread of a definite theory of history running through them; not only is their significance bound up with particular historical configurations, but their full significance becomes apparent only when what Weber regarded as the total historical configuration is held in view. (We shall refer to this point again when discussing theories of the total process of historical change.)

Culture Case Study Exemplified. —A striking example of successful culture case study, similarly pervaded by a theory of the total historical configuration, is afforded by Arnold J. Toynbee's *A Study of History.* Three massive tomes (1st ed., 1934; 2nd, 1935) of the projected twelve-volume work have appeared, and they are sufficiently self-contained to be dealt with by themselves.

The adjective " successful " has just been applied to Toynbee's enterprise — and it undoubtedly is warranted in so far as *culture case study* is concerned. In other respects a number of flaws are evident, and of these we must first take account. Most important of these defects is Toynbee's adherence to a universal and transcendent philosophy of history (one of the " rejected types " shortly to be discussed). He has taken over seriously Goethe's conception of evil as a force that in spite of itself makes for good.

This is but an echo of the far older belief that " All things work together for good for them that love God." *Sub specie aeternatis,* such a belief may indeed be true, but it has nothing to do with science. Second among the blemishes is a vague mysticism that leads Toynbee to play with terms such as *yin* and *yang* in a way that results in emotional exaltation rather than intellectual clarity. Third is a shortcoming common to historians who manufacture their sociology *ad hoc,* in entire ignorance of the critical sociological literature. For example, Toynbee has adopted a number of Huntington's most dubious doctrines — doctrines that were demolished long ago. This is the more regrettable in view of the fact that the merits of Toynbee's analysis are relatively independent of the truth or falsity of Huntington's theories. Fourth, Toynbee wastes a great deal of energy and space in attacking racial dogmas that are entertained seriously only by Nazis, English colonels in India, and a number of sub-Mason-Dixon Americans; here again his lack of acquaintance with the critical literature has led him to home-brew his sociology. (This defect, by the way, is common among British writers; the reasons for it are set forth in Chapter Twenty-One.)

In spite of these and many other flaws, however, there can be no contesting the profound significance of Toynbee's work. He begins with a telling attack on extreme historicism, and goes on to consider, very circumspectly and thoroughly, a number of vital questions of method. After formulating a plan of operations centering about several societies shown to be " intelligible fields of historical study," he isolates twenty-one comparable entities to which a method of culture case study can be applied. (Needless to say, he does not use the terminology of this chapter!) These are: Egyptiac, Andean; Sinic, Minoan, Sumeric, Mayan; Syriac; Indic, Hittite, Hellenic; Western; Orthodox Christian (in Russia), Far Eastern (in Korea and Japan); Orthodox Christian (main body), Far Eastern (main body); Iranic; Arabic, Hindu; Mexic; Yucatec; and Babylonic.

We cannot stop to present Toynbee's reasons for the peculiar juxtapositions evident in the above classification; suffice it to say that he makes good his case. The problem which the comparison of these societies is designed to solve is that of the genesis and growth of civilizations (these being regarded as distinct from " primitive societies "). His next step is to consider a number of " possible negative and positive factors " which would help to account for the traits which civilized groups manifest as over against more " primitive " types. He concludes, not without a strong admixture of value-judgment, that the negative factors of " psychic inertia " and "inferior race " provide no satisfying explanations. Turning then to the natural environment as a possible positive factor, he quite conclusively demonstrates, through the skillful dissection of several culture cases, that favorable natural environments do not necessarily engender civilizations. In fact, Toynbee renders plausible the theory that peculiarly *un*favorable natural environments have in some cases been among the significant factors in initiating the transition from " primitivism " to civilization. For Egypt, the challenge of drought; Sumeria, trackless marsh; China, flood; Mayan civilization, tropical forest; Andean, bleak climate and grudging soil; Minoan, sea; and so on for many of the twenty-one culture cases. In other instances, where challenges from the natural environment have been conspicuously lacking, there have been challenges from the human environment, and especially from what Toynbee calls external and internal proletariats (of which proletariats instances are afforded by the Germanic barbarians and the early Christians respectively).

The similarity of all this to what Thomas has called " crisis " is plain to every informed American sociologist. The likeness is rendered more striking by Toynbee's masterly survey of " the range of challenge-and-response." The stimulus of hard countries; the stimulus of new ground; the stimulus of blows; the stimulus of pressures; the stimulus of penalizations — all are analyzed with amazing dexterity and with an abundance of comparable culture cases. So great is the scope of Toynbee's knowledge of history that he is often able to select cases in which only the crucial factors vary; he therefore provides virtually experimental setups for many of his generalizations. The upshot is that the vital rôle of challenge-and-response in the *genesis* of civilizations is incontestably demonstrated; here culture case study has won a veritable triumph.

We can be much less sure of the adequacy of Toynbee's researches with regard to the *growth* of civilizations. To be sure, his analysis of the factors in arrested growth carries conviction, based as it is on the adroitly chosen cases of the Eskimos, the Mongols, the 'Osmanli Janissaries, and the Spartiates. The conclusion is inevitable that machine-like or ant-like perfection of adaptation inevitably checks further change. When Toynbee turns to the positive factors in civilizational growth, however, he is much less convincing. The soft mystical note that merely confuses the earlier parts of his work becomes so loud toward the end of the third volume that it almost drowns out the systematic-empirical strain. We therefore do not discuss his concepts of "etherialization" and "withdrawal-and-return," largely because we do not fully understand them. Perhaps the volumes planned to follow those we have so briefly discussed will set affairs right again.

No matter what the flaws in tne first three volumes may seem to be, Toynbee has given to sociologists a magnificent specimen of the possibilities of culture case study. It remains only for us to be inspired by his example.

Theories of the Total Process of Historical Change. — And thus our second question forces itself on our attention, "What has been the general trend of the whole process of social and cultural development?" In other words, Max Weber's and Toynbee's emphases on the total historical configuration make it necessary for us to survey the various philosophies of history, i.e., the many attempts that have been made to determine the trend of the development of culture, or of "the historical movement" as a whole. Only a few of these attempts can justifiably be designated as historical sociology; what is currently called the philosophy of history includes a great deal that the critical sociologist must summarily reject. Before discussing the type of philosophy of history that is sociologically acceptable, therefore, it is advisable to run over the list of the rejected varieties.

Exceedingly prominent in the ranks of the philosophies of history to be excluded from the field of historical sociology are several of the universal and transcendent sort. By "universal" is meant purpose or meaning or value toward which not only all mankind but the entire universe strives, that "one far-off divine event toward which the whole creation moves." The occurrence of the word "divine" in the foregoing quotation hints at what is meant by "transcendent" — the universal meaning or purpose or value is not the more or less fortuitous outcome of a cosmic process itself essentially meaningless, but is to be attributed to God's will, or to the progressive unfolding of the Absolute Idea, or to a beneficent Nature. The lineage of this type of philosophy of history is a long one: it begins with the earliest cosmogonies and cosmologies, takes in Plato and Polybius, Isaiah and John, Chrysostom and Orosius, Augustine and Thomas Aquinas, Bossuet and Paley, Vico and Turgot, DeBonald and DeMaistre, Drummond and Wallace, Lilienfeld and Schäffle, and finally, reckons among its recent progenitors Branford, Ellwood, the early Scheler, and Toynbee, to name only a few.

In the space at our disposal it is useless to attempt to justify the exclusion of universal and transcendent varieties of the philosophy of history from the field now being delimited; suffice it to say that they are excluded.

In the same way we must bar the universal and immanent (i.e., non-transcendent) species. Even though transcendent sanction is not sought, the assertion of a goal or purpose toward which the development of the cosmos and of human society not only *does* tend but *ought* so to tend places this type outside our field because one of the basic assumptions not only of historical sociology but of all scientific sociology is that *ultimate* value-judgments, such as the word " ought " necessarily implies, cannot be passed upon by any scientific means whatsoever. And here again a long, diverse, and impressive lineage confronts us: Condorcet, Burke, Comte, Spencer, Ward, Giddings, Müller-Lyer, Hobhouse, Marx, Burckhardt, Breysig, Wells — and how many more!

Third in the row of excluded varieties is the relative but transcendent philosophy of history of which the writings of Troeltsch afford the clearest example,[30] but of which traces are also to be found in Schlegel, Müller, Nietzsche, DeLagarde, Theodor Lessing, Klages, Bäumler, and Spengler. To confine ourselves to the writer first mentioned: Troeltsch approximates the position of many extreme historicists (numbering among their ranks many American ethnographers) in maintaining that there can be no philosophy of history applicable to all mankind because there is no such thing as mankind. Great cultural totalities there are, to be sure, but each has its own peculiar set of values and, *by the same token,* its own peculiar set of causal sequences. Not only is there no way of determining what *ought* to be the universal or even the common-human trend of development, but there is no way of determining what *is* that trend. At the most one can discover the meaningful and the causal sequences in particular cultures to which one wholeheartedly adheres (or to which one can cultivate full allegiance by long participation, mediated through the written record or otherwise). This seemingly complete relativity of values Troeltsch saves for a sort of transcendental sanction by invoking the aphorism of Ranke, *Jede Epoche ist unmittelbar zu Gott* — " Every epoch is in direct communion with God." Even though the values of the Chinese are not our values, they are God's values, for the Chinese, as it were, are God's children. What *we* must do, said Troeltsch, is to strive to realize the values of the great European *Kulturkreis* to which we are inseparably bound, and hope that God will ensure the absoluteness, the transcendence, of what to mortal eye is wholly relative. Here, it seems, is the *reductio ad absurdum* of this incongruous amalgam of extreme historicism and longing for the absolute. At any rate, relative but transcendent philosophies of history are beyond the pale, so far as we are concerned.

An Acceptable Theory of History: Max Weber. — But enough of these excluded types; let us now turn to those which can justifiably be included under the head of historical sociology. The plural pronoun " those " has just been used, but the contrast between the excluded and the included sorts is so great that we might properly regard the latter as sub-varieties, differing merely in minor points, of only one major form.

This form is not cosmically universal, for it is not built about an assumed purpose or meaning or value toward which the cosmos strives. Further, it is not socially universal, for it presupposes no supreme ideal, end, or norm toward which mankind as a whole ought to or does struggle. Neither is it transcendent, for it embodies no intuition or revelation of nor insight into the workings of the Divine Mind, the Absolute, Nature, or Progress. Once more, it is not relative in the sense of extreme historicism, inasmuch as its exponents maintain that certain generalizations can be made that are not entirely limited to specific historical complexes at specific times and places.

The two sub-varieties into which this major form can be divided differ only in the degree to which the theoretical implications of such a philosophy of history are explicitly formulated. In the first, comprising the less thorough formulations, we may place the theories of Shotwell, Robinson, Durkheim, Woodard,[31] and more especially Tönnies and Teggart; in the second, the theories of Max Weber and Alfred Weber.

The writers of the first group agree, roughly speaking, that the trend of social development has been and will be toward a greater measure of accessibility, differentiation, integration, and secularization, paralleled on the personal plane by an increase in individuation, compartmentalization, and rationality. Tönnies, for example, shapes his entire theory in terms of the transition from community to society — i.e., from primary grouping to secondary grouping — and as an inseparable corollary, from essential will to arbitrary will; which is to say, in our terminology, from mental immobility to mental mobility.[32] Teggart follows a similar line of analysis, but is more interested in the *modus operandi* of the transition than is Tönnies; he finds it in the breakdown of isolation following upon migrations and communication, which in turn brings about the clash of contending idea-systems and eventual release from traditional inhibitions.[33]

With much of this Max Weber is in essential agreement, but he qualifies his agreement by the methodological precision of culture case study and the ideal-typical method. A historian commanding a simply stupendous array of data,[34] Weber was properly sceptical of all-inclusive formulas. From his early agrarian history of the ancient world to his posthumous articles on Pharisaism, Weber was an unflagging advocate of intensive culture case study; he opposed, with fitting acerbity, all efforts to find modern capitalism in the Greek world, or to equate the Middle Ages with the era of the Eupatrids, or to extract illustrations for a rigid sequence of stages of industrial evolution, à la Bücher, from the Greek household or workshop. Nevertheless, he did not fall into the abyss of extreme historicism; he not only succeeded in finding *comparable* aspects in analyses primarily intended to render possible the sociological comprehension of particular historical configurations, but he was also able to make some of those aspects *generalizable* through his use of the ideal-typical method. This method makes use of various personality types, types of social processes and structures, and relatively self-contained configurations of such personalities, processes, and structures which are rarely if ever found in an unmixed or " pure " form, but which for purposes of clarity and systematization are dealt with *as if* they so existed.[35] The " rational man," for example, is such an ideal type in the writings of the advocates of "understanding " or " interpretative " sociology (see Chapter Twenty-Three); he is an abstraction *never* concretely embodied, and yet considerable insight into social processes can be gained by thus operating with what is after all a *fiction*. An ideal type, moreover, is never a statistical mode or mean; it is a deliberate accentuation or even distortion of empirical reality for the purpose of gaining scientific control over that reality. In short, an ideal type is a device made of the full particularity of history, shaped in such a way that such particularity can be at least partially generalized. To take our "rational man" again: only in particular historical epochs can even relatively well-marked conduct of the kind he represents be found, *and without knowledge of the non-comparable and comparable particularities of human behavior in those epochs we should not be able to construct our ideal type.* Once he is constructed, however, he may be of great aid in revealing the presence and further ramifications of his conduct in other

eras and cultures; moreover, if he has been well constructed the
fact that a particular culture does *not* reveal his presence is in
itself of great significance — ideal types have negative as well as
positive utility.

Now the interesting thing about Max Weber's ideal-typical
method, in the present context, is the fact that it makes use of
and is made use of by a non-universal, non-transcendent, non-
relative philosophy of history. For Max Weber the prime fact
of social evolution was the continuous growth of the rational
habit of mind, the habit of abstraction from the concrete and
personal, the habit of which *Homo oeconomicus* and *Homo scien-
tificus* are such striking instances. But although he devoted his
life to the further perfection of *Homo rationalis,* Weber made no
explicit value-judgment about rationality; as he so trenchantly
said, " Secularization (*Entzauberung der Welt*) and its concomitant rationalization may be good, or it may be bad, but it is
our destiny. . . . To him who cannot manfully bear this destiny . . . the doors of the old churches stand forgivingly open
. . . if he will but make ' the sacrifice of the intellect.' " [36] That
sacrifice Max Weber never made or could make, but he cast no
scorn on those who did; the vials of his wrath he saved to cast
upon the heads of those who fondly fancied they could rationally
blend " the best features of both science and religion."

The growth of the rational habit of thought and of its attendant secularization of society, then, was for Weber the strand
upon which all sociological concepts must be strung, regardless of
the religious or ethical value of that strand. At the same time, he
refrained from absolutizing this ideal-typical generalization; it
merely appeared as the most easily comparable and generalizable
trait of all the manifold culture case studies upon which he had
so successfully labored. Moreover, he was under no delusions as
to the scope of rational conduct, for he regarded many phases of
life as quite beyond the reach of rationality. Further, his ethical
standpoint was that of unqualified individual autonomy and responsibility on a wholly *non*-rational basis: " [The ethical task]
. . . is plain and simple when each of us finds and obeys the
daimon [in the Socratic sense] that holds the thread of *his* life." [37]
In short, for Max Weber the conception of rational conduct was
merely a tool of analysis, not the demand of an apostle of " enlightenment."

It must be granted, however, that many of the implications of
Max Weber's theory of history, and even some of the major
premises, were never clearly formulated by him; his work had a

torso-like, fragmentary character. Let us therefore turn to the analysis presented by his younger brother, Alfred Weber, in which there is a persistent effort to be highly explicit.

Society, Civilization, " Culture": Alfred Weber. — In spite of the fact that this writer aims at a sociology and not a philosophy of history, there are many connections with the abiding problems of social philosophy dealt with in the great systems of Herder, Hegel, and others. From another angle, his endeavor may be regarded as the culmination of *Kulturgeschichte.* The details it has laboriously accumulated he subjects to a generalizing, ideal-typical analysis, best exemplified in his *Kulturgeschichte als Kultursoziologie* (1935), along lines not unlike those projected by his elder brother.[38]

These and other traditional tendencies are complicated, however, by the influence of historical materialism. Indeed, in one sense it is not unfair to characterize Alfred Weber's sociology of culture as an attempt to apply certain Marxian formulas to historical happenings as far as they can be applied, and then to point out their inadequacy in the explanation of the generically " cultural " achievements of man (taking " cultural " in a special sense — to be defined later). The undeniable *conditioning* of these achievements by the framework of social structure and intellectual climate does not *determine* their essences.

Considerations of this kind lead to the conclusion that Alfred Weber not only aims at a sort of synthesis of idealism and historical materialism, but also unites within his inclusive system the opposites of Romanticism and rationalism. Hence he maintains that there really is such a thing as progress, but limits it to the domain of the rational, of the intellect, of civilization. On the other hand, he joins the Romantics in affirming the uniqueness and mystery of genius and human creativeness as manifested in music, sculpture, poetry, and other " cultural emanations."

Alfred Weber's conceptions of the nature, aim, and method of sociology must therefore be viewed in the light of this background and of the related methodological disputes current in Germany. He holds that sociology cannot be limited to analysis of the processes of sociation and of the structure of plurality patterns — herein taking issue with Wiese. Sociology must be of the " material " type, going beyond the structural shells of art, philosophy, and religion, for example, to investigate the essences that lie within. Moreover, it must relate these essences, when discovered, to all the other facts entering into the underlying pattern of the given period. This type of investigation is partially but splendidly exemplified by Max Weber's studies in the sociology of religion (of which the early chapters of the present volume give some inkling). Alfred Weber maintains that this program is closely in accord with that advanced by " the founders of sociology — Saint-Simon, Comte, and Marx " — for they attempted to synthesize both trans-societal and societal facts within the framework provided by a systematic structural analysis of history.

These early attempts were vitiated, however, by several biases, chief among which were naturalism and evolutionism. The naturalistic bias led its adherents to assign priority to material factors and to stress societal influences, thereby rendering much less than justice to the non-material achievements of man. The result was that the non-material came to be regarded as derivative and even as epiphenomenal — as " a mere shadow cast by the wheels of an onrushing locomotive." The evolutionistic bias led to the assumption of teleological development and continuous progress in all phases of man's activity. It was blandly assumed that everything was " getting bigger and better " because Evolution, that nineteenth-century Mumbo-Jumbo, had so ordained.

The purpose of Alfred Weber's work is the construction of a sociology of culture. This of course is not the same as the " universal " histories or the philosophies of history found among our rejected types; it is, however, an attempt at a unitary *interpretation* of the processes of history. This interpretation is possible only because it is inseparably bound up with ultimate cultural values, in spite of the fact that value-*judgments* are excluded. (Clearly manifest here are close connections with Rickert's philosophy, and also with Scheler's ideas about the primacy of metaphysical knowledge.) The task of this sociology is the systematic analysis of the totality of history. To what end? Nothing less than the *understanding and interpreting,* in all their diversity, of the various cultures that have emerged within that totality. Rephrasing: the aim of the sociologist of culture is to survey the total course of history synoptically in order that he may " understand " its cultural aspects or emanations in their general functional relations within their given historical complexes.

The analysis preliminary to such understanding leads Alfred Weber to distinguish, within the totality of historical processes, three focal points; namely, society, civilization, and culture. These distinctions, presently to be explained, reflect his conception of sociology. Although he does not state his position in so many words, it is clear that for Alfred Weber, as for Rickert, Dilthey, Max Weber, Znaniecki, and others, sociology is not a natural but a cultural science. He holds that its object-matter is indissolubly embedded in " vital aggregations," and hence cannot be fully known if naturalistic methods alone are used. Fundamental to his whole procedure is a definite theory of culture and of its changes and functions in the totality of life. This theory is based on a rejection of the naturalistic method and an espousal of an essentially vitalistic view insisting on the rootedness-in-life (*Lebenseingefügtheit*) of the cultural enterprise. In fine, the aim of the sociology of culture is to analyze ideal-typically (*not* individually, which is the aim of history) the structure, dynamics, and rhythms of the relations between society, civilization, and culture.

The processes of history may from one point of view be regarded as sequences, coexistences, and interdependences of various great historical entities; e.g., Babylonian, Hindu, Chinese, Hebrew-Persian, Greco-Roman, Byzantine, Islamic, and Occidental. Each has its own unique essence, its characteristic life-attitude (*Schicksalshaltung*) and mode of expression, and its unmistakable appearance; moreover, each has its own rhythm of change, its own peaks and valleys.

Every great historical entity embodies a culture; i.e., exhibits an absolutely distinctive patterning of vital energies. This culture is crystallized out of the reaction, manifested as a unique set of historical experiences, of a particular ethnic group to a particular environment. It is in a certain sense a unique effort on the part of a particular vital aggregation to impress its own appearance, its own " countenance," upon the world within which it has historically emerged.

Every " culture-countenance " is shaped and sustained by a unique attitude toward life which may be regarded as an expression of a sort of " psychical entelechy" (roughly equivalent to our term " mentality") that has arisen in and through the processes of history. There results a " unity of style" in the whole culture, permeating religion, philosophy, and art as well as the social and psychical realms. When decisive innovations in mentality take place, they are accompanied by corresponding shifts in the culture's style, as witness the vast changes that marked the Enlightenment and like " mobilizations." (The degree of dependence and interconnection of the various aspects of a culture depends, however, on the character of the time. Today an unusual degree of *independence* marks art, religion, and philosophy.)

Each of the great historical bodies in which the major cultures have become manifest has been integrated by its *own* historical life-process. Otherwise phrased: the chief factors in the development of historical entities such as Babylonia, Islam, or China have been *immanent,* in spite of the undeniable relations between these entities brought about by trade, war, migration, and other means of diffusion. These immanent forces of integration constitute the *societal* process. This process, or configuration of processes, has typical forms and stages of development; it channelizes the non-human and human forces issuing from certain necessary organizations of the population — generations, sexes, castes, classes, territorial groupings, and the like. (Marxian theory concentrates almost exclusively on this phase of the societal process.) Every significant society has its own specific structure. This is a generalized patterning or conditioning of the actualized native endowments of the members of the given group, and all changes within the society may be viewed as phases of the development of this general pattern. Indeed, it is by virtue of their distinctive societal structures that we recognize given historical entities to be closed forms. Otherwise put: The societal process results in the formation of typical societal structures. And, says Alfred Weber, these structures tend to follow in certain sequences — although, to be sure, no unilinear schema can be constructed. As an example he offers the well-nigh universal transition from kinship organization (clan, gens, and the like) to grouping based on territory (deme, nome, nation).

Closely connected with the formation and transformation of life-aggregates, and also with the sequence of forms of societal structure, is another and different process, the intellectual-cultural. It too is a unity and totality, taking place in the intellectual-" spiritual " sphere of every historical entity. (Note that the use of " soul," " spiritual," " salvation," and like terms does not carry with it the traditional Christian interpretation or evaluation!) It possesses a regularity which corresponds to that of the societal process and to some degree runs parallel to it throughout all phases.

On closer examination this whole (which influences the phenomena of the societal realm as it is influenced by them) is seen to be made up of two components. One is the purely intellectual, which differs sharply from the purely cultural and is much more closely and lastingly related to the corporeal, material aspects of the societal process. The secularization and rationalization of life and the world, most clearly demonstrated in the observation and control of external nature — i.e., in natural science — is the aim of the civilizing intellect. Alfred Weber calls this intellectual activity the process of civilization (in some respects an equivalent of our secularization, rationalization, mental mobilization). Its essence is the growth of rational, systematized knowledge and technical command over the forces of nature. This growth is coherent, and follows a regular order. Its fruits are transferable from people to people; they are generally valid for all civilized humanity. The process of civilization is based on rationally communicable, theoretical and practical knowledge of nature and man, culminating in modern science.

This process of increasing rationalization for the most part proceeds parallel with the societal process. But though there is an obvious dependence on various societal factors — e.g., on the emergence of a new class to be the bearer of knowledge — the movement is *in principle* irreversible (in spite of stagnations) and universal. (Here is a point of fundamental difference from Sorokin's cyclical theories, as well as from Spengler's radical relativism and Mannheim's *Wissenssoziologie*.) The world of rational knowledge revealed by the process of civilization is general, potentially accessible to all men, and necessarily takes possession of its rightful place in all historical entities as soon as the proper phases of development have appeared. Rationality, given the right conditions, *must* emerge. The universality of civilizational phenomena means that the great historical entities, differing vastly in their societal processes and their cultural movements, are nevertheless interdependent. They therefore tend toward a unitary civilization; and this, says Alfred Weber, will eventually incorporate a system of generally valid ideas, overarching all mankind.

We have considered, however, only one aspect of the intellectual-cultural world. The other side of this duality is the realm dominated by the cultural process. Unlike civilization, the phenomena of culture *per se* are not subject to logical-intellectual causality; they have not arisen in the course of intellectual and material organization of life. In brief, culture does not " progress," and it has no necessary connection with the rational control of the conditions of existence. MacIver, who presents a closely similar conception, says: " There is no ' march ' of culture. It is subject to retrogression as well as to advance. Its past does not assure its future." [39]

Culture springs from the inner resources of man as man; it transcends all intellectuality and the world view issuing therefrom. Its emanations bear the mark of the unique and unrepeatable. Culture is not a product of inferences preëxisting in the rational axioms basic to civilization, but is a *creation,* an irruption, an emergent. Specific cultural emanations cannot be predicted or explained. Hence there can be no talk of sequences or stages of development, but only of series of self-contained periods of productivity and sterility, stagnation, and decline. The only kind of " development " that can be mentioned at all is with reference merely to the exterior, technical means of expression; e.g., the series of naturalistic, classic, Romantic, and baroque art styles.

In the terminology of Alfred Weber, the " soul " strives to express and lend form to itself in the medium of the " stuff of life." It permeates this stuff, seeking to form it in its own image. Putting it differently: Man in his most exalted, truly human capacity struggles to liberate and " save " himself through and by means of the modes and conditions of life itself. These modes and conditions, embodied in the developing historical forms of the societal process, and providing the requisite scientific-technical means in the civilizational process, constitute for the cultural process the stuff that must be transformed if man is to be fully human. *Wer immer strebend sich bemüht, ihn können wir erlösen.*

Culture as culture can be dealt with only historically; each case must be studied in its individual character. Clearly, culture does not lend itself to the generalizing methods of science, whereas civilization does. Unlike Spengler, Alfred Weber does not regard the cultures of different peoples as in any sense homologous; each is necessarily unique. Accordingly, there can be no morphology of culture of the type Spengler proposes, and hence no prophecies. Civilizational developments can be forecast; cultural emanations can be understood once they have occurred, but defy prediction.

The function of the sociology of culture is to determine the rhythms of cultural movement; to analyze the typical, periodic, and transitory elements of cultural expressions and forms; and to understand their connection with the processes of society and civilization. Only those selected traits of cultural phenomena which can be viewed as projections of the general patterns of their particular society, and *vice versa,* can be offered by the sociologist as evidence of his understanding of cultural-societal interconnections.

Frequently temporal and spatial correspondence of the various general phases of the societal, civilizational, and cultural processes can be demonstrated; this would indicate a strong possibility of functional interdependence. But functional interdependence is not causality! Alfred Weber unhesitatingly proclaims that even as between societal and civilizational processes, to say nothing of societal and cultural or civilizational and cultural, it is virtually impossible to find simple causal relationships. To speak with Pareto and Sorokin, what is a dependent variable in one phase becomes an independent variable in another; to speak with Dilthey and Max Weber, to "understand" is not to "explain." [40]

Here, in the analyses of the total historical process set forth by Alfred Weber and Max Weber, some features of which are present in less clean-cut form in the theories of Tönnies, Teggart, and several other writers, we have theories that perhaps may be rightfully included in the field of historical sociology. After the dusty chaff has been blown away, the rewarding kernels remain.

The Ideal-Typical Conception of Stages and Its Utility. — Part and parcel of a great many theories of history, and especially of the varieties just discussed, is the conception of stages or phases of societal development — the attempted answer to our question, " By what sequences or stages have the various branches of the human race arrived at their present state of societal organization?"

Following Ginsberg [41] (in part), we may distinguish four ways in which the notion of stages has been employed; each of these has different roots in the history of social thought, and each possesses a very different value for a sound historical sociology.

First is the conception of stages set forth by social evolutionists such as Morgan. This, as we have seen, has been thoroughly discredited, and we shall pay no further attention to it.

Second is the idea of stages as describing particular phases of general trends of development in the social life of mankind taken as a whole. One of the chief nineteenth-century efforts along this line was the work of Auguste Comte. Comte did not rest satisfied, as so many have contended, with a purely intellectual theory of social development. His famous division of history into theological, metaphysical, and positive stages applied merely to his notion of intellectual progress, whereas his stages of social development were based upon a more comprehensive set of factors: they included a theological-military period, a metaphysical-legalistic age, and the modern scientific-industrial era. Durkheim viewed social development as primarily a passage from a social system based upon the mechanical and restraining solidarity of group repression of individuality to a social system founded upon the voluntary solidarity of the social division of labor and the functional organization of society. DeGreef asserted that the history of society could be most intelligently summed up as the transformation from a régime based on force to one characterized by voluntary contractual social relations. Novicow contended that social evolution was a process of substituting progressively higher for lower forms of social conflict: from the physiological, through the economic and political, to the intellectual or highest form. Ratzenhofer and Small suggested that the vital social transformation has been from a " conquest state " to a " culture state," carrying with it the realization of a progressively more adequate range of social interests. Hobhouse stated that the stages of social development were those in which kinship, authority, and citizenship have been the basis of social cohesion and organization. Giddings divided the general process of social development into the following stages: *zoögenic,* or animal society; *anthropogenic,* or the society of man in the stage of the transformation from animal to human tribal society; *ethnogenic,* or tribal society; and *demogenic,* or the society of the so-called " historic " period. This last era he further divided into the military-religious period, roughly corresponding to that of Oriental antiquity and the early Middle Ages, the liberal-legal period, or that of Greece and Rome and early modern history, and the economic-ethical period, or that since the Industrial Revolution.

These stage theories certainly owe something to social evolutionism, but they probably are most deeply in debt to those older philosophies of history already noted and *excluded* from the field of historical sociology. At the same time, these stage theories have a few features that are not entirely irreconcilable with the non-universal, non-transcendent, non-relative type of philosophy of history we have approvingly discussed, and in the section on " The Nature of Ideal Types " we shall try to show how they may be of use. The major weaknesses of these theories are their complacent optimism and the illustrative method usually invoked to support them; the names of Comte, DeGreef, and Giddings need but be mentioned to call these weaknesses vividly to mind.

Third are the much less ambitious attempts of those who frame schemas of change for one or more parts of a total social organization, using the method of culture case study. Theorists of this variety sometimes confine themselves primarily to the development of one culture case, although virtually all of them leave open the possibility that comparable schemas may be found to apply to other cases. Schmoller [42] and Proesler [43] are examples in point: the former worked out a sequence of stages of economic development chiefly applicable to Germany, and the latter made a somewhat similar venture with more explicit attention to the method of culture case study.

Most of the theories discussed under the three preceding heads implicitly or explicitly make use of the principle of genetic continuity; i.e., they involve the thesis that subsequent stages arise or evolve out of precedent stages. Writers representing the fourth point of view, thoroughly disillusioned by the excesses of the evolutionary independent originists — excesses plainly exposed by Ratzel and other early diffusionists — leave the question of genetic continuity entirely open. The stages distinguished are not supposed to be descriptive of sequences as they actually occurred; they are merely viewed as ideal types useful as devices for facilitating estimates of rank or quantity, for comparison, and for generalization. Here again the influence of Max Weber makes itself felt; even the severest historical critic of the usual theories of stages, Georg von Below, himself adopted the ideal-typical method.[44]

No modern sociologist need feel himself hypercritical when he views the first three types of stage theory with considerable scepticism. The old-fashioned type of unilinear evolution is entirely out of court; the theories dealing with general trends of social development are ramshackle, jerry-built hovels when composed of the miscellaneous scraps collected by the illustrative method; and stages based on the unrefined results of culture case studies alone provide no generalizations that bridge the gulf of extreme historicism. Only the ideal-typical method of conceiving stages includes everything of sociological value in the other conceptions, and in addition welds these contributions into a new tool of magnificent form and power.

The Nature of Ideal Types. — As already noted, ideal types are heuristic constructions, not definitions or averages. Max Weber recognized that in dealing with a historical configuration such as Christianity, for example, we cannot hope to seize and embody in a set of words the infinite variety and complexity of the phenomena intended to be called to mind by the term; the full historical reality as such yields nothing which the sociologist can directly utilize in his generalizations. It is necessary to give a special twist to certain characteristics of a set of historical occurrences, and to tie them up with others which may not always be found in such association or do not always take place in the same way, in order that they may be woven into a coherent whole, into an ideal type. In working with the medieval stage of Christianity, to modify our example, there is no sociological point in attempting to gather together the tremendously diverse and even contradictory beliefs, emotions, and modes of behavior of a gigantic congeries of persons alive at any one medieval date. The only way out of formless historicism is the weaving of a sort of limiting concept out of the warp and woof provided by certain dogmatic beliefs, moral ideas, maxims of conduct, and so on, with which the actual reality, as embodied in culture case studies, is then compared. Beyond doubt the strands we use in our weaving are all spun out of experience, and we certainly intertwine them in harmony with our ideas of what is objectively possible — nevertheless, the resulting fabric is confessedly a heuristic construct, a means of generalization, and is never exemplified in pure empirical form.

Max Weber applied this ideal-typical method in many ways, but one of the most important applications was in the study of societal and civilizational development, and Alfred Weber has followed a similar course. It is permissible — nay, desirable, because sociologically necessary — to construct an ideal-typical series or sequence-pattern, and then to use this series as a means of estimating the rate and trend of the actual historical occurrences, which in turn form a test of the validity of the ideal type. Instance: If intensive culture case studies of handicraft economies are made, it is then possible to build an ideal type of a handicraft economy, and from it to make deductions which may be verified or refuted by reference to culture case studies; e.g., we may deduce that in a social order of which such an economy is a constituent, the only source of capital accumulation is to be found in ground rent. From this we may infer that the influences leading to a transformation of the system would be found in limited supply of land, population increase, influx of precious metals, greater accessibility, and growth in secularization and rationalization (i.e., in one major phase of mental mobility). The deductions thus made must then be compared with the actual facts, and if they do not fit (as they do not in the so-called Middle Ages, for example), the inference that should follow is that the social order in question was not primarily constituted by a handicraft economy, and the investigation proceeds to a deeper level of analysis. If they do fit, the deductions may then be legitimately transferred to other cases having comparable features for further checking, and if repeated transference proves possible, a valid ideal-typical generalization has emerged.

The notion of stages, therefore, may be a very useful one, so long as a particular stage or sequence of stages is not absolutized, so long as room is left for changes brought by increasing knowledge. If great caution is practiced, it is sometimes even possible to make use of the schemas of stages formulated in and through the old illustrative method, provided they are checked by subsequent reference to culture case studies. In this way our researches into the history of social thought may be made to bear fruit, not only for our general appreciation of past thinkers but *for specific sociological theories of contemporary importance;* our information about the adumbrations of historical sociology to be found in Plato, Ibn Khaldūn, Turgot, or Durkheim may yield more than learned footnotes and the prideful preening of the erudite. To be sure, these writers were not scientists; we expect from them suggestion but not hypothesis. Suggestion, however, may be worth while — *vixere fortes ante Agamemnona!* — whereas neglect of the insights they offer may lead to that state of invincible ignorance upon which Goethe so bitingly commented:

> A pedant boasting said: " I follow none,
> I owe my wisdom to myself alone;
> Neither to ancient nor to modern sage
> Am I indebted for a single page."
> To set his boasting in its proper light,
> This author is — a fool in his own right!

Cyclical Theories: Small-Scale. — There are many conceptions of science, and it is not our present task to criticize any of them. We may, however, legitimately offer our own conception in order to show why we say that cyclical theories are perhaps the most scientific of all types of historical sociology. It may well be that the narrow definition of science which we shall set forth in the quotation to follow is too rigid for the historical sociologist to abide by at all times, but be this as it may, the cyclical theories we shall discuss conform most closely to it:

No science can justifiably offer intelligible explanation of all phenomena from ultimate source to ultimate goal; philosophers and religionists have attempted to do so — with what success the scientist *as scientist* cannot judge. He seizes the thread of knowledge at a point that seems likely to be heuristically usable, disregarding its beginning and all its ramifications outside his own field; his task is to follow it as far as it can be traced by the methods of his particular science. As a scientist he is interested only in (1) potential or (2) actual control of phenomenal recurrence: (1) potential in the sense that given such and such assumed conditions (which may be actually impossible of attainment at present or in the foreseeable future), he can predict the result of their interaction to a high degree of statistical probability; or (2) actual in the sense that he can set up the conditions, can control all the factors involved, and can *produce* the recurrence. Such control is his only concern; to a scientist, truth as such has no meaning.[45]

It should be clear that potential or actual control of this kind must provide the only satisfying answer to our fourth question: " Are there really cycles in social affairs which when discovered will demonstrate the truth of the maxim that 'History repeats itself'? "

Fortunately for the scientific standing of historical sociology, there is already a body of accredited theories, sometimes called social dynamics, which has successfully determined a large number of rhythms, process-series, sequence-patterns, cycles, and periodicities in social processes and structures. To be sure, these theories must often be cast in what are essentially ideal-typical forms, and hence the control attained is merely potential and probable, but they nevertheless conform to the strictest canons of scientific method. This conformity is rendered easier because they do not attempt to determine the trend of the *total* process of historical change; large-scale theories are manifestly very difficult if not impossible to subject to the criteria of potential or actual control. Small-scale cyclical theories can be more readily verified. Some examples are Simmel's " conflict cycle," Bogardus's " race relations cycle," Park's "ecological succession" series, Hiller's " strike cycle," Edwards's "natural history of revolution," many of the Marxian theories concerning revolutionary tactics, and Pareto's " speculator-rentier " sequence-pattern (analyzed in Chapter Twenty-Five). Of the scientific legitimacy of this kind of historical sociology there can be little doubt. Whatever the hardened sceptic may think of the types considered in other sections, he can scarcely fail to give his support to this more limited variety, even though he may think that *attested* results to date are meager, unless he is a historicist so extreme that he does not believe in the possibility of any sociological generalizations whatsoever. In the latter case, however, he probably will not concern himself with the problems of this chapter.

All-Inclusive Cycles: Spengler and Sorokin. — We can be much less certain of the scientific warrant of the large-scale cyclical theories, and particularly of those which take in all phases — societal, civilizational, "cultural" — of the total processes sustaining and changing all historical entities. Prediction is always a supreme test, and it can be applied most readily to phenomena of limited scope in time and space, such as " strike cycles " and " race relations " cycles. For one thing, it is relatively easy to determine whether or not the phenomenon which is supposed to have recurred is really the " same "; i.e., whether it falls within the ideal-typical limits previously established. When whole epochs and continents are the objects of massive cyclical generalizations, any frame of reference strong enough to carry the load is likely to be so cumbersome that fine adjustments are not possible.

A good example of a cyclical theory of this unduly overweening type is afforded by Oswald Spengler's *Der Untergang des Abend-landes* (vol. I, 1917; vol. II, 1922). It has already been included among our " rejected types," but must none the less be considered here as well. Spengler makes no *effective* use of distinctions such as Alfred Weber's society, civilization, and " culture "; everything is dealt with *en bloc.* Basic to the Spenglerian schema of the historical cycle is a sort of Hegelian idea of an " oversoul " of historical entities, complicated by crude organismic notions. Each of the great units he isolates — Egyptian, Chinese, Classical, Magian, Mayan, Faustian, Russian, and several others — has gone or will go through a cycle of birth, vigorous maturity, and senile decay that is the same for all and is determined by immanent organismic laws which nothing can alter. Each has its own mathematics, science, religion, and art, and each develops in absolute independence of every other; there is no genuine interaction whatsoever. Moreover, nothing can either accelerate or retard the ripening, withering, and decay.

No space can here be devoted to pointing out the egregious specific errors and general distortion of history perpetrated by Spengler; we shall merely say that in spite of the praise bestowed by Eduard Meyer on Spengler's work and the theories it contains,[46] few historians of repute have accepted his basic theses. Moreover, historical sociologists, among them Max and Alfred Weber, regard *The Decline of the West* as nothing more than a journalistic *tour de force* executed by a man of some erudition and undeniable literary ability. Whatever importance it possesses for the sociologist does not lie in the antiquated organismic version of all-inclusive cyclical theory which it reawakens, but in the excellent

analyses of rural and urban culture which are found in the second
volume, " World-Historical Perspectives." Spengler does not
give the sources of his distinctions, but plentiful internal evidence
shows that he borrowed his basic conceptions in this field from
Tönnies. At the same time, it cannot be denied that he has added
a great deal to the already fruitful antithesis between sacred and
secular societal types.

A recent cyclical theory somewhat resembling Spengler's, but
which its originator prefers to call a theory of trendless fluctuations, is embodied in the ideational-idealistic-sensate triad forming the framework of Sorokin's *Social and Cultural Dynamics*
(first three volumes, 1937). Ideational societies and cultures
(using the latter term in the ordinary sense) closely resemble our
sacred societies; Sorokin uses as one of his outstanding examples
of an ideational structure the Brahman-dominated, *dharma*-con-
trolled Indian world. (His stress on abstraction, however, di-
verges strongly from our analysis.) At the opposite pole stand
the sensate societies and cultures, and these in turn are closely
similar to our secular societies. Instance the fact that for Sorokin
the past six hundred years of Euro-American history have been
marked by a steady increase of sensate traits; this fits hand and
glove with our analysis of post-Middle-Ages secularization.
Many other parallel antitheses are to be found: Sparta-Athens
of the late fourth century B.C. is merely the most obvious of a
dozen or more.

Sorokin's middle term, however, has no analogue in the present
work; we make no use of anything equivalent to his conception
of idealistic societies and cultures. These are relatively rare, however, even in Sorokin's analysis; they are balanced configurations
in which certain ideational and sensate traits are proportioned in
such a way that they form a harmonious whole. Two of Sorokin's
examples are fifth-century Athens and thirteenth-century Western
Christendom. The balance seems to be delicate, for throughout
by far the greater part of the historical record, relatively one-
sided ideational or sensate conditions prevail. The prospectus of
Social and Cultural Dynamics contains this statement: " In the
history of culture Sorokin finds that either the Ideational or the
Sensate system flourishes at the expense of the other, except at
rare intervals in the beginning of Ideational declines, when the
two maintain precariously an Idealistic balance." [47]

In the following statement, written especially for the present
chapter, Sorokin has summed up the main features of his work
(here and there we add comment or explanation in []):

1. Method. Formulation and application of the logico-meaningful and causal-functional methods [somewhat akin to Alfred Weber's ideas of understanding, interpretation, and functional interdependence].

2. Main field of study: Greco-Roman and Western cultures during some twenty-five hundred years (600 B.C. to the present time), with brief excursions into Egyptian, Arabic, Hindu, Chinese, and Babylonian cultures . . . almost all the chapters represent a research monograph [executed by skilled assistants under the supervision of the author] in which the specialists in the respective fields will possibly find a great deal that is new to them.

3. The cultures studied are found to be tangibly integrated (logico-meaningfully and functionally), and each of their compartments is also found to be integrated, as a system within a system. [This is a much higher degree of integration than is found by Alfred Weber.]

4. In the changes traced during the twenty-five hundred years, each current of culture-mentality undergoes an immanent change, and the phases of the change are also immanent. But in every swing in a given direction there is a limit, after which the direction of the change reverses. . . . This means that no linearism in any form is found to be valid, and likewise no Spencerian or other formula of increasing differentiation and integration. The principle is an ever new recurrence of the same patterns: materialism — idealism; determinism — indeterminism; ethics of absolute principles — ethics of happiness; realism — nominalism; Ideational art — Visual or Sensate art; and so on.

5. In these transformations, each current of culture, being a system, shows a margin of independence in its movement, but at the same time they change together, in appreciable degree, where long-time waves are concerned. In this sense the cultures studied show themselves notably (but not perfectly) integrated.

6. In the leading and lagging of many cultural variables there is no uniform sequence; e.g., now music changes in a certain direction earlier than painting and sculpture, now it lags somewhat behind them.

7. All the essential " swings " of the currents of culture-mentality in each compartment of culture (science, philosophy, religion, art in all forms, ethics, law, economic, political, social forms — including disruption of social relationships, war and revolutions) cannot be understood properly without consideration of the main types of culture.

Such types — the veritable key to the comprehension of these changes — are the types of culture: Ideational, Sensate, and Mixed (of which Mixed forms the Idealistic is particularly important). When the essentials of each of these types is properly understood, then the main swings in each compartment of the cultures (Greco-Roman and Western) appear to be but a manifestation of the passage of these cultures from one of these main phases to another. When culture passes from, say, Ideational to Sensate form, its science, philosophy, art, ethics, law, economic, etc. organization undergo a related change: all move in the Sensate direction.

8. Such " swings " — the most fundamental of all the transformations — occurred several times during the twenty-five hundred years studied.

Greek culture before the sixth century B.C. appears to be predominantly Ideational; with the end of the sixth century its Ideationalism declines, its Sensate forms appear and grow. In the fifth and first part of the fourth century they give the Idealistic form of Greek culture (as a harmonious equilibrium of Ideational and Sensate elements). After the fourth century B.C. it becomes predominantly Sensate, and with several complications and minor swings remains so up to roughly the third century A.D.

After the third century Sensate forms definitely decline and Ideational forms become dominant and monopolistic from the sixth century A.D. up to about the end of the twelfth century. Then Sensate forms reappear again and mingle with declining Ideational forms to give the organic synthesis in the form of the Idealistic culture of the thirteenth and fourteenth centuries (similar to Greek Idealistic culture of the fifth century B.C.). After the fifteenth century up to the present time we witness a rising tide and domination of the Sensate forms. These reached their climax, up to date, in the nineteenth century.

With the end of the nineteenth and in the twentieth century all compartments of our culture manifest unmistakable symptoms of revolt against the Sensate forms, from painting and science to economic and social relationships. This unmistakable crisis may be a short-time reaction or — what seems to me more probable — it may be the beginning of the long-time decline of our overripe Sensate culture. After the period of transition, it is altogether likely that a rise of Ideational forms will occur. As you see, I am an anti-Spenglerist, and claim the decline of the Sensate forms of our culture, but not its end or decay. [The difference between Spengler and Sorokin, although evident, does not seem to the writers sufficiently great to warrant the use of the prefix " anti- ".]

9. In the light of this theory all the main fluctuations of each compartment of the cultures studied (and I give as complete quantitative-qualitative material as is available) become comprehensible and " logical." They are all but manifestations of the change of the system of the whole culture, *somewhat analogous to many anatomical, physiological, and mental changes which occur when an organism passes from, say, childhood to maturity.* [Italics ours; here the organismic analogy becomes explicit.]

10. In the same way as in this passage a certain manifestation — say, growth of beard — is neither cause nor effect of other changes (glandular, muscular, mental), so in the fundamental transformation of culture from Sensate to Ideational or *vice versa,* none of the cultural variables are either causes or effects, either leaders, laggards, or led. All are parts of one system that has its own immanent law and logic of change. [This would seem to imply that any measure of prediction and control whatsoever is wholly impossible, but perhaps Sorokin does not intend to draw this radical conclusion.]

11. Even systems of truth and knowledge, including so-called science, are but manifestations dependent on the type of culture. [At this point the crucial question comes to mind that is inevitably addressed to Spengler: "How then do you know anything about other cultures and the diverse systems of knowledge occurring in your own? How do you know that what you say is true?" Alfred Weber avoids this difficulty, it will be recalled, by asserting the potential universality of civilizational ideas.]

This succinct digest and the brief comments thereon of course give only a very hazy idea of the multifarious problems raised by Sorokin's remarkable work. Beyond any doubt it will cause a whirlwind of controversy comparable to the *Streit um Spengler* which swept over Germany from 1917 to 1923. On the American scene are now to be found most of the major types of historical sociology, and battles that will wipe out many of them and signalize the emergence of new types are even now under way. And not even the strongest will remain unscathed.

The Need for Historical Data. — Further, these battles will probably bring in a far more extensive use of historical data in systematic sociological generalization than our stultifying ethnographization has heretofore permitted. To assail theories of social and cultural dynamics that build their walls with the materials of history requires the systematic use of historical missiles. The resulting improvements in method cannot but be beneficial to American sociology, and we shall probably be thankful for provocative cyclical theories, large-scale or small-scale, when the rattle of machine-guns and the crash of shells has died away. In the realm of the mind, at least, "Conflict is the father of all things."

Moreover, it is in this cyclical subdivision of the field we have been surveying that the mutually beneficial natures of historical sociology and systematic sociology, rightly understood, become most evident. Without the problems set by systematic sociology, historical sociology becomes a trackless maze; while without the check on unbridled abstraction afforded by culture case study and ideal-typical method, systematic sociology becomes nothing more than verbal jugglery. As Wiese fittingly says, "It is not a question of either-or, but of the complementary function of two different viewpoints." [48]

In spite of general agreement as to this complementary function, however, a curious and injurious paradox makes itself evident in most if not all contemporary American sociology of the small-scale cyclical type. It is this: In studying cycles, rhythms, and so forth, we are prone to restrict ourselves to data of the present and the immediate past. In other words, we are given to generalizing in what is from at least one aspect historical sociology without properly availing ourselves of historical data!

This failing is in part due to the general ahistoricity of American thinking, as already noted, but a contributory factor is the belief, quite widespread even in countries with more abundant historical humus, that it is easier to check the present than the past, easier to view events *sub specie aevi nostri*. Hence, runs the inference, the good sociologist should do his best to gather contemporary material as basis of his theories, and if historical sources are used at all, an apologetic shrug should avow the fact of an inferior substitute.

No such apology is necessary. Without going into all the reasons for this statement, let us adduce a few without comment. Most important, the present, as even the most widely experienced person knows it, covers a very limited range; if one wishes to know even a fairly wide sector of the present, recourse must be had to sources of precisely the same type as those made use of by the historian — written records, interviews, traveler's tales, and similar accounts. Moreover, many of the sources indispensable for anything like adequate knowledge of the present will not become available until this present is the historical past — diaries, memoirs, confessions, autobiographies, secret archives, covert diplomatic agreements, uncoördinated statistical material, undercover trade agreements, " cold-storaged " inventions, and countless other buried data vitally affecting this present day and generation are beyond our present reach. Again, almost any hypothesis concerning process-series, cycles, or periodicities one cares to name cannot be adequately checked by reference to the present alone; there must either be a wait for verification in the indefinite future, or the past must be searched for phenomena presenting comparable and generalizable similarities — no matter how advanced sociology may become, contemporary sources will never provide data in sufficient volume for checking the majority of cyclical hypotheses. And last of all: inasmuch as it is exceedingly difficult to lift oneself by one's cultural bootstraps, generalizations based on contemporary data and suggested by contemporary theories alone are likely to be much more relative, short-lived, and fallacious than generalizations in historical sociology have any right to be.

Summary of the Chapter. — There was a great deal of historical sociology before the time of Spencer and Darwin — indeed, virtually every social thinker whom we have considered offered some generalizations falling in this category — but it became much more important after evolutionary theories were generally accepted. The classical school of ethnology was especially active in setting forth theories of unilinear social evolution, using for this purpose a so-called comparative method which did violence to the facts. Among sociologists, Spencer was the most flagrant offender, but his errors were repeated, on a smaller scale, by many others. Durkheim was the first to reject the comparative method as it was then practiced, but his substitute was almost equally erroneous. Hobhouse and some of his associates endeavored to apply statistical techniques to the problem of comparison, but were not notably successful, although they did avoid some of the pitfalls of the older method.

Among ethnologists themselves the classical school was soon challenged by the diffusionists, and later by the critical or historico-analytical school under the leadership of Ehrenreich and Boas. The deflation of social evolutionism was most effectively carried out in studies of the relation of the family to the political aspects of social organization, the key point of Morgan's theory. Lowie and others succeeded in showing that the social history of any particular people could not be reconstructed on the basis of any general evolutionary scheme.

The after-effects of the collapse of social evolutionism were in some respects harmful to ethnology and to historical sociology. There developed a hypercritical historicism that eschewed all generalizations, however modest, thus presumably making sociology impossible. The solution seems to lie in making more use of data gleaned from the history of peoples having a longer known course of development than is the case with preliterates — in other words, in making more use of strictly " historical " information.

The relation of history and sociology should be closer than it has been or now is; by making use of a genuinely comparative method it is possible to derive valid generalizations in historical sociology without distorting or disregarding the context of historical occurrences. This new comparative method, in part attributable to Max Weber, Park, and Toynbee, is based upon intensive culture case study; i.e., upon the most careful kind of historical research into the specific context and conditions of a given problem in widely varying societies. The abyss of extreme historicism is avoided by making use of the ideal-typical method of generalization.

This ideal-typical method may also be used to work out an

acceptable theory of the general trend of historical development. Such a theory, to be included in the category of historical sociology, must be non-universal, non-transcendent, non-relative, and non-evaluative. Only the ideal-typical method of formulation can fully meet these requirements. Max Weber never worked out an explicit, connected theory of the process of historical change; this was left for his younger brother, Alfred Weber. The latter's conceptions of society, civilization, and "culture" have already proved their worth.

Not only is it possible to develop historical sociology along the general lines just noted, but it is also possible to salvage a good deal that is ideal-typically valid in some of the older theories of stages of social development. These theories were discredited by the débâcle of social evolutionism, but a few of them have points that can still be utilized by a sound historical sociology.

Even though some doubt may still remain as to the complete conformity of the foregoing varieties of historical sociology to scientific canons there is another kind that can hardly be denied that claim: namely, the small-scale cyclical type. A number of sociologists have already developed theories of this sort, but usually without being aware of the additional validity to be derived by ideal-typical formulation. It is to be hoped that this field will be further cultivated, and in particular, that American sociologists will make more use of historical data and ideal-typical method when so doing. If some effort is made to pass beyond the chaos of "raw empiricism" and the limitations of purely contemporary material, the outlook for this variety of historical sociology seems very bright.

Large-scale cyclical theories, of which Spengler's "Hegelian organicism" provides a scientifically unacceptable example, are in a somewhat less promising situation. Sorokin, however, is making vigorous efforts to rehabilitate historical sociology of this type, and in his *Social and Cultural Dynamics* has presented a large-scale cyclical theory that will undoubtedly have to be reckoned with for a long time.

American historical sociology is just beginning to get under way; it has every prospect of a brilliant future.

Although Weber himself did not perpetrate the errors to which some of his formulations laid him open, some of his followers did. Indeed, Becker feels that in this treatise he has occasionally been guilty of the faults of which he accuses others! He has endeavored to correct some of these, as the comment on p. 42 of Vol. I indicates. See also his article, "Culture Case Study and Greek History: Comparison Viewed Sociologically," *ASR,* vol. xxiii, 5 (Oct., 1958), pp. 489-504.

Commentary on Value-System Terminology

Lament and Thanksgiving.—Many years and the Hitler war have passed since this treatise first took form; it is now being reprinted in the midst of the intertwined cold and Korean wars. The entire typescript, with the exception of the final chapter, epilogue, and preface, was delivered to the then publishers in the early fall of 1934, and the remainder in the summer of 1935, but the book did not come off the press until the early spring of 1938. The delay was the result of the fact that other books, judged to be better bets from the sales standpoint, time and again received priority; composition therefore proceeded slowly and by fits and starts. In order to take account of the new literature that was appearing almost daily, large portions of both volumes were rewritten on the margins of the galley proofs. Then came the Hitler war, the plates were melted for military purposes, and the treatise that had been so painstakingly altered and expanded went out of print. It reappears in its original form in 1952, thanks to the enterprise of the new publisher in utilizing modern photographic processes relying on the printed pages instead of the nonexistent plates. The reader may properly inquire, "If the book had been set up afresh, what changes in terminology would have been made?"

The answer is, "Very few." The theoretically interlinked terms that had been woven into the material from 1930 on by the editor-coauthor, and that gave what might otherwise have been a featureless web or even formless tangle some semblance of pattern, had been inspected time and again before the typescript was turned in. Moreover, they could have been changed during the galley-proof alteration and expansion period of three or four years referred to above. There is no faintest intention of implying that their theoretical and research potentialities were fully exploited, or even that the remoter potentialities were adequately envisaged, but it is to say that sacred and secular societies, mental mobility and immobility, vicinal, social, and mental isolation and accessibility, and several other key terms seemed to stand up under scrutiny. Further, that scrutiny has been continued ever since, and in addition numerous researches conducted by graduate students, full-fledged professional sociologists, and the writer himself have apparently demonstrated the utility of the substantive theory, as yet not completely available in print, with which the terms are integrally connected. Some of them have even reached the elementary textbook level, as the reader can see by referring to Martindale and Monachesi's 1951 product.

Rejection and Retention.—One term, however, would unquestionably be changed were the job being done over again from scratch; namely, "ideal type." "Constructed type" has none of the epistemological and other ambiguities or unacceptable commitments that "ideal" drags with it, as has been pointed out at several places in the writer's *Through Values to Social Interpretation* (1950, hereinafter abbreviated as *TVTSI*; periodicals, etc., for which abbreviations are given are listed on pp. iii and iv of the Notes.) The time when "ideal type" was first coined is now almost fifty years in the past, and advances in epistemology, the logic of science, probability theory, and configurational psychology make its denotations and connotations liabilities far too great to be willingly borne today. "Constructed type" has none of these liabilities, is bound up with a much more explicit method, has many more possibilities for quantitative formulation while at the same time doing full justice to qualitative demands, and in general should come to be the preferred term. But after all, it is only one of many in the array of which this treatise makes use.

Two other key terms, "sacred" and "secular," most frequently appearing in conjunction with "society," would be retained in the majority of instances. Here and there, however, subordinate terms would now be used for the sake of greater precision: folk-sacred, prescribed-sacred, principled-secular, normless-secular, or simply folk, prescribed, principled, and normless. Similarly, where there is likelihood of confusion or ambiguity, terms that are in other respects subordinate to sacred and secular would today be used: holy, ritualistic, loyalistic, intimate, commemorative, moralistic, fitting, appropriate, pursuant, consequent, comfortable, and thrilling. This is a long list, and the reasons for calling attention to these subordinate varieties of sacred and secular are by no means self-evident. It therefore seems wise to expand this commentary a good deal, in part for a survey of similar concepts now in use and the warrant for choice of sacred and secular, and in part for analysis of the subordinate items and their referents.

Sacred and Secular, Holy and Profane.—Let us begin with the concept of the sacred. This is quite comprehensive, taking in as it does far more and other than religion, for example, in any customary sense. Etymologically, religion can of course be shown to have once included a great deal that is today outside its meaning, as noted in the present treatise, pp. 37-39. These earlier senses are interesting but hardly worth reviving, for the English language has become so rich in words expressing fine shades of meaning that synonyms exist for virtually every one of the ways in which the term religion and its qualifying auxiliaries can be used. Moreover, the concept of the sacred comprises much that religion has never fully included. It is therefore advisable to use sacred as the *general* term and religion and its equivalents as only *one* aspect thereof.

It follows that sacred and secular are by no means synonymous with holy and profane. This is one of the most frequent errors, and is chiefly the result of failure to consult original sources or lack of attention to finer shades of meaning in ordinary English.

First, let us take up the failure to consult original sources. In American sociological literature, for example, one occasionally finds references to "Durkheim's sacred and secular." Durkheim used *sacré* and *profane* in his *Les Formes élémentaires de la vie réligieuse* and elsewhere. Swain, the translator, used "sacred-profane," which is loose or obsolescent English, but at least he did *not* use "sacred-secular."

Second, let us consider the lack of attention to ordinary English usage. We may begin with the old standby, Webster's: "Sacred, not holy, is opposed to secular," *New International Dictionary,* 2nd ed. (1943).

This not does carry us quite far enough. Consulting another Webster source, we find this: "In . . . *general* [italics ours] use, *sacred* applies chiefly to that which one treasures as a thing apart, not to be violated or contaminated by being put to vulgar or low uses or associated with vulgar or low ends," *Webster's Dictionary of Synonyms,* 1st ed. (1942), p. 145.

Again from the same Webster source: "*Sacred* as meaning having such a character that it is protected by law, custom, tradition, human respect, or the like, against breach, intrusion, defilement. . . . *Sacred* implies either a setting apart for a special and, often, exclusive use or end (as, among civilized peoples, property is regarded as *sacred* to its owner; a fund *sacred* to charity; the study was *sacred* to the father of the family) or a special character or quality which makes the person or thing held sacred an object of almost religious veneration or reverence (as '[Louis XIII] . . . saw that things which happened increasingly strengthened the Royal Office which was *sacred* to him' —*Belloc*. . . .

"[Analogous words] Protected, shielded, defended, guarded . . . : revered, reverenced, venerated . . ." (pp. 721-722).

Let us explore further, this time in a widely recognized "non-Webster": "*Holy* is a stronger and more absolute term than *any other* [italics ours] of similar meaning. That which is *holy* is of a divine nature, or has its sanctity directly from God or as connected with him; that which is *sacred,* while *sometimes* [italics ours] accepted as entitled to religious veneration, may derive its sanction from man; hence we speak of the *Holy* Bible, and of one's *sacred* duty to his country," *The New Century Dictionary,* section on Synonyms, Antonyms, and Discriminations (1940 ed.), p. 2319.

The conclusion to be drawn from these and many other considerations is essentially this: "sacred-profane," although not strictly incorrect, is loose or at best obsolescent usage in view of the fact that "profane" is a more absolute term than "sacred," and hence should be used as the antonym of "holy." "Sacred," a more inclusive and less absolute term, should be used as the antithesis of the similarly general term "secular."

When we take properly into account the fact that Durkheim was writing about the elementary forms of the *religious* life, it is clear that the translator should have used "holy-profane," not "sacred-profane," and certainly not "sacred-secular." (Incidentally, it may be noted that in French *sacré* must perform many tasks, for the French language lacks the wide range of terms here available in English. "Secular," on the other hand, divides into *séculaire* and *séculier,* with *laïque* thrown in for good measure. Additional comment on "secular" will be made later.)

The Importance of Terminological Precision.—Close attention to the standard authorities, then, supports the present use of sacred as distinctly different from religious, holy, divine, spiritual, supernatural, sacrosanct, blessed, and related terms. Science of course freely disregards authority when occasion warrants, but if ordinary English words can be used in standard senses, only the careless or pretentious scientist will bandy those words about in unwarranted ways, coin neologisms, or flash the fine feathers of a foreign tongue. Granted, it is *possible* to do all of these things, and in particular to use sacred in senses roughly equivalent to many other words, but in science the "roughly equivalent" will not do. We want to look at the societies most important in weaving the contexts of social thought, and in order to do this most effectively we must use precise terms.

Precise terms, however, must be used scientifically, i.e., without connotations of praise or blame. Sacred already has praiseworthy connotations for many if not most persons; these must be resolutely excluded if analysis is not to be perpetually hampered. It therefore would seem wise, on this ground alone, to use secular instead of profane as its polar opposite. Not only does profane have its own highly colored connotations, but by contrast it heightens the coloring of sacred. Secular, on the other hand, is relatively colorless, and it therefore diminishes the irrelevant contrast effect.

What Might Have Been.—The essential colorlessness of the sacred-secular antithesis, as it occurs in the pages of this treatise, may perhaps be underscored by the statement that if certain other terms did not have irrelevant connotations of potentially misleading character, or did not too sharply limit the range of phenomena to be observed, these other terms could well be used. We might speak of traditive and transitive, conservative and conversive, ritualistic and casual, retrospective and prospective, immobile and mobile, perpetuative and alterative, hallowed and hedonic, prohibitive and permissive, conventional and sophisticated, lore-holding and law-making, customary and innovative, usage-limited and utilitarian, venerative and varietal, ceremonial and functional, misoneistic and philoneistic, neophobiac and neophiliac, and so on and on.

Further, there are many antitheses in the literature of sociology that *seem, at first glance,* to point at identical phenomena. Primitive and civilized, established and adaptive, component and constituent, folk society and urban society, primary group and secondary group, communal groups and associational groups or fellowships and affiliations or community and society (*Gemeinschaft und Gesellschaft*), societies with mechanical solidarity and societies with organic solidarity, constraint and normlessness (*anomie*), traditional and rational, ideational and sensate, cumulative and disintegrated, status-maintaining and contractual, preliterate and literate, ancient and modern, static and dynamic, residues of the persistence of aggregates and residues of combination, organic and critical, organic and atomic, particularistic and universalistic, kinship society and political society, societies with custom-imitation and societies with mode-imitation, *yin*-state and *yang*-state, and other explicit or implicit distinctions of the same general character abound.

The qualification, "seem, at first glance," must nevertheless be held in view. For example, Redfield's folk-urban dichotomy is *not* identical with sacred-secular, for many urban societies are strongly sacred in either folk or prescribed senses, or both, and many rural societies have distinctly secular traits. Moreover, folk is only one of the subdivisions of sacred. Similar comments might be made about the other paired terms.

The Sacred and Changelessness.—Enough and more than enough has now been said, the writer feels, to justify the use of sacred in this treatise to designate all social phenomena with regard to which a certain emotionalized reluctance to change is manifested, as well as to designate that reluctance itself. Thus a given clan system that is clung to with tenacity in spite of pressures making for its alteration or breakup can properly be called a sacred clan, and the unwillingness or inability to change, or both, that is felt and manifested by the clan members can also be termed a sacred reluctance.

Not every unwillingness or inability to change comes under the sacred heading; there may be social arrangements, such as demonstrably efficient work routines, so thoroughly expedient in attaining their ends that change to less expedient methods is resisted. Change as such, in other words, is not viewed with disapproval; it is only the inexpedient change that is opposed. "Until you can show us how to do it better, we'll do the job as we have been doing it" is the essence of this state of affairs. The emotions involved are merely those that, e.g., make up the craftsman's contempt for the bungler. There is no zealous defense of the inviolability of the holy of holies, no righteous indignation at sacrilege, nor even amused disdain for the "socially impossible" who are forever doing what "isn't done." Standard practices that are changed only when necessary may be current in principled secular and, on occasion, normless secular societies, as has been pointed out in *TVTSI,* chapter v. The basic point is that there is none of that "certain emotionalized reluctance to change" that is so definitely an essential of the sacred, phenomenologically and otherwise considered.

The Intensity Range of the Sacred.—The broadly general character and at the same time the clear denotations and connotations of the concept of the sacred can perhaps best be indicated here by listing and now and again commenting on a wide array of relevant terms, phrases, sayings, and other assorted utterances drawn from ordinary English. These lists are by no means all-comprehensive, however, even for English; space forbids. The writer has also prepared lists for Greek, Latin, French, German, and "Lallans" (the *corpus* of Lowland Scots in its many varieties), but again space forbids more than bare mention here. Even the limited lists show how seriously we must take Dewey's aphorism, "Society exists in and through communication," to say nothing of Mead's "taking the role of the other, through vocal gesture, toward one's own conduct." Language and symbolic systems functioning like language are not epiphenomena having merely external connection with social action; they are part and parcel of the essence of social action.

The list of formulations included in the concept of the sacred can conveniently be presented in a few main groups. These range from the most intense and qualitatively differentiable phenomena to the least intense and "almost-but-not-quite" secular. Frequently, but not always, an antonym of the word or phrase will also be listed; we shall therefore take note of the sacred in both its "positive" and "negative" aspects.

One of the main criteria of the intensity of the sacred in these groupings is the extent to which reluctance to change may manifest itself. At one extreme are the words dealing with matters for the sake of which life itself—one's own and, when need be, one's fellows—would be sacrificed. At the other are those indicating some emotionalized preference for the continuation of the conduct in question, which preference, however, would be set aside if serious inconvenience were to result from insistence on it. The range, in effect, is from potential or actual martyrdom to shoulder-shrugging capitulation to "bad taste" or the like.

Simple Folk May Make Subtle Distinctions.—Capacity for martyrdom, given the historical and contemporary evidence available, is implicitly indicated in our first group: holy-profane, hallowed-unhallowed, blessed-cursed, religious-irreligious, godly-ungodly, godlike-devilish, reverent-sacrilegious, consecration - desecration, saintly - worldly, pious-impious, awesome-commonplace, sacrosanct-defiled, "clean"-"unclean," spiritual-temporal, and the fairly extensive collection of words and phrases relating to taboos, positive and negative, of the more vital sort.

Confusion in both psychology and sociology of value-systems is almost certain to result if this first grouping, here termed the holy-profane, or simply the holy, is not distinguished from other groupings when the context requires such distinction. The concept of the sacred includes all the groupings, to be sure, and on occasion no great harm is done by using the most general rather than the specific term—in fact, there are contexts in which sacred, i.e., the most general term, *should* be used. More often than many of us like to think, however, scientific purposes are best served by taking account of the finer shades of meaning so abundantly available in the everyday language of those possessing a modicum of general education, and sometimes even in the vernacular of the relatively uneducated.

As the writer ascertained in his war and postwar field work, even certain simple-minded German peasants, limited in linguistic resources, refused to follow those Party intellectuals who would persuade them that the *Führer* was in some way holy. For them Hitler lacked "the beauty of holiness," even though ecstatic city women often referred to him as "beautiful Adolf." Invocations to the Nazi hero stopped short of "Holy, holy, holy, Lord God Almighty," even though by Party decree children were taught:

> Fold your hands,
> Bow your head,
> Hitler thank
> For daily bread.

Men walked reverently in his presence, but they had not

reached the point of "Take thy shoes from off thy feet, for the spot whereon thou standest is holy ground." Poets such as Baldur von Schirach conveyed quivers of exaltation at the preternatural qualities of their master to admiring throngs, yet no one ventured to echo:

> The thrill of holy dread
> Is the best trait of mankind.

This was not because of lack of familiarity with Goethe's words; peasants who had left school at twelve could nevertheless quote the passage from *Faust;* in the original it runs thus: *Das Schaudern ist der Menschheit bestes Teil.* Those with more learning also knew it as the title-page motto of Rudolph Otto's *Das Heilige,* translated as *The Idea of the Holy.* The careful reader will here note that the writer has exercised the freedom of translating the single word, *Schaudern,* as "the thrill of holy dread," herein taking account of the full idiomatic meaning as well as of the content of Otto's book. "Holy dread" obviously comes from Coleridge's *Kubla Khan:*

> Weave a circle round him thrice,
> And shut your eyes with holy dread,
> For he on honey-dew hath fed,
> And drunk the milk of Paradise.

In short, the Nazi leader and his movement lacked the essential attribute of holiness where many Hessian peasants were concerned, hence they remained relatively unaffected by Nazism, and in some instances became openly although impotently anti-Nazi. When this occurred, the available evidence, to be presented at length in a projected book, *Yesterday's Hessians Today,* seems to show that established Roman Catholicism and Lutheranism, basically holy in character, were chiefly responsible. If we may descend to the vernacular at this point, and at the risk of seeming paradoxical, the peasants really swayed by such religions regarded Hitler as a holy terror and his Nazis as an unholy outfit.

The Holy Is Held to Be the Supernatural.—If the writer's analysis—here presented in summary so brief as to be grotesquely inadequate—is correct, phenomena labelled "holy" were of great importance in this German peasant case at least. Many other studies, from which the few examples of holy-profane formulations that have been listed above were taken, show that the importance of such formulations far transcends any single instance. Such formulations demonstrably relate to what many students of comparative religion regard as the basic criterion of religion; namely, the *sensus numinis* of which so much is made in Otto's *The Idea of the Holy,* "the thrill of holy dread" evoked by "something apprehended but not comprehended." The power or powers, being or beings, held to be the "objective" ground for this quiver of awe may be worshipped in love or fear, ecstatically or sedately, in religious humility or with assertive confidence in ability to control by magic, alone or in the midst of fellow-devotees, with voluptuous abandon or with stern restraint, with torture or with kindness, as a disembodied force or as "having parts and passions like unto man's"—but the orientation is essentially toward that which is held utterly and completely to transcend the human and even the natural.

The holy "object" and the holy "thrill" are alike of superhuman and supernatural reference—in brief, supernaturalistic. The Holy Ghost, the Holy Mass, His Holiness the Pope, the Holy Bible, the Holy of Holies, the Ark of the Covenant that was holy unto the Lord, Holy Communion—how many are the instances of the supernaturalistic orientation in the Judaic and Christian traditions alone! And by taking account of the evidence from other traditions presented by Tylor, Robertson Smith, Frazer, Marett, Spencer and Gillen, Preuss, Schmidt and Koppers, Van Gennep, and literally scores of others, how might these instances be multiplied!

Ritual Is Repetitive.—Next among our groupings comes one that is closely related to the holy, although it may be of less intensity in some cases. Many of the formulations placed in the holy rubric refer to the holy object, the thrill it engenders or which engenders it, or both. Several of those now to be listed refer, at least indirectly, to what is "done" or believed in conjunction with object and thrill: ritual, liturgy, solemnization, creed, orthodoxy-heterodoxy, and so on.

Where what is "done" is concerned, it is entirely possible, as Jane Harrison long ago pointed out, that the holy *dromenon,* the ritual activity, may evoke both the holy object and its thrill—but we are not here dealing with problems of origins.

What does concern us is that the repetitive character of ritual, liturgy, creed, and the like may help to introduce another aspect of the sacred that sometimes has little if any connection with the holy; namely, the strong reluctance to change that threatened or actual disturbance of deep-set habits evokes. Men have died for the sake of preserving inviolate certain ways of performing a ritual, intoning a liturgy, repeating a creed. In what we shall henceforth call the ritualistically sacred, the form becomes as important as the content, if not more so.

From here to traditionalism having no definite connection whatever with the holy except emotionalized reluctance to change is no impassable gulf; phrases such as "hallowed by time" may be used to refer to practices of admittedly mundane, everyday, and utilitarian beginnings. English life notoriously abounds in ceremonials of quite matter-of-fact origin that have become "time-honored" and hence "unalterable." Change in these practices not infrequently produces uneasiness, a state of being "all upset," and in the aged at least, marked disorientation. Traditionalistic unwillingness and/or inability to change tinge a large part of the sacred spectrum—but it should by now be plain that the sacred is not merely the traditionalistic.

Loyalties to Social Entities.—It is fairly well known that Émile Durkheim, as a French anticlerical, was deeply involved in the Third Republic struggle over lay control (*laicïsme*) of the schools. He attempted to counter the assertion that lay education would inevitably lack moral guidance by developing a theory of religion in which "society" becomes an entity *sui generis* and an ultimate source of moral values.

What he really did, throughout a large part of his "scientific" effort, was to substitute or attempt to substitute *la patrie, la belle France,* the French nation, for the Roman Catholic conception of the holy and its enshrining church. This was too much even for French Protestants; Gaston Richard joined his powerful voice, in *L'Athéisme dogmatique en sociologie réligieuse* and other writings, to the denunciations coming from clerical circles to which he was ordinarily opposed—although, to be sure, he did not second the clerical outcry of "Talmudic sociology."

This is not the place, however, for a lengthy presentation of "the Durkheim problem"; it is enough to have pointed out the fact that a sincere and earnest sociologist could regard (1) the holy and (2) the ethnocentric, "societo-centric," patriotic, and nationalistic as basically the same. He was mistaken in this identification, but he called attention to an aspect of the sacred for which men have died in droves.

An important grouping, third in our set, therefore comprises sacred words and phrases such as loyal—disloyal, faithful—faithless, patriotic—traitorous, dutiful—shirking (Nelson and "England expects every man . . ."), clan-leal—clan-false, "to the last man"—defeatist, allegiance—subversion, class-conscious—class-indifferent, and a host of others. Once a social unit has been reified or hypostatized, has become an abstract collectivity or corporate group, it can be an object of sentiments that lead to great reluctance to change in either object or sentiments. This is not mere traditionalism, although traditionalism may come to play a large part in such loyalistic sacredness; class-consciousness, for example, may arise quite suddenly and in defiance of traditional fealties.

Intimacies May Not Be Taken Lightly.—Further, the loyalistic may sometimes run counter to those aspects of the sacred indicated by words in our fourth grouping, which we may call the intimate: brotherly, sisterly, fatherly, motherly, "kindly" (in the sense of "Let never living mortal ken That a kindly Scot lies here"—i.e., one united with his fellows of Scottish kind), friendly, neighborly, the wealth of terms relating to "true love" of all varieties, the almost equally large number of companionship words such as "buddy," "chum," "pal," "side-kick," "matey," other "positive" primary group terms, and so forth.

The intimately sacred may not only encounter opposition from the loyalistic (as when brothers fight against each other in civil war), but also from the holy. The latter is well illustrated by the passage in the New Testament where the would-be disciple is told that he must abandon his family, and even neglect the sacred duty of burying his father, if he is to be true to his holy obligations (Luke 9: 59-60). Similar conflicts with other aspects of the sacred may appear, as with what we shall later call the commemorative, the moralistic, the fitting, or even the appropriate.

In many cases, however, Antigone-like or similar dilemmas do not make themselves evident; on the contrary, the holy more often than not reinforces the ritualistic, the loyalistic, the intimate, and the various other aspects mentioned. Moreover, any or all of these may reinforce one another.

Such mutual reinforcement often produces sacred bonds of great intensity, but the intimate alone sometimes elicits striking results. Folk tales equivalent to that of Damon and Pythias occur among many peoples. Life may be willingly sacrificed on the altar of the intimately sacred.

Commemoration Need Not Be Supernaturalistic.—The intertwining of the holy, the ritualistic, and the intimate is particularly apparent where our fifth grouping, the commemorative, is concerned. It includes "pious care" (in one of the original senses of *pietas*) of the dead with whom one has been on terms of intimacy, perpetuation of memory, demonstration of persisting affection, expression of "everlasting fidelity," many aspects of Van Gennep's "ceremonies of transition" (*rites de passage*), and so on. Several such practices have received attention from Malinowski and others as "rites of tendance." So multifarious is the reinforcement of sacred reluctances to change in the realm of the rites of tendance that, as Malinowski pointed out, the relatively independent character of such rites is ordinarily obscured. We are so accustomed, in the Western world at least, to seeing, in churchyards and similar holy places, tombstones bearing "Sacred to the Memory of" that we think of such commemoration as never occurring except under holy auspices. The available evidence shows, however, that commemoration, rites of tendance, and so on frequently take place in separation from the holy and even the ritualistic. A belligerent atheist, to choose a drastic illustration, may profanely reject proposals for performing masses or erecting angelic headstones, but may nevertheless commemorate his deceased friends, mate, children, or parents in his own way.

Primary group intimacies, by their very nature, call for perpetuation. The results are "In Memoriam" items on the front page of the London *Times,* "perpetual care" cemetery lot contracts, the setting up of tombstones or plaques, the laying out of Prince Albert's clothing every day, by Queen Victoria's order, for decades after his death, and even a Rudolph Valentino shrine with a commemorative retinue headed by "the woman in black."

Sacred intimacies subject to perpetuation may not have been interrupted by death, of course: birthday ceremonials abound, absent friends or relatives may be commemorated at specified times, honeymoons may be "repeated," there is a thriving business in electroplating baby shoes symbolizing the continuance of parent-child intimacies, and Bossard and Boll have shown how rich may be the store of family memories that are "ritually" (in their readily comprehensible terminology) perpetuated.

In one of his early studies, the writer was handicapped by the fact that no accepted terminology enabling easy distinction between the needs and values associated with rites of tendance or commemoration, on the one hand, and those involved in apotropaic or placatory conduct, on the other, was discoverable in the literature. The present distinction between the holy and the more clearly religious aspects of the ritualistic, as over against the intimate and the commemorative, represents an effort to fill this gap. The former, particularly in their "negative" varieties (cursed, etc.) help to account for practices aimed at pacifying or preventing the return of the presumably malevolent dead, whereas the latter have to do primarily with efforts to continue the expression of love, fellowship, and devotion. Supernaturalism is not *inseparably* linked with the needs and values incorporating the tender emotions, although we must grant that it often acts as a powerful bond.

Commemorative sacredness is probably a less intense form than the others discussed, although on occasion it too may bring about, metaphorically speaking, a kind of martyrdom. The death of the Douglas in the act of commemorating his departed leader—the famous "Heart of the Bruce" episode—is but one example among many.

Sumner and the Moralistic.—Of a somewhat lower degree of intensity, in many although not all instances, than most aspects of the sacred heretofore discussed, and yet strongly supporting all other aspects as well as receiving support from all, is the moralistic, our sixth grouping. This comprises a large proportion of those formulations which were epitomized by Sumner in his well-known *mores:* among them are moral—immoral, ethical—unethical, lofty—base, noble—low, honorable—dishonorable, principled—unprincipled, and many others. They loom so prominently in the literature of sociology that little space need be devoted to them here. They and the conduct bound up with them play a leading part in most of those reluctances to change ordinarily called traditionalistic, although it should be noted that some traditionalism has few *overtly* moralistic accompaniments: "That's the way it is and always has been, and that's that. Them as doesn't like it can lump it."

"It Jest Ain't Fittin'."—Such traditionalism still comes with the ambit of the sacred, for there is some measure of emotionalized reluctance to change. This evidences itself in the list of what we here call the "fitting" terms, our seventh grouping: fitting—out of place, proper—improper, seemly—unseemly, "done"—"not done," good form—bad form, gentlemanly — caddish, respectful — disrespectful, polite—uncouth, refined—boorish, and a great number of others. (Many of those just listed refer primarily to "social" ceremonial, but there are equivalents for all the realms of conduct.)

On occasion there may be intense reluctance to change even in the merely fitting; men may not die for the sake of good form, but they may undergo extreme discomfort, and sometimes danger. Those of us who saw certain Londoners refuse, during the buzz-bomb blitz, to go to air raid shelters until they had quietly finished their afternoon tea have a vivid realization of the power of the proper.

Folkways Are Still Appropriate.—Lowest in intensity, and yet sacred enough to play a part in traditionalism, are the social actions linked with words in our eighth grouping, the appropriate. *The line between this and the fitting is admittedly a vague one,* and yet it seems worth drawing.

The fitting lies in the twilight zone between the *mores* and the folkways; there is not much overt moralism, but feelings of outrage at conduct that is "out of place" may nevertheless manifest themselves quite definitely. "Sending to Coventry," ostracism, the cold shoulder, the raised eyebrow if not the curled lip, the sudden although perhaps not persistent silence when the "bounder" enters the room are moral judgments even though unspoken.

Where the merely appropriate is concerned, the zone of the folkways *per se* has been reached; there is an absolute minimum of moral judgment—and yet the transition to sheer expedient rationality has not been effected. Appropriate, suitable, customary, in good taste, workmanlike, and similar expressions indicate that there is still held to be a "right" and a "wrong" way of doing things, but that those who choose the wrong are not necessarily unworthy in the moralistic sense. They are simply uninstructed, and there may be no more than mild and concealed amusement at

xvi   COMMENTARY ON VALUE-SYSTEMS

their remediable ignorance. The American in London who
is obviously distressed because his breakfast coffee is poor
or not to be had at all will eventually learn that the appropriate drink is tea; he is not beyond the moral pale, but
simply not yet conversant with the customary amenities of
civilized life. Righto!

Implicitly and Explicitly Sacred.—We have now glanced
at eight groupings of "positive" and "negative" formulations. This number is somewhat arbitrary. It might be possible, for many purposes, to get along with only three or
four; in other cases, a dozen or so might prove quite usable.
But whatever the number, these formulations are integrally
related with various intensities of that emotionalized reluctance to change here called sacred. Phenomenologically,
many qualitative and, in other contexts, crucial differences
are apparent, but for some purposes a rough arrangement
according to gradations in readiness to sacrifice life in
resisting change is usable. Hence our eight groupings run
as follows: holy, ritualistic, loyalistic, intimate, commemorative, moralistic, fitting, and appropriate.

What the writer has termed folk-sacred and prescribed-
sacred societies (in *TVTSI*) differ primarily in the extent
to which the sacred expressions and their related conduct
have been explicitly schematized or symbolically integrated.

In a folk society there is no dearth of sacred lore, but
it is not cast in the form of catechism, creed, legal code,
deductively patterned political or religious doctrine. Instead, the idiom, proverb, folk-poem or song, seasonal
round, work routine, and "ceremonies of transition" provide the stuff of the sacred value-system, and that system
is largely *implicit.*

In a prescribed society, however, the sacred system is
stated with the utmost attainable clarity and consistency;
every one of its eight aspects is explicitly linked with every
other to the fullest extent possible to persevering ingenuity.
There necessarily remains a good deal that is difficult and
perhaps impossible to integrate successfully, but effort to
make the pattern *explicit* and *total* is rarely relinquished.

A folk society may without intention be in effect totalitarian; a prescribed society is avowedly totalitarian without
admitted limit, and in actual practice may go a long way on
its chosen road. Peronist Argentina and Stalinist Russia are
but two contemporary instances of extensive prescription;
George Orwell's *1984* is a futuristic *reductio ad horrendum.*

Pursuant to Principle, But Not Blindly Obedient.—In listing the sacred formulations many antithetical formulations were also listed, and the discussion necessarily dealt to some extent with both. It is therefore unnecessary to deal with secular phenomena in quite so much detail, for although the secular is not the mere antithesis of the sacred, it does have many "negative" aspects. Some attention must be still given to the secular, however, if only in order to clear the ground for consideration of the various bearings of the phenomenon of *charisma,* inasmuch as this in turn is of the utmost importance for further penetration into crucial aspects of both sacred and secular.

Following the same procedure of word-and-phrase grouping, for the same reasons, we first distinguish what may be termed the pursuantly secular: pursuant to principle, due process of law, "keeping in channels," following established procedure, using good current practice, being systematic, "taking appropriate action consistent with directives"—in short, everything that has a governing rule determining the extent and direction of change.

The "expedient rationality" that is characteristic of pursuant and related kinds of secularity is in many respects akin to what Mannheim has termed "substantive rationality." The deductive logic evident in many value-systems pervading prescribed-sacred societies, on the other hand, frequently makes Mannheim's "formal rationality" almost equivalent to the writer's "sanctioned rationality." Please note, however, the "in many respects" and "almost," and compare the relevant passages in *TVTSI.*

It has already been mentioned that there may be secular resistance to change if such change is regarded as inexpedient for the attainment of secular ends, but with this exception (which is only apparent), willingness and/or ability to change is central to secular conduct. Pursuant secularity is limited, however, in the extent of its secularity; the supreme principle, pursuant to which all derivative conduct follows and is justified, may not be subject to considerations of expediency or affective appeal, and hence may not be secular.

"The rule of reason," for example, may be based on an elevation of reason into the realm of the sacred, as in Roman law of the early period, where the holy, the ritualistic, and the loyalistic all played prominent parts. The same, *mutatis mutandis,* is true of supreme principles such as "the greatest good of the greatest number," the "unalienable rights" of "life, liberty, and the pursuit of happiness" vouchsafed by "the laws of Nature and of Nature's God," "that government is best that governs least," and "the welfare of all in the welfare state."

Nevertheless, pursuant secularity is distinct from the sacredness of a prescribed society, for in the latter the prescriptions themselves are sacred and hence unalterable, whereas in the former only the principle is fixed—the regulations, etc., are not unalterable *as* regulations. Naturally, they often develop traditionalistic rigidities, sometimes quite rapidly, but these are continually undercut by the expedient rationality that is at least periodically applied to them, and some flexibility results.

The Constitution of the United States of America, for example, contains a supreme principle of "liberty under law" from which its subordinate "regulations" derive. No provision is made for alteration of the principle; it is in effect sacred, and sometimes intensely so. Provision is made, however, for alteration of the "regulations"; amendment, although difficult because of traditionalism and cumbersome procedure, has taken place many times in the century-and-a-half since ratification.

Consequences Count.—A second grouping, here designated the consequently secular, includes scores of phrases such as "anything to get the job done," "don't work with your hands tied behind you," "rules were made for the right man to break," "why try to fill a tank with a teaspoon?" "any fool can tell me what the law is, but I hire lawyers to tell me how to get around the law lawfully," "inefficiency is a crime," "he'd sooner get licked by rule than win by brains," "do it regardless," "results, not precedents," and numerous maxims of scientific experiment.

Consequent secularity pushes expedient rationality to the extreme—so far, in fact, that means tend to become ends. Sheer efficiency for efficiency's sake is not uncommon in secular societies. Anything whatever, even supreme principles, will be changed if efficiency is thereby increased; pursuant secularity yields to consequent secularity.

Having dealt with two of the ways, one limited and one unlimited, in which expedient rationality may exert its secularizing force, it is now advisable to shift attention to affective non-rationality and its role in secularization. It is a residual category, or in less fancy language, a catchall for leftovers, and would take a long time to delve into thoroughly. For present purposes, just two batches of the more easily grouped sayings bound up with their relevant social actions will be considered: the comfortable and the thrilling.

"Why Not Be Comfortable?"—We are still dealing with the secular, hence the comfortable is called the third grouping: it includes "doin' what comes naturally," "you might as well relax and enjoy it," "shirt-sleeves is good enough," "work gives you ulcers," "let somebody else do the worryin'," "morals is for them that can afford 'em," "you only got one life to live," "come day, go day, God send plenty beer," and scores of similar phrases stressing absence of sacred compulsions and restraints, and of pursuant and consequent secularity as well.

No effort is made to justify the comfortable by appeal to anything other than the comfortable itself; "I like it because I like it" is the final answer. What Thomas and Znaniecki called "the sensual- and vanity-values" are those chiefly involved; few if any demanding norms are at work. To be sure, all societies have their ostensibly disapproved but tacitly tolerated relaxations. When relaxation becomes general, however, the society tends toward the normless-secular type; there is much "social disorganization" that causes the disorganized no particular concern.

Thrill as Be-All and End-All.—Our fourth grouping, the thrilling, likewise has to do with relatively normless conduct, but may sometimes be the outcome of latent uneasiness (insecurity) that the normlessness has evoked. Stress on such insecurity as the sole source of what has recently come to be styled *anomie* results, however, in the overlooking of much thrill-seeking conduct that has no traceable relation with insecurity. Drug addiction, for example, may come about among *déclassé* aristocrats who want to find forgetfulness in a new thrill, but there is plenty of evidence to show that children may initially be attracted to drugs for reasons essentially similar to those that lead to "hooking" and eating green apples or enjoying the delicious taste of stolen watermelon. (No general theory of the actual physiology, psychology, and sociology of drug addiction, *à la* Lindesmith or otherwise, is here advanced; what is said is strictly limited to the present context.) "Forbidden fruit" is an old metaphor applicable to conduct of many kinds.

Of course not all thrill-seeking is of the "forbidden fruit" sort. The charm of novelty, of experience going beyond everyday humdrum, can be found in much that is not under ban. Gambling, horse-racing, cock-fighting, and the like are attractive in societies that are in no way "puritanical." Moreover, the thrill of witnessing and perhaps participating vicariously in extraordinary feats of memory, skill, strength, asceticism, fortitude, bravery (and even foolhardiness), endurance, oratory, or holy exaltation is a perennial source of the attraction of *charisma* and the persons who "incorporate" it.

But let us turn to our fragmentary list: "I'll try anything once," "we don't know where we're going but we're on our way," "something hid beyond the ranges," "for to admire an' for to see," "Germany, awake!" "Leader, we follow thee and shout 'Yea!'" "the word is 'Forward!'" "believe and act!" "God wills it!" "he spake as never man spake," "the lion hath roared, who can but hear? The Lord Jehovah hath spoken, who can but prophesy?" "for only drunk is man divine, and only mad can he forget," "that sends me," "His flashing eyes, his floating hair," "get high and get happy," "ho, ho, honey, have a sniff on me," "Brodie took a chance," "ride 'em, cowboy!" "we have nothing to fear but fear itself," stirring, spine-chilling, blood-curdling, hair-raising, pulse-quickening, breath-taking, inspiring, and so on indefinitely! This jumble of words, phrases and slogans testifies to the amazingly varied character of thrill-evoking and thrill-seeking conduct, and also to the fact that it is frequently evoked and sought in normless situations—or at least, situations for which ordinary norms provide little guidance.

When Extremes Meet.—Having now glanced at four groupings of formulations having secular bearing: the pursuant, the consequent, the comfortable, and the thrilling, it is now possible to take account of an important matter; namely, the circumstances under which the secular may become in certain respects sacred. Elsewhere (in *TVTSI*) the writer has made brief mention of "the normative reaction to normlessness," i.e., of the fact that extreme social disorganization and its attendant unpredictability of conduct often call forth efforts at reorganization, either around a surviving sacred core or a new set of norms. The charismatic leader in political, economic, moral, religious, or other fields may here find content for his message and conviction in his mission. Many such "prophets" of regeneration are disavowed or go unrecognized; only a favorable conjunction of circumstances enables an occasional "extraordinary man" to win a sufficient following.

Even when the charismatic leader secures a following, however, he is confronted with the task of ensuring continuity beyond his own life span. The vexed question of succession arises, which is to say that the problem of effective transmission of *charisma* must be confronted. Sometimes reliance is placed on "blood will tell"; the family line, the clan, the race, and similar hereditary channels (in the biological sense) are held to be assurances of "legitimate *charisma*." Even here, however, reinforcement is usually vouchsafed, and often deliberately sought, in those aspects of the sacred that can readily become traditional. Holy, loyalistic, and commemorative are most amenable and effective.

The holy, however, requires a special state of affairs if it is to become an essential part of the *"charisma* of office" or even of "hereditary *charisma*." Those who succeed the original leader are often unable, even though themselves "extraordinary" in their own way, to elicit the thrill that moved the first followers. This may occur because the crisis situation in which the leader first emerged has passed, perhaps because his mission has at least partially succeeded, or because the successor's extraordinariness is of different kind, or because the thrill of *charisma* was never sufficiently "the thrill of holy dread."

Let us consider the last of these reasons for failure of effective transmission in more detail. The holy, it will be recalled, is based on the *sensus numinis,* on the quiver of awe at something "apprehended but not comprehended," on action oriented toward what is held to be a supernatural object. The preternatural, i.e., the natural in hitherto unprecedented degree of power, concentration, or the like, is not sufficiently dissociable from the natural to be in and of itself a sufficient basis for continuing holy regard. Wizards become toothless, prophets turn into dotards, soothsayers fail to remember what they foretold last week, the warrior with a charmed life has a vulnerable spot or can be pierced by a silver bullet, a near-omniscient ruler can still be misled by favorites, and even a Father Divine may be plagued by bunions.

The qualities of a charismatic leader must somehow be projected on an object "that is not of the things that pass away." If *charisma,* which is to say "the gift of grace," is to endure, it must be genuinely grace—that it, it must be held to come from some source of grace, and that source must be regarded as one that possesses "the kingdom, the power, and the glory *forever.*" Indefinitely transmissible *charisma* is perennially renewable only from a supernatural spring, as it were. It is no accident that, in the New Testament, men do not possess grace in their own right, but are vouchsafed *charisma,* "the *gift* of grace"; they are thought of as cisterns, not as fountains.

What has been said amounts to this: the renewing, reviving, or relatively innovating extraordinariness that is manifested ever and again in any society, even at the level of supreme values, has the best chance of gaining a following if there is a considerable amount of normlessness and its incipient normative reaction. The message soon loses its appeal, and the mission comes to nothing, however, if in the faith of the followers "the time, the place, and the man" are not transcended; *charisma* must be fused with holiness, the preternatural with the supernatural.

And when that fusion takes place, the normlessness that permitted the emergence of the charismatic leader has begun to give ground to a new or revived set of norms. The phoenix springs from its own ashes; the chaos of today is the cosmos of tomorrow. Whether or not, given the increasingly naturalistic viewpoint of our time, a genuinely new holy era can appear in the future is an open question. That the sacred in *some* form can readily reassert itself is, in the writer's estimation, beyond doubt. The final comment of this commentary is that value-systems go, but value-systems come.

At the end (p. 42) of the first chapter of Volume I, attention was called to a number of terminological modifications that have been made since 1938. The present commentary dates from 1951, and since that time terminology and, in some respects, analytic categories have been altered, shifted, or telescoped. Here too the remarks on p. 42 are relevant.

Supplementary Bibliography for Volume Two

It is of the utmost importance that the reader bear in mind the fact that this bibliography, as the items in the Prefaces, the Notes, the Third Edition Comments (in small type at the end of each chapter) the Value-System Commentary, and the Appendix on Sociological Trends, *is not indexed.* In other words, the Name Index and the Subject Index deal only with the names and subjects appearing in the First Edition (1938) text *as such,* and this text, with the exception of minor corrections, is presented unaltered.

Reviewers the world over evidenced remarkable kindliness in dealing with the 1938 version, in spite of the extremely wide coverage that the nature of the treatise made necessary. Only with such encouragement would the present writer have ventured to present the original text again in 1952; thereafter the earlier goodwill was once more manifested. Now, in 1960, the risk is once more taken, with the hope that tolerance, at least, will be encountered.

Given the tremendous amount of contemporary scholarly activity, full up-to-dateness could not conceivably be achieved within any reasonable space limits, even if the present writer felt competent to achieve it. The list here provided is intended merely to offer a means whereby the reader can delve deeper in the direction of his intrests, guided by searching investigators, than this treatise alone would ever have made possible.

Stress is on the fairly recent, but a few references of earlier date are given when it seems obvious that they should have been included in the first place. Now and again, items listed elsewhere in this treatise are included here if the present writer's orientation is indicated or has been markedly influenced by them; some of his own books and articles, understandably enough, fall in this category! Apart from such considerations as these, preference has often gone to works that contain bibliographies, in footnotes or otherwise. Further, articles and books that survey the various works of given authors, grouped in "schools" and the like (albeit singly now and again), rather than the writings of the authors themselves, figure prominently—need for brevity forced this in *most* cases. In addition, there has been an effort to list convenient "paperbacks"; in some cases passages or entire books that would otherwise be hard to come by, will thus become available. Had it seemed advisable to list well-known standard writings, such as those of Plato, Hegel, Max Weber, and others, the bibliography would have been in some respects more useful (*many* "paperbacks" are in print), and certainly more lengthy—but a line somewhere was unavoidable.

Abbreviations of journals, etc., follow the keys at the beginning of the Notes; what is not to be found in the keys is not abbreviated. The abbreviation bib. or bibs. is used for bibliographies, n. for notes, fn. for footnotes, sel. for selected, I or III for "also very useful for Volume I" (or III), PB for paperback, ext. for extensive, and so on.

Acton, H. B.,
The Illusion of the Epoch: Marxism-Leninism as a Philosophical Creed (Boston: Beacon, 1957). III.

Aiken, H. D., ed.,
The Age of Ideology: the 19th Century Philosophers (Boston: Houghton Mifflin, 1957). Mentor PB. Useful compend.

Antoni, Carlo,
foreword by Croce,
Benedetto,
From History to Sociology: the Transition to German Historical Thinking, trans. by H. V. White (Detroit: Wayne Univ. Press, 1959). III.

Arendt, Hannah,
"Tradition and the Modern Age," *Partisan Review,* vol. xxi, 1 (Jan.-Feb., 1954), pp. 53-75. I and III.

Barber, E. G.,
The Bourgeoisie in 18th Century France (Princeton: Princeton Univ. Press, 1955).

Becker, Carl,
The Heavenly City of the Eighteenth-Century Philosophers (New Haven: Yale Univ. Press, 1932). Yale PB. Imp. as indic. non-rat. el. in thought of "philosophes."

Becker, Howard,
"Les theories du conflit et l'origine de l'Etat" (with Leon Smelo), *Revue de synthèse,* I, 1 (March, 1931), pp. 15-38. Imp. re Oppenheimer *et al.* I and III.

————, "Forms of Population Movement, Part I," *SF,* ix, 2 (Dec., 1930), pp. 147-160; Part II, *ibid.,* 3 (March, 1931), pp. 351-361. I and III.

————, "Pastoral Nomadism and Social Change," *SSR,* vol. xv, 5 (May-June, 1931), pp. 417-427. I and III.

————, "Origines possibles de l'animisme" (with D. K. Bruner), *RIS,* vol. xxxix, 11-12 (Nov.-Dec., 1931), pp. 569-580. I.

————, "Early Generalizations Concerning Population Movement and Culture Contact" (in Japanese), *Sociology* (ed. by H. Juri Tanabe and Kiyoto Furuno), 3 (July-Aug., 1932), pp. 39-80. I.

————, "Le part du sentiment dans les origines de la croyance a l'immortalité," *RIS,* vol. xli, 9-10 (Sept.-Oct., 1933), pp. 487-511. I and III.

————, "Historical Sociology" (in Czech), *Sociologická Revue,* vol. lv, 3 (1933), pp. 346-367. I and III.

————, "Sociologie historique," *Revue de synthèse,* vol. v, 3 (Dec., 1933), pp. 237-250. I and III.

————, *German Youth: Bond or Free* (London: Routledge Kegan Paul, 1946). Ext. bib. Effects of Romant. III.

————, *Vom Barette Schwankt die Feder* (Wiesbaden, Germany: Verlag Der Greif, 1949). Trans. of prev. item, with 2 new chs.

——————————, *Through Values to Social Interpretation* (Durham, N. C.: Duke Univ. Press, 1950). Bibs. for chaps. and secs., sel. Imp. for disc. of "hist. sociol." III.

——————————, "Sacred and Secular Societies Considered with Reference to Folk-State and Similar Classifications," *SF*, vol. xxviii, 4 (May, 1950), pp. 361-376. I and III.

——————————, "In Defense of Morgan's 'Grecian Gens': Ancient Kinship and Stratification," *Southwestern Journal of Anthropology*, vol. vi, 3 (Autumn, 1950), pp. 309-339. I and III.

——————————, "Max Weber, Assassination, and German Guilt," *American Journal of Economics and Sociology*, vol. x, 4 (July, 1951), pp. 401-406. III.

——————————, "Anthropology and Sociology," ch. 5 in John Gillin, ed., *For a Science of Social Man: Convergences in Anthropology, Sociology and Psychology* (New York: Macmillan, 1954). Other surv. in vol. also useful. III.

Barzun, Jacques, *Darwin, Marx, Wagner* (New York: Doubleday, 1958). Anchor PB.

Bendix, Reinhard, *Max Weber: An Intellectual Portrait* (Garden City, L. I.: Doubleday, 1960). Useful. Bib. III.

Berlin, Isaiah, ed., *The Age of Enlightenment: the 18th Century Philosophers* (Boston: Houghton Mifflin, 1956). Mentor PB. First-rate ed. of useful compend.

——————————, *Karl Marx: His Life and Environment* (London: J. Butterworth, Ltd., 1949). Galaxy PB. Stand. work.

Bernard, L. L., and Bernard, Jessie, *Origins of American Sociology: the Social Science Movement in the United States* (New York: Crowell, 1943). Det. bibs. in fn. Esp. val. for 19th cent. III.

Brinton, Crane, *The Anatomy of Revolution*, rev. ed. (New York: Prentice-Hall, 1952). Not method. profound, but good pop. surv.

Bruno, F. J., *Trends in Social Work, 1874-1956*, 2nd ed. (New York: Columbia Univ. Press, 1957). III.

Bryson, Gladys, *Man and Society: the Scottish Inquiry of the Eighteenth Century* (Princeton: Princeton Univ. Press, 1945). Det. bibs., chiefly in fn.

Bury, J. B., *The Idea of Progress*, introd. by Charles Beard (New York: Macmillan, 1932). Dover PB. Highly imp. stand. work. III.

Canu, Jean, *The Religious Orders of Man* (London: Burns and Oates, 1960). I.

Cassirer, Ernst, *The Philosophy of the Enlightenment* (Princeton: Princeton Univ. Press, 1951). Beacon PB. I.

Charlton, D. G., — *Positivist Thought in France During the Second Empire 1852-1870* (Oxford: Oxford Univ. Press, 1959).

Comte, Auguste, — *A General View of Positivism,* trans. by J. H. Bridges (Stanford: Academic Reprints, 1958).

Crawford, W. Rex, — *A Century of Latin-American Thought* (Cambridge: Harvard Univ. Press, 1944). Bib. III.

Curti, Merle, — *The Growth of American Thought* (New York: Harper, 1943). Ext. bib. n. III.

Dunayevskaya, Raya, — *Marxism and Freedom: from 1776 until Today,* with a preface by Herbert Marcuse (New York: Bookman Associates, 1958). III.

Durkheim, Émile, — Foreword by Henri Peyre, *Montesquieu and Rousseau: Forerunners of Sociology* (Ann Arbor: Univ. of Michigan Press, 1960).

Evans-Pritchard, E. E., — *Social Anthropology* (Glencoe, Ill.: Free Press, 1950). sel. bib. III.

Gerth, H. H., and Gerth, H.I., — "Bibliography on Max Weber," *SRE* (March, 1949), pp. 70-89. Exc.

Glass, Bentley, Temkin, Owsei, and Straus, W. L., eds., — *Forerunners of Darwin, 1745-1859* (Baltimore: Johns Hopkins Press, 1960). Useful compend., well ed.

Gregoire, Franz, — *Aux sources de la pensée de Marx: Hegel et Feuerbach* (Louvain: Institut supérieur de philosophie, 1947). Bib. in fn.

Gross, Feliks, — *European Ideologies: a Survey of 20th Century Ideas* (New York: Philosophical Library, 1948). Classif. bibs. Not restr. in 20th cent. in view backgr. III.

Hall, E. W., — *Modern Science and Human Values: a Study in the History of Ideas* (Princeton: D. Van Nostrand Co., 1956).

Hare, Richard, — *Pioneers of Russian Social Thought* (New York: Oxford Univ. Press, 1951). Exc. brief surv. Good bib.

Haskins, C. H., — *The Rise of Universities* (New York: Holt, 1923). Great Seal PB.

Hauser, Arnold, — *The Social History of Art,* 4 vols. (New York: Knopf, 1951). Vintage PB. Marxist interp.; very pop. I and esp. III.

Hayek, F. A., — *The Road to Serfdom* (Chicago: Univ. of Chicago Press, 1944). Phoenix PB. Att. on socialism, etc. Stim.; widely read. III.

Herbertson, Dorothy, — Ed. by Victor Branford and Alexander Farquharson, *The Life of Frederic LePlay* (Ledbury, Herefordshire, England: LePlay House Press, 1952).

Hertz, Frederick,   *The Development of the German Public Mind* (New York: Macmillan, 1957).

Himmelfarb, Gertrude,   *Darwin and the Darwinian Revolution* (Garden City, N. Y.: Doubleday, 1959).

Hofstadter, Richard,   *Social Darwinism in American Thought* (New York: George Braziller, 1959). Beacon PB. III.

Honigsheim, Paul,   "The Roots of the Soviet Social Structure: Why and Where It Has Spread," *Agricultural History,* vol. xxv (July, 1951), pp. 104-114. Exc. bib. in fn. III.

——————————,   "Max Weber as Historian of Agriculture and Rural Life," *Agricultural History,* vol. xxiii (July, 1949), pp. 179-213. Ext. bib. in n. III.

——————————,   "The Roots of the Nazi Concept of the Ideal German Peasant," *RUS,* vol. xii, 1 (March, 1947), pp.3-21. Exc. bib. in fn. III.

——————————,   "Max Weber: His Religious and Ethical Background and Development," *Church History,* vol. xix, 4 (Dec., 1950), pp. 3-23. III.

Iggers, G. G.,   *The Cult of Authority: A Political Philosophy of the Saint-Simonians. A Chapter in the Intellectual History of Totalitarianism* (The Hague: Martinus Nijhoff, 1958).

——————————,   *The Doctrine of Saint-Simon: An Exposition—*
trans. and annot.,   *First Year, 1828-1829* (Boston: Beacon, 1958). Imp.

Jacobs, Norman,   *The Origin of Modern Capitalism and Eastern Asia* (Hong Kong: Hong Kong Univ. Press, 1958).

Kolaja, Jiri,   "Sociology in Poland," *ASR,* vol. xxiii, 2 (April, 1958), pp. 201-202.

Lacroix, Jean,   *La Sociologie d'Auguste Comte* (Paris: Presses Universitaires de France, 1956). Crit.

Latourette, K. S.,   *A History of Christianity* (New York: Harper, 1953). One of best rec. treat. Exc. bib.

Lehmann, W. C.,   *John Millar of Glasgow: (1735-1801): His Life and Thought and His Contributions to Sociological Analysis* Publications of the Dept. of Social and Economic Research, Univ. of Glasgow: Social and Economic Studies: 4. (Cambridge: Univ. Press, 1960). Very imp. for soc. strat. I and III.

Leming, A. (Mrs.),   "The Origin of the Popularization of Science," *Impact of Science on Society,* vol. iii (1952), pp. 233-257.

Mann, F. K.,   "Albert Schäffle als Wirtschafts- und Finanzsoziologe," in G. L. Duprat *et al., Gründer der Soziologie* (Jena: Fischer, 1932). III.

Manuel, F. E.,   *The New World of Henri Saint-Simon* (Cambridge: Harvard Univ. Press, 1956).

Mead, G. H.,   *Movements of Thought in the 19th Century* (Chicago: Univ. of Chicago Press, 1936). Val. for anteced. of pragmat. III.

Meisel, J. H.,   *The Genesis of Georges Sorel: an Account of His Formative Period Followed by a Study of His Influence* (Ann Arbor: Wahr, 1951).

Mensching, Gustav,   *Soziologie der Religion* (Bonn: Ludwig Röhrscheid Verlag, 1947). Bib. in fn. and at end. III.

Merton, R. K.,   "Priorities in Scientific Discovery: A Chapter in the Sociology of Science," *ASR*, vol. xxii, 6 (Dec., 1957), pp. 635-659. III.

Merz, J. T.,   *A History of European Thought in the Nineteenth Century* (Edinburgh and London: Blackwood, 1903). New York: Reprint, Humanities Press, esp. vols. iii and iv; bib. in fn.

Michels, Robert,   *Political Parties: a Sociological Study of the Emergence of Leadership, the Psychology of Power, and the Oligarchical Tendencies of Modern Democracy* (New York: Hearst, 1915). Dover PB. Major stand. work; highly imp. for sociol. of pol. III.

Morais Filho, Evaristo de,   "A Sociologia do Jovem Comte," *Sociologia*, vol. xvii, 3 and 4 (Aug., and Oct., 1955), pp. 269-323 and 371-422.

Mühlmann, W. E.,   *Geschichte der Anthropologie* (Bonn: Universitäts-Verlag, 1948). Sel. bib. III.

Nef, J. U.,   *Industry and Government in France and England, 1540-1640* (Philadelphia: American Philosophical Society, 1940). Great Seal PB. Valuable contrib.

————,   *War and Human Progress: an Essay on the Rise of Industrial Civilization* (Cambridge: Harvard Univ. Press, 1950). I.

Niebuhr, H. Richard,   *Social Sources of Denominationalism* (New York: Holt, 1929). Meridian PB. Imp. work in sociol. of rel.

Ortega y Gasset, José,   *Man and Crisis*, trans. Mildred Adams (New York: W. W. Norton & Co., 1958).

Parrington, V. L.,   *Main Currents in American Thought*, vol. I, The Colonial Mind, 1620-1800; vol. II, The Romantic Revolution in America, 1800-1860; vol. III, The Beginnings of Critical Realism in America, 1860-1920 (New York: Harcourt, Brace, 1939). Harvest PB. Doctrinaire Marxist. III.

Penniman, T. K.,   *A Hundred Years of Anthropology* (New York: Macmillan, 1936). Ext. bib. Pedest. but useful. III.

Pirenne, Henri,   *Economic and Social History of Medieval Europe* (London: Kegan Paul, 1936). Harvest PB. Stand. work. I.

Proesler, Hans,   "Chladenius als wegbereiter der Wissenssoziologie," *Kölner Zeitschrift für Soziologie,* vol. vi, 3, 4 (1953-54), pp. 617-622.

Rose, E. A.,   *Social Control: A Survey of the Foundations of Order* (New York: Macmillan, 1924). Perh. best book by this auth. Bib. in fn. I and III.

Rossi, Pietro,   "La Sociologia di Max Weber," *Quaderni di Sociologia* Parts I and II, vol. xiii (1954), pp. 114-140, with ref. to earlier part.

Russell, Bertrand,   *A History of Western Philosophy and Its Connection with Political and Social Circumstances from the Earliest Times to the Present Day* (New York: Simon and Schuster, 1945). I and III.

Salomon, Albert,   *The Tyranny of Progress: Reflections on the Origins of Sociology* (New York: The Noonday Press, 1955). III.

Schelting, Alexander von,   *Russland and Europa* (Bern: Francke, 1948). Bib. in n. Very useful.

Schmidt, Wilhelm,   *The Culture-Historical Method of Ethnology,* trans. by S. A. Sieber and Franz Müller (New York: Fortuny's, 1939). III.

Schumpeter, Joseph,   *Imperialism and Social Classes* (New York: Kelley, 1951). Meridian PB. III.

Sohm, Rudolf,   *Outlines of Church History* (London: Macmillan, 1895). Beacon PB. Preced. of Max Weber in disc. of charisma. I and III.

Sorokin, P. A.,   "Sociological Trends in Euro-American Culture during the Last Hundred Years," in Robert S. Rankin, ed., *A Century of Social Thought* (Durham, N. C.: Duke Univ. Press, 1939). III.

———, *Social and Cultural Dynamics: a Study of Change in Major Systems of Art, Truth, Ethics, Law and Social Relationships,* one-vol. ed. (Boston: Porter Sargent, 1957). I and III.

Stein, Lorenz von,   *Begriff und Wesen der Gesellschaft* (Köln und Opladen: Westdeutscher Verlag, 1956). III.

Sumner, W. G.,   *Folkways* (Boston: Ginn, 1907). Dover PB. Good examp. of Soc. Darw. among sociol. III.

Tawney, R. H.,   *Religion and the Rise of Capitalism* (London: Murray, 1922). Mentor PB. III.

Timasheff, N. S.,   "Comte in Retrospect," *American Catholic Sociological Society Review,* vol. xiii (1952), pp. 224-232.

Udy, S. H., Jr.,   " 'Bureaucracy' and 'Rationality' in Weber's Organization Theory: An Empirical Study," *ASR*, vol. xxiv, 6 (Dec., 1959), pp. 791-795.

Wach, Joachim,   *Sociology of Religion* (London: Keegan Paul, *et al.*, 1947). Phoenix PB. Very full bib. in fn. Still most imp. work in field.

Weber, Max,   *From Max Weber: Essays in Sociology,* trans., ed., with intro. by H. H. Gerth and C. Wright Mills (New York: Oxford Univ. Press, 1946). Galaxy PB. Very useful. III.

————————, *The Protestant Ethic and the Spirit of Capitalism* (London: Allen and Unwin, 1930). Scribner PB. In spite of 5th ed. qualif., doctrinaire; ex., disreg. of Arminianism e.g. Methodism, etc. III.

————————, *The Rational and Social Foundations of Music,* trans. and ed. by Martindale, Riedel, and Neuwirth (Carbondale, Ill.: Southern Illinois Univ. Press, 1958).

White, Morton, ed.,   *The Age of Analysis: 20th Century Philosophers* (Boston: Houghton Mifflin, 1955). Mentor PB. Useful compend.

————————, *Social Thought in America: The Revolt against Formalism* (New York: Viking Press, 1949). Beacon PB. Useful compend. III.

Willey, Basil,   *The Eighteenth-Century Background: Studies on the Idea of Nature in the Thought of the Period* (New York: Columbia Univ. Press, 1941). Bib. in fn.

Williams, M. J.,   *Catholic Social Thought: Its Approach to Contemporary Social Problems* (New York: Ronald Press, 1950). Ext. bibs. in fn. and in classif. form. III.

Williams, Raymond,   *Culture and Society: 1780-1950* (New York: Columbia Univ. Press, 1958).

Williams, R. M., Jr.,   "Continuity and Change in Sociological Study," *ASR*, xxiii, 6 (Dec., 1958), pp. 619-633. Rec. surv., primar. Am.

Wish, Harvey,   *Society and Thought in Early America: a Social and Intellectual History of the American People through 1865.* (New York: Longmans Green, 1950). Bib.

Zilsel, Edgar,   "The Sociological Roots of Science," *AJS*, vol. xlvii, 4 (Jan., 1942), pp. 544-562. III.

NOTES

The reader should be made aware of the fact that, as mentioned elsewhere, *names and topics occurring in these Notes are not indexed*. Valuable bibliographic resources will be overlooked if those wishing to make use of such resources do not pore through the Notes. The same is true of the comments at the ends of all chapters; references appearing therein are not indexed.

Other bibliographical resources are provided in the Supplementary Bibliography for Volumes I, II, III. These bibliographies contain references to other bibliographies. As DeMorgan said:

Great big fleas have little fleas upon their backs to bite 'em,
  And little fleas have lesser fleas, and so *ad infinitum*.
And the great fleas themselves, in turn, have greater fleas to go on;
  While these again have greater still, and greater still, and so on.

Levity aside, now, it may be well to direct attention to the present state of the history of social thought and, for that matter, of sociological theories. Less and less reading in these fields, to say nothing of research, is today being done by professional sociologists, and this might be viewed as justifiable if it were not for the fact that picayune notions are perpetually being swallowed as the latest novelties by the gullible. Perhaps no one need worry about the gullible; the poor, in our present economy of abundance, may not be always with us (although the writer here coughs discreetly), but the gullible certainly will. Nevertheless, there are good grounds for worry; the gullible sometimes control the sinews of research, with the result that the veriest quacks and/or ignoramuses inflict on us their pompously formulated trivialities. "Paper is patient; anything can be impressed on it"—but should not *we* begin to be impatient with the fools, charlatans, semi-literates, and "scientistic" dogmatists?

Apart from this, it seems clear that those who have recently become interested in sociology of knowledge might gain a good deal for us all by dealing with the history of social thought and of sociological theories from that standpoint. If sociology is ever to transcend its ethnic, religious, class, national, chronological, technological, and other limitations, there must be relentless probing into basic assumptions with a view to discovering what can be relied on as suitable foundations for research leading to conclusions that hold despite those ethnic... to the *n*th limitations. Circularity of this kind is the only way out of circularity of that kind; only sociology of knowledge can lay bare our basic assumptions thoroughly enough for the logic of science to be effectively applied to them. And what better materials for sociology of knowledge investigation can be found than man's ideas about life with his fellows, from the years when the sages whose very names have long since been forgotten dispensed their lore to the days when the columnists who have themselves forgotten what they said last year peddle their wares?

I pause for a reply, and not only from the columnists. "My fires are banked, but still they burn..."

Notes and Suggestions for Further Reading

LIST OF ABBREVIATIONS

A   *The Annals of the American Academy of Political and Social Science*
AA   *American Anthropologist*
AAS   *Archiv für angewandte Soziologie*
ADS   *Archives de sociologie*
AESS   *Archives of the Economic and Social Sciences* (modern Greek)
AFLB   *Annales de la faculté des lettres de Bordeaux*
AGA   *Allgemein statistisches Archiv*
AGPS   *Archiv für Geschichte der Philosophie und Soziologie*
AHR   *American Historical Review*
AIIS   *Annales de l'institut international de sociologie*
AJS   *The American Journal of Sociology*
APM   *Archives of Philosophy and Methodology* (modern Greek)
ARGB   *Archiv für Rassen- und Gesellschaftsbiologie*
ARW   *Archiv für Rechts- und Wirtschaftsphilosophie*
AS   *L'Année sociologique*
ASGS   *Archiv für soziale Gesetzgebung und Statistik*
ASPS   *Archiv für systematische Philosophie und Soziologie*
ASR   *American Sociological Review*
ASSSR   *Archives of Social Science and Social Reform* (Roumanian)
ASUP   *Archiv für Sozialwissenschaft und Sozialpolitik*
BMCPEE   *Bulletin mensuel du centre polytechnicien d'études économiques*
BNJ   *Byzantinisch-neugriechische Jahrbücher*
BSFP   *Bulletin de la société française de philosophie*
BSSR   *Bulletin of the Society for Social Research*

BWC   Harry Elmer Barnes, *History of Western Civilization*
CAH   *Cambridge Ancient History*
CH   *Current History*
CM   *Communist Monthly*
ConR   *Contemporary Review*
CR   *Cambridge Review*
CSPSR   *The Chinese Social and Political Science Review*
E   *Economica*
EA   *Encyclopedia Americana*
EB   *Encyclopedia Britannica*
EI   *Enciclopedia Italiana*
ER   *Educational Review*
ES   *Encyclopedia Sinica*
ESS   *Encyclopedia of the Social Sciences*
GE   *Grande Encyclopédie*
GGE   *Great Greek Encyclopedia* (modern Greek)
HERE   Hastings's *Encyclopedia of Religion and Ethics*
HO   *Historical Outlook*
HWBS   *Handwörterbuch der Soziologie*
IJE   *International Journal of Ethics*
JA   *Journal asiatique*
JAFL   *Journal of American Folk-Lore*
JAS   *Journal of Applied Sociology*
JASA   *Journal of the American Statistical Association*
JASP   *Journal of Abnormal and Social Psychology*
JCCL   *Journal of Criminology and Criminal Law*
JCP   *Journal of Comparative Psychology*
JDP   *Journal de psychologie*
JFS   *Jahrbuch für Soziologie*
JNCBRAS   *Journal of the North China British Royal Asiatic Society*
JP   *Journal of Philosophy*

JPE   *Journal of Political Economy*
JPNP   *Journal de psychologie normale et pathologique*
JPPSM   *Journal of Philosophy, Psychology, and Scientific Methods*
JRAI   *Journal of the Royal Anthropological Institute*
JRAS   *Journal of the Royal Asiatic Society*
JRD   *Journal of Race Development*
JSM   *Japanese Sociological Monthly*
JSP   *Journal of Social Philosophy*
JSPS   *Journal of Social Psychology*
KVS   *Kölner Vierteljahrshefte für Soziologie*
M   *The Monist*
MEM   *Mensch en Maatschappij*
MF   *Mercure de France*
MP   *Modern Philology*
MSOS   *Mitteilungen des Seminars für orientalische Sprachen*
PA   *Pacific Affairs*
PASS   *Publication or Proceedings of the American Sociological Society*
PR   *Philosophical Review*
PSM   *Popular Science Monthly*
PSQ   *Political Science Quarterly*
RASI   *Reports of the Archaeological Survey of India*
RAST   *Royal Asiatic Society Transactions*
RB   *Revue bleue*
RDI   *Rivista d'Italia*
RDIS   *Revue de l'institut de sociologie*
RDP   *Revue de Paris*
REO   *Revue de l'Europe orientale*
RHES   *Revue d'histoire économique et sociale*
RIS   *Revue internationale de sociologie*

RMM   *Revue de metaphysique et de morale*
RP   *Revue philosophique*
RPP   *Revue de philosophie positive*
RS   *Rivista di sociologia*
RSe   *Revue socialiste*
RSH   *Revue de synthèse historique*
RSICP   *Report at Sixth International Congress of Philosophy*
RUBB   *Revue universitaire belge: Bruxelles*
RUS   *Rural Sociology*
S   *Sociologus*
SBKAWPH   *Sitzungsberichte der kaiserlichen Akademie der Wissenschaften, philosoph.-histor. Klasse*
SF   *Social Forces*
SJ   *Schmollers Jahrbuch*
SLR   *Slavische Rundschau*
SM   *Scientific Monthly*
SPSSQ   *Southwestern Political and Social Science Quarterly*
SR   *Sociological Review*
SRE   *Social Research*
SS   *Social Science*
SSR   *Sociology and Social Research*
SSSQ   *Southwestern Social Science Quarterly*
UTQ   *University of Toronto Quarterly*
VFWP   *Vierteljahrsschrift für wissenschaftliche Philosophie*
VWPS   *Vierteljahrsschrift für wissenschaftliche Philosophie und Soziologie*
ZP   *Zeitschrift für Politik*
ZSF   *Zeitschrift für Sozialforschung*
ZVS   *Zeitschrift für Völkerpsychologie und Soziologie*

Each author is responsible for the notes bearing on the chapters or sections marked with his symbol in the Table of Contents, with two exceptions: (1) all references in Barnes's notes to books and articles dated 1927 or later have been inserted by Becker; and (2) all the notes have been edited by Becker.

Books and articles likely to be of interest and value beyond their specific reference function are marked with an asterisk.

NOTES

CHAPTER XII

1. The outstanding authority on this subject is the philosopher Arthur O. Lovejoy, and the second, third, and fourth sections of this chapter lean heavily on the *Documentary History of Primitivism and Related Ideas in Antiquity*, the first volume of which, " Primitivism and Related Ideas in Antiquity," edited by Professors Lovejoy, Boas, Chenard, and Crane, has recently appeared (Baltimore, Johns Hopkins Press, 1935). **2.** *Ibid.*, p. 2. **3.** *Ibid.*, p. 7. **4.** *Ibid.*, pp. 9 ff.
5. *Ibid.*, pp. 447 ff. **6.** *Ibid.*, pp. 111–12. **7.** *Ibid.*, pp. 14–15.
8. *Ibid.*, p. 15. **9.** *Ibid.*, p. 16. **10.** *Ibid.*, p. 17. **11.** *Ibid.*, p. 17.
12. W. H. R. Rivers, *History of Melanesian Society* (1914); G. Brown, *Melanesians and Polynesians*, chap. xiv.
13. W. R. Smith, *Religion of the Semites* (1894); J. H. Breasted, *The Development of Religion and Thought in Ancient Egypt* (1912); M. Jastrow, *The Religion of the Babylonians and Assyrians* (1898); F. Cumont, *Oriental Religions in Roman Paganism* (1911); F. Delitzsch, *Babel and Bible* (Eng. trans., 1903).
14. J. H. Breasted, *Ancient Records of the East* (1906); R. W. Rogers, *Cuneiform Parallels to the Old Testament* (1912).
15. *See the remarkable summary by G. Santayana, *Reason in Religion*, pp. 92–97.
16. W. F. Albright, " Primitivism in Ancient Western Asia (Mesopotamia and Israel)," in *ibid.*, pp. 429 ff. The following account draws heavily on this supplementary chapter. **17.** *Ibid.*
18. *J. B. Bury, *The Ancient Greek Historians* (1909), p. 187.
19. *Ibid.*, p. 118.
20. See *ibid.*, chap. v, especially the summary on pp. 167–68, of which our text is merely a paraphrase. **21.** Plato, *Philebus*, 16 c, quoted in *loc. cit.*
22. Plato, *Laws*, 890 d, quoted in *ibid.*, p. 166. **23.** *Ibid.*, pp. 189 ff.

24. *Ibid.*, p. 176.

25. *Nichomachaean Ethics*, VII, 1145 a, 30 ff., quoted in *ibid.*, p. 179.

26. Polybius, *Histories*, VI, 5–6.

27. Cf. *H. F. Osborn, *Men of the Old Stone Age* (3rd ed., 1923), Appendix IX, p. 504. **28.** Tacitus, *Germania* (1874), *passim*.

29. A. J. Carlyle, *A History of Medieval Political Theory* (1903), vol. i, p. 172; Isidore, *Etymologies* (1493), XV, 2. **30.** Carlyle, *op. cit.*, pp. 211–12.

31. Carlyle, *op. cit.*, vol. ii, pp. 56–74. **32.** *Ibid.*, pp. 143–44.

33. W. A. Dunning, *A History of Political Theories, Ancient and Medieval* (1923), pp. 197–98; R. L. Poole, *Illustrations of the History of Medieval Thought* (2nd ed., 1920), pp. 242–46.

34. Marsiglio, *Defensor pacis*, Bk. I, chap. iv, given in F. W. Coker, *Readings in Political Philosophy* (1914), p. 161.

35. *Machiavelli, *Discourses on the First Ten Books of Titus Livius*, Bk. I, chap. ii. (Detmold ed., vol. ii, pp. 99–101.)

36. Dunning, *A History of Political Theories from Luther to Montesquieu* (1905), p. 47. **37.** Coker, *op. cit.*, pp. 210–11.

38. Dunning, *op. cit.*, p. 57 and note. **39.** *Ibid.*, pp. 87–88.

40. Bodin, *The Six Bookes of a Commonweale*, done into English by Richard Knolles (London, 1606), p. 47. (As here quoted the English has been modernized to some degree.) **41.** *Ibid.*, pp. 262–63.

42. Hooker, *The Laws of an Ecclesiastical Polity*, Bk. I, chap. x, par. 3; cf. the first hundred pages of *Hooker's Ecclesiastical Polity*, Bk. VIII, with an introduction by R. A. Houk (1931).

43. A. Franck, *Reformateurs et publicistes de l'Europe, dix-septième siècle*, pp. 52–53; 71–73.

44. Mariana, *De rege et regis institutione*, Bk. I, chap. i, pp. 12–16 *et passim*.

45. *John Laures, *The Political Economy of Juan de Mariana* (1928), pp. 27–30. Cf. Scherger, *op. cit.*, p. 115; Dunning, *A History of Political Theories from Luther to Montesquieu*, pp. 68–69. **46.** Dunning, *ibid.*, p. 180, note.

47. *Ibid.*, pp. 180–81. **48.** *Hobbes, *Leviathan*, chap. xi.

49. *Ibid.*, chaps. xii–xiii. Cf. *Philosophical Rudiments concerning Government*, chap. i; and *De Corpore Politico*, Part I.

50. Hobbes, *op. cit.*, chaps. xiii, xvii.

51. Milton, *The Tenure of Kings and Magistrates* (1649), reprinted in Coker, *op. cit.*, p. 281.

52. *Spinoza, *A Theologico-Political Treatise* (Bohn), chap. xvi. See also *ibid.*, chap. v and *A Political Treatise*, chap. ii. Something of Spinoza's contemporary obscurity may be gleaned from the statement of Pufendorf that his authorship of the work which Pufendorf criticized could not be determined with certainty.

53. *Pufendorf, *The Law of Nature and of Nations* (1729), Bk. II, chap. ii, sec. 1. **54.** Pufendorf, *op. cit.*, Bk. II, chap. i, sec. 8, p. 101. **55.** *Ibid.*, sec. 3.

56. Locke, *Two Treatises of Government*, Part II, chap. ii, sec. 6; chap. iii, sec. 19; chap. vii, secs. 77–78.

57. Bossuet, *Discours sur l'histoire universelle* (4th ed., 1892). Janet has summarized his conception as follows: " Bossuet admet, comme Hobbes, une sorte d'état de nature antérieure au gouvernement civil, où tout était en proie à tous. ' Où tout le monde veut faire ce qui'il veut, nul ne fait ce qui'il veut; où tout le monde est maître, tout le monde est esclave.' Dans cet état, il est bon que chacun renonce à sa propre volonté et la transmette au gouvernement. Ainsi toute la force est dans le magistrat souverain, et chacun l'affermat au préjudice de la sienne propre. On voit ici que Bossuet donne au gouvernement la même origine que Hobbes lui-même, le besoin d'une force souveraine qui résume et accable toutes les forces particulières " (P. Janet, *Histoire de la science politique*, vol. ii, p. 278).

58. R. Flint, *Vico* (1884), pp. 200–204, 206.

59. Montesquieu, *The Spirit of Laws*, Bk. I, chap. ii.

60. *A. C. Haddon, *History of Anthropology*, pp. 27–28. Cf. *Myres, " The Influence of Anthropology on the Course of Political Science," in *Publications of the University of California*, 1916.

61. Hume, *A Treatise of Human Nature* (Green and Grose ed.), vol. ii, pp. 265–66.

62. Rousseau, *Discourse on the Origin and Foundation of Inequality among Mankind* (Cole trans., 1913), especially pp. 194–203, 214–17.

63. H. Taine, *L'Ancien Régime*, translated by John Durand (1876), Part IV. Compare with Pufendorf's " mere state of nature."

64. *Rousseau, *The Social Contract* (Cole trans., 1913), chap. vi, p. 14; chap. viii, pp. 18–19.

65. *Rousseau, *Discourse on the Origin of Inequality*, p. 203.

66. *Social Contract*, pp. 14, 18–19.

67. Blackstone, *Commentaries on the Laws of England* (Cooley, ed., 1872), vol. i, pp. 46–47.

68. *H. Higgs, *The Physiocrats* (1897), p. 70; Gide and Rist, *History of Economic Doctrines* (2nd ed., 1912), pp. 7–8.

69. Of course, we refer merely to his doctrine of the natural as the normal and as tending toward perfection.

70. Ludwig Stein, *Die Soziale Frage im Lichte der Philosophie* (3rd and 4th eds., 1923), pp. 350, 354, 423. See also Janet, *op. cit.*, vol. ii, p. 564; and the excellent monograph by *W. C. Lehmann, *Adam Ferguson and the Beginnings of Modern Sociology*, 1930. For an opposite view see L. Stephen, *English Thought in the Eighteenth Century* (3rd ed., 1927), vol. ii.

71. *Ferguson, *An Essay on the History of Civil Society* (4th ed., 1773), Part I, sec. I. As all of Ferguson's chapter on the state of nature is almost equally pertinent and yet far too long to quote, any direct citation from his work will be omitted.

72. For an extreme modern statement of this tendency, see *Paul Radin, *Primitive Man as Philosopher* (1927).

73. Burke, " A Vindication of Natural Society," in *Works* (London, 1852), vol. ii, pp. 520–51.

74. *A. K. Rogers, " Burke's Social Philosophy," *AJS* (July, 1912), pp. 71–72.

75. Burke, *op. cit.*, pp. 520–21.

76. Paine, *Common Sense*, given in Coker, *op. cit.*, p. 523.

77. F. Paulsen, *Immanuel Kant*, pp. 349–53; Kant, *On the Common Saying*, edited by Hastie as *The Principles of Political Right*, p. 1.

78. *Bentham, *A Fragment on Government* (2nd ed., 1823), chap. i, pars. x–xi. **79.** Bacon, *Advancement of Learning* (1904).

80. See Flint, *Vico*; and Croce, *The Philosophy of Vico*, translated by R. G. Collingwood (1913).

81. *See J. Morley, *Critical Miscellanies* (1913), vol. ii; and *Flint, *The History of Philosophy of History* (either edition).

82. Kant, *Idea of a Universal Cosmo-Political History*.

83. See *Bury, *Idea of Progress* (1932); and Morley, *op. cit.*

84. *Ibid.*, and *Godwin, *Enquiry Concerning Political Justice* (1793).

85. See Dunning, *Political Theories from Rousseau to Spencer* (1928); and our Chapter Fifteen.

CHAPTER XIII

1. Quoted in James Harvey Robinson, *Readings in European History*, vol. i, p. 461.   **2.** Basil Montagu, *The Works of Francis Bacon*, vol. i, p. 170.
3. *F. J. Teggart, *Readings in the Idea of Progress*, pp. 65–67.
4. *Ibid.*, pp. 99, 105.   **5.** *Ibid.*, pp. 94, 96–98.
6. *Ibid.*, pp. 107, 109, 110, 112.
7. Robert Flint, *Vico*, pp. 164–65. Cf. the recent study by Elio Gianturco, *Joseph DeMaistre and Giambattista Vico* (1937).
8. *Ibid.*, p. 213.   **9.** *Ibid.*, p. 214.
10. W. A. Dunning, *A History of Political Theories from Luther to Montesquieu* (1905), p. 388.   **11.** Flint, *op. cit.*, pp. 217–18.   **12.** *Ibid.*, p. 218.
13. *Ibid.*, pp. 223–24.   **14.** *Ibid.*, pp. 224–28.
15. *Benedetto Croce, *The Philosophy of Giambattista Vico*, translated by R. G. Collingwood (1913), pp. 131–32.
16. *McQuilkin DeGrange, *Turgot on the Progress of the Human Mind* (1929), p. 6; cf. also *John Morley, *Critical Miscellanies*, 2nd series, vol. ii, p. 187; Teggart, *op. cit.*, p. 116.
17. Teggart, *op. cit.*, p. 115.   **18.** *Ibid.*, pp. 116–17.
19. *The Life and Writings of Turgot* (W. Walker Stephens ed), p. 181.
20. Teggart, *op. cit.*, p. 117.   **21.** J. B. Bury, *The Idea of Progress*, p. 157.
22. John Morley, *Critical Miscellanies*, 2nd series, vol. ii, pp. 193–94.
23. Teggart, *op. cit.*, pp. 140–42, 148.
24. James Bonar, *Philosophy and Political Economy in Some of Their Historical Relations*, pp. 204–05.
25. Teggart, *op. cit.*, pp. 175–76. For a penetrating little sketch of the eighteenth-century optimists in general, see *Carl Becker, *The Heavenly City of the Eighteenth-Century Philosophers* (1932).
26. H. S. Salt, ed., Godwin's *Political Justice*, pp. 1–2.
27. Bonar, *op. cit.*, p. 203.   **28.** *Ibid.*, pp. 199–200.   **29.** *Ibid.*, p. 201.
30. William Godwin, *An Enquiry Concerning Political Justice* (Dublin, 1793), vol. ii, Bk. VIII, pp. 326–27.   **31.** *Ibid.*, vol. i, Bk. I, pp. 47–48.
32. *Raymond A. Preston, ed., *Godwin's Enquiry Concerning Political Justice and its Influence on General Virtue and Happiness* (1926), vol. i, Introduction, pp. xxi–xxiii.   **33.** Teggart, *op. cit.*, pp. 178–81.
34. William Hastie, trans., *Kant's Principles of Politics* (Edinburgh, 1891), pp. 10–12.   **35.** *Ibid.*, pp. 18, 21.   **36.** *Ibid.*, pp. 68–69.
37. Robert Flint, *The Philosophy of History in France and Germany* (London, 1874), p. 381.   **38.** Bury, *The Idea of Progress*, pp. 240–41.
39. Flint, *The Philosophy of History in France and Germany*, p. 386.
40. Comte Joseph Marie DeMaistre (1754–1821). His principal works are the following: *Considerations sur la France* (1796); *Essai sur le principe générateur des constitutions politiques* (1814); *Du pape* (1819); *Les Soirées de Saint-Petersbourg* (1821). On DeMaistre, see John Morley, *Critical Miscellanies*, pp. 113–94; Georges Cogordan, *Joseph DeMaistre*; Peter Rohden, *Joseph DeMaistre als politischer Theoretiker*; Frédéric Paulhan, *Joseph DeMaistre et sa philosophie*; and see particularly H. J. Laski, *Studies in the Problem of Sovereignty*, pp. 211–38, and Émile Faguet, *Politiques et moralistes du dix-neuvième siècle*, vol. i, pp. 1–50, to which the present sketch is especially indebted. Cf. the work by Elio Gianturco cited in note 7.   **41.** No pejorative connotations are intended.
42. Quoted by Faguet, *op. cit.*, p. 34.

43. Louis Gabriel Ambroise, Vicomte DeBonald (1754–1840), author of *Théorie du pouvoir politique et religieuse dans la société civile, démontrée par de raisonnement et l'histoire* (3 vols., 1796); *Essai analytique sur les lois naturelles* (1800); *Législation primitive* (2 vols., 1802). On DeBonald see: R. Mauduit, *Les conceptions politiques et sociales de DeBonald;* H. Moùlinié, *DeBonald;* C. Sainte-Beuve, *Causeries du lundi*, vol. iv, pp. 324–41; and especially H. J. Laski, *Authority in the Modern State*, pp. 123–89, and Émile Faguet, *op. cit.*, vol. i, pp. 69–121, to which this sketch is particularly indebted.

44. Dunning, *A History of Political Theories from Rousseau to Spencer* (1928), pp. 164–66. **45.** Bury, *The Idea of Progress*, pp. 255–56. **46.** *Ibid.*, p. 282.
47. Dunning, *A History of Political Theories from Rousseau to Spencer*, p. 357.

CHAPTER XIV

1. William L. Gage, *Geographical Studies*, pp. 247–48, 242–43. See also W. Z. Ripley, "Geography as a Sociological Study," *PSQ*, vol. x (1895), pp. 636–55.
2. A. W. Small, "Sociology," *EA*, vol. xxv (1920), pp. 209–10. Cf. *F. L. Nussbaum, *A History of the Economic Institutions of Modern Europe. An Introduction to* Der moderne Kapitalismus *of Werner Sombart* (1933), especially "The State as Economic Organization," pp. 61–79.
3. Henry Higgs, *The Physiocrats* (1893), p. 70. The writers sponsoring this point of view, in opposition to Mercantilism, were the so-called Physiocrats. Most of them were Frenchmen, and their chief works appeared about 1755–1780. There has been some difference of opinion as to who were the chief representatives of the school, but some general agreement can be found. It has been the custom to name as the leaders, Quesnay (1694–1774), Gournay (1712–1759), and Turgot (1727–1781), but only the first can be classed as a true Physiocrat, though the others held many ideas resembling his. Hancy, in his *History of Economic Thought*, says that the three men above mentioned were the chief representatives of the school, but points out that Gournay wrote but little, being mainly an adviser, and that Turgot kept himself formally separate from the sect in general. Ingram holds practically the same idea. Bonar takes the ground that Quesnay and Gournay were Physiocrats, but that Turgot should not be reckoned among their number. Higgs asserts that Gournay should not be classified with this school, and maintains that Turgot was not properly a Physiocrat, though his views were in substantial accord with theirs. Gide classifies Turgot as one of the school, but not Gournay. Morley differentiates the fundamental doctrines of Turgot from those of the Physiocrats. It therefore seems best to accept the unanimous opinion that Quesnay was the leader of the school, and to reject the idea that Gournay and Turgot were properly members. The minor adherents are not disputed: the most important of them were Mercier de la Rivière, whose work *L'ordre naturel et essential des sociétés politiques*, published in 1767, is the best concise statement of Physiocratic doctrine; Abbé N. Baudau, whose *Première introduction à la philosophie économique* was published in 1771; Le Trosne, who published his *De l'ordre social* in 1777; Mirabeau, whose *Philosophie rurale ou économique générale et politique de l'agriculture* appeared in 1763; and finally, the man whose work gave the name to the school, Dupont de Nemours; his treatise, *Physiocratie ou constitution naturelle du gouvernement le plus advantageux au genre humain*, came out in 1767.
4. *Gide and Rist, *A History of Economic Doctrines*, pp. 7–9.
5. *Higgs, *op. cit.*, p. 67.
6. J. Bonar, *Philosophy and Political Economy* (3rd ed., 1923), p. 141.
7. Cf. J. K. Ingram, *A History of Political Economy* (1844), p. 66.

8. Henry Thomas Buckle, *History of Civilization in England* (1913 ed.), vol. i, p. 154. **9.** *Walter Bagehot, *Economic Studies* (2nd ed., 1895), p. 1.
10. *A. W. Small, *Adam Smith and Modern Sociology*, pp. 1, 235, 238.
11. J. B. Bury, *The Idea of Progress*, pp. 165–67.
12. W. A. Dunning, *A History of Political Theories from Rousseau to Spencer* (1928), p. 102.
13. *H. N. Brailsford, *Shelley, Godwin, and Their Circle* (1913), pp. 163–64, 166–67.
14. *Wesley C. Mitchell, " Bentham's Felicific Calculus," *PSQ*, vol. xxxiii (June, 1918), pp. 164, 172–76.
15. *J. H. Randall, *Making of the Modern Mind* (1926), pp. 395–96.
16. See the interesting list given in Jakob Baxa, *Einführung in die romantische Staatswissenschaft* (Jena: Fischer, 1931).
17. B. Spinoza, *Ethics,* translated by W. H. White (1894), Part III, Proposition XXVII.
18. D. Hume, *A Treatise of Human Nature* (Green and Grose ed., 1874), vol. ii, p. 111.
19. Franklin H. Giddings, *The Principles of Sociology* (1896), Preface, p. x.
20. Howard Becker, review of Eckstein's translation of *The Theory of Moral Sentiments, AJS*, vol. xxxiii (Jan., 1928), pp. 637–38.
21. Cf. Jessica Peixotto, *The French Revolution and Modern French Socialism.*
22. Edmund Burke, " Reflections on the Revolution in France," in *Works* (1910), vol. ii, pp. 368–69.
23. *W. C. Lehmann, *Adam Ferguson and the Beginnings of Modern Sociology* (1930), pp. 26–27.
24. H. C. Engelbrecht, *Johann Gottlieb Fichte: A Study of His Political Writings with Special Reference to His Nationalism* (1933), p. 190.
25. G. W. F. Hegel, *Philosophy of History* (Sibree trans.), p. 164.
26. *Ernest Barker, *Political Thought in England from Herbert Spencer to the Present Day* (1915–16), pp. 10–11.
27. Quoted in *Albion W. Small, *Origins of Sociology* (1924), p. 320.
28. Quoted in Small, *Origins of Sociology*, p. 57.
29. *Ibid.*, pp. 43–45. **30.** *Ibid.*, pp. 61–62.

CHAPTER XV

1. Wiese-Becker, *Systematic Sociology* (1932), p. 666.
2. See W. H. Schoff, " A Neglected Chapter in the Life of Comte," in *Annals*, vol. viii (1896), pp. 491–508. See also J. F. Normano, " Saint-Simon and America," *SF*, vol. xi (Oct., 1932), pp. 8–14.
3. For a list of Comte's works see M. Defourny, *La Sociologie positiviste* (1902), pp. 19–22. An excellent brief survey of Comte's life is to be found in *John Morley's article (revised) " Comte " in *EB*, 14th ed. The best recent brief biography in English is F. S. Marvin's *Comte* (1937). The definitive biography of Comte's youthful period promises to be that by Henri Gouhier, *La Jeunesse d'Auguste Comte*, 2 vols. (1933–35).
4. Cf. L. Chiappini, *Les Idées politiques d'Auguste Comte* (1913), Introduction; *McQuilkin DeGrange, *The Curve of Societal Movement* (1930), pp. 5–6.
5. See Schoff, *op. cit.*, p. 506. Morley, *op. cit.*, also takes a negative attitude toward it.
6. J. Devolvé, " L'histoire mentale d'Auguste Comte," *JPNP*, vol. xxviii (Nov. 15–Dec. 15, 1931), pp. 749–68.

7. F. Alengry, *La Sociologie chez Auguste Comte*, pp. 389 ff.; Defourny, *op. cit.*, pp. 35–54; H. Michel, *L'Idée de l'état*, pp. 451–58. For studies of Comte's thought, see E. Littré, *Auguste Comte et la philosophie positive* (1864); Depuy, *Le Positivisme d'Auguste Comte* (1911); L. Lévy-Bruhl, *The Philosophy of Auguste Comte* (1903); G. H. Lewes, *Comte's Philosophy of the Sciences* (1904); *E. Caird, *The Social Philosophy and Religion of Comte* (1893); De Grange, *op. cit.*; and *J. P. Lichtenberger, *The Development of Social Theory* (1923), pp. 236–62.

8. Excellent attempts to estimate Comte's contribution to social science have been made in French by Defourny, *op. cit.*; Alengry, *op. cit.*; and DeGrange (later in English, *op. cit.*). A more special treatment of his political theories is attempted by Fezensoc, *Le Système politique d'Auguste Comte*; and by Chiappini, *op. cit.* In German we have H. Waentig, *Auguste Comte und seine Bedeutung für die Socialwissenschaft* (1894), and Alexander Marcuse, *Die Geschichts-Philosophie Auguste Comtes* (1932). Excellent bibliography.

9. Martineau, *The Positive Philosophy of Comte* (1853), vol. ii, pp. 241–57.

10. *Ibid.*, vol. i, chaps. i–ii, particularly pp. 8, 29. Cf. G. H. Lewes, *op. cit.* See the discussions of this classification by H. Spencer, *Classification of the Sciences*; F. H. Giddings, *Principles of Sociology* (1896), pp. 45 ff.; L. F. Ward, *Pure Sociology* (1903), pp. 65 ff. For a vigorous criticism of the notion that sociology is peculiarly complex, see *Read Bain, " The Concept of Complexity in Sociology," I and II, *SF*, vol. viii (Dec., 1929, and Mar., 1930), pp. 223–31 and 369–78.

11. *F. W. Coker, *Organismic Theories of the State* (1910), pp. 123–24; L. T. Hobhouse, *Social Evolution and Political Theory* (1911), p. 204.

12. *Polity*, vol. ii, pp. 240–42.

13. Martineau, *op. cit.*, vol. ii, pp. 258–62, 299–301; *Philosophie positive* (5th ed., 1893), vol. iv, pp. 469–81.

14. Martineau, *op. cit.*, pp. 140–41, 218, 258; vol. iii, pp. 383–85.

15. *Ibid.*, vol. ii, pp. 140–41.

16. *Philosophie positive*, vol. iv, pp. 430, 498.

17. *Polity*, vol. ii, pp. 242–44. Cf. Wiese-Becker, *op. cit.*, p. 290.

18. Martineau, *op. cit.*, vol. i, pp. 1–3, and vol. iii, *passim*. See also Hobhouse in *SR*, vol. i, pp. 262–79. Max Scheler's trenchant criticism of the " law " of the three stages should be consulted: " Über die positivistische Geschichtsphilosophie des Wissens (Dreistadiengesetz)," *Moralia* (Leipzig, 1923), pp. 26–40.

19. *Polity*, vol. iv, translated by Congreve, General Index, pp. 558–60.

20. Cf. Michel, *op. cit.*, p. 432; Martineau, *op. cit.*, vol. ii, pp. 232–34. This doctrine of the relativity of the excellence of institutions was not an original conception, as Bristol would seem to indicate (*Social Adaptation* [1915], pp. 20–21), for it was perhaps the central feature of Montesquieu's philosophy.

21. *Polity*, vol. ii, pp. 235–39. 22. *Ibid.*, vol. iv, p. 157.

23. *Ibid.*, vol. iii, pp. 55 ff. Cf. Ward, *op. cit.*, chaps. vi, xvi.

24. Cf. Giddings, *op. cit.*, pp. 303–04.

25. *Philosophie positive*, vol. iv, pp. 17 ff., 578–87; *Polity*, vol. iii, pp. 44–45 *et passim*. Cf. Dunning, *Political Theories from Rousseau to Spencer* (1928), pp. 393–94: " Whatever addition it may receive, and whatever corrections it may require, this analysis of social evolution will continue to be regarded as one of the greatest achievements of the human intellect "; and Morley, *loc. cit.* For a contrary view, see Scheler, *op. cit.*

26. C. A. Ellwood, *Sociology and Modern Social Problems* (1910), pp. 74 ff.; *Sociology in its Psychological Aspects* (1915), pp. 186–87, 356–58; *The Social*

Problem (1915), pp. 189 ff.; *The Reconstruction of Religion*. Kirkpatrick's assault on "the ministerial mind" in sociology should perhaps be consulted (*Religion in Human Affairs*, chap. x to end.)

27. *Polity, passim*, particularly vols. ii and iv.

28. Martineau, *op. cit.*, vol. ii, pp. 241–57. 29. *Ibid.*, pp. 225–26.

30. Cf. Wiese-Becker, *op. cit.*, pp. 45, 671, 693–700.

31. Martineau, *op. cit.*, vol. ii, pp. 210–22, 235. *Polity*, vol. iv. pp. 558–60, General Appendix, 3rd part, "Plan of the Scientific Operations Necessary for the Scientific Reorganization of Society."

32. *Polity*, vol. ii, pp. 224, 241. Cf. *Philosophie positive*, vol. iv, pp. 485–95.

33. Cf. Chiappini, *op. cit.*, pp. 97 ff.

34. *Polity*, vol. ii, p. 237, 241. For his excessive emphasis on this point he is criticized by Defourny, *op. cit.*, pp. 133–36, 301–02, but Oppenheimer (*Der Staat*, 2nd ed., 1926) upholds Comte throughout.

35. *Polity*, vol. ii, pp. 247–49. 36. *Ibid.*, p. 241.

37. *Philosophie positive*, pp. 431–47; Martineau, *op. cit.*, vol. ii, pp. 157–58.

38. *Polity*, vol. i, pp. 511–13. Cf. Giddings, *op. cit.*, Bk. III, chaps. i–iii; J. Fiske, *Outlines of Cosmic Philosophy* (1875), vol. ii, pp. 340–44, 360–69; Wiese-Becker, *op. cit.*, pp. 139–49.

39. *Polity*, vol. ii, pp. 153, 183; *Philosophie positive*, vol. iv, pp. 447–69.

40. *Polity*, pp. 234, 242; *Philosophie positive*, vol. iv, pp. 469–81.

41. *Philosophie positive*, vol. iv, pp. 469–87; *Polity*, vol. ii, pp. 243–44; Chiappini, *op. cit.*, pp. 102–03.

42. *Philosophie positive*, vol. iv, pp. 487–93; *Polity*, vol. ii, pp. 245–46. Cf. Spencer's doctrine of the military and industrial orders in society, and our discussion of combat theories of the origin of the state in Chapter Nineteen.

43. Cf. the doctrines of Von Haller and Simmel.

44. *Philosophie positive*, vol. iv, pp. 493–95. Cf. *Polity*, vol. ii, p. 244; and Giddings's theory of "protocracy" in his *Responsible State* (1918), pp. 17 ff. Some relevant passages are also to be found in Wiese-Becker, *op. cit.*, pp. 303–309, 354–56, 594–98. 45. *Polity*, vol. ii, pp. 247–51.

46. Cf. Martineau, *op. cit.*, vol. ii, chap. vi; *Polity*, vol. i, pp. 540–93.

47. *Polity*, vol. ii, pp. 251–53, 304. This independence of the church is possible only when its realm of domination is more extensive than that of the political group; see *Polity*, vol. ii, pp. 252–53. Such domination is possible only to an international "ecclesia"; cf. *Wiese-Becker, *op. cit.*, pp. 624–25.

48. Cf. Dittman, "Die Geschichtsphilosophie Comtes und Hegels, ein Vergleich," in *VFWP*, vol. xxxviii, pp. 281–312; vol. xxxix, pp. 38–81.

49. E.g., G. P. Gooch, *History and Historians of the Nineteenth Century* (1913), p. 585.

50. One should look for Comte's philosophy of history not exclusively in the last volumes of his *Philosophy*, but in the third volume of his *Polity*, for he himself tells the reader (*Polity*, vol. iii, p. 5) that his complete theory is to be found only in that volume. For Comte's most compact summary of his philosophy of history, see *Polity*, vol. iii, pp. 421–22. 51. *Polity*, vol. iii, pp. 154–60.

52. *Ibid.*, vol. i, p. 507; vol. iv, p. 157. Cf. Ward, *op. cit.*, chaps. vi, xvi. Social evolution, as a whole, is a combination of all three of these special types of evolution. Defourny well summarizes this point; cf. *op. cit.*, p. 151. Cf. also Dunning, *Political Theories from Rousseau to Spencer* (1928), pp. 393–94.

53. Hobhouse, "Comte's Three Stages," in *SR* (1908), p. 264. For Wundt's arguments supporting fetishism as the most primitive cult see his *Völkerpsychologie: Mythus und Religion*, vol. ii. Modern students of comparative religion, it should

be noted, have abandoned the attempt to find *the* origin of religion; their theories are pluralistic. Cf. Howard Becker and D. K. Bruner, " Origines possibles de l'animisme," *RIS* (Nov.-Dec., 1931), pp. 569–80; and also their " Some Aspects of Taboo and Totemism," *JSPS* (Aug., 1932), pp. 337–53.

54. *Polity*, vol. iii, pp. 91–92, 118–23, 156–61, 171–78, 201–02.

55. *Ibid.*, vol. iii, pp. 216–31. For an unrelievedly pessimistic view of Greek political life, see R. Pöhlmann, *Geschichte der antiken Kommunismus und Sozialismus*. Jacob Burckhardt's *Griechische Kulturgeschichte* (1898) is only a shade less somber.

56. *Polity*, vol. iii, pp. 305–11. 57. *Ibid.*, pp. 336, 350–51, 353, 387–88.

58. *Ibid.*, pp. 409, 412–13, 434–36. 59. *Ibid.*, pp. 487–89.

60. *Ibid.*, pp. 423–24. 61. *Ibid.*, pp. 526–30.

62. Caird, *op. cit.*, p. 35. For Flint's rather unsympathetic treatment of Comte's philosophy of history, see his *History of the Philosophy of History in France* (1894), pp. 575–615; a popular discussion in a somewhat similar vein is to be found in *Will Durant, *The Story of Philosophy*, pp. 383–84.

63. *Polity*, vol. ii, p. 344. 64. *Ibid.*, vol. iii, *passim*.

65. Cf. Chiappini, *op. cit.*, pp. 97 ff. 66. *Polity*, vol. i, pp. 106–10.

67. *Ibid.*, vol. ii, pp. 247–49. 68. *Ibid.*, vol. i, pp. 106–10.

69. Lévy-Bruhl, *op. cit.*, pp. 320–21. 70. *Ibid.*, pp. 328–29.

71. *Ibid.*, pp. 329, 331.

72. *Polity*, vol. ii, pp. 225–28, 266, 291–92. There are here certain anticipations of the modern socio-political theory of the functional reorganization of the state. Cf. F. Pécanut, " Auguste Comte et Durkheim," in *RMM* (Oct.–Dec., 1921), pp. 64 ff.

73. Cf. Chiappini, *op. cit.*, p. 18. " En dernière analyse, les princes de la science, ou sociologistes, et les princes de la finance, ou banquiers, seront les chefs de gouvernement " (Defourny, *op. cit.*, p. 193).

74. Cf. Chiappini, *op. cit.*, pp. 134 ff. 75. *Polity*, vol. ii, pp. 286, 343.

76. *Ibid.*, vol. iv, pp. 222–25.

77. *Ibid.*, vol. ii, pp. 337–39; vol. iv, pp. 64, 266–70. Comte might have expressed himself more confidently had he lived in the age of mental testing.

78. *Ibid.*, pp. 262, 289–90, 309–10, 338–42.

79. *Ibid.*, pp. 336–39; vol. iv, pp. 71, 301. During the decade of unbounded and touching faith in the supreme wisdom of the banker which the United States underwent in the 1920's, it seemed that this requisite of Positivism had at last arrived.

80. *Polity*, vol. ii, p. 338. Apparently Comte failed to realize the social benefits of unregulated competition! 81. *Ibid.*, pp. 328–31, 334–36; vol. iv, p. 291.

82. *Ibid.*, vol. ii, pp. 255–56, 338 ff. 83. *Ibid.*, vol. i, pp. 187–96.

84. *Ibid.*, vol. ii, pp. 251, 304.

85. Chiappini, *op. cit.*, pp. 64 f., 186. " Cette substitution des devoirs aux droits est vraiement l'idée centrale du système politique d'Auguste Comte " (*ibid.*, p. 46). 86. Cf. Chiappini, *op. cit.*, pp. 107 ff.

87. *Polity*, vol. i, pp. 110–12, 114–15, 117–20.

88. *Ibid.*, vol. ii, pp. 234–35; vol. iv, pp. 536, 558–61; General Appendix, 3rd part, " Plan of the Scientific Operations Necessary for Reorganization of Society " (1822).

89. *Ibid.*, vol. iv, pp. 536, 558–60. For Ward's appreciation of Comte's beginnings towards a doctrine of social telesis, see *Dynamic Sociology*, vol. i, p. 137.

90. E.g., Defourny, followed by Bristol.

91. For another summary of Comte's theories, see *F. H. Hankins's treatment

in H. E. Barnes, ed., *The History and Prospects of the Social Sciences* (1925), pp. 292–97.

CHAPTER XVI

1. Sombart has shown how early this transition began; see **Frederick L. Nussbaum, A History of the Economic Institutions of Modern Europe: An Introduction to Der moderne Kapitalismus of Werner Sombart* (1933), pp. 80–89.

2. Silas Bent, *Machine Made Man* (1930), *passim*.

3. **Nussbaum, op. cit.*, "The Transformation of Industry," pp. 204–31.

4. Sidney and Beatrice Webb (hereafter cited as The Webbs), *The History of Trade Unionism* (1911 ed.), chap. i, "The Origins of Trade Unionism," pp. 1–56.

5. **Nussbaum, op. cit.*, "The Rationalization of Business Organization," pp. 357–72. **6.** **Ibid.*, "Population and Labor Supply," pp. 312–26.

7. Albion W. Small, *General Sociology* (1905), pp. 36–37.

8. Robert Flint, *Historical Philosophy in France, French Belgium, and Switzerland* (1894), p. 35.

9. **Nussbaum, op. cit.*, "The Transformation of the Market," pp. 165–203.

10. Gide and Rist, *History of Economic Doctrines*, (2nd ed., 1913), Bk. I, chap. ii, "Adam Smith."

11. Warren S. Thompson, *Population Problems* (1930), "The Population Doctrines of Malthus," pp. 14–27.

12. Gide and Rist, Bk. I, chap. iii, "The Pessimists."

13. *Ibid.*, Bk. III, chap. ii, "Stuart Mill."

14. *Ibid.*, Bk. III, chap. i, "The Optimists."

15. Othmar Spann, *Die Haupttheorien der Volkswirtschaftslehre* (16th ed., 1926; **English translation now available), pp. 100–11.

16. Gide and Rist, *loc. cit.* **17.** Spann, *op. cit.*, p. 112.

18. **H. N. Brailsford, Shelley, Godwin, and Their Circle* (1913).

19. Leslie Stephen, *The English Utilitarians* (3 vols., 1900).

20. *Ibid.*, vol. i. Cf. Graham Wallas, "Bentham as Political Inventor," *ConR* (1926), pp. 308–19.

21. Gide and Rist, *op. cit.*, Bk. II, chap. i. **22.** Spann, *op. cit.*, pp. 91–98.

23. **Small, Origins of Sociology* (1924), pp. 194–233.

24. Sombart's great work, *Der moderne Kapitalismus*, is based on "historicist" assumptions.

25. The Webbs, *op. cit.*, chaps. ii and iii, "The Revolutionary Period," and "The Struggle for Existence," pp. 57–161.

26. *Ibid.*, chap. iv, "The New Spirit and the New Model," pp. 162–214.

27. **Harry W. Laidler, A History of Socialist Thought* (1927), pp. 651–69. An excellent collection of readings, giving excerpts from the writings of many of the reformers dealt with in this chapter, is **Donald Wagner's Social Reformers* (1934).

28. Ashcroft and Preston-Thomas, *The English Poor Law System* (1902), p. 7.

29. ***"Thomas Chalmers," *EB*, 14th ed.

30. For some of the points in sections 15–19 we are indebted to Philip Klein of the New York School of Social Work, who placed at our disposal the MS of his chapter on "Social Work Theory," which is to appear in a *Contemporary Social Theory* (about 1939). See also **Stuart Queen, Social Work in the Light of History* (1922), *passim*.

31. **Jane Addams, Philanthropy and Social Progress* (1893), p. 2.

32. J. L. Gillin, *Poverty and Dependency* (1921), p. 526.

33. W. Rex Crawford, mimeographed material used in Soc. 2, " Social Problems," University of Pennsylvania.

34. For an extensive collection of excerpts from the literature of aesthetic protest, see *Upton Sinclair, *The Cry for Justice* (1st ed., 1915), *passim.*

35. Laidler, *op. cit.*, pp. 61–69. Cf. for all *early* utopian socialism the excellent work by *W. B. Guthrie, *Socialism before the French Revolution* (1907).

36. Laidler, *op. cit.*, pp. 69–74. 37. *Ibid.*, p. 74.

38. The Webbs, *op. cit.*, pp. 139–61.

39. Max Beer, *History of British Socialism* (1919), vol. i, p. 130.

40. E. V. Zencker, *Anarchism* (1897), pp. 60–82.

41. *C. H. Driver, " Thomas Hodgskin and the Individualists," in F. J. C. Hearnshaw, ed., *op. cit.*, pp. 191–219.

42. *Esther Lowenthal, *The Ricardian Socialists* (1911).

43. Laidler, *op. cit.*, pp. 75–80.

44. *Ibid.*, pp. 133–35. 45. *Ibid.*, pp. 278–94.

CHAPTER XVII

1. *A. W. Small, " Socialism in the Light of Social Science," *AJS*, vol. xvii (May, 1912), pp. 809–10.

2. *Norman Sykes, " The Age of Reaction and Reconstruction," in F. J. C. Hearnshaw, ed., *The Social and Political Ideas of Some Representative Thinkers of the Age of Reaction and Reconstruction* (1932), pp. 9–28.

3. *Bertrand Russell, *Proposed Roads to Freedom* (1919), p. 3.

4. *Harry W. Laidler, *A History of Socialist Thought* (1927), pp. 279–346.

5. *A convenient discussion of the *Communist Manifesto* is to be found in J. P. Lichtenberger, *Development of Social Theory* (1925), pp. 291–302. Mention should also be made of the treatment in E. S. Bogardus, *A History of Social Thought* (2nd ed., 1929), pp. 251–64. The *Manifesto* itself has appeared in countless editions, of which the Kerr version is most widespread in the U. S. The edition published by the Rand School, New York, is fairly good for *ordinary* purposes. The scholar will of course wish to work with the original text, of which the best edition is that of D. Ryazanoff (David Goldendach). The English translation of Ryazanoff is also of high quality and is to be preferred to the Rand School version if exegetical studies *must* be made without reference to the original German.

6. *J. L. Gray, " Karl Marx," in F. J. C. Hearnshaw, ed., *The Social and Political Ideas of Some Representative Thinkers of the Victorian Age* (1933), pp. 146–47. Italics ours.

7. Marx and Engels, *Die deutsche Ideologie*, quoted in Rühle, *Karl Marx*, p. 97. 8. Marx, *Capital*, vol. iii, p. 953. 9. *Ibid.*, vol. i, p. 49.

10. Marx, *Revolution*, etc., pp. 22–23.

11. *Marx and Engels, *Communist Manifesto*, pp. 24–25.

12. Marx, *Revolution*, etc., p. 14. 13. Marx, *The Eighteenth Brumaire*, p. 9.

14. Marx, " On Feuerbach," in Engels, *Feuerbach: The Roots of the Socialist Philosophy*, p. 133, as quoted in *Chang, *The Marxian Theory of the State* (1931), pp. 35–36.

15. *Marx, *Civil War in France*, p. 165. (This is the title of the Kerr edition, which for lack of a better version we have been forced to use.)

For the possible influence of Lorenz von Stein on Marx, see Heinz Nitzschke, *Die Geschichtsphilosophie Lorenz von Steins* (1932), pp. 135–136, especially the bibliography in note 4, p. 135.

16. Marx, Letter to Kügelmann, Apr. 17, 1871, translated in *CM* (Mar., 1927), p. 52.

17. Lenin, *Complete Works*, vol. xviii, p. 42, " Marx's Teaching."

18. Marx, *Revolution*, etc., pp. 161–62.

19. Marx, *The Eighteenth Brumaire*, p. 18. 20. Marx, *Civil War*, p. 5.

21. *Manifesto*, p. 28. 22. *Ibid.*, pp. 38, 58. 23. *Ibid.*, p. 58.

24. Marx, *Criticism of the Gotha Program*, p. 38.

25. From Marx on the conclusion of the Congress of the International at the Hague in 1872, in *Kautsky, *The Dictatorship of the Proletariat*, pp. 9–10.

26. Engels, *Principles of Communism*, p. 17, as quoted in Chang, *Marxian Theory*, p. 71. 27. Quoted in Kautsky, *The Labor Revolution*, p. 25.

28. Marx, *The Poverty of Philosophy*, pp. 190, 191. Italics his.

29. A letter from Marx to Kugelmann, Apr. 12, 1871, quoted in Kautsky, *The Labor Revolution*, p. 64. 30. Marx, *Eighteenth Brumaire*, pp. 103–04.

31. Quoted in Lenin, " A Letter to the Workers of Europe and America," (Jan. 12, 1919), *CM* (Jan., 1928), p. 5.

32. Marx, *Capital*, vol. i, p. 552; *Poverty of Philosophy*, p. 188; quoted in *Lenin, *The State and Revolution*, p. 71; Marx, " Address to the Communist League, 1850," in " Two Speeches by Karl Marx," pp. 8–9, quoted in Chang, *Marxian Theory*, p. 84. 33. Marx, *Civil War in France*, pp. 173–74.

34. " Address to the Communist League, 1850," pp. 6–7; *ibid.*, as quoted in Rühle, *Karl Marx*, pp. 173–74. 35. *Ibid.*, pp. 5, 8–9.

36. Marx, *Revolution*, etc., pp. 63–64. 37. *Manifesto*, p. 58.

38. " Address to the League of Communists in 1850," quoted in Beer, *The Life and Teaching of Karl Marx*, pp. 87–90. 39. *Manifesto*, pp. 30–31.

40. Otto Rühle, *Karl Marx*, pp. 300–303.

41. Marx, *The Poverty of Philosophy*, p. 190, quoted in Chang, *op. cit.*, p. 34.

42. *Manifesto*, p. 38.

43. Quoted in Beer, *The Life and Teaching of Karl Marx*, p. 92.

44. Marx, *Civil War in France*, p. 76. 45. *Manifesto*, p. 35.

46. *Engels, *Landmarks of Scientific Socialism*, p. 129.

47. *The Origin of the Family*, p. 216.

48. Marx, *Class Struggles in France*, p. 118. 49. *Manifesto*, pp. 33–34.

50. Engels, *Landmarks of Scientific Socialism*, p. 144.

51. ——, *On Feuerbach*, etc., p. 87. 52. Marx, *Civil War in France*, p. 87.

53. *Manifesto*, p. 42. 54. Marx, *Capital*, vol. i, p. 822.

55. Marx, *Civil War in France*, p. 40. 56. Rühle, *Karl Marx*, p. 78.

57. Marx, *Eighteenth Brumaire*, p. 50.

58. Engels, *Origin of the Family*, p. 214, quoted in Chang, *op. cit.*; Engels, " Introduction " to the third German edition of Marx, *Civil War in France*.

59. Marx, *Eighteenth Brumaire*, pp. 57–58.

60. *Manifesto*, pp. 40–41. 61. Marx, *Civil War in France*, p. 40.

62. *Ibid.*, p. 56. 63. *Ibid.*, p. 39.

64. Quoted in Beer, *The Life and Teaching of Karl Marx*, pp. 90–91.

65. *Manifesto*, pp. 41–42.

66. Engels, letter to Bebel, quoted in Bebel, *My Life*, vol. ii, p. 322, as quoted in Lenin, *The State and Revolution*, pp. 170–71. 67. *Manifesto*, p. 42.

68. Extract from a letter by Marx to Weidmeyer, quoted in Lenin, *The State and Revolution*, p. 140.

69. *Engels, *Socialism, Utopian and Scientific*, pp. 127–29.

70. Marx, *Criticism of the Gotha Program*, p. 31, quoted by Lenin in *The State and Revolution*, p. 199. 71. Engels, *op. cit.*, p. 129.

72. Engels, *The Origin of the Family*, quoted in Lenin, *The State and Revolution*, pp. 122–23. **73.** Laidler, *op. cit.*, pp. 215–77.
74. *Ibid.*, pp. 295–320. See also *Sidney Hook, *Towards the Understanding of Karl Marx: A Revolutionary Interpretation* (1933), pp. 35–43.
75. Laidler, *op. cit.*, pp. 619–50.
76. Gray, *op. cit.*, p. 125. **77.** *Ibid.*, p. 146.

CHAPTER XVIII

1. See *Spencer's *Essays, Scientific, Political, and Speculative* (1891), vol. ii, pp. 118–49, essay entitled " Some Reasons for Dissenting from the Philosophy of M. Comte." **2.** O. Michel, *L'Idée de l'État* (1896), p. 462.

3. For a brief statement of the sources of Spencer's doctrines see *Ernest Barker, *Political Thought in England from Herbert Spencer to the Present Day* (1915), pp. 86–90. For Spencer's own account of his early years see his *Autobiography*, vol. i, pp. 48–142.

4. For a brief but incisive summary of the significance of this work see Giddings, *Sociology, a Lecture* (1908), pp. 26–28.

5. See *A. G. Keller, *Societal Evolution* (1st ed., 1929), pp. 5 ff. The *First Principles* was followed by the *Principles of Biology*, 1864–67; the *Principles of Psychology*, in 1872; the *Study of Sociology*, in 1873; the *Principles of Sociology* from 1876 to 1896; the *Principles of Ethics* from 1879 to 1893; and *Man versus the State*, in 1884. In addition to these systematic works, Spencer published a large number of articles which were collected in numerous volumes of *Essays*. For a complete list of Spencer's works, see the article " Spencer," in *EB*, 14th ed., and in W. H. Hudson, *An Introduction to the Philosophy of Herbert Spencer* (1894), Appendix, pp. 231–34.

Spencer produced this mass of material under conditions far from conducive to its execution. He was a chronic neurasthenic during the entire period of the development of his sociological system, and his pecuniary resources were not always sufficient to keep his plan in a normal state of progress. The preface to the third volume of his *Principles of Sociology*, published in 1896, which completed the work to which he had devoted practically a lifetime, sums up the difficulties of the writer and expresses his satisfaction at his final success. To an understanding reader there are few more inspiring pages in literature than these few paragraphs.

Four good works dealing with Spencer's system are: W. H. Hudson, *op. cit.*; Josiah Royce, *Herbert Spencer, an Estimate and Review* (1904); Hector Macpherson, *Spencer and Spencerism* (1900); and H. Elliott, *Herbert Spencer* (1916). An authorized and approved digest of his system as a whole is to be found in *F. H. Collins, *An Epitome of the Synthetic Philosophy* (1889). Finally, no one should consider himself thoroughly acquainted with Spencer unless he has read his *Autobiography*, which appeared posthumously in two volumes in 1904, and Duncan's *Life and Letters of Herbert Spencer* (1908).

6. W. G. Sumner, *The Forgotten Man and Other Essays* (1918), p. 401.

7. This latter fundamental doctrine was taken from the German writer, Von Baer. See Spencer, *Progress, Its Law and Cause* (1857), and *First Principles*, sec. 43. **8.** Spencer, *First Principles* (edition of 1867), p. 396.

9. For Spencer's summary of his system, see his Preface to Collins, *op. cit.*, pp. viii–xi. Cf. also Mackintosh, *From Comte to Benjamin Kidd* (1899), chaps. viii–ix. **10.** F. H. Giddings, *Sociology, a Lecture* (1908), pp. 29–30.

11. See O. Gierke, *Political Theories of the Middle Ages* (Maitland trans., 1913), pp. 22–30, and notes, 66–100.

12. Spencer, *The Social Organism* (1860); *Specialized Administration* (1871); *Principles of Sociology*, vol. i, Part II; citations from the *Principles of Sociology* are from the New York edition of 1896.

13. ——, *Principles of Sociology*, vol. i, Part II, chaps. ii–ix, particularly chap. ii. More detailed analyses of Spencer's organismic theory of society are to be found in F. W. Coker, *Organismic Theories of the State*, pp. 124–39; and Ezra T. Towne, *Die Auffassung der Gesellschaft als Organismus, ihre Entwickelung und ihre Modifikationen* (Halle, 1903), pp. 41–48.

14. See Carver's review of Spencer's *Principles of Sociology* in Peabody, *A Readers' Guide to Social Ethics and Allied Subjects*, p. 29.

15. A. W. Small, *General Sociology* (1905), p. 130. For estimates of Spencer's importance for sociology, see Giddings, *Principles of Sociology*, Bk. I, chap. i, and his adaptations of Spencer's doctrines in all his works; Ward, *Dynamic Sociology* (1883), vol. i, pp. 139–219; Small, *op. cit.*, pp. 109–53; Ross, *Foundations of Sociology* (1905), pp. 42–47; and above all Leopold von Wiese, *Zur Grundlegung der Gesellschaftslehre, eine kritische Untersuchung von Herbert Spencer's System der Synthetischen Philosophie* (Jena, 1906).

16. *Spencer, *The Study of Sociology* (1874), pp. 265 ff.

17. ——, *Principles of Sociology*, Part II, pp. 253 ff.

18. ——, *The Study of Sociology*, pp. 270–71. **19.** *Ibid.*, p. 403.

20. Cf. *ibid.*, chaps. vii, xi.

21. A. W. Small, *op. cit.*, p. 153.

22. For Spencer's account of his ambitious plan to make a study of the effect of so-called " reform legislation " during the whole period of medieval and modern English history, see *Various Fragments* (1898), pp. 136–40, essay entitled " A Record of Legislation." **23.** Cf. Barker, *op. cit.*, pp. 112 ff.

24. For Spencer's own account of the development of his political theories, see his *Autobiography*, vol. ii, pp. 431–36. This seems to be somewhat of a " rationalization after the fact."

25. *Spencer, *Social Statics*, pp. 103 ff. In this connection the edition of 1850 is used. Citations other than those in this paragraph are from the abridged edition of 1892. **26.** *Ibid.*, pp. 206 ff.

27. These prohibited activities are retained practically unchanged in the abridged edition of 1892.

28. *Ibid.*, pp. 66–72, 250 ff. For Spencer's own estimate of the doctrines expressed in *Social Statics* in later years, see *Autobiography*, vol. i, pp. 415–21, and the preface to the abridged edition of 1892.

29. Spencer, *The Study of Sociology*, pp. 285–86.

30. ——, *Essays*, vol. iii, p. 440.

31. *Ibid.*, pp. 445–70. This was originally written as an introduction to a composite work, *A Plea for Liberty*, attacking socialistic doctrines.

32. Spencer, *Man versus the State* (1884). Citations are from the revised edition of 1892, published with the abridged *Social Statics*.

33. Spencer, *Justice* (1891); *Principles of Ethics*, Part IV.

34. ——, *Man versus the State*, pp. 401–11. Cf. also *Justice*, p. 46, and chap. xxv; *The Study of Sociology*, p. 286.

35. A new edition of *Man versus the State*, edited by Truxton Beale (1916), contains critical comments on Spencer's doctrines by leading conservative American statesmen and political writers with the obvious purpose of combating " progressive " tendencies. For the relation between Spencerian doctrines and anarchism, see *E. Zencker, *Anarchism: A Criticism and History of the Anarchist Theory* (1897), pp. 245–59.

36. For a full discussion of Spencer's political theories, see *Harry Elmer Barnes, " Some Typical Contributions of English Sociology to Political Theory," *AJS*, vol. xxvii (Nov., 1921), pp. 302–22.

37. Spencer, *Principles of Sociology*, pp. 106–08.

38. ——, *The Study of Sociology*, chap. iii, " Nature of the Social Science."

39. ——, *Principles of Sociology*, Part I.

40. E. B. Tylor, *Primitive Culture* (1871).

41. See the discussion in Chapter One of the present work, section on " Religion." **42.** See Spencer's *Autobiography*, vol. ii, chaps. xvii, xviii, and xix.

43. *F. H. Hankins, " Sociology," in H. E. Barnes, ed., *The History and Prospects of the Social Sciences* (1925), pp. 297–302.

44. Ezra T. Towne, *Die Auffassung der Gesellschaft als Organismus, ihre Entwickelung und ihre Modifikationen* (1903), pp. 15–24; E. Barker, *The Political Thought of Plato and Aristotle* (1906), pp. 127, 138–39, 276–81.

45. O. Gierke, *Political Theories of the Middle Ages*, pp. 22–30, notes, pp. 103–04, 112, 122–23, 129–37. Other writers in the Middle Ages expressing this point of view were Thomas Aquinas and Marsiglio of Padua. See F. J. C. Hearnshaw, ed., *The Social and Political Ideas of Some Great Medieval Thinkers*.

46. T. Hobbes, *The Leviathan* (1881, reprint of 1651); J. J. Rousseau, *The Social Contract*. Cf. *F. W. Coker, *Organismic Theories of the State* (1910), pp. 14–16. In this section we rely largely on Coker's excellent monograph.

47. Coker, *op. cit.*, pp. 26–42. **48.** *Ibid.*, pp. 62–82.

49. *Ibid.*, pp. 49–60. The most thorough English statement of Rohmer's theory is found in Bluntschli's article on " Political Parties," in Lalor's *Cyclopedia of Political Science, Political Economy, and United States History*.

50. *Ibid.*, pp. 82–114. **51.** *Ibid.*, pp. 116–190.

52. *Ibid.*, pp. 123–24. A recent version of this same doctrine, explicitly claiming Comte among its antecedents, is A. J. I. Kraus's *Sick Society* (1929), a work of almost unparalleled obscurity and " word-polishing."

53. A. Comte, *Principles of a Positive Polity*, vol. ii, pp. 240–42; Martineau, *Philosophy of Comte*, vol. ii, pp. 258–62, 299–301.

54. Spencer, *The Social Organism* (1860); *Specialized Administration* (1871); *Principles of Sociology*, vol. i, Part II (citations from the *Principles of Sociology* are from the New York edition of 1896).

55. ——, *Principles of Sociology*, vol. i, Part II, chaps. ii–ix, particularly chap. ii. More detailed analyses of Spencer's organismic theory of society are to be found in Coker, *op. cit.*, pp. 123–39; and Ezra T. Towne, *op. cit.*, pp. 41–48. See also A. W. Small, *General Sociology* (1905), pp. 109–30.

56. Spencer, *Principles of Sociology*, vol. i, Part II, p. 592.

57. Coker, *op. cit.*, pp. 139–54, *passim*.

58. Howard Becker, " Pavel Fedorovich Lilienfeld-Toailles," *ESS*, ix (1933), pp. 473–74.

59. A revised two-volume edition of the *Bau und Leben* appeared in 1896. A good critical review of Schäffle's system is given by Paul Barth, *VWPS* (1907), pp. 468 ff. See also Small, *General Sociology* (1905); *Jacobs, German Sociology* (1909), *passim*; and Wiese-Becker, *Systematic Sociology* (1932), pp. 694–95.

60. Coker, *op. cit.*, pp. 154–69, *passim*.

61. Other pertinent works of Fouillée are *L'Évolutionisme des idées-forces* (1898); and *Psychologie du peuple français* (1898).

62. This was essentially the attitude of DeGreef, the famous Belgian syndicalist-sociologist, on this point. See the definitive treatise by *Dorothy Wolff

Douglas, *Guillaume de Greef: the Social Theory of an Early Syndicalist* (1925), especially pp. 295–307.   **63.** Coker, *op. cit.*, pp. 181–89, *passim.*

64. Worms's main ideas on this subject are to be found in his work, *Organisme et Société* (1896); and in the *AIIS*, vol. iv (1898), pp. 296–304.

65. Coker, *op. cit.*, pp. 171–79. For Towne's treatment of Worms, see *op. cit.*, pp. 61–66.

66. Cf. the biting comment of Paul Leroy-Beaulieu, *L'État moderne et ses fonctions*, pp. 27 ff.

67. J. S. Mackenzie, *Introduction to Social Philosophy* (rev. ed., 1916).

68. *Ibid.*, pp. 147–48.   **69.** *Ibid.*, p. 293.

70. *Ibid.*, pp. 157–58; cf. pp. 244–49.

71. The official status of organismic sociology can best be understood by an examination of the arguments advanced in the discussion which appeared in the *AIIS*, vol. iv (1898), pp. 169–339. A list of the main works which criticize the organismic doctrine is given in Coker, *op. cit.*, p. 209.

72. Cf. *L. T. Hobhouse, *Liberalism* (1911), pp. 125 ff.

73. Cf. MacDonald, *Socialism and Government* (1909) and *Socialism and Society* (1906).

74. Hobhouse, *Social Evolution and Political Theory* (1911), p. 87.

75. René Worms, *La sociologie, sa nature, son contenu, ses attaches* (2nd ed., 1926), p. 55, footnote 2.   **76.** *Ibid.* pp. 54–55.   **77.** *Ibid.*, p. 37.

CHAPTER XIX

1. John Masefield, " The Everlasting Mercy," in *Collected Poems*, vol. i (1923), pp. 152–53.

2. J. K. Ingram, *History of Political Economy* (2nd ed., 1907), p. 113.

3. This summary has been drawn from a number of sources, of which the most important are: Erik Nordenskiöld, *The History of Biology* (1917; English trans., 1928); and *William A. Locy, *Biology and Its Makers* (3rd rev. ed., 1915).

4. *Charles Emil Stangeland, *Pre-Malthusian Doctrines of Population* (1904), pp. 353–54. This book is far and away the best treatise on the topic.

5. *Parallel Chapters from the Two Essays of Population by Malthus* (1909).

6. *Ibid.*, pp. 77–78.   **7.** *Ibid.*, pp. 89–90.

8. *Ibid.*, pp. 100–101. For an excellent critical exposition of Malthusianism and an anthology of recent views of the theory, see *W. S. Thompson, *Population Problems* (1930), chaps. ii–iii.

9. *J. P. Lichtenberger, *The Development of Social Theory* (1925), p. 276. This text contains a brief biographical study of Darwin which should be consulted by the student. The article in *EB* is fuller and gives an outline of all of Darwin's major hypotheses.

10. Charles Darwin, *The Voyage of the Beagle* (1909), *passim.*

11. Frances Darwin, ed., *The Life and Letters of Charles Darwin* (1887), p. 68, quoted in Lichtenberger, *op. cit.*, pp. 276–77. Italics ours.

12. *Ernest Barker, *Political Thought in England from Spencer to the Present Day*, p. 133. Cf. J. G. Schurman, *The Ethical Import of Darwinism* (1887), especially chap. v.

13. A. W. Benn, *History of Ancient Philosophy* (1912), p. 20. Cf. E. Zeller, *Greek Philosophy to the Time of Socrates* (1881), " Heraclitus."

14. *Cf. J. B. Bury, *The Ancient Greek Historians* (1909), pp. 44–45.

15. Aristotle, *Politics* (Jowett's translation), Bk. I, 1–2; Bk. VII, 4–15.

16. Polybius, *History of Rome* (Schuckburgh's trans., 1889), Bk. VI, 5–6.

17. E. Zeller, *Stoics, Epicureans, and Sceptics* (1870), pp. 490–98; Ludwig Stein, *Die Soziale Frage im Lichte der Philosophie* (3rd and 4th eds., 1923), pp. 178–79. **18.** Cf. H. Peter, *Wahrheit und Kunst* (1911).

19. A. J. Carlyle, *A History of Medieval Political Theory* (1903), vol. i, pp. 211–12; vol. ii, pp. 56–74, 143–44; *J. M. Littlejohn, *The Political Theory of the Schoolmen and Grotius* (1894), pp. 26–33.

20. Thomas Aquinas, *De regimine principum*, Bk. I, p. 1; F. W. Coker, *Readings in Political Philosophy* (1914), pp. 129 ff.

21. W. Cunningham, *Western Civilization* (1898), vol. ii, Bk. V; *C. J. H. Hayes, *Political and Social History of Modern Europe* (1st ed., 1916), vol. i, pp. 27–72; W. C. Abbott, *The Expansion of Europe* (rev. ed., 1924), vol. i.

22. Machiavelli, *Discourses on the First Ten Books of Livy* (Detmold trans., 1882), Bk. I, chap. vi.

23. Jean Bodin, *The Six Bookes of a Commonweale* (Richard Knolles trans., 1606), pp. 47 ff., 262 ff.

24. Johannes Althusius, *Politica methodice digesta* (Friedrichs ed., 1932), chaps. i, vi–ix, xix. See also the excellent introduction by Friedrichs to this edition, as well as the older work, O. Gierke, *Johannes Althusius und die Entwickelung der naturrechtlichen Staatstheorien* (1880), chaps. i–iii.

25. Thomas Hobbes, *Leviathan*, chap. xvi.

26. *David Hume, *A Treatise of Human Nature* (1874), vol. ii, pp. 111, 114, 140, 259–65; *Essays, Moral, Political, and Literary* (1880), vol. i, pp. 113–17, 447 ff.; vol. ii, pp. 197 ff.

27. *Adam Ferguson, *An Essay on the History of Civil Society* (1767), Part I, secs. 2–3, *et passim*. The book by W. C. Lehmann, *Adam Ferguson and the Beginnings of Modern Sociology* (1930), should be consulted on this head. *Gladys Bryson of Smith College has the best treatment in her unpublished *Man and Society in Eighteenth-Century Thought*, chap. iii, " Adam Ferguson's System of Moral Philosophy," *et passim*.

28. Ludwig Gumplowicz, *Die sociologische Staatsidee* (1902), pp. 77–80.

29. *Robert Flint, *The Philosophy of History in France and Germany* (1875), pp. 496–541.

30. Auguste Comte, *The Principles of a Positive Polity*, vol. ii, pp. 247 ff.

31. Herbert Spencer, *Principles of Sociology*, vol. ii. pp. 241 ff., 265 ff., 331 ff., 568 ff., 603 ff., 646 ff.

32. See the more thorough study by *Harry Elmer Barnes, " Some Typical Contributions of English Sociology to Political Theory," Part III, sec. 1, " Walter Bagehot and the Psychological Interpretation of Political Evolution," *AJS*, vol. xxvii (Mar., 1922), pp. 573–581.

33. Spencer, *op. cit.*, vol. ii, pp. 241–646, *passim*.

34. *Ludwig Gumplowicz, *Outlines of Sociology* (Moore trans., 1899), pp. 110–12, 130. **35.** *Ibid.*, pp. 112–13.

36. *Ibid.*, pp. 106 ff.; Jaques Novicow, *Les Luttes des races*, pp. 167–68, 210 ff., 217. **37.** Gumplowicz, *op. cit.*, p. 123.

38. Novicow, *op. cit.*, pp. 161–62; Gumplowicz, *op. cit.*, pp. 117–19.

39. *Ibid.*, pp. 116–21; Novicow, *op. cit.*, pp. 218 ff.

40. Gumplowicz, *op. cit.*, p. 119. In another part of this work the author rather grudgingly admits that it is conceivable that in extremely rare instances a state may have originated through the peaceful division of labor and the differentiation of classes, but maintains that even in such cases its history as a scene of the conflict of divergent interests would be the same as though it had originated in group conflict. *Ibid.*, p. 136. This anticipates part of the criticism leveled at the theory by Sorokin and MacLeod. **41.** *Ibid.*, pp. 117–144, *passim.*

42. Howard Becker and Léon Smelo, " Conflict Theories of the Origin of the State," *SR*, vol. xxiii (July, 1931), pp. 65–79.

43. Gumplowicz, *op. cit.*, pp. 146–53, *passim.* For a more detailed study of Gumplowicz and a list of his more notable works, see *Harry Elmer Barnes, " The Struggle of Races and Social Groups as a Factor in the Development of Political Institutions: An Exposition and Critique of the Sociological System of Ludwig Gumplowicz," *JRD*, vol. ix (Apr., 1919), pp. 397–419. *Lichtenberger, *op. cit.*, has an excellent chapter on Gumplowicz and Ratzenhofer in which the importance of the Austro-Hungarian background is stressed. Not enough attention is paid, however, to the fact that Gumplowicz was a Jew with Social-Democratic leanings. See Bernhard J. Stern, ed., " The Letters of Ludwig Gumplowicz to Lester F. Ward," *S*, supplement 1 (1933).

44. *Albion W. Small, *General Sociology* (1905), pp. 425–42.

45. *Ibid.*, Parts IV and V, " Society Considered as a Process of Adjustment by Conflict between Associated Individuals; An Interpretation of Ratzenhofer," and " Society Considered as a Process of Adjustment by Co-operation between Associated Individuals: Further Interpretation of Ratzenhofer." This is by far the best epitome in English of Ratzenhofer's system.

46. Lester F. Ward, *Pure Sociology* (1903), p. 193. **47.** *Ibid.*, p. 224.

48. Ward, " Mind as a Social Factor," *Mind*, vol. ix (Oct., 1884), p. 573. See also his *The Psychic Factors of Civilization* (1896), *passim.*

49. C. A. Ellwood, quoted in Lichtenberger, *op. cit.*, p. 395.

50. *Franz Oppenheimer, *The State* (Gitterman trans., 1912), pp. 27–46.

51. *Ibid.*, pp. 56–81. **52.** Ward, *Pure Sociology*, p. 204.

53. Oppenheimer, *op. cit.*, pp. 16–17.

54. *Pitirim Sorokin, *Contemporary Sociological Theories* (1928), pp. 485–86.

55. W. C. MacLeod, *The Origin of the State*, University of Pennsylvania thesis, 1924. See also his more recent work, *Origin and History of Politics* (1931).

56. R. H. Lowie, *Origin of the State* (1926), pp. 20–21.

57. A. Loria, *The Economic Foundations of Society* (1899); M. A. Vaccaro, *Les Bases sociologiques du droit et de l'État* (1898); Oppenheimer, *op. cit.*

58. G. Tarde, *L'Opposition universelle* (1895); S. Sighele, *Psychologie des sectes* (1898); and J. M. Williams, *Principles of Social Psychology* (1922).

59. G. DeGreef, *Introduction à la sociologie* (1886).

60. Herbert Spencer, *First Principles*, Part II; G. Tarde, *La logique sociale* (1895); M. A. Vaccaro, *op. cit.*, especially Introduction, pp. v–vi, 178 f., 188 ff.

61. G. Ratzenhofer, *Wesen und Zweck der Politik* (1893); *Die sociologische Erkenntnis* (1898); A. W. Small, *General Sociology* (1905), pp. 190 ff.

62. Harry W. Laidler, *History of Socialist Thought* (1927); Charles Gide, *Selections from the Works of Fourier*; O. D. Skelton, *Socialism: A Critical Analysis* (1911), pp. 69–70.

63. Novicow's *La Politique internationale* was first published in Paris in 1886.

64. For a brief analysis of the earlier plans for international organization see S. P. Duggan, *The League of Nations* (1919), chap. ii.

65. Novicow's *Les Luttes entre sociétés humaines et leurs phases successives* was first published in 1883. Citations and quotations in this chapter are from the second revised edition of 1896. His later works are primarily an expansion of some of the theses partially stated in *Les Luttes*. If this work and its successor, *La Guerre et ses prétendus bienfaits* (1894), had been familiar to English readers, Norman Angell's *The Great Illusion* would have attracted far less attention, as it contained few ideas that had not been developed with great vigor by Novicow a decade and a half before. So far as we know, the best short summary of this major work of Novicow's in English is to be found in *L. M. Bristol, *Social Adaptation* (1915), pp. 268–82.

66. Novicow, *Les Luttes*, Bk. I, *passim*; Bk. III, chap. viii.

67. Novicow's detailed exposition of this fundamental aspect of his system is to be found in pp. 51–402 of *Les Luttes*, and is summarized in chap. viii of Bk. III of that work.

68. *Ibid.*, table opposite p. 403. A translation of this table is given in Bristol, *Social Adaptation*, p. 278. **69.** *Ibid.*, p. 404.

70. *Ibid.*, p. 407. This is of course a proposition drawn from the partially discredited hedonistic psychology of Epicurus, Machiavelli, Hobbes, Helvétius, Bentham and the utilitarians, and the sociologists Ward and Patten.

71. *Ibid.*, pp. 330–35, 424–55, 481 ff., 485–86, 498. Novicow makes the analysis of justice from this standpoint the subject of a detailed exposition in his work entitled *La Justice et l'expansion de la vie* (1905). This work is briefly summarized by Hecker, *Russian Sociology* (1934).

72. Novicow's *Les Gaspillages* was published in 1894; it has some resemblance to Spencer's *Social Statics*.

73. An English translation of this work by Thomas Seltzer appeared in 1911; the original in 1894. The work is reviewed by E. V. D. Robinson, *AJS* (Nov., 1898), pp. 408–10. In 1897 Novicow published his *Conscience et volonté sociales*, which ranks next to *Les Luttes* among his contributions to sociological theory. (Reviewed by G. E. Vincent, *AJS* [Jan., 1898], pp. 544–45.) This is devoted to an elaboration of his psychological interpretation of society, which is in turn based upon a modified version of the organismic theory of society. His chief thesis is that the *élite* in society, and not the government, are the social sensorium — the brain of the social organism. He attempts to compute the numerical proportion of the *élite* in modern society and to estimate their importance in social progress. Like LeBon, he finds the English aristocracy to be particularly worthy of the admiration of the sociologist. The latter part of the work is essentially a psychological analysis of present European social problems, particularly militarism and socialism, both of which naturally fail to secure from him any enthusiastic support. Novicow's elaboration of the organismic theory of society, which is briefly referred to in his *Politique internationale* and his *Conscience et volonté sociales*, is to be found in his contribution to the symposium on the organismic theory published in the *AIIS*, vol. iv (1898), and in his work, *Théorie organique des sociétés* (1899). In general, Novicow's organismic theory of society is based upon the proposition that the identity between society and the organism consists chiefly in the fact that both are living entities comprehending a unified and organized system of vital processes. It is among the least objectionable of the classic expositions of the organismic theory, and may in some respects be classed with the organic or strictly psycho-sociological type.

74. This telling critique of extreme social Darwinism is a piece of special pleading, but it is marked by great vigor and logical clarity. It was published in 1910.

75. An English translation by S. P. Otis, edited by C. A. Ellwood, appeared in the *AJS* (Nov., 1917). The subtitle is " The Foundation of a Society of Peace." The original dates from 1912.

76. J. H. Huxley, " Evolution and Ethics," in *Methods and Results* (1893), p. 33. **77.** *Ibid.*, pp. 34–35. **78.** Barker, *op. cit.*, p. 135. **79.** *Ibid.*, p. 136.

80. *Ibid.*, p. 140. Huxley's main essays dealing with political subjects are: " Administrative Nihilism " (1870) — an attack on Spencer's *laissez faire* individualism; "Government: Anarchy or Regimentation" (1890) — a critical and historical analysis of the weaknesses of extreme individualism and socialism; "Social Diseases and Worse Remedies" (1891) — a criticism of the tenets of the Salvation Army; and "Evolution and Ethics," particularly pp. 28 ff. (1893) — an analysis of the main points of divergence between natural selection and moral evolution. The majority of Huxley's social and political writings are to be found in a collected form in his *Methods and Results* (1893). His political theories are splendidly summarized by Barker, *op. cit.*, pp. 133–41. Cf. Read, *English Evolutionary Ethics*, chap. iii.

81. Cf. Wallace's *On Miracles and Modern Spiritualism* (1875), and his *Studies, Scientific and Social* (1900), vol. ii, chap. xxi.

82. Wallace, *op. cit.*, vol. ii; *Social Environment and Moral Progress* (1913); *Letters and Reminiscences* (James Marchand ed., 1916), Part V.

83. J. P. Lichtenberger, *op. cit.*, p. 284.

84. *F. H. Giddings, "Darwinism in the Theory of Social Evolution," PSM* (July, 1909), p. 75, quoted in Lichtenberger, *op. cit.*, p. 287.

85. Alexander Sutherland, *Origin and Growth of the Moral Instinct* (2 vols., 1898), vol. i, p. 2. **86.** *Benjamin Kidd, *Social Evolution* (1894).

87. *Ibid.*, chap. ii, particularly p. 37. For a rather supercilious but keen criticism of Weismann on this point, see Mackintosh, *From Comte to Benjamin Kidd*, chaps. xviii–xix. **88.** Kidd, *op. cit.*, pp. 65–286, *passim*.

89. Giddings, *op. cit.*, pp. 80–81, quoted in Lichtenberger, *op. cit.*, p. 291.

CHAPTER XX

1. Paul Barth, *Die Philosophie der Geschichte als Soziologie* (3rd and 4th eds., 1922).

2. J. K. Ingram, *History of Political Economy*, chap. vi.

3. Cf. *Alexander Goldenweiser, "Four Phases of Anthropological Thought," PASS*, xvi (1921), pp. 50–55.

4. Cf. *Franz Boas, *The Mind of Primitive Man*, pp. 155 ff.

5. Herbert Spencer, *An Autobiography*, vol. ii, pp. 324–26.

6. W. I. Thomas, *Source Book for Social Origins*, pp. 3–26, 316–17, 530–34, 733–35, 856–58.

7. It is only fair to say that Hobhouse was much more critical of the crude comparative method in the second edition of his *Morals in Evolution*.

8. Alexander Goldenweiser, review, *AA*, xvii (Oct.–Dec., 1915), p. 723.

9. See the splendid discussion of the defects of Durkheim's method in *Goldenweiser, *op. cit.*, pp. 719–35; and by the same author in *JPPSM* (Mar. 1, 1917), pp. 113–24.

10. E. B. Tylor, "On a Method of Investigating the Development of Institutions: Applied to the Laws of Marriage and Descent," *JRAI*, xviii (1889), pp. 245–72.

11. *Hobhouse, Wheeler, and Ginsberg, *The Material Culture and Social Institutions of the Simpler Peoples* (1915), pp. 1–2.

12. See Tylor's comment on a related point in *op. cit.*, pp. 270 ff.

13. Hobhouse, *et al.*, *op. cit.*, pp. 7–8.

14. *Ibid.*, pp. 30–44. A comparison of Hobhouse's results with those of *R. H. Lowie in his *Primitive Society* is instructive.

15. Cf. Lowie, *op. cit.*, chap. i.

16. See Morgan, *Ancient Society*; D. G. Brinton, *The Basis of Social Relations*; *Edward Westermarck, *Origin and Development of the Moral Ideas*.

17. See F. Graebner, *Methode der Ethnologie*; G. Elliot Smith, *Migrations of Early Culture* and *Human History*; W. H. R. Rivers, *History of Melanesian Society*, vol. ii. See the discussion in Goldenweiser, *Early Civilization*, chap. xiii.

18. F. Boas, *The Mind of Primitive Man*, chaps. v–vii; Goldenweiser, " The Principle of Limited Possibilities in the Development of Culture," *JAFL*, xxvi; R. H. Lowie, " The Principle of Convergence in Culture," *ibid.*, xxv. It is true, of course, that there are differences in theory between members of the American "critical school." Cf. *Paul Radin, *Method and Theory of Ethnology* (1933).

19. *Westermarck, *History of Human Marriage* (5th ed.). It should be noted, however, that by the use of the same antiquated method, R. E. Briffault has challenged virtually every one of Westermarck's conclusions. Questions of method apart, however, it has recently been shown that for the early Aegean world Briffault was right.

21. One of the best examples is afforded by Murdock's recent attempt to disinter Lippert's *Kulturgeschichte*, a work that was creditable enough in the last quarter of the nineteenth century, but that is utterly anomalous at present. In general, the modern Sumner-Keller school represents the most objectionable type of " ethnographized sociology " extant. This is no criticism of Sumner, but merely of his less critical or unduly reverential followers. Although to be classed among the latter in his earlier translations and articles, it should be noted that G. P. Murdock has freed himself of many of the disadvantages mentioned, and has done relatively independent work of great promise.

22. R. H. Lowie, *Primitive Society*, p. 185.

23. Paul Radin, *Method and Theory of Ethnology*, p. vii.

24. *Howard Becker, " Forms of Population Movement: Prolegomena to a Study of Mental Mobility," *SF*, ix, 3 (Mar., 1931), p. 360.

25. Hans Freyer, *Soziologie als Wirklichkeitswissenschaft* (1930), pp. 189–99; ——, *Einleitung in die Soziologie* (1931), pp. 112–16.

26. Wiese-Becker, *Systematic Sociology* (1932), pp. 624–42; Ernst Troeltsch, *Die Soziallehren der christlichen Kirchen und Gruppen* (1923), *passim* (now available in English translation).

27. One of them, on which Chapter Four of the present work is based, will appear about 1939 under the title of *Mental Mobility in Hellenic History*, or something similar. Abstracts of others, dealing with certain types of pastoral nomadism, Spartan society, the society of Renaissance Florence, and so on, have appeared in *SSR, SSSQ, SS*, etc. See the critique of culture case study by Louis Gottschalk, "The Potentialities of Comparative History," *BSSR*, March, 1936.

28. A step in this direction has been taken in Howard Becker's " Processes of Secularisation," *SR*, xxiv, 2 and 3 (April-July and October, 1932), pp. 138-54, 266–86. Cf. also Wiese-Becker, *op. cit.*, pp. 319–44.

29. *Karl Löwith, " Max Weber und Karl Marx," *ASUP*, lxvii, 1 and 2 (March and April, 1932), pp. 59–99, 175–214.

Toynbee's culture case studies are briefly criticized by M. Postan, " A Study of History: A Review of Professor Toynbee's Book," *SR*, xxviii, 1 (Jan., 1936), pp. 50–63.

30. Ernst Troeltsch, *Der Historismus und seine Probleme* (1922); *Eugene Lyman, " Ernst Troeltsch's Philosophy of History," *PR*, xli, 5 (September, 1932), pp. 443–65.

31. *Émile Durkheim, *The Division of Labor in Society* (Simpson trans., 1933), esp. Bk. II, chaps. i–ii.

32. Ferdinand Tönnies, *Fortschritt und soziale Entwicklung* (1926); ——, *Gemeinschaft und Gesellschaft* (1935 ed.). Cf. Wiese-Becker, *op. cit.*, " Tönnies," " isolated sacred structure," " mental mobility," etc. (use index).

33. *F. J. Teggart, *Theory of History* (1925); ——, *The Processes of History* (1918); ——, *Prolegomena to History* (1916).

34. The tremendous scope of Weber's historical knowledge is evidenced by his amazing agrarian history of the ancient world, contained in *Die römische Agrargeschichte in ihrer Bedeutung für das Staats- und Privatrecht* (1891), his *Gesammelte Aufsätze zur Sozial- und Wirtschaftsgeschichte* (1924), his *Gesammelte Aufsätze zur Religionssoziologie* (2nd ed., 1922–23), and his almost superhuman *Wirtschaft und Gesellschaft* (2nd ed., 1925).

35. One of the best brief discussions of the method to be found in English is that given by *Theodore Abel in his *Systematic Sociology in Germany* (1929), pp. 140–56. Weber himself gave no single connected exposition; his methodological analyses are scattered here and there in writings called forth by special occasions. The greater number have been collected in the *Gesammelte Aufsätze zur Wissenschaftslehre* (1922). The outstanding secondary source for his methodology is *Alexander von Schelting, *Max Webers Wissenschaftslehre* (1934). This, however, is a trifle prolix and involved; absolutely essential for the specialist in systematic sociology, it offers serious difficulties to the uninitiated. Talcott Parsons, *The Structure of Social Action* (1937) is also a bit difficult, but has the advantage of being in English and being relatively brief. An excellent elementary presentation is *L. J. Bennion, *Max Weber's Methodology* (1931). Unfortunately, this is a doctoral dissertation, University of Strasbourg, and only a few copies are to be found in the United States. Other good discussions in English are *Albert Salomon, " Max Weber's Methodology," *SRE*, i, 2 (May, 1934), pp. 147–68; ——, " Max Weber's Sociology," *SRE*, ii, 1 (Feb., 1935), pp. 60–73; and ——, " Max Weber's Political Ideas," *SRE*, ii, 3 (Aug., 1935), pp. 368–84. There is of course an enormous German literature on Max Weber, and a few of the more significant titles may be listed:

Andreas Walther, " Max Weber als Soziologe," *JFS*, ii (1926), pp. 1–65; Bernhard Pfister, *Die Entwicklung zum Idealtypus* (1928); Hans Oppenheimer, *Die Logik der soziologischen Begriffsbildung, mit besonderer Berücksichtigung von Max Weber* (1925); and Werner Bienfait, *Max Webers Lehre vom geschichtlichen Erkennen* (1930).

Some attention is paid to ideal-typical method in Wiese-Becker, *op. cit.*, pp. 21–22, 57, *et passim*.

36. *Max Weber, " Wissenschaft als Beruf," *Gesammelte Aufsätze zur Wissenschaftslehre*, p. 554. 37. *Ibid.*, p. 555.

38. See the bibliography in *HWBS*, p. 294.

39. R. M. MacIver, *Society: A Textbook* (1937), p. 275. See also his more extended discussion, *"Civilization versus Culture," *UTQ*, Apr., 1932; and " The Historical Pattern of Social Change," in *Authority and the Individual*, Harvard Tercentenary Publications (1937). James W. Woodard has made use of similar distinctions in his *Intellectual Realism and Culture Change* (1935).

40. The foregoing exposition of Alfred Weber's theories owes much to a research paper prepared especially for this volume by Dr. Ephraim Fischoff of Pennsylvania State College. Cf. *Albert Salomon, " The Place of Alfred Weber's *Kultursoziologie* in Social Thought," *SRE*, iii, 4 (Nov., 1936), pp. 494–500.

41. *Morris Ginsberg, " The Conception of Stages in Social Evolution," *Man*, xxxii (Apr., 1932), pp. 87–91. Cf. also his *Studies in Sociology*. A good German presentation is that by Hans Freyer, " Typen und Stufen der Kultur," *HWBS*, pp. 294–308.

42. Gustav Schmoller, *Grundriss der allgemeinen Volkswirtschaftslehre*, Part I.

43. H. Proesler, *Die Epochen der deutschen Wirtschaftsentwicklung*.

44. Georg von Below, *Probleme der Wirtschaftsgeschichte.*
45. Wiese-Becker, *op. cit.,* p. 105.
46. August Messer, *Spengler als Philosoph* (1922). For a vigorous defense of Spengler which also provides a conspectus of the literature pro and con, see Manfred Schröter, *Der Streit um Spengler: Kritik seiner Kritiker* (1922). A fair-minded but brief discussion in English is James T. Shotwell's " Spengler, a Poetic Interpreter of History," *CH*, May, 1929, pp. 283–87.
47. Pitirim A. Sorokin, *Social and Cultural Dynamics* (1937), prospectus, p. 2. During the interval of going through the press, Sorokin's treatise has appeared, and at the last minute we can therefore give references direct. See vol. ii, pp. 29–33, 44–45; vol. iii, pp. 233, 238, 244, 247. See also Sorokin, "A Survey of the Cyclical Conceptions of Social and Historical Process," *SF*, vi, 1 (Sept., 1927), pp. 28–40; and " Forms and Problems of Culture-Integration and Methods of Their Study," *RUS*, i, 2 and 3 (June, 1936 and Sept., 1936), pp. 125–41 and 344–74. **48.** Wiese-Becker, *op. cit.,* p. 676.

Name Index for Volumes One and Two

Literary allusions, and names occurring on pages numbered in roman are not indexed. Volume One comprises pages 1 through 422, and Volume Two comprises pages 423 through 790.

Subject Index for Volumes One and Two

Volume One comprises pages 1 through 422, and Volume Two comprises pages 423 through 790.

Inasmuch as a very full Table of Contents has been provided, the Subject Index deals chiefly with matters not clearly recognizable in the section and chapter headings. For a full set of references, the Table of Contents, Name Index, and Subject Index should be used in conjunction.

SUBJECT INDEX lxxiii

criminology, 551–52
crisis, 141, 750, 765
cross-fertilization of cultures, 258
"crowd that acts," 259
Crusades, 257–65, 280, 341, 617, 618, 762
cult, 760
cultural: fixity, 8–9, 411; process, 775–76; science, sociology a, 773
culture, 452, 771–77; case study, 273, 759–66, 769, 770, 779, 780–81, 787; complex, functional unity of, 488; conflict, 118–19; contact, 114, 142–43, 165–75, 216–17, 219–20, 224, 252, 257–65, 341, 348–50, 370, 406–410, 472, 561, 706–707, 753–54, 762; relation of to social change, 760–63; cross-fertilization of, 258; hero, 26–27; material, 258, 262–63, 753; morphology of, 776; non-material, 262–63; non-material, relation of to material, 642
cyclical theory: of social dynamics, 184, 198–99, 274–77, 349–50, 411–21, 455, 458–59, 504, 643, 708, 743–90, 775, 781–87; large-scale, 781–82; small-scale, 781–82
Cynics, 194
Cyrenaics, 194

danda, 79–80
Danubian iron culture, 140–41
Darwinism: social, 661, 692; social, and militarism, see militarism
Day of Doom, 260
deism, 361–68, 561–62, 604
Deluge, 445
democracy, 67, 113, 151, 199, 253, 375, 378–79, 492, 544, 598, 615, 625–27, 653; social, 639, 642
denomination, 760
determinism: economic, see economic determinism; geographic, see geographic determinism; historical, 270, 421, 571
development, historical, three-stage theory of, 467
dharma, 72, 74, 76–77, 116, 123, 236, 784
dialectic method, 642
Diaspora, 219–20
dictatorship of the proletariat, 653–57
differentiation, 175
diffusionism, 753–54
Discovery, Age of, 265, 351
discrimination: age, 18–19; sex, 19–20, 89, 93, 189, 237–38, 249–50, 283
disorganization, 13, 103, 104–105, 106, 108, 137, 141, 151–53, 170, 174, 225,

252, 259–61, 279–80, 349, 409, 498–99, 762
divine: law, 246–50; right of kings, 24–26, 50, 80–81, 125, 210, 214–15, 242, 328–39, 377
division of labor, 19, 39, 180–83, 186, 190, 251, 278, 289, 316–19, 356, 389, 403, 480, 497, 506, 525, 571, 578, 602, 710
divorce, 89, 93
dominance and world-organization, 414
Dominican order, 246
domination: charismatic, 22–23, 49, 86–87, 712–13, 763; rational, 27–30, 51, 79, 87, 93, 111, 122, 276, 371, 550, 712–13, 715, 720, 763; traditional, 49, 74, 86–87, 95, 116, 218, 263, 319, 704, 712–13, 763
"drive toward objectivity," 540, 561, 600–601
dualism, cosmic, 35, 130
dualistic ethic, 122
duty, innate sense of, 481–82
dynamics, social, 265, 568, 572–73
dynastic succession, 50
dynasty: Ch'in, 69–70; Chou, 50, 51, 67; Han, 70; Hohenzollern, 373; Hsia, 49, 50; Merovingian, 298; Shang, 49, 50; Thinite, 97

ecclesia, 760
eclecticism, 203–204
economic: basis of state, 392; determinism, 387, 421, 564, 642, 657, 714, 726; doctrine, sociological significance of Smith's, 525–26; individualism, 604–661; interpretation of history, 641; liberalism, 365, 523–26, 604–634, 699; nationalism, 514–17
economics, 564; as an abstract and objective science, 607, 611; classical, see economic liberalism; historical school of, 612; institutional, 641; sociological aspects of early, 514–26; welfare, 611
education, 282–83; of women, 283
egalitarianism, 431, 475–76, 481, 633
egocentricity, 348
egoism, 483–84, 537
elders, 11–13, 96, 116, 148, 179
élite, circulation of, 110, 277
"emblems," 46, 54, 56
emissary prophet, 123, 228
emotion, 481, 526, 574, 581, 746
"emotional halo," 10, 87
Empire, Holy Roman, 240, 242, 244, 279, 286

A CATALOGUE OF SELECTED DOVER BOOKS
IN ALL FIELDS OF INTEREST

AMERICA'S OLD MASTERS, James T. Flexner. Four men emerged unexpectedly from provincial 18th century America to leadership in European art: Benjamin West, J. S. Copley, C. R. Peale, Gilbert Stuart. Brilliant coverage of lives and contributions. Revised, 1967 edition. 69 plates. 365pp. of text.
21806-6 Paperbound $3.00

FIRST FLOWERS OF OUR WILDERNESS: AMERICAN PAINTING, THE COLONIAL PERIOD, James T. Flexner. Painters, and regional painting traditions from earliest Colonial times up to the emergence of Copley, West and Peale Sr., Foster, Gustavus Hesselius, Feke, John Smibert and many anonymous painters in the primitive manner. Engaging presentation, with 162 illustrations. xxii + 368pp.
22180-6 Paperbound $3.50

THE LIGHT OF DISTANT SKIES: AMERICAN PAINTING, 1760-1835, James T. Flexner. The great generation of early American painters goes to Europe to learn and to teach: West, Copley, Gilbert Stuart and others. Allston, Trumbull, Morse; also contemporary American painters—primitives, derivatives, academics—who remained in America. 102 illustrations. xiii + 306pp. 22179-2 Paperbound $3.00

A HISTORY OF THE RISE AND PROGRESS OF THE ARTS OF DESIGN IN THE UNITED STATES, William Dunlap. Much the richest mine of information on early American painters, sculptors, architects, engravers, miniaturists, etc. The only source of information for scores of artists, the major primary source for many others. Unabridged reprint of rare original 1834 edition, with new introduction by James T. Flexner, and 394 new illustrations. Edited by Rita Weiss. 6⅝ x 9⅝.
21695-0, 21696-9, 21697-7 Three volumes, Paperbound $13.50

EPOCHS OF CHINESE AND JAPANESE ART, Ernest F. Fenollosa. From primitive Chinese art to the 20th century, thorough history, explanation of every important art period and form, including Japanese woodcuts; main stress on China and Japan, but Tibet, Korea also included. Still unexcelled for its detailed, rich coverage of cultural background, aesthetic elements, diffusion studies, particularly of the historical period. 2nd, 1913 edition. 242 illustrations. lii + 439pp. of text.
20364-6, 20365-4 Two volumes, Paperbound $6.00

THE GENTLE ART OF MAKING ENEMIES, James A. M. Whistler. Greatest wit of his day deflates Oscar Wilde, Ruskin, Swinburne; strikes back at inane critics, exhibitions, art journalism; aesthetics of impressionist revolution in most striking form. Highly readable classic by great painter. Reproduction of edition designed by Whistler. Introduction by Alfred Werner. xxxvi + 334pp.
21875-9 Paperbound $2.50

A History of Costume, Carl Köhler. Definitive history, based on surviving pieces of clothing primarily, and paintings, statues, etc. secondarily. Highly readable text, supplemented by 594 illustrations of costumes of the ancient Mediterranean peoples, Greece and Rome, the Teutonic prehistoric period; costumes of the Middle Ages, Renaissance, Baroque, 18th and 19th centuries. Clear, measured patterns are provided for many clothing articles. Approach is practical throughout. Enlarged by Emma von Sichart. 464pp. 21030-8 Paperbound $3.50

Oriental Rugs, Antique and Modern, Walter A. Hawley. A complete and authoritative treatise on the Oriental rug—where they are made, by whom and how, designs and symbols, characteristics in detail of the six major groups, how to distinguish them and how to buy them. Detailed technical data is provided on periods, weaves, warps, wefts, textures, sides, ends and knots, although no technical background is required for an understanding. 11 color plates, 80 halftones, 4 maps. vi + 320pp. 6⅛ x 9⅛. 22366-3 Paperbound $5.00

Ten Books on Architecture, Vitruvius. By any standards the most important book on architecture ever written. Early Roman discussion of aesthetics of building, construction methods, orders, sites, and every other aspect of architecture has inspired, instructed architecture for about 2,000 years. Stands behind Palladio, Michelangelo, Bramante, Wren, countless others. Definitive Morris H. Morgan translation. 68 illustrations. xii + 331pp. 20645-9 Paperbound $2.50

The Four Books of Architecture, Andrea Palladio. Translated into every major Western European language in the two centuries following its publication in 1570, this has been one of the most influential books in the history of architecture. Complete reprint of the 1738 Isaac Ware edition. New introduction by Adolf Placzek, Columbia Univ. 216 plates. xxii + 110pp. of text. 9½ x 12¾. 21308-0 Clothbound $10.00

Sticks and Stones: A Study of American Architecture and Civilization, Lewis Mumford.One of the great classics of American cultural history. American architecture from the medieval-inspired earliest forms to the early 20th century; evolution of structure and style, and reciprocal influences on environment. 21 photographic illustrations. 238pp. 20202-X Paperbound $2.00

The American Builder's Companion, Asher Benjamin. The most widely used early 19th century architectural style and source book, for colonial up into Greek Revival periods. Extensive development of geometry of carpentering, construction of sashes, frames, doors, stairs; plans and elevations of domestic and other buildings. Hundreds of thousands of houses were built according to this book, now invaluable to historians, architects, restorers, etc. 1827 edition. 59 plates. 114pp. 7⅞ x 10¾. 22236-5 Paperbound $3.00

Dutch Houses in the Hudson Valley Before 1776, Helen Wilkinson Reynolds. The standard survey of the Dutch colonial house and outbuildings, with constructional features, decoration, and local history associated with individual homesteads. Introduction by Franklin D. Roosevelt. Map. 150 illustrations. 469pp. 6⅝ x 9¼. 21469-9 Paperbound $4.00

THE ARCHITECTURE OF COUNTRY HOUSES, Andrew J. Downing. Together with Vaux's *Villas and Cottages* this is the basic book for Hudson River Gothic architecture of the middle Victorian period. Full, sound discussions of general aspects of housing, architecture, style, decoration, furnishing, together with scores of detailed house plans, illustrations of specific buildings, accompanied by full text. Perhaps the most influential single American architectural book. 1850 edition. Introduction by J. Stewart Johnson. 321 figures, 34 architectural designs. xvi + 560pp.
22003-6 Paperbound $4.00

LOST EXAMPLES OF COLONIAL ARCHITECTURE, John Mead Howells. Full-page photographs of buildings that have disappeared or been so altered as to be denatured, including many designed by major early American architects. 245 plates. xvii + 248pp. 7⅞ x 10¾.
21143-6 Paperbound $3.00

DOMESTIC ARCHITECTURE OF THE AMERICAN COLONIES AND OF THE EARLY REPUBLIC, Fiske Kimball. Foremost architect and restorer of Williamsburg and Monticello covers nearly 200 homes between 1620-1825. Architectural details, construction, style features, special fixtures, floor plans, etc. Generally considered finest work in its area. 219 illustrations of houses, doorways, windows, capital mantels. xx + 314pp. 7⅞ x 10¾.
21743-4 Paperbound $3.50

EARLY AMERICAN ROOMS: 1650-1858, edited by Russell Hawes Kettell. Tour of 12 rooms, each representative of a different era in American history and each furnished, decorated, designed and occupied in the style of the era. 72 plans and elevations, 8-page color section, etc., show fabrics, wall papers, arrangements, etc. Full descriptive text. xvii + 200pp. of text. 8⅜ x 11¼.
21633-0 Paperbound $5.00

THE FITZWILLIAM VIRGINAL BOOK, edited by J. Fuller Maitland and W. B. Squire. Full modern printing of famous early 17th-century ms. volume of 300 works by Morley, Byrd, Bull, Gibbons, etc. For piano or other modern keyboard instrument; easy to read format. xxxvi + 938pp. 8⅜ x 11.
21068-5, 21069-3 Two volumes, Paperbound $8.00

HARPSICHORD MUSIC, Johann Sebastian Bach. Bach Gesellschaft edition. A rich selection of Bach's masterpieces for the harpsichord: the six English Suites, six French Suites, the six Partitas (Clavierübung part I), the Goldberg Variations (Clavierübung part IV), the fifteen Two-Part Inventions and the fifteen Three-Part Sinfonias. Clearly reproduced on large sheets with ample margins; eminently playable. vi + 312pp. 8⅛ x 11.
22360-4 Paperbound $5.00

THE MUSIC OF BACH: AN INTRODUCTION, Charles Sanford Terry. A fine, nontechnical introduction to Bach's music, both instrumental and vocal. Covers organ music, chamber music, passion music, other types. Analyzes themes, developments, innovations. x + 114pp.
21075-8 Paperbound $1.25

BEETHOVEN AND HIS NINE SYMPHONIES, Sir George Grove. Noted British musicologist provides best history, analysis, commentary on symphonies. Very thorough, rigorously accurate; necessary to both advanced student and amateur music lover. 436 musical passages. vii + 407 pp.
20334-4 Paperbound $2.25

JOHANN SEBASTIAN BACH, Philipp Spitta. One of the great classics of musicology, this definitive analysis of Bach's music (and life) has never been surpassed. Lucid, nontechnical analyses of hundreds of pieces (30 pages devoted to St. Matthew Passion, 26 to B Minor Mass). Also includes major analysis of 18th-century music. 450 musical examples. 40-page musical supplement. Total of xx + 1799pp.
(EUK) 22278-0, 22279-9 Two volumes, Clothbound $15.00

MOZART AND HIS PIANO CONCERTOS, Cuthbert Girdlestone. The only full-length study of an important area of Mozart's creativity. Provides detailed analyses of all 23 concertos, traces inspirational sources. 417 musical examples. Second edition. 509pp. (USO) 21271-8 Paperbound $3.50

THE PERFECT WAGNERITE: A COMMENTARY ON THE NIBLUNG'S RING, George Bernard Shaw. Brilliant and still relevant criticism in remarkable essays on Wagner's Ring cycle, Shaw's ideas on political and social ideology behind the plots, role of Leitmotifs, vocal requisites, etc. Prefaces. xxi + 136pp.
21707-8 Paperbound $1.50

DON GIOVANNI, W. A. Mozart. Complete libretto, modern English translation; biographies of composer and librettist; accounts of early performances and critical reaction. Lavishly illustrated. All the material you need to understand and appreciate this great work. Dover Opera Guide and Libretto Series; translated and introduced by Ellen Bleiler. 92 illustrations. 209pp.
21134-7 Paperbound **$1.50**

HIGH FIDELITY SYSTEMS: A LAYMAN'S GUIDE, Roy F. Allison. All the basic information you need for setting up your own audio system: high fidelity and stereo record players, tape records, F.M. Connections, adjusting tone arm, cartridge, checking needle alignment, positioning speakers, phasing speakers, adjusting hums, trouble-shooting, maintenance, and similar topics. Enlarged 1965 edition. More than 50 charts, diagrams, photos. iv + 91pp. 21514-8 Paperbound $1.25

REPRODUCTION OF SOUND, Edgar Villchur. Thorough coverage for laymen of high fidelity systems, reproducing systems in general, needles, amplifiers, preamps, loudspeakers, feedback, explaining physical background. "A rare talent for making technicalities vividly comprehensible," R. Darrell, *High Fidelity*. 69 figures. iv + 92pp. 21515-6 Paperbound $1.00

HEAR ME TALKIN' TO YA: THE STORY OF JAZZ AS TOLD BY THE MEN WHO MADE IT, Nat Shapiro and Nat Hentoff. Louis Armstrong, Fats Waller, Jo Jones, Clarence Williams, Billy Holiday, Duke Ellington, Jelly Roll Morton and dozens of other jazz greats tell how it was in Chicago's South Side, New Orleans, depression Harlem and the modern West Coast as jazz was born and grew. xvi + 429pp.
21726-4 Paperbound $2.50

FABLES OF AESOP, translated by Sir Roger L'Estrange. A reproduction of the very rare 1931 Paris edition; a selection of the most interesting fables, together with 50 imaginative drawings by Alexander Calder. v + 128pp. 6½x9¼.
21780-9 Paperbound $1.25

POEMS OF ANNE BRADSTREET, edited with an introduction by Robert Hutchinson. A new selection of poems by America's first poet and perhaps the first significant woman poet in the English language. 48 poems display her development in works of considerable variety—love poems, domestic poems, religious meditations, formal elegies, "quaternions," etc. Notes, bibliography. viii + 222pp.
22160-1 Paperbound $2.00

THREE GOTHIC NOVELS: THE CASTLE OF OTRANTO BY HORACE WALPOLE; VATHEK BY WILLIAM BECKFORD; THE VAMPYRE BY JOHN POLIDORI, WITH FRAGMENT OF A NOVEL BY LORD BYRON, edited by E. F. Bleiler. The first Gothic novel, by Walpole; the finest Oriental tale in English, by Beckford; powerful Romantic supernatural story in versions by Polidori and Byron. All extremely important in history of literature; all still exciting, packed with supernatural thrills, ghosts, haunted castles, magic, etc. xl + 291pp.
21232-7 Paperbound $2.00

THE BEST TALES OF HOFFMANN, E. T. A. Hoffmann. 10 of Hoffmann's most important stories, in modern re-editings of standard translations: Nutcracker and the King of Mice, Signor Formica, Automata, The Sandman, Rath Krespel, The Golden Flowerpot, Master Martin the Cooper, The Mines of Falun, The King's Betrothed, A New Year's Eve Adventure. 7 illustrations by Hoffmann. Edited by E. F. Bleiler. xxxix + 419pp.
21793-0 Paperbound $2.50

GHOST AND HORROR STORIES OF AMBROSE BIERCE, Ambrose Bierce. 23 strikingly modern stories of the horrors latent in the human mind: The Eyes of the Panther, The Damned Thing, An Occurrence at Owl Creek Bridge, An Inhabitant of Carcosa, etc., plus the dream-essay, Visions of the Night. Edited by E. F. Bleiler. xxii + 199pp.
20767-6 Paperbound $1.50

BEST GHOST STORIES OF J. S. LEFANU, J. Sheridan LeFanu. Finest stories by Victorian master often considered greatest supernatural writer of all. Carmilla, Green Tea, The Haunted Baronet, The Familiar, and 12 others. Most never before available in the U. S. A. Edited by E. F. Bleiler. 8 illustrations from Victorian publications. xvii + 467pp.
20415-4 Paperbound $2.50

THE TIME STREAM, THE GREATEST ADVENTURE, AND THE PURPLE SAPPHIRE— THREE SCIENCE FICTION NOVELS, John Taine (Eric Temple Bell). Great American mathematician was also foremost science fiction novelist of the 1920's. *The Time Stream,* one of all-time classics, uses concepts of circular time; *The Greatest Adventure,* incredibly ancient biological experiments from Antarctica threaten to escape; The *Purple Sapphire,* superscience, lost races in Central Tibet, survivors of the Great Race. 4 illustrations by Frank R. Paul. v + 532pp.
21180-0 Paperbound $3.00

SEVEN SCIENCE FICTION NOVELS, H. G. Wells. The standard collection of the great novels. Complete, unabridged. *First Men in the Moon, Island of Dr. Moreau, War of the Worlds, Food of the Gods, Invisible Man, Time Machine, In the Days of the Comet.* Not only science fiction fans, but every educated person owes it to himself to read these novels. 1015pp.
20264-X Clothbound $5.00

THE RED FAIRY BOOK, Andrew Lang. Lang's color fairy books have long been children's favorites. This volume includes Rapunzel, Jack and the Bean-stalk and 35 other stories, familiar and unfamiliar. 4 plates, 93 illustrations x + 367pp.
21673-X Paperbound $2.50

THE BLUE FAIRY BOOK, Andrew Lang. Lang's tales come from all countries and all times. Here are 37 tales from Grimm, the Arabian Nights, Greek Mythology, and other fascinating sources. 8 plates, 130 illustrations. xi + 390pp.
21437-0 Paperbound $2.50

HOUSEHOLD STORIES BY THE BROTHERS GRIMM. Classic English-language edition of the well-known tales — Rumpelstiltskin, Snow White, Hansel and Gretel, The Twelve Brothers, Faithful John, Rapunzel, Tom Thumb (52 stories in all). Translated into simple, straightforward English by Lucy Crane. Ornamented with head-pieces, vignettes, elaborate decorative initials and a dozen full-page illustrations by Walter Crane. x + 269pp.
21080-4 Paperbound $2.50

THE MERRY ADVENTURES OF ROBIN HOOD, Howard Pyle. The finest modern versions of the traditional ballads and tales about the great English outlaw. Howard Pyle's complete prose version, with every word, every illustration of the first edition. Do not confuse this facsimile of the original (1883) with modern editions that change text or illustrations. 23 plates plus many page decorations. xxii + 296pp.
22043-5 Paperbound $2.50

THE STORY OF KING ARTHUR AND HIS KNIGHTS, Howard Pyle. The finest children's version of the life of King Arthur; brilliantly retold by Pyle, with 48 of his most imaginative illustrations. xviii + 313pp. 6⅛ x 9¼.
21445-1 Paperbound $2.50

THE WONDERFUL WIZARD OF OZ, L. Frank Baum. America's finest children's book in facsimile of first edition with all Denslow illustrations in full color. The edition a child should have. Introduction by Martin Gardner. 23 color plates, scores of drawings. iv + 267pp.
20691-2 Paperbound $2.25

THE MARVELOUS LAND OF OZ, L. Frank Baum. The second Oz book, every bit as imaginative as the Wizard. The hero is a boy named Tip, but the Scarecrow and the Tin Woodman are back, as is the Oz magic. 16 color plates, 120 drawings by John R. Neill. 287pp.
20692-0 Paperbound $2.50

THE MAGICAL MONARCH OF MO, L. Frank Baum. Remarkable adventures in a land even stranger than Oz. The best of Baum's books not in the Oz series. 15 color plates and dozens of drawings by Frank Verbeck. xviii + 237pp.
21892-9 Paperbound $2.00

THE BAD CHILD'S BOOK OF BEASTS, MORE BEASTS FOR WORSE CHILDREN, A MORAL ALPHABET, Hilaire Belloc. Three complete humor classics in one volume. Be kind to the frog, and do not call him names . . . and 28 other whimsical animals. Familiar favorites and some not so well known. Illustrated by Basil Blackwell.
156pp. (USO) 20749-8 Paperbound $1.25

EAST O' THE SUN AND WEST O' THE MOON, George W. Dasent. Considered the best of all translations of these Norwegian folk tales, this collection has been enjoyed by generations of children (and folklorists too). Includes True and Untrue, Why the Sea is Salt, East O' the Sun and West O' the Moon, Why the Bear is Stumpy-Tailed, Boots and the Troll, The Cock and the Hen, Rich Peter the Pedlar, and 52 more. The only edition with all 59 tales. 77 illustrations by Erik Werenskiold and Theodor Kittelsen. xv + 418pp. 22521-6 Paperbound $3.00

GOOPS AND HOW TO BE THEM, Gelett Burgess. Classic of tongue-in-cheek humor, masquerading as etiquette book. 87 verses, twice as many cartoons, show mischievous Goops as they demonstrate to children virtues of table manners, neatness, courtesy, etc. Favorite for generations. viii + 88pp. $6\frac{1}{2}$ x $9\frac{1}{4}$.
22233-0 Paperbound $1.25

ALICE'S ADVENTURES UNDER GROUND, Lewis Carroll. The first version, quite different from the final *Alice in Wonderland*, printed out by Carroll himself with his own illustrations. Complete facsimile of the "million dollar" manuscript Carroll gave to Alice Liddell in 1864. Introduction by Martin Gardner. viii + 96pp. Title and dedication pages in color. 21482-6 Paperbound $1.25

THE BROWNIES, THEIR BOOK, Palmer Cox. Small as mice, cunning as foxes, exuberant and full of mischief, the Brownies go to the zoo, toy shop, seashore, circus, etc., in 24 verse adventures and 266 illustrations. Long a favorite, since their first appearance in St. Nicholas Magazine. xi + 144pp. $6\frac{5}{8}$ x $9\frac{1}{4}$.
21265-3 Paperbound $1.75

SONGS OF CHILDHOOD, Walter De La Mare. Published (under the pseudonym Walter Ramal) when De La Mare was only 29, this charming collection has long been a favorite children's book. A facsimile of the first edition in paper, the 47 poems capture the simplicity of the nursery rhyme and the ballad, including such lyrics as I Met Eve, Tartary, The Silver Penny. vii + 106pp. 21972-0 Paperbound $1.25

THE COMPLETE NONSENSE OF EDWARD LEAR, Edward Lear. The finest 19th-century humorist-cartoonist in full: all nonsense limericks, zany alphabets, Owl and Pussycat, songs, nonsense botany, and more than 500 illustrations by Lear himself. Edited by Holbrook Jackson. xxix + 287pp. (USO) 20167-8 Paperbound $2.00

BILLY WHISKERS: THE AUTOBIOGRAPHY OF A GOAT, Frances Trego Montgomery. A favorite of children since the early 20th century, here are the escapades of that rambunctious, irresistible and mischievous goat—Billy Whiskers. Much in the spirit of *Peck's Bad Boy,* this is a book that children never tire of reading or hearing. All the original familiar illustrations by W. H. Fry are included: 6 color plates, 18 black and white drawings. 159pp. 22345-0 Paperbound $2.00

MOTHER GOOSE MELODIES. Faithful republication of the fabulously rare Munroe and Francis "copyright 1833" Boston edition—the most important Mother Goose collection, usually referred to as the "original." Familiar rhymes plus many rare ones, with wonderful old woodcut illustrations. Edited by E. F. Bleiler. 128pp. $4\frac{1}{2}$ x $6\frac{3}{8}$. 22577-1 Paperbound $1.25

TWO LITTLE SAVAGES; BEING THE ADVENTURES OF TWO BOYS WHO LIVED AS INDIANS AND WHAT THEY LEARNED, Ernest Thompson Seton. Great classic of nature and boyhood provides a vast range of woodlore in most palatable form, a genuinely entertaining story. Two farm boys build a teepee in woods and live in it for a month, working out Indian solutions to living problems, star lore, birds and animals, plants, etc. 293 illustrations. vii + 286pp.

20985-7 Paperbound $2.50

PETER PIPER'S PRACTICAL PRINCIPLES OF PLAIN & PERFECT PRONUNCIATION. Alliterative jingles and tongue-twisters of surprising charm, that made their first appearance in America about 1830. Republished in full with the spirited woodcut illustrations from this earliest American edition. 32pp. 4½ x 6⅜.

22560-7 Paperbound $1.00

SCIENCE EXPERIMENTS AND AMUSEMENTS FOR CHILDREN, Charles Vivian. 73 easy experiments, requiring only materials found at home or easily available, such as candles, coins, steel wool, etc.; illustrate basic phenomena like vacuum, simple chemical reaction, etc. All safe. Modern, well-planned. Formerly *Science Games for Children*. 102 photos, numerous drawings. 96pp. 6⅛ x 9¼.

21856-2 Paperbound $1.25

AN INTRODUCTION TO CHESS MOVES AND TACTICS SIMPLY EXPLAINED, Leonard Barden. Informal intermediate introduction, quite strong in explaining reasons for moves. Covers basic material, tactics, important openings, traps, positional play in middle game, end game. Attempts to isolate patterns and recurrent configurations. Formerly *Chess*. 58 figures. 102pp. (USO) 21210-6 Paperbound $1.25

LASKER'S MANUAL OF CHESS, Dr. Emanuel Lasker. Lasker was not only one of the five great World Champions, he was also one of the ablest expositors, theorists, and analysts. In many ways, his Manual, permeated with his philosophy of battle, filled with keen insights, is one of the greatest works ever written on chess. Filled with analyzed games by the great players. A single-volume library that will profit almost any chess player, beginner or master. 308 diagrams. xli x 349pp.

20640-8 Paperbound $2.75

THE MASTER BOOK OF MATHEMATICAL RECREATIONS, Fred Schuh. In opinion of many the finest work ever prepared on mathematical puzzles, stunts, recreations; exhaustively thorough explanations of mathematics involved, analysis of effects, citation of puzzles and games. Mathematics involved is elementary. Translated by F. Göbel. 194 figures. xxiv + 430pp.

22134-2 Paperbound $3.00

MATHEMATICS, MAGIC AND MYSTERY, Martin Gardner. Puzzle editor for Scientific American explains mathematics behind various mystifying tricks: card tricks, stage "mind reading," coin and match tricks, counting out games, geometric dissections, etc. Probability sets, theory of numbers clearly explained. Also provides more than 400 tricks, guaranteed to work, that you can do. 135 illustrations. xii + 176pp.

20338-2 Paperbound $1.50

"ESSENTIAL GRAMMAR" SERIES

All you really need to know about modern, colloquial grammar. Many educational shortcuts help you learn faster, understand better. Detailed cognate lists teach you to recognize similarities between English and foreign words and roots—make learning vocabulary easy and interesting. Excellent for independent study or as a supplement to record courses.

ESSENTIAL FRENCH GRAMMAR, Seymour Resnick. 2500-item cognate list. 159pp.
(EBE) 20419-7 Paperbound $1.25

ESSENTIAL GERMAN GRAMMAR, Guy Stern and Everett F. Bleiler. Unusual shortcuts on noun declension, word order, compound verbs. 124pp.
(EBE) 20422-7 Paperbound $1.25

ESSENTIAL ITALIAN GRAMMAR, Olga Ragusa. 111pp.
(EBE) 20779-X Paperbound $1.25

ESSENTIAL JAPANESE GRAMMAR, Everett F. Bleiler. In Romaji transcription; no characters needed. Japanese grammar is regular and simple. 156pp.
21027-8 Paperbound $1.25

ESSENTIAL PORTUGUESE GRAMMAR, Alexander da R. Prista. vi + 114pp.
21650-0 Paperbound $1.25

ESSENTIAL SPANISH GRAMMAR, Seymour Resnick. 2500 word cognate list. 115pp.
(EBE) 20780-3 Paperbound $1.25

ESSENTIAL ENGLISH GRAMMAR, Philip Gucker. Combines best features of modern, functional and traditional approaches. For refresher, class use, home study. x + 177pp.
21649-7 Paperbound $1.25

A PHRASE AND SENTENCE DICTIONARY OF SPOKEN SPANISH. Prepared for U. S. War Department by U. S. linguists. As above, unit is idiom, phrase or sentence rather than word. English-Spanish and Spanish-English sections contain modern equivalents of over 18,000 sentences. Introduction and appendix as above. iv + 513pp.
20495-2 Paperbound $2.00

A PHRASE AND SENTENCE DICTIONARY OF SPOKEN RUSSIAN. Dictionary prepared for U. S. War Department by U. S. linguists. Basic unit is not the word, but the idiom, phrase or sentence. English-Russian and Russian-English sections contain modern equivalents for over 30,000 phrases. Grammatical introduction covers phonetics, writing, syntax. Appendix of word lists for food, numbers, geographical names, etc. vi + 573 pp. 6⅛ x 9¼. 20496-0 Paperbound $3.00

CONVERSATIONAL CHINESE FOR BEGINNERS, Morris Swadesh. Phonetic system, beginner's course in Pai Hua Mandarin Chinese covering most important, most useful speech patterns. Emphasis on modern colloquial usage. Formerly *Chinese in Your Pocket*. xvi + 158pp.
21123-1 Paperbound $1.50

How to Know the Wild Flowers, Mrs. William Starr Dana. This is the classical book of American wildflowers (of the Eastern and Central United States), used by hundreds of thousands. Covers over 500 species, arranged in extremely easy to use color and season groups. Full descriptions, much plant lore. This Dover edition is the fullest ever compiled, with tables of nomenclature changes. 174 full-page plates by M. Satterlee. xii + 418pp. 20332-8 Paperbound $2.75

Our Plant Friends and Foes, William Atherton DuPuy. History, economic importance, essential botanical information and peculiarities of 25 common forms of plant life are provided in this book in an entertaining and charming style. Covers food plants (potatoes, apples, beans, wheat, almonds, bananas, etc.), flowers (lily, tulip, etc.), trees (pine, oak, elm, etc.), weeds, poisonous mushrooms and vines, gourds, citrus fruits, cotton, the cactus family, and much more. 108 illustrations. xiv + 290pp. 22272-1 Paperbound $2.50

How to Know the Ferns, Frances T. Parsons. Classic survey of Eastern and Central ferns, arranged according to clear, simple identification key. Excellent introduction to greatly neglected nature area. 57 illustrations and 42 plates. xvi + 215pp. 20740-4 Paperbound $1.75

Manual of the Trees of North America, Charles S. Sargent. America's foremost dendrologist provides the definitive coverage of North American trees and tree-like shrubs. 717 species fully described and illustrated: exact distribution, down to township; full botanical description; economic importance; description of subspecies and races; habitat, growth data; similar material. Necessary to every serious student of tree-life. Nomenclature revised to present. Over 100 locating keys. 783 illustrations. lii + 934pp. 20277-1, 20278-X Two volumes, Paperbound $6.00

Our Northern Shrubs, Harriet L. Keeler. Fine non-technical reference work identifying more than 225 important shrubs of Eastern and Central United States and Canada. Full text covering botanical description, habitat, plant lore, is paralleled with 205 full-page photographs of flowering or fruiting plants. Nomenclature revised by Edward G. Voss. One of few works concerned with shrubs. 205 plates, 35 drawings. xxviii + 521pp. 21989-5 Paperbound $3.75

The Mushroom Handbook, Louis C. C. Krieger. Still the best popular handbook: full descriptions of 259 species, cross references to another 200. Extremely thorough text enables you to identify, know all about any mushroom you are likely to meet in eastern and central U. S. A.: habitat, luminescence, poisonous qualities, use, folklore, etc. 32 color plates show over 50 mushrooms, also 126 other illustrations. Finding keys. vii + 560pp. 21861-9 Paperbound $3.95

Handbook of Birds of Eastern North America, Frank M. Chapman. Still much the best single-volume guide to the birds of Eastern and Central United States. Very full coverage of 675 species, with descriptions, life habits, distribution, similar data. All descriptions keyed to two-page color chart. With this single volume the average birdwatcher needs no other books. 1931 revised edition. 195 illustrations. xxxvi + 581pp. 21489-3 Paperbound $3.25

AMERICAN FOOD AND GAME FISHES, David S. Jordan and Barton W. Evermann. Definitive source of information, detailed and accurate enough to enable the sportsman and nature lover to identify conclusively some 1,000 species and sub-species of North American fish, sought for food or sport. Coverage of range, physiology, habits, life history, food value. Best methods of capture, interest to the angler, advice on bait, fly-fishing, etc. 338 drawings and photographs. 1 + 574pp. 6⅝ x 9⅜.

22383-1 Paperbound $4.50

THE FROG BOOK, Mary C. Dickerson. Complete with extensive finding keys, over 300 photographs, and an introduction to the general biology of frogs and toads, this is the classic non-technical study of Northeastern and Central species. 58 species; 290 photographs and 16 color plates. xvii + 253pp.

21973-9 Paperbound $4.00

THE MOTH BOOK: A GUIDE TO THE MOTHS OF NORTH AMERICA, William J. Holland. Classical study, eagerly sought after and used for the past 60 years. Clear identification manual to more than 2,000 different moths, largest manual in existence. General information about moths, capturing, mounting, classifying, etc., followed by species by species descriptions. 263 illustrations plus 48 color plates show almost every species, full size. 1968 edition, preface, nomenclature changes by A. E. Brower. xxiv + 479pp. of text. 6½ x 9¼.

21948-8 Paperbound $5.00

THE SEA-BEACH AT EBB-TIDE, Augusta Foote Arnold. Interested amateur can identify hundreds of marine plants and animals on coasts of North America; marine algae; seaweeds; squids; hermit crabs; horse shoe crabs; shrimps; corals; sea anemones; etc. Species descriptions cover: structure; food; reproductive cycle; size; shape; color; habitat; etc. Over 600 drawings. 85 plates. xii + 490pp.

21949-6 Paperbound $3.50

COMMON BIRD SONGS, Donald J. Borror. 33⅓ 12-inch record presents songs of 60 important birds of the eastern United States. A thorough, serious record which provides several examples for each bird, showing different types of song, individual variations, etc. Inestimable identification aid for birdwatcher. 32-page booklet gives text about birds and songs, with illustration for each bird.

21829-5 Record, book, album. Monaural. $2.75

FADS AND FALLACIES IN THE NAME OF SCIENCE, Martin Gardner. Fair, witty appraisal of cranks and quacks of science: Atlantis, Lemuria, hollow earth, flat earth, Velikovsky, orgone energy, Dianetics, flying saucers, Bridey Murphy, food fads, medical fads, perpetual motion, etc. Formerly "In the Name of Science." x + 363pp.

20394-8 Paperbound $2.00

HOAXES, Curtis D. MacDougall. Exhaustive, unbelievably rich account of great hoaxes: Locke's moon hoax, Shakespearean forgeries, sea serpents, Loch Ness monster, Cardiff giant, John Wilkes Booth's mummy, Disumbrationist school of art, dozens more; also journalism, psychology of hoaxing. 54 illustrations. xi + 338pp.

20465-0 Paperbound $2.75

MATHEMATICAL PUZZLES FOR BEGINNERS AND ENTHUSIASTS, Geoffrey Mott-Smith. 189 puzzles from easy to difficult—involving arithmetic, logic, algebra, properties of digits, probability, etc.—for enjoyment and mental stimulus. Explanation of mathematical principles behind the puzzles. 135 illustrations. viii + 248pp.

20198-8 Paperbound $1.25

PAPER FOLDING FOR BEGINNERS, William D. Murray and Francis J. Rigney. Easiest book on the market, clearest instructions on making interesting, beautiful origami. Sail boats, cups, roosters, frogs that move legs, bonbon boxes, standing birds, etc. 40 projects; more than 275 diagrams and photographs. 94pp.

20713-7 Paperbound $1.00

TRICKS AND GAMES ON THE POOL TABLE, Fred Herrmann. 79 tricks and games— some solitaires, some for two or more players, some competitive games—to entertain you between formal games. Mystifying shots and throws, unusual caroms, tricks involving such props as cork, coins, a hat, etc. Formerly *Fun on the Pool Table*. 77 figures. 95pp.

21814-7 Paperbound $1.00

HAND SHADOWS TO BE THROWN UPON THE WALL: A SERIES OF NOVEL AND AMUSING FIGURES FORMED BY THE HAND, Henry Bursill. Delightful picturebook from great-grandfather's day shows how to make 18 different hand shadows: a bird that flies, duck that quacks, dog that wags his tail, camel, goose, deer, boy, turtle, etc. Only book of its sort. vi + 33pp. 6½ x 9¼.

21779-5 Paperbound $1.00

WHITTLING AND WOODCARVING, E. J. Tangerman. 18th printing of best book on market. "If you can cut a potato you can carve" toys and puzzles, chains, chessmen, caricatures, masks, frames, woodcut blocks, surface patterns, much more. Information on tools, woods, techniques. Also goes into serious wood sculpture from Middle Ages to present, East and West. 464 photos, figures. x + 293pp.

20965-2 Paperbound $2.00

HISTORY OF PHILOSOPHY, Julián Marias. Possibly the clearest, most easily followed, best planned, most useful one-volume history of philosophy on the market; neither skimpy nor overfull. Full details on system of every major philosopher and dozens of less important thinkers from pre-Socratics up to Existentialism and later. Strong on many European figures usually omitted. Has gone through dozens of editions in Europe. 1966 edition, translated by Stanley Appelbaum and Clarence Strowbridge. xviii + 505pp.

21739-6 Paperbound $3.00

YOGA: A SCIENTIFIC EVALUATION, Kovoor T. Behanan. Scientific but non-technical study of physiological results of yoga exercises; done under auspices of Yale U. Relations to Indian thought, to psychoanalysis, etc. 16 photos. xxiii + 270pp.

20505-3 Paperbound $2.50

Prices subject to change without notice.
Available at your book dealer or write for free catalogue to Dept. GI, Dover Publications, Inc., 180 Varick St., N. Y., N. Y. 10014. Dover publishes more than 150 books each year on science, elementary and advanced mathematics, biology, music, art, literary history, social sciences and other areas.